Religion Among the Folk in Egypt

Religion Among the Folk in Egypt

Hasan M. El-Shamy

PRAEGER

Westport, Connecticut
London

Library of Congress Cataloging-in-Publication Data

El-Shamy, Hasan M., 1938–
Religion among the folk in Egypt / Hasan M. El-Shamy.
p. cm.
Includes bibliographical references and index.
ISBN: 978–0–275–97948–5 (alk. paper)
1. Islam—Egypt—History. 2. Folk religion—Egypt. 3. Islam—Egypt—Customs and practices.
I. Title.
BP64.E3E4 2009
297.0962—dc22 2008022562

British Library Cataloguing in Publication Data is available.

Library of Congress Catalog Card Number: 2008022562
ISBN: 978–0–275–97948–5

First published in 2009

Praeger Publishers, 88 Post Road West, Westport, CT 06881
An imprint of Greenwood Publishing Group, Inc.
www.praeger.com

Printed in the United States of America

The paper used in this book complies with the Permanent Paper Standard issued by the National Information Standards Organization (Z39.48–1984).

10 9 8 7 6 5 4 3 2 1

Contents

Acknowledgments xi

Alphabet and Note on Transliteration xiii

Arabic Language: Classical and Vernacular (Dialectical) xv

Abbreviations and Signs xvii

INTRODUCTION 1

I. CREATION AND COSMOLOGY: CHARACTERS AND THEIR FUNCTIONS 11

ALLAH, CREATION, AND WORSHIP 11

I.A. 'Allâh (i.e., God) 11

I.A.1. *zìkr* (Remembrance [of God]) 20

I.B. Cosmology (*el-wùgûd, el-koan*) 24

I.B.1. Creation of *al-qadàr, el-qismah/en-naṣîb* (Destiny, Kismet): *al-qalàm* (the Pen), *al-làwḥ al-maḥfûẓ* (The Safeguarded Tablet) 24

I.B.1a. *al-¿arsh* (The Throne), *al-ḥàyyah* (The Viper), *es-samâwât* (The Skies, Heavens), Nûn (The Whale) 25

I.B.1b. Creation of Time: Establishment of night, day, and related temporal phenomena 27

I.B.2. Paradise, Hell, the Isthmus, and the Straight-Path 29

I.C. Heavenly Bodies 36

I.D. *el-'Arḍ* (Earth) 37

I.E. *el-Ḥigâb* (The Veil, Barrier-to-Gnosis) 39

I.F. *el-bàrzàkh* (The Isthmus, Purgatory) 41
I.G. *Sìdràt al-Mùntahâ* (The Lote-Tree of the Extremity) 42

II. SUPERNATURAL BEINGS 45
II.A. *malâykah/malâ'ikàh* (Angels) 45
II.A.1. Other Categories of Angels 50
II.A.1a. Angels as components of a person (self/psyche, etc.) 51
II.A.1b. Nâkir and Nakîr, the two interrogative angels 52
II.A.2. Eblis and Other Fallen Angels 52
II.A.2a. Hârût and Mârût 55
II.B. *el-gìn* (The Jinn, Fairies) 56
II.B.1. *gìnnìyyât* (Female Jinn) 62
II.B.1a. Unstratified female jinn 64
II.B.2. Harnessing the Jinn and Minor Angels 65
II.B.2a. *fàtḥ el-màndàl* (oracle, detective-divination via jinn) 72
II.B.3. *sìḥr* (Magic): *sìḥr-sùflî* (Nether-Magic, Witchcraft, Sorcery): *ḥàlb-en-nugûm* (Milking-the-Stars); *shàbshabàh* ([Sorcery Via] Use of Slipper); *ràbṭ* (Induced Impotence) 74
II.B.3a. Magic (*sìḥr*) or folk para-religious ritual? 78
II.C. Jinn as Components of the Individual: Supernatural Counter-Spirits and Siblings 79
II.C.1. The *Qarîn* and *Qarînàh*: A Human's Counter-Spirit, Correlative, or Spouse 80
II.C.1a. The *'ukht* (sister), and *'akhkh* (brother) 83
II.C.2. The Cult of Supernatural Illness, Possession, and Healing 87
II.C.2a. *'asyâd ez-Zâr* (*zâr* spirits/possessing-jinn) 89
II.C.2b. *'asyâd ez-Zâr* pantheon 95
II.D. Zoological Supernatural Beings 103
II.D.1. *ghîlân* (Ogres) and Similar Creatures 104
II.D.2. Supernatural Animals: The Mare and the Stallion 106
II.D.2a. "*Dâbbàt al-'àrḍ*" (the "earth's animal") 108
II.D.3. Supernatural Reptiles 109
II.D.4. Supernatural Birds 111
II.D.5. The Cat and Other Creatures with Ties to the Supernatural (Ant, Bee, Mantis) 114
II.E. *er-roaḥ* (The Soul), and *en-nàfs* (The Self) 116
II.E.1. *¿àfrît* (Ghost, Cf. Spook/Revenant) 129
II.E.2. Summoning the Soul (Seance, "Ouija Board") 130

III. *AL-'INCE* (HUMANS) 133
III.A. Social Stratification in *'ince* Society 139
III.B. Specific Classes 141
III.B.1. *rusùl* ([God's] Messengers) and "*anbiyâ*" (Prophets) 141
III.B.2. *ṣaḥâbàh* (The Prophet's Companions) 143
III.B.3. Saints: Moslem *'awliyâ* ("God's Favorites") and Coptic *shuhadâ* ("Martyrs") 144
III.B.3a. *Ṣûfî* brotherhoods and other religious organizations 152
III.C. *en-nâs* (People), and Folk Theories of Personality 155

IV. DEIFIED HUMANS 161
The Arch-Saints 161
IV.A. *el-'arba¿ah el-'aqṭâb* (The Four Axes [of the World]) 161
IV.B. *el-Khiḍr* (The Green-One), St. George, Elijah 163
IV.C. *Imam* ¿Alî 164
IV.D. Organization among Arch-Saints 165
IV.D.1. The Concept of Power and the Right to Rule: The Parallel Government 166
IV.D.2. *ed-Dîwân* (the Divan/Council), and the Cult of Martyrdom 167
IV.E. *jihâd*: Righteous-Struggle and Greater Martyrdom 171

V. POWERS AND ABSTRACTS 175
V.A. Sacred Powers 175
V.A.1. God's Power 175
V.B. *al-¿ilm*, (Gnosis, Knowledge) 176
V.B.1. Sources of Knowledge and Truth 178
V.B.2. Instructive Dreams (Sleeper's Vision, *manâm*) 179
V.C. Concepts and Abstract Forces 182
V.C.1. *barakàh* (Blessing/Grace/Benediction) 183
V.C.2. *la¿nàh, ghaḍàb/sùkhṭ, niqmàh*: ([God's] Curse, Anger/Wrath, Vengeance) 186

VI. NONSACRED FORCES AND CONCEPTS 189
VI.A. Temporal Forces, Quasi Powers of Fate: *ez-zamàn/ez-zamân* (Time), *ed-dàhr* (Time-Epochs), *el-'ayyâm* (Days), *el-¿îshàh* (Life), *ed-dùnyâ/dìnya* (World, Life) 189
VI.B. Chance: *ḥaẓẓ/bàkht* (Luck), *zàhr* (Dice), *el-yâ-naṣîb/lutariyyah* (Lottery), *ṣùdfah* (Accident, Chance), and *ṭâli¿* (One's Place in the Horoscope) 190
VI.C. Learning of the Unknown: *el-kàff* ([Reading] the Palm of the Hand); *el-fìngân/fingâl* ([Reading the Residuals in a Coffee]

Cup); Divination through *er-ràml* ("[Cutting] Sand"); *el-wadà¿* (Sea Shells), *eṭ-ṭâlì¿* (One's Horoscope) 190
VI.C.a. Soliciting God's Choice (*'ìstikhâràh*), and Bibliomancy (*fàtḥ el-kitâb*) 190
VI.D. Risks and Gambles: *miqàysàh/muqâyasah* (Risk-Taking, Venturing), *muqâmarah* (Gambling, or Taking a Gamble), *'ìstibyâ¿* (Venturing Everything Out of Desperation) 191

VII. ANTI-SACRED FORCES 193
VII.A. *shàrr* (Evil) *khair* (Goodness) 193
VII.B. Eblis (Satan), Other "Satans." Cf. *shàrr* (Evil) 194

VIII. MECHANICAL ASSOCIATIONS WITHIN THE SUPERNATURAL 197
VIII.A. *khuzà¿balât* (Superstitions) 198
VIII.B. *mushâhràh, kàbsàh* or *sàkt* (Induced Loss of Fecundity, Barrenness, Infertility) 199
VIII.C. *el-ḥasàd* ([Malicious] Envy) and *el-¿Ain* (The [Evil] Eye) 205
VIII.C.1. *el-¿ain* (The Eye) 207
VIII.C.2. *el-kelmàh* (The Word) 210

IX. APPENDIXES 213
God/Allâh and Creation 213
Appendix 1: The Ninety-Nine Names of God 213
Appendix 2: Reasons for Creation 214
Appendix 3: The Tablet and the Pen (Reed) of Destiny 215
Appendix 4: Creation of Earth and the Mountains 216
Appendix 5: Resuscitation in Answer to Prayer: Image of the Universe 216
Appendix 6: Tour of Sky-Worlds 217
Angels 221
Appendix 7: Love Song for a Dead Sweetheart 221
Appendix 8: A Turk Is Introduced to the Two Angels 222
Appendix 9: Chain of Command among Archangels 223
Appendix 10: Crumbs as Fee for Admission into Paradise 223
Jinn and Familiars 224
Appendix 11: How Shâkir Became a Shaman-*Shaikh:* "Working from the Books" 224
Appendix 12: How Shamaness-*Shaikhah* 'Âmnah Acquired Her Supernatural Powers: Working with a Jinni-Familiar 229
Appendix 13: How Was the Temperamental Father Handled: A Psychodrama 231
Appendix 14: The Value of Dying in the Holy Land 236

Appendix 15: Why It Is Preferable to Seek Reconciliation with the Jinn 236
Appendix 16: Pregnancy via Artificial Insemination 238
Appendix 17: How Shâkir Cured a Case the Medical Doctor Couldn't 238
Appendix 18: Miscarriage: A Problem of a Young Bride Addressed 241
Appendix 19: Detective-Divination by *màndàl*: A Successful Case 243
Appendix 20: Detective-Divination via Pottery Water-Bottle: A Failure 250
Appendix 21: A Case of Missing Jewelry 253
Appendix 22: A Jinni-Woman Pays an *'încî*/Human Friend a Visit 254
Illness 255
Appendix 23: The Thigh of the Duck 255
Appendix 24: "Mari" Girgis, The Devil Slayer 257
Zâr 258
Appendix 25: *Zâr 'asyâd*: A Pantheon (I, II, III) 258
Appendix 26: How the *Zâr*-Ritual Solved a Childless Woman's Problem 260
Appendix 27: Marûma's *nidâ* 262
Appendix 27A: Safînah's *nidâ* 263
Appendix 28: Saints in *Zâr*-Like Ritual ("The Love for el-Ḥasan and al-Ḥusain") 264
Appendix 29: The Possessed Husband and His *Zar* 265
Appendix 30: Moslem Woman Possessed by Christian *Zâr*-Spirit 267
Zikr and Worship 267
Appendix 31: *dhikr* Worship: "O Moḥammad, You Are My Beloved" 267
Martyrdom: Advantageous Death 269
Appendix 32: "In Order Not to Gain Martyrdom" 269
Suffering 269
Appendix 33: The Blind Man and Satan 269
Nether-Magic 270
Appendix 34: How Za¿zû¿ Can Be Summoned to Perform a Task: A Case of Nether-Magic 270
Appendix 35: How Shâkir Was Pressured into Leaving His Village and Giving Up His Craft 273
Appendix 36: Magic Fix Written on a Catfish 276
Prophets and Saints 276
Appendix 37: God's Messengers (Apostles) 276

Appendix 38: The Generating of a Saint for a "Saint-Less" Community: A Dead Person Demands Recognition 277
Appendix 39: The Death of *Shaikhah* Shafîqah's Brother 278
Appendix 40: The Shaman-*Shaikh*'s *Barakàh* Produces the Lost Wallet 279
Appendix 41: Can a Woman Be More Beautiful than the Moon? Ibrâhîm ed-Disûqî and the Ulama 280
Appendix 42: Arch-Saint as Deity: ed-Disûqî's Power Display 282
Appendix 43: Bes, El-Badawî, and St. Nicholas: From Ancient Egyptian Deity to Moslem *waliyy*, to Christian Saint 284
The Evil Eye 287
Appendix 44: *el-¿Ain* (The Eye): Incantation (*ràqwàh*) 287
Appendix 45: The Source of Illness Was the Eye 288
Appendix 46: The New Car 289
Appendix 47: The Stone in Bed 290
Instructive Dreams and Other Visions 290
Appendix 48: A Widow's Dream—Sayyidah's Dream 290
Appendix 49: El-Sayyid el-Badawî Cures a Case of Heart-ailment 291
Appendix 50: A Utopia and Mental Illness 292
Appendix 51: Unfulfilled *nàdhr* (Pledge) to Saint 293
Appendix 52: The Benefit of Friday 294
Luck 295
Appendix 53: Luck: Playing with Dice 295

Notes to Appendixes 297

Register of Tale-Types 309

Register of Motifs 313

Bibliography 357

General Index 369

Acknowledgments

To the informants and tradition bearers, who adhere to the beliefs and practice the rituals depicted in this work as a matter of typical daily folkloric behavior, no amount of thanks is sufficient. The majority of the individuals cited in this study are my relatives, friends, colleagues, and acquaintances. They strove to be as fair and accurate in reporting what they practice and know as humanly possible.

I am also indebted to Ms Jane Garry, my esteemed former editor who first acquired this book, and Ms Elizabeth Potenza, dedicated editor with Praeger Publishers. Their support for this book addressing *Religion among the Folk in Egypt* from a folkloristic perspective has been indispensable.

Alphabet and Note on Transliteration

The transliteration system adopted in this work is as follows:[1]

'/a	ا/ء	ḍ	ض
b	ب	ṭ	ط
t	ت	ẓ	ظ
th	ث	¿[1]	ع
g/j	ج	gh	غ
ḥ	ح	f	ف
kh	خ	q	ق
d	د	k	ك
dh	ذ	l	ل
r	ر	m	م
z	ز	n	ن
s	س	h	ه
sh	ش	w	و
ṣ	ص	y	ي
Short vowels:		**Long vowels:**	
a	*fatḥah*	â	aa
i/e	*kasrah*	î	ee/ii
o/u	*ḍammah*	û	uu/oo
ai/ä	*'imâlah*		

[1]For the rationale for using ¿ in lieu of the letter c/superscript (e.g., ^{c}Alî) or the open single quote ('), see H. El-Shamy, "A Response [to H. Jason's Review of *Folk Traditions of the Arab World: A Guide to Motif Classification*]," *Asian Folklore Studies*, Vol. 57, No. 2 (Nagoya, Japan: 1998), pp. 345–355, p. 352 ("*Issue six*").

Arabic Language: Classical and Vernacular (Dialectical)

Islamic religious literature is intimately associated with *fuṣḥâ* (classical) Arabic; it is the language used in liturgy. However, a number of Arabic dialects constituting levels of speech are spoken in various regions of Egypt. Verbal communication through these dialects represents the typical ("normal") level of speech used in daily life in a culture area. On the whole, informants did not use classical Arabic, nor attempt to do so, except when they cite a written document (e.g., the Koran, a passage from a school book, etc.) or parts of religious services and sermons they had heard in mosques or churches. Arabic names and labels are cited here as closely as practically possible to the way they are commonly (vernacularly) pronounced. I have used, with some modifications, the transliteration system adopted by *Al-¿Arabiyyah* and the *International Journal of Middle Eastern Studies*, which is more suited for classical Arabic. The changes are necessary to allow for an approximation of the pronunciation of colloquial words, and for easier typing and printing.

In most dialects in which data were acquired, some phonetics are indicated by letters indicating different sounds in classical Arabic. These include the following:

j is pronounced as a **g** in the English word: **Go**

dh (*Zâl*) is pronounced as the English **z** (rather than the initial phonetic in the English word **This**)

q is mostly pronounced as an **'a** (*Hamzàh*, as in the English word **And**) rather than a *Qâf.*

Vowels with an accent (**ì**, **à**, **ù**) are pronounced as short with stress, as in the English: s*i*t, men*a*ce, and h*u*t, respectively.

Abbreviations and Signs

Tale-type: AT/AaTh: Antti Aarne and Stith Thompson_s *The Types of the Folktale*: A Classification and Bibliography, *Folklore Fellows Communications* No. 184. Helsinki, 1961, 1964. See *DOTTI*, below.

GMC: Hasan El-Shamy, *Folk Traditions of the Arab World: A Guide to Motif Classification*, 2 vols. (Bloomington, IN: Indiana University Press, 1995).

DOTTI: Hasan El-Shamy, *Types of the Folktale in the Arab World: A Demographically Oriented Approach.* (Bloomington, IN: Indiana University Press, 2004).

MITON: A Motif Index of The Thousand and One Nights. (Bloomington, IN: Indiana University Press, 2006).

Motif: Stith Thompson, *Motif-Index of Folk Literature*, 6 vols. (Bloomington, IN: Indiana University Press, 1955–1958), first published between 1932–1936; or Hasan El-Shamy, *GMC (Folk Traditions of the Arab World: A Guide to Motif Classification)*.

§: (Section sign) at the end of a number indicates a new motif added by Hasan El-Shamy to the Thompson motif system or a new tale-type added to the Aarne-Thompson tale-type system. (This replaces the dysfunctional practice of indicating an addition by an asterisk to the left of the number.)

‡: (Double dagger) indicates a newer motif developed or added after the publication of El-Shamy's, *Folk Traditions of the Arab World* (1995).

[??]: Doubtful or ambiguous.

Introduction

A prototype of the present work was first introduced at the IX International Congress of Anthropological and Ethnological Sciences, held at Chicago, Illinois in September 1973 (see Abstract No. 0637, p. 61) as part of the Brother–Sister Syndrome theory advanced by the present writer. The manuscript for the work was expanded and made available to students at Indiana University and elsewhere in successive mimeographed prepublication editions (Folklore Forum Monograph Series (Mimeographed). Bloomington, IN, 1973, 1974, 1975, 1984, and 1997) as a textbook in my Middle Eastern folklore classes taught from 1974 to the present. Segments of the system were published by the author in *Annual Review of Sociology*. (Hasan El-Shamy, "Belief Characters as Anthropomomorphic Psychosocial Realities." In: *al-Kitâb al-sanawî li-¿ilm al-'igtimâ¿* (*Annual Review of Sociology*), Department of Sociology, Cairo University, Vol. 3 (1982), pp. 7–36, Arabic Abstract, pp. 389–393.)

The outline depicting the general structural schema of this system was published along with relevant motifs in 1995 in Hasan El-Shamy, *Folk Traditions of the Arab World: A Guide to Motif Classification*, in two volumes. (Bloomington, IN: Indiana University Press, 1995), vol. 1, pp. 443–444. Since then data presented concerning four subfields were grouped together as subcategories of the system. These are:

I.B.1b. Creation of Time

II.C.2b. *'asyâd ez-zâr* Pantheon

IV.E. *jihâd*: Righteous-struggle and Greater Martyrdom

VI.Ca. Soliciting God's Choice (*'ìstikhâràh*), and Bibliomancy.

The main objective of this work is to structure the entire field of supernatural beliefs and related practices in the folk communities of Egypt. These beliefs are treated as constituting a cognitive system on the one hand and as behavioral experiences felt, thought, and lived by individuals and social groups on the other.

The systemic[2] structure of the beliefs involved is represented by the empirical fact that the components are interconnected: even a peripheral belief is connected to others and, ultimately, attributed to a central component. The cognitive nature of the system is due to the fact that the individual "believer" is aware of its components and the interrelationships among these components. The cognitive behavioristic nature of a belief or a piece of knowledge within the system is manifested through the actions of the individual or a social group.[3] These actions, or social practices, are, to varying degrees, motivated by these beliefs and are made in response to, and within the confines of, the beliefs.

A major component of a belief is its affective[4] (or feeling) quality; from the viewpoint of the believer, a religious belief is associated with a certain type of sentiment:

---

[2]A cognitive system may be seen as an interrelated complex of separate cognitions about objects and persons. Cognitive systems differ from one another in a number of ways. Among these are whether a system is composed of a few components (i.e., *simplex*) or a large number of components (i.e., *multiplex*); whether a system is *interconnected* with other cognitive systems, or whether it stands alone (i.e., is a cognitive isolate). Systems may vary also in the degree of internal agreement among their parts, and in the degree of their external agreement with the other cognitive systems, which constitute an individual's cognitive constellation (i.e., everything that the individual knows). A system in which all parts are in agreement is characterized by a high degree of *consonance*, whereas a system in which parts do not agree is characterized by *dissonance*. *Pervasiveness* indicates the degree to which a trait is manifested in the behavior of an individual or group. Traits that are highly pervasive are manifested in a wide variety of situations; traits of low pervasiveness manifest in only a restricted number of situations. See David Krech et al., *Individual in Society* (New York: McGraw Hill, 1962), pp. 40–42; see also H. El-Shamy, *Brother and Sister. Type 872* A Cognitive Behavioristic Text Analysis of a Middle Eastern Oikotype* (Folklore Monograph Series No. 8, Bloomington, IN, 1979) pp. 3, 49.

[3]El-Shamy, writes:

> It is important that we differentiate between mere "knowledge" and "belief." Not all supernatural beings, which are usually classified as "belief characters" in a culture necessarily involve a feeling on the part of all members of that culture. In certain cases a member of a culture may know about a character which is believed in by others, and which evokes in those believers a specific sentiment, such as fear, but that member himself does not experience this sentiment at all. Some intellectuals, for example, who just emerged from traditional cultures have knowledge of a belief character in that culture without experiencing the feeling which the character normally evokes. ("Belief-Characters as Anthropomorphic Psychosocial Realities," p. 8)

[4]A belief is treated as a close equivalent to a psychological "attitude."

First, both a belief and an attitude involve a cognition: something which the individual knows about. [. . .].

Second, a belief and an attitude both include a feeling component: fear, love, hatred, reverence and so forth. [. . .]

Thirdly, beliefs and attitudes impel the individual to act in the direction of the feeling involved. (El-Shamy, "Belief Characters as Anthropomorphic Psychosocial Realities," pp. 7–8).

For applications of this concept of "attitude", see El-Shamy, "African World View and Religion," p. 211; "Belief-Characters," pp. 7, 21; *Brother and Sister. Type 872**, pp. 3–4; *Tales Arab Women Tell, and the Behavioral Patterns They Portray*, collected, translated, edited, and interpreted (Indiana University Press,

awe, reverence, fear, love, hate, and so forth. Such feelings (sentiments) are learned and lead the individual to act in a certain manner and direction congruent with his/her feelings. In the present inquiry the sentiments involved are predominantly of a religious nature.

Although the folk belief–practice system derives its credibility from formal religion—as delineated in *al-Qur'ân* (Koran) and directly related religious sources, it does not totally stem from, nor agree with formal sacred dogma (ecclesiastical religion).[5] The folk system only partially overlaps with the formal religion. Folk beliefs and practices, however, represent real behavioral patterns that influence the thoughts, feelings, and actions of individuals and tradition-bound groups in daily living; in many respects it is *the real*[6] religious culture, while formal religion represents the "ideal," or the supposed form of that culture.

Data used in this presentation are drawn almost exclusively from folk sources, chiefly from stylized unrehearsed expressions and discussions; even the texts of quotations from the Koran cited here were elicited orally in the field by typical bearers of *folk* traditions as they accounted for specific aspects of their own experiences (behavior). (See Appendixes, pp. 217–295) A number of other sources are also used for purposes of comparison and further documentation, unless otherwise specified. These sources may be classified into four groups:

1. The Koran, and the "Prophet's Tradition" (*sunnah-nabawiyyàh*, which consists of *ḥadîth*, i.e., sayings, and deeds attributed to Prophet Mohammad).[7] These sources will be referred to as "sacred dogma" or "formal religious teachings."
2. Older, traditional literary works written by the "learned" or the elite, which include Ṭabarî's (AD 838–932) History;[8] al-Kisâ'î's (eleventh century) *Qiṣaṣ al-'anbiyâ'* (*Vita Prophitorum*);[9] al-Tha¿labî's (d. 1035 or 1037), *Qiṣaṣ al-'anbiyâ'* (*Stories of Prophets*);[10] and Ibn Khaldûn's (1332–1406) *Muqaddimah* (Prologue).[11] Such works, though of

Bloomington, IN, 1999) p. 8; "Emotionskomponente." In: *Enzyklopädie des Märchens*, Vol. 3 (1981), Nos. 4–5, p. 1393.

[5]See Anthony F.C. Wallace, *Religion: An Anthropological View* (New York, Random House, 1967) pp. 84, 87–88.

[6]Within the broader field of folkloric behavior, these concepts occur as components of verbal lore. They are designated by the following new Motifs: J6§, ‡"Ideal culture (learned ways and values for social living as they are supposed to be: good, bad, or neutral);" J250§, ‡"Choice between the supposed (presumed) in life and the actual ('ideal culture,' and 'real culture');" U1§, ‡"Not every thing (practice, value) that one is instructed exists really exists as presumed."

[7]Typically cited in abbreviated form *ḥadîth* ("Tradition"). The reference used in the present work to comment on these primary religious edicts is ¿Abdul-Galîl ¿Îsa Abu al-Naṣr, *Ṣafwat ṣaḥîḥ al-Bukhârî* (The Choicest from Bukhari's Authenticated [Utterances of Prophet Muhammad]; Cairo, 1953).

[8]Muḥammad ibn Jarîr al-Ṭabarî, *Târîkh al-rusul wa al-mulûk* (The History of Prophets and Kings) 10 vols. (Cairo: 1960–1969).

[9]Muḥammad ibn ¿Abdallâh al-Kisâ'î, *Qiṣaṣ al-'anbiyâ' (Vita Prophitorum)*, Isaac Eisenberg, ed. (Brill, Leiden, 1922).

[10]Aḥmad Ibn Muḥammad al-Tha¿labî, *Kitâb qiṣaṣ al-'anbiyâ' al-musammâ bi al-¿arâ'is* (The Book of Prophets' Stories, Labelled: *al-¿arâ'is*). Cairo, n.d.

[11]Ibn Khaldun, ¿A. *The Muqddimah*, Franz Rosenthal, tr., ed., 3 vols. (New York, Pantheon: 1958).

varying degrees of intellectual sophistication, will be referred to as "learned sources" or literary "para-religious" traditions. Of these and comparable works, al-Tha¿labî's *Qiṣaṣ* seems to have had significant impact on current oral traditions in Egypt (and other Arab and Islamic countries). A number of informants named this book as the source from which some of their data had been derived; it is readily available at booksellers in traditional city quarters, and is fairly inexpensive. Yet, most informants seem to be "passive bearers" of such literary para-religious accounts; they know of them, but usually are unable to present them fully.[12]

3. Works written by literate individuals, but are viewed here as not belonging to the traditions of the scholarly, learned elite. Two such works are Aḥmad al-Bûni's (d. AD 1225) *Manba¿ 'uṣûl al-ḥikmah*, and *Shams al-ma¿ârif al-kubrâ*, which serve as "magic" manuals or handbooks explaining "How-to." Practitioners seeking to harness the powers of the supernatural seem to have relied on these "reference" works for more than seven centuries.[13]
4. Modern academic (folkloristic, anthropological, historical, sociological, and psychological) critical studies. Such works—as those by the pioneering Edward E. Lane (1801–1876),[14] and the distinguished orientalist–folklorist Enno Littmann (1875–1958).[15]

A few semiliterary sources citing authentic folk traditional practices were consulted. One of these works treated as a source of primary data is the biographical index of saints and their *karâmât* (miracle-like manifestations, thaumaturgic divine gifts) compiled by Yûsuf Ibn Ismâ¿îl al-Nabhânî (1849 or 1850–1932).[16] This important work was

---

[12]By contrast, the term "active bearer" of tradition designates a person who knows traditions and presents them socially (by word of mouth, practice, or the like). On the differences in psychological processes involved in "active" and "passive" bearing of traditions, see El-Shamy, "Folkloric Behavior," pp. 39, 95–96, 123, 138–139. Also see El-Shamy, *Tales Arab Women Tell*, p. 9. Cf. n. 476.

[13]Aḥmad bin-¿Alî al-Bûnî, *Manba¿ 'uṣûl al-ḥikmah* (The Source of the Foundation for Wisdom) Cairo, 1956; and *Shams al-ma¿ârif al-kubrâ* (The Great Sun of Knowledge) Cairo, n.d.

For an example of al-Bûnî's far-reaching influence on neighboring countries, see ¿Abd-al-Laṭîf M. al-Barghûthî, *ḥikâyât jân min Banî-Zayd (Jinn-Tales from Bani-Zayd [Palestine])*. (Jerusalem, 1979). Also see Mohamed M. al-Gawhary, "Die Gottesnamen im magischen Gebrauch in den al-Buni Zugeschriebenen Werken." Ph.D. Dissertation (Bonn, 1968).

It is worth noting here that the owner of the bookshop that markets these and similar works seemed not to believe in their usefulness. When I visited his shop (across from al-Azhar Mosque in Cairo) in 1970, dressed in western clothes, he did not take notice since many of his customers come from secular educational ranks. However, when I asked for these two books by title, he was clearly both intrigued and amused. He asked in disbelief: "Do you really think that you will *tìsḥir* (bewitch) with these books!?" In spite of assuring him that I had no intention of practicing magic, he did not seem to be persuaded of the legitimacy of my quest.

[14]*The Manners and Customs of the Modern Egyptians*, written in Egypt during the years 1832–1835 (London: Ward, Lock and Co., 1902; Dover, NY, 1973).

[15]*Arabische Geisterbeschwörungen aus Ägypten* (Leipzig: Otto Harrassowitz, 1950).

In 1982, the present writer noted:

> "It is surprising that this invaluable work by Littmann has not received any attention from scholars in this field of scholarship." (Hasan El-Shamy, "Belief Characters," p. 35 n. 35).

[16]*Gâmi¿ karâmât al-'awliyâ'* ([An Inclusive] Collection of Saints' [Miracle-like] Manifestations). 2 vols. (Cairo, 1962).

As will be shown, translating the word *karâmàh* (sing. of *karâmât*) as miracle is inaccurate. (See Section III.B.3.)

derived mainly from folk oral traditions; the author's introduction articulates the traditional folk beliefs about the subject of sainthood during the latter part of the nineteenth century. Much of the esoteric views expressed in that work still circulate orally among various contemporary groups.

In numerous instances, orally transmitted data—especially concerning God, cosmology, higher angels, and the basic belief in the existence of jinn—stem directly from, and are largely congruent with formal or learned (i.e., elite) written sources. Yet, folk traditions in numerous situations reflect distinct characters markedly different from their literary or sacred religious counterparts. As such, the present study reflects the actual composition of the system as recognized by nearly all men and women who practice para-religious or "magical" rituals and are typically referred to as [shaman-] *mashâyìkh* (sing.: [shaman]-*shaikh*; i.e., faith healers, "magicians," etc.).

In order to focus more directly on the integrated behavioristic nature of the belief–practice (motivation-organism-response) systems, I have cited certain practices in their appropriate positions within the broader system without elaborating on their own systemic qualities, contents, or meanings. References for further readings are provided for those who wish to study these secondary systems more closely.

The structure of this presentation reflects the overall pattern agreed upon by hundreds of informants from all levels of life in Egyptian communities and subcultures, and is derived almost exclusively from field observations, oral folk reports, and text performances. In its present size and format, the system is an ideal construct; no individual layman or specialist has demonstrated full knowledge of *all* its aspects. As will be shown individual adherents manifest only varying amounts of knowledge of the majority of its components. Among other factors, differences in age, gender, profession, religious denomination, and social class typically correspond to various levels of knowledge of the system as a whole. Nevertheless, with reference to these categories informants agree unanimously on (1) the hierarchical stratification of their major belief components, (2) the intellectual (logical mentalistic, i.e., knowledge) aspects of the beliefs, and (3) on the cognitive affective (i.e., feeling) significance that accompany a belief or ritual.

Major differences occur only in regard to the positions of lesser characters or forces within single categories or strata of the hierarchy; some variations in views are also occasionally found concerning the strength of the feeling associated with a belief, especially a peripheral one (e.g., the majority of the educated city dwellers do not *fear* ogres as strongly as do many of their rural and nomadic counterparts).

The present study also refers frequently to the stand taken by formal religious and modern "scientific" circles vis-a-vis folk practices and beliefs. The official viewpoint of al-Azhar, the foremost formal religious institution, is usually voiced through fatwas (*fatâwî*: deliverance of religious legal edicts, opinions, and judgments, sing.: *fàtwâ*). These viewpoints are typically published in al-Azhar's official journal titled *al-Azhar* (which was later renamed *Nûr al-Islâm*).[17] In most instances these opinions were

Cf. Motifs: V220.0.6§, "Miracle-like manifestation by saint (*karâmah*);" A170.1§, ‡"Miracle. Supernatural deed or manifestation by God."

[17] *Majallt al-Azhar* was issued first in 1930. Vols. 7–43 (1936–1972) published by Mashyakhat al-Azhar, Cairo.

given as replies to concerned readers who had written to inquire from *ulama* (the authoritative references), about "*mawqif al-dîn min*... (the position taken by [formal] religion toward...)" specific practices, and whether a practice is "sinful" or "legitimate." Many inquiries revolved around folk rituals and beliefs such as possession and exorcism, soul-summoning visitation to saints' shrines, and communicating with the dead. In this respect, al-Azhar represents the formal Sunni (orthodox) viewpoint.

The Present Writer and the Belief–Practice System

Having been born in Cairo, raised since late infancy in Zagazig—a provincial city in the easternmost part of the Nile Delta, spending extended periods of numerous summer school breaks with relatives in the village (in Qalyûbiyyah province in central Delta), the present writer has experienced a significant portion of the concepts, beliefs, and rituals described in this work. Yet, as a member of a typical urban, "white-collar," middle-class family, he became aware of the existence of numerous components of the system for the first time only after embarking on the academic study of folklore (in 1960); these components include the astronomical size of angels, "the-Divan" of the arch-saints, *mushâhràh* (supernaturally induced barrenness), the nether-magic rituals of "milking-the-stars," and "*shàbshabàh*" (sorcery [through] the use of a slipper), among others. Subsequently, on several occasions while conducting fieldwork, the recording sessions were attended by "educated" friends of the writer. To the majority of those observers who were members of the cultural elite, numerous vital folk beliefs and practices elicited by informants as a matter of common knowledge, or shared folk practices proved completely alien and astonishing. This phenomenon points to the duality, or even dichotomy, between the subcultures practiced by the majority of the population of Egypt (i.e., folk groups) and those practiced by the elite. (See App. 42 and 46)

For the present author, typical religious experiences associated with such formal aspects of faith as God, prophets, angels and other supernatural beings, prayers, fasting, pilgrimage, and the "legitimate" and the "sinful" can always be readily identified and recalled. However, memories concerning certain salient experiences seem to have proven indelible. These include the following folk beliefs and practices listed here chronologically as he grew toward adulthood:

1) Innumerable cases—mostly during children's play—of "encounters" with fear-evoking *¿afàrît* (afrits), jinn, ghosts, and female water spirits (*gìnnìyyât*) residing in a river where he and friends secretly went swimming during summer vacations; fear of folktales' ogres. Fear of ghosts of dead ancient Egyptians residing in Tàll-Basṭah (Bubastis) to which he and friend made a number of summertime visits for entertainment (the ruins lie just a few kilometers from Zagazig). (Also see 700).
2) Angels, many of whom seemed to reveal to his mother in her dreams—according to her—most of the "unruly" and "sinful" acts he is supposed to have committed. (However, most of these angels proved later to be neighbors or tattletale siblings; cf. No. 8, in this list).
3) A fearsome landlady—a widow and a matriarch of family of uneducated low-class but well-to-do tradesmen—who, although a Moslem, was possessed by a Copt *zâr*-spirit. But the present writer was forbidden to watch the *zâr* appeasement ritual that was

held periodically, due to the fact that "these are things good people do not do." Yet, on few occasions he managed to catch a glimpse of some of the *tàfqîr* (ritual dancing) that landlady did. That image still lingers in his mind depicting that lady dressed in a priest's vestments: black robes, black priest's turban, and a heavy chain around her neck supporting a huge silver cross that reached down past her waist, her forearms raised upward at the elbows, with her upper arms horizontally aligned with her shoulders and both index fingers pointing upward—and swaying at the waist from side to side while standing in place. (See App. 30)

4) Reading of the Koran *at* that landlady once, for having horrified his family while his father was abroad. The reading was meant as a plea (prayer) for divine punishment for having forced her way into the family's apartment, threatening his mother, and demanding either to raise the rent or be evicted by force.

5) Recitations from the Koran against Satan, "evil," and the harmful—in general, and occasionally against the evil eye.

6) Innumerable reports on the effects of *barakàh* (blessedness). These accounts included the blessedness associated with a Christian physician, and a Jewish radio shop-owner.

7) Use of nonprofessional charms, incantations, and amulets.

8) Dream interpretations (cf. No. 2 in this list).

9) Serving as a medium in *màndàl* ("magic liquid-mirror") ritual to detect the guilty party in a case of stolen money. (See Section II.B.2a, and App. 19 and 20)

10) Witnessing numerous cases of *nudhûr* (conditional vows) to saints, pledged mostly by his friends or his friends' relatives. (But he was forbidden to attend saints' festivals; see App. 51.)

11) Practicing soul summoning once or twice during the 1950s, according to an article published in a weekly *al-Gîl al-Gadîd* (*The New Generation*). He and two friends tried to summon a deceased teacher's soul to get information on the final examination. The results were near disastrous. (See Section II.E.2)

12) Being a party to a case of "lost money," resolved by the owner's mere declaration of intent to resort to a certain shaman-*shaikh*: the money was found by the owner (actually, anonymously returned by the "thieves" to the location where they had found it). (See App. 40)

13) One case of *ràbṭ* (induced impotence), when a member of the elite class came from Cairo to the village—where the writer was visiting once in summer (in 1956)—so as to be treated by its famous shaman-*shaikh*. (See App. 36)

14) Witnessing the practice of *ìstikhâràh* (prophesying via sleeper's vision, asking God's counsel) through a dream, according to which a recipient of a graduate fellowship to study sociology in Germany declined the award (1956–1957). Future events caused the "sociologist" to regret his decision; he developed hostile attitudes toward the person who performed the ritual on his behalf, but he himself continued to uphold the validity of the practice.

15) Witnessing, while undertaking fieldwork in New York City (in 1961), the reaction of a Cairene doctoral student in physics—a member of Egypt's National Science Research Center—upon receiving a letter from his fiancée's family informing him that she—also a research scientist—has broken their engagement due to a *¿amal* ("fix," magical "charm")

done to her. The friend gave some credence to the excuse and expressed his belief in the efficacy of magic.

16) Witnessing the addressing of the dead, when his recently deceased grandmother was informed by one of her sons of current family events, including the present writer's return from his studies abroad (in 1968).

Scope of Relevance

This work points out some of the strong similarities between ancient Egyptian belief systems and contemporary ones. In so doing, this study does not seek to surmise the origins of contemporary beliefs and practices, but simply to establish the seeming continuity of their active existence. As shown in Hasan El-Shamy's examination of current folk narratives in Egypt, the impact of ancient Egyptian culture on Africa, south of the Sahara, and the rest of the Red Sea basin is quite pronounced.[18] This finding is reinforced by data provided in Gaston C. Maspero, *Popular Stories of Ancient Egypt* (Hasan El-Shamy, ed., Santa Barbara, CA, 2002, and Oxford, 2004), and *Types of the Folktale in the Arab World: A Demographically Oriented Approach* (Indiana University Press, 2004; henceforth: *DOTTI*).

Although this presentation is limited to the folk culture of Egypt, the system is also found, with local variations, in other Arab and Moslem culture areas.[19] Similarly, beliefs found in numerous areas of sub-Saharan Africa,[20] where Islam and Arab influences are pronounced, show strong resemblances to the system outlined below.

Various societies in Somalia, Ethiopia, Sudan, Tanzania, Uganda, Chad, Mali, Mauritania, Senegal, Guinea, Ghana, Nigeria, and several other nations have been influenced in various degrees by these Arab and Islamic folk (as well as formal) religious and para-religious beliefs and practices. It should be borne in mind that western Christianity and Judaism are essentially variations on Middle Eastern sacred belief systems. Thus, Euro-American religious beliefs may be assumed to have direct historical connections to their counterparts in the present schema.

Motifs and Tale-Types

The comparative aspect of this study can best be presented through application of the "motif" as an analytical and classificatory device. The assigning of a motif number,

---

[18] *Folktales of Egypt: Collected, Translated and Annotated with Middle Eastern and [sub-Saharan] African Parallels* (Chicago, IL: University of Chicago Press, 1980), pp. 258–259.

[19] For a basic description of the culture areas of the Middle East before the advent of the current socioeconomic and demographic transformations, see Raphael Patai, *Golden River to Golden Road: Society Culture and Change in the Middle East* (Philadelphia, PA, 1969), pp. 60–72. Naturally, the conditions have changed drastically since the book was first written, but the psychological effects of the environment, natural and sociocultural, of regions still persist.

[20] See Hasan El-Shamy, "Belief and Non-Belief in Arab, Middle Eastern, and sub-Saharan Tales: the Religious–Non-Religious Continuum. A Case Study." In: *al-Ma'thûrât*, Vol. 3, No. 9 (Doha, Qatar, January, 1988), pp. 7–21.

For folk narratives commonly found in both segment of Africa, see Hasan El-Shamy, *DOTTI*.

according to Hasan El-Shamy's, *Folk Traditions of the Arab World: A Guide to Motif Classification* (*GMC*) and Stith Thompson's *Motif-Index of Folk-Literature*, to a specific belief or practice places the item concerned in a broader cultural and geographical matrix, and should enable a researcher to peruse questions of interconnectedness, convergence–divergence, distribution, diffusion, origin, etc., not addressed as a primary objective in this study. Yet, since ancient Egyptian beliefs seem to have received only skeletal representation in the *Motif-Index*, and because of their significance for establishing the degree of strength of a practice, a special effort—though not comprehensive—has been made to point out basic aspects of similarities between ancient and "modern" beliefs and rituals. For this purpose, an augmentation and adaptation of Thompson's *Motif-Index* has been devised so as to allow for more accurate treatment of Arab cultural materials.[21] The same argument may be applied to the "tale-type" as a classificatory device of narrative plots. A tale-type index addressing Arab and related materials has been developed. Relevant data are incorporated in the present work.[22]

---

[21] Stith Thompson, *Motif Index of Folk-Literature*, 6 vols. (Bloomington, IN: Indiana University Press, 1955–1958; CD-ROM edition, 1993). Also see the following indexes by Hasan El-Shamy, *Folk Traditions of the Arab World: A Guide to Motif Classification*, 2 vols. (Bloomington, IN: Indiana University Press, 1995); *Types of the Folktale in the Arab World: A Demographically Oriented Tale-Type Index* (Bloomington, IN: Indiana University Press, 2004); and *Motif Index of the Thousand and One Night* (Bloomington, IN: Indiana University Press, 2006).

These reference works provide data concerning the occurrence of motifs/themes in various regions of the Arab world. For example, *GMC* gives the following data concerning the theme of "'The balance' of Judgment Day: for weighing religious exercise (soul, heart, etc.)" (Mot. A464.5§): It is a component in Tale-type: 802A,* *His Faith in the Balance*; and that it occurs in the following sources:

> "Lit.:- al-Tha¿labî 188, Basset *Mille* I 177 No. 49; EGYPT:- Ions 107 134–136, al-¿Idwî 264–265, Lane 66."

Similarly, the theme of "*sakhṭ, maskh* (devolution): creation of animals through degeneration to present forms" (Mot. A1737§), appears in the following sources:

"Basset *Mille* II 408 No. 129, III 498–499 No. 301; Morocco: Stumme 194 No. 34; Palestine: Schmidt-Kahle 6–7 No. 3.

[22] Reference here is to El-Shamy's *DOTTI*. For example, the recurrence of Tale-type 830C, *If God Wills*. [Successive misfortunes because of forgetting to say, "If God wills"] (cited in n. 153) is indicated as follows:

(A) Literary: _**1**_ Basset *Mille* I, 421, No. 128; _**2**_ Marzolph, *Ridens*, No. 481.

(B) Iraq: _**3**_ K. Sa¿d-al-Dîn, *Turâth* III:10, 21.

(C) Palestine: _**4**_ Stephan, "Fables," 184, No. 14; _**5**_ Bushnaq, *Arab*, 284–285, [No. 87]; _**6**_ Schmidt/Kahle, *Palästina* I, 12–15, No. 9; _**7**_ Schmidt/Kahle, *Palästina* II, 43–45, No. 81.

(D) Egypt: _**8**_ AUC: 41, No. 11; _**9**_ Elder, *Reader*, pt. 2A, 12–13, No. 3.

(E) Sudan: _**10**_ Mitchnik, *Egyptian and Sudanese*, Intro., p. X.

(F) Morocco: _**11**_ Loubignac, *Zaër*, Pt. I, 271–272, No. 22.

Clearly, the data in the sample entry cited above can assist students of culture and society develop a more inclusive image of the worldviews of individuals and social groups.

CHAPTER I

Creation and Cosmology: Characters and Their Functions

As realities lived in the daily lives of believers, the constituents of the belief–practice system may be grouped into two major divisions: "Characters" (or beings) on the one hand, and "Powers and Abstracts" on the other. Each division may be analyzed further into smaller components. Since characters are perceived in terms of their presumed nature, capabilities, and deeds, they will be treated in combination with the functions they are believed to perform.

ALLAH, CREATION, AND WORSHIP

I.A. 'Allâh (i.e., God)

Islam may be characterized as a theocentric sacred ideology, with applied social programs that regulate virtually all aspects of social life: familial, economic, political, educational, in addition to other facets of life. The central point in all Islamic belief systems is the concept of *'Allâh* (God, Allah)[23] and His powers. The perceiving of God on both the formal religious level as well as on the popular and folk levels is uniform and well defined. This perception stems mostly from the Koran and directly related formal tenets of the faith. God has ninety-nine praise names, known as "God's beautiful names" (*'asmâ' 'Allâh al-ḥusnâ*).[24] Each name corresponds to, and describes,

[23]The word "'Allâh" by itself is pronounced with dark double "l", as in the English words "love", "like" or "luck"). However, the pronunciation will vary morphologically. For example, in the phrase "by God" the pronunciation would be "*bi* Illâh," (i.e., *bi* 'Allâh).

[24]See Appendix 1. For other lists see, E. Doutté, *Magie et réligion dans L'Afrique du Nord* (Algér: Jourdan, 1908), p. 199; R. Kriss, and H. Kriss-Heinrich. *Volksglaube in Bereich des Islams*, 2 vols. (Wiesbaden: Harrassowitz, 1960–1962), Vol. 2, p. 68; and Helmut Gätje, *Koran und Koranexegese*, (Zürich, Artemis:

one of God's attributes. The first and the most important trait, which apparently developed in contradistinction to the doctrine of Trinity in Christianity, is that of God's oneness and unity. "Allah is *Wâḥid* (One), [He] has no *thânî* (second)," and "God is one, [He] has no *sharîk* (partner)" are powerful truisms that recur on the lips of people in various daily situations, thus constantly reinforcing the concept of the absolute oneness of God. One such situation is to be encountered in marketplaces where giving out or receiving bills of money is often done in the formulaic manner of stating, as bills are changing hands, "God is One, has no second, three, four, etc." Additionally, as some of His names indicate, God is The Creator, The Beginning and The End, The Everlasting, The Omnipotent, The Compassionate, The All-knowing, The Justice, The Forgiving, The Mighty, The Peace, The Protector, The Life-Giver ("*al-Mùḥyî*"), The Death-Giver (*al-Mumît*, lit.: The–One–who–Makes-Die), The Avenger, and The Holy-One (*al-Quddûs*). With respect to the latter name—The Holy-One (*al-Quddûs*), it is noteworthy that God and the "Holy Spirit" (*rûḥ al-Qudùs*) are the only two entities Koran associates with the concept of "holiness."[25] (In the Arabic language, the word *rûḥ* is perceived as feminine.)

1971), pp. 197–221. Richard F. Burton, *Arabian Nights: The Book of the Thousand Nights and a Night* (London, 1894), Vol. 2, p. 28, note 1 provides an early reference on the subject. Edwin Arnold, *Pearls of the Faith, or Islam's Rosary, Being the Ninety-Nine Beautiful Names of Allah* ([al-] *Asma-el-Husnâ*) etc. (London: Trubner, 1883).

[25]The Name "al-Qùddûs" appears only twice in Koran (Koran, 50:23, 62:1; also cf. Koran, 2:30). Meanwhile, *Rûḥ al-Qudùs* (the "Holy Spirit"), which is commonly thought of as the archangel Gabriel, appears infrequently (Koran, 2:87, 2:253, 5:110, 16:102). Similarly, Koran characterizes only two locations as "holy;" these are: *al-wâdî al-muqàddàs* (the Holy Valley) in Sinai (Koran, 79:16), and *al-'arḍ al-muqàddàsah* (The Holy Land, i.e., Palestine; Koran, 5:23). Significantly, Abdallah Yousuf Ali translates "al-Qur'ân al-majîd" as *The Glorious Kur'ân*, ([Beirut], 1973), and *al-wâdî al-muqàddàs* as "the *sacred* valley" [emphasis added]. Currently, other translations that eschew the concept of holiness include "Great" and "Noble Qur'ân."

This scarcity of the use of the concept of "holiness" is also reflected in other facets of daily life: the name "¿Abd-al-Qùddûs," when compared to other proper names that use the prefix "¿Abd- . . . ," appears only rarely. In common parlance, the phrase *al-'arâḍî al-muqaddasàh* (Holy land*s*) signifies Mecca, Medina, and other sites in Hejaz/Saudi Arabia connected with "pilgrimage" as a required service. Meanwhile, when used as a noun, the word "al-Qùds" (holiness) designates "Jerusalem." A Christian pilgrim to the Holy Land is titled: *muqaddìs* (typically pronounced "*mi'addìs* in vernacular," i.e., one who has performed pilgrimage to Jerusalem), a title also applied to a Moslem who has undertaken this optional service after having fulfilled the required pilgrimage to Mecca.

Occasionally, the concept of *tàqdîs* (bestowing holiness or sacredness) appears as a prayer soliciting God's favor for an asset, but not a person. An example of this usage appears in connection with *shaikh* al-Bûnî, "*qàddàsa rûḥah* (May [God] bestow holiness/sacredness on his soul)" (*Shams*, title page/p. 1); another example is to be found in a folk epic about an arch-saint where those who doubt his powers tell others "let us not *nuqaddìs maqâmùh* (hold his shrine holy [i.e., venerate])" (see H. El-Shamy, "The Story of El-Sayyid Aḥmad El-Badawî with Faṭma Bint Berry, An Egyptian Folk Epic, part II, text and explanatory notes." In: *Folklore Forum*, Vol. 11, Nos. 3–4 (1976), pp. 140–163, verse/line/num. 61, p. 143). It is significant that the word *nuqaddìs* ("hold as holy") does not appear in the oral Arabic rendition of the epic; the oral text uses "*ne¿aẓẓàm maqâmùh* (i.e., *nu¿aẓẓimu . . .*)," which I translated as "show grand respect for his shrine," a statement indicating being worthy of exaltation but not of "holiness." Also see data associated with Section III.B.3, n. 241, 242, and 527.

Among Copts, the phrase *al-kitâb al-muqàddàs* (The Holy Book), stands for the Bible.

Regrettably, at present (2000s) the word "holy" appears frequently and indiscriminately on Web sites

God's names and corresponding traits portray God as all-mighty, all-powerful, and all-capable. Some pairs of God's names reflect opposites: manifest/hidden, first/last, life-giver/death-giver, rewarding/punishing, honorer/abaser, exalter/humbler, etc.[26] God is also perceived as beautiful: *'Allâhu gamîlun yuḥibbu al-gamâl* ("God is beautiful and likes beauty") is an adage that is often-cited to promote interest in beautiful things and in maintaining one's own attractiveness through cleanliness, neatness, and elegance without excessive adornment. It is also often used to defend oneself if criticized for displaying what may be perceived as sinful interest in the looks of a beautiful person.[27] God, however, may not be perceived in corporal terms as an adage states: *kùllù ma-khaṭara bi-bâlìk, fa-huwa bi-khilâfi dhâlìk* (in other words, "Whatsoever [notion] may occur to your mind, He is unlike that!"). The recurrent idioms: "God's [helping] hand," and "God's [watchful] eye" are thought of as mere rhetorical expressions.[28] God created both the *'înce* (humans) and the *gìnn* (jinn) solely to worship Him (Koran, 51:56). This relationship between man and God is represented by the prefix: *¿àbd* (lit.: slave of; i.e., worshipper or servant of . . .) that functions as an adjective. Common names such as ¿Abd-'Allâh, ¿Abd-er-Raḥîm, ¿Abd-el-Ghafûr, and ¿Abd-es-Salâm, mean: "Slave/Servant-of-The-God," "Slave-of-The-Compassionate," "Slave-of-The-Forgiver," and "the-Slave-of-The-Peace," respectively.

It is significant to note here that names that include the "¿Abd- . . . " suffix are given only to males. This phenomenon suggests that the maleness of a human being is perceived as corresponding, noncognitively, and as necessitated by the nature of the Arabic language, to that of the name of the God. There is no rule against giving such names to females; nonetheless, a name beginning with the feminine form of *¿àbd* (i.e., *¿Àbdàt- . . .* or *'amàt- . . .*) does not occur, and seems not to be assigned to a female as the given-name. Yet, in literary sources a female may occasionally be referred to or addressed as *'amàtu-llâh* (God's she-slave or servant); this form of address is a polite

---

and other publications in English language; some sites speak of the "holy Prophet." Clearly, such a characterization is incongruent with the basic tenets of Islam.

[26] Motif: Z183.7§, ‡"Personal names formed from one of God's names (deus-nymics)—e.g., ¿Abd-Allâh, ¿Abd-al-Karîm, 'Amatu-Allâh, etc.". Cf. Yassin M. Aziz, "Personal Names of Address in Kuwaiti Arabic." In: *Anthropological Linguistics*, Vol. 20, No. 2 (1978), pp. 53–63.

For a discussion on this concept from a Jungian archetypal perspective, see Hasan El-Shamy and Gregory Schrempp, "Union of Opposites, or Coniunctio Oppositorum." In: *Archetypes and Motifs in Folklore and Literature*, eds. Jane Garry and Hasan El-Shamy (M.E. Sharpe: Armonk, NY, 2005), pp. 481–488.

[27] Motifs: T481.0.2§, ‡"Lustful regard—('fornication-with-eye');" A462.3§, ‡"God is beautiful and likes beauty;" J2203.1§, ‡"Sinful interest in a beautiful person rationalized: 'God is beautiful and loves beauty;'" J1768.2.1.1§, ‡"Youth thought to be a man's lover (actually his son);" J2215.7.1§, ‡"God created temptation but ordered worshippers not to give in."

See El-Shamy, "A Motif Index of *Alf Laylah wa Laylah*: Its Relevance to the Study of Culture, Society, the Individual, and Character Transmutation." In: *Journal of Arabic Literature* (Brill, Leiden), Vol. 36, No. 3, pp. 235–268; p. 266 n. 111.

[28] On *al-tajasîm* and *al-mushabbihàh* (anthropomorphism, i.e., thinking of God in corporal, human-like terms), see Ibn Khaldûn/Rosenthal, *The Muqddimah*, Vol. 3, p. 16. Also see: Merlin Swartz, tr. ed., *A Medieval Critique of Anthropomorphism: Ibn al-Jawzî's Kitâb Akhbâr aṣ-ṣifât: A Critical Edition of the Arabic Text with Translation, Introduction and Notes* (Leiden, Boston: Brill, 2002).

manner to signify that the speaker does not know, or is refraining from voicing the name of the female concerned.

God's name, like every last thing in the universe, is believed to have been created by God and has real existence apart from the verbal utterance. Knowledge of the properties of God's names—and of all other names and of letters of which they are composed—is known as *¿ìlm el-ḥùrûf* (the science of letters).[29]

Before God there was God. No branch of Arab-Islamic belief systems—formal or folk, sacred or antisacred—attempts to go so far as to ask the question "How did God come to be?" Such a thought is considered a sign of impiety, if not sheer blasphemy, and is invariably attributed to the instigation of *'Iblîs* (Eblis)—who is also labelled *esh-Sheṭân* (i.e. *al-Shàyṭân*, Satan, or the Devil)—and is therefore judged as sinful, or at least inadvisable. Typically, children who ask the question are instructed that the mere thought is sinful and therefore must not be repeated.

Moslems, particularly those who are members of traditionary groups, view their world and their actions in it as comprising two types of objects and deeds. There are certain objects that God created as *ṭâhìr* (i.e., immaculate, pure, clean) and others that God created as *negìs* (i.e., *najìs*, impure, defiled, or profane). A cow's milk, for example, is "pure," while a cow's dung or urine, is *negìs* (defiled, impure). Also certain animals, especially the pig and the dog, are considered *nagâsàh* (i.e., *najàs*, defilement). Some objects are viewed as neutral in themselves, but may acquire a different character when man interacts with them. Blood, for example, may be considered *ṭâhìr* (pure); however, if blood touches a human it becomes *nagâsàh* (defilement)[30] and the contaminated person must ritually cleanse self before performing prayers or similar rituals (see Section II.B.2). Likewise, all human deeds or actions are viewed as either *ḥalâl* (legitimate, permissible, or "lawful"—in a religious sense) or *ḥarâm* (sinful, illegitimate, "unlawful," or tabu). *El-ḥalâl* is what God legitimized for man to do or consume, while *el-ḥarâm* is what God prohibited man from doing or consuming. The considerations according to which the two realms of that what is legitimate and what is sinful are perceived as central and very powerful; they pervade virtually every aspect of individual and group behavior.[31]

Violation of God's commandments concerning the legitimate and illegitimate constitutes a sin (*dhànb*, *'ithm*, *khaṭî'àh*).[32] Sins are ranked as either *ṣaghâ'ìr* (minor

---

[29]For a description of "the science of letters," see: Ibn Khaldûn/Rosenthal, *The Muqddimah* (1958), Vol. 3, pp. 171–182. Also see: al-Bûnî, *Manba¿* and *Shams* (treated in M. El-Gawhary, "Die Gottesnamen;" and E. Lane, *Modern Egyptians*, 260–262. On the use of the "letters" by Shiites, see n. 235.

[30]Motif: C1.1.1§, ‡"The profane (*najiss/najass/*"*nagâsah*"): the opposite of the pure/immaculate (*ṭâhir/ṭuhr*)."

[31]Motif: A608§, ‡"Determination of *al-ḥalâl* (the licit, legitimate) and of *al-ḥarâm* (the illicit, sinful) for man."

[32]The word *'ithm* seems not to occur in folk parlance—presumably due to the fact that the *thâ'* (phonetic: "th" as in the English "*th*ick") is pronounced as an "s;" thus "*'ithm*" would be confused with *'ism* (i.e., name). Meanwhile, the word "*dhànb*" has been incorporated in psychological literature as a term designating "guilt;" in its new academic milieu, it is usually qualified as "*shu¿ûr bi al-dhànb*" (guilt feeling); see: A. Alhefnee, *Encyclopedia of Psychology & Psycho-analysis*, 2 Vols. in 1 (Cairo:, Madbouli, 1969) Vol. 1,

infringements), or as *kabâ'ir* (cardinal sins).[33] A good deed (e.g., charity, benevolence) is termed *ḥasanàh*, and constitutes credit for the individual; a sinful act is termed *sàyyi'àh*, and counts as debit against the person who commits it. In certain contexts the word *ḥasanàh* is also used to indicate alms or charity such as giving money, food, or the like to the needy without expecting reciprocity. Beggars typically solicit "*ḥasanàh* for God's sake!" a loss at a business deal or loan to a less fortunate person may be considered "veiled *ḥasanàh* (charity)" provided it is not based on deception. This concept may urge a person to buy from a needy vendor at a slightly higher price than from a prosperous merchant at a lower price so as to benefit the needy without causing him loss of face.[34] Good deeds consume or nullify sinful ones. Thus, it is possible for a person to redeem a sin by performing additional credit-worthy deeds (e.g., fasting, praying, feeding the poor, helping the weak, etc.); when such a deed is intended as an expiating act, it is labeled *kàffàràh*.[35] It is also possible for the living to perform a religious duty and grant the credit gained to a deceased person; such an act is labeled *wàhb* (granting). If the deceased were remiss in the performance of a *fàrḍ* (required or obligatory service, e.g., prayers, pilgrimage, fasting, giving alms-tax) due to disability or lack of means, he/she would receive the full benefit of the granting-act; the performer of the expiatory act receives credit as well. With reference to a deceased person who had sinned, it is permissible to perform an expiating act—also called *ràḥmàh* (mercy) in this context—as a compensatory deed so as to benefit the deceased; however, these redeeming acts are believed to apply only to minor infractions, but not to cardinal sins.[36] A similar concept is that of *al-mùnaggiyât* (i.e., *al-mùnjiyât*, [soul]-rescuers/savers), which may be defined as a category of good deeds, of which a single act would outweigh all sinful ones theretofore committed, and consequently would save its "owner" from hell. These soul-savers are multiple, varied, and recurrent especially in cycles of didactic religious narratives. A Prophet's

---

p. 341. Meanwhile, the word *khaṭa'* simply designates a "wrong," whereas *khaṭî'ah* is a misdeed within a religious context.

[33]Motifs: U230.0.2§, "Cardinal sins (*kabâ'ir*), and minor sins (*ṣaghâ'ir*);" U230.0.2.1§, ‡"Hierarchy of sins: great, greater, and greatest sin." See Lane, *Modern Egyptians*, p. 525, n. 1–2.

[34]"el-ḥasanàh el-màkhfiyyah fi-l-bai¿ wì-esh-shirâ": Motif: P775.2.0.2.1§, ‡"The veiled charity (*ḥasanah*) is [given] through buying-and-selling."

[35]Motifs: V6§, "Expiatory-deed (*kaffârah*): negligence in religious exercise made up for by additional good deeds;" V6.0.1§, ‡"Minor good-deeds erase cardinal misdeeds (sins)."

For an example of a *kàffàràh*, see "The Man Who Didn't Perform His Prayers," in El-Shamy, *Folktales of Egypt*, No. 19, pp. 123–125.

[36]See Muḥammad ¿Abd-al-Ḥamîd al-Bûshî, "hal yantafi¿u al-mayyitu bi-¿amali al-ḥayy?" (Would the Dead Benefit from the Deeds of the Living). In: *al-Azhar*, Vol. 31 (1959) pp. 707–715; also see Lane, *Modern Egyptians*, p. 525. On the *thawâb* (reward) of *dhìkr*, and whether it benefits the dead, see Muḥammad ¿A. Khalîfah, *Kitâb al-dâr al-barzakhiyyah, min al-mawt 'ilâ al-ba¿th* (The Book of Isthmusian-life: From Death to Resurrection) (Cairo, 1974), pp. 292–294.

Cf. Tale-type 1872§, "*Jokes on Sale of Redemption (Admission to Heaven, Forgiveness)*. Sold by beggars, clerics, undertakers, etc.". Also see Tale-types: 809§, *One Act of Charity Redeems All Sins*; 809,* *Rich Man Allowed To Stay in Heaven* for *Single Deed of Charity*; 0809X§, *One Uncharitable Act Erases All Benevolent Deeds*.

saying (*ḥadîth*) lists seventeen such acts.[37] All of these soul-saving practices rest on the belief that the soul is eternal and that the body of a deceased person will be reunited with its soul at Resurrection Day. (See Section II.E)

When one performs a *ḥasanàh* (a benevolent act), it is often reported that a single freckle-like mole (also called "*ḥasanàh*") appears on one's skin as a permanent sign of having done that act of goodness.[38] Yet, this lasting physical marking of a good deed does not seem to have a folkloric counterpart indicating that a sin (*sàyyi'ah*) has been committed.[39]

The sinful (*el-ḥarâm*), therefore, includes disregarding or disobeying God's commandments as well as the mere thinking of evil thoughts. Acts such as failing to perform the five prayers, lying, stealing, cruelty to animals, needless destruction or

---

[37] See *mùnaggiyât*, in Khalîfah, *al-Dâr al-barzakhiyyah*, pp. 197–200.

Motifs: V4.5§, *"munjiyât/'munaggiyât'* (soul-savers): deeds that serve as 'intercessors' to spare person from hell;" V4.5.1§, ‡"Dutifulness toward parents as intercessor;" V4.5.2§, ‡"Mentioning God as intercessor"; V4.5.3§, ‡"Prayers (ritual) as intercessor;" V4.5.4§, ‡"Ramadan-fasting as intercessor;" V4.5.5§, ‡"Cleansing self of effects of (by bathing) coition as intercessor;" V4.5.6§, ‡"Pilgrimage and *¿umrah* as intercessor(s);" V4.5.7§, ‡"Almsgiving as intercessor;" V4.5.8§, ‡"Kindness to relatives (other than parents) as intercessor;" V4.5.9§, ‡"Preaching the exercise of *ma¿rûf* (benevolence, kindness) and the avoidance of *munkar* (malevolence, the sinful) as intercessor;" V4.5.10§, ‡"Being mild mannered as intercessor;" V4.5.11§, ‡"Fearing God as intercessor;" V4.5.12§, ‡"Deceased offspring (children) as intercessor;" V4.5.12.1§, ‡"Pious (saintly) offspring as intercessor;" V4.5.13§, ‡"Placing one's hope (faith) in God as intercessor;" V4.5.14§, ‡"Shedding a tear due to experiencing awe toward God as intercessor;" V4.5.15§, ‡"Assuming that God is compassionate as intercessor;" V4.5.16§, ‡"Praying on behalf of the prophet as intercessor;" V4.5.17§, ‡"*tashahhud* (uttering the testimony that 'there is no god but God') as intercessor."

Compare the recurrent saint's legend in which ninety-nine murders are forgiven for one more justifiable killing: Tale-types 756C, *The Greater Sinner*. [One more cardinal sin (murder) brings redemption]; and 756C1§, *Forgiveness Indicated by the Blooming of a Dry Rod (Staff)*. For a full text, see "The Killer of Ninety-Nine," in El-Shamy, *Folktales of Egypt*, No. 22, pp. 132–134, 270.

[38] Motif: F545.3.3§, ‡"Mole (*khâl, ḥasanah, shâmah*) on cheek."

It is not clear whether this idea is actually a religious belief or simply a marginal explanation of the physiological phenomenon. This etiological account seems to be based on the linguistic fact that both the act and the object—which is considered a mark of beauty—are both labeled "*ḥasanàh*" (a word that may denote: good, beautiful, fair, etc.): a cleft-chin is referred to as *ṭâbi¿ el-ḥùsn* (mark-of-beauty or handsomeness), a moderately large freckle-like mole, a trait of greater beauty, is called *shâmàh*, and the name "Abu-Shâmàh" or "Abu-esh-Shâmât" designates a handsome person with a *shâmah*. (See, for example, the folk-story of "¿Alâ'-iddîn Abu-Shshâmât," in V. Chauvin, *Bibliographie*, Vol. 5, No. 43.)

The occurrence of the explanation for the *ḥasanàh* seems to be confined to nonreligious contexts, and is addressed mainly to children. Yet, an erotic joke—(a man grants sexual intercourse to a beggar as an act of benevolence, and, consequently, receives a "mole" (*ḥasanah*) on the organ involved in the "giving" act)—suggests some degree of interconnectedness between this seemingly isolated concept-cluster and the broader belief system.

The above-described physical features are to be differentiated from *wàḥmah* ("birthmark") due to craving by a pregnant woman prior to the birth of her child. Although the appearance of such a mark on the body of the newborn is believed to be caused by the mother's desire for a certain food (or a similar object) during pregnancy, no supernatural agent or force is believed to be involved in forming it. (Motif: T570.2.1§, ‡"Appearance of '*waḥmah*' (birth-mark) as result of mother's craving.")

[39] Motif: C910: "Permanent sign of disobedience for breaking tabu."

A parallel belief concerning sinful acts that blacken the face is alluded to in Koran, 3:106, 39:60. Also, a common curse recurrent in daily life begs that God would blacken someone's face. (See Section V.C.2)

spoiling of Earth or natural resources, excessive consumption or wasting of goods (such as water or food), unfair or inconsiderate treatment of another person, lending money with any interest whatsoever (i.e., usury), and unfairly making too much profit in a business deal (i.e., price gouging) are all considered illegitimate or sinful. These and similar acts constitute sins (*'âthâm*, sing.: *'ìthm*) and must not be committed (*tùrtakab*). It is also sinful for a person to intend (*yanwî*) committing a sinful act, even if he fails to carry out his intention. "Acts (deeds) are [judged by God] according to the intentions [behind them]. . . . "[40] If a person becomes aware of harboring or openly considering sinful intentions or fantasies, he should dismiss them by stating *Allâhùmma 'ikhzîk, yâ Sheṭân* ("O Satan, May God dishonor you!"), or the like.[41]

God's support may be acquired through worship and obedience to religious precepts, as prescribed by formal religious teachings, and by strict observance of the required *furûḍ* (sing.: *Fàrḍ*, i.e., sacred ritual services, forms of worship), which are also called "The pillars of Islam." These are five: *shahâdàh* (testimony, i.e, declaring that "There is no god but God/'Allâh, [and that] Mohammad is the messenger of God"), *ṣalâh* (prayers, five times a day—at dawn, midday, mid-afternoon, sunset, and late evening), *zakâh* (alms-tax or tithe, annual giving to the poor of "one-fourth-of-one-tenth" of money and some other specified items of property still in one's name), *ṣiyâm Ramaḍân* (fasting from dawn to sunset during the lunar month of Ramaḍân—abstention from food, drink, smoking, erotic activities, violence, etc.), and *ḥàgg* (i.e., *ḥàjj*, hajj, pilgrimage to Mecca once during one's lifetime, provided one is able to do so physically and financially).[42] Observance of these five "services"—in addition to other commandments (e.g., dutifulness toward parents and neighbors, honesty, truthfulness, etc.)—is the form of worship recognized by formal religious institutions. Going beyond the prescribed amount and recommended intensity of worship earns a person additional *ḥasanât* (credits), and makes one closer to God. In this respect, the mere "mentioning" of God's name, and the recitation of passages from the Koran bring *barakàh* (blessedness, grace, benediction) and drives away *esh-Sheṭân*

---

[40] A Prophet's utterance; see: ¿Abd-al-Raḥmân M. ¿Uthmân, ed., *Sunan al-Tirmidhî* (*Sunan [according to] al-Tirmidhî's*) (Cairo: al-Madanî, 1964), Vol. 3, p. 100. Motif: V301.1§, ‡"Deeds are [judged] according to intent (*niyyât*)."

For the *sharia* stand on the intent behind learning "magic," see Yûsuf al-Digwî, "ta¿allum al-siḥr wa al-ḥukm fîh (The Learning of Magic, and [How it is] Judged [in Islam])." In: *al-Azhar*, Vol. 12, No. 8 (1941), pp. 490–491.

[41] Motifs: V90§, "Miraculous effects of invoking God's attributes (*basmalah, ḥasbanah, ḥawqalah*, etc.);" V90.1§, "Unintentional curse: accidental calling on God's name destroys tyrant (devil etc.)."

For cases where this motif occurs in folk literature, see Hasan El-Shamy, *Motif Index of the Thousand and One Nights* (Bloomington, IN, 2006); henceforth *MITON*.

[42] Motif: V3§, "Required religious services ('pillars,' corners, *arkân, furûḍ*) and fundamental beliefs."

These services recur in all facets of daily life and traditional folk expressions. For example, among most traditionary social groups prayer time is the standard means for setting an appointment, e.g., "before/after Dawn-prayers, or before/after Noon-prayers." Motif: U265.1§, ‡"Prayer times as timing devices (they marks times of day)."

(Satan).[43] A widespread belief pronounces that if a person performs pilgrimage seven times, it becomes "sinful" for hell to touch his body in the hereafter;[44] also an adage states, *en-ni¿àm timna¿ en-niqàm* ("Almsgiving prevents [God's acts of] wrath"). God hears all prayers, curses, and pleas, and answers them, especially those emanating from the weak, the afflicted, the oppressed, the pious, and the parents. A parent's plea, especially of mother's, is believed to be particularly effective even if the parent is a disbeliever.[45] God also sees whatsoever any creature does, and knows whatsoever a creature is thinking or intending to do. There is no place in the universe where an act or occurrence can be concealed from God.[46]

Frequently, going beyond what formal religion requires—especially with reference to alms giving—is offered on a conditional basis. This practice is known as *nàdr* (i.e., *nàdhr*, conditional vow, or pledge made to God or a saint).[47] A person may appeal to God: "O Lord, grant me such and such, and I will do such and such." Typical pledges include performing prayers or fasting, establishing a public service such as a free waterstand or school, giving to the needy (money, food, clothing, etc.), as well as the *dàbḥ* (slaughtering) of a bird or an animal and feeding its meat to the poor. In this latter context, the "slaughtering" is not viewed as a *ḍaḥiyyàh* or *qùrbân* (a sacrifice),[48] it is simply considered a more persuasive form of soliciting God's help through performing the good deed of giving generously to the needy (cf. *ḥasanât*).

---

[43]For an example of the occurrence of the ritual in family context, see El-Shamy, *Folktales of Egypt*, No. 27, especially p. 144. The ritual is practiced by both Muslims and Copts. Also, see Hamed Ammar, *Growing Up in an Egyptian Village: Silwa, Province of Aswan* (London, 1954/1966), p. 73. On *barakàh* (Motif: D1705§), see n. 660.

[44]Motifs: V7§, "Religious exercise (fasting, pilgrimage, prayers, etc.) performed by proxy (surrogate);" V8§, ‡"Divine commandments (as prescribed in formal religious dogma)."

Aḥmad Amîn observes that pilgrimage is a religious service that "usually elevates the status of its owner/doer within the community, more than prayers, fasting, or *zakâh*—giving—do." He also refers to cases of establishing of a *waqf* (endowment) for ten persons to perform the service by proxy. See his *Qâmûs al-¿âdât wa al-taqâlîd wa al-ta¿âbîr al-miṣriyyah* (*Dictionary of Egyptian Customs, Traditions and Expressions*) (Cairo, 1953), p. 155.

For a case of "mental illness" in which the economic consequences of repeated pilgrimage by the family patriarch seems to have played a significant role in generating negative sentiments among other family members, see: App. 13 and 14.

[45]Motifs: M411.1, "Curse by parent;" and P245§, "Parent's prayer (blessing or curse) always answered."

[46]See Tale-type: 827C§, *No Place Secret Enough for Sin*: (God is All-Seeing, Omnipresent) (El-Shamy, *DOTTI*). Motifs: A102.2, "All-seeing god;" A102.5, "Omnipresent god;" T331.4, "No place secret enough for fornication."

This didactic religious narrative is also taught at secular schools.

[47]Motifs: M117.0.1§, "*nadhr/nadr*: conditional vow: pledge to perform certain (good) act if prayer is answered (request is granted);" M209§, "Reminder of unfulfilled (forgotten) vow: recipient must execute own part of pledge (bargain)."

For an example of a vow involving the begetting of a child, see "Louliyya, Daughter of Morgan," in El-Shamy, *Folktales of Egypt*, No. 8, pp. 54–63. Also see n. 344.

[48]A cleric, working as Enno Littmann's assistant and field collector on his behalf, observed that in the *zâr* ritual the slaughtered animal is offered as "*shibh-qurbân*" (i.e., a semi-sacrifice, sacrifice-like) to a possessing spirit (see: Littmann, *Geisterbeschwörungen*, pt. 12, pp. 21, 92; cf. pt. 7, pp. 18–19).

Compare the act of "slaughtering" before the corpse of a deceased person is carried out of the house as

Another form of vowing is to pledge not to do or enjoy specific things until a certain desired event is brought to pass. Examples of such a vow include abstaining from sexual activity until revenge has been accomplished, not shaving one's beard until a lost relative has been found, and the like.

Pledges are also made to saints in order to secure their aid in asking for God's grace. In this context, the pledge would be stated as "If such and such would happen, I would 'make an eve' for the sake (benefit) of God's people" (. . . *lailàh li-'ahl-i-llâh*, i.e., the poor and other needy believers [who follow the saint's path]), or "I would visit the saint's shrine" along with promising to light up candles or give money to be left in the box of pledges (*nudhûr*) at the shrine. A ceremony of this sort would typically include public performances of religious rituals such as recitations from the Koran by a professional "Koran-recitalist" (*mùqrì'*), or holding a *zìkr*-circle (*ḥàlqàt-dhìkr*: group "kinetic-hymns"), and feeding the participants along with the onlookers (see Section I.A.1). Failure to fulfil one's end of the pledge is believed to anger God or the saint and may result in some punishment, especially if the cheated party is a saint (see App. 51). Although the *nàdr* has all the characteristics of a "bargain" between an individual and God or saint, it is not thought of as such. No incident of a *nàdr* made to Satan or a jinni has so far been reported from oral traditions.[49]

God is just. However, God's justice may not always be readily discernible to man (i.e., "The Lord moves in mysterious ways").[50] Thus, seemingly unfair, Divine acts should not be so interpreted, for behind them there are just reasons that may have escaped the comprehension of average men at the time of passing the judgment. Natural and manmade disasters are typically viewed as Divine "trials and tribulations" or justly deserved heavenly punishments or rewards. Similarly, God's justice may not take place at the same moment a sin is committed; a recurrent truism states: *'Allâhu yùmhìl walâ yùhmìl* ("God gives respite, but does not neglect"); another truism—derived from a Prophet's tradition—promises that *az-zânî yùznâ bìh, walàw bi-gidâri dârìh* ("A fornicator will have fornication committed against him—even [if it had to be done] to the wall of his house"); while a third asserts that *al-qâtìl yùqtàl wa-làw bà¿da ḥîn* ("A killer will be killed even after a [long] while").[51] Thus, it is believed that the effects (credit or debit) of good and evil deeds by parents "remain" for their children's benefit or misfortune. A Koranic narrative accounts in part for a hermit

---

reported by Khalîfah, *al-Dâr al-barzakhiyyah*, pp. 327–328; and Blackman, *Fellâhîn*, p. 110. Also cf. n. 307, Section II.C.2a; and App. 11, 23, and 29.

[49]Motif: cf. M210, "Bargain with devil." A unique case in Arab traditions may be cited in this regard: Tale-type AaTh 361, "*Bear-skin.* [bargain with the devil]." However, the text concerned is borrowed from western sources and claimed to be Arabic (see El-Shamy, *DOTTI*).

[50]Motif: V540.0.1§, ‡"Providence (God's wisdom) is behind seemingly apparent injustice (i.e., 'The Lord moves in mysterious ways')."

[51]Motif: Q550.0.3.1§, ‡"'A killer will (inevitably) be killed [i.e., die by violence] even after a [long] while.'"

An Egyptian lawyer accounted for the death of President Anwar El-Sadat by murder in terms of the principle of divine justice. Mindful of the fact that as a young officer El-Sadat was involved in an assassination plot, the lawyer stated the truism: "*al-qâtìl yùqtàl*. . . (A killer will be killed. . . . "). (Told in August 1991. Informant: Mr. ¿.S., elite, convert to Islam.)

(thought to be al-Khiḍr, a benevolent spirit) companion of Moses kills a young boy without apparent justification. Disturbed by this inexplicable act in the Koranic narrative, a reader sought an explanation from al-Azhar, the highest Islamic authority. The answer was as follows: "The approximate interpretation of the story of al-Khiḍr, 'May peace be upon him,' [is that he was] a *mùlhàm*-prophet (i.e., receiving [Divine] revelations from God . . .)." Since the child was predestined to cause great hardship to his pious parents when he grew up, the seemingly unjustifiable murder was actually an act of mercy carried out on God's command.[52]

I.A.1. *zìkr* (Remembrance [of God])

Another means of achieving "closeness to God" (*taqàrrùb 'ilâ 'Allâh*) is a group-ritual labeled *zìkr* (i.e., *dhìkr*), a word that literally means "remembrance" or "mentioning." Formal religion endorses the mere "remembrance" of God as a form of quiet dignified worship and means to finding peace and "bestowing serenity on hearts" (Koran, 3:41, 7:205, 13:28, 18:24, etc.). In daily life, an exhortation "to mention God" (i.e, to utter words of "remembrance"), "to testify to His Oneness," or to "praise His Prophet" are common occurrences that constitute calls for calm in tense situations, or used as an aphorism intended for breaking an uneasy silence. Another appellation for this quiet form of worship is *tàsbîḥ* (exaltation of God), which is often done with a *sìbḥàh* (i.e., *misbaḥàh*, rosary). Due to the fact that God has 99 beautiful praise names, the number of beads in a rosary corresponds to God's praise names: 33, 66, or 99 (i.e., constituting one-third, two-thirds, or all the names, respectively). (See App 1)

However, the label *zìkr* stands more specifically for a special ritual exercised mainly in rural areas and urban folk quarters by members of various Sufi-brotherhoods. In this context, *zìkr* may be described succinctly as the performing of religious kinetic hymns that often climax in altered state of consciousness for performers. When performed casually, it combines melodic chants and vehement body movements labeled as *tàfqîr*. On special occasions, a certain category of indigenous music associated with religious events accompanies the performance. Consequently, this ritual is described by outsiders as "singing" and "dancing."[53] However, since "singing," "music-making," and "dancing" are, generally speaking, negatively valued in formal

---

[52] *al-Azhar*, Vol. 31 (1959–1960), p. 647. The narrative belongs to Tale-type 759, "*God's Justice Vindicated.* (The Angel and the Hermit)—[apparent misdeeds explained]." For a Koranic counterpart, see El-Shamy, *Folktale of Egypt*, No. 12, p. 259. It includes Motifs: A194.2.1§, "'God may give respite, but never neglect;'" V540.0.1§, ‡"Providence (God's wisdom) is behind seemingly apparent injustice (i.e., 'The Lord moves in mysterious ways');" J225.4.1§, "Hermit (al-Khiḍr) kills boy: predestined to cause grief to his pious parents;" J675.0.1§, "Preemptive actions: anticipatory treachery countervailed by treacherous acts;" P794.2.1§, ‡"Murder committed (war waged) to ensure one's own survival;" cf. P528§, ‡"Euthanasia: mercy killing. Person (animal, demon, etc.) put to death so as to relieve his suffering."

Stith Thompson reports the theme from Spanish religious literature under Motif J225.4, "Angel (Jesus) kills man. Done because man is plotting a murder."

[53] For a brief description of the entertaining aspect of *zìkr*, see Amîn, *Qâmûs*, p. 389, where he describes a performance by a troupe of the "Mawlawiyyah" Sufi-brotherhood of "whirling dervishes." Amîn expresses

Islamic dogma, this characterization is rejected by those who partake in the ritual, especially when musical instruments are not used.[54] (See, Section I.A.1, and n. 64)

This special ritual developed at a fairly late stage of the history of formal Islamic worship.[55] It is closely linked to the emergence of *taṣawwùf* (Sufism, Islamic mysticism) and related mystic practices, many of which—it is argued—seem to seek escape the harsh social realities of daily life.[56] As a Sufi ritual, *zìkr* is typically performed by a throng of men led by a lead-chanter (*mùnshid* or *'zàkkîr'/dhakkîr*); notably, the participant in the ritual is never designated as *mughannî* (singer) or *shâ¿ìr* (poet, bard). The lead-chanter does not participate fully in the physical activity, but controls the entire event and the behavior of the participants who echo his words and match the tempo of his chant in terms of speed and intensity of expression.[57] Typically, the ritual begins in a relaxed tempo and is gradually escalated to higher levels of intensity and speed. The verbal component is expressed in the form of a poetic piece referred to as *madîḥ, nashîd,* or *muwashshàḥ* or—simply—as *zìkr* (these labels correspond roughly to the forms, or genres, designated in English as "spirituals," "gospel

---

his own pleasure with the atheistic aspect of the ritual as a dance. Also see, Burton, *Arabian Nights*, Vol. 2, p. 28, note 1. For a detailed description of a "*zikr*" performance on the occasion of the Prophet's Birthday, see Lane, *Modern Egyptians*, pp. 444–453.

[54]The main instruments used are the *nây* (nire, reed flute), *dùffl bàndîr* (bandir drum), *darabùkkàh* (small goblet-shaped drum, usually held under arm). Typically, participants describe the *zìkr*-event as *ḥalqìt zìkr* (*dhìkr*-circle), *ḥaḍrìt zìkr* or simply as *ḥaḍràh* (["remembrance" in God's] Presence). See Lane, *Modern Egyptians*, pp. 355–376.

[55]A notable representative of Islamic mysticism (Sufism) is Ḥusayn ibn-Manṣûr (858–929) nicknamed al-Ḥallâj (the Wool-Carder). He was born in Persia, began a life of wandering and preaching that led him through Persia, Turkestan, India, and Mecca, and finally to Baghdad, where he settled and attracted many disciples.

Al-Ḥallâj conceived God as the essence of love, and the aim of all human life as the union with God by loving God alone and by the close adherence to the divine will. Jesus, according to al-Ḥallâj, achieved this spiritual transformation in the fullest measure. He incarnates the Creator; and impersonates and reveals from within himself the Divine Spirit. Al-Ḥallâj was convinced that he had attained this state of holiness, and that he expressed by his acts the will of God. This conviction he formulated in the word: "*'anâ al-Ḥaqq*" ("I am the Truth," i.e., God).

From the point of view of the secular law Ḥallâj's doctrine involved the negation of all state authority. He was accused of heresy and pantheism but remained true to his faith. He was imprisoned and tried by a religious court and sentenced to death. (Motifs: Q221.3, "Blasphemy punished;" Q221.3, "Blasphemy punished;" Q411.16§, ‡"Death as punishment for blasphemy.")

His martyrdom gave rise to numerous legends and down to this day his alleged tomb in Baghdad is venerated as that of a saint. (See: Stephan and Nandy Ronart, *Concise Encyclopaedia of Arabic Civilization.* 2 vols. Amsterdam, 1966), Vol. 1, p. 199.

For a similar expression in current folk traditions, see App. 42 (Motif: A595.1§, "Arch-saint proclaims himself a divinity: 'I am God'"). (Cf. n. 630, and Sections 4.D.2 and 4.E.)

[56]Hasan El-Shamy, "The Story of El-Sayyid Aḥmad El-Badawî with Faṭma Bint Berry," Part I, "An Introduction." In: *Folklore Forum*, Vol. 10, No. 1 (1976), pp. 1–13, esp. p. 4.

[57]For an application of the process of "matched dependent behavior" in the learning of traditional culture, see Hasan El-Shamy, "Folkloric Behavior: A Theory for the Study of the Dynamics of Traditional Culture." [A case study of the stability and change in the lore of the Egyptian community in Brooklyn, NY.] Doctoral dissertation, Indian University, Bloomington, 1967, p. 74.

songs," "hymns," or "psalms").[58] The spoken part may range in intricacy from the simple *'All-â-â-âh! 'All-â-â-âh! 'All-â-â-âh!* or *'Allâ: ḥayy! 'Allâ: ḥayy! 'Allâ: ḥayy!* ("God [is] Alive! God . . . "), to the highly elaborate epic-like narratives accounting for an arch-saint's miracle-like feats.[59] Notably the words *ràqṣ* (dancing), *ghùnâ* (i.e., *ghinâ'*, singing), *mazzîkàh* (i.e., *mûsîqâ*, music), and their derivatives are not used in folk circles to designate any kinetic or melodic aspect of the ritual. The chants revolve around exalting God, His prophets, and His saints by "mentioning," enumerating, describing, and exalting their attributes and deeds; the chants also speak in highly esoteric mystic terms of such themes as "love," "fusion of one's self with the Beloved God (Prophet)," "beauty," "power," "drinking Divine liquor," mystical "inebriation," "sin," and "forgiveness."[60] *Zìkr*-circles are held at mosques, clubs, private homes, or even at street corners or public squares.

The expressed intent of the person who partakes in the ritual is to place himself directly in the *ḥaḍràh* (Presence) of God. Through swaying the body sidewise, back, and forth while remaining stationary, jolting the head in semicircular movements and generating appropriate mental images, a participant may reach one of the number of levels of being closer to God. These levels correspond to stages of altered consciousness. The highest level, typically referred to as the "deepest" (labeled as *el-ghamîq*, i.e., *al-¿amîq*), toward which the participant strives is a dissociated mental and emotional state known as *'ìngizâb* (i.e., *'ìngidhâb*, the state of being pulled toward God), *tagàllî* (the state of "seeing" [God]), *khadìtuh el-galâlàh* (taken by [God's] Majesty), or *wùṣûl* (arriving at, or reaching [God via a state of dissociation]). In this state, the soul of the person is believed to have freed itself from its human body and, consequently, the *Ḥigâb* (Veil, or Barrier-to-gnosis) between man and God would have been removed or its effects overcome, thus, man (i.e., the soul) experiences being in the immediate presence of God. In such a state, ecstatic and dissociative patterns of intense behavior are emitted, and a state of physical comfort and spiritual serenity (presumed to be unconsciously induced, or nondeliberate) is to follow.[61]

---

[58] Lane notes the similarities between *zìkr*-songs and parts of Solomon's song (see *Modern Egyptians*, pp. 448–449). Also see Earle H. Waugh, *The Munshidîn of Egypt: Their World and Their Song*. (Colombia: University of South Carolina Press, 1989).

[59] For a case in which the poems of an epic-like saint's legend is used as *zìkr*-chants, see El-Shamy, "The Story of El-Sayyid Aḥmad El-Badawi with Fâṭma Bint-Birry: an Introduction," Part I, p. 8.

[60] For a description of this art form see: Martin Hartmann, "Über die Muwashshaḥ genannte Art der Strophengedichte bei den Arabern." In: *Actes der X congres international des Oreintalists*. (Geneva, 1894), Vol. 2, pt. 3, pp. 47–67 (Ktaus reprints—Nendeln-Leichtenstein, 1972); Louis Ibsen al-Faruqi, "Muwashshaḥ: A Vocal Form in Islamic Culture." In: *Ethnomusicology*, Vol. 19, No. 1 (January 1975), pp. 1–29. Also see Lane, *Modern Egyptians*, pp. 171, 446, 506; and Ahmad I. Osman, "In Praise of the Prophet: A Structural Analysis of Sudanese Oral Religious Poetry" (Ph.D. Dissertation, Indiana University, Bloomington, 1990).

[61] See Ibn Khaldûn/Rosenthal, *The Muqddimah*, Vol. 3, pp. 81–83, 87. Hasan El-Shamy, "Mental Health in Traditional Culture: A Study of Preventive and Therapeutic Folk Practices." In: *Psychiatry and the State*, Mark C. Kennedy, ed., *Catalyst*. (Fall, 1972, Trent University Press, Petersborough, Ontario) pp. 13–28.

With reference to a case he had seen, Lane described the physical aspects of this state:

A young junior police officer (*'amîn shurṭah*), who participates regularly in a public *zâr*[62] held in his home village described his own experience with this spiritual activity. At his workstation in Cairo, he always felt unhappy, fatigued, and unmotivated. He sought medical and psychiatric help through governmental services offered by his employer and was examined by a number of medical commissions (*qomsyoanât*), but the treatment he received did not improve his condition. Then, he and a friend from *el-mukhâbrât* (secret-service, intelligence) began to participate in *zìkr* rituals and felt immediate relief. He described his own experiences with a private form of *zìkr* custom-tailored to him as follows:

> Every once in a while, [I would travel to the village and] get ¿Abdu *es-safârtî* (¿Abdu the-flutist [in the village's *zâr/zìkr* troupe]) and tell him, "Give me *ḥittâh* ('a piece'). If you can make me *'àwṣàl* ('reach' [dissociation]), I'll give you a pound [a considerable some]." We would come to my house; he and . . . the drummer would play certain beats. I, and a friend of mine, . . . , would *nifàqqàr* (perform the physical part of *zìkr* by swaying to and fro).[63] When I hear the music, words [of the associated poems] would come to my mind. Then I would weep, and I would laugh [at the same time]! When I weep, I'd weep *bi-ḥurqàh* (intensely, bitterly). Afterwards, I would feel great relief. I also compose Sufi poems. Sometimes I perform *zìkr* to chants of my own composition.
>
> Whenever my work circumstances [in Cairo] permit, I try to return to the village every Tuesday so as to participate in the *zìkr*. Without it, I would be *mit¿àknìn* (feeling cranky); it is *'afyùntî* (lit.: it is my opium, i.e., I am addicted to it, it is my daily [drug]—"fix").[64]

Formal orthodox Islam, while endorsing the principle of *dhìkr* ("remembrance") of God and His names as means of worship, frowns upon this form of *dhìkr*, and

---

"... he fell on the ground, foaming at the mouth, his eyes closed, his limbs convulsed, and his fingers clenched over his thumb. It was an epileptic fit: no one could see it and believe it to be the effect of feigned emotions: it was undoubtedly the result of a high state of religious excitement." (Lane, *Modern Egyptians*, pp. 449–450).

Also compare M. Ḥusayn Haykal's literary portrayal of this general affective state, in his autobiographical novel: *Zaynab: manâzir wa 'akhlâq rîfiyyah* (*Zaynab: Rural Scenes and Manners*), pp. 258–259.

[62] Also labeled "*zìkr*" by some, due to the fact that the two rituals overlap significantly in terms of chants, music, physical activities. The public *zâr* is open to all for a modest fee. (See n. 336)

[63] The ritual dancing in both *zìkr* and *zâr* is typically referred to as *tàfqîr*. (See Section I.A.1)

[64] Informant: Maḥmûd . . . , a young man in his thirties, a graduate of a junior police-officers college, works as *'amîn shurṭah* (policeman, higher in rank than a sergeant and lower than a lieutenant), married, and has one son. Uncharacteristically, he volunteered the information: "I drink," and "smoke [hashish]."

Motifs: F689.1§, ‡"Ecstacy from immersion in music (song);" F689.1.1§, ‡"Madness from listening to marvelous music or song (violent reactions: ecstatic convulsions, clothes slit, self-injury, etc.);" F959.7§, ‡"Music as therapy: marvelous cure (healing) by music;" F956.7.2.1§, ‡"Curative effects of strenuous physical activity (till exhaustion);" V93.1§, "Ecstasy (trance) through religious dancing (*dhikr*, '*zikr*');" V462.8.0.2§, "*shaṭḥ*: philosophical unorthodoxy due to ascetic immersion." (See n. 642)

On the value of the fee, see n. 335.

views it as an indignity to the faith and the individual; consequently, the ritual as it is practiced by Sufis and non-Sufis is condemned as *bìd¿àh mùnkaràh* ("irreverent innovation"/deviant fad) and is, therefore, sinful.[65] Yet, the ritual persists on a very wide scale, and has expanded to include members of the urban middle and upper classes. In the recent past, participants in *zìkr*-circles were mostly peasants, carpenters, mechanics, grocers, vendors, lower clerks and clerics, and others of fairly lower social ranks; currently, participants include government ministers, university professors, engineers, medical doctors, and others of high social rank. Additionally, women *zìkr*-circles emerged and are spreading. In its current expanded format, *zìkr*-circles overlap with the modernized "public" forms of *zâr* rituals, which seek to appease possessing-jinn. However, in the *zìkr* performance, possession is not manifestly presumed to be a factor from which relief is sought. (See Section II.C.2a)

I.B. Cosmology (*el-wùgûd, el-koan*)

The typical image of the universe is that of a flat Earth on which humans and other beings live, the sky in which God, angels, Paradise, and hell exist, and the atmosphere in between Earth and the sky where various planets and stars are located. The atmosphere is also believed to contain some supernatural beings and certain sites relevant to human life.

I.B.1. Creation of *al-qadàr, el-qismàh/en-naṣîb* (Destiny, Kismet): *al-qalàm* (The Pen), *al-làwḥ al-maḥfûẓ* (The Safeguarded Tablet)

Creation and Creator are perceived inseparably. In the beginning there was God (*'Allâh*): creation began when God created *al-Qalàm* (The Pen) and commanded

> "Write!" The Pen asked, "My Lord, what should I write?" God answered, "Write '*b-ìsm-i-llâhi ar-Ràḥmân ar-Raḥîm*' ('In the Name of God the Merciful the Compassionate'), [then] continue with what is *kâ'ìn* ([would be] in existence) till the Day of *Qiyâmàh* (End of the World)."[66]

---

[65]The principle is that "Every *bìd¿àh* (deviant-innovation/fad) is a *ḍalâlàh* (corrupting act), and every *ḍalâlàh* is to Hell." (*al-Azhar*, Vol. 31, p. 377).

Some writers view the ritual as *makrûh* (near-tabu, "disliked," i.e., to be discouraged; see ¿Abd al-Salam Khiḍr al-Shuqayrî, *al-sunan wa al-mubtada¿ât al-muta¿alliqah bi-al-'adhkar wa al-ṣalâwât (Prophet's Traditions and Deviant Fads in Remembrances and Prayers)* (Cairo, 1969).

Thus, orthodox Muslims merely tolerate Sufis and their ways whereas fundamentalists censure them. They are accused of being interested mainly in *¿âlam al-ghaib* (the transcendental world or the unknown) and *¿ilm al-ghaib* (occult knowledge); they are also condemned for rejecting the physical world and of not observing strictly Islamic laws (*sharî¿ah*).

The sufi ritual is regarded with more respect than *zâr*, since those who practice the former base their arguments on Koranic texts inviting "the mentioning of God." (Cf. n. 53)

Gerda Sengers, in her *Women and Demons: Cult Healing in Islamic Egypt* (Leiden: Brill, 2003), concludes that in "the eyes of some Egyptians the *dhikr* is [. . .] a sort of 'middle way.'" (p. 28, note 1). Also see el-Aswad, *Religion and Folk Cosmology* (Westport, CT: Prager, 2002), pp. 125–143.

[66]al-Tha¿labî, *Qiṣaṣ*, p. 10. *Qiyâmah* literally signifies: [the day of] standing up.

The Pen, which is made of light (*nûr*), registered in light *al-Qadàr* (destiny): whatsoever was, whatsoever is, and whatsoever will be, until eternity. *al-màktûb* ("What is written") is registered on *al-Làwḥ al-màḥfûẓ* (The Safeguarded Tablet), which is kept in Heaven. The Tablet is often described as constituted from a single white gem, with a red-ruby frame, its width is equal to the distance between the sky and Earth.[67] Similarly, each individual is believed to have his destiny written on the forehead: "What is written on the forehead will [inevitably] be witnessed by the eye" (i.e., will take place) is a compelling truism that explains and occasionally anticipates the inevitability of fate. From the perspective of the individual, whatsoever occurs takes place only because God willed it to be so; likewise, whatsoever does not occur fails to transpire for the same reason. A central belief asserts that caution cannot prevent the predestined.[68] (See Section V.A.1, God's Power)

Knowledge (gnosis) and deeds were created *a priori* and, therefore, are ever present in the universe in which human beings live; this is a major thesis of Sunni (orthodox) philosophy.[69] Man along with other creatures only enact what God has ordained. Knowledge (gnosis) and the sciences—commonly referred to as "of the light of God" (Koran, 24:35, 24:40, 39:22, and 66:8.)—are granted by God to people, usually, but not necessarily, on the basis of their piety. The same characterization is applied to Jewish and Christian scriptures (e.g., Koran, 5:44 and 5:46) respectively (see Section V.B).

I.B.1a. *al-¿arsh* (The Throne), *al-ḥayyah* (The Viper), *es-samâwât* (The Skies, Heavens), Nûn (The Whale)

After having created destiny, God created *al-¿Arsh* (The Throne) and the rest of the universe (*el-wùgûd, el-koan*) in seven days. God did not rest on the seventh day, for God does not tire; this doctrine apparently constitutes a counter-belief that countervails the Jewish and Christian beliefs concerning the Sabbath.

Literary tradition quotes Ka¿b al-Aḥbâr ("Ka¿b of the Rabbis," d. 652 AD), the Yemenite-born Jewish convert to Islam and a contemporary of Prophet Mohammad,

---

67 Motifs: A604§, "Creation of destiny (*al-qadar, al-'aqdâr*: determination of fate);" A604.1§, "Tablet of destiny (fate);" A604.1.0.1§, ‡"Attributes of the Tablet of destiny (size, substance from which it is made, etc.);" A604.1.1§, ‡"Tablet of destiny 'filled' after fate has been determined at creation;" A604.2§, ‡"The Pen of destiny;" A604.2.0.1§, ‡"Attributes of the Pen of destiny (size, substance from which it is made, etc.);" A604.2.3§, ‡"Pen of destiny writes with light (produces luminous writing)."

On the Tablet of Destiny see: al-Ṭabarî, *Târîkh*, Vol. 1, pp. 32–36; Ibn Kathîr, *al-Bidâyah wa al-nihâyah fî al-târîkh* (*The Beginning and the End in History*). (Cairo [1928 or 1929]), Vol. 1, p. 15; and, al-Tha¿labî, *Qiṣaṣ*, p. 10. Also see J.E. Hanauer, *Folk-lore of the Holy Land: Moslem, Christian and Jewish* (London, 1910), pp. 3–8. Also see App. 3.

68 Motifs: N101.0.2§, ‡"'What is written on the forehead will [inevitably] be witnessed by the eye;'" N101.5.1§, ‡"'Caution does not prevent [(alter)] fate.'"

For folk literary examples that reinforce these beliefs, see El-Shamy, *MITON*.

69 Ignác Goldziher, *Madhâhib al-tafsîr al-'islâmî*. Translation of *Die Richtungen der Islamischen Koranauslegung*, ¿Abd al-Ḥalîm al-Naggâr, tr. ed., (Cairo, 1955), p. 172.

as stating that God's throne is surrounded by a "great *ḥayyàh* (viper) that has seventy thousand wings, each wing has seventy thousand feathers, every feather has seventy thousand sides. . . . " The viper coils around the throne and holds it together.[70] A similar belief in the existence of a serpent, responsible for the stability of the universe and described in a like manner, appears as a god of the underworld in an ancient Egyptian religious system.[71]

Days of the week represent names of the sequence of acts of creation. Most literary accounts written by the learned report Sunday (*al-'aḥàd*), not Saturday (*as-sàbt*), as the first day of Creation. Friday constitutes the day of rest (Sabbath) in the Islamic calendar, while Saturday is the first day of the Islamic week. Creation lasted for six days and was concluded with the creation of Adam ('Âdam) on Friday.[72]

Heavens (*es-samâwât*) were created from steam or vapor, but are typically perceived to be "solid," God "raised the sky" and suspended it without pillars—a feat often cited as testimony to God's power and as an evidence of His existence. According to some accounts, Earth was created on the back of a great whale called *Nûn*; a chain of beings, one on top of the other in a stratified manner, hold the Earth in its place within the universe. In one of these sequences an angel and an ox are reported to support the Earth; in another, an angel, a gem, and water are the agents. Mountains were created to stabilize the Earth on the back of the whale.[73] Another folk conceptualization of this cosmological stratigraphy goes as follows:

> God [. . .] created the whole world on top of water, the water is in a sea, the sea bottom is resting on the horns of an ox, the ox is resting on a rock, the rock is resting on ground, the ground is resting on the back of a whale, the whale is in water, underneath the water there is wind [. . .]
>
> The world is surrounded by an ocean [. . .]. The whale encircles the world [i.e., planet Earth] like a doughnut, except that between his eyes and tail there is about 100 centimeters. He is trying to catch his tail and this [act of the whale chasing its tail] causes the movement of the Earth. If he does catch it, the Day of *Qiyâmàh* [the End of World] would commence.[74]

---

[70]al-Tha¿labî, *Qiṣaṣ*, pp. 9–10.

[71]Motifs: A876, "Midgard Serpent. A serpent surrounds the earth;" B3§, ‡"Viper (*ḥayyah*, female serpent) as animal central to supernatural beliefs (religious records)."

See John Anthony West, *Serpents in the Sky: The High Wisdom of Ancient Egypt* (New York: Harper, 1979), pp. 70–71. Also cf. Ions, *Egyptian Mythology*, p. 26 (plate: "a mythical creature of the Underworld," a hybrid with human head, jackal-headed tail, four human legs and winged sun disk.

[72]al-Ṭabarî, *Târîkh*, Vol. 1, p. 45; al-Tha¿labî, *Qiṣaṣ*, p. 9.

Cf. Motif: A1541.8.1§, ‡"Why Friday is the 'chieftainess' of the days [of the week];" Z122.8§, ‡"Certain day personified."

[73]al-Tha¿labî, *Qiṣaṣ*, p. 3. Cf. App. 4.

[74]Informant: recorded on June 24, 1972 from A. Shâkir, about 45 years old, from el-Bargî, Minya Governorate; he is a retired shaman-*shaikh*, literate, recently wed, works as janitor in Cairo (see App. 11). Literally, the word *Qiyâmah*, means Day-of-Rising (i.e., Resurrection).

Motifs: A651.3.1, "Seven worlds above and below. An angel upholds the Seven Worlds on his shoulders. Under him in turn are: rock, bull, fish [(whale)], vast sea, air, fire, and serpent;" A650.1.1§, ‡"The world is suspended within the universe by the movement of a celestial animal (whale, serpent);" A1082.3.2§,

Both Earth and the sky (heavens) are believed to be stratified into seven layers; these layers are known according to their place within the strata (e.g., second or third sky, second or third earth). Each has its own inhabitants and characteristic physical qualities. Angels inhabit the skies, while humans inhabit the first earth (i.e., the surface). Jinn inhabit all seven layers of earth and the atmosphere as well, but they do not dwell in the skies.

Koran states that the skies and Earth were joined together before God clove them asunder (Koran, 21:30). In a literary para-religious tradition, this statement is taken to mean that Earth and Heaven were one solid mass, but God divided each into seven separate layers.[75] In folk tradition, this is understood to mean that heavens were peeled off or ripped apart from Earth. This belief had its counterpart in ancient Egyptian creation myths, where goddess Nut and her brother Geb [i.e., "Heaven" and "Earth"] formed a single body before they were separated.[76]

I.B.1b. Creation of Time: Establishment of night, day, and related temporal phenomena

God created time: the days, the weeks, the months, and the years. He also created darkness and light, night and day, usually in that order. Among tradition-bound social groups, a day begins with the sunset of the previous day; thus, for example, Friday night, as it is known in western cultures, is known as *lailît es-sàbt* (the eve of Saturday) that would be followed by the daytime of Saturday. Then Saturday ends with the sunset of its day, which signals the beginning of the day known as Sunday. At the beginning of the nineteenth century, Lane reported that at every sunset Egyptians reset their watches at 12:00 (the time believed to be the beginning of a new day).[77] Currently, this practice is not found in Egypt and seems to have vanished completely. On Friday, the last day of creation, God created the stars, the sun, the moon, and the angels. Three hours were still left. In the first of these left hours, God created *al-'à¿mâr* (life spans), that is, who would live and for how long, who would die, as well as when and where death will take place. In the second, He made the *'âfàh* (pestilence) and cast it over things that would benefit man. Although no reason is given for this Divine act, some informants seem to think that it designates "God's plan to make man's life on Earth laborious and that one must expect both the good and

---

"End of world comes when Leviathan (whale) encircling the world catches its tail (its movement stops);" A1002.0.1§, ‡"Doomsday: Day of End of World ('*Qiyâmah*'—to be followed by Resurrection Day, and then Judgment Day)."

For other signs of the End of the World see Sections, I.D, II.D.2a, and n. 122.

[75] al-Tha¿labî, *Qiṣaṣ*, pp. 3–4.

[76] Motif: A625.2.1.1§, ‡"Heaven and earth originally layers of one mass: ripped (peeled) apart by deity."

For comparable cosmological beliefs in ancient Egypt, see Ions, *Egyptian Mythology*, pp. 46–47; and West, *Serpents*, p. 97; cf. pp. 139–140; Motif: A626.1§, ‡"Embrace of twin brother Geb (the earth) and his twin sister Nut (the sky) broken by jealous brother Shu (the atmosphere)."

[77] Lane, *Modern Egyptians*, p. 220.

the evil to occur in *ed-dùnyâ* ('worldly life')," or that the act "says that everything is of God's creation, including sickness, the weevil, and the like."[78] In the third hour, He created Adam and ordered the angels to "prostrate themselves (*yàsgudû*)"[79] before His newest creation. In spite of their earlier expressed apprehensions concerning man's predestined propensity toward violence and sin (Koran, 2:30), all angels complied with the divine order except Eblis, then the chief angel, who refused on the grounds of his physical (racial) superiority to Adam. Eblis was cast out of Paradise at the last hour of the creation week (see Section II.A).

One of God's days is worth one thousand years in the time schema of mortal humans. Certain days and certain times of a day are believed to have special significance. Tradition-bound groups and individuals often plan their activities with reference to these beliefs concerning times of Creation or a closely related event believed to have been characteristic of a sacred person's behavior and social conduct. There are auspicious times and inauspicious times for performing certain acts, especially important ones, such as getting married, building something, or taking a trip.[80] The observation of these limitations is not always strict but some general knowledge of the linkage between a day and an activity is often seen among various levels of social classes. Strict observance is more frequently encountered in the sphere of marriage and related activities. Most such observances are typically traceable to learned religious traditions and characterized as *sunnah* ("Tradition," i.e., things done by the Prophet in such a manner).

An inherent aspect of the creation of things is the creation of names. The name, as is the case with God's names, is believed to be organically integrated with the "thing" that it designates—be it person, plant, animal, inanimate object, or abstract entity such as "blessedness," "goodness," or "evil." Letters of the Arabic alphabet and numerals were also created. Aḥmad al-Bûnî (d. 1225 AD), an authoritative source and teacher of the para-religious ritual of the science of letters, sheds light on the practical aspect of applying the hidden attribute of letters and names toward performing certain tasks with the aid of supernatural beings and forces. He states,

---

[78]Informant: a Cairene man named ¿A.I. Ḥasan, (nicknamed Farûz), grocer and owner of a notions shop in a Cairo suburb. Others from various regions of Egypt expressed the same view.

[79]In other words, *yàsjudû* (Koran, 2:34): to perform the *sajdâh* (prostration, kneeling with knees, palms of hands, and forehead resting on the ground. This event was cited by numerous informants as signifying God's ordaining of man's superiority over all other creatures including angels.

Although this religious ritual is restricted to formal prayers to God, it is also used as an act of paying homage to powerful persons (Motifs: Z179.1.2.1.1§, ‡"Submission: kneeling;" cf. Z179.1.2.1.1.1§, ‡"Submission: kissing ground (before a certain person);" A1213.2§, ‡"God orders angels to prostrate themselves before Adam (as acknowledgment of his privileged status);" A54.3.1.1§, "Eblis refuses to prostrate himself before Adam." (See also n. 167; and El-Shamy, *MITON*.)

[80]Motifs: N127, "The auspicious (lucky) day (days);" N127.3, "Thursday as lucky day;" cf. A789.2.1§, ‡"Certain day controls certain planet."

See El-Shamy, *MITON*; cf. n. 114. Also see al-Bûnî, *Manba¿*, pp. 7–9; Lane, *Modern Egyptians*, pp. 261–262; Amîn, *Qâmûs*, p.189–190; Sayce, *Folk-Lore*, Vol. 11:4, p. 394. Cf. Maspero/El-Shamy, *Ancient Egypt*, Intro. p. lvi.

> Be advised, may the Lord guide me and you, that the letter *'alîf* ["A"] is *'awwalu makhlûq khuliqa min al-ḥurûf* (the first letter-creature that was *created* [of the Alphabet]); and that it [the letter *'alîf*] is [identical form-wise] with the numeral [-creature] "one" [i.e., the number "1"]. . . . [81]

This constitutional concept is central to the belief–practice system, and has far reaching effects on how certain para-religious rituals (e.g., "magic," "incantations," and the like) are perceived and applied in various situations in actual social life; it also underlines the social attitudes toward "the word," spoken or written (see Section VIII.C.2).

I.B.2. Paradise, Hell, the Isthmus, and the Straight-Path

Paradise and hell are perceived as two infinite places existing in *es-samâ* (the sky). Although some early literary reports placed hell "in" the seventh earth,[82] the established recurrent perception is that hell is in the sky and is spanned by a "Straight-path" leading to Paradise.[83] In the hereafter, both Paradise and Hell will be populated by humans and jinn.[84]

El-gànnàh (Paradise) is typically characterized as the place of *¿àdn* (Eden), *khùld* (eternal-life), *na¿îm* (luxuriousness), etcetera; it is thought of as a garden with fruit trees and ponds.[85] A contemporary religious folk ballad about the deeds of a saint portrays Paradise simply and in the same experiential terms of daily life in the village: a walled in "*ghaiṭ*" (cultivated field, farm), or *gnainâh* (i.e., *junáynáh*, grove, lit.: little paradise), whose fruit-laden trees are out of the immediate reach of the outsider.[86] Paradise is a place of absolute sinlessness, satisfaction, comfort, bliss, and peace. Special categories of human-like beings, typically thought of by laymen as minor angels or angel-like, will serve the inhabitants of Paradise. These include "*wìldân mukhàlladûn*"

---

[81] al-Bûnî, *Shams*, pt. 4, p. 1, emphasis added. In Arabic script, the letter *'alîf* (A) and the numeral 1 look identical (as in the case of the numeral 1 and the letter l in English).

See "God's Language and Man's Parlance: Arabic Language and the Stratification of Narrative Traditions," in El-Shamy, "Oral Traditional Tales and the *Thousand Nights and a Night*: The Demographic Factor," pp. 65–67. Also see J.R.T.M. Peters, *God's Created Speech* (Leiden, the Netherlands, 1976); and Anwar G. Chejne, *The Arabic Language: Its Role in History* (Minneapolis, MN, 1969).

[82] In his *Qiṣaṣ* (p. 5), al-Tha¿labî, an eleventh century author, cited an earlier source as stating: "Hell, today, is in the lowest earth; [but when] tomorrow comes, God may place [it] wherever He wills."

Motifs: A671.0.1.1.3§, "Hell is located in the seventh earth;" cf. A671.0.1.1.1§, "Hell is located in the sky."

[83] For a humorous example reflecting this worldview concerning Hell being in the sky, see the joke titled "Foreigner and Citizen," in El-Shamy, *Folktales of Egypt*, No. 65, pp. 229–230. Also see App. 6 and 42.

[84] See: Sayyid ¿A. Ḥusayn, *al-Ginn (Jinn)* (Cairo: al-Ḥalabî, n.d.) pp. 77–80.

[85] Koran, 2:25, 3:15, 3:195, 4:13, 85:11, etc. Similarly, Koran (18:32) refers to two groves as "two paradises." See also Lane, *Modern Egyptians*, p. 66 n. 2.

[86] For an example reflecting this view of Paradise, see App. 6. Cf. Paradise in ancient Egypt; see E.A. Wallis Budge, *Egyptian Ideas of Future Life* (New York, 1976).

(boys [granted] eternal life/youth),[87] and *ḥûrìyyât* (houris, sing.: *ḥûrìyyàh*: a female counterpart to the *wîldân*).[88] The *wìldân* will go around serving food and drink to the human inhabitants of Paradise, in a manner that evokes the image of waiters in a restaurant in modern terrestrial living; the *ḥûrìyyât* will provide companionship, presumably to men. Some literary sources interpret these basic concepts to include amplifications of "sensual pleasures," such as "seventy-two wives" for each man.[89] However, other informal accounts of creation tend to describe a houri's anatomy in a manner that would preclude any possibility of association with sexual desires or feminine functions.[90] Additionally, the word *Ḥûrìyyàh* (sing.: *Ḥûrìyyât*) is used as a female's given name at all levels of society; parents would be disinclined to name

---

[87]Koran 56:17. In his English rendition of *The Glorious Kur'an*, A.Y. Ali translates the name of this category of minor angels as: "Youths of perpetual (freshness)." Other literary sources describe them as neither angels nor jinn nor human.

Motifs: F499.9.1§, ‡"Serving-boys of Paradise (wildân);" F499.9.1.1§, ‡"Beardless waiters of Paradise are for serving foods and drinks only." See: Burton V 161–162 (El-Shamy, *MITON*).

[88]Koran (52:20, 44:54, 56:22–23) labels these beings "*ḥûr ¿în*." The name signifies a person with eyes that combine stark blackness on bright whiteness (Motif: F499.2, "Nymphs of Paradise (houris [*ḥûriyyât*]))." See App. 6.

In some oral traditions in Egypt, these celestial beings are occasionally labelled *banât el-ḥûr*, especially in a children's rhyme that begs them to release the moon during a lunar eclipse (*khusûf al-Qamar*); this appellation tends to confuse them with *banât el-bàḥr* (sea-nymphs/mermaids).

Motifs: A737.1.2§, ‡"Eclipse of moon due capture (imprisonment) by supernatural being;" A737.1.2.1§, ‡"Houris (nymphs of Paradise) capture moon, thus causing eclipse."

[89]For such a description, see Lane, *Modern Egyptians*, pp. 67–68.

However, It may be stated here that as of yet (1973, 1991, 1997, 2001), the present writer has not come across an oral folk tradition in which Paradise is perceived or described in such carnal terms. This total absence of excessive eroticism with reference to Paradise also applies to the genre of the "urban joke." Typically, joke-tellers recognize no theme or character as "tabu" lying outside the "joking" realm, or beyond their own all-encompassing "joking" reach. Clearly, within the folk belief–practice system, Paradise and satyriasis/nymphomania are not interconnected.

In his *Religion and Folk Cosmology*, el-Aswad reports the belief that *hûrîs* are created of light; in this respect they are like angels (see p. 74). For a debate in literary lore on the functions of the "wuldân," see Burton, Vol. 5, pp. 156, 160 (see also El-Shamy, *MITON*).

[90]al-Tha¿labî, *Qiṣaṣ*, pp. 26–27. This myth may be summarized as follows:

> God made Adam and Eve descend to Earth, and formed a union between the two of them. A daughter was born to Adam [by Eve]; he named her ¿Unâq [(Lilith)]. She became outrageously wicked and was the first human to commit wicked-injustice (*bághy*) on Earth. God set against her [a being] that killed her. Subsequently, Adam had borne to him Cain, and after him Abel was born.
>
> When Cain reached puberty, God caused the surfacing of a female-jinni named ¿Imâlah[??], who was of the [Earth]-jinn; she assumed the shape of a human female. God created for her a womb, and inspired a revelation to Adam: 'Marry her to Cain!' So Adam married her to him. However, when Abel reached puberty, God sent down [from Paradise] a Houri-maiden in the image of a human-female, and created for her a womb; her name was Tarkah[??]. When Abel looked at her admiringly, God inspired a revelation to Adam: 'Marry her to Abel!' So, he married her to him.
>
> [Hurt,] Cain complained and wondered, "O father. Am I not older than my brother, and more deserving than he of what you have done for him!?"
>
> Adam replied, "Son, *faḍl* (boon) is in God's Hand. He bestows it on whomsoever he chooses!"
>
> Abel replied, "No! You favored Abel over me, in accordance with your own whim (*hawâk*)!"

their daughters after a supernatural being that functions exclusively as a sex object for males.

Things that a person did not attain in the worldly life—because of disability, lack of financial means, or abstinence due to obedience to religious prohibitions—can be instantly realized in Paradise by the mere thinking of them. This belief in receiving compensation in the hereafter from worldly suffering and deprivation has been associated with strong fatalistic attitudes toward acquisition of material possessions and secular power. When comparing their own poor lot in life with that of the more wealthy, especially of non-Moslems, numerous groups and individuals state: "The here-and-now belongs to them; the hereafter belongs to us." (Other narrative accounts—presumably of a humorous nature—cite error, or dishonesty on the part of a non-human messenger between God and man; the messenger assigns the wrong lot to Muslims).[91]

By contrast, *en-Nâr* (Fire, or *Guhànnàm*, i.e., *Jahannàm*, hell)[92] is perceived as an infinite, bottomless fire pit; it is a place of absolute agony, sorrow, and torture in which life for those who have committed certain cardinal sins may be eternal (or beyond eternal). Hell is divided into strata, and is tended by a special category of angels labeled *khazanàh* (keepers, i.e., hell's angels; Koran, 39:71 and 67:8); they are also called *zabâniyàh* or *malâ'ikat al-¿adhâb* (angels-of-torture).[93] These angels will administer punishments to sinners. The "doors of Hell" (*'àbwâb Guhànnàm*) are guarded by Mâlik, a cardinal angel mentioned in this context mainly in literary sources.[94]

Thus sibling rivalries began.

Designated as new Tale-type 758C§, *Origin of Sibling Rivalry*; conflict between siblings of the same sex began when one was favored over the other. (See El-Shamy, *DOTTI*)

Motifs: A1228§, ‡"Man remodeled to provide for terrestrial (earthly) life needs;" A1228.1§, ‡"Adam remodeled: body orifices (for urination and defecation) added;" A1278.1.2§, ‡"Remodeled angel: given physical and emotional attributes suited for life as member of mankind (on Earth);" A1278.1.2.1§, ‡"Remodeled houri: given physical and emotional attributes of human female;" A1278.1.2.1.1§, ‡"Abel given remodeled houri (from paradise) as wife—(favoring treatment)."

91 Motif: A1689.11.3§, "Disbelievers more powerful (rich) than believers since former have the here-and-now, but not the hereafter." Cf. new Tale-type: 774M2§, *Why One Group (Nation) Is Poor while Another Is Rich: Bad or Careless Messenger.*

It is not clear whether this mythological folk account reported mostly from North Africa is taken seriously, or told humorously. (See: *DOTTI*)

92 Other appellations for Hell circulate only within formal religious literature; these include: "ḥùṭamàh," "sa¿îr," "qàswaràh," and "saqàr" (Koran, 104:5, 54:48, 74:26). See n. 106. With reference to the latter name, cf. the ancient Egyptian "Seker," the necropolis deity of Memphis; see: Ions, *Egyptian Mythology*, p. 29, 116.

93 Koran, 96:18. Motif: A671.1.5§, "*zabâniyah*: Hell's angels; they administer punishments (torture)."

Khalîfah (*al-Dâr al-barzakhiyyah*, pp. 197, 198) cites a Prophet's tradition that speaks of "Angels-of-torture," (No. 3), and *zabâniyàh* (No. 9). For examples of the occurrence of these beings in jocular context, see "Foreigner and Citizen," in El-Shamy, *Folktales of Egypt*, No. 65; see also *DOTTI*, Tale-type 1872§, "*Jokes on Sale of Redemption (Admission to Heaven, Forgiveness)*. Sold by beggars, clerics, undertakers, etc." (See App. 10)

94 Motif: A671.1.1§, "Archangel Mâlik: porter (guardian) of hell."

This description of Hell is very similar to its ancient Egyptian counterpart labeled "Taut." See Budge,

Koran speaks repeatedly of *a* "Straight-path" (*ṣirâṭ mùstaqîm*) euphemistically to signify a righteous, correct, or clearly delineated manner of appropriate conduct in the here-and-now that would presumably earn those who follow it admission to Paradise in the hereafter. Being on a Straight-path is contrasted to going aimlessly or into uncharted wilderness.[95] Yet, nowhere among these Koranic occurrences is there a reference to the concept of the Straight-path as a soul bridge or a means for trial by ordeal. This abstract concept of following a well-defined path seems to have acquired concrete dimensions in the broader religious systems. A narrow one-way path also known as *aṣ-ṣirâṭ al-mùsatqîm* (the Straight-path) is believed to span over hell and lead to Paradise. The Path is often reported to be "sharper than a razor's edge and narrower than a hair." Sinners will fail to maintain their balance while crossing the Straight-path and thus will fall into hell.[96] A closely related concept in ancient Egyptian beliefs is that of "the terrifying stretch of country between the land of the living and the kingdom of the dead,"[97] which the deceased had to cross before reaching the hereafter—so to speak—and undergoing the subsequent assessment ("weighing") of the worth of his/her deeds in life. In contemporary daily social life the Straight-path does not seem to occur overtly as a major concern of individuals or groups. Yet, it is frequently cited as a proverbial phrase with reference to disciplining the wayward in a severe manner to the extent that he "will be made to [behave as if] walking on Straight-path (*al-ṣirâṭ al-mustaqîm*)," with absolutely no room for even the most minute deviation. An equivalent of this proverbial utterance that is reflective of a female's homemaking duties is "to make someone walk on dough without disturbing its surface."

A concept paralleling that of the Straight-path as an instrument for judging innocence or guilt, and consequently worthiness for admission into Paradise or deserving

Egyptian Heaven and Hell, Vol. III, p. 159; also see "The Story of Khamuas and his Son" in Budge's *Romances*, No. A: XI, p. 173. Cf. El-Shamy, *Folktales of Egypt*, pp. 248–249.

[95]It is in this allegorical sense that Koran mentions the *ṣirât* forty-five times; see Koran, 1:6–7; 2:142, 213; 3:51, 101, 5:16, etc.

[96]Lane, *Modern Egyptians*, p. 66.

Motifs: H220, "Ordeals. Guilt or innocence thus established;" A661.0.5.2§, "Soul-path (*aṣ-ṣirâṭ al-mustaqîm*): sharper than razor's edge, thinner than a hair;" A661.0.5.2.1§, "‡Soul-path spans over Hell and leads to Paradise: sinners will fall off before reaching Paradise;" A661.0.5.2.2§, ‡"Traversing the Soul-path (*ṣirâṭ*) requires 3000 years descending, 1000 years ascending, and 1000 years of leveled travel."

Similar trials by ordeal recur in oral tradition of the region.

cf. Tale-type AaTh 136A*, "*Confession of Animals*. [The unjust (thieving) partner swears falsely: fails trial]." (See "The Biyera Well," in El-Shamy, *Folktales of Egypt*, No. 51, pp. 201–203, 293–296. Also cf. Motif H221.2.3§, ‡"Ordeal by hot-iron placed on tongue of accused (*'al-bashʿah'*).")

[97]See Ions, *Egyptian Mythology*, 135. This concept is comparable to the theme of Motif A661.0.5.1, "Soul-bridge: easy for righteous to cross, more difficult for others."

It is worth noting here that ancient Egyptian religious beliefs, typically mislabelled "mythology," are not taken into account when assessing similarities between early Islam and other belief systems of the region. Burton (*Arabian Nights* Vol. 10, p. 128) concludes that "the Bridge over the Great Depth" is "either Talmudic or Iranian."

punishment in hell, is that of the weighing of deeds in *al-mîzân* (the Balance Scale).[98] God has set up the Balance simultaneously with His raising of the sky. In daily life, the Day of Judgment is also referred to as the "Day the Balance will be set up." This traditional utterance is a truism that carries the same admonition as "Fear God!" and is applied in situations where it is thought that injustice is being committed (Koran, 55:7). Typically, the Scale is perceived as similar to the traditional common instrument used in trade in traditional marketplaces for weighing groceries, meats, or the like: with two "palms" (*kàffatân*, i.e., shallow dishes or pans)—each as broad as a layer of heaven—and a *lisân* (lit.: tongue, i.e., needle-indicator); the pan in which good deeds are placed is constituted of light, the other in which sinful acts are placed is of darkness; the first side is suspended over Paradise while the second is over Hell. On Judgment Day, archangel Gabriel will be in charge of holding the handle of the Balance, while archangel Mîkâ'îl will stand by as *'amîn* (trustee, supervisor, observer) and the "weighing" of a creature's deeds would begin. God's Messengers, prophets, founders of schools of sharia (*sharî¿àh*, Islamic law, religious jurisprudence), and—according to some views—heads of Sufi-brotherhoods, will be in the forefront, each heading his nation or followers and serving as an observer, intercessor, or advocate (see Section III.B.3a). During Judgment (*ḥisâb*, lit.: account settling), a human's good deeds will be weighed against the sinful ones. Sufficient good deeds ("heavy," weighty) will tip down the scales in favor of the individual being judged; conversely, insufficient good deeds ("light") will tip up the scales against the person.[99] This manner of evaluation in the hereafter reflects the general perception of receiving a good or fair deal in the marketplace—where it is still until nowadays expected that the scales should tip down (*yiṭobb*) in the buyer's favor. In principle, the same procedure applies to jinn; yet, no actual accounts of such a final judgment for this category (or species) of creatures have been reported from traditionary folk groups.

The scales as perceived in Islamic accounts are virtually identical with their ancient Egyptian counterpart as depicted in the "Hall of the Two Truths" or "Hall of Double [i.e., Dual] Justice" where the heart of the deceased was weighed. A number of deities stood by the scales, including Anubis who observed to see if the pans of the scales were balanced and to make sure that "the heart used no trickery."[100] However, in the ancient Osirian system, the heart (i.e., deeds) of a sinless person would be "light" when weighed while that of a sinner would be "heavy." Still, this viewpoint is compatible with its contemporary counterpart.

During Judgment, the record of deeds for each creature will be handed over to its owner; some accounts add that the deeds *tùgassàm* (i.e., are to be rendered into

[98]Motif: A464.5§, "'The balance' of Judgment Day: for weighing religious exercise (soul, heart, etc.)." See also n. 100.

[99]Koran, 7:8–9, 23:102–103, 101:6–8. See Lane, *Modern Egyptians*, p. 66. For description of the Balance, see al-¿Idwî, *Mashâriq*, pp. 264–265.

[100]Ions, *Egyptian Mythology*, pp. 108, 134–136. Cf. n. 98, above. With reference to the role of Anubis in the ritual of accompanying the deceased to the "nether-world," and the weighing of the heart, E.A.W. Budge has observed: "The belief that this god acted in this capacity survived for some centuries after Christ." See *The Mummy*. (New York, 1974) p. 279.

corporal or tangible form) before they are shown to the person being judged.[101] "Those who are given their record in their right hand . . . " will rejoice (Koran, 17:71, 69:19, and 84:7), but, "Those who are given their record in the left hand . . . " will wail over their negligence and sins during their lifetime (Koran, 69:25).[102] A comparable concept characterized ancient Egyptian traditions of judging the dead; according to that concept the pure hearted were depicted with two right hands so that they may "receive" more rewards.[103] During the Day of Judgment, every person will be in utter absorption with his/her very own affairs, and will "run away" from own parents, spouse, children, and friends (Koran, 80:34). Furthermore, the soul and the body will act independently of each other. Consequently, one's own limbs will testify as to the exact nature of the deeds done during one's life-time and the intent behind them (Koran, 24:24); also an "adversarial relations between the soul and the body" (a *takhâṣum ar-roaḥ wa al-gasàd*) may occur, and each would accuse the other as to which of the two was responsible for instigating or executing the commission of a sinful act.[104]

Once in Paradise, a person will live in it eternally. By contrast, the length of a person's term in hell will depend on the seriousness of the sins committed by that person. For example, *kùfr* (disbelief, being an infidel), *shìrk* (associationsim, polytheism, idolatry), and premeditated murder are punishable by endless life in hell. Deliberate implacable sinners will be sent to hell *ḥàdf* (i.e., hurled or flung immediately into hell with little or no deliberation); meanwhile lesser sins will require shorter term of punishment by fire.

The community of the inhabitants of Paradise and that of hell are characteristically presented as stratified. In Paradise, an individual will occupy a higher or lower *daragàh* (i.e., *darajàh*, stratum, or level) according to the extent of that person's religiosity, purity, and sufferings in worldly life. The highest strata are those closest to God and afford the beholder a vantage point that would allow for seeing "His

---

[101] al-¿Idwî, *Mashâriq*, pp. 264–265. Motif: Z129§, "Religious exercise personified: 'benefit of' alms giving, prayers, fasting, pilgrimage, etc."

[102] Motif: cf. D1708.1§, ‡"Use of right side blessed."

[103] West, *Serpents*, p. 20; see also p. 146, note "A." Also, Raymond Faulkner states that

> the concept of the left hand being unclean or bad was captured in ancient Egypt in tomb and temple carvings and inscriptions. The artists endeavored to reproduce all deities, pharaohs, and subjects with two right hands. This would ensure that they possessed clean hands with which to present or receive objects such as the book of their lives, offerings, and gifts. (*The Egyptian Book of the Dead: The Book of Going Forth by Day*. plates 2, 3. San Francisco, CA: Chronicle Books, 1998)

Also, cf. el-Aswad, *Religion and Folk Cosmology*, p. 9 (after Dumont 1986 277, 228, 252).

[104] Khalîfah, *al-Dâr al-barzakhiyyah*, p. 241.

Motifs: Z129.9§, ‡"Deeds (acts) personified—miscellaneous;" cf. F1042§, "Mania: compulsion—uncontrollable (involuntary) behavior."

On the concepts of "compulsion," and "mania" in a folkloric contexts, see Tale-type 1366§, *Groom Traumatized by his Maniac Bride* (insane wife terrorizes husband). (See: El-Shamy, *DOTTI*.) Also see "The Man Who Didn't Perform His Prayers," in El-Shamy, *Folktales of Egypt*, No. 19, p. 123.

Face"—(a parallel ancient Egyptian belief is being close to Osiris in the afterlife).[105] The occupants of these favored ranks are God's messengers (apostles), prophets, martyrs, and the sinless and pure hearted. Meanwhile, the lowest *daràk* (level of a pit) in hell, presumed to be the hottest and most torturous (Koran, 5:145), will be occupied by *al-munâfiqûn* ([religious] hypocrites) and disbelievers; while murderers, thieves, usurers, liars, the wicked, etc. will be placed on various levels depending on the severity of their sins.[106]

In daily life, the typical believer is constantly concerned with whether an act is legitimate or sinful and whether the act will lead to Paradise or to hell. Thus, Paradise and hell represent a system of delayed rewards and punishments in a religious behavioristic formula. In this formula, the motivation (a person's needs and God's commandments) and the responses (the person's actions) are closely timed; the greatest effect (reward or punishment) is deferred until the hereafter. Lesser rewards or punishments are also received in worldly life. Fortunate and unfortunate occurrences are typically interpreted as being rewards or punishments from God for an act done earlier by an individual or group.[107] It is a common practice to console a person whose right to a reward for an accomplishment in worldly life cannot be met by stating "God will make it up for you in the hereafter," or "May He *'yiqà¿¿adùh làk fì 'awlâdàk'* ('spare it [in your behalf]' and bestow it on your children)." By the same token, a person who commits an offense but his guilt cannot be proven will be warned: "May He *'yiṭàlla¿uh fì'* ('take it out on') your children."

[105]al-¿Idwî, *Mashâriq*, pp. 301–303.

Motif: A698.6.1.1§, ‡"The highest strata in paradise are those closest to God."

For ancient Egyptian counterpart of paradise, see: Budge, *Romances*, 175; Maspero/El-Shamy, *Ancient Egypt*, No. 8, pp. 150–151; and El-Shamy, *Folktales of Egypt*, pp. 259–260.

[106]al-Kisâ'î, *Qiṣaṣ*, pp. 18–19; al-Tha¿labî, *Qiṣaṣ*, pp. 4–5, 32.

Motifs: A671.0.2, ‡"Creation of hell;" A671.0.5, "Size and arrangements of hell;" A671.0.5.1§, "Hell has seven doors (gates);" A671.2.4.11, ‡"Fiery columns in hell;" A671.2.4.14§, "Seven strata of hell's fires."

al-Kisâ'î, *Qiṣaṣ* (pp. 18–19), labels these strata as follows: The first is *Jahannam*; the second is *Laẓâ*; the third is *Ḥuṭamah*; the fourth is *Sa¿îr*; the fifth is *Saqàr*; the sixth is *Jaḥîm*; the seventh is *Hâwiyah*.

In his *Qiṣaṣ* (pp. 4–5), al-Tha¿labî states that the sixth contains the compartments ("divans") for hell-bound people, their [sinful] deeds, and their wicked souls. Its name is *sijjîn* [. . .].

Cf. Motif: Z127, "Sin personified." See also n. 92.

[107]Motif: Q172.0.3§, ‡Reward in the hereafter (Heaven) preferred to that in the here-and-now." (See: El-Shamy, *DOTTI*, and *MITON*)

In his explication of the "Fraction of Decision" principle, David K. Berlo concluded by a reassessment of the validity of the maxim: "'it is more blessed to give than to receive,'" stating, ". . . man does not behave on this principle unless he gets more from the giving than he does from receiving." See D.K. Berlo, *The Process of Communication* (New York, 1961), pp. 98–99.

The maxim complies with the general rule of the effect of reward, the degree of giving being affected by the greatness of the reward to be gained. If, for example, the state of grace falls to individuals who have lived righteously, an individual's giving is not giving at all, but merely the discarding of minor rewards in expectation of the major reward—eternal joy in the afterlife. Thus, an individual's "giving" is actually an exchange of rewards, determined by the type of reward that he values most highly. See El-Shamy, "Folkloric Behavior," p. 100.

I.C. Heavenly Bodies

God subjugated (*sàkhkhara*, subordinated) all of his creations to man; accordingly, man is to use the rest of God's creatures but only as God has ordained. The sun and the moon, the night and the day, are to be exploited by humans. Originally, the sun and the moon—according to some beliefs—were equal in light and heat intensity (or that the moon had "three times the heat of the sun").[108] They shine over Earth from behind a "sea" [of water] suspended between the sky and Earth; that body of water reduces the intensity of their light and heat. Some literary sources state that in order to enable people to run their economic, religious, and legal affairs, God ordered archangel Gabriel (Jibrâ'îl, Gibrîl) to pass his wing over the surface of the moon, thus dimming it.[109] The sun—which is invariably perceived as feminine—derives her light from God's Throne, while the moon, which is perceived as masculine, derives his from God's Chair. Another folk account with limited frequency for this natural fact attributes the cause to sibling conflict. It states that the sun and the moon are sister and brother; they had a fight and the sun struck the moon and put out one of his eyes, thus dimming his lights.[110] According to written sources, both the sun and the moon are harnessed to a great wheel with three hundred and sixty notches, each representing a day. Each notch is assigned to an angel to pull.[111] A match to this belief is found in ancient Egyptian cosmology where a scarab and "the gods of hours of the night" performed the task of rolling the sun along its course.[112]

Every dawn, the sun, and the moon receive God's command to rise from the east. At the time predestined to be the Day of End of World, they will be ordered to rise from the west. This reversal of the sun's course is one of five major signs heralding the End of World. (See n. 122)

Many of the beliefs about cosmology and heavenly bodies as cited are not well known in systemic or holistic manner in folk circles. Consequently, these beliefs appear only separately mostly as cognitive isolates, and do not seem to play central roles in daily life. Fuller knowledge of them is typically derived from written para-religious sources, and is maintained and circulated by the lower-clergy.

Each human being has a corresponding star, which falls to Earth at his death; this belief is a key doctrine of astrology. Also, stars are believed to serve as sentries to prevent

---

[108] al-Thaȥlabî, *Qiṣaṣ*, p. 11.

It is interesting to observe that al-Thaȥlabî uses the word *ḍàw'* (light) to denote heat or fire and the word *nûr* to denote ("light"). Such usage of the word *ḥàw'* as denoting heat/fire rather than "light" is characteristic of the Arabic dialects of the Gulf region of the Arabian Peninsula, but does not appear in the Nile Valley culture area. Cf. n. 473.

[109] al-Thaȥlabî, *Qiṣaṣ*, p. 11. Motif: A755.8.1§, "Creation of night by making moon dim: Archangel Gabriel wipes moon with his wing."

[110] Motif: A755.8.2§, "Sun puts out an eye of her brother moon: made dim."

See A.Ḥ. Ṣâliḥ, "al-'Âthâr al-ȥulwiyyah fî al-muȥtaqdât al-ȥarabiyyah (Upper [Celestial, solar] survivals in Arabic Beliefs)." In: *Al-Turâth*, Vol. 3, Nos. 5–6 (1970), p. 42.

[111] Motif: A726.0.1§, ‡"Sun drawn (pulled) across sky by supernatural beings (angels, deities, etc.)." See al-Ṭabarî, *Târîkh*, Vol. 1, p. 66; and al-Thaȥlabî, *Qiṣaṣ*, pp. 11–12.

[112] Motif: A726.3.1§, ‡"Sun drawn across sky seated on wheel." See Ions, *Egyptian Mythology*, p. 26; also see plate p. 27.

Satan from eavesdropping on angels in heaven. A comet or meteorite is ordinarily viewed as a fallen star; it may signify the death of a person (usually a notable), a stellar attack on an eavesdropping Satan,[113] or a foretelling of other significant happenings. In all instances the doors of Heaven (*'àbwâb es-samâ*) would be opened and the time is perfect for a prayer to be heard and answered (i.e., "wishing on a shooting star"). Knowledge of stars and planets in their relationships to one another, on the one hand, and to human affairs, on the other, is called *tangîm* or *¿ìlm en-nùgûm* (astrology).[114] Although references to stars and planets may occur in the course of other practices dealing with the supernatural, astrology is mostly a specialized traditional profession, with little circulation among laymen in folk communities.

I.D. *el-'Arḍ* (Earth)

el-'Arḍ (the planet Earth) is believed to be composed of four quarters.[115] Only one is inhabited; the other three quarters are the Empty (*khâlî*), the Ruined (*kharâb*), and the Dark (*ẓalâm*). The Ruined quarter is inhabited by *qùṭb* (axis, or arch-saint) er-Rifâ¿î. It is also thought of as the breeding ground for reptiles; axis er-Rifâ¿î has control over them and so do his followers of the Sufi-brotherhood called "er-Rifâ¿iyyàh" many of whom are believed to be snake charmers.[116]

Two marvels are to be found in the Dark quarter: *¿ain el-ḥayâh* (the fountain of life, i.e., "Fountain of Youth"), and precious stones. Both are of little recurrence in folk traditions except in association with the Alexander the Dual-horned legend cycle and its companion account about the origin of precious stones.[117] Available data indicate that the quadruple division of the surface of Earth seems to have its widest circulation in Egypt and to be little known in adjacent countries.

Earth is surrounded by a chain of mountains called Qâf Mountains; on the surface of Earth, these mountains resemble "blood veins on a human's arm." When God

---

[113] Motifs: A157.8§, ‡"Shooting star (*shahâb*) as god's weapon;" A157.8.1§, ‡"Shooting star destroys satan (devil, demon) flying near (spying on) heavens."

See Lane, *Modern Egyptians*, p. 223; and S. Ḥusayn, *al-Ginn*, p. 31.

[114] See Lane, *Modern Egyptians*, p. 264; and Amîn, *Qâmûs*, p. 84, pp. 275–276.

Motifs: A789.2.1§, ‡"Certain day controls certain planet;" A789.2.1.1§, ‡"Sun controlled ('owned') by Sunday);" A785§, ‡"'Residence' (location) of major planets within the seven skies;" A785.1§, ‡"Saturn (Zuḥal) resides in the Seventh Sky;" A785.2§, ‡"Jupiter (al-Mushtarî/Mushturâ) resides in the Sixth Sky;" A785.3§, ‡"Mars (al-Marrîkh/Mirrîkh) resides in the Fifth Sky;" A785.4§, ‡"Sun (al-Shams) resides in the Fourth Sky;" A785.5§, ‡"Venus (al-Zahrah) resides in the Third Sky;" A785.6§, ‡"Mercury (¿Uṭârid) resides in the Second Sky;" A785.7§, ‡"Moon (al-Qamar) resides in the First Sky;" A787, "Relation of planets to human life;" A787.5§, ‡"Character (nature) of the twelve signs of the Zodiac;" A787.5.1§, ‡"Three signs correspond to (four) personality types;" etc. See n. 80, and El-Shamy, *MITON*.

[115] Motif: A871.4§, ‡"Four corners of earth."

[116] Motifs: D2156.5.0.1§, "Saint has control over reptiles. ('er-Rifâ¿iyyah' Brotherhood);" F709.5.3.1§, ‡"The Ruined quarter of earth: faraway."

[117] I.e., Alexander the Great (356–323 BC). See Section III.B.1, especially n. 520.

Motifs: F709.5.3.3§, ‡"The Dark quarter of earth: faraway;" F756.8§, ‡"Valley of precious metals and stones." See "How El-Khidr Gained Immortality" in El-Shamy, *Folktales of Egypt*, No. 23, pp. 137–138. On the Rifâ¿iyya, see Section IV.A; and n. 597.

wants to punish a city, He sends earthquakes to it from the Qâf Mountains.[118] Earth is also viewed as composed of seven provinces and to have seven seas—an apparent legacy from medieval Arab geography.[119] Adam, and consequently all other humans as well, were created from clay of Earth's crust (Koran, 55:14). The physical and psychological characteristics of humans are believed to reflect the attributes of Earth's clay from which Adam was created (see Section III.C). Humans were made from Earth and they will return to it when they die. This doctrine explains the Islamic practice of burying the dead "in the ground," unseparated from Earth except by shrouds. Other burial practices that isolate the corpse from Earth—such as placing the corpse in a casket, freezing it for an extended period beyond what is required for quick burial, or cremation, are incongruent with this belief, and are considered sinful.[120]

Earthly paradises, or utopias, in which ideal lifestyles prevail are believed, especially by many Sufis, to exist in hidden terrestrial locations, or even in "other dimensions" within ordinary human communities. One such utopia is reported as part of the Alexander legend cycle, where Alexander comes across a community in which there are no conflicts, dishonesty, usury, illness, injustice, or social stratification into royalty and commoners; every one in the community is a believer and enjoys total freedom and full equality.[121] For the majority of people such utopias do not seem to play a significant role in actual daily living. However, a utopian otherworld is occasionally cited to account for the disappearance of certain men from their home communities, or to explain how a "village idiot" incurred his mental illness after having lived happily in such a utopia but evicted for breaking one of its tabus (see App. 50).

Associated with the concept of life on Earth is that of the termination of that life at *yoam el-Qiyâmàh* (i.e., *yàwm* . . . , the Day of End of World, Doomsday, Apocalypse),

---

[118] Motif: A1145.5§, "Earthquakes from movements of Qâf mountains."

Recorded in January 1969 from "Little Farûz" (see n. 78). He heard the account from his father and also read it in al-Tha¿labî's *Qiṣaṣ* (see p. 4). Also see Lane, *Modern Egyptians*, pp. 221–222. Cf. C.E. Padwick, "Notes on the jinn and ghoul in the peasant mind of Lower Egypt." In: *Bulletin of School of Oriental and African Studies*, Vol. 3 (1923), pp. 421–446.

[119] Ibn Khaldûn/Rosenthal, *The Muqddimah*, Vol. 1, pp. 109–166.

[120] Khalîfah, *al-Dâr al-barzakhiyyah*, pp. 170–171.

Motifs: V61.8.2§, "Moslem buried into earth (in shroud) without coffin;" V61.8.2.1§, ‡"Burial into earth returns man (Adamite) to place of origin (from where he had come: Ashes to ashes, dust to dust;" C898.1§, "Tabu: indignities to corpse (beating, cremation, etc.)." (See also n. 167 and 400)

On the state of the soul between death and Judgment, see Lane, *Modern Egyptians*, p. 52; also cf. El-Sayed El-Aswad, "Death Ritual in Rural Egyptian Society: A Symbolic Study." In: *Urban Anthropology and Studies of Cultural Systems and World Economic Development*, Vol. 16 (1987) pp. 205–241. On use of the casket, cf. "Why the Copts Were Called 'Blue Bone,'" in El-Shamy, *Folktales of Egypt*, No. 25, pp. 139–140. Also see *tàlqîn*, n. 432.

[121] Motifs: F9§, "Utopian otherworld;" cf. F701.2, "Land of the blessed. Everything as it should be." In this respect, the legend may be viewed as a utopian community (Cf. Tale-type: 470C§, *Man in Utopian Otherworld Cannot Resist Interfering: Meddler Expelled.* ("It Serves me Right!"); see: El-Shamy, *DOTTI.*

For texts of this narrative account, see al-Damîrî, *Ḥayât al-ḥayawân al-kubrâ*, 2 vols. (Cairo, 1963). Vol. 2, p. 183; and Burton, *Arabian Nights*, Vol. 5, pp. 252–254. Also, see Yuriko Yamanaka's "Alexander in the *Thousand and One Nights* and the Ghazâlî [i.e., Gazzâlî] Connection." In: *The Arabian Nights and Orientalism: Perspectives from East and West*, Yuriko Yamanaka and Tetsuo Nishio, eds. (London, I.B. Tauris, 2006), pp. 93–115.

also referred to as the day of *qiyâm as-sâ¿àh* (the coming of the Hour). Fear of that day is a central component of the daily concerns of practically every "God-fearing" person and all other living creatures. On the Day of End of World, apocalyptic occurrences—such as the rupturing of the sky, the splitting of the moon, the implosion of the mountains, the scattering of the stars, and the boiling over of the oceans—will take place. Five "major" and numerous "minor" signs (*¿alâmât*) will herald that day. One account specifies the major signs as (1) the appearance of the Antichrist; (2) the second coming of Christ; (3) escape of Gog and Magog from their prison; (4) the appearance of the *dâbbàh min al-'àrḍ* (i.e., "animal from earth"—referred to in folk circles as *Dàbbìt el-'àrḍ*); (5) the sun's rising from the west.[122] Meanwhile, the "minor signs" revolve around the themes of "abandonment of God's edicts and laws," "prevalence of impiety," "decay of morality," "lack of justice" "reversal of the established social order" especially with reference to the division of labor between men and women (e.g., females riding warhorses and doing battle), and battle at the Latter Days (cf. Armageddon).[123]

I.E. *el-Ḥigâb* (The Veil, Barrier-to-Gnosis)

The word *ḥigâb* designates a Veil or curtain that blocks one's vision from seeing what is behind it, as in the case of veiling the face in public. This concept is applied to the supernatural sphere to account for the inability of humans to know certain aspects of the universe.[124]

---

[122]al-¿Idwî, *Mashâriq*, pp. 200–205; and Khalîfah, *al-Dâr al-barzakhiyyah*, pp. 330–337. Khalîfah points out that he is citing these beliefs as they occur among people (folk groups) in his home region of Asyût in southern Egypt.

Motifs: A1070.2§, "Speaking-monster (*'dâbbat al-'arḍ'*) as sign at end of world;" B15.7.17§, ‡"'*dâbbat al-'arḍ'*: hybrid animal with ox's head, pig's eyes, elephant's ears, stag's antlers, lion's chest, tiger's color, cat's waist, ram's tail, camel's legs—with twelve cubits between each two joints (*mifṣalayn*);" A1063, "Extraordinary wind at the end of the world,"

Other motifs associated with the signs of Doomsday are A1002.2, "Signs before the Day of Judgment;" A1002.2.0.1§, ‡"Latter days (*'Âkhir al-Zamân*);" A1002.2.4, ‡"Unusual migration of birds as sign of Doomsday;" A1002.2.4.0.1§, ‡"Change in habitual behavior of animals (birds, insects) as sign of Doomsday;" A1002.2.4.1§, ‡"Extinction (disappearance) of creature as sign of Doomsday;" A1002.2.4.1.1§, ‡"Failure of locusts to appear as sign of Doomsday;" A1002.2.4.3§, ‡"Talking animal as sign of Doomsday;" A1002.2.6§, ‡"Abandonment of 'God's ways' (violation of sacred tabus) as sign of Doomsday;" A1002.2.7§, ‡"Coming of the 'Seal of Prophets' as sign of Doomsday;" A1002.2.7.1§, ‡"Appearance of the False-Messiah (Antichrist, 'al-Masîkh', *al-Daggâl*) as sign of Doomsday;" A1002.2.7.2§, ‡"Return to Earth of the Messiah (al-Mahdî) as sign of Doomsday;" A1002.2.8§, ‡"Excessive adornment of Earth (high civilization, luxurious development) as sign of Doomsday."

See also n. 74 and 362. Also see sections II.D.2a.

[123]J. Seldon Willmore, *Spoken Arabic of Egypt* (London, 1901) XVIII, p. 358.

Motifs: A1080, "Battle at end of world. Armageddon;" A1088§, "Black ('Abyssinians') and White races kill each other at end of world."

See n. 380.

[124]Cf. "The Cosmos, the Visible and the Invisible," in el-Aswad, *Religion and folk Cosmology*, pp. 60–85.

Since the entire universe—supernatural and natural, abstract and concrete—is believed to be organically interconnected, knowledge of the past, present, and future is believed possible from a spiritual (theoretical) standpoint. Before Adam and Eve were evicted from Paradise, existence (life) was one continuous and timeless entity. Clairvoyance, so to speak, characterized all living beings as a matter of fact bestowed upon them by the Creator. At a later stage, after Adam's fall and the developments of its accompaniments, God established the Veil (*Ḥigâb*, Barrier-to-gnosis) between heavens and the rest of the universe so as to prevent Eblis, jinn, and humans from approaching heavens, spying on its inhabitants, and learning its secrets. Consequently, the unknown came into existence as a characteristic of all living things outside the sky world. The difference in the ability of humans and the jinn to know the past, the present, or what is in heaven, is one of degree rather than of kind. Some creatures are believed to know more than others, but no one knows the future or what God intended to be veiled. Jinn, for example, are believed by some to know the future; this belief is countervailed by a Koranic assertion that they do not (Koran, 34:14, also see n. 190). Jinn's capabilities differ from those of humans only in degree rather than in type; jinn's knowledge is greater because they are believed to live longer, travel from place to place faster, and occupy a larger area of the world than humans do. The universe may, therefore, be viewed as divided into two realms or moieties. From a human's standpoint, there is a worldly realm that exists outside the Veil, and there is a spiritual or heavenly realm on the other side of the Veil, where everything is clearly seen, with no temporal or physical boundaries or barriers to timeless and infinite perception.

It is firmly believed that there are situations where the effects of the Veil are temporarily suspended for a human being. This suspension is spiritual (or soul-wise). Since the soul (*rûḥ*), unlike the Earth-bound body, is thought of as eternal and from God's "breath" it is entitled to all the capabilities of a heavenly entity. When within the body, the soul is barred from the larger, transparent universe. The Veil is raised off a human being when the soul is released from the body during sleep or upon death because the body ties the soul to the Earth, or worldly life, and shackles it to the nontransparent side of the Barrier-to-gnosis (see also, "The Soul," in Section II.E). Additionally, God grants certain individuals, it is believed, the boon of clairvoyance (*kàshf*) or the power to penetrate the Veil with their vision or soul; such a person would be referred to as "the Veil has been lifted off him" (*makshûf/marfû¿ ¿annùh el-Ḥigâb*).[125]

This belief in Barrier-to-gnosis plays an important role on all levels of the belief–practice system and among all levels of social groups and classes. A number of rituals, such as *zìkr* (remembrance-ritual, kinetic-hymns) and *khàlwàh* (i.e., *khùlwàh*: deep meditations, or ascetic immersions) seek to help the soul penetrate the Veil and enter into the other transparent, timeless, and infinite realm (moiety) of the universe.

[125] On the contradiction between this common belief and formal Koranic doctrine, see Lane, *Modern Egyptians*, pp. 232–234.

I.F. *el-Bàrzàkh* (The Isthmus, Purgatory)

Among the folk, as well as the "learned," one of the numerous suggested abodes for souls during the interval between death and burial of a deceased person and the Day of Resurrection is *el-Bàrzàkh* (the Isthmus, Purgatory; lit.: a barrier between two things).[126] In folk traditions, the Isthmus is vaguely perceived as a place between Earth and the sky. Some sources speak of two separate abodes, one "designated for the residence of good souls until the last day," and another, that is, "the designated prison in which wicked souls await their final doom."[127] Other writers name the site without specifying its nature.[128] A theologian issuing a formal opinion quoted Imam Mâlik (715–795 AD) as stating, "It has been reported to me that the soul [of a dead person] is free-moving in an isthmus of land thus going where it ['she'] wishes."[129]

Another writer reports that the Isthmus is "... a road connecting *al-'ûlâ* (the here-and-now) and *al-'âkhiràh* (the hereafter)." *Al-ḥayâh al-bàrzakhìyyàh* ("isthmusian life," or life in the isthmus) is believed to begin at the moment of death (final departure of the soul from the body) and lasts until the first blowing of the "Horn" (signalling Resurrection and the end of that intermediate life). It also believed that life in the Isthmus is neither an extension of worldly life nor a prelude to life in the "hereafter," but an intermediate life with its own laws, rules, and regulations. Death is perceived to be *màkhlûq* (created, or a creature) just like life, and each of life and death is an independent *dùnyâ* (world, cf. *¿âlàm*: world).[130] The Isthmus, however, does not seem to occupy an important position in folk cognitive systems and is not associated with any required rituals; it is mostly cited to account for the whereabouts of the soul of a deceased person.

The word *bàrzàkh* is also used to refer to the abode for each of the four arch-saints who are believed to support Earth, each is cited to currently be "in his own *bàrzàkh*,"[131] and would descend (*yìnzìl*) to Earth to undertake a certain mission such as helping a follower or addressing an injustice. In this context, the *bàrzàkh* may be simply assumed to be a private compartment (stratum, level) of the Isthmus occupied

---

[126] Motif: A691§, "*al-barzakh* (Isthmus): Intermediate world between heavens and earth." (See Ibn Khaldûn/Rosenthal, *The Muqddimah*, Vol. 3, pp. 70–71.)

[127] Lane, *Modern Egyptians*, p. 525. Although Lane did not use the word *bàrzàkh* (isthmus), his description of "the places" concerned corresponds to that belief-site. Also see his résumé of opinions on the subject, p. 525 n. 3.

[128] A.M.J. Ḥigâb, *al-¿Iẓah wa al-'i¿tibâr fî ḥayât al-Sayyid al-Badawî al-dunyawiyyah wa ḥayâtihi al-barzakhiyyah (The Moral [Lesson] and Example in al-Sayyid al-Badawî's Worldly and Isthmusian Life)*. Cairo, 1966 or 1967.

[129] Yûsuf al-Digwî, "'ayna maqarru al-'arwâḥ ba¿da al-mawt? ("Where Is the Abode of Souls After Death?" In: *Nûr al-Islâm*, Vol. 3, No. 4 (1932), p. 265.

[130] Maḥmûd Ibn al-Sharîf, *al-Ḥayâh al-barzakhiyyah (Isthmusian Life)* (Cairo: al-Sha¿b, 1972), pp. 27 and 89. The author, an MD, dedicates the book to his "companion on the road of life" who passed away suddenly while still at the age of a flower (i.e., very young).

[131] Motif: A416.1§, ‡"*Mudarrak*-axis: Arch-saint with assigned *daràk* ('precinct,' post—also referred to as *bàrzàkh*)."

See "Why There Is a 'Saint the Forty' In Every Town," in El-Shamy, *Folktales of Egypt*, No. 26. pp. 141–143, 274–275. Also see n. 593.

by the soul of the arch-saint. It may also mean an arch-saint's domain located some place between Earth and the sky, and thus would be similar to the concept of a saint's *daràk* (precinct, domain—which is not identical with the abode of souls after death; see Section IV.A).

I.G. *Sìdràt al-Mùntahâ* (The Lote-Tree of the Extremity)

A tree known as *Sìdràt al-Mùntahâ* marks a location near which "the Garden of Abode" (i.e., Paradise) is situated.[132] Although the name of the tree and its location are mentioned in the Koran, no further information is provided. However, literary sources describe it as

> [. . .] a tree in the seventh heaven, next to Paradise, its roots are fixed in Paradise and its limbs are under the Chair [. . .], each leaf shades one of the nations; angels enter it like golden butterflies; on it are angels whose number is known only to God; the residence of Gabriel (May peace be upon him) is in its midst. ("And God is more knowing.")[133]

Clearly, in this learned elaboration on the Koranic concept, the association between the Lote tree on the one hand, and angels on the other is made on the basis of perceiving angels as flying supernatural beings who, like birds, have wings and dwell in trees. The notion that Gabriel dwells in a tree has not been encountered in oral folk traditions. In current folk traditions, the Lote tree of extremity is typically perceived as marking the uppermost limits beyond which no average human being can reach.[134]

At the beginning of the nineteenth century, Lane observed that "The Sidr (or Lote tree) of Paradise [. . .] is more commonly called *Shegeret al-Muntahâ* (or the Tree of the Extremity) [. . .];" consequently, he linked *Sìdràt al-Mùntahâ* to rituals concerning life and death exercised by the serious and considerate Muslims on the night of the Middle of the lunar month of Sha¿bân ("eve of the fifteenth"). Thus, he reported that the Tree of the Extremity

> [. . .] in Paradise, is believed to have as many leaves as there are living human beings in the world; and the leaves are said to be inscribed with the names of all beings; each leaf bearing the name of one person, and those of his father and mother. The tree [. . .] is

---

[132]Koran, 53:14–16. Cf. Lane, *Modern Egyptians*, p. 471 n. 1.

[133]al-Tha¿labî, *Qiṣaṣ*, p. 10.

Cf. Motifs: A151.7.1, ‡"Deity resides in tree;" and Z13.11.1§, ‡"Uncertainty about accuracy of truthful report: 'And God knows best,' 'And God is omniscient' (or the like)."

[134]During the 1960, 1970, and 1980s most members of folk groups viewed the news of Western-man's landings on the moon with considerable suspicion and general disbelief. Commenting on recent successes in space exploration, a group of university-educated professionals commented: "Maybe they did [reach the moon]. But *Sìdràt al-Mùntahâ* is the one place they [space-explorers] will never, ever, reach." Also, an interpretation of the destination of the spaceship in the movie "Space Odyssey: 2001" was: "They think they reached *Sìdràt al-Mùntahâ* [but they actually did not]." (Col. H. El-Shamy, 1969, and 1981)

> shaken on the night above mentioned, a little after sunset; and when a person is destined to die in the ensuing year, his leaf, [. . .], falls on this occasion: if he be to die soon, his leaf is almost wholly withered, [. . .], if he be to die later in the year, a larger portion remains green [. . .].[135]

As such, the "Tree of Extremity," seems not to be the same as *Sìdràt al-Mùntahâ* (the Lote tree of extremity); it is more likely that the two names given by Lane designate two distinct trees assigned to separate locations on the Extremity of the universe. "*Shegaret al-Muntahâ*"—as cited by Lane—seems to be a belief-tree (existing only in the believers' minds) labeled in contemporary lore *shagaret el-'a¿mâr* (the tree of life-spans). The theme of life-spans of humans corresponding to fruits, or leaves, on a tree (commonly a sycamore-tree), harvested by an old man symbolizing the Angel of Death, occurs frequently in philosophical and instructional folktales pondering "the nature of life," and utopias.[136] Currently, however, there is no evidence relating this tree of life spans to active matters of sacred faith, or to consequent rituals in the manner described in Lane's account.

---

[135] Motifs: A652, "World-tree. Tree extending from lowest to highest world;" A652.3, "Tree in upper world;" A652.3.0.1§, ‡"'Tree of Heaven.' Its fruits are the foods of the gods and give them immortality;" A652.3.1§, "*Sidrat-al-Muntahâ*: the Lote-tree of the extremity of the universe. (Zizyphus lotus);" A652.3.2§, "Tree of life-spans in upper world. (Has as many leaves as there are living persons, when a leaf falls the corresponding person dies.)"

See Lane, *Modern Egyptians*, p. 471; and Burton, *Arabian Nights*, Vol. 5, p. 393 n. 2; cf. Ions, *Egyptian Mythology*, p. 87.

[136] Motifs: Z167§, "Tree (plant) symbolism;" Z111, "Death personified."

See "'It Serves Me Right!'" in El-Shamy, *Folktales of Egypt*, No. 12, pp. 86–93, especially pp. 92–93; and "Belief Characters . . . ," esp. pp. 9–11, n. 6, p. 31.

CHAPTER II

Supernatural Beings

In addition to the Creator (God), six broad categories of this major subdivision of the supernatural may be identified. These are: Angels, Jinn in general and Jinn as components of a person (self/psyche), zoological beings, the soul, and ghosts.

II.A. *malâykàh/malâ'ikàh* (Angels)

The word *malâk* (pl.: *malâykah*, i.e., *malâ'ikàh*) designates the same supernatural being known in the English language as an angel. Belief in angels stems directly from the Koran and, along with belief in God's messengers and God's books (scriptures), is considered a basic requirement for being a Muslim (Koran, 2:98, 285; 4:136). Secondary information about the nature and attributes of angels is mostly para-religious. The creation of angels preceded that of Adamites; they were created of pure light. Their normal habitat is the seven layers of heaven, where God has placed them in an ascending manner according to rank: the higher the rank, the higher the sky assigned as habitat—ranging from the first, which is the lowest and closer to Earth to the seventh, which is the highest and closer to God's throne. Angels are pure spirit and intellect; they praise God eternally. Unlike humans and jinn, angels do not eat, drink, marry, procreate, or die; they also lack the organs associated with such biological functions.[137] However, all angels (with few exceptions) will die when

[137] S. Ḥusayn, *al-Ginn*, p. 111; ¿A. Nawfal, *¿Âlam al-ginn wa al-malâ'ikah* (*The world of Jinn and Angels*). (Cairo, 1968), pp. 102–103; and Gätje, *Koran und Koranexegese*, pp. 220–222.

Motifs: A52.3.1§, "Material of which angels are created is: pure light—(angels created from light);" V230.5.1§, "Angels dwell in the seven heavens;" V230.5.2§, ‡"Angels (regardless of class) can go anywhere in the universe;" V230.0.2§, ‡"Angels do not have mortals' basic needs (e.g., sex, food, etc.)." Cf. n. 437.

the "first" blowing of the "Horn" (*ṣûr*)[138] is sounded, signaling the advent of the Day of End of World. Four main archangels play instrumental roles on both the formal and the folk levels; literary traditions labels them *al-ro'asâ'* (the cardinals, the chiefs, and the principals).[139] They are: 'Isrâfîl (Israfil), Gibrîl or Gibrâ'îl (Gabriel), ¿Izrâ'îl (Azrael), and Mîkâ'îl (Michael).

The angel closest to God, at least in spatial terms, is 'Isrâfîl. He is the angel that will blow the Horn declaring the arrival of the Day of End of World; this first blowing is labeled *nafkhàt aṣ-ṣa¿q* (the Blowing of Thunderbolt-Striking) for all creatures will die instantly as if stricken by thunderbolt. He also will blow the Horn later declaring the arrival of the Day of Resurrection and the Day of Judgment (*yàwm al-bà¿th, yàwm al-ḥisâb*); this second blowing is named *nafkhàt al-ba¿th* (the Blowing of Resurrection) by which all creatures that are required to observe religious precept are resurrected. With few exceptions from among animals associated with major religious events, these creatures are the Adamites and the jinn. Some sources report that resurrection occurs when special water flows from under God's throne forty years after the Day of End of World.[140] Azrael is the angel of death; in addition to the awe-evoking appearance common to all cardinal angels, he has a frightful face.[141] Azrael is the angel most frequently encountered in daily life and social exchanges (such as curses);[142] he also appears frequently in various branches of folk traditions—serious and nonserious. Although angels are invincible, Azrael is occasionally portrayed in para-religious literature as momentarily vulnerable. One literary account reports that when the Angel of Death went to collect Moses' soul, Moses struck him with his fist, thus punching out his eye; another account describes how Prophet Idrîs (Henoch/Enoch) deceived the angel of death.[143] Azrael is reported to be the last of God's creatures—including all angels and God's messengers—to die after the first *nafkhah* (trumpet

---

[138]Described as a great trumpet of light, and with holes equalling the number of all the "creatures" that existed [from Creation to the Resurrection]. See Khalîfah, *al-Dâr al-barzakhiyyah*, p. 341.

Motifs: A1093, "End of world announced by trumpet;" A1093.1§, ‡"Archangel Isrâfîl will blow the trumpet, announcing commencement of End of World;" cf. D1221, ‡"Magic trumpet."

[139]Khalîfah, *al-Dâr al-barzakhiyyah*, p. 31.

[140]Motifs: E178.0.1§, ‡"Resurrection at Judgment Day when horn (trumpet) is sounded;" E178.0.4§, ‡"Resurrection at Judgment Day by water of life that flows from under God's Throne. ('mâ' al-ḥyawân');" Z71.12, "Formulistic number: forty."

See: Khalîfah, *al-Dâr al-barzakhiyyah*, pp. 341–343.

[141]Motif: A487.2§, "Azrael (¿Izrâ'îl, '¿Azrâ'îl,' '¿Uzrâ'în', etc.): angel of death."

As the motif indicates, there are several dialectical variations as to how the name ¿Izrâ'îl is pronounced. Unlike the names of other archangels such as Ruḍwân and Gibrîl, ¿Izrâ'îl is never used as a person's given name. Some informants reported that the name means ¿Abd-al-Jabbâr (the Slave-of-The-Mighty). One salient physical characteristic of Azrael is that he has multiple eyes in front and back of his face. (Motif: V233.0.1.1.2§, ‡"Angel of death has multiple eyes;" see Khalîfah, *al-Dâr al-barzakhiyyah*, pp. 30–33). Of the four archangels Azrael will be the last to die; cf. Motif: A487, "God of death."

It may be noted that Azrael is comparable to the ancient Egyptian "'Savage-faced Messenger,' which [... Osiris] had at his disposal, whom he could send to fetch the heart of any god or mortal who performed evil deeds." (Ions, *Egyptian Mythology*, p. 75.)

[142]E.g., Motif: M412.4.1§, ‡"Curse: A: 'Take!' B: 'May you get taken by Azrael!'"

[143]al-Tha¿labî, *Qiṣaṣ*, p. 139; also see "The Contract with Azrael", and "When Azrael Laughed, Cried, and Felt Fear," in El-Shamy, *Folktales of Egypt*, Nos. 17, p. 122, and 18, pp. 121–122, respectively.

blow); also, at resurrection, God will resurrect all cardinal angels, with the exception of Azrael.[144] Archangel Gabriel—labeled *al-'amîn* (the honest or the trusted)—is God's emissary to the messengers and prophets. He is empowered to instruct or reform the people. Gabriel appears in oral folk traditions frequently in roles compatible with this perceived "office" of communicating God's instructions to man.[145] Michael (Mîkâ'îl), about whom reports seems to be confined mostly to the older learned traditions, controls nature, particularly phenomena associated with the weather such as rain and storms.[146] References to two other cardinal angels, Rudwân and Mâlik, appear sporadically in literary traditions, and even less frequently in folk expressions. Ràḍwân, (i.e., Ruḍwân) is perceived as the guardian and gatekeeper of Paradise; he appears in that role in folk oral traditions, especially in religious legends. Yet, in daily life Paradise is often described as *gànnit Ràḍwân* ("Rudwân's Paradise").[147] Meanwhile, Mâlik is the chief *khâzìn* (warden, keeper) of hell.[148]

Each of the main archangels is typically referred to as *sàyyìdnâ* (i.e., *sàyyìdunâ*, our lord/master), a title used also to refer to prophets but not applied to designate a saint.[149] Angels, with the possible exception of the angel-like *ḥûriyyât* (houris), are invariably perceived as males; no feminine form for the word *malâk* (angel) exists in the Arabic language. In daily life, even when a human female is compared to an angel, the analogy is drawn in terms of her being as kind as a *malâk* ([masculine]

---

[144]Khalîfah, *al-Dâr al-barzakhiyyah*, p. 341.

[145]Motif: A165.2.3.1.1§, ‡"Archangel Gibrîl (Gabriel) as the 'spirit trusted by God' (*al-rûḥ al-'amîn*)."

[146]al-Thaؘlabî, *Qiṣaṣ*, p. 46, p. 110. Motif: V249.9§, "Angels with specific assignments: 'Angel of such and such.' Angel controls the elements, insects, disease, etc."

[147]The word *ruḍwân* appears in Koran associated only with God's *ruḍwân* (contentment) with believers—not as the name of an angel. The only case in which Prophet Muhammad is reported to be the guardian of Paradise appears in Inea Bushnaq, ed., tr., *Arab Folktales* (New York, 1986), No. 13, pp. 55–56. Bushnaq does not accredit her tales to the printed sources from which she extracted them. If authentic—which is doubtful—this theme would be a radical deviation from the established traditional beliefs.

On the issue of lack of accuracy in published folk materials, see H. El-Shamy, "Towards A Demographically Oriented Type Index for Tales of the Arab World." In: *Cahiers de Littérature Orale*, No. 23: *La tradition au présent (Monde arabe)*, Praline Gay-Para, Ed. (Paris, 1988), pp. 15–40; also see El-Shamy, *MITON*, pp. 9–15.

[148]Perhaps the most noted case where Archangel Mâlik plays a role—though peripheral—is the religious "folk" ballad: "The story of *sayyidî* 'Ibrâhîm ed-Disûqî . . . ," p. 8 (see App. 6). For additional occurrences of the theme of Mâlik as porter of Hell, see El-Shamy, *GMC*, Motif: A671.1.1§, "Archangel Mâlik: porter (guardian) of hell."

[149]For an example of editorial "improvement" (without consulting the author), see: El-Shamy, *Folktales of Egypt*, p. 7, where the word "*sidi*" was substituted for "*sayyidna*" in identifying el-Khidr (Motif: F440.3§, "al-Khiḍr (the Green-one): benevolent spirit associated with vegetation and water)."

Yet some published literature cited names of prophets described as *sîdî*. These incidents are, probably, not representative of native informants' utterances. Sengers (*Women and Demons*, p. 115) cites "sidi Hussein" as one of the saints. If accurately reported, this label is uncommon: typically, al-Ḥusain/al-Ḥusayn, or el-"Hussein" is referred to as "*sayyidnâ* (Our Lord/Master)." (See App. 28)

Similarly E. Laoust, *Contes berbères du Maroc*, 2 vols. (Paris, 1949–1950) , No. 138, pp. 292–293) gives a text in which the word "*sidna*" is used in the title applied to Jesus ("ؘÎsâ"); yet, the table of contents cites (*sîdî* Aîssa [*sic*]).

However, a cleric may occasionally be *addressed* as "O *sayyidnâ*;" yet he would not be referred to as "*sayyidnâ* so-and-so."

angel), or as beautiful as a "*ḥûrìyyàh* (houri) from Paradise." Names of most cardinal angels are used as proper names for humans. Gibrîl, Ruḍwân, and Mâlik are fairly common names for Moslem males (however, in the case of "Mâlik," the association with the angel bearing that name is not certain); while Mîkhâ'îl—a variation on the name Mîkâ'îl—is a recurrent male name among Copts only, along with the name ¿Abd-el-Malâk (lit.: "Slave-of-the-Angel"). By contrast, neither "'Isrâfîl" nor "¿Izrâ'îl" occurs as a proper name among members of either denomination. With reference to Moslem females, only "Ḥûrìyyàh" (houri) is used as a given name; in this context, the name is perceived as a variation on other names that denote being pretty (e.g., Gamîlàh, Badî¿àh; cf. "Julie"). Another female name with possible association to angels (or to royalty) is "Malàk," which may signify "angel-like," "peacefulness," or "serenity."

Learned traditions portray the organization of angels as reflecting political stratification and military-like chains of command similar to those found in human society. Strict rules of royal court protocol govern angels' interaction with one another and God,[150] who seems to be accessible only to a few select archangels. It is reported that angel Ḥizqyâ'îl, who is located at the feet of God's throne, got a notion (*khâṭìr*) to merely catch a glimpse of the throne; with God's permission to try, he still failed to attain his goal after a total of fifty thousand years of upward flight.[151]

Prior to the creation of Adam, Eblis had led armies of angels in battles against rebellious Earth jinn (then called *Bìn* or *Ḥìn*) and subdued them. Success corrupted the powerful victorious "general" and led him to conceit and defiance that became more pronounced when Adam, predestined to be God's preferred creature, was being created. Such a happening in which a war hero rebels against his supreme commander-in-chief is common in actual life; numerous examples can be found in various human societies. Angels also fought on the side of God's prophets; in such cases angels are referred to as *'agnâd 'ilâhiyyàh* (divine soldiers, soldiers of God). In contemporary social life, manifestations of self-confidence are often equated with the behavior of Eblis, and are hardly differentiated from arrogance and conceit, which are condemned in the Koran (Koran, 31:18; cf. 2:34, 38:74). A good person must express humility and profess inability, even when he (or she) is fully aware of his (or her) own high competence and capabilities. Recurrent truisms stressing this fact state "No one would praise himself except Eblis!" and "*el-¿ìgb* (self-admiration, i.e., conceit) is from Satan!" Such moralistic truisms are further reinforced by literary religious accounts (exempla) presenting the same principle in graphic terms.

> As a man in a [fine] mantle was walking around haughtily, looking at his hips with admiration for himself, God caused earth to swallow him, [. . .] and there he shall remain until the Day of End of World [or Day of Resurrection].[152]

---

150 See al-Bûnî, *Shams*, p. 3. (Motif: V247.1.2§, "Chain of command among angels.")

151 al-Tha¿labî, *Qiṣaṣ*, p. 9.

152 al-Tha¿labî, *Qiṣaṣ*, p. 5. Motifs: Q331.3§, ‡"Conceit (arrogance) punished;" Q 552.2.3.2.6§, ‡"Earth swallows arrogant (vain, proud) person."

Consequently, even experts at a craft or an art always express inability, or—to the perplexity of many European foreigners—adopt a noncommittal attitude toward the performance of a task (e.g., a mechanic repairing an automobile, or a medical doctor executing a surgical operation). Typically, they refuse to specify the possible outcome, or insist that the outcome cannot be discussed since all matters, especially futuristic events, are in God's hands. Neglecting this rule is believed to invite failure.[153]

Literary traditions list numerous other angels, their names, their powers, and qualities; however, these angels have little or no currency in the daily orally circulated lore. Even a recently retired practicing shaman-*shaikh* (faith healer, "magician") stated his need to refer to written manuals and records for specific information on the lesser angels. (See Sections II.B.2, 2.B.3a)

The physical characteristics of certain classes of angels are described in secondary literary sources. Some angels are reported to have the faces of cows, or eagles, or horses, or men, according to the layer of heaven that they inhabit.[154] The size of some angels is reported to be of cosmological dimensions and is therefore beyond a layman's comprehension. Early Moslem writers often described the measurement of an angel in terms of a walk or flight of hundreds or thousands of years. For example, al-Tha¿labî reported that

> God created heaven [as] seven [layers], and Earth [as] seven [layers]. Underneath each [layer of] earth [there is a distance of] five hundred years [of travel], and underneath each heaven exists a sea whose depth equals all of these distances; an angel is standing in this sea with water not [even] approaching his heel.[155]

Similarly, Gabriel is described as having wings, which block the east and the west; his feet touch the seventh earth while his head reaches the corners of God's throne. Yet, Gabriel flew the distance between 'Isrâfîl's ear and lip in three hundred years. Likewise, Ḥizqyâ'îl, who originally had eighteen thousand wings before God doubled them to become thirty-six, each separated from the other by a distance of five hundred years' travel, succeeded only in reaching the [knob] of the foot of God's throne after fifty

---

For an example, see "'Imamu' ¿Ali and ¿Antar," in El-Shamy, *Folktales of Egypt*, No. 31, especially p. 156.

[153]Cf. Tale-type 830C, *If God Wills*. [Successive misfortunes because of forgetting to say, "If God wills."]

For an example where planning for the future is discouraged, see "The Twelfth Month," in El-Shamy, *Folktales of Egypt*, No. 32, especially p. 157. Also cf. Amîn, *Qâmûs*, p. 376, where he presents the expression "*balâsh muqâṭ¿ah*" (without interrupting/protesting [fate]) as a protective measure against the negative effects of making such plans.

[154]al-Tha¿labî, *Qiṣaṣ*, pp. 8–9; al-Qazwînî, *¿Ajâ'ib al-makhlûqât*. . . , Vol. 1, pp. 101–102.

Motifs: V231, "Appearance of angel;" V231.1.0.1§, "Angel with bird face;" V231.7§, "Angel with animal-face;" V231.9.1§, ‡"Angel in human form (shape)—general."

[155]al-Tha¿labî, *Qiṣaṣ*, p. 8.

Motifs: A651, "Hierarchy of worlds. [Cosmological stratification];" A704§, "Seven strata of sky, ('seven skies');" A651.1.4, "Seven heavens."

thousand years of flight.[156] Clearly, the perceiving of angels as illustrated in literary sources is the representation of astronomical concepts in concrete terms that can be grasped by the layman. In current folk traditions, however, angels are presented in human-like measurements. A number of folk drawings depict angels simply as winged human-like beings.[157] Numerous belief narratives (i.e., legends, myths, exempla, etc.) depict angels, including archangels, in their encounter with humans mostly in human form, mannerisms, and garb (cf. App. 7 and 9).

In modern academic studies on the subject of angels, there is considerable confusion stemming from the similar forms but different meanings of the names assigned to angels on the one hand, and to jinn on the other. Jinn are often called "*mulûk el-ginn*" or "*mulûk el-gân*" (kings of the jinn), or simply *mulûk* (kings). In folk speech an angel is referred to as *malâk* (angel) or "*malìk*" (a word that in other contexts means "king"). When the word "*malìk*" is used to denote an angel, it is always qualified as "*màlìk min es-samâ*" (lit.: king from the sky, i.e., angel).[158] In the plural form, however, angels are referred to as *malâykàh* (i.e., *malâ'ikah*) and hardly ever as *mulûk* (kings). The word *mulûk* refers only to jinn, not to angels. The inability of several scholars to differentiate among these folk usages has led to some misunderstanding concerning the exact nature of a supernatural being and, consequently, its relation to a human individual with whom the supernatural being interacts.[159]

II.A.1. Other Categories of Angels

Angels with lesser cosmological functions and stature, but with greater relevance in everyday life, are assigned to humans. Some of these may be viewed as components of

---

[156]al-Thaꜥlabî, *Qiṣaṣ*, p. 9.

Motifs: A53.1§, "Astronomical size of angels;" Z92.2§, "Formulas of astronomical (celestial) distances (thousands of years walk or flight)."

[157]It is in this human form that archangel Gabriel appeared to Virgin Mary to inform her of God's command that she will become pregnant with Christ (Koran, 19:17–21).

For an example of folk representation of an angel, see the cover of the sixteen-pager: *Qiṣṣat Sârrah wa al-Khalîl* (The Story of Sarah and [God's] Bosom Friend)—a folk religious ballad; also see, *Alf Laylah*, Vol. 3, p. 163 (drawing).

[158]In her *Women and Demons*, p. 98, Sengers quotes a "zar leader" (i.e., *kudyah*/*zâr*-priestess) named Zahra, aged 54, as follows:

> I have a *zar* sultan who belongs specially with me and he helps to determine what is wrong with the sick person. The sultan is not a *jinn*. Every time Zahra says "*jinn*" she immediately adds "*dastur*" to protect herself. "He is one of the *malayka ardiyya* (good demons, who are also called angels). It is not *jinn—dastur*—that help me; people are not allowed to deal with *jinn—dastur*. *Malayka ardiyya* live underground, but they are *min 'andi Allah* (from God), they are not *jinn* but *qurana'* (*qarins*). And God says that every person on earth has a *qarin* under the earth. The *qarin* and the 'sister under the earth' are the same thing."

From Zahra's confused description, the spirit that she refers to as "*zar*-sultan" is more likely a familiar rather than a zâr-spirit/jinni, and the "malayka ardiyyah" are jinn-counter-spirits, not angels, who can be very injurious as well. (See Section II.C)

[159]See El-Shamy, "Belief Characters . . . ," p. 20, 26.

a person and do not relate to other individuals; others have a transitory relationship with all humans.

II.A.1a. Angels as components of a person (self/psyche etc.)

Every person is believed to have two "attendant" angels "sitting" on his shoulders.[160] The "Angel of the Right [side]" registers *el-ḥasanât* (good deeds, acts of benevolence) that the person performs, and the "Angel of the Left [side]" registers *es-sàyyi'ât* (bad deeds, sinful deeds).[161] The latter is subordinate to the former, for the right side is always preferred over the left. These two angels also act as guardians who protect at all times the individual to whom they belong. However, at certain moments they may temporarily leave their posts; at such a time the person would be vulnerable, and it would be possible for an external force or entity, such as a jinni, to enter the body of that person and affect it. According to some accounts, the two guardian angels fall off when the person trips or falls on the ground and thus become in the jinn's domain; as one shaman-*shaikh* explained, " . . . because the earth (i.e., the ground) belongs to them [i.e., to the jinn]" (see App. 15). The two angels also leave the person when he/she sins and thus he/she becomes vulnerable to intruding supernatural beings during the commission of the sinful act. Other instances of such temporary departure of the two angels are commonly designated by the truisms: "Whenever God wills for a [harmful] matter to occur" to the individual concerned.[162] This temporary vulnerability, or relaxation of defenses, is often cited by healers (clerics, shaman-*mashâyìkh*/*shaikhs*) as a key factor in accounting for the occurrence of supernatural illness, possession, and numerous aspects of "magic fright."[163]

The human eye is also believed to have its own guardian angel. The rapid reflexes of the eyelid, that usually shield the eye against fast-moving debris or other objects that may injure the eye, are typically attributed to the protective role of that guardian. This belief is expressed in the recurrent folk truism "el-¿ain ¿laiha *ḥârìs* (there is guardian-[angel] set for the eye.") (Cf. Section II.C)

---

[160]Motif: A189.8.1§, "Angel-keepers (*ḥafazah*) of a mortal. They also act as accountants of deeds."

See: Ibn Kathîr, *al-Bidâyah wa al-nihâyah*, Vol. 1, p. 55; S. Ḥusayn, *al-Ginn*, pp. 80–81. In *Modern Egyptians* (p. 78, n. 3), Lane states that some of his informants reported that the number of those angels is two, while others reported five, six, or 160.

[161]Motif: A189.8.1.1§, "'Angel of the Right' registers mortal's good deeds, 'Angel of the Left' registers mortal's sins."

See el-Aswad (*Religion and Folk Cosmology*, p. 108 n. 21), where these two angels are assigned the names "*raqîb*, the supervisor" and "*'atîd*, the prepared," respectively. However, these names seem to be a learned clerical interpretation of a Koranic verse (50:18); significantly, A.Y. Ali, (*The Glorious Kur'an*), p. 1413 translates the two words (names) as adjectives or traits of one entity: "A sentinel by him, Ready (to note it)."

Cf. The ancient Egyptian concept of "Hall of Double Justice" and the roles of Anubis and Ammut (see Ions, *Egyptian Mythology*, pp. 135–136).

[162]S. Ḥusayn, *al-Ginn*, p. 81.

[163]Motifs: A189.8.1.0.1§, ‡"Angel-keepers abandon mortal during commission of sin;" V238, "Guardian angel;" V238.0.1§, ‡"Guardian angel abandons mortal (under certain circumstances);" cf. E723, "Wraith [guardian angel] of person separate from body."

II.A.1b. Nâkir and Nakîr, the two interrogative angels

Nâkir and Nakîr are the commonly used names for two interrogating angels who are believed to question the dead in the tomb in order to evaluate the deeds they had performed during their lifetime.[164] This interrogation is typically labeled *ḥisâb al-qàbr* ("tomb trial"); it is not the final judgment, for the "Day of Judgment" will come at once for all. It is also believed that these two angels will administer some punishment in the grave to sinners; cries of pain that may issue from the deceased being punished are believed to be audible to animals but not to humans. Nâkir is occasionally reported to be the scribe for good deeds, while Nakîr records sinful deeds; one places himself at the head of the corpse and the other at the corpse's feet.[165]

Believing in this preliminary judgment is reported to be a fundamental aspect of faith; a person who rejects the belief in "tomb trial" is often considered a *kâfir* (infidel).[166] Consequently, passing this interrogation successfully constitutes a significant concern for a person anticipating death, and for the family of a deceased person as well. The term *tàlqîn* ("prompting"—as in the case of prompting an actor on stage) stands for a major graveside burial ritual in which the officiating cleric instructs the deceased (or the soul) as to how to answer and what to say when the two angels come into the grave to conduct the interrogation. (See Section II.E, especially n. 448, cf. App. 7)

The transparent realm of *Ḥigâb* (the Veil, barrier-to-gnosis), in which the "secrets" of heaven are wholly, clearly, and accurately perceived, ends with the angel category. Beings with lesser powers are found in the nontransparent realm; these include the jinn and "Adam's children" (i.e., human beings, Adamites), both of whom are thought to be mortal. Generally speaking, those beings have no direct contact with the universe behind the Veil (the transparent realm); cases in which a human being may be in touch with the sphere (moiety) that exists on the other side of the Veil are found, but as exceptions to the rule.

II.A.2. Eblis and Other Fallen Angels

God created angels from light and jinn (al-Jân) from pure smokeless fire flame (Koran, 55:15). Eblis, now a *sheṭân* (i.e., *shayṭân*, satan), was the head of the angels and chief guardian of Paradise. (In other accounts, he was from a tribe called Jinn and assigned to guard Paradise; or, as indicated earlier, he headed a group of angels who fought destructive jinn on Earth.) When God ordered all angels to "prostrate

[164] Motif: A679§, "Interrogative angels (Nâkir and Nakîr, Munkir and Nakrân, etc.) question the dead at time of burial."

Other name variations are also reported from other Moslem groups, see for example "Munkir and Nakîr" (Khalîfah, *al-Dâr al-barzakhiyyah*, pp. 163–164; Ibn al-Sharîf, *al-Ḥayâh al-barzakhiyyah*, pp. 65–66); "Munkar and Nakir" (Burton, *Arabian Nights*, Vol. 5, p. 111 n. 2); "Nâkir and Nekeer," "Munkar and Nekeer" (Lane, *Modern Egyptians*, p. 68 n. 2, 522–525). Cf. n. 432, below.

[165] Khalîfah, *al-Dâr al-barzakhiyyah*, pp. 167–168. Also see n. 443 and 444.

[166] Ibn al-Sharîf, *al-Ḥayâh al-barzakhiyyah*, p. 62.

themselves" before Adam, Eblis refused. When asked about the reason for disobeying God, Eblis declared that "fire" from which he was created is superior to clay from which Adam was created (Koran, 2:34).[167] As learned interpreters elaborate and laymen believe, he became conceited because of his power and knowledge. Eblis was cast out of Paradise after he secured for himself God's promise of eternal life—till the Day of Resurrection. He vowed to corrupt the children of Adam (i.e., mankind). Eblis, or *esh-Sheṭân* (the Devil), causes humans to sin. According to an often-cited tradition attributed to Prophet Moḥammad, Satan is so close to a human being that he may be considered circulating in the human blood.[168] A literal interpretation of this utterance can be misleading.[169]

The constant attempts by Satan to lead people astray are referred to as *wàzz* (inciting), or *wàswasàh* (instigation). This latter term was adopted by psychiatrists to signify "obsessive-compulsive neurosis."[170] Just as everything occurs only if God wills, every sin or evil committed is believed to be instigated by Satan and takes place only because God willed its occurrence[171] through the cunning of Eblis and the weakness of human beings. Due to the belief that it was Eve who succumbed first to Eblis' temptation, she and "her daughters" (*banât* Ḥawwâ, i.e., females) have become weaker and more easily corruptible than the "sons" of Adam (i.e., males). Consequently, Eblis is regarded as the "*shaikh*" (headman, leader) of women. In order

---

[167] Motifs: A2905.1§, "Jinn created from fire." See S. Ḥusayn, *al-Ginn*, p. 8; al-Gindî, *al-Ginn*, p. 21; Nawfal, *¿Âlam al-ginn wa al-malâ'ikah (The World of Jinn and Angels)*, pp. 102–103.

Motif: A1241.0.1§, ‡"Adam made from clay brought from earth crust (*'adîm al-'arḍ*)." See also n. 79 and 120.

There is some ambiguity here: Eblis was presented as an angel; angels were created of light, whereas jinn were created of fire. This incongruence led to the view that Eblis was actually a jinn. See Lane, *Modern Egyptians*, p. 222. S. Ḥusayn (*al-Ginn*, pp. 8, 19) concludes that "The correct view is that Eblis was of the jinn, not of the angels."

[168] "*'inna al-shayṭâna yajrî min 'ibn 'Âdam majrâ al-dàmm* (In deed, Satan runs within an Adamite in the same manner as blood [runs])." See Ibn Kathîr, *al-Bidâyah wa al-nihâyah*, p. 64; S. Ḥusayn, *al-Ginn*, p. 87.

[169] Citing J. Robson's "Hadith," in *Encyclopaedia of Islam*, 1971, Vol. 1, 1129, and Dutch literature, Sengers states:

> "The idea that *demons* have to *leave the body through a drop of blood* is based on a *hadith*, which says that 'demons go through the veins like a blood-clot.'" (*Women and Demons*, p. 130 n. 3; italics added).

This inference is inaccurate, and is based on the fallacious academic perception that confuses Satan (Shayṭân/'Iblîs, Lucifer) with other belief-characters that Sengers and others designate as "demons" and satans. See n. 173, 325, and Section II.C.2a. S. Ḥusayn (*al-Ginn*, p. 87) clarifies the euphemism,

> "In deed, the *mafhûm* (concept) [of the *ḥadîth*] is that [Satan] is in total control of the Adamite—externally and internally—including his *mashâ¿ir* (feelings) and *'aḥâsîs* (sensations); no one escapes him [Satan] except whomsoever God has granted immunity."

[170] Okasha, *Contemporary Medical Psychology* (in Arabic), p. 107; Alhefnee, *Encyclopedia of Psychology & Psycho-analysis*, p. 45.

[171] S. Ḥusayn, *al-Ginn*, p. 91. Also cf. the data concerning the determination of true magic and *kùfr* (disbelief) cited in n. 216.

to better escape temptation, Sufis state that "He who has no *shaikh* [i.e., does not follow a religious leader], has Satan as his *shaikh*;" similarly, a folk truism proclaims that "He who has no senior [or, leader] must buy [i.e., find at any cost] one for himself." The impact of the beliefs expressed in these truisms on the dynamics of social organizational setup is considerable; they also shed light on the systemic nature of the female–male stereotypes, and the need on the part of many "believers" to be followers of a leader who would shield them from temptation.[172] (Also see Section III.B.3a)

An unbeliever or evil jinni may also be hyperbolically called a *sheṭân* (i.e., *shàyṭân*, satan) or an *Iblîs* (i.e., Eblis, pl.: *'abâlisàh*, "Eblises"—recurring only in folk speech); such beings constitute Eblis' soldiers. Literary traditions, however, refer to such beings as *maradàh* (giants, or *mârids*) or *¿utât al-ginn* (the evilly intrepid jinn).[173] Sometimes it is argued that Eblis, the principal satan, was not an angel but one of the jinn that existed on Earth before the creation of Adam and Eve.[174] Since jinn are thought to be similar to humans in many respects, procreation in both species is perceived to be through coition, conception, and parturition (childbirth). This explanation seems to have developed so as to account for the incongruent fact that although angels do not marry or reproduce, Eblis—himself once the foremost angel—has *shayâṭîn/'abâlisàh* (devils, "eblises/satans") as sons and descendants; it may also account for the Koranic passage in which Eblis states that he was created from fire (see n. 167). Another answer to this dilemma of perceived incongruity is that Satan—who is invariably perceived as male—had sexual intercourse with himself and laid four eggs out of which came his offspring.[175]

Under Sunni (orthodox) Islam and folk beliefs, predestination and Eblis' instigation (*wàswasàh*) provide the most powerful defensive mechanism for an individual. Because the commission of personal "sins" are normally attributed to external entities and

---

[172]Motif: P352.1.1§ "'He who has no *shaikh* has Satan for a leader.'"

For an occurrence of the concept and the cliche in a literary work, see M. Ḥusayn Haykal's *Zaynab*, p. 258; also see al-Nabhânî, *karâmât al-'awliyâ'*, Vol. 2, p. 535.

[173]al-Tha¿labî, *Qiṣaṣ*, p. 5; cf. ¿Alî al-Gindî, *al-Ginn bayna al-ḥaqîqah wa al-'asâṭîr (Jinn Between Fact and Legends)*, 2 vols. (Cairo, maktabat al-Anglo, 1969), Vol. 1, pp. 28, 29. See n. 169, and cf. n. 325.

[174]al-Ṭabarî, *Târîkh*, Vol. 1, p. 88; al-Gindî *al-Ginn*, Vol. 1, p. 12; S. Ḥusayn, *al-Ginn*, pp. 18–19; Gätje, *Koran und Koranexegese*, pp. 223–225.

[175]al-Tha¿labî, *Qiṣaṣ*, p. 25. (Motif: A2924§, ‡"Hermaphroditic Eblis (Satan) begets he-satans and she-satans"). The theme of a progeny through the male alone appears in the religious beliefs of the ancient world. The Egyptian deity Atum, who in order to produce offspring without a mate, had union with his shadow (see Ions, *Egyptian Mythology*, p. 26); cf. Motif: T512.6, "Conception from drinking sperm."

The cognitively salient theme of male pregnancy due to eating or drinking appears also in contemporary folktales (Tale-type 705). It is also found in the ancient Egyptian account of the conflict between Horus and Seth for the rule. Seth—who had made homosexual advances towards Horus—was tricked by Horus' mother, Isis, into eating lettuce that had Horus' semen on it; he became pregnant and gave birth to moon. See El-Shamy "Hermaphroditism," in *Archetypes and Motifs*, Garry and El-Shamy, eds., pp. 57–63. Also see El-Shamy, "Vom Fisch geboren (AaTh 705)." In: *Enzyklopädie des Märchens* (Göttingen) Vol. 4 (1984), Nos. 4–5, pp. 1211–1218. (For a full text of the tale, see: "The Daughter of the *Khuddârî*-bird," in H. El-Shamy, *Tales Arab Women Tell*. No. 5, pp. 83–89, 416–417; and "The Falcon's Daughter," in *Folktales Told Around the World*, R.M. Dorson, gen. ed. (Chicago, 1975, pp. 159–163).

forces—such as sacred higher powers (i.e., God, fate), or to irresistible coaxing by the anti-sacred (i.e., Satan, devils)—the actual experiencing of guilt by an individual and its emotional consequences are minimal.[176]

II.A.2a. Hârût and Mârût

Hârût and Mârût are two fallen angels; their names do not appear in any other usage beside designating them.[177] They were sent in human form by God to preach to corrupt people (the Babylonians) during the time of Prophet Idrîs (Henoch/Enoch). A recent account adds that their mission also included the task of teaching people magic so as to be able to countervail the powerful witchcraft of jinn. Evidently, the two angels were to teach people magic as a preventive measure along with warning them against unwittingly slipping into *kùfr* (disbelief, being infidel) by succumbing to the temptation of using magic for the purpose of harming others (i.e., sorcery, or "nether-magic").[178] But the two angels were themselves seduced by a woman named *az-Zàhràh* (Venus); moreover, they taught witchcraft and committed murder. They became aware of the magnitude of their sin when they tried to ascend to heaven but their wings failed (or refused) to carry them aloft (see n. 727). God punished the female seducer, Venus, by transforming her into the Planet bearing that name.[179] Meanwhile, Hârût and Mârût sought the aid of Prophet Henoch; he interceded with God on their behalf. God gave them the choice between receiving their retribution in this world or in the hereafter. Realizing the severity of the punishment in the hereafter and that it would be eternal, they chose the former. Thus, it is believed that they are still in human form they had assumed for the mission and receiving their punishment somewhere on Earth (where ancient Babylon used to be). It is reported that they are chained and hung upside down by their feet over a pool of water, which they cannot reach in order to quench their thirst; only a distance of four karats (*qarârîṭ*, i.e., equal to the width of four fingers) separates their mouths from the pool's surface.[180] They will remain in that position until God wills an end to their worldly punishment.

---

[176] For a discussion on the differences between "shame" and "guilt" as agents of social control, see "Guilt in Folk Culture" in El-Shamy, "Mental Health . . . ," pp. 24–27, where it is stated:

> "[. . .] shame being a reaction to actual or anticipated sanction by members of the immediate social group, i.e., the significant other. Conversely, guilt is viewed as a negative self-evaluation with a regretful feeling arising from experiencing deviation from an internalized ethical or religious norm. As such, guilt is viewed as the basic instrumental factor in emotional or mental disorder." (p. 24).

Also cf. data associated with n. 632.

[177] Koran, 2:102. See al-Thaʿlabî, *Qiṣaṣ*, pp. 30–32. (Motif: V236.5§, "Hârût and Mârût as fallen angels.")

[178] al-Digwî, "taʿallum al-siḥr (The Learning of Magic)," pp. 490–491; and S. Ḥusayn, *al-Ginn*, pp. 93–94.

[179] For the role planet Venus plays in contemporary Iraqi beliefs, see: Hasan El-Shamy, "Belief and Non-Belief in Arab, Middle Eastern and sub-Saharan Tales: the Religious–Non-Religious Continuum. A Case Study." In: *al-Ma'thûrât*, Vol. 3, No. 9 (January 1988), pp. 7–21.

[180] al-Thaʿlabî, *Qiṣaṣ*, p. 31. Motif: Q501.2.4§, "Punishment of Hârût and Mârût. Hung upside down over pool, tongues cannot reach water."

Hârût and Mârût are cited occasionally in contemporary folk traditions but do not play an important role in active folk beliefs. Knowledge of them in folk communities seems to constitute a cognitive isolate, for they do not appear in other contexts including active magical rituals.

Before their downfall, Eblis, Hârût, and Mârût used to have angel names. They were stripped of their former names because of the sins they committed.

II.B. *el-gìn* (The Jinn, Fairies)

It is commonly stated that jinn have their own world (*¿âlàm*); it is a part of *¿âlàm al-'athîr* (world of ether-like beings) whose members may exist side-by-side with human beings but are invisible to humans. It is a sphere that constitutes another dimension, so–to speak, of the world in which human beings exist.[181]

Jinn, like Eblis, were created from fire. They inhabited the Earth before humans. God placed some of them under the command of Prophet Solomon. He commanded them to manufacture for him inimitable buildings, images (statues), and similar artifacts (Koran, 34:12–13). According to some literary traditions interpreting and elaborating on sacred dogma, jinn were also ordered by Solomon to dig out the seas and pile up the mountains.[182] (This belief seems incongruent with the idea that God created the mountains at the initial stage of creating the universe in order to stabilize the shaky Earth—thus mountains are described as *rawâsî*, i.e., "stabilizers.") However, the Earth jinn became despotic, and God sent angels to drive them off to remote areas of the Earth where they remained till the advent of Adamites. With the exception of their "ethereal," nonmaterial substance and their great capabilities, jinn are very similar to humans. Jinn, like men, have a strong inclination toward sin and evil.[183] Jinn societies mirror human societies especially with reference to social and cultural institutions: social structure, political, legal, economic, educational, and

---

[181] S. Ḥusayn, states that the word "ginn" is a name that applies to whatever is hidden and is beyond the observation of a human being (*al-Ginn*, p. 14). Similarly, in answers to questions from readers, *Al-Ahram* newspaper (No. 34101, 4/24/1980, p. 2) asserts in a brief reply titled "*ḥaqîqat al-ginn* (The Reality of Jinn)" that "the origin of the word "gin" is a derivative of [the root] "gnn," which means "becoming concealed or hidden."

For general information on the jinn in Egyptian society, see Lane, *Modern Egyptians*, pp. 222–226; Almut Wieland, *Studien zur Ginn-Vorstellung im modernen Ägypten* (Würzburg: Ergon, 1994); ¿Abd al-Mun¿im Shumays, *al-Ginn wa al-¿afârît fî al-'adab al-sha¿bî al-Miṣrî* (Jinn an Afrits in Egyptian Folk Literature) (Cairo: al-Hay'ah, 1976). Also see: Ernest Zbinden, *Die Djinn des Islam und der altorientalische Geisterglaube* (Bern: P. Haupt, 1953).

[182] Koran, 13:3, 15:19, 21:31, 50:7, etc. See al-Tha¿labî, *Qiṣaṣ*, p. 4. Also see n. 75.

In Islamic literature and lore, Prophet Sulaymân is typically referred to as "*sàyyidunâ* Sulaymân;" the designation of "King Solomon" is associated only with western literature.

[183] al-Gindî, *al-Ginn*, Vol. 1, p. 12; Gätje, *Koran und Koranexegese*, p. 226.

Sengers asserts that "Islamic spirits *can never* be bad of course, since this would go against all religious convictions" (*Women and Demons*, p. 105, emphasis added). This claim is incongruent with numerous field cases. For an example, see App. 13, where a jinn woman reported to be from Islam's holy land plays a "bad" role in the life of a young man. Also cf. App. 29, where Bedouin female spirit plays a similar "bad" role in the life of a butcher.

familial institutions, industries, and religions. Also, like humans, jinn are *mukàllafîn* (obligated to observe the precepts of religion); they will undergo the preliminary tomb-trial,[184] and will be resurrected and tried on the Day of Judgment. Thus Koran (55:31) refers to both Jinn and humans as *al-thiqalân* (the two with burdens, or the two with religious duties). By contrast, nature (e.g., thunder, lightening, clouds, wind, and the like), inanimate objects and animals pray to God constantly but are not "obligated." They will expire or die and will *not* be resurrected (with few exceptions).[185] However, angels will die at the blowing of the Horn for the beginning of Day of End of the world.[186]

Jinn, though less powerful than angels, are far more powerful than humans. It is believed that any jinni can fly, dive, go through solid barriers (rock, wood, steel, or the like), and undergo metamorphosis or shape-shifting at will; but it is also believed that these powers are proportionate to a jinni's race, tribe, and social position within his or her group. Sometimes the various capabilities of the jinn are expressed in the titles assigned to them. Categories labeled *ghàwwâṣ* ("Diver") and *ṭàyyâr* ("Flyer") signify jinn from groups perceived on the basis of the special power of diving into seas or flying in the air, respectively. More commonly, the folk perceive two more powerful groups (tribes, races) of jinn in terms of colors: these are the red jinn and the blue jinn, the red often presented as being the more powerful (jinn of the green or yellow colors have not been reported).[187] If a jinni transforms himself (or herself) into an animal—especially a cat, dog, or snake—and is killed, that jinn's body remains in the animal form.[188]

Like humans, jinn have no knowledge of the future. A shaman-*shaikh* emphatically declared:

> A jinni is just like a human: he [the jinni] knows only the past and the present; unlike the human, the jinni knows more. But a jinni does not know the future. Koran states, "... had they [the jinn] known *al-ghàyb* [(destiny, the unknown, the unseen)], they wouldn't have tarried in the humiliating punishment.... [Koran: 34:14]."[189]

---

[184]Khalîfah, *al-Dâr al-barzakhiyyah*, pp. 177–178; S. Ḥusayn, *al-Ginn*, pp. 68–69.

[185]The exceptions are animals associated with major religious events or sacred persons:

> "Jacob's wolf and the Seven Sleepers' dog and Esdras's ass and Salih's she-camel and Duldul the mule of the Prophet. . . . " (Burton, *Arabian Nights*, Vol. 5, p. 235.

Motifs. Q172.0.4§, "Animal admitted to heaven;" B811, "Sacred animals;" B811.3.5.1§, "Sacred she-camel (*nâqah*);" etc.

For a narrative account of the she-camel event, see al-Thaꜥlabî, *Qiṣaṣ*, pp. 40–41.

On the concept of a "religious universe," see n. 398.

[186]Khalîfah, *al-Dâr al-barzakhiyyah*, pp. 341–343; al-Gindî, *al-Ginn*, Vol. 1, pp. 39–40. Also see n. 141.

[187]An exception is to be found in Sengers (*Women and Demons*, pp. 104, 105), where she reports a "yellow" *zâr* spirit. Cf. Motif: F233.0.1§, "Color of jinni (fairy) is one of its racial (ethnic) attributes."

[188]S. Ḥusayn, *al-Ginn*, p. 56.

For additional information on jinn assuming forms of animals, see n. 196–197.

[189]Informant: Shâkir: see n. 74. Also see App. 11.

The informant went on to explain the latter part of his statement as follows:

> '*Sàyyìdnâ'* [i.e., *sàyyidunâ*, our lord, Prophet] Sulaymân [Solomon], for some reason, wanted to punish the jinn. He ordered them to dig the seas and pile up the mountains. To make sure that they did their work, he sat on his throne, leaning forward on his cane, and kept an eye on them. "Our lord" Sulaymân died [(prophets's bodies do not decay, so they did not know of hi death)], but whenever the jinn got tired [and wished to relax], they would take a peek at him [only] to find him seated on his throne, and leaning against his cane [staring at them]; so, they would work harder. Finally, the cane rotted away; the *sûsàh* (mite) bored holes in it, and the cane could not support the weight of "our lord" Sulaymân: he collapsed. When the jinn saw that he fell down, they stopped working. That is why it is stated that the jinn do not know the future; meaning: that which God intended for them not to know.[190]

Generally, jinn are believed to exist everywhere on Earth. Yet, they are also believed to have their own natural habitats or domains. One informant stated

> God—glory be to Him—created angels, jinn, and humans. He divided the universe into ten portions; He assigned nine portions to the angels, and only one to both jinn and humans. Then he divided that tenth portion into ten portions: nine for the jinn and only one for the humans.[191]

Jinn are believed to be partial to desolate areas, but they can also be found within households in such odd places as ovens, staircases, toilets, baths, and dark abandoned rooms. Most people often take special precautions when entering these places or when they seem to be speaking about jinn. These precautions include asking permission (or forgiveness) from the inhabiting jinn by stating out loud *dàstûr*! (i.e., *dùstûr*: "Permission!" or "Apology!"), and "May God render our talk bearable to them" (*yig¿al kalâmnâ khafîf ¿alaihum*), or simply uttering the *bàsmalàh* (i.e., saying "In the name of God, the Merciful the Compassionate").[192] Failure to do so may offend the jinn who would retaliate by causing physical illness, possession, or damage to property (see App. 23). The very concept of mental or emotional disorder (*gunûn*) is clearly related to belief in jinn's ability to "possess" human body and mind. An animal that seems to act uncharacteristically in violent ("crazy") manner may thought to be possessed by jinn; however, reported cases of such animal possession are rare. The word *gunûn* (i.e., madness or mental disorder) is a derivative of the word "gin," (i.e., jinn); a mentally ill person is referred to as *màgnûn*, (i.e., jinn-stricken or ridden).

---

[190]Informant: Shâkir, see n. 74. Several other sources cited these "facts" almost verbatim. Also see, al-Tha¿labî, *Qiṣaṣ*, p. 181; Hanauer, *Holy Land*, Pt. VIII, pp. 49–50.

Motifs: F200.0.1§, ‡"Solomon as supreme ruler of all jinn and similar beings (afrits, dwarfs, elves, etc.);" R181.3§, "Demons (jinn) escape forced labor through accidental knowledge of captor's (Solomon's) death;" Z167.2.2.1§, "Symbolism: carob tree—decay;" cf. D1711.1.1, "Solomon as master of magicians."

[191]Informant: hajji Draihem, middle age, from a village in middle Nile Delta; see App. 13. Also see S. Ḥusayn, *al-Ginn*, pp. 9, 62.

[192]Lane, *Modern Egyptians*, 223; Amîn, *Qâmûs*, pp. 199–200.

In spite of this linguistic association, mental illness on the one hand and possession on the other are perceived separately in current traditional cultures. Evidently, in the minds of members of the culture, each of these two forms of abnormality belongs to a separate cognitive subsystem. Jinn have often been described as fond of filth and dirty places (toilets, commodes).[193] This view is sometimes countervailed by the idea that jinn also love "beautiful," "clean," "uncontaminated," or "pure" human beings; this belief is a key element in diagnosing and treating cases of possession. One practitioner stated emphatically

> Jinn are enamored with beauty . . . they pay attention only to a person with a *ṭâhìr* (ritually pure) body. [. . .] As for the *nigìs* (profane) body, the jinn do not like it.[194]

In numerous instances of possession, the intruding spirit gave "the beauty" and/or "the purity" of the afflicted person as the reason for choosing to enter the body and affect the mind. This belief in the purity of a possessed person plays a key role in maintaining a positive attitude on the part of the community toward the afflicted person; such a person is not considered profane and thus, does not lose status or face. By contrast, a person whom psychiatrists diagnose as mentally disturbed is viewed largely in negative terms; in folk parlance such a person is commonly labeled *màgnûn* (crazy), *màkhlûl* (i.e., *mùkhtàl al-¿àql*, mentally dysfunctional), or addressed by one of a number of derogatory and taunting euphemisms, such as *sarâyâ ṣafra* ("yellow-palace," i.e., "funny farm," mental asylum) or "¿Abbâsiyyah."[195]

A special category of jinn are perceived as household spirits; they are referred to as the *¿ùmmâr* (dwellers or inhabitants; sing.: *¿âmìr*). They coexist with humans in the same living quarters and are viewed as the keepers and defenders of the home against malevolent jinn and other intruding spirits who do not belong (a similar function is also carried out by a snake found in many homes and viewed as a protector against outside snakes). Reptiles may also be jinn (or other supernatural beings) assuming the form of an animal.[196] When such a snake (or other animals, notably a cat or

---

[193] Padwick, *Notes on the Jinn*, pp. 430ff. Winifred S. Blackman, *The Fellahin of Upper Egypt* (London, 1927), pp. 15ff.

[194] Informant: Shâkir (see n. 74). This viewpoint is also expressed by others. See App. 11, where a woman's "purity" was cited as one of the reasons her male [jinni] familiar became attracted to her. Also see El-Shamy, "Belief-Characters . . . " (p. 17), where the purity of the body of a young man attracted a possessing female jinn-woman (App. 13).

[195] A district of Cairo where the mental institution is located. Yellow is the presumed color of the mental asylum/hospital.

A change of attitudes toward mental illness is heralded in a report titled "The Mentally Ill Outside the Fences of el-¿Abbâsiyyah [Asylum]. For the First Time: Cairo Tries the Treatment of the Ill Mentally and Psychologically in Public Hospitals Amidst People and Society," in *Al-Ahram*, 8/17/1970. Also see A. ¿Abd al-Mun¿im, "Educated Women Become Oriented Toward the zâr, While Non-Literate Women Turn to Psychiatry," in *Al-Ahram*, 16/2/1971, p. 3. The article reports that of a sample of zâr-female customers, 8 percent are university graduates, some of whom hold major [administrative] positions; it also reports that all their psychiatric problems are attributable to marital discord.

[196] S. Ḥusayn, *al-Ginn*, p. 56; Amîn, *Qâmûs*, pp.141–143; Sayce, *Folk-Lore*, Vol. 11, No. 4, p. 390; Lane, *Modern Egyptians*, pp. 224–225; Nöldke, "Die Schlange nach arabischen Volksglauben," in: *Zeitsch*

a dog, particularly if black in color) is encountered, especially during nighttime, precautionary measures should be taken before one would cause the animal harm or drive it away in a harsh manner.[197]

Jinn may also steal a healthy human infant and leave in its stead a sickly child of their own. If a human infant is left alone or its crying ignored, the infant is believed to attract the jinn who will be tempted to make the substitution. In such a case the jinn infant is labeled *badàl* (a substitute, i.e., changeling). The changeling may be recognized by its full set of teeth, insatiable appetite for food, and being incurably sick. Therefore, parents in many folk quarters do not like to leave their infants unattended or let them cry.[198] Consequently, as soon as an infant starts crying, it is immediately attended to so as not to draw the jinn's attention and allow them a chance to undertake/complete the substitution. Such a practice associated with the process of enculturation (socialization) has far-reaching consequences on character development, especially during the early years of his or her life.

Until relatively recently, certain physical disorders were believed to be caused by jinn. As reported by a physician, these illnesses were numerous and included serious diseases as syphilis and jaundice, which were reported to be caused by supernatural agents and to be cured by magical means, including the "Fear Cup" ritual.[199] It is worth noting here that some scholarly movements that attempt to offer rational explanations of certain religious dogma reinterpret "jinn" to mean "jerms" or microbes.[200] Although the scope of such jinn-generated ailments seems to have shrunk considerably during the past few decades, residuals still linger actively. Additionally, in many "enlightened" communities the old beliefs are being revitalized under the impact of neo-fundamentalism that came into power during the 1970s.

An undefined female supernatural creature typically called *esh-Shàmmâmàh* (the she-sniffer) is reported to cause the cold sore known as *kàrfàh*; it is believed that she comes during the night and sniffs unwashed mouths of sleeping humans, especially children. Thus, children are instructed that if they don't wash their hands and mouths

---

für Völkerpsychologie und Sprachwissenschaft, Vol. 1 (1860), pp. 412–416; see also "Killing Vipers." In: al-Gindi, *al-Ginn*, Vol. 2, pp. 53–71, esp. p. 58.

In folktales, jinn appear in the form of snakes. Typically, a jinni female assumes the form of "viper" (female) while a male assumes the form of a snake (male); Motifs: F337.3§, "Fairy (in viper form) saved from pursuer (unwanted suitor): grateful;" F337.3.1§, ‡"Jinni-maiden (woman) grateful for protection from sexual assault (rescuing her sexual honor or modesty)." For examples from folk literature, see El-Shamy, *MITON*, pp. 11–12; also see n. 364.

[197] See al-Gindî, *al-Ginn*, Vol. 2, pp. 53–77, 89–105. For a case where a jinni in a form of cat bites a girl and makes her ill, see App. 23 (cf. App. 22). Also, *The Fellahin*, p. 75) cites a case in which a woman beat a cat that proved to be her supernatural *'Ukht* (sister).

Cf. "Agathodaemon" in Lane, *Modern Egyptians*, p. 226; Motif: A416.2§, ‡"Patron saint of city or district (guardian-genius, or Agathodaemon)." See n. 367.

[198] See El-Shamy, "The Changeling," in *Folktales of Egypt*, No. 43, pp. 179–180; Walker-Ismâ¿îl, *Folk Medicine*, p. 48; Amîn, *Qâmûs*, p. 324; also cf. Amîn, p. 267, where measures against the "changeling" are given under "*ḍabbah*" ([old-fashioned] door-bar or wooden-lock), i.e., "barring-out" the jinn.

[199] See Walker-Ismâ¿îl, *Folk Medicine*, p. 69.

[200] See *al-Manâr*, Vol. 9 (1909), p. 335; Goldziher/al-Naggâr, *Madhâhib*, pp. 383–385; cf. Nawfal, *¿Âlam al-ginn wa al-malâ'ikah* (The world of Jinn and Angels) pp. 84–88.

after a meal, the "she-sniffer" will come during the night and "sniff" at them, and leave them with the bothersome sore. In this respect, the she-sniffer is comparable to—and is also likely to be member of—another category of minor zoological beings used for socializing and other disciplining purposes.[201] (See Sections II.B.1a and II.D.1)

With reference to jinn in general, names such as "*mârid*" (giant), "*¿àfrît*" (afrit), "*¿oan*" (giant/afrit), and "*sheṭân*" (devil) often refer to different types of jinn with various personal capabilities. The words "*qabîlàh*" (tribe) and "*ṣaff*" (line, file, platoon) refer to a group of jinn; meanwhile, "*màlik*" (king) and "*sulṭân*" (sultan) refer to jinn with potent political powers. The sultan of all the jinn is commonly known as *Shàmhûrìsh*. Professional shaman-*shaikh*s report that he is dead and has been succeeded by his son, Abu-l-Walîd.[202] Other names, such as *khâdim* (servant), *Qarîn* (counter-spirit, spouse, correlative, familiar), *'Akhkh* (Brother) and *'Ukht* (Sister) refer to jinn in their relationship to humans. (See Section II.C)

Practicing shaman-*mashâyìkh* dealing with this category of the supernatural always consult lists of the names, characteristics, and powers of the jinn. Such sources are professionally compiled and represent trade manuals and handbooks that circulate mainly in print and, occasionally, in manuscript form.[203] In this context of using the jinn, they are referred to as *'à¿wân* (helpers, aids) or *khùddâm* (servants). They may serve a certain individual (e.g., a shaman, a "magician," a devout person), or they may be in the service of an object (e.g., brick from old tomb, ring, lamp) and become obliged to obey the commands of the person who possesses or controls that object.[204] (See Section II.B.3)

---

[201] S. Ḥusayn (*al-Ginn*, pp. 61–62) reports the phenomenon of *kàrfàh* [cold sore], as proof that jinn consume food, but attributes the occurrence of the sore to Satan. He cites a Prophet's *ḥadîth* describing Satan as "*jassâsun[-]laḥḥâsun*" (feeler-licker, i.e., one who touches and licks [sleepers]), and adds:

> that is what happens to the fellahin's children, who eat stew [cooked] with fat then go to bed without having washed their hands. Satan comes and licks their mouths and hands. . . .

Evidently, S. Ḥusayn substitutes Satan for the she-sniffer. Also see Walker-Ismâ¿îl (pp. 68, 113), where "*impetigo* (*kàrfàh*)" is reported to appear "when a viper blows its poison into the body," and is, therefore, believed to be cured by snake charmers.

A concept likely to be related to Satan being a "licker" is expressed in the vernacular word "malḥûs." It recurs in daily life in describing a person who is extremely silly, or whose behavior is bordering on lunacy.

[202] Informant: Shâkir, June 24, 1972 (see n. 74). It seems that the sacred Hebrew name of God—"Shem hamme forash" (the unspoken name of God), has become "Shamhûrish," the king of all the jinn in Muslim folk traditions. Cf. Walker, 1934, p. 38 note 1; Winkler, 1930, p. 142; Samja Jahn, ed., tr. *Arabishe Volksmärchen* (Berlin, 1970), p. 472.

[203] On the attitudes toward manuscripts, see Amîn's comment in n. 230.

[204] The recurrent examples of this power are to be found in folktales: Tale-types AT 560, "*The Magic Ring*. [Lost, but recovered by grateful cat, dog, and mouse];" and 561, *Aladdin*. [Magic wishing lamp (ring) from treasure trove stolen and subsequently recovered by means of another magic object.]

However, the theme seems to be restricted to fantasy tales where a "magic ring" (also labelled "Solomon's ring") appears frequently. There are no reports of a person in contemporary actual life in possession of such a wish-fulfilling magic object.

Compare the religious belief in "Wishing by *ṭâqàt al-qàdr* ('[Light-]Halo of Power')," (Motif: D1761.3.1§). (See n. 663)

The presumed utilitarian functions of jinn extend to language. Every letter of the Arabic alphabet, every word, verse, or chapter of the Koran; every number, figure, proper name, time period, second, hour, day, month, etc., is viewed in Sunni orthodox philosophy to have been created by God *a priori*. For practitioners of the craft of harnessing jinn, each of these created things has its own *khùddâm* (servants), a *khâdim ¿ùlwî* (upper servant) who is typically a minor angel, and a *khâdim sùflî* (lower or nether servant) who is typically a jinn. The former is a good angel (or occasionally a *good believing* jinn), while the latter is an *evil*, infidel, and unbelieving jinn. This concept is crucial in magico–religious rituals that seek to harness the *khuddâm* through knowledge of their names and other personal attributes, and through the belief in the hierarchical power structure of jinn community.[205] The organization of the jinn in this respect is similar to that of angels and reflects, but to a lesser extent, the same type of military-like discipline and power hierarchies. Jinn are also perceived in terms of political organization of tribes and kingdoms headed by kings.[206]

II.B.1. *gìnnìyyât* (Female Jinn)

Jinn, like humans, are either males or females, young or old; they also are of all races, social classes, and religions. The word *gînnìyyàh* (pl.: *gìnnìyyât*) may denote a female jinni in the broadest sense. Yet, in oral traditions, the word *gìnnìyyàh* seems to be used mainly to refer to a female water spirit; a female member of the general jinn is usually referred to as "*wàḥdàh min el-gìnn*," (a female-one of the jinn) or "*wàḥdàh min tàḥt el-'àrḍ*" (a female from underground), or in a similar descriptive manner. (Informants sometimes use the word "*gìnnìyyàh*" to designate a female jinni merely for convenience, mainly when trying to clarify the nature of that creature to an outsider.) A female jinni may help a person, or she may possess, or cause illness to a human individual; yet, female jinn are practically never used as "servants" or "aids" in "magical" practices. Also, a female jinni may marry, and/or establish a *mikhawìyyàh* (*mu'âkhâh* meaning brotherly/sisterly relationship with a human being, i.e., a human male becomes the "brother" of a jinn female, or a human female becomes the "sister" of a jinn male; henceforward, this concept will be designated as foster-sibling). In

---

[205]al-Bûnî (*Manba¿*, pp. 81–82) proposes "*nàṣb al-màndàl* (setting up of the màndàl)" so as to ask about the chief of the tribe of the *¿âṣ* (defiant/rebellious-[jinni]) who refuses to abide by the *shaikh*'s commands to exit the body of the person it has entered.

Cf. Motifs: F252, "Government of fairies [(jinn)];" F405.15§, "Spirit leaves when exorciser threatens to resort to its government." (See n. 169; and Section II.B.2a) For a case in which such a threat of resorting to a more senior jinni, the king, was made by a contemporary shaman-*shaikh*, see El-Shamy, "Belief Characters . . . ," p. 19 (App. 13).

[206]Cf. the following image from fictitious folk literature, where a jinn-servant of a magic wishing ring describes his domain:

> I am Sultan over two-and-seventy tribes of the Jinn, each two-and-seventy thousand in number every one of which thousand ruleth over a thousand Marids, each Marid over a thousand Ifrits, each Ifrit over a thousand Satans and each Satan over a thousand Jinn: and they are all under command of me and may not gainsay me. (Burton, *Arabian Nights*, Vol. 10, p. 28.)

theory, these two types of interaction—a female of the jinn becoming the wife of a human male, on the one hand, or becoming his sister, on the other—are distinguished from each other. Nonetheless, in most reported cases, the borderlines between the two types of relationships tend to be very hazy.[207] Scholars view supernatural foster-sibling (*el-mikhawìyyàh*, bebrothering) as establishing a mere *friendly* relationship.[208] A broader systemic consideration of field data, however, indicate that this bond is much more serious and has broader and more significant psychological implications than mere "friendship," or "friendliness" would suggest. (See Section II.C, and App. 11 and 12)

A *gìnnìyyàh* seems to become implicated in the lives of Adamites mostly as a female water spirit. It is frequently reported that certain men are married from under the water or from *el-bàḥr* (sea, i.e., river).[209] In this context—as is the case in marriage to the female jinn who is not associated with water—a marriage contract is concluded at the outset of the relationship. A man should not be foolish enough to offer to support the *gìnnìyyàh* because she would ruin him with her demands. When he, contrary to the "ideal" situation in human society, chooses her to support him, he will lead a prosperous life and usually remain a bachelor. This belief is often cited to account for the bachelorhood of those few men who remain unwed (or celibate) in a folk community. It is possible, however, for a married man to negotiate with a *gìnnìyyàh* a prenuptial agreement that would allow for his marrying a human woman as well. The terms of such an agreement depend on the strength of the attraction and attachment the *gìnnìyyàh* has to that man. Children born out of this sort of wedlock belong to the mother. If the man were to reveal the secret, the *gìnnìyyàh* would drown him. This aspect of the belief also accounts for the disappearance of numerous men from folk communities.[210]

---

[207]On the topic of marriage between jinn and humans see al-Gindi, *al-Ginn*, Vol. 2, pp. 157–170. Cf. Tale-type 470E§, *Man in Utopian Otherworld Punished for His Desire to Marry Foster-Sister(s).*

See Hasan El-Shamy, "Sibling in *Alf laylah wa laylah*." In: *Marvels & Tales: Journal of Fairy-Tale Studies*. Special Issue: *The Arabian Nights: Past and Present*, U. Marzolph, Guest Ed. (Wayne University Press), 2004: Vol. 18 No. 2, pp. 170–186, especially pp. 177–181.

[208]Littmann, for example, translated "*mikhawiyyah el-gân*" as "mit den Geistern befreundet war" (*Geisterbeschwörungen*, pt. B1, p. 16, Arabic, p. 86). Yet, the context in which his informant accounted for the origin of the *zâr* involved a jinni falling in love with pharaoh's daughter and the jinni's desire to marry her. An old woman named "Zârah" acted as healing priestess, hence, the name. Clearly, the relation involved is more than mere friendliness.

[209]For an example, see "The One Sesame Seed," in Hasan El-Shamy, *Folktales of Egypt*, No. 3, pp. 25–28, 244–245 (Tale-type AaTh 465, *The Man Persecuted Because of His Beautiful Wife*. [supernatural wife helps husband perform impossible tasks]). Also cf. the story of "Jullanâr of the Sea," in *'Alf laylah wa laylah*, Vol. 3, pp. 247–270 (Burton, Vol. 7, pp. 264–308). This belief harkens back to Egyptian antiquity, see Maspero/El-Shamy, *Ancient Egypt*, p. 12 note 4.

[210]Informant: An elderly Kenûzî Nubian woman named Zainab G.; she stated emphatically: "Our men were married from underwater. . . . " She, like all members of her community, believes that the inexplicable disappearance of some men from the village scene is due to abduction by underwater people (i.e., *jinniyyât*).

Motifs: F420.6.1, "Marriage or liaison of mortals and water-spirits;" cf. T198.3.4§, ‡"Unhappy (angered) husband leaves marital home;" S11.9§, "Runaway father (deserts family)."

II.B.1a. Unstratified female jinn

Other minor female jinn or jinn-like beings called *gìnnìyyât* seem to belong to a less integrated and unstratified subsystem of the supernatural community. The degree of interconnectedness between a member of this amorphous group and the larger jinn category is minimal. Among these is *¿Arûsìt-el-Bàḥr* (sea-bride or sea-maiden), sometimes called *'Omm-esh-Shu¿ûr* (the one-with-[long-]hair); she sits at river banks or wells and captivates men with her beauty, especially her extraordinarily long hair. *el-Mùzayyaràh* is another female water spirit, seldom reported in any other context beside water sources; she stands by river banks pretending to be a stranded human female and then kills those who approach her by squirting them with fire from her iron breast.[211] *En-Nàddâhàh* (the she-caller) seems to be a dry-land spirit; she calls on people to follow her, and when they respond, she leads them astray. Sometimes those who follow *en-Nàddâhàh* return in a state of bewilderment after a period of time; occasionally, they are never to be found.[212]

It is interesting to note that no male component of any of these supernatural female beings was ever reported; moreover, the masculine forms for these feminine names do not exist in the active vocabulary of the concerned Arabic dialects. All these beings appear in various Egyptian communities and often simultaneously in the same community. In numerous cases, different names of *gìnnìyyât* (female jinn) were given by informants to designate the same being, but in different roles. This multiple identity of a supernatural being is also recognized in semi-learned writings.[213]

Members of these groups of the individualized female jinn constitute a separate cognitive subsystem. As pointed out earlier, they are never used as "servants" or "aids"

For a fictitious case depicting the life of a human woman wed to an under water human-like character, see "The Sultan of the Underwater" in El-Shamy, *Tales Arab Women Tell*, No. 23, pp. 195–199, 433 (Tale-type AaTh 425L, *The Padlock on the Enchanted Husband*. [Human wife cast out for discovering supernatural husband's secret: forgiven]).

In this context, Sengers Sates:

> In Upper Egypt in particular it is believed that demons living in the water (the Nile) are the souls of the deceased (they are generally called ʿafarit). People who come close to the river can be pulled into the depths by the spirits. (*Women and Demons*, p. 133.)

This conclusion does not specify what sort of "demons" are involved in pulling people into the depth. The supernatural beings involved in such an act may belong to the category of general jinn labelled "ginn ghawâṣah" (Divers), or the "unstratified female jinn" designated here in Section II.B.1a; however, none of these beings would normally be labelled "ʿafrit." The "demons" of which Sengers speaks may also designate the ghosts (*¿afârît*) of persons who died *by drowning* (or a similar violent death; i.e., ghosts) rather than, the indiscriminate, "souls of the deceased" she gives in her statement.

[211] For a text illustrating an encounter with this supernatural character, see "El-Muzayyara," in El-Shamy, *Folktales of Egypt*, No. 44, pp. 180–181, 286; also see Sayce, *Folk-Lore*, Vol. 11 No. 4, p. 387; and Amîn, *Qâmûs*, p. 91.

[212] Informant: Nabawiyyah Y., a middle-aged Cairene housewife (in October 1969). For more information, see El-Shamy, *Tales Arab Women Tell*, No. 9, p. 113, and n. 324, below. For a treatment of this theme in literature, see Yûsuf Idrîs, *al-Naddâhah* (Cairo: Maktabat Gharîb, 1978).

[213] See I. Rushdî, "maraḍ al-'iklimbsia" (Eclampsia). In: *al-Muqtaṭaf* [magazine], No. 22 (Cairo, April 1898), pp. 293–294. Also cf. Amîn, *Qâmûs*, 1953, p. 324.

in shamanistic or "magical" practices; also, they do not appear in the roles of "foster-sisterly relation," wife, or possessing-spirit (see Section II.C.2). Even when a person, usually a male, is reported to be "married from underneath the water," the being he is believed to be married to would *not* be one of those four water spirit categories, but rather a female jinn from the "general jinn" category who just happened to be a resident of an aquatic habitat.

II.B.2. Harnessing the Jinn and Minor Angels

Apart from using religious service—such as reciting verses from the Koran so as to exert pressure on the angels, jinn, or Satan in order to influence their conduct,[214] a person may resort to other rituals that clearly lie outside the realm of formal religion. Only a limited number of such rituals may be labeled *sìḥr* (magic). However, available academic literature has been uncritical in treating such nonformal rituals and their underlying beliefs by lumping their various categories and branches under the heading of *sìḥr* (magic)—an undiscriminating word that may denote magic, witchcraft, or sorcery, as well as—occasionally—some nonmagical healing rituals that lie in the realm of the para-religious rituals.

For early Moslem jurists, not all practices that may have been labeled *sìḥr* (magic) were indeed so from a judiciary's (*shrî¿ah*) standpoint. Consequently, different penal codes were devised for the various types of "magic." For example, "Imam" Moḥammad ibn Idrîs al-Shâfi¿î (AD 767–820) founder of the Shâfi¿ite-*màdhhàb*, one of the four recognized orthodox schools of Sunni Islamic jurisprudence,[215] stated that

> . . . if a person is accused of having learned *sìḥr* ("magic/witchcraft"), we would ask him, "Describe your magic for us." If he describes what would constitutes *kùfr* (unbelief, being an infidel)—as [for example], that which people-of-Babel had believed concerning *at-taqarrùb 'ilâ* (venerating) the Seven Planets and that these planets do what is begged of them—then that person is an "infidel," but if [that person's description of the "magic"] does not constitute infidelity, he would become an infidel [only] if he believes that [true magic] should be allowed (*'ibâḥatàh*, i.e., considered legitimate).[216]

---

[214]See 'Usâmah 'al-Karm, *ḥiwâr ma¿a al-ginn. 'asra¿ ṭuruq ¿ilâg al-'amrâḍ al-musta¿ṣiyah bi al-Qur'ân* (*Discourse with Jinn. The Fastest Methods for Treating Incurable Illnesses with Koran*; Cairo: Madbûlî, 1990). Cf. Sengers "*'ilâg bi-al-qur'ân* (Koran Healing)." In: *Women and Demons*, pp. 22, 123–155. Also see n. 306 and 332.

[215]The other three *màdhhab*s are the Mâlikî, founded by Anas ibn Mâlik (ca 715–795); the Ḥanafî, founded by Al-Nu¿mân ibn Thâbit, nicknamed Abû Ḥanîfah (700–767); and the Ḥanbalî founded by Aḥmad ibn Ḥanbal (780–855). The latter, with the smallest numerical following, is recognized as the most strict and rigid; the common expression (a proverbial phrase): "to be a *ḥabalî*" signifies being too dogmatic or intolerant. See also n. 569.

[216]As quoted in Yûsuf al-Digwî's *ta¿allum al-siḥr* (The Learning of Magic), pp. 490–491. Cf. n. 171.

Another viewpoint asserts that a human being may not trespass on the jinn sphere and interact with a jinni (male or female). Violation of these boundaries may result in the loss of mind (i.e., madness) and religious faith. The fact that God granted Prophet Solomon power over jinn was in response to Solomon's prayer to be granted kingship that has not been allowed before, or would be given, any one after himself

Likewise, applying the same judicial considerations, Ibn Khaldûn did not consider the science of letters *siḥr* (magic/witchcraft).[217]

In more recent times, this basic distinction still characterizes how "magic" is perceived. Thus, Lane reported

> The more intelligent of Muslims distinguish two types of magic which they term "Er-rooḥânee" [...] and "Es-Seemiyâ:" the former is *spiritual* magic, which is believed to effect its wonders by agency of angels and genii, and by the mysterious virtue of certain names of God, [...]: the latter is *natural* and *deceptive* magic; and its chief agents, the less credulous Muslims believe[,] to be certain perfumes and drugs, which affect vision and imagination nearly in the same manner as opium [...].
>
> "Er-rooḥânee," which is universally considered among Egyptians, as *true* magic, is of two kinds: "¿ilwee" (or high) and "suflee" (or low); which are also called "raḥmânee" (or divine, or, literally, relating to "the Compassionate," which is an epithet of God) and "shayṭânee" (or satanic).[218]

Similarly, A. Amîn identifies the types of "magic" along the same lines specified by Lane. He, however, relates the practice to the supernatural servants as "*¿ùlwî*" (upper) and "*sùflî*" (nether) servants.[219]

Students of "magical" practices have applied various descriptive terms to characterize the specifics of the ritual under examination. For example Ismâ¿îl—an MD and a social reformer—labeled such rituals "enslavement" of jinn;[220] Amîn, a distinguished historian, speaks of "*taskhîr al-gân*" (coercing jinn into forced labor or subjugation);[221] El-Gawhary (Gohary) addresses the use of "God's Names in Magical Practices in al-Bûnî's Written Works."[222] In this respect, the criterion according to which scholars have determined that a certain practice is "magical" seems to be the presence in a ritual of the element of coercing or subjugating supernatural beings, especially jinn, for utilitarian objectives in the same manner in which wild beasts are domesticated and their powers harnessed.[223] This concept is similar to the Koranic description of how God has subjugated (*sákhkhara*) to man numerous entities (e.g., sun and moon, day and night, wind and sea, riding and farming animals, edible

(Koran, 38:35). Thus, Solomon's case is unique and cannot be extended to any other human beings (See: Fawqiyyah al-Kouly, "Islam Prohibits Magic and Contact with, and [Secular] Law Considers these acts Crimes of Impostery," *Al-Ahram* (9/8/1978, p. 11). See also n. 181.

[217] Ibn Khaldûn/Rosenthal, *The Muqaddimah*, Vol. 3, pp. 171–182.

[218] Lane, *Modern Egyptians*, p. 263.

[219] See S. Ḥusayn, *al-Ginn*, p. 103. Amîn does not include an entry for "siḥr" (Magic/Witchcraft). See: "bùrg" (Zodiac), and the upper/nether servant for each *bùrg* in his *Qâmûs*, p. 84.

[220] As expressed by Ismâ¿îl (see, Walker-Ismâ¿îl, *Folk Medicine*, p. 98).

[221] Amîn, *Qâmûs*, pp. 116–119.

[222] M. El-Gawhary, "Die Gottesnamen". (See n. 13)

[223] This objective is specified in the title *al-Kawâkib al-lammâ¿ah fî taskhîr mulûk al-gin fî al-waqt wa al-sâ¿ah* (The Shimmering Planets in [How to] Instantly Coerce Jinn into Forced Labor), of a magic manual composed by "The *sháykh/¿âlim, ḥâkim al-gìn, waliyy Allâh* (The Shaikh, the ¿Âlim, the Ruler over Jinn, Protegee of God) ¿Abd-Allâh al-Maghâwrî."

In his *Qâmûs* (p. 119), Amîn cites this work as: "*al-Bahgah al-lammâ¿ah fî [...]*" (The Shimmering Delight in [...]).

animals and birds, etc.). God's placing the jinn under Prophet Solomon's control, and Solomon's use of the jinn for accomplishing certain tasks that seem to lie beyond human capabilities, are perceived as part of that subjugation (Koran, 21:82). Yet, due to the facts that Solomon is a prophet, and that the jinn and the other creatures were coerced into carrying out his orders by God's command, this very situation is never thought of as constituting "magic," characterizing it as such would be considered a sacrilege.

Occasionally the terms "white magic" and "black magic" are used to distinguish between rituals used for "good" purposes and those used for "evil" purposes, respectively; such labels, however, do not specify what is meant by "magic." Nonetheless, the rationale and the mechanisms involved in the folk practices do not seem to coincide with the idea of the "enslavement" of jinn.

An academic study proposed the use of the term *sìḥr ràsmî* (formal magic) to refer to rituals performed by trained, mostly literate or semiliterate practitioners who are usually—but not necessarily—professional and belong to exclusive groups generally referred to as "*mashâyìkh*" (shamans, faith-healers), or—as branded by their critics—*dàggâlîn, mùshà¿withîn* (impostors, charlatans, quacks). The study also proposes the term *sìḥr shà¿bî* (folk magic) to refer to rituals performed by laymen (e.g., a mother applying an incantation to her child so as to cure or protect).[224] This distinction—though useful in that it differentiates between two sets of the nonformal rituals, does not recognize the folk *religious* nature of the so-called "formal magic." The proposed distinction would merely set apart two types of rituals according to the level of specialization of the practitioner and that of the consumer of the ritualistic service.[225]

[224] M. al-Gawhary/Gouhary, "al-siḥr al-rasmî wa al-siḥr al-sha¿bî." In: *The National Review of Social Sciences*, Vol. 7, No. 2, (Cairo, 1970), pp. 3–23, p. 6. And El-Gawhary, "al-ginn fi al-mu¿taqad al-sha¿bî (Jinn in the [Egyptian] Folk Beliefs)." In: *The National Review of Social Sciences*, Vol. 9, No. 1, (Cairo, 1972), pp. 95–131.

[225] Anthony F.C. Wallace addressed the issue of differentiating among various categories of rituals. He classified religious and related practices into four types, which he labelled "cult institutions": "individualistic," "shamanistic," "communal," and "ecclesiastical."

1. In the individualistic the ritual is conducted by layman for himself (luck cult, making one's own amulet, or the like).
2. In the shamanistic, workers of magic and diviners work for laymen (the fortune-teller cult, faith healer for an individual, etc.).
3. In the communal, lay officials who act as priests for particular groups at prescribed times (e.g., heads of Sufi associations officiating at a saint's celebration, public *zar*-cult, etc.).
4. In the ecclesiastical, professional clergy organized into bureaucracy, denominations, sects, etc. (Christianity/"Catholicism," Judaism, Islam, etc.; the cleric officiates for the entire nation in situations such as sending troops to war, celebrating peace treaty, opening of a parliamentary session, or the like).

The proposed "folk magic," as defined by El-Gawhary (see n. 222), would fall under the "individualistic," while "formal magic" would fall under "shamanistic" or "communal" cult institutions according Wallace's schema. See Wallace, *Religion*, pp. 84–101. For a detailed analysis, see Hasan El-Shamy, "Al-dîn wa al-thaqâfah: naẓrah anthropoalojiyyah (Religion and Culture: an Anthropological View)." In: Majallat al-khiṭâb al-thaqafî (*Journal of Cultural Discourse*). Vol. 1, No. 1 (Fall, 2006), pp. 1–24. (King Saûd University, Riyadh, Saudi Arabia).

As will be pointed out below, the so-called "formal magic" is actually a segment of the religious system as it is practiced among the folk; it may also be seen as para-religious rituals (or even a "folk" component of a religion). From the perspective of native practitioners and their clients, rituals that may be designated as "formal magic" are not perceived as *sìḥr* (witchcraft or sorcery), nor are they referred to as such. The person who practices this craft is not called *sâḥìr* or *sàḥḥâr* (magician, sorcerer, witch, wizard, warlock, etc.) but is normally referred to as shaman-*shaikh*, or shaman-*shaikhàh* (if a female practitioner); the plural form for both male and female practitioners is *mashâyìkh*. These folk appellations are characteristically used to designate clergymen, community notables or elders, or saints and persons marked for sainthood upon their death, and carry the same connotations the English title "Reverend" may signify. However, until relatively recently, women had not been frequently reported to be actively involved in this branch of specialized form of the craft, presumably due to the fact that the execution of its rituals relies heavily on literacy, and the ability to write and perform arithmetical calculations, a rare commodity among members of folk groups, and even more scarce among females. (Currently, however, this situation is changing mainly due to the effects of mandatory elementary education through secular schooling for members of both sexes; consequently, the number of literate female shamans has been steadily increasing.)

These practitioners (shaman-*mashâyìkh*) derive their power from reliance on actual or assumed formal religious dogma. In folk communities the title *sâḥìr* (i.e., sorcerer, magician, or witch) is applied to a practitioner who derives his/her powers from sacrilegious means and antisacred agents (see App. 34). Beliefs in the hierarchical stratification of both angel and jinn communities, the "organic" connection between their names and their constitution as nonhuman entities, and in the accountability of both communities of supernatural beings before higher powers, provide the rationale for the possibility of controlling or harnessing them through various ritualistic procedures.

Proceeding from the premise that magic is a form of pseudoscience that seeks to "control" the supernatural, as compared to religion, which "solicits" the aid of the sacred supernatural (deity),[226] we will have to conclude that within the context of monotheism the so-called "formal magic" is not magic at all. It is rather a form of institutionalized but not formalized folk religious subsystem.[227] It relies on para-religious beliefs and on the old "science of letters" (*¿ìlm al-ḥùrûf*) for its procedures; this subsystem revolves around the concept of God, and rests on certain formal religious doctrines that explain its efficacy and provide the basis for its development and continued open existence in a community. Al-Bûnî (d. 1225 AD, see n. 13)—who is perhaps the most prominent figure in the practice of the so-called "formal magic"—characterizes that "science" as follows:

---

[226] Bronislaw Malinowski, *Magic, Science, and Religion* (Garden City, NY: 1925).

[227] See J.D.J. Waardenburg, "Official and Popular Religion as a Problem in Islamic Studies." In: Peter Henrik Vrijhof & Jacques Waardeburg, eds., *Official and Popular Religion, Analysis of Themes for Religious Studies*. Religion and Society 19. (The Hague/Paris: Mouton 1979), pp. 340–386.

Be advised that the science of letter is a *sharîf* (glorious, honorable [i.e., sacred]) and *nûrânî* (light-bound) science; it is [also] a spiritual, soul-bound, delicate secret [that] has been trusted by those who are knowledgeable and relied upon by the virtuous among the ulama.[228]

Al-Bûnî specifies the conditions under which this type of ritual that addresses the supernatural is managed.

First: the practitioner must be of utterly pure (*ṭâhìr*) soul and attire.

Second: when the proper angel is contacted, this angel will first get from God permission to go to the aid of the person who summoned him.

Third: the practitioner "must not apply [. . . his power] except to that [i.e., to achieve goals] that would please God."

Fourth: al-Bûnî declares that it would be sinful to show a book of his composition (of "magic"-manuals) except to those who are *'àhlihi* (lit.: its family, i.e., worthy and protective of it), or expose it in a location unworthy of its merits.

In concluding his instructions, al-Bûnî reminds the potential user of his manuals that he must also not harbor sinful notions, since "deeds are [judged by God] according to [man's] intentions" behind them.[229] These perceived attributes of the "science of letters," as well as their consequences in terms of actions (rituals) are virtually identical with those assigned to "*al-mùṣḥàf ash-sharîf*" (*The Glorious Koran* [as a sacred book]).

The practitioner of the so-called "formal magic" undertakes "upper works" (i.e., "white magic") and is also capable of performing "nether-works" (i.e., black magic, sorcery). However, he/she normally refrains from trafficking with the latter because of its inherent sacrilegious and sinful (*ḥarâm*) nature. A number of practicing *mashâyìkh* (shaman-*shaikhs*) informed this writer that a pious "*khâdìm*" (i.e., a jinn or an angel who acts as servant or aid) would disobey the command of the practitioner if committing a sinful act is involved. Also, a shaman-*shaikh* is always aware of the limitations that formal religion imposes on such "servants." The shaman does not, for example, try to set the jinn to "read" the future, but he typically asks them to report on the past and the present since they are presumed to have lived during the time when past events took place. Yet, a practitioner may occasionally ask the jinn to foretell how a certain event will turn out. The answer the jinn give in this situation

---

[228]The Arabic text cited as description of the "science of letters" is as follows:

[. . .] *¿ilm sharîf nûrânî, wa sìrr laṭîf rûḥanî ¿awwala ¿alyhi al-'akâbiru min al-'awliyâ' al-¿ârifìn wa 'i¿tamada ¿alyhi al-'afâḍilu min al-¿ulamâ'.* (al-Bûnî, *Shams*, p. 52)

Also see Lane, *Modern Egyptians*, pp. 263–264.

[229]al-Bûnî, *Shams*, pt. 1, pp. 3–4. Also see "Sharḥ al-Barahtiyyah" (The Exegesis of the Barahtiyyah). In: al-Bûnî, *Manba¿*, p. 90.

would be considered a highly skilful deduction or inference rather than foretelling the future (see App. 21); by contrast, a prophet or saint's answer would be based on reading the unknown off the Tablet of Destiny safeguarded in heaven due to the gift of clairvoyance (see Section I.E). Accounts of incidents of jinn—"servants" being commanded to perform tasks through the *sùflî* (nether, satanic) rituals show that the jinn involved are of infidel or rebellious categories. (See n. 248, and App. 34)

The practitioner constructs a *¿amàl* (lit.: "work," i.e., fix, spell, gramerye, hex, charm, etc.), which is assumed to produce the desired effect under prescribed conditions. The Arabic word *¿amàl* simply signifies "work" or "deed;" however, as a technical term in the jargon of the shamanistic craft, it denotes a written spell in material form—an artifact; the plural form of this term is the ungrammatical "*¿amalât*" (fixes, charms, hexes), but *never* the correct form *'a¿mâl*, a word that signifies "deeds," "actions," or "doings." Typically, the *¿amàl* is in written form; in this context, the words *yiktìb* (to write) and *kitâbàh* (a writing, an inscription) signify "to produce a charm" and "a charm, or a gramerye" respectively.[230] When compared with other artifacts produced by practitioners, the charm/gramerye is of active, "on the offense" nature; it is intended for making desired things happen. By contrast, a *ḥigâb*, *ḥirz*, or *tàḥwîṭàh* (lit.: [protective] barrier/veil, seal/sanctuary, or encirclement, respectively—i.e., an amulet, talisman, etc.), is of passive, "on the defensive" nature; it is meant to prevent undesirable things from occurring or getting to the subject under their protection. An example of the first (the *¿amàl*) would be a writing that generates love or hatred between two individuals; while an example of the second (the *ḥigâb*) would be the wearing of a blue bead or a similar ornament that is believed to protect against the evil eye.[231]

Two "things" are used to identify the person at whom the "fix" will be aimed and applied: an *'aṭàr* (i.e., *'athàr*: trace, vestige, residual), and the name of that person identified through matrilineal descent. The identifying—"trace" is an object that had been in intimate contact with that person and carries a "trace" from him/her.

---

[230]Motif: D1266.1, "Magic writings (gramerye, runes)." In this respect, the following idioms are recurrent: *yiktìb li* (writ for), *yiktìb bi*... (write so as to generate...); *yiktìb ¿alâ* (write for/against, or write on an object such as paper or skin); *yiktìb ḍiḍ* (write against).

For a sample of books typically found in a traditional village before the establishment of "village libraries" and "culture centers," see: Ammar, *Growing*, pp. 222–223.

Earlier, Ismâ¿îl, had observed that during the late 1890s, one-fourth of the books in the Khedival Library [...] constituting almost a quarter of its contents were of "terrifying" [(i.e., magical]) nature (Walker-Ismâ¿îl, *Folk Medicine*, p. 98); Amîn (*Qâmûs*, pp. 116, 378) also points out that in the public library the dominant and more frequently borrowed works are manuscripts (rather than printed works); the reason is the belief that new books and recent publications have less *barakàh wa fâ'idàh* (blessedness and utilitarian benefit) than do the old. (Cf. n. 203.)

Some fixes go beyond the mere "writing" by offering practical solutions as well: cf. Motifs: T531.2§, "Conception from 'wearing' semen-stained clothing item;" T591.5.1.1§, ‡"'*ṣûfah*': inseminating agent placed on ball of wool (cotton or the like) and 'worn' by woman (i.e., placed in vagina as love-philtre). Typically, it contains human semen."

See App. 13; cf. El-Shamy, *MITON* (Mot.: T591.5.1.1§).

[231]Motifs: D1344.3, "Amulet renders invulnerable;" D2071.1.4.0.1§, ‡"Amulet guards against Evil Eye;" D2071.1.4.1§, "Blue as guard against Evil Eye." See App. 11 and 35.

The more intimate the contact, the more efficacious that object is believed to be in representing its owner. Locks of clipped-off hair, disposed of bodily hair—shaven or "plucked/waxed," cast away after birth—residuals from circumcision operations (e.g., placenta, skin excised from genitalia), unwashed pieces of used underwear or handkerchiefs, dust upon which the target person has trodden barefoot, are typical "traces." The process involved may be described as "contagious magic."[232] Knowledge of the names of the persons and objects involved, it is believed, leads to pinpointing the exact "servants" suited for carrying out the task to be performed. A human being is identified through his or her mother, mother's mother, and so on; in this respect the practice runs contrary to the actual norms in social life where descent is reckoned patrilineally and identifying a man via his mother's name is considered an insult.[233] The rationale for this practice is that the organic relationship between a mother and her offspring is verifiable and thus indisputable, while that between a father and his child is not so. As one informant explained: "No one sees a person [i.e., a sperm] going into the mother [at conception], but everyone sees him coming out [at birth]."[234]

The entire operation rests on some sacred beliefs and on the "science of letters." The use of the "letters and numerals" technique was formalized into certain branches of the Shiite sect and persisted in early forms of Bahaism, thus becoming integrated into the greater body of the *formal* teachings of these religious systems.[235] However, for Sunni Muslims, although this ritualized practice is usually accepted as valid in numerous religious circles, it is not a part of the formal religion ("ecclesiastical cult institutions," to use A.F.C. Wallace's term).[236] It has not been formalized, and the ritual remains outside the bounds of formal Sunni religious dogma.

It is in this sense outlined above, and within that context of accommodating the objectionable yet tolerable—or the "normal abnormality"—that members of

---

[232]This technique was identified by Sir James Frazer (in *The Golden Bough*). It is the standard technique in "magical" ritual in Egypt. (Motifs: D1789§, "Contagious magic. Magic results obtained by contact or touch;" D1789.0.1.1§, "'Trace-measuring': magic diagnosis from a person's residuals.") Contagious magic is differentiated from "Homeopathic"/"sympathetic," which relies on the similarity of one object to another—as exemplified by the Voodoo-doll. The latter type plays only a secondary role in Egyptian practices. (Motifs: D1782, "Sympathetic magic. Magic results obtained by imitating desired action;" D1782.0.1§, "Magic result from effigy in the likeness of target for magic ritual (Voodoo doll).") (Cf. App. 45.)

[233]Motif: Z84.1.1§, "Insult: mention of mother's name."

The significance of the mother's line of descent is further enhanced by the belief that a person may acquire the status of a *sharîf* (descendant of the Prophet) "after mother, even if father is not [a sharîf]." (al-¿Idwî, *Mashâriq*, p. 159). See also n. 573.

[234]Informant: A.M.A, 60, former deputy mayor of Qirshah village (See El-Shamy, *Folktales of Egypt*, p. 75). Motif: T149.1.1§, "Maternity (childbirth) is indisputable, paternity (impregnation) is not."

The concept is extended to the relation between a man in his role of "maternal-uncle" as compared to that man's role as "paternal-uncle". As expressed by a Nubian village notable cited above (October 1969), it is stated: "The maternal-uncle can swear, 'This is my sister's son, but a paternal-uncle . . . can not swear 'This is my brother's child.'" (Motif: P297.0.1§).

[235]See A. Bausani, "Bahâ'ism". In: *EI*², Vol. 1, 915–918; and Ignác Goldziher, *Vorlesungen über den Islam*, Andras and Ruth Hamori, trs. (Princeton, NJ: Princeton University Press, 1981), pp. 250–254.

[236]Motif: D1766, "Magic results produced by religious ceremony."

See Ibn Khaldûn/Rosenthal, *The Muqddimah*, 1958, Vol. 3, pp. 171–182, 263–264. Also see n. 219.

folk groups speak of "*sìḥr ḥalâl*" (legitimate magic), as opposed to mere *sìḥr* (sorcery, witchcraft), which is *ḥarâm* (sinful).[237] Thus, the so-called "formal magic" (or "applied *¿ìlm al-ḥùrûf*") is actually an unformalized para-religious ritual, or—in terms of Wallace's schema—it is a "communal" but *not* an "ecclesiastical cult institution."[238] (Also see Section I.A)

II.B.2a. *fàtḥ el-màndàl* (oracle, detective-divination via jinn)

A specialized oracular ritual known as *fàtḥ el-màndàl* (the opening of *màndàl*, also called *ḍarb el-màndàl*) seeks aid of the jinn in providing information about past events. This detective practice is based on the belief that jinn have greater power of knowledge and capability to observe the locale or sphere they share with humans. Through an intermediary (labeled *nâẓûr*, lit.: viewer, or one who sees), the operator of the *màndàl* ritual—typically labeled *shaikh*, or *shaikh* el-*màndàl*—summons the appropriate jinn and asks them to provide the desired information.

The *màndàl*-operator performs the rituals that lead to the summoning of the jinn to be used as a source of information but does not address them directly.[239] He conducts the process of communicating with them through the intermediary (the *nâẓûr*, lit.: the one who looks or sees) who is typically a young girl or boy, or an adult of low social status and of "whimsical" personality (see Section III.C). The intermediary will "see" the jinn reflected on the surface of a small cup full of liquid, usually oil, ink, or water and will convey instructions from the operator to the jinn and relay information from the jinn to the operator. The answer the jinn give is taken as an eyewitness' testimony of past events.[240] (Cf. Section II.E.2; also see App. 19)

---

[237]The concept appears frequently in folk poetry; for example, a chapbook (pamphlet) is titled, "*kitâb as-siḥr al-ḥalâl fî naẓm al-mawwâl* (*The Book of the Legitimate Witchcraft* . . .) (Gumhûriyyah Bookshop: Cairo, n.d.), pp. 3–10. Similarly, an elite culture cliché states "*'inna min al-bayâni la-siḥran* (magic does indeed exist in some of the rhetorical)."

On the concept of "normal abnormality," see El-Shamy, "Mental Health . . . ," p. 23.

[238]Wallace, *Religion*, pp. 87–88.

[239]al-Bûnî specifies the process as follows:

> . . . take the number [involved] in His saying: *wa kadhâlika nùrî 'Ibrâhîm malkût al-samâwâti wa al-'arḍ . . . 'ilakh.* (So also did We show Abraham the Power and the Laws of the Heavens and the Earth . . . etc. [Koran 6:75]); place it in a china dish, put ṭayyib-oil, [and then] command a *nâdhûr ṣaghîr hawâ'iyy aṭ-ṭab¿* (a young medium of the aerial/whimsical nature) to look into it then *¿azzìm* (recite as verbal incantation) by the Surah of 'wa al-shamsî wa ḍuḥâhâ (By the Sun and [. . . her] splendor) [Koran: 91:1] along with the oath till the servants come, then give them the command of sweeping and spraying till the end of what is [well] known (*Manba¿*, p. 308).

In his translation of *The Glorious Kur'ân*, Ali designates the genders of the sun as masculine ("his") and the moon as feminine ("her"). This translation is incorrect. Typically, the sun is perceived as feminine, and the moon as masculine, a fact evident in the morphology of the Koranic words.

[240]Motif: D1810.0.4.1.1§, "*mandal* ('magic liquid-mirror'): knowledge from jinn shown on surface of ink (or oil) in cup." See Lane, *Modern Egyptians*, pp. 268–275.

In his presentation of "Soul-summoning," Amîn (*Qâmûs*, pp. 381–382) attributes the presumed efficacy of the ritual to *al-'îḥâ'* ([hypnotic] suggestion) and cites Lane's account.

A variation on this ritual, known as *màndàl b-el-qullàh* (divination via pottery—water bottle), asks the jinn to provide detective information by showing the way to a sought-after person or object: typically that person would be someone who had committed a theretofore unsolved crime or is missing, while the object would have been stolen or misplaced. A jinn (in the form of a spirit) is assumed to temporarily occupy the water bottle, and upon being allowed free movement accommodating his/her etherial incorporeal constitution, would seek and point out the site where that person or object happened to be located at that time and can be found.

An identical practice was reported from ancient Egypt in a recent work by Egyptologist John Romer. As is the case with the modern ritual, the ancient one also occurred among the common people as a para-religious oracular service. The instrument used then—outside the realm of the powers of the official Gods—was a statue of the deity King Amenhotep, rather than the water bottle utilized in modern times for the same purpose. The time period was the days of foreman Nekhenmut, during

> [. . .] the last decades of the Theban Kingdom, when the kings had retreated to the north of Egypt, far away from the High Priests of Amun and their fearful statues, [via which] all major decisions were sanctioned by the oracular gods.

The ability to look into people's hearts was assigned to the deity king. "As he [i.e., his statue] was carried through the village, questions were asked and the statue would answer by 'nodding its head' or moving backward and forwards." In a case of a workman whose clothes had been stolen, a suspect was pointed out by three different such oracles, but he continued to deny his guilt. Upon being beaten by the priests, he confessed and "was even made to swear an oath [. . .]" not to go back on his confession. Breaking an oath made to the formal deity "Ptah, Lord of the Truth" resulted in severe divine punishment, such as blindness.[241]

It is interesting to observe in this context that one of the requirements for a successful *màndàl*-opening is that on the day of the execution of the operation, the chief operator "[. . .] inescapably, must 'fast from' [i.e., abstain from consuming] whatsoever has a soul and whatsoever comes out thereof."[242] As a shamanistic-ritual, this type of fasting is not practiced by Moslems including those of Egypt; but it is the

[241] See John Romer, *Ancient Lives* (New York, Holt, 1984), Chapter 15, "The Oracle," pp. 100–105, especially pp. 102–103. It may be noted that Romer compares this ancient practice with the flying bier in modern Luxor; however, this analogy is applicable only to the aspect of how the wishes of the "spirit" (i.e., soul) may be expressed. Each of the two practices belongs to a separate belief subsystem.

Motifs: D1654.9.1, "Corpse cannot be moved;" cf. E405§, "Uncontrollable corpse ('flying bier'): bearers compelled as to speed and route."

For a local legend illustrating this belief, see "The Death of *shaikhah* Shafîqah's Brother," in El-Shamy, *Tales Arab Women Tell*, No. 43, pp. 313–314 (App. 39). Also cf. "The Grave That Wouldn't Dig," in El-Shamy, *Folktales of Egypt*, No. 38, pp. 166–167, 283; and n. 439.

[242] " . . . *walâ bùdda min ṣàwmi yàwmi al-¿àmàl ¿àn kùlli mâ bihi rûḥ wamâ kharaga minhâ.*" (al-Bûnî, *Manba¿*, p. 308). Motif: C222§, ‡"Tabu [taboo]: eating or drinking during Lent whatever comes from a creature-with-soul—(e.g., cow, chicken, fish, etc.)—('Christian's fasting')."

This stipulation suggests the existence of a link between the ritual and former religious systems

typical official mode for "fasting" (Lent) among Egyptian Copts.[243] It may therefore be argued that the roots of the *màndàl*-ritual seem to reach back to the pre-Islamic Coptic period, and, very likely, to the Pharaonic oracular service described above.

II.B.3. sìḥr (Magic): sìḥr-sùflî (Nether-Magic, Witchcraft, Sorcery): ḥàlb-en-nugûm (Milking-the-Stars); shàbshabàh ([Sorcery Via] Use of Slipper); ràbṭ (Induced Impotence)

A *sâḥìr* (i.e., sorcerer or true magician) in folk ideology and worldview is a person who has secured the support of Satan, and the infidel or evil jinn for his/her activities. This support is achieved as a result of the desecration of the holy book (the Koran for Moslems, and the 'Ingîl for Copts) and other sacred or "immaculate/pure" entities. Washing with milk, for example, or committing cardinal sins, such as fornication and adultery, are acts of desecration. Reports from female field workers state that the most powerful magician in Cairo in the 1970s—especially among female clients—was a former monk who had been defrocked from a monastery in Ethiopia. Not only did he desecrate the Holy Book, but he also required the same of his clients. Some of his other procedures included having sexual intercourse with female clients. Such extreme sacrilegious acts make the violation of sacred tabus complete and unequivocal, please Satan who seeks to corrupt humans, and thus guarantee his full support and cooperation. In cases of "high class" women who do not want to commit the illicit sexual act with the magician, another less scrupulous female may be hired to substitute for the actual client. The former monk–magician charged exorbitant fees that ran as high as several hundred pounds (worth thousands by today's value and purchasing power).[244]

More recently (in 2001), some thirty years later, the situation remains basically unchanged. This very sacrilegious ritual came into full public view with drastic political and interreligious consequences that affected the entire nation. The location

---

(Christianity). It is also significant to observe the use of the supplication for holiness: "*qàddàsa rûḥah*," which is recurrent among Copts but virtually unused by Moslems (see n. 25).

[243]Motifs: C677§, ‡"Compulsions during performing magic-ritual (is required);" C677.2.1§, ‡"Abstinence from eating or drinking whatever comes from a creature-with-soul (e.g., milk, eggs, meats, etc.) during preparation for magic-ritual (is required)."

[244]Information provided by Miss Hâdya S. and Cherifa M., both university students majoring in anthropology (spring 1972). During the 1980s wealthy Arab clients have been making extensive use of this craft. Mr. Ḥâzim Ḥ., a tourism agent, reported that some of his customers pay "thousands" of pounds for the shaman's services; in one case a client "purchased a house" and gave it to the shaman-shaikh as fee.

In 1990, Mr. ¿Â.S., a Copt, reported the following incident that took place during the late 1940s, when he was a district attorney in Alexandria:

A "priest" in Alexandria named Ghaṭṭâs was arrested and investigated for performing *siḥr bi es-suflî* (nether magic, sorcery). His residence was searched, and many items of his belongings seized as evidence. [He was guilty as charged.]

However, shortly afterward the police and the D.A.'s office were instructed by higher authorities to "close the case." This was due to the fact the names of female relatives of high-ranking government officials were found at the sorcerer's residence—all of whom were his clients.

Therefore, the sorcerer–priest was given a beating and released. (Also see n. 700)

and names of participants may have changed but the beliefs and rituals remain unaltered. In this case the location was the ultra conservative Middle-upper Egypt, and the persons involved were a defrocked Coptic monk, his brother, and hundreds (or perhaps "thousands," according to some reports) of their female clients who were sexually violated. In this case, the supposed rituals for treatments of barrenness were secretly videotaped and sold to the general public, or used to further blackmail the hapless victims.[245]

A newspaper acquired one of the tapes and published some of the scandalously obscene photographs ("*ṣuwar fâḍiḥah*") of the treatments. Copts, especially youth, rioted in the streets against the affair, the heads of the church, and the newspapers involved; rioters suspected that the matter was a conspiracy orchestrated by Moslems. The head of the Church, Pope Shenouda, addressed the rioters and the nation appealing for quiet but resolute deliberations. State agencies confiscated the newspapers and magazines that contained reports of the incident. Publishers and reporters involved were formally charged with conspiracy, sedition, and threatening national unity. Thus, the affair involved Christian–Moslem relations, journalism and freedom of the press, police procedures, and jurisprudence and objectivity of law courts. The political and religious issues were addressed to the satisfaction of some parties to the conflict; however, others continued to be offended and remained disappointed. Yet, the belief–practice system that makes resorting to such profane and fallacious practices, namely nether-magic, were left untouched. Thus, desperate women and immoral predatory "magicians" and clerics who peddle their craft among all social groups of the population continue to thrive.

Two additional rituals may be viewed as subcategories of true *sùflî*-magic, sorcery, or black magic. These are: *ḥalb en-nùgûm* (milking-the-stars), and *shàbshabàh* (lit.: "slippering," i.e. [sorcery through] use of a *shìbshìb*, a slipper—casual footwear).[246]

"Milking-the-stars" is a procedure that seeks to acquire the powers of certain stars (or planets) by receiving their "milk" in the same manner in which one would milk

---

[245]The affair (by A. Mûsâ, et al.) appeared under the headlines: "The Deforked Monk Usurped 400,000 [Egyptian Pounds], and 4 Kilograms of Gold From Blackmailing Women." (In: *Al-Ahram*, June 18, 2001, p. 30; No. 41832), and "What *al-Naba'* [Newspaper] Published is Injurious to the Church and Offends the Hollies of Christianity," in *Al-Ahram*, (June 19, 2001 No. 41833; June 20, 2001 No. 41834; June 21, 2001 No. 41835).

Cf. Tale-types: 1424, *Friar Adds Missing Nose* (fingers [added to fetus]). [Gullible woman thus seduced]; 1424A§, *Seduction by Pretending to Show (Instruct, Teach) Husband how it is Done*; 1424B§, *Seduction by Other Tricks*. Sexual intercourse under pretence of strengthening, increasing eyesight (or the like).

Motifs: K1397.1§, "Seduction (rape) by threatening woman with defamation and causing scandal: woman fears for her reputation and surrenders;" T429.1.1§, ‡"Faith-healer (exorcist, etc.) seduces (seeks to seduce) client;" P230.0.1.1§, "Misery of childlessness (person weeps);" K1339.6.1§, "Priest seduces woman (at confession);" P426.0.8§, ‡"Immoral (corrupt) cleric (judge);" D1925, "Fecundity [(fertility)] magically induced;" D2161.3.11, "Barrenness magically cured;" T591.5.2.1§, ‡"Barren (childless) woman sacrifices her honor to become pregnant."

(See also n. 561 and 700)

[246]Motifs: D759.3.1§, "*ḥalb en-nugûm* (milking the stars): magic ritual performed by naked virgin at dawn;" G303.22.5.2§, "*shabshabah*: sorceress beats own vulva with slipper so as to please devil."

a cow. This ritual, by its very nature, is a female specialty; a pubescent virgin must perform it at the beginning of her puberty stage (immediately after first menstruation). Stark naked, she would begin the ritual at dawn, usually on the flat top of a house so as to be directly under the stars, she would kneel before the desired star, then anoint all her feminine organs with the milk of a she-donkey while pleading the stars to give their milk—which would be deposited on her feminine organs where the she-donkey's milk was placed. The mixture would be used later to produce a "work" that would give the girl an irresistible hold over a targeted male.[247] Although jinn do not seem to be directly involved—at least on basis of the scanty information currently available—the power of the stars or planets plays the role typically assigned to jinn in other "magic" rituals. Clearly, this rite fits Imam al-Shâfi¿î's depiction of the type of magic that constitutes *kùfr* (disbelief, being an infidel; see his opinion, n. 215–216).

In spite of its daring and highly sensational nature—for the ritual is supposedly performed by a solitary female, acting both as the priestess (shamaness or sorceress) as well as the client, it represents mostly an "individualistic cult institutions," to use Wallace's term. (See n. 225)

Similarly, *shàbshabàh* is a magic ritual that is conducted by females. Although the word *shàbshabàh* appears frequently in stereotyped phrases used to level an accusation at a woman as employing this ungodly ritual at a man (e.g., *bi-tshàbshib-lùh*, "she slippers for [controlling] him"), the actual execution of its phases seems less widespread. Like "milking-the-stars," "slippering" requires commission of sacrilegious acts such as using milk instead of water for cleansing the latrine, or treading on the Holy Book; once these acts have been committed, the practitioner would use a slipper (*shìbshìb*) to slap her vulva repeatedly (hence the name of the ritual). It may be assumed that the abuse of genitalia—particularly female's—is an additional Satan-pleasing act, and consequently, he would come to the aid of the ritual performer.

At the end of the nineteenth century, Ismâ¿îl reported attending a ritual involving "milking-the-stars" (Venus), and *shàbshabàh* in which a woman practitioner ("shaman-*shaikhàh*," or sorceress) performed the ritual addressing herself to a jinn named Sindâs the one who is "*¿âlìm bi al-'aksâs*" ("all-knowing" of vaginas) as well as to the evil jinn who are "*mukhâlifìn* Sulîmân" (disobedient to [Prophet] Solomon). The target for this "love-generating" ritual was the husband who had forsaken his wife, and the goal was to cause his return by awakening his sexual desires for her.[248]

---

[247] Information given here is based on A.R. Ṣâliḥ's in his *al-'Adab*, Vol. 1, p. 125.

[248] Walker-Ismâ¿îl, *Folk Medicine*, pp. 96–98. (It would seem that the practitioner could not have been a "pubescent virgin," a requirement cited in data related to n. 247.)

With the help of additional homeopathic magic rituals the *shaikhah*-shamaness " . . . names the person in the case, and casts the fruits upon an image of a person made of clay which is in front of her." (Walker-Ismâ¿îl, *Folk Medicine*, p. 96 note 3). Also see A.R. Ṣâliḥ, *al-'Adab*, Vol. 1, pp. 124–125; and Amîn, *Qâmûs*, p. 153.

Amîn reports cases of contagious magic used by women to evoke "love" between married couples; these include hair baked in bread or cake, and menstrual blood in drink (Motif: D1355.3.0.1§, "Carnal love charm: made from human menstrual blood, pubic hair, milk, semen, etc.)."

Due to the blatant sexual and offensive nature of these rituals in addition to their illegal pagan character, it is virtually impossible for an outsider—man or woman—to observe the ritual while it is being actually performed. Most informants deny the existence of these practices in their communities and describe them as "things from the old past and *gâhilyyah* (pre-Islamic paganism)." Thus, actual cases of "slippering" and "milking-the-stars" have not been frequently reported in recent times. Occasionally, the names of these sacrilegious rituals are merely cited but no description would be provided.[249] It is, therefore, difficult to assess the degree to which they are currently in use. Available data seem to indicate that both rituals have drastically declined in frequency, or, perhaps, are on the verge of becoming extinct.[250]

The techniques used in all these practices are generally referred to as *sùflî* (nether, subterranean, i.e., satanic); regardless of whether the objective is benevolent (to help) or malevolent (to hurt), the operation is thoroughly sacrilegious. A comparison between an erotic ("love-generating") *¿amàl* (hex, charm) by applying "nether-magic" rituals as described above on the one hand, and a typical erotic *¿amàl* ("fix," "work") through the para-religious ritual (upper-"magic," or the so-called "formal magic") on the other, reveals the stark differences between the types of powers addressed, and the psychological attitudes of the practitioners vis-a-vis these powers.

One folk "love-generating" *¿amàl* ("work") of the non-*sùflî* type uses three of God's names denoting affection, kindness, and mercy, written seventy times on a piece of red leather in a prayer-like style to evoke the desired result; the names are: Wadûd (affectionate, caring), ¿Aṭûf (kind, compassionate, gentle), and Ra'ûf, (merciful, sympathetic).[251] Another para-religious "work" provided in a literary manual uses four Archangels for the same purpose. The author writes:

> If you wish to *tùhayyìg* (excite, arouse) with love someone, write down the "seal" provided here: [Gibrîl, 'Isrâfîl, ¿Izrâ'îl, Mîkâ'îl] on a rag of the *'athàr* ("trace," a residual) of the sought after [target] person or [. . .] on a raw (*nayyi'àh*, [i.e., not kiln-dry or burnt]) potsherd, then set the [identifying]-"trace" on fire with *ṭîb*/*ṭayyib*-oil [. . .], or bury the potsherd in fire, and read the oath seven times while incensing (fumigating, sending incense smoke) with the benzoin (*gâwî*): the target becomes excited with love and will come to you in the shortest time.[252]

---

[249]Amîn (*Qâmûs*, p. 175), for example, mentions *shàbshabàh* but does not define it and refers the reader to "*ḥàlb en-nùgûm* (milking-the-stars);" yet, in the latter, the reader is referred to the former "sorcery through use of slipper (*shàbshabàh*")*.* However, Amîn adds the significant observation that "milking-the-stars" was cited by the Syrian-Iraqi poet of *zùhd* (asceticism) Abu-al-¿Alâ' [al-Ma¿arrî] (973–1057 AD) in his anthology of poems titled "*Luzûmiyyât.*"

[250]For example, addressing the theme of "love" in 1953, Amîn (*Qâmûs*, p. 153) spoke of *shàbshabàh* in the past tense as a ritual that "was famous in that [love-generating] connection."

[251]Amîn, *Qâmûs*, p. 153. See also the *khâtàm* ("seal") he diagrams for this formula.

On the concept of cognitive association (clustering), cf. Motif Z108§, ‡"Sound (name) symbolism: association based on sound similarities (homophony)." (See n. 739, and App. 34)

[252]Bûnî, *Manba¿*, p. 79. The oil mentioned may be *ṭîb* (fragrant nut) or *ṭayyib* (which is sweet and is extracted from lettuce).

Within the context of attempting to affect erotic behavior, induced impotence is a "magical" ritual that targets a male's physical capability to have an erection. A man may be "excited with love" (to use al-Bûnî's words) but rendered impotent to experience the physical effect of sexual arousal (erection). The ritual is labelled *ràbṭ,* literally, "tying" (as in tying a knot); a man who is believed to be under its spell is referred to as *màrbûṭ* (tied). With rare exceptions, "tying" is viewed as harmful. The practitioner who would generate "tying" is viewed as working for evil ends (*shàrr*), without necessarily utilizing *sùflî* (nether) magic. Unlike the intent behind causing a female to become barren (*mushâhràh/kàbsàh*), "tying" (or rendering a male impotent) is *not* manifestly assumed to render a male sterile. (For amplifications of this issue, see Section VIII.B)

II.B.3a. Magic (*sìḥr*) or folk para-religious ritual?

Formal Islamic institutions tolerate the para-religious practitioners whose practice would not constitute *kùfr* (unbelief, being an infidel), but condemn the *sùflî*-sorcerer (*sâhìr*) as a *kâfir* (infidel, unbeliever). Both old and recent systems of Islamic jurisprudence state that such a sorcerer *may* be executed "even if he hasn't committed murder with his magic—for matters are [to be judged] according to the intentions behind them."[253] A contemporary religious authority states: "Many of the ulama prohibit learning *sìḥr* (magic) in any of its forms." They, however, are of divergent views concerning standing of a person who learns magic and uses it only for defensive purposes so as to avert its effects. For the majority of ulama, such a person—in contrast to the person who learns it believing its efficacy and that it would benefit him—would not become infidel.[254]

Yet, it is believed that any type of magic works only if God wills; for, according to the principle of *'ìstìdrâg* (leading on), God grants power even to infidels and sinners for specific reasons (see n. 530). Formal religious sources state that a person who believes "that magic works without God's permission is a *kâfir* (i.e., infidel)."[255]

The attitudes of members of folk communities toward practitioners of both types of "magic" correspond to those articulated by formal religious institutions. The practitioner of *sùflî*-magic is both despised and resented; but for those who require

For further illustrations of the technique of magic squares, see *badûḥ*, and *'awfâq* in Amîn, *Qâmûs*, p. 82; and Yûnus, *Mu¿gam al-fûlklûr* (Dictionary of Folklore). Beirut: Maktabat Lubnân, 1983, p. 84.

[253] Ibn Khaldûn/Rosenthal, *The Muqddimah*, Vol. 3, p. 169; and al-Digwî, "ta¿allum al-siḥr (The Learning of Magic)," pp. 490–491.

[254] *al-Azhar*, Vol. 12, No. 8 (1941), pp. 490–491. In this context, Sengers reports,

> But there are all sorts of black magic, such as for instance: "*'amal bis-sufli* (magic with the aid of lower/common demons), but this is forbidden because you are doing something bad to someone this way." But does it work? "O yes, if you want to have it done, you generally go to a priest or a Christian *sheikh*, since they are the best at this sort of magic. (*Women and Demons*, p. 48)

This viewpoint is inaccurate. As pointed out, *suflî* (nether-[magic]) need not be undertaken by "a priest or Christian sheikh." See n. 248, and App. 34 and 35.

[255] al-Digwî, "ta¿allum al-siḥr (The Learning of Magic)," pp. 490–491; and S. Ḥusayn, *al-Ginn*, p. 91.

his services, he is viewed as a necessary evil. Meanwhile the regular practitioner of the so-called "formal magic" is, generally speaking, esteemed and viewed—perhaps apprehensively—as an atypical yet still "normal" member of the community. (See App. 35, and also see the concept of "normal abnormality," in Section II.B.2)

Secular legal systems have recently (1980) sanctioned the fundamental belief premises on the basis of which "magic" is believed to operate. A practitioner of "magic through contact with jinn" was tried in civil court for defrauding his female clients and practicing medicine without a license. The trial judge—in congruence with formal religious dogma—asserted that jinn do exist and that they may indeed gain control of a person. Consequently, like crimes committed while being "drunk," "insane," or "under duress," a person under the influence of *al-quwâ al-khafiyyàh* (invisible powers/forces, i.e., jinn) is, legally, not responsible for his own actions. The accused was pronounced "Innocent."[256]

II.C. Jinn as Components of the Individual: Supernatural Counter-Spirits and Siblings

The larger, more general category of jinn, described above, is believed to exist independently of human beings. Occasionally, a jinni may interact with a man, woman, or child, but such interaction—though occurring frequently—is considered coincidental and is usually transient. Particular categories of jinn are, however, more closely linked to a person. Some of these jinn, or jinn-like beings, are believed to constitute a permanent component of the individual. The "Counter-spirit" (that may be a male-spouse or a female-spouse), and the "sibling" (that may be a "Brother" or a "Sister") are such beings.[257] These supernatural entities are perceived as permanent

---

[256]Motifs: P526.3.1§, ‡"Conditions that render a person not responsible for consequences of own actions (e.g., being a minor, insanity, drunkenness, etc.);" cf. E724.3.0.1§, ‡"Counter-spirit forces its human counterpart to express (act) its will—(person acts involuntarily, and is not responsible for own actions)."

This affair, came to be known as the case of "Abu-Kaff"—(a nickname signifying "The man with[out] a palm of hand"), generated considerable public interest and controversy. A civil court judge found the accused "Innocent." The verdict evoked resentment on the part of numerous professional organizations, especially the Egyptian Medical Association (*Naqâbat al-'Aṭibbâ'*).

"The Medical Association of Physicians appealed the verdict and called for a conference so as to block the loopholes in the [present law] which allows such 'importers' (shaman-*shaikhs*) to practice medicine." However, legal scholars took an opposing view and asserted that the "Medical Association" had no right to interfere.

The judge who issued the "Innocent"-verdict clarified his position by stating "Innocent" does not mean [a permission] for the accused to practice medicine. He further explained that the verdict rested on "The realness [of the existence of] the jinn" since they are cited frequently in the Koran (p. 2).

See Riyâḍ Tawfîq, and Muṣṭafâ el-Ṭarâbîshî, "An Objective Pause Concerning the Innocent-[Verdict] for An Accused of Contact with *gânn*" (Arabic). In: *Al-Ahram*, No. 34101 (Sunday, April, 24, 1980) p. 3.

[257]Names of these supernatural belief characters are treated here as proper names; therefore, the initial letter will be capitalized (e.g., supernatural *S*ister, supernatural *S*pouse, supernatural *B*rother, etc.).

Motif: E724§, "A person's counter-spirits (Qarînah, Qarîn, 'Ukht, 'Akhkh, 'Umm-eṣ-Ṣubyân, etc.)".

components of a person just like the soul, but they may not be identified with it. (Compare Section II.A.1a)

II.C.1. The *Qarîn* and *Qarînàh*: A Human's Counter-Spirit, Correlative, or Spouse

Among numerous groups, especially in rural areas, it is believed that each person acquires at birth a supernatural entity perceived as that person's counter-spirit, correlative, or spouse. This being is labeled *Qarîn* (feminine: *Qarînàh*; the plural is *'Aqrân* or *Quranâ*). The counter-spirit has same experiences that the person goes through: health–sickness, happiness–sorrow, marriage–divorce, success–failure, etc.; it also dies when its human counterpart dies. As such, the *Qarînàh* is identical with the ancient Egyptian supernatural entity called "*Ka*," which is described as "a double of a person."[258] One major difference between the modern *Qarîn/Qarînàh* and the ancient *Ka* is that the *Qarînàh* dies along with the person, whereas the *Ka* was believed to continue living inside the mummy and also to be able to move about.[259]

The sex of the supernatural entity in relation to that of a human being is controversial. Some reports cite the *Qarînàh* (counter-spirit) is of the same sex as that of the person to whom it belongs.[260] Meanwhile, early Moslem religious literature quotes Prophet Mohammad as having stated that he had a *Qarîn*, i.e., a male counter-spirit.[261] It was *not* mentioned, however, that the Prophet did *not* have a female counter-spirit as well; also, contrary to the conduct of the counter-spirits of others that cause harm, the Prophet's *Qarîn* urged him to do *khàyr* (benevolent acts). Recently, field workers have reported the existence of the belief in counter-spirits opposite in sex to the humans to whom they belong.[262] In current linguistic usage

---

[258] E.A.W. Budge, *The Gods of the Egyptians* (London: Methuen, 1904) Vol. 1, p. 34. Motifs: E724.0.1§, ‡"The Ka as a person's counter-spirit ('Double');" cf. E732, "Soul in form of bird."

In her *Egyptian Mythology* (p. 109), Ions identifies the *Ka* in contradistinction to the "body," as the "soul." Similarly, other scholars have pointed out that the modern belief in *'Ukht* or *Qarînàh* is different from *rûḥ* (soul). For a discussion on the possible origins of the *'Ukht*-belief in Helwân, see G.D. Hornblower, "Traces of a Ka Belief in Modern Egypt and Old Arabia." In: *Islamic Culture* (1927), pp. 426–430.

[259] Motif: V311.4.1.1§, ‡"The tomb as a person's home ('everlasting house') till the hereafter."

Budge states:

> The [ancient] Egyptian called the tomb [. . .] "the everlasting house," and he believed that the *ka* [. . .] or "genius" of the deceased resided there as long as the mummy of his perishable body, [. . .] *cha*, was there. The *ka* might go in and out of the tomb, and refresh itself with meat and drink, but it never failed to go back to the mummy with the name of which it seems to have been closely connected; the [. . .] *ba* or *soul*, and the [. . .] *chu* or intelligence did not live in the tomb. (*The Mummy*, p. 328)

[260] Blackman, "The Ḳarîn and Ḳarîneh." In: *Journal of the Royal Anthropological Institute*, Vol. 56 (Jan. 1926), pp. 163–169., *The Fellâhîn*, pp. 74–75.

[261] S. Ḥusayn, *al-Ginn*, pp. 86–87.

[262] Blackman, *The Fellahin*, p. 74; and Sayyid Quṭb *Ṭifl min al-qaryah* (A Child from the Village), as cited in Lyman H. Coult, *An Annotated Bibliography of the Egyptian Fellah*. (Coral Gables, FL: University of Miami Press, 1958) p. 81.

the word *qarînàh* is a polite and dignifying term for "wife;" one for example, speaks of "the *qarînàh* of the president," the male form, *qarîn*, is not used in this context, though recent sociological literature uses both words to refer wife and husband. The verb *yaqtarìn* means "to get married," and the noun *qirân* is "marriage." The notion that the relationship between a human being and the counter-spirit is similar to marriage was expressed by a number of informants. An adult male from southern Egypt stated that the tie between a man and his *Qarînàh* "is exactly like that between a [human] husband and his wife;"[263] four other participants in the interview session agreed. Thus, the *Qarînàh* may also be referred to as supernatural "spouse." Because of its implicit erotic nature, this usage that identifies a *Qarînàh* as a "spouse" lends support to the academic argument that the names *Qarînàh* (spouse, counter-spirit, or correlative) and *'Ukht* (Sister) may stand for "the same thing." (See App. 18)

The informant quoted above explained:

> A man acquires a *Qarînàh* as an *'Ukht* (spirit-Sister), and a woman acquires a *Qarîn* as an *'Akhkh* (spirit-Brother).

It should be pointed out, however, that the name and role assigned to the supernatural entity are relativistic and contextual;[264] its exact nature is determined by the frame of reference, which guides a person's perception. Therefore, how the spirit is perceived depends on who is characterizing it and judging its actions vis-a-vis the person with whom the supernatural belief being is involved. Its exact character emerges in a dynamic process of application to a specific situation.[265] A retired shaman from Upper Egypt, who moved to live and work in Cairo, described the counter-spirit and the personal experience of his own human sister with that spirit as follows:

> A woman has a *Qarîn*; a man has a *Qarîn* and a *Qarînàh*. . . . However, my [real human] sister, who lives in the village, saw a [friendly] *Qarîn* in a dream. Village people said to her, "This is your [human] Brother," meaning me [i.e., the speaker himself].[266]

---

[263]Informants: Ḥesain-Abu-Aḥmad (also nicknamed Abû-¿Âdil), age 46; Shâkir, a retired shaman-*shaikh*, and two other adult men from el-Bargi in middle Southern Egypt. All four work and live in Cairo.

[264]Motif: U300§, "Relativity of perception: "adaptation level" (judgment depends on circumstances, objects of comparison, frame of reference, or context)."

On the psychological implications of the concept of "contextualism," see Hasan El-Shamy, *Folkloric Behavior*, p. 47.

[265]See El-Shamy, "Belief Characters . . . ," p. 20; Amîn, *Qâmûs*, p. 324; Rushdi, "maraḍ al-'iklimbsia (eclampsia)," 1898, pp. 292–293 (see n. 213).

Lexicographers El-Said Badawi and Martin Hinds point out: "male's female counterpart thought to exist in the spirit world (also called qarîna)." See *A Dictionary of Egyptian Arabic: Arabic-English* (Beirut, 1986), p. 9.

[266]Informant: Shâkir in June 24, 1972 (see n. 74). See App. 17, where the informant attributed a newly wed woman's illness to "the Qarînah." However, it is not clear whether the Qarînah was her, her husband's, or just a mischievous spirit of the general jinn.

Thus, the informant's human actual sister "saw" a benevolent supernatural male *Qarîn* (male counter-spirit); because of the fact that the spirit was of an opposite sex to that of the person who encountered it and it was benevolent to that person, villagers identified it as her "Brother." A woman's *Qarînàh* (female counter-spirit) is invariably malevolent and injurious to that woman. It is significant to note here that in colloquial Egyptian Arabic, the word *miqârnàh* (i.e., *muqâranàh*) signifies [verbal] "harassment," or "constant quarrels."[267] The same view about the gender of the spouse/counter-spirit is voiced by Copts:

> A man has a *Qarînàh*; a woman has a *Qarîn*. [. . .] My mother told me: "You used to have a very beautiful *khâl* (maternal-uncle [i.e, the speaker's mother's brother]); his *Qarînàh* became enamored with him. When he expressed his desire to marry [a human girl], she [his *Qarînàh*] treated him tyrannically [by causing him all sorts of physical and emotional problems]. Thus, he became very sick, and continued to *yensàll* [lit.: suffer the effects of tuberculosis, i.e., become emaciated and pale] until he was finished and died."[268]

With reference to available academic literature on the *Qarînàh*, inability to recognize the relativistic nature of such a being has led to considerable confusion.[269] Furthermore, writers have derived information from at least two distinctly diverse sources: contemporary oral traditions from Egypt on the one hand, and historical written traditions on the other. The latter sources—gleaned mostly from ancient Arabia—belong to an earlier time period and subsequently to a different community and phase of Arab culture. In literary traditions the *Qarîn* is also called *Tâbi¿*

---

[267] Perhaps meaning, "horn-locking;" *munâqarah* also is referred to as matching one's *nì'r* (i.e., *nìqr*) against another, an idiom that signifies faultfinding, or pecking.

[268] Informant: Mr. Lewîs T., librarian, about 50 years of age, "Engineer," a Copt, from Abnûb, Upper Egypt; recorded on Sat. June 24, 1972.

Almost a century earlier, Walker reported,

> [There is another instance of the widespread belief in the *Ḳarîna* . . .]. Dr. Klunzinger (formerly physician at Kosseir [Quṣeir] on the Red Sea coast) in his work, *Upper Egypt, its People and its Products* (London, 1878), deals with popular medicine on pp. 397–400. On p. 383 he writes, "Even in the official register of death kept by the physicians the *ḳarîna* was till lately a regular variety of disease, exactly corresponding to our convulsions.]." (Walker-Ismâ¿îl, *Folk Medicine*, p. 47, note 2)

The same remark was made by I. Rushdî, "maraḍ al-'iklimbsia" (eclampsia), in n. 213.

Motifs: E724.3.5.1§, ‡"Counter-spirit harms human counterpart;" E724.3.5.2.1§, ‡"Counter-spirit causes death to human children;" E724.3.5.2.1.1§, ‡"'SIDS' (Sudden Infant Death Syndrome, '*khunnâq*', etc.) caused by suffocation by malevolent counter-spirit (Qarînah, 'Ukht, etc.)." (See also n. 286)

[269] For example, Walker labels this being "mate" and, as is case the with our present Coptic informant, reports—but with some uncertainty—that in "most cases, it appears, the 'mate' is of the opposite sex [of the human]." (See: Walker-Ismâ¿îl, *Folk Medicine*, p. 44, note 1.) Meanwhile, C.E. Padwick ("Notes on the Jinn . . . ") argues that the sex of the *qarîn*/*qarînah* corresponds to that of their human counterparts. This is also the viewpoint Blackman expresses in her article titled "The Ḳarîn and Ḳarîneh." In: *Journal of the Royal Anthropological Institute*, Vol. 56 (Jan. 1926), pp. 163–169. Similarly, B. Seligman, G.D. Hornblower among others are of the opinion that *qarîn*/*qarîah* are of same sex as of the human counterpart (see Coult, *Annotated Bibliography* . . . , pp. 117–118).

(Follower; feminine: *Tâbi¿àh*). According to older Arabian beliefs, the *Tâbì¿* is a jinni or a satan (*shayṭân*) who inspired poets.[270] A *Tâbì¿* does not exist in contemporary oral traditions of Egypt, yet, a *Tâb¿àh* (she-Follower) is recurrent. A *Qarînàh* (counter-spirit) may be referred to as "*Tâb¿àh*," "*'Omm-eṣ-Ṣùbyân*" (Mother-of-male-children), and "*'Omm-Mulgàm*" (Mother-of-Mulgam [a masculine name]);[271] within certain contexts a female counter-spirit (*Qarînàh*) may also be perceived as the *'Ukht* (spirit-Sister). (See App. 18)

II.C.1a. The *'ukht* (sister), and *'akhkh* (brother)

As pointed out earlier, a human being may—usually after reaching adulthood—develop an intimate and affectionate relationship with a jinni of the opposite sex; this type of bond is labeled as *mikhawiyyàh* (bebrothering, supernatural foster-sibling; see Section II.B.1). A spirit referred to as *'ukht* (Sister) and another called *'akhkh* (Brother) are also found as independent entities and are believed to have a lifelong association with the involved human being. Some scholars reported that the supernatural *Akhkh* (spirit-Brother) for a human female does not exist.[272] This viewpoint has been openly challenged. Commenting (in 1934) on Blackman's conclusion (published in 1927) in light of the field data provided earlier by Ismâ¿îl (published in 1892 and 1894), Walker concludes that "Miss Blackman [. . .] is seemingly wrong when she states that there is no Brother (*akhkh*)."[273]

In 1892, Ismâ¿îl reported

> Some [. . .] claim that every male child has a sister (*ukht*) among the jinn, and every female child a brother (*akhkh*); [. . .] and since the sister loves her brother, this Jinn-sister tries to destroy her real brother so that she may enjoy his love. And that is why whenever a mother curses her son she says to him *Ḥabbatak ukhtak* (may your [S]ister love you). [. . .] The only object in cauterizing the child, or scarifying his head with a razor, is to punish him so that his sister may have pity on him and betake herself to her lover among the Jinn that he [i.e., the sister's Jinn-brother] may leave him [i.e., the human boy/brother] to them.[274]

---

[270] In classical Arabic, *tâbi¿* is a *shàyṭân* ("satan") that inspires poets (Motifs: E724.1.2.1§, ‡"A poet's counter-spirit: inspires poetic creativity. Also labeled a poet's 'satan', *tâbi¿* ('follower'), etc.;" cf. G225, "Witch's familiar spirit [(*tâbi¿*)])." Meanwhile, *zawba¿ah* is whirlwind; such a wind is commonly associated with jinn and afrits.

A literary example that uses these two themes is Abû ¿Âmir Aḥmad Ibn Shuhyd's (d. 1035), *al-Tawâbi¿ wa al-zawâbi¿: the treatise of familiar spirits and demons*, James T. Monroe, tr. ed. (Berkeley, CA: U. of Cal. Press: 1971). Also see al-Gindi, *al-Ginn*, Vol. 2 (1970), pp. 3–8.

Motifs: cf. F411.1, "Demon travels in whirlwind;" F559.9.1.2§, ‡"Whirlwind is 'afrit's fart';" and F401.0.1.1.1.1§, ‡"Jinni named 'Whirlwind' ('*Zawba¿ah*')." Also cf. whirlwind (*zàwba¿àh*), n. 404.

[271] Informant: Shâkir, as in n. 74.

[272] Blackman, *The Fellâhîn*, pp. 74–75; El-Gawhary, "*al-Ginn fi al-mu¿taqad al-sha¿bî* (Jinn in the [Egyptian] Folk Beliefs)," p. 111.

[273] Walker-Ismâ¿îl, *Folk Medicine*, p. 47, note 1.

[274] Walker-Ismâ¿îl, *Folk Medicine*, pp. 46–47.

This writer's own field observations and data (gathered during a period extending from the 1960–1990s) substantiate the continued presence of the belief in the existence of the spirit-Brother, but on a comparatively limited scale. Belief in the spirit-Brother seems to be confined to females. One female informant from the Nile Delta stated:

> Every human male has a [spirit] Sister who exists underground; and every human female has a [spirit] Brother. When the [human] male or female suffers the Sister or the Brother who exists underground also suffers.[275]

A verbal incantation invoked to protect children—and similar to the curse cited by Ismâ¿îl—confirms that the belief in a supernatural sibling consists of a "Brother" for the human female, and a "Sister" for the human male. If a little boy trips and falls, the charm is: "May God's name protect you and your Sister;" meanwhile if a girl trips, the charm states: "May God's name protect you and your Brother."[276] More recently (1986), lexicographers Badawi and Hinds identified *akhkh* (Brother) as a "female's male Counterpart thought to exist in the spirit world. . . . " They, however, add parenthetically, "(also called *qariin*)."[277]

It is important to observe that the attitude expressed toward a boy's supernatural "Sister" and a girl's supernatural "Brother" is a positive one; the person who invokes the verbal incantation—typically a female—wishes that the supernatural being also be protected. By contrast, a girl's supernatural Sister plays a harmful role toward that girl (who is her human sister); normally, the supernatural Sister of a human sister is cursed.

Also, a recent field report includes data confirming the existence of the belief in both the spirit-"Sister" as well as the spirit-"Brother" and highlights the underlying erotic nature of this belief:

> One of the strongest and most salient beliefs in Abu-l-Maṭamîr [a town in the Nile Delta] is the belief that every human being has a [supernatural] Brother [for a female] or Sister [for a male]. An indication of the strength of this belief is that they report that there are some men of whom one would ask his wife to leave the [bed]room because: "This is the night for my Sister."[278]

An old parallel to the *'Ukht* (spirit-Sister) is cited in a tenth-century Arabic work. According to al-Mas¿ûdî (d. ca 956 AD), ¿Unâq was a deformed daughter of Adam and Eve who was born without a twin brother, and therefore could not have a husband by exchanging her twin brother for the twin brother of another sister. Frustrated and

---

[275] Informant: Galîlah ¿A., she was in her twenties, hails from the Nile Delta, and works in Cairo as a housemaid. For a detailed presentation on the life of this young woman and the centrality of the "brother" in her life, see "Profile of a Typical Household Tale Teller, 1969–1972." In: El-Shamy, *Tales Arab Women Tell*, pp. 32–56.

[276] Amîn, *Qâmûs*, p. 324.

[277] Badawi and Hinds, *A Dictionary of Egyptian Arabic: Arabic-English*, p. 9, pt. 4.

[278] ¿Abd-al-Ḥamîd Ḥawwâs, and Ṣâbir el-¿Âdily, *Mulâḥaẓât ḥawla ba¿ḍ al-ẓawâhir al-folkloariyyah fî muḥâfaẓat al-Beḥairah* (Observations on some Folkloric Phenomena in Behairah Governorate)." In: *Al-Funûn*, No. 12 (Cairo, March 1970), p. 75.

alienated, she became a witch and "misled a great many of Adam's sons [i.e., her brothers]." Thus, Adam cursed her and Eve said, " *'âmîn* ('Amen')." God sent a lion that devoured her and relieved Adam and Eve of her.[279]

Beliefs concerning ¿Unâq are similar to the beliefs concerning Lilith, which are found in Jewish and Christian traditions.[280] The connection between a supernatural Sister (or Brother) and emotional instability is implicitly expressed in some aspects of folk speech in Egypt. An emotionally disturbed person may be labeled *makhwût*; an extremely disturbing affair or noise is referred to as *khàwtàh* or *khawàt*; a curse states: *gatàk khàwtàh* ("May you become *khawàt*-stricken"). These folk expressions seem to be derivatives of the words *'akhkh* (Brother) or *'ukht* (Sister). With the possible exception of the curse cited by Ismâ¿îl,[281] Egyptian folk groups do not seem to cognitively associate these words with the beliefs about the supernatural brother or sister. In some other Arab culture areas the link is explicit; in regions of Syria and Lebanon, mental illness, especially epilepsy, is called *khawàt*.[282] In south Arabia and the Gulf regions, a love affair between a man and a woman is often labeled *mikhawiyyàh* (lit.: bebrothering, taking a brother), and a woman's *¿ashîq* (paramour) is identified as *khùwàyy* (lit.: "little-brother," i.e., brother in the diminutive form).[283]

Currently, the use of the folk terms *'Ukht*, *Qarînàh*, *Tâb¿àh*, etc., in referring to a supernatural being seems to be a function of how a particular person perceives the supernatural being's role in a given situation. The exact nature and characteristics of the spirit at a given time emerge only under the conditions of a dynamic encounter. The title *'Ukht* (spirit-Sister) is used to refer to this entity in its role of love and affection for the human male; an adult male informant cited a truism to illustrate this relationship: " *'Ukhtùh widdùh*" (His Sister/sister [is] his affection/fondness).[284] On the other hand, the titles *Qarînàh*, *Tâbi¿àh*, *'Omm-eṣ-Ṣùbyân*, as well as "Sister"

---

[279]Motif: A1388.2§, "Hatred begins when a daughter of Adam and Eve (¿Unâq, Lilith) discovers that she cannot marry because she has no twin brother to exchange for a husband with other brother-sister twins."

Abu-al-Ḥasan ¿Ali al-Mas¿ûdî, *'Akhbâr al-zamân* [*The Events of Time*] (Beirut: Dâr al-'Andalus, 1966), pp. 116–117; also cf. al-Tha¿labî, *Qiṣaṣ*, 26–27.

[280]Motif: A1599.10.1§, "Origin of witchcraft due to hatred: ¿Unâq (Lilith) as the first witch." See Hanauer, *Holy Land*, p. 19.

[281]Walker-Ismâ¿îl, *Folk Medicine*, pp. 47–48. See n. 274.

[282]See Rhodokanakis, Nikolaus, *Der vulgärarabische Dialekt im Dofâr (Ẓfâr)*, *Südarabische Expedition*, Vol. 8 (Vienna, 1908) No. 89, pp. 113–14.

[283]These are archival field tape-recorded texts in which the word *khùwàyy* signifies "paramour" or lover. All were narrated by adult females: AGSFC: QTR 87-3ff., 683-x-No. 9; AGSFC: QTR 87-3ff., 698-2-No. 7; AGSFC: QTR 87-3ff., 700-1-No. 7; AGSFC: QTR 87-3ff., 700-2-No. 4.

[284]Informant: Ḥesain (Abû-¿Âdil) from Bargî, Minya, see n. 263. It is not clear whether the informant was specifically describing the spirit-Sister, or the human sister. The context of the conversation suggests that the reference is to the supernatural entity.

One of Sengers informants (Umm Mohammed) explained:

> The *qarina* is *min 'andi rabbina* (from our Lord) and sits in your body and the "sister" belongs in the world of the *ginnis*. But she does not necessarily only do bad things. Children do not have a *qarina*, but a "sister" who protects them. Only adults have a *qarina*. It is only when children get older, cry a lot, or are sick that they get one too. The sister protects them against evil from others, [. . .]. (*Women and Demons*, pp. 40–41).

are used to refer to the same being in its injurious role toward a human female. This supernatural character threatens a human female, challenges her role as the human wife of that supernatural entity's human brother, and threatens her capacity as a human mother who is capable of giving male children to her human husband. This viewpoint can be substantiated by pointing out that in actual social life, especially in rural areas, a new wife has a shaky position in her husband's family; the wife's status can be strengthened only by bearing male children, which earns her the title *'omm-eṣ-ṣùbyân* (mother of male children).[285] The most injurious role of the supernatural *'Ukht*, *Qarînàh*, *Tâbi¿àh*, or *'Omm-eṣ-Ṣùbyân* is that of suffocating human infants; thus undermining the position of a new wife within her husband's family.

Blackman reports a case in which a woman beat a cat that proved to be her own supernatural *'Ukht* (Sister). Moreover,

> it also transpired that the woman's *ukht* and also the *ukht* of her husband were both very jealous, because the man and his wife were always laughing together. The *'ikhwât* (plural of *ukht*) said they did not like it, and that if that merriment between the pair continued all their children should die.[286]

Thus, a man's supernatural Sister separates ("protects") him from his human wife with whom he is affectionate, and a woman's supernatural sister injures her by destroying her affectionate ties with her human husband and threatens to bring death to their children. The net result is that with either supernatural entity ("Sister") the human wife/sister is the loser, while the human husband/brother is more endeared by the two supernatural sisters.

---

[285] This practice is explained by Mr. Muḥammad ¿A.—a clerk in a Governmental office, from Shebin al-Qanaṭir, Qualyubiyyah Governorate, Nile Delta (Saturday, July 1, 1972). Speaking as if a member of a husband's family, he stated:

> [A woman/wife is considered] a wife as long as she begot a child—she becomes ours [i.e., member of the husband's family]. If she has not begotten (children), then she is not ours [i.e., member of the husband's family]: there is no dispute about this [fact]. However, if the family into which she has married is a weak one, and the family to which she belongs happens to be a big [and powerful] family and would says, "We will take our flesh back!" here they [the wife's in-laws] will not be able to [refuse]. [. . .].

El-Shamy: This means that giving birth to a child. . . .

Muh. [Interrupting. The rule is that:] [If] she begets a child, the matter is settled: she "became" the wife of so-and-so [of our family]; [for] she has produced. As long as she has produced, she has become ours, and (must) be buried in our own soil or earth.

[286] Blackman, *The Fellâhîn*, p. 75. Motifs: E724.3.1.1.1§, ‡"'Ukht (Sister) protects her human brother;" E724.3.5.1.1§, ‡" *'Ukht* (Sister) injures her human sister." (See n. 268)

This theme of the death of children at the hands of jealous supernatural counterspirits and siblings recurs in folktales. For examples, see: El-Shamy, *Brother and Sister: Type 872** pp. 70–71; and Prym and Socin, *Ṭûr ¿Âbdîn*, Vol. 2, No. 2, pp. 8–12. Also cf. Quṭb, *Ṭifl min al-qaryah* (A Child from the Village)—see anti n. 262; Amîn, *Qâmûs*, p. 286; Walker-Ismâ¿îl, *Folk Medicine*, pp. 44–45; and Rushdî, "maraḍ al-'iklimbsia (Eclampsia)," 1898, (as in n. 213). Also see "Barrenness": Section VIII.B and App. 18).

II.C.2. The Cult of Supernatural Illness, Possession, and Healing

That jinn and other supernatural beings can cause a person to become ill is an established and widespread belief. Emotional and physical malfunctions that are attributed to the various categories of jinn are viewed as separate from illnesses that God may inflict on an individual in order to punish that individual or test the strength of his faith (as is the case with Job, for example).[287]

The concept of jinn-caused illness involves belief in a coincidental relationship between a person and a jinni, usually of the opposite sex. Unlike human being's lifelong association with his or her supernatural spirit-"Sister," spirit-"Brother," or "Counter-spirit/Spouse," this relationship is usually transient; occasionally, however, it may become a long-lasting bond between that person and the jinni involved. Numerous shamans (*mashâyìkh*) claim to derive their powers from such a liaison between themselves and spirits (jinn) who had once intruded into their lives so as to injure or possess. In academic English literature such an intruding-helper is commonly designated as "familiar." In native parlance, this being is, significantly, sometimes labeled "*nazîl*,"[288] a "term" denoting a guest, or resident in public facility (such as a hotel, hospital, or prison). By contrast, a supernatural being who intrudes into the life of a human being in an offensive or injurious, harmful manner is labeled *¿âriḍ* (pl.: *¿awâriḍ*),[289] a "term" denoting an unexpected encounter or an intruding matter; the symptoms of an illness are also referred to by physicians as *'a¿râḍ*.

Two different levels, or classes, of such illness may be recognized. Professional healers distinguish between illness caused by *làms* or *màss* (i.e., a mere touch), or the relatively stronger *ṭaṣṣ* or *ḍàrb* (i.e., dealing a blow) on the one hand, and *lìbs* (lit.: wearing, as if a gown) or *rùkûb* (riding as if a riding animal) on the other. In cases involving disorders on the first level, a localized illness occurs due to a contact initiated by a jinni. The contact may be slight in which the jinni touches that person or deals him/her a blow; in such cases the illness is perceived as localized in one part of the body or one aspect of behavior (see App. 23). On the second level an inclusive state of abnormality occurs when a jinni is believed to actually enter and reside in the body of a person. A practicing healer illustrated this concept by pointing out that the jinni "wears a person like one would wear a gown" or "rides that person like one would ride a horse"[290] (see App. 12 and 22). In such cases the abnormality is inclusive, usually affecting the whole person—body and mind—and is characterized by severely aberrant behavior on the part of the afflicted person. In formal Islamic dogma, and its Coptic (Christian) counterpart as well—it is possible for a mere *màss* (touch) from al-Shayṭân (Satan) to cause sickness (Koran, 2:275). Yet, a situation

---

[287] Motifs: W26.1§, "Job's patience;" Q550, "Miraculous punishments."

See el-Sayed el-Aswad, *Aṣṣabr fi at-turath ash-sha'bî al-miṣ[r]î dirdsah anthropolojiyyah* (The Concept of Patience in Egyptian Folklore) (Alexandria: Munsh'at al-Mar'âf[??] 1990).

[288] Walker-Ismâ¿îl, *Folk Medicine*, p. 98.

[289] al-Bûnî, *Manba¿*, pp. 80, 282. Also see App. 12.

[290] Motif: F381.0.5§, ‡"Fairy (jinni, spirit) possesses by 'riding' ('mounting,' 'wearing') victim;" cf. Z186.4.3.1§, "Symbolism: wearing (slipping on, pounding "it" into, etc.) a shoe or garment—sexual intercourse."

in which Satan is believed to actually enter the body of a person and possess it, is believed to be possible only in Coptic beliefs and rituals. In actual folk practices among Moslem shamans, Satan may mislead and corrupt a person but has *never* been cited as an illness-causing agent. A number of practitioners stated that if Satan were to *enter* the body of a human being, that person would not be worth saving.[291] Although some academic studies on Moslem groups report "Satan" as a possessing agent,[292] these reports are in error—or inaccurate in labeling the intruding spirit. One source of confusion is the multiplicity of meanings designated by the word "Satan": an especially evil and powerful jinni is often, euphemistically, referred to as *sheṭân* (Satan) or an *'Iblîs* (Eblis). Also, folk expressions such as "*râkbu esh-Sheṭân*" (Satan has ridden him), and "*dakhalùh esh-Sheṭân*" (Satan entered into him) do not refer to a state of possession but signify only excessive, sinful, or erroneous actions that a person arrogantly, deliberately, and persistently or defiantly commits. An especially naughty boy or girl may be labelled *sheṭân* (a he-satan) or *sheṭânah* (a she-satan), respectively; likewise, hyperactivity is referred to as *shàyṭanàh* (devilish behavior); an adult may agree to take along a young boy or girl to a place or a public event on the condition that he/she would not "*yitshàyṭan/titshàyṭan*" (act irresponsibly). Yet Moslem shamans-*mashâyìkh*—like learned writers—cite the Koranic passage (Koran, 2:275), cited above, as an irrefutable proof that a "spirit" can and indeed does cause illness. In this respect they use the passage to merely justify and lend credence to the claim of the legitimacy of their craft.

In cases of possession by jinn, the sex of the possessing jinn is invariably the opposite of that of the *malbûs* (possessed person). Frequently, more than one jinn will possess a person. In such cases, the possessing spirits are related to one another, and one of them, usually *not* the main spirit, may be of the same sex as the person afflicted.[293] Within the context of illness and possession, the intruding spirit accounts for a change in the behavior and the overall character or temperament of the afflicted person. In this respect the possessing jinni is similar to the *'Ukht* (Sister) and the *Qarînàh* (counter-spirit/spouse/correlative). Thus, the spirit becomes what may be viewed as a component of the individual's "personality" or "self," or a "personality-spirit."

Familial, economic, and personal factors, especially self-esteem, usually underlie the conditions under which a person becomes spiritually "ill" or emotionally disturbed. Such an illness would be manifested in maladaptive behavior patterns such as depression (feeling "*makbûs*," "sick at heart," etc.), dissociation with social reality

---

[291] El-Shamy, "Belief Characters . . . ," pp. 29–30.

[292] Motif: cf. G303.0.1§, ‡"Other entities labeled 'satan.'"

See Okasha, "A Cultural Psychiatric Study of el-zar in U.A.R." In: *British Journal of Psychiatry*, Vol. 112 (1966) p. 1217. The same viewpoint is expressed by Nathan S. Kline, "Psychiatry in Kuwait." In: *British Journal of Psychiatry*, Vol. 104 (1963), pp. 766–774, especially p. 768; Sengers, *Women and Demons* (see for examples pp. 31, 39); also cf. R. Critchfield, "The Persistent Past: Passing the Buck to Demons," In: *The New Republic*, November 8, 1975, p. 15.

On the problems of attributing possession to "satan," see El-Shamy, "Belief Characters . . . ," especially p. 29. Also cf. Budge's usage of the word "devil" in n. 299.

[293] Informant: a young woman named Galîlah, see n. 275. Cf. the case cited by her in *The Fellâhîn*, pp. 185–186.

(being detached or "in another world"), and lack of interest in life (to "wish one were dead" or "taken away by God").[294] Among traditionary groups such abnormalities of behavior, especially in the absence of visible physical symptoms of malady, are attributed to possession by jinn. In great many cases, the underlying factors for "supernatural illnesses" are sexual. The erotic nature of possession was observed as early as in the eighth century; al-Jâḥiẓ (777–869 AD), a rationalist of the Mu¿tazilah school of Islamic philosophy,[295] recognized the hallucinatory origins of the concept of the jinn among Arabs. He attributed the emergence of the belief in these supernatural beings to what may be labeled in today's psychological jargon "sensory deprivation,"[296] which characterized life in the empty desert and pointed out the intimate relationship of possession to sexual needs.[297] Yet, we find that believers treat the sexual liaison between jinn and humans as a reality; the older Sunni orthodox legal systems—that still govern contemporary sharia (*sharî¿àh*)—legislated for cases in which humans are married to jinn.[298] Meanwhile, in contemporary folk communities established traditions regulating such marital relations are strongly observed in a manner that may be viewed as paralleling those of *qânûn ¿urfî* (customary law).

II.C.2a. *'asyâd ez-Zâr* (*zâr* spirits/possessing-jinn)

Reports of "evil" spirits possessing human bodies, and of the expulsion of such spirits are found in ancient Egyptian literature dating back to at least the fourth or fifth century BC.[299] The cult of possession and exorcism in various formats and under differing rationales is widespread among all ethnic and religious groups throughout Egypt. One form of this cult has come to be known as the *zâr* and the jinn involved

---

[294] Motif: V52.16§, ‡"Prayer (to God) for one's own death—'O God, take me away!' 'O God, grant me death!', etc."

[295] See "al-Jâḥiẓîyah," in Stephan and Nandy Ronart, *Concise Encyclopaedia of Arabic Civilization*, Vol. 1, p. 261; and C.H. Pellat, "Al-Jâh^iz^." In: *EI*. Vol. 2, pp. 385–387.

[296] Motifs: A2909§, "Origin of jinn: generated by hallucination caused by sensory deprivation;" F1043.1§, "Hallucinatory experiences from sensory deprivation;" U303§, "Relativity of perceiving physical attributes (size, shape, form, etc.)."

See: El-Shamy "Arab Psychiatry," p. 316.

[297] Motif: Z186.4.3.4§, ‡"Symbolism: spirit-possession (being 'epileptic,' worn or ridden by spirit)—sexual desire (lust)."

al-Jâḥiẓ, 'Abû-¿Uthmân ¿Amr ibn Baḥr, *al-Ḥayawân (Animal[s])*, ¿Abd-al-Salâm Muḥammad Hârûn, ed., 7 vols. (Cairo: al-Ḥalabî, 1938–1945), Vol. 1, p. 180, and Vol. 6, p. 260. See: El-Shamy "Arab Psychiatry," p. 316; and Walker-Ismâ¿îl, *Folk Medicine*, p. 47, note 2.

[298] Motif: F300, "Marriage or liaison with fairy." See al-Gindî, *al-Ginn*, Vol. 2, pp. 157–170; and Goldziher, *Vorlesungen über den Islam*, A. and R. Hamori, trs., pp. 63–64, esp. n. 88.

[299] See: "The Daughter of the Prince of Bakhtan and the Possessing Spirit," in Maspero/El-Shamy, *Ancient Egypt*, No. 10, pp. 141–147 (1917 ed.: pp. 172–179).

A text entitled "The Legend of the Possessed Princess," that claims to date back to a period corresponding to the thirteenth century BC but is dated only to the fourth or third century BC is reported in James Bennett Pritchart, ed., *Ancient Near Eastern Texts Relating to the Old Testament* (Princeton, 1950), p. 29; see also Budge's introduction to "How the God Khonsu expelled a Devil from the Princess of Bekhten" in his *Egyptian Tales and Romances*, No. 9, p. 142.

As already pointed out in "The Possessed Husband and His *Zar*."

as *'asyâd-ez-zâr* (masters or lords of the *zâr* [jinn]). The aggregate of the spirits that constitute this form of possession may be referred to as a pantheon; many of them are related to one another by blood or marriage and have specific names and characteristics that are better known among members of the population than the names of the general jinn. It should be noted that although the title *'asyâd* is etymologically related to the adjective: *sayyìd* (pl.: *sâdàh*, i.e., honorables or masters)—used to refer to a descendant of Prophet Mohammad, and to *sîdî* (my master/lord)—used to refer to a saint (see Sections III.C and III.B.1), a *zâr*-spirit is not referred to as *sayyìd* or *sîdî*, nor are *zâr*-spirits labeled *sâdàh*. Such a possessing being is typically referred to as "*sîd m-el-'asyâd*" or "*wâḥid m-el-'asyâd*" (i.e., one of the *'asyâd*). Similarly, a female member of the *zâr* pantheon of spirits is not referred to as *sàyyidàh*, but as "*wàḥdah m-el-'asyâd*" (a female of the *'asyâd*). In the case of a major possessing female *zâr*-spirit, such as Mustaghîtah, she may be simply described as *es-sitt el-kibîràh* (the grand, or the senior lady; see App. 25 and 26).

In spite of the intensity of its rituals, the involvement of scores of participants in its ceremony and its fame (or infamy), the *zâr* sub-cult has a relatively limited distribution. *Zâr* is not practiced by the Copts—though some Copts have been reported to attend ceremonies held by Moslems; the practice is less known in the countryside; some western desert communities (Oases) do not practice it at all, as stated by a female elder: "As for us, *zîrân*: we do not have!"[300] Yet, *zâr* practices have been spreading (see below).

Zâr-'asyâd constitute a special category of jinn and are associated exclusively with the *zâr* sub-cult, which is a part of the broader cult of supernatural illness, possession, healing, and exorcism. Unlike the more general categories of jinn or minor angels, *zâr*-jinn are never used as "helpers" or "servants" in shamanistic practices seeking to harness the lesser categories of supernatural beings. Also, they do not become overtly involved in sexual liaisons with the afflicted person (though such a relationship is presumed to exist symbolically). In this respect, *zâr*-jinn are perceived under the same terms as the supernatural "Counter-spirit" and "spirit-Sibling."

The *zâr* sub-cult has received considerable academic attention. Most scholars seem to agree that the word *zâr* originated in Ethiopia, where it refers to the possessing spirit itself;[301] the same usage is also found in some western desert communities in Egypt.[302] In most regions of Egypt, however, the word *zâr* refers to the ritual or ceremony through which the possessing spirit is addressed. As will be shown the *zâr-'asyâd* are typically appeased and pacified rather than expelled or "killed."

"Clearly Budge's use of the word 'devil' is an approximation influenced by Western views of possession; modern psychiatrists make the same error of equating local possessing spirits with the devil" (El-Shamy, *Folktales of Egypt*, No. 41, pp. 284–285).

However, Maspero correctly labels this supernatural entity "possessing spirit." (Cf. n. 292)

300 "*'iḥnâ zîrân ma¿andinâsh.*" Note the uncommon pl. form: "*zîrân.*" (Source: Archives: CFMC, New-Valley, Western Desert, March 1971, Col.: Miss Su¿âd Ḥasan.)

301 E.g., Littmann, *Geisterbeschwörungen*, pp. 38–62, esp. p. 48; C.B. Klunzinger, *Upper Egypt*, pp. 55–56.

302 New-Valley, Western Desert; as in n. 300.

The *zâr* sub-cult seems to be a relatively newcomer to the Egyptian scene, where it converged with an already established indigenous belief in possession, equipped with its own magico-religious procedures of appeasing and exorcising. The indigenous, more widely spread ritual concentrates on expelling the possessing spirit through punishment, or by resorting to a higher, more powerful spirit that can force the offending possessing spirit to comply.[303] Appeasement and peacemaking are also common, though still under the threat of punishment by the higher spirit or other powers, which can be evoked by the shaman-*shaikh* (healer). The prevalent indigenous and presumably older process is exemplified in one aspect of the Mar Girgis (Saint George) belief complex (see Section III.B.3); it is a part of an ecclesiastical ritual aimed at "slaughtering evil spirits" that possess the bodies of human beings in the same manner that the Saint had slain a dragon. This event takes place during an annual mass performed at the Mar Girgis Church at Mît Damsîs, a little town in the Nile Delta. A number of Coptic informants[304] reported that possessed persons attend the mass wearing white garments. Many Moslems participate in this healing ritual as well. At a certain moment a flash of light is seen, indicating that the Saint has passed through; he "slaughters" the possessing "evil spirits" with his sword. A stain of blood shaped like a cross or a crescent, depending on the religious affiliation of the possessed and that of the possessing spirit, appears on the white garment. The appearance of blood signifies that the "slaughtering" was accomplished (see App. 24).

The same procedure that involves resorting to a more powerful supernatural agent in order to compel or expel the possessing spirit is extensively used by local shamans—Moslem and Copt—particularly in rural areas. Their practices, however, lack the mass ritual aspect and the direct sponsorship of formal religious institutions, which characterize the Saint George's "devil-slaughtering" ritual. *Zâr* cultic rituals, by contrast, concentrate on appeasing the possessing spirit—not on expelling or punishing it.

The actual treatment ritual is usually constituted of two major phases: diagnostic and therapeutic. In the first, i.e., diagnostic phase, the healer attempts to identify the specifics of the intruding spirit, induce it to give its reasons for interfering in the life of the afflicted person, and to stipulate its conditions for ceasing to harm the patient. The intimate knowledge the healer acquires about the patient and the community

---

[303] In cases where a spirit refuses to cooperate, and/or refuses to divulge his/her name to the practitioner, al-Bûnî (*Manba¿*, pp. 81–82), prescribes the use of *màndàl* in order to acquire this information necessary for reporting the case to the spirit's superiors (see n. 205, 206). Also see El-Shamy, "Belief Characters . . . ," pp. 18–19 (App. 13).

With reference to the hierarchy among shaman-*shaikhs*, Sengers writes:

> "Higher *sheikh*" here means "higher in the demonic ranking" since [*shaikh*] Abu Musa too works with demons whose help he calls upon in healing his patients (thus, speaking in healers' terms, he is really using the "not-permitted path").(*Women and Demons*, p. 132, note 4)

In the case Sengers cites here, no *sùflî* (or as she reports, "non-permitted") means were used; therefore, the evoking of the high–low ranking is inapplicable. Moreover, not every practitioner of nether magic is necessarily seen as of "higher" ranking than a practitioner of the permitted (*nûrânî*) magic.

[304] Informants: Mr. Lewîs T. (see n. 268); Mr. Ibrahîm Ḥ., 64, public scribe (see El-Shamy, *Folktales of Egypt*, No. 2, p. 14); and Mr. Gamâl B.B., 25?, from Asyout, Engineer.

in which the patient lives is critical. In several treatment rituals, especially those that are private and individualized (such as the true *zâr*), the diagnostic phase requires the practitioner and assistants to move in and live with the afflicted person for a period of time that can be as long as seven days and observe the context of the client's typical family life. The amount of information gleaned through this procedure is usually immense and becomes germane to the healer's identification of the sources of the stress and, subsequently, the treatment. Identification of the details of the treating ritual (e.g., sacrificial animals, types of incense, foods and drinks, the name and characteristics of the likely possessing spirit, etc.) allows the afflicted to have some input in the process and facilitates the requirements of role-playing during the performance of actual ritual.

In the second phase, the healer prescribes the proper treatment and administers the remedy to the patient. Usually the family, friends, and neighbors of the afflicted person participate in both phases, along with the healer and the patient. In so doing, the healer utilizes several techniques that serve as healing prescriptions. Two of these techniques seem to be quite effective. The first is to induce the patient to express publicly his or her most threatening and anxiety-generating ideas and sentiments. The expressing of these negative feelings is presumed to be impersonal and is done within the safety provided by the belief that it is the possessing spirit that is speaking, not the patient (see App. 13). This frank and uninhibited identification of sources of conflict allows for the conversion of vaguely sensed *anxiety* into specified *fear* or anger that can be addressed and treated. The second is the ability of the healer to *re*organize the social system in order to accommodate the needs of the afflicted person, which are usually in conflict with the common practices and the ideals of the community. The processes of dissipating *anxiety* and *re*organizing the social system are totally dependent on the shared beliefs (along with the attitudes emanating thereof) among members of the community, the intimate knowledge the healer has of all parties involved, and the role that the community as a whole plays in the healing process. In this respect, a shaman's potential for publicly disgracing an oppressive party such as a father or husband and ability to get that party to experience "shame" seem to be powerful healing mechanisms through nonconfrontational, gentle coercive techniques. (See App. 13, 14, and 18; cf. App. 26)

Numerous folk and traditionary groups recognize a number of healing rituals within the broader context of faith healing and exorcism. These rituals may involve verbal expressions (incantations) and gesture, music and song, dance, or other forms of vehement body movements, use of incense—and in certain cases—hallucinatory drugs (such as hashish and alcoholic beverages), and offering a sacrifice with specific characteristics on behalf of (or as an offering to) the possessing spirit.[305] On an ascending scale of their perceived magnitude, these rituals may be classified as follows:

---

[305] Motif: N207.4§, ‡"Task can be performed only by using animal (bird) with certain physical qualities (e.g., color, size, age, etc.);" cf. H1379.1§, "Fool's errand: quest for the 'orphan chick;'" H1379.2§, Fool's errand: quest for the he-sparrow's milk." Also see n. 587.

Examples of typical identifying markings of the sacrificial animal or bird are: being "... with no markings [whatsoever]," "all-black ...," "all-white ...," "an orphan. ... " Among groups whose members

1. The *ràqwàh* (i.e., *rùqyàh* or *rùqwàh*, an incantation composed of sacred and other religious formulaic texts): It employs only verbal expressions and gestures. This ritual is often accompanied by *tàbkhîr* (burning of incense), presumed to drive away evil spirits. Reciting certain verses from the Koran is applied both as preventive measure as well as therapeutic. Professional recitalists are retained to perform this sacred blessedness bringing ritual on daily basis at businesses and homes. Recently, this practice has acquired new professional dimensions through low-ranking clerics who came to be known as "*mu¿âligîn bi-al-Qur'ân*" (healers through Koran).[306]
2. The *dàqqàh* (lit.: pounding, i.e., beat): It is the music produced mostly by membrane instruments and the flute. It is a ritual that includes the components found in the *ràqwàh* in addition to the music, song, and body movement. When performed within a religious context the "beat" is very similar to the male-oriented *zìkr*-ritual. The so-called public-*zâr* is essentially a variation on this ritual that allows for relatively open participation by interested parties (see n. 65 and 336).
3. *The ¿àqd* (lit.: tying, as tying a knot, i.e., contract), also called *¿ùqâd*: It is a sacrificial ritual, the purpose of which is to conclude an agreement with the jinn not to harm a person or disrupt the lives of the inhabitants of a residence. Within a context of exorcism, it involves the slaughtering of an animal or bird; blood-related practices such as smearing the body of the afflicted with blood, verbal incantations, and burning of incense are typically used. No music, song, or dance are applied. A number of sources, especially in areas where *zâr* is not practiced, described the *¿àqd* as "*zâr ¿a-s-sâkìt*" (a *zâr* on the quiet, a silent *zâr*), or "a very light form of *zâr*." As is the case with the true *zâr*, sacrificing a living being to jinn is deemed sinful.[307]

---

do not accept beliefs of the *zâr*-cult, these demands (usually made by women) are subject for ridicule, especially bringing "an orphan chick," and "young chicken that has not been mounted by a rooster [i.e., virgin]."

From the perspective of the practitioner, the assignment of these seemingly impossible, but indispensable, tasks gives the client a sense of the importance of the treatment. As one female practitioner (*shaikhah*-shamaness) put it:

> "Just like buying a medicine (drug). There is one that you can get for a piaster in every pharmacy or grocery store, and another that you must look hard for it, and may even have to get from abroad at a costs of a hundred pounds. The first may make [. . . you] sicker, while the second will cure you."

Cf. Sengers, *Women and Demons*, Case No. 2, p. 136, where she reports the exorbitant price a native healer claims he had to pay for the required incense imported from Yemen—(as for the treatment: it was "free"). Also see n. 335.

[306]Motifs: D1273.0.6§, "'*raqwah*'/*ruqwah*: charm containing sacred words renders invulnerable (protects);" cf. D1707.1.5.1§, ‡"Sacred words (from holy book) blessed."

A common practice among the various religious groups in Egypt is the "*raqwàh*" by professional low-ranked clerics acting also as incense-fumigators; the ritual is applied to shops, homes, equipment, or the like. See "Blow for Blow," in El-Shamy, *Folktales of Egypt* No. 27, pp. 143–145. Also see: Amîn, *Qâmûs*, pp. 80–81; and Lane, *Modern Egyptians*, pp. 138–139. (See n. 729)

Koran recitation is also used as a curing agent; see 'Usâmah 'al-Karm, *Ḥiwâr ma¿a al-ginn. 'asra¿ ṭuruq ¿ilâg al-'amrâḍ al-musta¿siyah bi al-Qur'ân (Discourse with Jinn. The Fastest Methods for Treating Incurable Illnesses with Koran)*. Compare Sengers' "*¿ilâg bi-al-Qur'ân* (Koran healing)," in *Women and Demons*, pp. 22, 123–161. See n. 214 and 332.

[307]Informant: Ḥesain/Abû Aḥmad/¿Âdil, from Bargî, southern Egypt. See n. 263.

Motifs: D1016.1§, ‡"Magic ritual requires slaughtering of certain animal (bird);" F385.2.2§, "Possessing

4. The *zâr*: It utilizes all the rituals involved in the three above-cited practices with the exception of sacred texts that must be excluded. In addition, it is perceived—at least from an ideal viewpoint—as situated outside the realm of religion and other sacred institutions. Thus, *zâr*-rituals are never held during sacred times (especially Ramaḍân, the lunar month of fasting). The rationale for this exclusion is that all jinn, devils, and similar supernatural creatures—except for angels—would be "chained" or otherwise prohibited from interacting with humans in any manner. Also, God's name must not be mentioned upon slaughtering the sacrificial animal being offered to the *zâr-'asyâd*. Failure to observe this rule will evoke the *'asyâd*'s anger and cause them to retaliate by harming the afflicted ("the *zâr*-bride") and the priestess.[308]
5. The *raḍwàh* (reconciliation, appeasement), or *ṣulḥàh* (peacemaking act): It is a ritual that may follow the *zâr*; it is held in situations where the effects of the *zâr* on the possessing spirit, as perceived by the afflicted, are thought to be wearing off or weakening. The *raḍwàh* would invigorate the state of accommodation granted by the possessing spirit. It consists of all the components of the *zâr*, but is performed on a much reduced level of intensity and with fewer participants.[309]

The true-*zâr* ritual is normally conducted by a female priestess (shamaness), known as *kùdyàh*—a word that suggests being the root-cluster of a wild leafy plant out of which offshoots grow (such as dandelion).[310] She may also be referred to as *shaikhìt-ez-zâr* (the she-shaikh of the *zâr*). In addition to the predominantly female members of her troupe, the *kùdyàh* is accompanied by an effeminate male practitioner labeled *'ùdyàh*.[311] Usually, an *'ùdyàh* lets his hair grow long, wears it hanging down behind his back, in addition to wearing feminine ornaments such as gold earrings; yet, many still wear a moustache. The *'ùdyàh*'s role as a music maker and participant in the physical movements (cf. ritual dancing) is clearly erotic (see al-Azhar's objections Nos. 8–9).

---

zâr-jinn (*asyâd*) placated by sacrifice;" C92.1.0.1, "Tabu: killing animals for sacrifice;" C92.1.0.1.1§, ‡"Tabu slaughtering animal as offering for jinn."

Occasionally, in tasks requiring drastic disturbing of earth (e.g., laying the foundation of a house, or digging a well) an animal or bird is slaughtered as an offering to the jinn-inhabitants of the site. (Motif: F385.2.8.1§, "Initiation sacrifice (for site): animal (bird) slaughtered as offering to jinn-dwellers (*¿ummâr*)," see also n. 48 and 446. See "*dhabâ'iḥ al-gìnn*" (lit.: jinn's slaughtered animals/birds, i.e., animals slaughtered [as offering for] the jinn). On the "slaughtering" at a certain site to appease its jinn inhabitants, see al-Gindi, *al-Ginn*, Vol. 2, pp. 90–94.

308 Littmann, *Geisterbeschwörungen*, p. 67, note B12; Ar. p. 92, pt. 12. (See also n. 504)

309 Informant: as in n. 284. Cf. *ṣulḥah*, in Littmann, *Geisterbeschwörungen*, p. 64, note A9. See also Blackman, *The Fellâhîn*, pp. 186, 199–200.

310 These plants bear the local names of *gu¿daiḍ* (dandelion), *sirîs* [??], or the like. Peasants in the countryside eat these plants, which grow in fields as wild weeds.

Motif: F561.14§, ‡"Social groups who live on weed-like greens (leek, radish, watercress, dandelion, etc.)."

311 ¿Aabd al-Mun¿im Shumays, "*al-Zâr masraḥ ghinâ'î lam yataṭawwar* (The Zar[:] a Lyric Drama That Did Not Evolve)." In: *Al-Funûn*, No. 17 (Cairo, 1971), pp. 72–83.

It is likely that the word *'ùdyàh* is a feminine derivative of "kùdyàh" signifying endearment or familiarity. In this respect it is a form of "Baby talk (by an adult)" (Motif: T604.4.1.1§). Also cf. Motifs: W202.1.1.1§, ‡"Indicator of femininity: women's speech-tone (soft, low-key);" and Z66.4.1§, ‡"Endearment: to be referred to (or addressed) in the diminutive."

Much of the traditional nomenclatures used in wedding ceremonies are utilized in *zâr* jargon; the afflicted person—often an adult female—is referred to as *¿arûsàt-ez-zâr* (bride of the *zâr*-[ceremony]), the main procession that represents the climax of the ritual is labeled *zaffàh* (i.e., [bridal or wedding]-procession), the following morning is labeled *eṣ-ṣabâḥiyyàh* (the morning after [the consummation of marriage]). Thus, the "bride" of the zâr-ritual is the focal point for the entire activity. Only selected peers of the "bride"—many of whom share the same condition and mindset of being (or having been) possessed—are invited to take part in the rituals that are normally held at the home of the "bride." Typically, a true *zâr* lasts for several days. According to three female informants, upon completion of the various phases of the ritual, the "bride" would be vulnerable to supernatural dangers. "She is to remain at home for seven days; if she were to go out [of her home], she would *titshâhìr*" (i.e., becomes infertile through *mushâhràh*) and, therefore, precautionary measures must be taken to ensure her safety.[312] (See *mushâhràh*, Section VIII.B)

II.C.2b. *'asyâd ez-Zâr* pantheon

Zâr-shamanesses (priestesses, *kùdyât*) usually claim that there are sixty-six members, or a similar high numbers of the *zâr* category of jinn (*'asyâd*); each has its own characteristics, *nidâ* (call) and *dàqqàh* (beat), and related rituals. Yet, in actual practice far fewer characters are cited. Most practitioners agree on the names and major traits of a core number of major *zâr*-spirits, but wide variations concerning the perceived nature of many of these spirits do exist. In this respect, the differences among the various practitioners may be viewed as reflecting the diverse nature and backgrounds of the practitioners themselves, and consequently the effectiveness with which the specific needs of a client can be addressed. Numerous regular users of the *zâr* ritual stated that they tried more than one *zâr*-priestess (*shaikhah*) before getting genuine relief through the professional nuances peculiar to the performative craft of a specific practitioner. A middle-aged Cairene woman—who held true private *zâr*-rituals on regular basis—addressed this point.

> I tried *shaikhàh* Zakiyyah, and another, and another; but I did not get any comfort. But with *shaikhàh* Faṭnàh [i.e., Fâṭimah to whom I resort now], I get relieved right away; *el-'asyâd 'illi m¿âhâ* (the *zâr*-jinn who are *with* her [i.e., which she offers]) are more agreeable with me.[313]

[312]Informants: Nabawiyyah Y., a Cairene middle-aged woman (see n. 212); and an elderly woman named 'Âmnah, aged 68, from el-Miyna, middle Upper Egypt (October 20, 1968); also 'Omm Shindî, settled Bedouin woman, in her fifties, married, has only one son (Cairo, Summer 1969).

[313]Informant: Mrs. K.S. middle-aged 55, married, childless, one adopted son (September 1968). (See App. 25 and 26)

On the efficacy of the familiar(s) a healer or a shaman-*shaikh* is presumed to offer, cf. the use of the phrase "with her are *nâs* (people) . . . " in n. 315.

Within the context of a public-*zâr*, a middle-aged female client, responding to the question as to why she was participating in a ritual conducted chiefly by a male practitioner, explained that the reasons were the pleasure and relaxation she experienced. She alluded to the personal characteristics and skills of the shaman-*shaikh*. When asked, "What is your name?" she replied in a rebuking manner:

> I am here to release pressure off my "self" (*'afdfàḍ ¿an nàfsî*); and you—(may God's Name protect your status)—can see [that]. Are a pleasant face and a gloomy face alike!? (*huwwa el-wìshsh es-simìḥ zàyy el-wìshsh el-¿ikìr!?*) Now, why should you be asking me as to what my name is, and what am I here for!?

Her response implied that she felt safe under conditions of anonymity and that the unpleasant face represents the atmosphere of family life at home (most likely her husband's ill temper), while the pleasant one is the *shaik*' and his troupe's.[314]

Addressing the issue of a shaman's proficiency and the effectiveness of his/her treatment of an afflicted person, one shaman-*shaikh* characterized a female competitor as being endowed with spirits that seem to be efficient; thus he stated: "With her are good people [i.e., jinn/familiars] (*me¿âhâ nâs kuwayyìsîn*)."[315] In this respect, a shaman's proficiency is judged according to the extent to which the spirits he/she offers appeal to clients, and the clients' responsiveness to the various facets of the rituals as described and performed by the shaman: the *'asyâd* and their attributes, music/beat (*nidâ*), chant/song, sympathy and helpfulness from other participants, and the like.

Available data indicate that *zâr*-spirits, like the general jinn, are perceived in terms of a socially organized community. Hierarchical power, social stratification, religious and ethnic identities, and kinship relationships are the most recurrent traits in this organization. Among *zâr*-spirits there are rulers and subjects, nobility and slaves, blacks and whites, Arabs and non-Arabs, Moslems, Christians, and—more recently—Jews and other faiths, as well as individual spirits representing significant economic and professional activities (i.e., sailor, peasant, policeman, etc.). As such, *zâr*-spirits represent a projective demographic model of the actual community in which the human participants in the *zâr* sub-cult actually live. Naturally, major changes in the cultural and social conditions in the community precipitate corresponding changes in the *zâr* characters. Currently, there is, for example, a noticeable decline in the incidents

---

[314] Informant: Anonymous woman, probably in her late fifties, she was partaking in a public *zâr*, in Kafr el-Zaytûn village, Gharbiyyah Governorate (April 1969). On the issue of anonymity in the public-*zâr*, see n. 336. (Cf. Vincent Carapenzano, *The ḥamadsha: A Study in Moroccan Ethnotherapy.* Berkeley, CA, 1973).

Here, an aging woman's concerns (anxiety) in a society dominated by adult male's preferences and privileges are expressed (Motif: P219§, "Aging wife's fears (anxiety)"). See: El-Shamy, *DOTTI*, Tale-type: 909§, *Taming the Disgruntled (Shrewish) Husband Is Like Taming a Lion: with Patience and Tenderness (Appeasement).* For an elaboration on this tale-type, see El-Shamy, "*A Motif Index of* Alf Laylah wa Laylah: Its Relevance to the Study of Culture, Society, the Individual, and Character Transmutation" as in n. 27.

[315] Informant: Shâkir (see n. 74). Note the use of *nâs* ("people"/"folks") to designate a shaman-*shaikhàh*'s familiars (jinn aids).

in which the Turkish spirits occur; this decline corresponds to the diminishing force of the once powerful Turkish roles in Egyptian society and culture. The familial aspect of *zâr*-spirits seems to be specified by more specialized practitioners, under less threatening interviewing circumstances. The symbolic significance of this aspect of the *zâr* cult seems to have eluded the scholars who have studied the *zâr* phenomenon.

Enno Littmann published two lists of *zâr*-spirits he had obtained from a native "collector" who assisted him and gathered field texts on his behalf.[316] In the first list, given by a professional *kùdyàh* (*zâr*-priestess), there are twenty-two characters; since two of these spirits were cited in double roles (i.e., "son of" and "sibling of"), twenty-five identities may be reckoned. Two of these spirits have a collective nature; they represent ethnic identities and class status rather than particular personal characteristics. They are "*es-Sûdân/mawâlî*" (the Sudanese/slaves), and "*el-hawânìm 'awlâd el-ḥabàsh*" (The ladies Children-of-the-Abyssinians, i.e., Abyssinian-ladies). Of the remaining twenty-three, twelve are given in pairs of brother and sister, two are presented as a pair of father and son, and two (slaves) are portrayed as a pair consisting of mother and son. The remaining seven are individual spirits with no identifying kinship relations; however, one of these is simultaneously perceived as a male slave to one of the sisters and as the son of a female spirit.[317] The dominance of the brother–sister relationship is also found in other published lists,[318] and in a number of this writer's own interviews with informants from different parts of Egypt. In these lists, the husband–wife relationships are near *unanimously* absent; yet parent–son relationships were present.[319]

The main and most powerful *zâr*-spirit is called Sultan Màmmàh (in urban communities this name suggests the word *mâmàh*, i.e., [my] mother). Màmmàh's sister is Mùstaghîtàh (i.e. Mùthtagîthàh, the one who is "Crying-out-for-help"), and his son is Yosaih.[320] The sister of Yosaih is 'Omm-Ghulâm (Mother-of-the-lad). Thus, as perceived by the *kùdyàh*, Màmmàh has a sister and a son, but he has no wife; Yosaih has a father and a sister. Yosaih's sister is not associated with Màmmàh, who logically should also be her father. Evidently, in this context, the brother–sister bond overrides the father–daughter relationship.[321] It may also be argued that an incestuous tendency underlies the brother–sister relationship; the issues of how Màmmàh fathered a son without having a wife and how Yosaih's sister acquired the name "Mother-of-the-lad" without having a husband are always left in a state of inarticulateness. Numerous

---

[316] Littmann, *Geisterbeschwörungen*, pp. 35–36. For lists of *'asyâd*, see App. 25; El-Shamy, "Belief Characters . . . ," pp. 27–28; cf. Sengers, *Women and Demons*, pp. 104–107.

[317] El-Shamy, "Belief Characters . . . ," p. 28 and 27, respectively.

[318] Shumays, "*al-Zâr masraḥ ghinâ'î lam yataṭawwar* (The Zar[:] a Lyric Drama that Did Not Evolve)," pp. 77–79. (For details of the list, see App. 25, pt. II)

[319] See El-Shamy, "Belief Characters . . . ," p. 27 (see App. 25). A rare case of husband–wife *'asyâd* (*shaikh* ¿Abd-el-Salâm and *al-sayyidah* Ruqayyah) is cited in Shumays (p. 74). However, this occurrence is casual and inconsequential.

[320] Probably a distortion of Yûsuf, i.e., Joseph (typically pronounced "Yûsìff" in vernacular).

[321] El-Shamy "Belief Characters . . . ," p. 27; and "Sibling in *Alf laylah wa laylah*," pp. 177–181. For occurrences of the phenomenon in literary lore, see H. El-Shamy, *A Motif Index of The Thousand and One Nights*. (Bloomington, IN: Indiana University Press, 2006), p. 12.

other folkloric expressions tend to substantiate this postulate of an incestuous tendency between brother and sister. This perception of familial relationships depicts more accurately the real structure of sentiments within the traditional Egyptian family, and—more generally—the Arab family than established academic postulates do.[322]

In the *zâr* cult, and to a lesser extent in other cultic practices, each spirit or group of spirits has its own representative symbols; the afflicted respond to these symbols in a manner that may be described as free association[323] under conditions controlled by the head practitioner (*kùdyàh*). The most important of these, at least from a folk therapeutic viewpoint, is the musical piece to which the possessing spirit is believed to respond. Each piece is called *nidâ* (a "call" or summons) or *dàqqàh* ("beat"). The title of the *nidâ* is the same as the name of the possessing spirit it calls; the accompanying words describe its acts. Other symbolic objects used to represent the possessing spirit include costumes, colors, jewelry, incense, and sacrificial animals or birds. The afflicted person responds to the specific *nidâ* (music) as well as to the other objects, presumably according to their symbolic and affective experiential significance to that afflicted person. (See App.27)

From the information gained about the afflicted through intimate conversations, keen observation, and other related traditional diagnostic techniques (as mentioned above) the practitioner (*kùdyàh*, shaman-*shaikhàh*) steers the activities toward inducing the client to express herself freely with less inhibitions. By participating in the ritual dance (*tàfqîr*) and often with the help of drugs such as hashish and alcohol, the afflicted reaches a dissociative state in which the possessing spirit, it is believed, takes over the body and the mind of the possessed.[324] Direct verbal communication can then be established between the practitioner and the possessing spirit via the patient. Through dialogues between the spirit and the practitioner, the "possessing

---

[322] For examples, see Tale-types: 932§, 933, *Brother-Sister Incest: the Sethian Complex (Syndrome)*; 932A§ (formerly 932§), *The Sister who Desires a Son Sired by Her Brother Achieves Her Goal: the Unsuspecting Brother*; 932B§, "*A Mother's Own Daughter as Her Daughter-in-Law; Bride Behaves as a Daughter-in-Law*. Brother–Sister Marriage (Sister as Wife)." See El-Shamy, *Tales Arab Women Tell*, No. 44, No. 49. Cf. Tale-type 450, "*Little Brother and Little Sister*. [They flee from home; brother transformed into deer, sister nearly murdered by jealous rivals.]" See *Tales Arab Women Tell*, Nos. 36–47; Cf. n. 588.

Also see Hasan El-Shamy, "The Brother-Sister Syndrome in Arab Family Life. Socio-cultural Factors in Arab Psychiatry: A Critical Review." In: *International Journal of Sociology of the Family*, Special Issue, *The Family in the Middle East*, Mark C. Kennedy, ed. Vol. 11, No. 2 (July–December 1981), pp. 313–323; and El-Shamy "The Traditional Structure of Sentiments in Maḥfouẓ's Trilogy: A Behavioristic Text Analysis." In: *Al-ᶜArabiyya: Journal of the American Association of Teachers of Arabic*, Vol. 9 (October 1976), pp. 53–74; (Cf. App. 26).

[323] See Robert M. Liebert and Michael D. Spiegler, *Personality: An Introduction to Theory and Research* (Homewood, Ill., 1970), p. 80, pp. 87–93.

[324] Motifs: F950.0.1§, "Hallucinatory drugs (hashish, opium, etc.) used as cures;" F950.0.1.1§, ‡"Hashish (opium, etc.) used to treat pain (distress);" F950.0.2§, "Hallucinatory drugs used to induce state of altered consciousness in exorcism rituals;" F950.0.2.1§, ‡"Drug-induced illusion (hallucination);" ‡V93.2§, "Ecstasy (trance) through sacrilegious dancing (*zâr*-ritual)."

Mrs. Nabawiyyah Y., who spent a wealth on *zârs*, stated (in October 1969):

> "Without hashish or whisky a *zâr* would not be a *zâr*. Nowadays, [with new laws, scarcity and high prices of imported goods], the very least one should do is *bîràh* (beer)."

jinni" (or rather the patient who has identified with the possessing spirit and enacts the spirit's role) declares the spirit's reasons for entering the body and specifies his/her reasons for harming the possessed person. Many of these exchanges between the spirit (i.e., the afflicted), the practitioner, and others who may be involved in the process may be viewed as brief pieces of drama played on that therapeutic stage; only the patient assumes the pseudo-character (i.e., persona) of the source of affliction. In this respect, the traditional healing practice is identical with the modern diagnostic and therapeutic technique known as psychodrama[325] (see App. 13).

Under these conditions, the symbolic significance of each component of the healing ritual becomes clear. Even a casual glance at names and other characteristics of such spirits reveals that the names are not haphazard, but often are indicative of an aspect of the affliction. Such is the case in the *zâr* pantheon, where the brother–sister relationship dominates. Similarly, the musical "call," to which a specific possessing spirit responds, projects this symbolic association. In a *zâr*-like ritual (public-*zâr*) that this writer attended in 1969 and 1982,[326] the musical "call" for the Sudanese spirits was unmistakably identical with the melody of a well-known folk ballad. The music "said" what the words of the ballad do "say;" the traditional song dealt with a tragic love story involving a girl named Bahiyyàh and a young man named Yâsîn who was murdered because of their love; the song began as follows:

- Tell me, O Bahiyyàh, about who killed Yâsîn.
- The *Sudanese* killed him, while [he was mounted on] the back of bull-camel.[327]

For additional information on the informant, see El-Shamy, *Tales Arab Women Tell*, No. 9, p. 113; and n. 212, above.

On the consumption of drugs, see data related to n. 333. Also, Sengers reports the use of Whisky (see: *Women and Demons*, p. 92).

325 See Lewis Yablonsky, *Psychodrama: Resolving Emotional Problems Through Role-Playing* (New York, 1976); quoted in El-Shamy, "Belief Characters . . . ," p. 21, note 16. Also see *Tales Arab Women Tell*, No. 37, p. 289, and "Mental Health . . . ," pp. 20–21 by the same author.

Motifs: F405.14.1§, ‡"Possessing spirit leaves body of possessed person via wound (made by exorciser);" cf. F415.1§, "Invisible spirit negotiates terms of departure with healer (shaman, exorcist, holy man, etc.): healing psychodrama." See also n. 169.

Sengers imprecisely describes this idea as follows:

> [. . . .] there can be "negotiations" with Satan and demons. The existence of *al-shaytan* (the devil) and *jinn* (demons) with their leader *Iblis* is acknowledged in the Koran. Although interaction with humans (*al-Ahqaf* [46], *Muhammad* [47], and especially *al-Jinn* [72]) is mentioned, this is strongly discouraged. For most Egyptians, devils and demons are part of their religious conviction. (*Women and Demons*, p. 31)

It should be mentioned that "Iblis" is not believed to be the leader of "jinn (demons)," as Sengers argues. Believing or pious jinn are not led by Iblis (Motif: V334.1§, ‡"Moslem jinni (fairy)"); only "*¿utât al-ginn* (the evilly-intrepid jinn)," like evil humans, follow Iblis. (See n. 173)

326 Held regularly in Kafr el-Zaytûn village, April 1969; revisited in May 1982, and 1999. See n. 314.

327 This translation is one of the two possible readings of the Arabic word '*es-sûdâniyyàh* (the Sudanese)'. Through *tàzhîr*, play on words labeled in the field of the study of Arabic rhetoric as *ginâs làfẓî*, the phrase may also be perceived as *es-sûd ¿inayyàh* (my eyes: the black). However, this latter rhetorical interpretation has so far not been encountered in the context of *zâr* rituals.

The words of the song were not used in the ritual, yet the music conveyed the very message expressed in the traditional verbal utterance; however, as indicated earlier, the music evokes the words (see information associated with n. 64). The argument here is that when a possessed person responds to a musical "call" that summons a specific "spirit" during the free association and expression during the *zâr* process, the characteristics of that spirit may be assumed to be related to the source of the affliction. These personal spirits may therefore be considered concrete anthropomorphic representations of affective and intellectual states. References to abstract concepts, meanings, and forces in anthropomorphic or concrete terms are common occurrences in Arab folk culture.[328] For example, *ed-dùnyâ* (the world, i.e., life) is often encountered by Moslem saints as a woman.[329] The *'Ukht, Qarînàh,* and *zâr*-spirits, such as Mùstaghîtàh, Safînàh, and el-Ghàwwâṣ, represent psychosocial realities, expressed symbolically these spirits are not literary fictions.

The *zâr* cult and the general concept of possession have been studied by scholars from a variety of fields. Generally speaking, most of the studies have overlooked the symbolic relationship between the nature of the possessing spirit and the position of the afflicted person vis-a-vis the spirit. Even psychiatrists have simply referred to the possessing spirit as the "Devil" (see n. 292). Thus formal psychiatry has demonstrated western-bound inability (or reluctance) to account for local folk cultures and, consequently, the very nature of certain aspects of mental illness as perceived within the context of the broader worldview in such cultures.

An especially dysfunctional view held by academic mental health officials in Egypt relates to certain aspects of traditional religious beliefs. From its inception during the 1950s formal psychiatry understandably advocated fighting harmful customs and traditions. To use the words of M.K. Barakât, one of the founders of psychiatric services in Egypt, these "wrong beliefs" included belief in the malice of the "evil eye;" existence of jinn and other supernatural beings; efficacy of witchcraft, *zâr* rituals, amulets, and visitations to saints; and drug addiction and alcoholism. Thus, Barakât equates belief in the jinn, "evil eye"/envy, and the power of saints, which are part of formal Islamic tenets of faith, with *zâr* rituals, alcoholism, and drug addiction that are sinful (tabu).[330]

---

[328] Motif: Z110, "Personifications [of abstractions]." See El-Shamy, *GMC*, as in n. 21.

The present writer introduced this therapeutic technique in 1982 under the title: "Belief Characters . . . ," p. 21. More recently, Sengers presented a similar idea; she wrote:

> For the diagnosis "you are possessed by a *jinn*[i]," the healer gives a name to unconscious conflicts in the patient and thereby makes them manageable. (*Women and Demons*, p. 137)

[329] Motifs: Z113.1§, "Life (the world) personified as a beautiful young woman;" Z122.7.1§, ‡"Temporal forces ('Time') responsible for man's misfortune (troubles)."

See al-Nabhânî, *karâmât al-'awliyâ'*, Vol. 1, pp. 191, 412, 452; Vol. 2, p. 40. Also in folktales, beautiful worldly life is depicted as "the lady." See "The Sure News is Up Ahead," in H. El-Shamy, *Tales Told Around the World*, R.M. Dorson, Gen. Ed., pp. 149–159; and Motif Z113.1§, in El-Shamy, *MITON*.

[330] M.K. Barakât, *Al-¿Ilâj al-nafsî* (*Psychiatries*). (Cairo, n.d.), quoted in Hasan El-Shamy's "Mental Health . . . ," pp. 27–28. See "Koran healing," n. 214 and 306.

Conflict can be readily seen between psychotherapeutic western institutions opposing powerful religious beliefs and clients whose self concepts are congruent with these dominant religious and moral institutions. When incongruence between self and experience exists and the individual is unaware of it, he is potentially vulnerable to anxiety, threat, and disorganization. These characteristics are widespread among the middle and educated classes.

Formal religious institutions view the *zâr* cult as lying outside the bounds of the realm of the legitimate or permissible, and condemn individuals who practice it as guilty of *kùfr* ("sacrilege," disbelief, being infidels). In a reply to concerned readers inquiring about "the religion's stand" on the *zâr*, an Azharite authority (member of the "Council of Senior Ulama") summed up the situation by reiterating the formal religious beliefs and stated that harm can indeed be caused to humans by Satan or the jinn by the *màss* ("touch") of Satan and by evil jinn in the form of *rîḥ* (i.e., wind) who would "*yadkhùl*" (enter, possess) the human body; these beings can cause insanity and epilepsy. He concluded that

> "This is the observable tangible [fact] the denier of which could almost be considered *mùkâbìr* (arrogantly insisting on correctness of own views in spite of incontrovertible evidence to the contrary) and denier of that which is witnessed by the eye."

The religious authority recommended that treatment of such illnesses should be by "medical doctors specializing in neurological disorder, or by [. . . soul] doctors—those true believers and the pious," who have been endowed with healing powers.[331] Typically, the true believers and the pious try to heal through sacred Koranic and other sacred texts.[332] Then, the fatwa went on to declare that formal Islam condemns the *zâr* for being a cult (*¿ibâdah*, veneration [of spirits]), which violates numerous sacred prohibitions (tabus). Among these are the following:

> (1) Simulating a *¿ibâdàh* (worship); (2) offering a *qùrbân* (sacrifice) to a spirit; (3) killing a living creature illegitimately for purposes other than those permitted by God; (4) circumambulating the sacrifice [thus treating it as if sacred]; (5) drinking blood, or covering the human body with blood; (6) drinking liquor—"if the possessing jinni is supposed to be the one who is drinking it;" (7) boasting; (8) erotic dancing; (9) immodesty of mixing of men and women in compromising positions; and (10) the destruction and wasting of goods.[333]

All these practices are forbidden by Islamic law (*sharî¿ah*). They range from cardinal sins (*kabâ'ìr*)—as in the cases of simulating a worship (Nos. 1, 2, and 4) seen as

---

[331] Ṭâhâ Ḥabîb. In: *Nûr el-Islam Review*, Vol. 3, No. 3, p. 217.

[332] With reference to treatment with Koran, See n. 214 and 306.

[333] Beside the sacrifice, alcoholic beverages or drugs (hashish, opium), the true-*zâr* requires additional edibles such as nuts, fruits, crackers, and the like to be placed on a tray that sits on a low-rise table. This element is labelled *kùrsî-ez-zâr* (the *zâr*-chair/stool). See n. 324.

sheer disbelief (*kùfr*), to the *ṣaghâ'ir* (minor sins)—as in the case of conspicuous consumption and destruction of goods (No. 10) viewed merely as disdainful.

In spite of this unequivocal condemnation and prohibition, the *zâr* cult not only persists but is also spreading both vertically to more social classes, and horizontally into more regions and culture areas. Recent reports reveal that members of western-educated groups including females holding high governmental offices participate in "*zâr*" rituals.[334] It should be pointed out, however, that the ritual referred to in the reports is the "popularized" public form that may be characterized as pseudo-*zâr* or public-*zâr*. Yet, after the advent of the Islamic fundamentalism tide beginning in the 1970s, the practice of the true *zâr* has become less overt.

Most practitioners of the public-*zâr* deny, with some justification, that the activity they conduct commercially is a *zâr*, and insist on calling it *zìkr* (remembrance), *daqqàh* (beat), or simply *galsìt tafârîḥ* (a gathering for joyfulness, or merrymaking). These *zâr*-like gatherings are held regularly on a specific weekday, and are open to all. For a small fee[335] anyone may join in the *tàfqîr* (ritual dance) when her/his musical "call/beat" is played. More than one participant may simultaneously reach the dissociative stage in which the possessing spirit is believed to manifest its presence. Each participant receives some attention from friends, other participants, or the troupe leader (the shaman-*shaikh* or his assistants).

Thus, as a modernized ritual, the public-*zâr* lacks a number of healing conditions characteristic of the traditional true-*zâr*. These include the diagnostic phase, sacrificial offering and related applications of blood rituals (including physical massage), uncontested centrality of the possessed person (as the "bride" of the *zâr*), direct involvement of members of the family of the afflicted, the conspicuous consumption of goods and drugs including alcohol, and consequent reorganization of the community so that the afflicted may be accommodated. During a public-*zâr* ritual held every Tuesday evening at a shaman-*shaikh*'s home in a village in the Nile Delta I asked him about the clients who were present. He defensively stated

> I don't know the name of any of those persons who are here; I don't know where they come from, nor what ails them. I am like a [medical] doctor; the *zùbûn* (client, customer) comes, pays the '*fizîtàh*' (i.e., 'visit,' a doctor's fee), and participates [in the *táfqîr*, ritual dancing]. When the client is satisfied, he or she leaves. I don't ask about where they come from or where they go to [. . .]. Ladies may come together, if one of them requires attention, they are the ones who would take care of one another.[336]

---

[334]*Al-Ahram* (February 16, 1971), p. 3. Professional Women in *zâr* (university graduates constituted 8 percent); meanwhile, the study indicated that nonliterate women were beginning to visit psychiatries.

[335]Vendors of religious objects and services eschew the use of the words "price," "cost," or "fee" to refer to what they expect from a consumer. The word "*wahbàh*" (lit.: donation, grant) is preferred. In 1969 the admission fee typically ranged from ten to twenty-five piasters (quarter of a pound) for the entire session; in 1982 it was roughly three times that amount; in 2000 the fee became 5.00–10.00 pounds—(there are 100 piasters to a pound). Currently, some practitioners charge per *tàfqîràh* ([joining in] one ritual-dance to a beat/call). See n. 64.

[336]Informant: *'shaikh'* Ḥesain Abu- . . . , 35, the son of Kafr-Zaytûn's senior shaman-*shaikh*; a practitioner himself. Recorded in April 1969 and May 1982. (See also n. 314.)

In many respects the modernized public-*zâr* resembles the Euro-American "discotheque" or psychedelic musical activities, which have found their way into Egyptian westernized urban centers. The popularized *zâr* however, is practiced within the context of beliefs about the supernatural. The public-*zâr* (and *zìkr*) share with the true-*zâr* the vital function of allowing for expenditure of bent-in energies in a manner that communal ethos and puritan religious edicts do not accommodate. Such dissipation of energy and resulting exhaustion has both preventive and therapeutic effects on the individual.[337] Numerous recent studies on the *zâr* were based on observing these public, less personalized, commercial enterprises. The findings of such studies should not be automatically extended to the traditional true-*zâr* ritual.

II.D. Zoological Supernatural Beings

A number of animal-like creatures constitute a distinct category of the supernatural; these beings are commonly considered "not completely jinn or *afrits*" but as animal-like beings with supernatural characteristics. Ogres, mules, and donkeys, certain horses, reptiles, birds, and insects are members of this zoological category. Occasionally, an academic report may view jinn as having animal qualities, but such a view would be inaccurate. Jinn, as previously stated, are presumed to have the capability of shape-shifting and self-transformation into virtually any form they may wish; most frequently they are reported to assume the form of cats, snakes, dogs, and mules or donkeys. However, such an assumption by a jinn of the shape of another being is transient, but if killed in that assumed form the jinn's corpse remains in the assumed shape. (See n. 461)

Usually, public-*zârs* are conducted by male practitioners assisted by three or four assistants (musicians: flutists, drummers, or tambourine players). Usually one of the troupe members is a female. In the present case, the female assistant was the main practitioner's elder sister (a divorcee, in her mid or late thirties, named Nagafah); she played the drum and attended to emergency situations when an unaccompanied female required close physical contact of delicate nature. In this respect, the public-*zâr* differs from the true-*zâr* where the female priestess is the uncontested leader aided by other assistants, one of whom may be an *'ùdyàh* (effeminate male *zâr* practitioner).

Within such nonindividualized context, Sengers quotes one of her informants as stating,

> "These days, [...], the *zar* is no longer concerned with the *asyad*, but songs are sung for Allah and the saints." (*Women and Demons*, p. 115.)

However, Sengers' declares,

> "[... I do not] agree with those researchers who say that changes take place in the life of the women because an important network is created by the *zar*, which allows them to make new relationships operating outside their daily lives [...]. I have never noticed that women who attend the *zar* go and visit each other in daily life too." (*Women and Demons*, p. 119)

Clearly, her assertion, which is based on limited public-*zâr* situations, is inapplicable to the true-*zâr* ritual where the "bride of the *zâr*" is expected to be supported by women in her own situation (i.e., belonging to the club of the "afflicted").

337 On the preventive and therapeutic effects of true *zâr*-rituals, see El-Shamy, "Mental Health...," pp. 21–23, 28.

II.D.1. *ghîlân* (Ogres) and Similar Creatures

Older Arab literary sources often reported ogres (*ghîlân/'aghwâl*) as a category of the jinn or the "devils."[338] Ogres were also perceived as constituting a powerful class of supernatural beings called *sa¿âlî*; however, the exact identity of this latter group seems controversial. *sa¿âlî* were described as "the magicians of the jinn," "the females of the devils," and a female product of a union between angels who were cast out of heavens (such as Hârût and Mârût) and some of Adam's daughters (i.e., human females).[339]

In the oral traditions of Egypt, belief in the existence of ogres seems to be derived from such older Arab portrayals; yet, contemporary beliefs are less diverse, especially with reference to the nature of these creatures. The *ghûl* (ogre) and *ghûlàh* (ogress) are man-eaters (cannibals); except for their frightening appearance, peculiar habits, and magical powers especially as shape-shifters, ogres resemble humans. As a Bedouin woman put it while arguing with her husband over the difference between an ogress and a female jinn: "An ogress is a female-individual (*el-ghûlàh nafaràh*)."[340] Occasionally, ogres are thought to have goat- or donkey-like legs and hoofs instead of feet, a characteristic they seem to share with *afrits* (*¿afârît*), devils, and other demonic beings; they also are portrayed as having hideous and frightening appearances such as huge lips and ears (that male ogres use as bedding and cover when they go to sleep); meanwhile ogresses may have long breasts thrown over their shoulders, and display signs of anger or peacefulness that are opposite to the normal.[341] The most frequent occurrence of ogres is in *ḥawadît* (i.e, *Märchen*, fantasy tales, fairy tales) that are narrated with the intent to entertain. Reports of encountering an ogre or an ogress in real life are extremely rare.[342] Oral folk narratives typically present ogres as neighbors, spouses—husbands or wives—adoptive parents, teachers, or the like.[343]

---

[338] See for example Maḥmûd Shukrî al-'Âlûcî, *Bulûgh al-'arab fi ma¿rifat aḥwâl al-¿Arab* (*The Attainment of Goal in Knowing of the Affairs of the Arabs*). M.B. al-Atharî, ed. 3 vols. (Cairo, [1964]), Vol. 2, p. 341.

[339] al-'Âlûcî, *Bulûgh al-'arab*, Vol. 2, p. 341. Motifs: cf. G1§, ‡"Origin of ogres. (Where ogres come from);" B14.5§, "Ghoul (ogre) as hybrid of jinniyyah and hyena;" Cf. al-Gindî, *al-Ginn*, Vol. 2, pp. 96–109, esp. p. 96.

[340] Informant: Mrs. ¿Azîzah ¿., 38, nonliterate, married, has one daughter (for more information on ¿Azîzah, see El-Shamy, *Tales Arab Women Tell*, No. 31, p. 274).

[341] Motifs: G303.4.5.10§, ‡"Devil (afrit, ogre) has goat's (ass's) hooves (legs);" G2.1§, ‡"Hideous ogre (ogress);" F511.2.5.1§, ‡"'Lower ear as mat; upper ear as cover;'" cf. F531.1.5.1, "Giantess (fairy, mountain woman, [ogress]) throws her breasts over her shoulders;" G654.1§, ‡"Indicator of ogress' contentment (peacefulness): disheveled appearance;" G654.2§, ‡"Indicator of ogress' anger (foulness of mood): neat (groomed) appearance."

[342] "The ancient Arabian goddess al-¿Uzza was described in older sources as 'having her breasts thrown over her shoulders;'" see El-Shamy, *Folktales of Egypt*, p. 55. Also see Ibn al-Kalbî (d. AD 826), *Kitâb al-'Aṣnâm* (. . . *Idols*) (Cairo, 1960), p. 25; and al-Âlûci, *Bulûgh al-'arab*, Vol. 2, p. 204. Also cf. "bogeyman" in n. 349, and Sengers, *Women and Demons*, p. 39 ("bogey-man").

[343] For examples, see Tale-type complex: AaTh 327, *The Children and the Ogre*; 363A§, *Husband Discovers that His Wife Is a Ghoul (Witch)*; and 894, *The Ghoulish Schoolmaster and the Stone of Pity* [A maiden's long- sufferings caused by her accidental learning of teacher's secret]. For representative texts, see El-Shamy, *Tales Arab Women Tell*, Nos. 13–14.

In this context the ogre and the ogress appear in patriarchal and matriarchal roles and are referred to as *'abûna el-ghûl* (our father the ogre) and *'ommìna el-ghûlàh* (our mother the ogress).[344] For a child, these parental titles assigned to ogres, along with an ogre's frightful actions, indicate the stern and often cruel roles parents and teachers play vis-a-vis children, or husbands in dealing with their powerless wives.

Ogres also appear in fantasy tales as common adversaries of a hero or heroine often with hideous features and habits (as described above). Still, in congruence with the role of paternal or maternal figures, they may appear in the role of helper and sound advice giver.[345] Such tales are typically, but not exclusively, narrated by females to children or young adults.[346]

Among members of social classes with western education, the ogress is virtually unknown. If a situation arises and a clarification of what a *ghûlah* (ogress) is supposed to be, the word "gorilla" and the human-like general appearance of this animal are evoked.[347] The fact that gorillas, unlike ogres, are not carnivorous becomes irrelevant. The ogress (*ghûlàh*) is sometimes (especially in Nubia) called *sà¿luwwàh*, a label clearly derived from the classical Arabic *si¿lâh*. In colloquial Egyptian Arabic, the word *sala¿awwàh*, a derivative of the classical (unused) "*si¿lâh*," addressed at a female, is an insult pertaining to physical meagerness (thinness), hideous facial features, and aggressive character.[348]

Other ogre-like creatures include *Abu-Rìgl-Màslûkhàh* (the one-with-a-skinned-leg), the *bù¿bù¿*, a fearsome creature without any definable description (comparable to "Bogeyman"), and *¿àfrît nùṣṣ-el-lail* (Midnight-*afrit*).[349] All three are minor beings typically invoked by adults mainly to scare children and induce them to comply with the orders they issue, especially to stop crying or to go to sleep. These belief characters are comparable to the *Shàmmâmàh* (she-sniffer), but may not be identified with her. (See Section II.B, and n. 201)

Another category of man-eaters, often found in oral legendary traditions, is an ethnic/racial group labeled "*nàmnàm*" (i.e., cannibals). Typically, they are reported to dwell in Sudan, have short tails that can be hidden under ordinary clothes, and occasionally pose—as do ogres—as ordinary men so as to trap a prey (through

---

344 See the use of this expression in "Louliyya, Daughter of Morgan," in El-Shamy, *Folktales of Egypt*, No. 8; Tale-type: 310A§, *The Maiden in the Tower: Louliyyah*. Youth cursed to fall in love with ogre's (ogress, witch's) daughter: elopement, transformation (separation), and disenchantment (reunion).

345 Motifs: N812, "Giant or ogre as helper;" N812.2, "Giantess [(ogress)] as helper."

For an example from oral traditions, see n. 342.

346 See El-Shamy, *Folktales of Egypt*, p. lxviii; and "Women and the Telling of Fantasy Tales," in El-Shamy, *Tales Arab Women Tell*, pp. 9–10.

347 For an example of crosscultural perception combining Egyptian and American (U.S.) views, see El-Shamy, "Folkloric Behavior," pp. 195–207.

348 For examples of the various views of Islamic writers (from various parts of the Islamic world), see: al-'Âalûcî, *Bulûgh al-'arab*, Vol. 2, pp. 340–341. Cf. al-Gindî, *al-Ginn*, Vol. 1, pp. 110–120; also see Ammar, *Growing*, pp. 133–134, where "*Silwa*" (probably a misprint for *sà¿lùuwwàh/si¿lâh*) is the name for ogress (cf. the name "sala¿awwah" in App. 20).

349 Walker-Ismâ¿îl, *Folk Medicine*, p. 70, note 1.

proposing marriage, or the like). Such groups are, however, not viewed as part of the supernatural, but simply as savage, beast-like people, who relish human flesh.[350]

The concept of a demonic race underlies the belief in the existence "Yà'gûg wa Màg'ûg" (Gog and Magog).[351] Literary traditions portray these two groups as tribes of human-like monstrous warriors, descendants of Yâfeth, one of Noah's sons, and the ancestors of peoples who may be perceived as belonging to the Mongoloid race. They were contained behind a wall of iron that Alexander, the Dual-horned, built around them. Prior to imprisonment, their military ranks multiplied rapidly—for each man of them will have begotten one thousand warriors before his death. They terrorized their neighbors. In folk tradition they are commonly perceived as pygmy-like in physical stature—"only as high as a *shîbr*" (i.e., the distance from the tip of the little finger to the tip of the thumb of a stretched out palm of hand, but some literary accounts describe a branch of them as tall as cedar trees), with file-like tongues with which they are trying to lick the iron wall through. Other accounts add that they have lion's claws and teeth, and ears so large that "one of which serves as mat and the other as cover" when they go to sleep; they devour every animal and plant they come across, but certain branches of them feed on nothing but human flesh and drink only human blood.[352] The resurfacing of Gog and Magog among the rest of human beings is believed to be one of the "major signs" of the coming of the Day of End of World. (See n. 122)

II.D.2. Supernatural Animals: The Mare and the Stallion

Several supernatural animals are known in oral folk traditions; flying mares and stallions appear normally in fantasy tales (i.e., *Märchen*/fairy-tales), as fictitious beings that are not believed to exist. Two horse-like beings, however, appear as a part of the belief system; these are el-Bùrâq,[353] and el-Màymûn.[354] The first is described as a mare or mare-like animal associated solely with the formal religious accounts of "*al-'ìsrâ' w-al-mì¿râg*" (i.e., Prophet Mohammad's visit to Jerusalem, and ascent to heavens where he met and conversed with numerous sacred figures in a few moments' interval).[355] The Bùrâq is depicted in a folk drawing sold at old marketplaces as a

---

[350]Motifs. G11.18, "Cannibal tribe;" G11.18.0.1§, "Namnam as cannibal tribe (race)." For specific references, see El-Shamy, *GMC*; and *MITON*.

[351]Koran, 21:92–98; al-Tha¿labî, *Qiṣaṣ*, p. 205.

Motifs: A1303.2§, ‡"Gog and Magog as giant races;" F510.2§, "Gog and Magog as monstrous races."

See "Why the Turks Were Called 'Tùrk,'" in El-Shamy, *Folktales of Egypt*, No. 24, p. 139, 273–274. For traditional elaborations on the origin of human character and racial traits, see also n. 509.

[352]al-¿Idwî, *Mashâriq*, p. 201.

[353]Motifs: B41.3§, ‡"*al-Burâq*: Angel-horse;" B41.3.1§, ‡"*al-Burâq* as riding-animal with the speed of lightening (*barq*)."

See S. and N. Ronart, *CEAC*, Vol. 1, p. 104; Aḥmad Bahjat, *al-Burâq*. (Cairo: al- Zahrâ', 1989). Cf. "The Beast That Took a Wife," in El-shamy, *Folktales of Egypt*, No. 20, pp. 126–128.

[354]al-Tha¿labî, *Qiṣaṣ*, p. 18.

[355]For a detailed description of the sacred events, see Sa¿îd Muḥammad Ḥasan, *Haqâ'iq al-Isrâ' wa al-Mi¿râj* (The Facts about the *'isrâ'* and the *mi¿râj*). Cairo: 1977.

winged, white mare with a female human face; in some older accounts, however, the Burâq is viewed as an angel-horse or a riding-mule that is neither male nor female.[356] Meanwhile, el-Màymûn is a stallion believed to be the offspring of a union between an ordinary mare and a sea-jinn horse. In oral traditions references to this fabulous hybrid are few, but its most frequent occurrence is linked to Imam ¿Alî's heroic and military feats.[357] (See Section IV.C) The movements of al-Màymûn, just like the Imam's sword, called Dhu-l-Fiqâr, were controlled by the eyesight of the rider; the hoof of the stallion landed where the eyesight of Imam ¿Alî did, as did his sword.[358] Both the Bùrâq and the Màymûn recur only in historical religious folk legends; they do not play active roles in accounts of contemporary experience of personal nature on part of the narrators.

However, encounters with a jinn who appears in the form of a mule or donkey, and occasionally a stallion, are frequently reported, mainly by men as personal experiences. In such cases a lone nighttime traveler may find a splendid-looking lavishly saddled animal and decides to ride it, but when he mounts its back the animal flies upward or starts rising by lengthening its legs, thus proving to be a jinn. Only by driving a pack-needle in-between the shoulders of that animal would it be brought under control.[359] One of the most recurrent encounters with jinn in animal form is associated with the belief in "*bàghlìt-el-¿ashr*" (the she-mule of the tenths). According to this belief, which is more commonly reported by women, during the first ten days of the lunar

---

Also see Brooke Olson Vuckovic, *Heavenly Journeys, Earthly Concerns: the Legacy of the Mi¿raj in the Formation of Islam.* (New York: Routledge, 2005.)

Occasionally, the Bùrâq is mentioned as the means of transportation to be used by Prophet Mohammad to ascend to heavens at the Resurrection Day (see "The Beast That Took a Wife" in El-Shamy, *Folktales of Egypt* No. 20, p. 128).

356 al-Damîrî, *Ḥayât al-Ḥayawân*, Vol. 1, pp. 116–117, cf. 311.

357 Motif: B184.1.3.1.1§, ‡"al-Maymûn: supernatural hybrid stallion whose movements are controlled by rider's thoughts (hoof lands where rider's eyesight aims)."

For a fictitious account of the supernatural hybrid, see Burton, *Arabian Nights*, Vol. 6, p. 8.

358 Motifs: D631.3.3, "Sword large or small at will," and D631.3.3.1§, ‡"Sword's strikes controlled by eyesight (thoughts) of striker." (In this respect, the stallion and the sword resemble the modern electronically guided aeroplane and laser guided bombs.)

359 Motifs: F401.3.1.1§, "Spirit in form of mule;" F384.3, "Iron powerful against fairies;" F384.3.1§, ‡"Driving iron needle into shoulders of jinni (afrit) assuming form of animal nullifies his power."

The belief has been reported by numerous informants from various regions of Egypt. Usually, it occurs as a belief legend or personal experience narrative. The present writer heard such accounts from other boys during his childhood. In the words of an adult Nubian man (Aḥmad T., in 1964, in Brooklyn, New York City):

> "A friend of mine in the old country said to me, 'When I was young, I was traveling alone toward[s] our village [Qirshah, Nubia]. All of a sudden a handsomely bedecked mule appeared as if from underground. He (the mule) weaved his head at me inviting me to mount it. I thought it belonged to someone [from our village] and it got lost. [So, I thought I'd take it back to the owner.] Once I mounted it, its legs begin to grow longer and I found myself at a considerable height. That mule was a 'one of them' [jinni]. It did not heed my imploring and kept on going up and up. I became very frightened. Finally, I remembered that I had a '*maibàr*' (long heavy-duty upholstery needle) with me. So, when I drove the needle between the animal's shoulders its legs began to grow shorter. I leapt off its back when I was at a safe distance from the ground and ran away.'"

month of Moḥarram (or the last ten days of the month of Ramaḍân) a jinn may appear in the form of a water carrier's she-mule. The mule carries a saddlebag filled with gold and a dead man's head on its back. The mule, or rather the jinn, visits a lucky person who—if wise enough—will not panic and keep the gold and put some other matter in its place. Occasionally, the she-mule is reported to be carrying onion and garlic skins, which will prove later to be gold. The gold is believed to be the *zakâh* (required alms-tax) that Muslim jinn pay in fulfillment of one of the five basic *furûḍ* (obligatory service) of the religion: giving to the poor "one-fourth-of-one-tenth" of money still in one's name.[360]

It is worth noting here that in active folk beliefs Eblis (i.e., the Devil)—unlike the jinn, is not associated with horses. Commonly the Devil is linked to mules and donkeys. This association between the ass, or donkey, and the Devil seems to hark back to ancient Egyptian religious beliefs where the ass was believed to be a Sethian animal. Some academic studies equate Seth, the trickster deity, with the Semitic Devil.[361]

II.D.2a. *Dâbbàt al-'àrḍ* (the "earth's animal")

Another supernatural being with animal characteristics is, surprisingly, amorphous and undefined even in the minds of those who spoke of it. Oral folk reports cite the anticipated, but dreaded, appearance "at the end of Time" of "*Dabbìt el-'àrḍ*" (i.e., *dâbbàt al-'arḍ*, "the Earth's Animal")[362] without describing its nature. Yet, this creature is typically perceived in feminine terms. This perception of the gender is apparently due to the fact that in classical Arabic the word *dâbbàh* ("animal") is feminine; in this respect, it is unlike the word *ḥayawân* (animal), which is masculine. The *dâbbàh* is immense in size, and is vaguely described as having viper-like characteristics but is not perceived to be a "viper." This association with the reptile may be due to the belief that "she will come out of a hole in the ground," and that "from the time her head appears on the surface of earth to the time its tail is completely out of the hole, several days will [*sic*] have passed." Numerous informants emphasize, that "she" will speak and argue with people. Some literary traditions portray the *dâbbàh* in more detailed, yet conflicting, terms as a talking hybrid of numerous birds and

---

[360] Motifs: V2.1§, "Jinn and humans are required to worship God;" V3.3§, ‡"Required alms-tax (*zakâh*, given out yearly—compare: tithe);" N182.2§, "Seemingly worthless objects (onion skin, garlic skin, etc.) turn into gold."

See Lane, *Modern Egyptians*, p. 427, 428; and Amîn, *Qâmûs*, pp. 91–92.

[361] Herman Te Velde, *Seth, God of Confusion* (Leiden, 1967), pp. 13–26, 109–152. Also see Hasan El-Shamy, *Folktales of Egypt*, p. 221.

[362] That is, *dâbbàh min al-'àrḍ* (an animal from the ground). Translated by A.Y. Ali, The Glorous Kur'an, p. 997:

> "We shall produce for them from the earth A Beast to (face) them: He will speak to them [. . .] [emphasis added]"). (Koran, 27:82.)

The general perception among laymen is that, contrary to Alî's translation, the *dâbbàh* (Beast) is feminine. Motifs: A1070.2§ and B15.7.17§. Cf. B99.2,‡"Mythical worm." (See also n. 122.)

animals—both ordinary and supernatural. In addition to her arguments, she will mark the believers and set them apart from the unbelievers. Meanwhile, other sources interpret the Koranic statement as merely a euphemistic designation of "a human being."[363]

References to "the Earth's Animal" seem to be strictly confined to the role assigned to it in formal religious dogma. As of yet, no mention of this being has been reported in any other branch of orally transmitted lore. The emerging of "the Earth's Animal" to the surface of earth is unanimously believed to be one of the "major signs" of the coming of the Day of End of World. (See Section I.D, and n. 122)

II.D.3. Supernatural Reptiles

Snakes in general, and vipers in particular, are believed to have supernatural powers. In Arabic, the words *tì¿bân* (i.e., *thù¿bân*) and *ḥanàsh* (snake) are invariably referred to in masculine, while the word *ḥàyyàh* (viper) is invariably feminine. Consequently, unless otherwise specified, snakes are always perceived as males and vipers as females. The similarity between the words *Ḥawwâ* (Eve) and *ḥàyyàh* (viper) is often noted by speakers of Arabic (in which the "w" and the "y" are interchangeable). In literary religious traditions the viper is associated with Eblis (i.e., Satan, the Devil). After Satan was cast out of heaven for refusal to honor Adam, he smuggled himself back into Paradise past Ruḍwân, the guardian, with the help of the viper who hid him inside her mouth. Subsequently, he was able to mislead Adam and Eve and cause their fall.[364]

Another literary account tells of Satan pausing in the form of a man as a cook and deceiving a king (al-Ḍaḥḥâk) known for his justice into hiring him for one year in return of granting him one wish as wages. At the end of the term, the cook (Satan) wished to kiss the king's shoulders. Two viper heads grew where Satan's kisses had been placed; they ate into the king's flesh and caused him excruciating pain. Whenever they are chopped off, the heads regrew. Satan then presented himself to the king as a doctor, and prescribed the applying of "human brains" to the vipers' heads so as to pacify them. Having no alternative, the once-just king tried the remedy made of

---

[363] For example, see Khalîfah, *ad-Dâr al-barzakhiyyah*, p. 235.

[364] al-Tha¿labî, *Qiṣaṣ*, p. 19. For more information on the gender of "snake" as compared to "viper," see n. 196.

al-Gindî (*al-Ginn*, Vol. 2, pp. 60–62), discusses the theme of "The Killing of Vipers" during the early Arab-Islamic period, and refers to them only in feminine terms. However, he includes a modern newspaper report from Egypt of a "*thu¿bân* (snake)" killing a bride as she sat on her bridal chair by biting her and then escaping. In this case the reptile is referred to in masculine terms. The snake is said to be a male jinni who was enamored with the human bride and killed her due to lover's jealousy, for he did not want an Adamite marrying his beloved. This event motivated the composition of a poem titled "*al-thù¿bân al-¿âshìq* (Snake-in-love)."

Motifs: F300.0.2§, ‡"Fairy (jinni) and human as rivals in love;" F499.4.1§, ‡"Jinni (fairy) kills human;" W180.1§, ‡"'If I cannot have it (him, her, etc.), no one else will!' Useful thing (object, person, etc.) destroyed so that others may not benefit from it."

brains of prisoners condemned to be executed, then of regular prisoners, and then of innocent people. Thus, the just king became a tyrant.[365]

In current folk beliefs, jinn may transform themselves into vipers or snakes.[366] Among traditionary groups, it is also believed that every house has its guardian snake which *may* be a good jinn; it drives away other reptiles and evil jinn thus contributing to the safety of the household. The belief in a beneficent snake that protects a certain locale was also current in ancient Egypt. In his accounting of widespread belief in jinn, Lane reported,

> a curious relic of ancient Egyptian superstition must here be mentioned. It is believed that each quarter of Cairo has its peculiar guardian-genius, or Agathodaemon, which has the form of a serpent.[367]

A number of specific reptiles with supernatural qualities are also known in current folk cultures. The *'âf*, a flying serpent, and the *tennîl* (or *tànnîl*, dragon-like serpent), are two related members of this category of the supernatural. The *'âf* seems to be best known in the oral lore of southern Egypt, while the *tennîl* is a variation on the more widely known *tennîn*, a fire-breathing serpent (i.e., a dragon). It is believed in some rural areas that "when a serpent grows old, it becomes wild, sprouts hair-like feathers, and flies away."[368] It also has a luminous gem over its head, a trait common to all vipers. The *'âf* is, evidently, a folk conception of the ancient Egyptian Uraeus: a winged viper or serpent with the sun disc on its head; the Uraeus was an emblem of pharaoh power.[369]

Another reptile appears in literary traditions; it is the *ṣùfàr*, a viper that is believed to exist in the stomach of every human being. The *ṣùfàr* causes a person to feel the pain of hunger when it bites the stomach.[370] Only residuals of this belief seem to have survived in current folk traditions. The metaphorical common expression, "to be bitten by hunger" and classical Arabic expression, "hunger bit him with its two fangs" seem to be related to the old belief in the *ṣùfàr*.

---

[365] Designated as new Tale-type 816A§, *Devil as a Skillful Cook, then Physician: Corrupts Just King*. It is linked to AaTh 985, "*Brother Chosen Rather than Husband or Son*. [A woman (a sister) may save only one from death]." For details see El-Shamy, *DOTTI*; and *Tales Arab Women Tell*, No. 45, pp. 318–319. Ismâ¿îl, gives a variant of this account, but his text lacks the satan–viper association (Walker-Ismâ¿îl, *Folk Medicine*, p. 99).

[366] S. Ḥusayn, *al-Ginn*, p. 75. For examples from narrative folk literature (Motif: F337.3§, "Fairy (in viper form) saved from pursuer (unwanted suitor): grateful;" see n. 196.

[367] See Lane, *Modern Egyptians*, p. 226.

Motifs: A132.1.2§, ‡"Deity in form of snake (serpent, viper);" A412, ‡"City-gods." (See n. 197)

[368] See "The Trip to 'Wag-el-Wag,'" in El-Shamy, *Folktales of Egypt*, No. 1, pp. 3–14, especially pp. 4, 8; Sayce, *Folk-Lore*, Vol. 11 No. 4, p. 380.

[369] Motifs: B91.2, "Plumed serpent;" B843.1.1§, "Wings grow on serpent (viper) when it becomes aged." See Ions, *Egyptian Mythology*, pp. 22ff.

[370] Motif: B784.5§, "*Ṣufar*: viper in man's stomach (intestines) causes hunger."

See al-'Âlûcî, *Bulûgh al-'arab*, Vol. 2, p. 313; al-Gindî, *al-Ginn*, Vol. 1, 136.

II.D.4. Supernatural Birds

Several common birds are assigned some supernatural qualities; these unusual characteristics can often be traced to the roles these birds are reported to have played in major religious events. Three common birds in particular are noteworthy for their association with the supernatural: the *ghurâb* (crow, raven), the *bûmàh* (owl, or "Omm-qwaiq"—sometimes translated as "Mother-of Screech"), and the *hùdhùd* (hoopoe bird). The crow and the owl are birds of ill omen; the cawing of the crow and the hooting of the owl are believed to signal an approaching disaster. The crow played a vile role in the religious account of the *ṭûfân* (Deluge); sent from the ark by Noah to search for dry land, the crow (raven) abandoned his mission and did not return.[371] Similarly, the owl was reported in some secondary religious sources to have denied the doctrine of predestination, a basic tenet of Islamic creed.[372] The hoopoe is a bird of good omen; this view may be due to the role the hoopoe played in informing Prophet Sulaymân of Belqais, the Queen of Sheba, and the fact that she and her nation worship the Sun as god.[373] The hoopoe's crown is often used in protective amulets. Under modern governmental rules, both the hoopoe and the ibis (*abu-qìrdân*) protected by law for secular reasons: they are considered "friends of the farmer" for feeding on harmful insects and worms that damage crops.

The dove/pigeon and the rooster are also viewed as endowed with some supernatural merits: the dove for her peacefulness and obedience to Noah, and the rooster for his crowing at dawn, thus awakening people for dawn prayers.[374] They are blessed birds and their presence in a household brings about blessedness (*barakàh*; see Section V.C.1).

Other supernatural birds also appear as unique beings. However, most of the birds seem to be largely confined to written sources. Two birds, the *rùkhkh* (roc) and *al-¿ànqâ'* (comparable to the Phoenix) are members of this category. The *rùkhkh* is a legendary bird that appears in some folk narratives; it is simply a huge bird with the capacity to carry a man for hundreds of miles, wreak havoc on ships on the high seas by dropping boulders on them, and be grateful or vengeful toward humans who help

---

[371]al-Tha¿labî, *Qiṣaṣ*, p. 30.

Motifs: B147.2.1.3§, "Hoopoe as bird of good omen;" B147.2.1.4§, ‡"Dove (pigeon) as bird of good omen;" B147.2.2.1, "Crow as bird of ill-omen;" B147.2.2.3, "Raven as bird of ill-omen;" B147.2.2.4, "Owl as bird of ill-omen;" A2221.7, "Dove returns to ark in obedience to Noah: receives sheen of raven [as reward]."

For the ancient Babylonian account of this theme, see Alexander Heidel, *The Gilgamesh Epic and Old Testament Parallels* (Chicago, 1970), pp. 80–88.

[372]al-Tha¿labî, *Qiṣaṣ*, p. 168. Motifs: A2491.2.1§, "Why owl lives in the ruins and is not seen during daytime. Because of her shame over rejecting predestination;" A2491.2.2§, ‡"Owl hides during daylight to avoid the evil eye (being envied for her beauty)."

[373]Koran, 27:20–28. See al-Tha¿labî, *Qiṣas*, p. 173. (Motif: V1.4.2, "Worship of the sun.")

[374]al-Tha¿libî, *Qiṣaṣ*, p. 25; al-Damîrî, *Ḥayât al-ḥayawân*, Vol. 1, p. 344; al-Gindî, *al-Ginn*, Vol. 2, pp. 88–89. Motifs: A156.7.4.1§, ‡"Cock (rooster) as God's bird (animal);" A1443.0.1.1§, ‡"Cock as first domesticated creature;" A2228.1§, ‡"Cock (chanticleer) from heaven: God-sent as timing-device so as to help Adam mark prayer-times;" A2228.1.1§, ‡"Cock crows when he sees an angel;" A2489.2§, ‡"Cock (chanticleer) as (dawn) prayer-crier."

or harm its young.[375] Meanwhile, *al-¿ànqâ'* is a female bird with human face and other human characteristics such as speech; she is occasionally cited in para-religious and related literary sources in connection with her disbelief in predestination. The reason this mythical bird is not seen today is that she, due to her shame for the blasphemous belief, has retreated to remote area of Earth and appears only once every 500 years.[376] In many respects, *al-¿ànqâ'* is similar to the ancient Egyptian Bennu bird and the Greek Phoenix and shares many traits with them.[377]

"*Ṭayr 'abâbîl*" (*'abâbîl* birds) is another category of supernatural birds that appears, but infrequently, in oral folk traditions. The name is cited in Koran, but is limited to only one chapter (Koran, 105:3); in this context, the name is interpreted to mean diverse birds or waves of birds.[378] In oral folk traditions the name is used only in the plural; there is no singular form of the word "*'abâbîl*" in active Arabic usage. No specific description for these birds is given in folk expressions except for the idea that they are birds that bring stones from hell and drop them on troops of unbelievers, thus decimating them.[379] Meanwhile, literary traditions portray these creatures in diverse images. Sources seem to agree that the birds were terrestrial, rather than from hell (located in the sky), and that they came from the direction of sea or that God created "them in the air" in order to defend the Kaaba against invaders—prior to the advent of Islam. The birds are also described vaguely as green in color with yellow beaks, having lion's heads, canine teeth, dogs' paws, and that they were capable of lifting huge boulders in their claws and beaks. It was also said that they had not been seen before that military event and never seen after it.[380]

Koran speaks of these birds in connection with an event that took place in the year 570 AD, some fifty years prior to the advent of Islam. An Abyssinian Christian ruler named "Abrahàh" (or Abraha, i.e., Abraham) attempted to conquer pagan Arabs' holy site that held their idols in Mecca. His troops employed war-elephants—a new war

---

[375] Motifs: B31.1, "Roc. A giant bird which carries off men in its claws;" B31.1.2, "Roc drops rock on ship. Rock is so large that it destroys ship."

For examples in *The Thousand Nights and a Night*, see El-Shamy, *MITON*.

[376] Tale-type: 930F§, *The Predestined Fornication* (The phoenix's foster daughter is reached and impregnated). Motif: V324§, ‡"Heresy: rejecting (doubting) predestination." See: al-Tha¿labî, *Qiṣaṣ*, pp. 165–168; also see El-Shamy, "Vom Fisch geboren (AaTh 705)," as in n. 175.

[377] Motifs: B32, "Phoenix. [(al-¿Aanqâ')];" B201.1§, ‡"al-¿Anqâ': human-like bird. Giant female bird (falconiform) with human face, breasts, and speech."

See El-Shamy, *Tales Arab Women Tell*, No. 5, p. 416. Cf. the description of "Bennu bird" in Ions, *Egyptian Mythology*, p. 124.

[378] According to the translation by Abdallah Yousuf Ali: *The Glorious Kur'an*, p. 1792.

[379] Historians cite an outbreak of smallpox as the reason for the decimation of Abraha's army. See Ronart and Ronart, *CEAC*, Vol. 1, p. 17.

Incidents in which a bird drops huge boulders on enemy recur in oral traditions: cf. "roc"—n. 376, above. Also see El-Shamy, "The Story of El-Sayyid Aḥmad El-Badawî with Faṭma Bint Berry, An Egyptian Folk Epic, part II, text and explanatory notes." In: *Folklore Forum*, Vol. 11, Nos. 3–4, (1976), pp. 140–163, p. 163, n. 30.

[380] al-Tha¿labî, *Qiṣaṣ*, p. 251. Motifs: P553.5.1§, ‡"Elephant used as weapon;" B268.3, "War-elephants;" B39.5§, "Bird from hell (*'abâbîl*);" B128.3.1§, ‡"Bird uses rock as tool (weapon);" cf. P553.3§, ‡"Flying device (air-plane, air-ship) as weapons. Air force."

machine unknown to his Arab adversaries. Many Arab tribes were quickly defeated in battles leading to the main encounter. Consequently, that year was labelled the "Year of the Elephant" (and a chapter in Koran bears the title "The Elephant," Koran, 105). As Abrahàh's army was about to enter Mecca, the troops were destroyed by a prodigy (natural catastrophe). Chroniclers of early Islam attribute the defeat of the superior Abyssinian army to divine providence. Following Koran's explanation, the credit for defeating the conquerors is assigned to the supernatural birds that dropped huge "*sijjîl*"-rocks ("stones of baked clay") on the invaders and their elephants. Among folk groups, both the birds and the rocks are thought of as being from hell.[381]

Another entity that may be viewed as bird like is the *hâmàh*. It is a being sometimes described as a person's soul in the form of a bird resembling a *bûmàh* (an owl). The *hâmàh*—or *bûmàh* as it is sometimes called in folk communities—is believed to issue out of the head of a person when that person dies;[382] if murdered the *hâmàh* will cry for revenge until the murderer is punished or revenge is accomplished by other means. The association between the *hâmàh* and vendetta seems to harken back to pre-Islamic Arabia where the word also denoted a male owl.[383] Meanwhile, the description of the *hâmàh* as owl-like being seems to be related to the ancient Egyptian *Ba* (i.e., soul), which was depicted as "a human-headed hawk."[384]

The *hâmàh*/*bûmàh* appears sporadically but mainly in the folk beliefs of southern Egypt; apparently it has been eclipsed by the concept of *¿àfrît* (i.e., ghost; see Section I.E) and that of *sarûkh* (i.e., *ṣârûkh*, a shooting flame), which may be seen as other appellations for the same bird-like entity. As a belief character, *hâmàh* is similar to *ṣarîkh* (i.e., screecher, or "shrieker"); meanwhile, the word *sarûkh* is colloquial for the classical Arabic *ṣarîkh*, a belief character, which parallels the *hâmàh*. In its vernacular form the *sarûkh* is a flame-like spirit (ghost).[385]

Belief in the existence of these creatures is closely associated with blood vendetta and calls for revenge. Such practices, which persist as part of traditions and contribute to intertribal violence, are condemned in formal Islam as "murder" punishable in the afterlife by eternal life in hell. As reported by authorities on Islamic law, it is sinful to believe that the *bûmàh* or *hâmàh* do exist.[386]

---

381 Probably because of misconstruing the Koranic word "*sijjîl*" to be "*sijjîn*," which is a certain lower stratum of Hell, usually the sixth. See al-Tha'labî, *Qiṣaṣ*, pp. 4–5; cf. the motif cited in n. 106.

382 See al-Gindî, *al-Ginn*, Vol. 1, pp. 138–152; Khalîfah, *al-Dâr al-barzakhiyyah*, p. 326; al-'Âlûcî, *Bulûgh al-'arab*, Vol. 2, p. 307; and Enno Littmann, *Tales, Customs, Names, and Dirges of the Tigré Tribes*. Publications of the Princeton Expedition to Abyssinia, Vol. 2 (Leiden, 1910). No. 112, p. 308.

383 al-Gindî, *al-Ginn*, Vol. 1, pp. 121–135; al-'Âlûcî, *Bulûgh al-'arab*, Vol. 2, p. 199.

384 West, (*Serpents*, p. 20) also points out that animals represented embodiments of principles rather than an exercise of zoolatry. In the plate the *ba*, depicted as free bird with human head, is the "spirit of a man or a woman."

385 On "*ṣârûkh*" and "*hâmah*", see al-Gindî, *al-Ginn*, Vol. 1, pp. 151–153. Also cf. al-'Âlûcî, *Bulûgh al-'arab*, Vol. 2, pp. 199–200, and Walker-Ismâ¿îl, *Folk Medicine*, p. 47.

386 Abu-al-Naṣr, *al-Bukhârî*, Vol. 4, p. 130; also see Khalîfah, *al-Dâr al-barzakhiyyah*, p. 326; cf. al-Gindî, *al-Ginn*, Vol. 2, pp. 138–150.

Motifs: P522.2§, "Vendetta: a life for a life, of equal (or higher) social rank;" E732.10§, ‡"Soul in the form of owl;" E473.1§, ‡"*ṣadâ*: ghost of murdered person in bird-form that cries at the *hâmah* for revenge;"

II.D.5. The Cat and Other Creatures with Ties to the Supernatural (Ant, Bee, Mantis)

A variety of animals and insects are often perceived as endowed with some quality of supernatural character. These beings do not constitute a distinct category of the supernatural, but rather an amorphous segment whose members are peripheral to the system; their supernatural traits are perceived only occasionally. Members include the cat, the ant, the bee, and the mantis; other miscellany such as the ichneumon and the weasel are infrequently included.[387]

The most salient member of this group is the ordinary cat (*qùṭṭàh* or *bìssàh*, classical: *qiṭṭâh/hirrâh/sinnàwràh*), which is typically perceived in feminine terms. A cat is valued as a natural enemy of snakes and rodents; it also evokes amazement as a survivor of life-threatening situations, and is said to have "seven souls" (i.e., life-spans).[388] Literary traditions attribute the origin of the pig and the cat to Noah's need to cleanse and safeguard the ark. Beset by animal waste, and fast-multiplying mice gnawing holes in the ark's bottom, Noah prayed for help. God commanded him to pull down the elephant's tail: the elephant dropped out of its rectum a pig and a sow; then, God commanded Noah to tap the lion between the eyes: the lion sneezed out of its nostrils a male and a female cats. Hence, the similarities in the physical and behavioral attributes (or, *raison d'être*) for each of the newest additions to the animal world and their respective points of entry (i.e., the pig's likeness to the elephant and its fondness of dirt and feces, and the cat's likeness to the lion and its enmity with mice).[389]

Although all creatures are believed to worship god in their own way and manner of communicating ("language"), the cat seems to be accorded this virtue more frequently. A cat's purring is usually thought of as its uttering of the word: "*Qùr-r-r-'ân, Qùr-r-r-'ân* . . . ," (i.e., "Kor-r-r-an, Kor-r-r-an"), and its perceptibly quiet demeanor is interpreted as that of sincere worshipper who should not to be disturbed.[390] The presence of a cat is occasionally cited as bringing *barakàh* (blessedness, grace) to a household or a business place, and as causing such domestic events as childbirth to go smoothly, and food stock to show the effects of blessedness by lasting longer (probably

---

E473.2§, ‡"*hâmah*: ghost of murdered person in owl-form that cries for revenge;" E451.9.1§, ‡"*hâmah* ceases to appear when revenge is accomplished;" Q560.5§, ‡"Eternal life in hell for certain cardinal sins (e.g., disbelief, murder, etc.)."

[387] Motif: B433.3.1§, ‡"Domesticated ichneumon ('*nimce*'—in Egypt) as snake killer." With reference of the *¿irsah* (ichneumon), see al-Jâḥiẓ, *al-Ḥayawân*, Vol. 4, pp. 120–121. Cf. Ions, *Egyptian Mythology*, p. 40, 118; and "The *Maghrabi's* Apprentice," in El-Shamy, *Folktales of Egypt*, No. 6, p. 39.

[388] Motifs: B844.1§, "'Cat has seven souls (lives);'" cf. E765.2.1§, ‡"Person to live as long as a certain eagle lives (Lubad: the seventh of seven eagles, or the third of three eagles)." On the vernacular *bìssàh* see n. 392.

[389] al-Tha¿labî, *Qiṣaṣ*, p. 35. Also see al-Jâḥiẓ, *Ḥayawân*, Vol. 1, p. 146; Vol. 4, pp. 49–50; Vol. 5, pp. 347–48. Motifs: A1811.2, "Creation of cat: sneezed from lion's nostrils;" A1871.0.2§, "Creation of pig (hog): discharged from elephant's anus." Cf. Tale-type AaTh 217, "*The Cat and the Candle.* [Trained cat drops lighted candle to chase mouse]." (Motifs: A2494.1.1, "Enmity between cat and mouse;" A2494.1.1.1§, ‡"Cat created to attack mice.")

[390] Motif: B251.4.3§, ‡"Cat prays when it purrs."

due to the fact that scorpions, snakes, rats, and similar harmful pests are driven away by the presence of a cat).

A preventive amulet made of cat's placenta is believed, especially among Nubians, to be effective against a variety of female-bound dangers, particularly barrenness.[391] In ancient Egypt, Bast (or Bastet)—the benevolent cat-goddess of Bubastis—performed similar services particularly for women, and "cats were treated as sacred in the honor of Bast."[392] The link between the ancient Bast and the modern blessed cat may be evident in the fact that in vernacular Egyptian-Arabic a cat is also referred to by the non-Arabic word "*bessàh*," a he-cat is labeled "*el-qùṭṭ Bésbés*" (Besbes-the-cat), and the sound "*béss-béss*" is the typical call with which a cat is to be summoned or its attention drawn. Thus, mistreatment of cats is viewed with considerable apprehension. Unlike dogs, cats are not chased away out of mosques, and are only gently steered away from customer's tables at restaurants; a dog catcher may be taunted by children as *dàbbâḥ el-quṭàṭ!* ("Slayer of Cats!"), rather than being the "Slayer of dogs."[393] By contrast, dogs are fiercely driven away from places of worship; the harshness with which dogs are treated in this situation is proverbial.[394]

A Cairene shoemaker—commenting on his own daughter's supernatural illness, triggered by her striking a thieving cat (that proved to be one of the jinn in cat's form) advised:

> A shoemaker, or any other leatherware craftsman, who would use a cat's skin would go bankrupt, for it is "sinful." A tannery that would deal in cats' hides would immediately go bankrupt; God would [cause the] closure of its doors. This is also true of [using] pig's and dog's hides [due to their being "impure"], but it is particularly so with cats![395] (See App. 23)

Conversely, cats are thought to play the harmful—but natural—act of "sucking an infant's breath" and causing crib death; therefore, a small infant must not be left

---

[391] Motifs: D1015.6§, ‡"Magic animal placenta (afterbirth);" D1015.6.1§, ‡"Cat's placenta has supernatural effects;" D1279§, ‡"Charm (amulet) of flesh. Made of human or animal flesh."

Informant: Kunûzî woman named Fanniyyah, from Dahmît but lives in Cairo, 44, widow, (Coll. El-Shamy: Bûlâq 69-3, No. 5); also "¿Abduh the Cook," a middle-aged man from Alexandria, living in New York, reported in 1964 that he wore such an amulet.

[392] Motifs: A131.3.0.1§, ‡"Deity in form of cat ('cat-goddess');" A131.3.1.1§, "Bast: goddess with cat's head." On the name Bast, cf. n. 388.

See Ions, *Egyptian Mythology*, p. 45; also see pp. 94, 103, 119, 126.

[393] Present writer's personal knowledge, during elementary school years (late 1940s).

[394] Motif: S481.3.1§, ‡"Animal cruelly beaten for desecrating place of worship."

The severity of a beating a person may have received for an offense is often expressed in the folk proverbial simile: "a beating the like of which a dog has not received inside a mosque." Other variations: ". . . the like of which a thief has not received," and ". . . the like of which a *miḍaqqarâtî* ('buttocks-presser,'molester')* has not received in a saint's birthday celebration." On dogs in Cairo, see Lane, *Modern Egyptians*, pp. 285–287.

*("*miḍaqqarâtî*," is a person who derives sexual pleasure by pressing his sex organs against the posteriors of others in crowded places.)

[395] For the account of the illness, and more information on the informant, see "The Thigh of the Duck," in El-Shamy, *Folktales of Egypt*, No. 40, especially p. 173.

unattended with a cat. A cat's selfish nature is often cited in proverbial similes; an ungrateful person is characterized as being "like cats: they eat but deny!"

Among other members of this peripheral group nebulously linked to the supernatural are the ant, the bee, and the mantis. All three insects—like the cat—are perceived in feminine terms.

Ants and bees are assigned some supernatural qualities on the basis of the roles in which they are cited in the Koran, each with an entire chapter bearing their name (i.e., The Bees, and The Ants). An ant (*nàmlàh*) "spoke" in the presence of Prophet Solomon as he was in "the Valley of Ants" to warn others against danger.[396] Likewise, Koran describes bees (*nàḥl*) as producing honey in which cures for people's maladies are to be found (Koran, 16:69 and 66:68). Consequently, honey is used as blessed natural medicine in numerous traditional medications, while discipline, work tenacity, and capabilities manifested by ants and bees are often viewed as divine gifts (*hidâyàh*; see n. 641).

Meanwhile, belief in the supernatural quality of the mantis (lit.: *farasìt en-nabî*, i.e., "the Prophet's mare") occurs in isolation. Among folk groups, the mantis is occasionally linked to Prophet Mohammad's ascent to heaven as the riding-animal on which he traveled; hence, the name of the insect. The apparent contradiction between this isolated belief and the more central one citing the Bùrâq as the creature involved, is typically noncognitive.[397]

As in the case with hoopoe, the association with sacred beliefs places these ordinary creatures within the realm of the supernatural. Yet, these beings, except the cat, play only marginal roles in oral traditions and seem to be absent in the performances of "magical" rituals.

II.E. *er-roaḥ* (The Soul), and *en-nàfs* (The Self)

The concept of *roaḥ* (i.e., *rûḥ*, soul) is central in both Moslem and Coptic supernatural belief systems. Beliefs about the soul manifest considerable stability. A soul is perceived to be the entity responsible for the presence of life in a "living creature," particularly a human being: when the soul is in the body the creature is alive, and when it is out of the body the creature is dead. Not every living thing, however, is believed to have a soul; a plant, for example, is perceived as having "life" but not a soul (also, in some mystical contexts inanimate objects are perceived as "living" and praising God, but are not endowed with souls responsible for their existence). By contrast, animals (birds, insects, fish, etc.) are believed to have souls, but they will not be resurrected at Resurrection Day because they are not *mùkallafîn* (obligated

[396] "*qâlat namlatun: 'yâ 'ayyuhâ al-naml. . .'* (An ant said: 'O ye ants . . .')," (Koran, 27:18).

[397] During his childhood, while the present writer was once engaged in catching dragonflies, he came upon the green insect. A farmer advised him not to interfere with it on the grounds that it was "the Prophet's Mare," and that after completion of the celestial trip she transformed herself into its present form. It is also perceived as masculine and called "faras en-nabî (The Prophet's Horse)," "gamàl el-yahûd" (Jews' camel), and "'Abu-Ṣalâḥ" (Father of Ṣalâḥ, or 'the righteous'); see: *Elias's Modern Dictionary: English-Arabic* (6th ed., Cairo, 1969).

to observe religious precepts). Although a soul is assumed to be invisible (etherial, incorporeal), some literary sources argue that it has distinctive features and character that conform to those of the person to whom it belongs.[398]

In daily usage, the word *nàfs* (i.e., self; also used as a psychological term to denote: "psyche," or "the principle of life")[399] occurs as a synonym of the word "*roaḥ* (soul, i.e., *rûḥ*)." Yet, Koran, as well as contemporary legal terminology, apply the two words to refer to different entities (or, perhaps the same entity in different contexts); in this respect the word *nàfs* typically appears in contexts involving "killing" of a [human] *nàfs*, a concept that would be inapplicable to the soul that is perceived as eternal and not susceptible to death or extermination. Thus, it may be inferred that as long as the human soul is within the body and is responsible for its being "alive," it may also be referred to as "*nàfs*" (self), but once it departs the body, it should be referred to only as "soul (*rûḥ*, typically pronounced '*roaḥ*')." This viewpoint is reinforced by the fact that an animal is spoken of as having a "soul" and never as being a *nàfs* (self). Theologians, however, seem not to be in agreement as to whether the "soul" and the "nàfs" are two independent entities, or one and the same.[400]

Moslem informants typically quote Koran concerning the belief that the soul originated when God "breathed" of his "Spirit" (Koran, 15:29, 38:72.) into the lifeless pottery-like figure of Adam, which He had made with "His own Hands," thus giving him life by creating the human "soul." They also cite Koran's (God's) description of the creation of Christ in Virgin Mary's womb through breathing "of Our Spirit"

---

[398] Khalîfah, *al-Dâr al-barzakhiyyah*, p. 240. Also, cf. n. 398.

Quoting an European source, M.F. Wagdî writes (*al-Azhar*, Vol. 12, No. 5 (1941), p. 375)

> Experiments and observable [results of] *mabâḥith rûhîyyah* (spiritual researches i.e., research on the soul) have proved that the soul has an etherial/incorporeal *gìsm* (body, shape) formed like the *gasàd* (body, corpse) in which it resides. This etherial/incorporeal body is not susceptible to decomposition nor to annihilation. This [finding] is similar to what the *madhhàb* (theological school of thought) of Mâlik Ibn-'Anàs [(715–795)] proposing that the soul is in the form of the body. 'ithbât al-rûḥ al-'insâniyyah ḥissiyyan. (Proving [the existence] of the human soul tangibly.)

On the belief of living inanimate objects, see Motifs: V310.1§, ‡"Religious universe (all of God's creation, animate and inanimate—worship);" V310.1.2§, ‡"Objects praise or worship God."

[399] In Arabic, the term *¿ilm al-nàfs* (science of the *nàfs*) stands for "psychology." However, the words *nàfs* and *rûḥ* are not used synonymously (see: Alhefnee, *Encyclopedia of Psychology & Psycho-analysis*, Vol. 2, p. 169; cf. "soul," p. 321.

[400] See Khalîfah, *al-Dâr al-barzakhiyyah*, pp. 227–231. Also see his discussion on the views of *Ṣûfîs* (mystics) on the subject (pp. 232–233).

In this respect Khalîfah reports that the *rûḥ* (soul) is *nûrâniyyah* (light-bound) and was the first to exist in the universe, while the body is *mùẓlim* (dim) and was created of Earth's elements to be the soul's residence. The "soul" constantly invites to the Divine Upper World, assisted by the enlightening mind, while the *nàfs* (self), aided by Satan and the earthly human nature, constantly entices to the nether Earthly World—having been constituted from planet Earth's different clays. Every Adamite, male or female, possesses both a "soul" and a "self.". However, the soul is more dominant in males while the "self" is more dominant in females; moreover, a female is more likely to be a sheer "self." (See Section I.D and n. 79, 120, and 494)

Since the "self" is Nether, it follows that [God's] prophets and their likes must be of wholly Upper nature, i.e., pure soul (*rûḥ*), without any influence whatsoever of the self (*nàfs*) on them (cf. n. 481).

(Koran, 66:12). Although Koran speaks of the *rûḥ* of God, as the source of the souls of Adam and Jesus Christ, God is, from an ideal culture perspective, not thought of a having a "soul" comparable to that of humans. The *rûḥ* of God is typically perceived as "spirit," "power," "omnipotence," and "will;" it is subject to God's command and is *not* viewed as responsible for God being "alive." Koran declines to expound on the nature of the "soul" on the grounds that God granted human beings only little knowledge; it only states that the soul is "of God's command."[401] In folk traditions the soul is often referred to as *es-sìrr el-'ilâhî* (the Divine secret), or simply "*es-sìrr*" (the secret).

Each human being is believed to have his or her own soul. Although some sources state that the word *roaḥ* (soul, pl.: *'arwâḥ*) may be in the feminine or masculine form,[402] the soul is typically perceived as feminine regardless of the gender of the person to whom it belongs. This is also the case with the *¿àfrît* (ghost) of a deceased person who suffered a violent death, which is invariably perceived as masculine. Thus, if reference is being made to a male who died violently, his ghost would be described as "*¿àfrît wâḥid,* (ghost of a male someone)," but if the reference is to a female, her ghost would be described as "*¿àfrît wàḥdàh* (ghost of a female someone/person)."

In actual daily usage, the word *roaḥ* specifically denotes a human "soul;" more generally, but less frequently in folk usage, it may refer to a "spirit" such as jinni or an angel. When used in the latter sense, the word *roaḥ* is always qualified as "benevolent" or "malevolent," "upper" or "nether." This broad application of the word *roaḥ* seems to stem from the fact that the soul is thought of as being composed of "non-material" substance (i.e., not solid) that resembles light or fire of which angels and jinn are, respectively, constituted. In modern literature, this nature is referred to as *'athîrî* (ethereal, intangible, incorporeal, invisible, etc.);[403] meanwhile, among folk groups the same quality is often explained as *rîḥ*, "wind-[like]." A person possessed by jinn is often described as *màryûḥ* (i.e., ridden/possessed by wind-like jinn). Further association between jinn and wind is revealed in other aspects of beliefs not related to possession: a whirlwind (*zàwba¿àh*, '*zoba¿àh*') that stirs up a dust funnel is typically labeled *fasyìt el-¿àfrît* (an afrit's fart or "let wind"); it is also often thought to be the wake of a rapidly departing jinni, or, as Lane presented it: the jinni "rides" the whirlwind.[404]

The duality of the meanings assigned to the word "*roaḥ*" has led some scholars to conclude that the soul of a dead ancestor may possess a living person.[405] This viewpoint is inaccurate and seems not to correspond to available field data. As will

[401] Koran, 17:85. See: al-¿Idwî, *Mashâriq*, p. 60.

[402] al-¿Idwî, *Mashâriq*, p. 60.

[403] Motif: E702.1§, "The soul is etherial." See S. Ḥusayn, *al-Ginn*, p. 9; cf. n. 398.

[404] Lane, *Modern Egyptians*, p. 223. See also n. 270. Cf. Motifs: F401.0.1.1.1§, ‡"Afrit (jinni) assumes form of wind or smoke;" F559.9.1.1.1§, ‡"'Broken wind causes whirlwind on earth and smoke-trail in sky;'" F559.9.1.2§, ‡"Whirlwind is 'afrit's fart.'"

[405] Hans Alexander Winkler, *Die reitenden Geister der Toten*; eine studie über die besessenheit des 'Abd er-Râdi und über gespenster und dämonen, heilige und verzückte, totenkult und priestertum in einem oberägyptischen dorfe. (Stuttgart, 1936)

be shown (see Section II.E.2), the soul is believed to be eternal; it does not change nor decay,[406] and has the power to see and hear those who are living. Thus, it is believed that a soul of a deceased person may visit a living person during his or her sleep (i.e., in a "vision"—typically labelled *manâm* (see Instructive Dreams, Section V.B.2); it may instruct, or verbally counsel, compliment, or reprove that person. It is also reported in religious literature that the souls of the dead may return home on occasions in order to visit or observe relatives, the soul of a dead person may ask the souls of recently deceased individuals about news from home,[407] and that the souls of the dead meet and hold conversations.[408] Occasionally, reports that souls, whether belonging to deceased or living persons, meet and socialize with one another, are encountered in folk communities.[409] The folk belief that the living are able to hear or communicate verbally with the dead and that the dead are able to hear the living holds considerable sway in actual social life. So powerful are these beliefs that their validity is maintained in spite of two verses in the Koran clearly stating the impossibility of such a communication taking place between the living and the dead. Yet, a fatwa by a religious authority asserts that when a Moslem addresses the community of the dead ("*'ahl al-qubûr*," lit.: tomb-people), his address would be an address or call by "the sane to those who are present" (i.e., it is not an act of mental deficiency aimed at the imaginary or the fantastic).[410]

Similar beliefs about the dead were at the heart of ancient Egyptian belief systems. Egyptologists report that belief in the existence of social life inside the grave was an integral aspect of ancient Egyptian views of life after death. Game boards and similar devices were placed with the mummified bodies so that the deceased can socialize with others inside the grave.[411]

According some cases reported from certain regions of modern Egypt, the soul of a dead person may assume the form of a snake, a bird, or a similar creature; this belief seems, however, not to be recurrent outside Nubia where dead *'awliyâ* (saints) are commonly believed to assume the form of birds and fly at certain times

---

[406] Khalîfah, *al-Dâr al-barzakhiyyah*, pp. 217–218.

[407] Khalîfah, *al-Dâr al-barzakhiyyah*, p. 250.

[408] Khalîfah, *al-Dâr al-barzakhiyyah*, pp. 245–247.

Motifs: cf. E545.1, "Conversation between the dead;" P790.0.1§, ‡"Need for interacting with others;" P790.0.1.2§, ‡"Invitation to have 'conversation.'"

[409] Khalîfah, *al-Dâr al-barzakhiyyah*, p. 249.

[410] al-Digwî, "*'ayna maqarru al-'arwâḥ ba¿da al-mawt?* (Where is the Abode of Souls After Death?)" p. 266 (as in n. 129). Also see Khalîfah, *al-Dâr al-barzakhiyyah*, p. 255. Motifs: E545.19, "Addressing the dead;" V61.0.2.1§, ‡"Inhabitants of graves (*'ahl al-qubûr*; the dead in graveyards, cemeteries)."

[411] Motifs: cf. E577.4§, ‡"Dead person plays the game of draughts (checkers, or the like);" E577.4.1§, ‡"Living person plays draughts with a dead person (mummy, ghost)."

Maspero states,

> the game of draughts was the favourite amusement of the dead; there was often deposited in the tomb with them a draughtsboard, draughtsmen, and some small knuckle-bones to regulate the movement of the pieces. (Maspero/El-Shamy, *Ancient Egypt*, No. 7 p. 133)

Also see Ions, *Egyptian Mythology*, p. 137.

as a flock. Consequently, shooting a flying bird during such times is a tabu.[412] In another Nubian case reported to me, a dead saint returned in the form of a camel and trampled his thieving son to death.[413] In a third case a deceased saint is reported to have punished his widow for agreeing to remarry; he assumed the form of a snake, crept into his widow's bridal chamber, and watched a flock of birds that he dispatched, peck the groom to death, and peck the bride until she became "like a red balloon."[414]

In oral traditions of Moslems, a human soul may haunt or obsess another living person, but that soul *can not* possess another person. Occasionally, the name of a dead saint may be casually mentioned by an informant as that of a possessing spirit. However, further scrutiny shows that the spirit involved is not the saint, but another possessing spirit (jinni), which is only identified by the same name. For example, a settled Bedouin woman living under rural-like conditions[415] reported that another woman "*¿alaiha* es-Sayyìd el-Badawî" (lit.: "*on her* is es-Sayyìd el-Badawî" i.e., "*Possessing* her is. . . . "[416] But upon asking the informant to describe the case, she explained that the possessing spirit responds to a musical "beat" labeled "el-Badawiyyah" (i.e., the Bedouin-woman, or that the beat, a feminine *word*, is titled "The Bedouin-[beat]"). Thus, the informant's use of the saint's name to identify that spirit proved to be merely an euphemism or an inaccuracy caused by word association. Other students of oral traditions have reached the same conclusion concerning possessing spirits; Littmann has observed that the names of dead saints uttered in the *zâr* ritual do not represent possessing spirits, and Sayce commented that the *afrît*, which he reported to possess a woman named Mostafa's-mother, "seems often to be little more than mischievous Puck."[417] None of the characters derived from formal religious beliefs and recurrent in the various forms of healing and exorcism rituals (e.g., al-Ḥasan, el-Ḥusain, Zainab, etc.) is perceived by a shaman or a client as a possessing spirit. A retired shaman emphatically stated,

[412]Informant: Mr. ¿U.¿U. K. Kunûzî Nubian, Teacher, folklorist, from Qirshah. Also, Archives: CFMC: Qulali 69-3A, No.1 (Collector: H. El-Shamy).

[413]Motif: E230, "Return from dead to inflict punishment."

Informant: young man, about 20, univ. student; Arch., CFMC: N-Nubia 69-10A, 1-2-19.

[414]Informant, as in n. 412. Motifs: F401.3.8, "Spirit in form of snake;" V220.0.8§, "Vengeful saint;" B256.5.1.1§, ‡"Flock of birds attack saint's adversary (at saint's command)."

[415]Informant: 'Omm Shindî, see n. 312 (recorded: Thursday, June 15, 1972; Col. El-Shamy).

[416]Motif: J148.2.1§, ‡"One word (phrase, sentence, idea) evokes another associated with it. ('Principle of polarity': stability of syntax, word sequence, word order)."

It should be noted that the word *sàyyid* is used here as a common proper name (i.e., "Sàyyìd," or "es-Sàyyìd") rather than as an adjective designating a descendant of the Prophet.

[417]Littmann, *Geisterbeschwörungen*, 1950, p. 53; Sayce, *Folk-Lore*, Vol. 11 No. 4, p. 390.

It may also be noted here that in vernacular Egyptian Arabic, when applied to a child—the phrases *yit¿afràt* or *yetshàyṭàn* denote acting like an afrit or a devil (i.e., to be naughty or unruly); thus a "naughty" child is typically labeled as "*¿áfrît/¿áfrîtáh* (an afrit/a she-afrit)" or "*sheṭân/sheṭânàh* (a satan/a she-satan or a devil/ a she-devil);" meanwhile when applied to an adult, the phrases mean to be crafty, devious, or mischievous. Cf. the use of the holophrase "*yi¿àfratùh*" ("He would bedevil/torment him") in App. 34; also see n. 456.

> let it be known to you that a human soul can *never* enter into another human soul and possess it. This cannot be! It cannot![418]

Sometimes the words *roaḥ* and *rîḥ* (wind, pl.: *'aryâḥ*, not to be confused with *'arwâḥ*, i.e., souls) are used synonymously by folk groups. This duality may be due to jinn being perceived as having "wind-like (i.e., ethereal)" consistency (see n. 404). Therefore, a possessed person may be labeled *maryûḥ* (possessed by winds), or—more accurately—*marwûḥ* (possessed by spirits), or *¿alaih 'aryâḥ* (ridden by winds, i.e., possessed by wind-like jinn). Similarly, a moody person—perceived as suffering from mild abnormality when compared to a possessed person—is described as *mràwḥàn* (i.e., motivated or mildly possessed by different spirits, each responsible for one of that person's contrasting moods).[419]

The soul is believed to be quite separate from the body to which it belongs and in which it resides. The perishable body ties the soul to earth, so to speak, and deprives it of the assets and capabilities of its nonmaterial spiritual nature. A soul per se is believed to be entitled, but on a lesser scale, to the same capabilities that angels and jinn enjoy by virtue of their bodily or physical constitution. The soul of a living prophet or saintly person, unlike that of an average human being, is believed not to be shackled to the body. This belief in the freedom of soul of the prophets and certain saints from the restrictions of the body accounts for their supernatural ability to perceive the unknown or the unseen, especially the future; such a capability is referred to as *kàshf* (unveiling, clairvoyance). A person with this capacity is described as having had "the Veil lifted off him" (see Section I.E). The soul of any person may temporarily leave the body during deep sleep—which is referred to euphemistically as *al-màwt al-aṣghàr* (the lesser death) or as "the brother of death;"[420] then that soul may assume the form of a green or blue fly commonly found around cemeteries, killing such flies is often reported to be sinful or tabu (*ḥarâm*). A well-hidden corpse is euphemistically referred to as, "not even the blue flies can find their way to it;" an underlying assumption here may be that not even that corpse's soul could find it so as to reanimate it.[421] Perceiving the soul in the form of a fly (or bird) seems to be related to the ancient Egyptian beliefs about the *Ba* (soul), which was depicted as a

---

[418] Informant: Shâkir, see n. 74. Emphasis added.

[419] A parallel, but unrelated, formulaic idiom is: *bi-ghazâlàh* (lit.: "[a person] with-a-gazelle"), meaning a person who is moody and unpredictable.

Motif: W124.0.1§, ‡"Moody person (*'bi-ghazâlah'*)."

[420] al-¿Idwî, *Mashâriq*, p. 282. (Motif: Z126.9.1.1§, ‡"Sleep as 'the lesser Death.'")

Also Ahmad H. Sakr states:

> In Islam a near death experience occurs every day. As the hadith states, the body actually dies each night, or participates in a "small death," during which God decides between those souls that will return to the body to awake in the morning and those whose time it is to die. (*Life, Death, and the Life After*. Lombard: Foundation for Islamic Knowledge, 1992, p. 52)

[421] Motifs: E734.7, "Soul in the form of fly;" E734.7.1§, "Soul in the form of blue (green) fly."

In certain Arbic dialects, the words "*ṭair/ṭairah*" may designate "flies/a fly" or "birds/a bird." Amîn, (*Qâmûs*, p. 176) reports that the soul may assume the form of bird of green color. Motifs: E732, "Soul in

human-headed hawk (see also the modern beliefs about the *hâmàh* in Section II.D.4). The soul leaves the body at death, which is a permanent departure but only until Resurrection Day. When the soul is out of the body, it is believed to be in touch with the rest of the universe in its entirety, including heavens. The rationale for this belief is that the body's limiting influence on access to the Barrier-to-Gnosis is nullified. An official fatwa states,

> A soul wanders to wherever it wishes. It has become an established fact that a sleeper's soul [leaves the body] and rises [toward heavens] until it has penetrated through the seven layers (strata) of the skies and reached God's Throne. It prostrates itself before God, and then, it reverts to the body. All of this takes place in the most minute amount of time.

The fatwa concludes by offering the following analogy:

> A soul is like a fetus, he does not like to get out of his mother's womb, but once he is out, he does not like to go back.[422]

For the ordinary individual, death is believed to be a harrowing experience. The act of wrenching (*nàz¿*, extracting) the soul from the body by the Angel of Death is presumed to be excruciating[423] and results in attempts on the part of the dying individual to elude the inescapable termination of his life. This latter phase of the process of dying is labeled "*menâz¿àh*" (i.e., *munâza¿ah*, contending, disputing, resisting), and is likened to a "tug-of-war" between death and the living creature over the soul. It is inevitably concluded in favor of the Angel of Death who succeeds in accomplishing his mission;[424] thus, the expression *bi-ynâzi¿* (lit.: "He is contending") signifies that a living creature is "breathing the last breath" of life and is trying to cling to it. Since the shape and size of the Angel of Death are horrifying, God ordained that Azrael becomes invisible to humans, and that no one would have foreknowledge of the place (or time) of one's own death (Koran: 31:34). However, as some reports indicate, it is also believed that death may come to true-believers in a soft peaceful

form of bird;" 722.1.4.1.1§, ‡"Soul out of its body in form of green bird;" cf. Z145.2§, "Green: auspicious color". See n. 635.

[422] al-Digwî "'Ayna maqarru al-'arwâḥ ba¿da al-mawt" (Where is the Abode of Souls After Death), p. 269.

[423] al-Digwî, "'Ayna maqarru al-'arwâḥ ba¿da al-mawt (Where is the Abode of Souls After Death)," p. 270.

Motifs: E722.0.1§, ‡"Gasping (*shahqah*) accompanies soul's departure from body at death;" E722.0.2§, ‡Soul struggles (contends) to remain in the body—(*munâza¿ah*);" E722.0.2.1§, ‡"Soul being extracted out of body emits scraping sound of excruciating pain—(*ḥashrajah*/*sakrât* al-mawt)."

A rural love-song (*mawwâl*) likens the separation between lovers as "*'aṣ¿ab min ṭulû¿ er-roaḥ* (more painful than the departure of the soul [from the body]." See: El-Shamy, "Folkloric Behavior," p. 236.

[424] al-¿Idwî, *Mashâriq*, pp. 18–20. See "The Contract with Azrael," in El-Shamy, *Folktales of Egypt*, No. 17, pp. 117–121.

form, and that certain persons may be granted knowledge of the time and/or place of their own death.[425]

God's prophets, and certain saints, seem to be exempt from some of these universally applied rules concerning dying. Prophets are usually thought of as having been granted the choice of the time and place of their deaths; typically, the Angel of Death asks permission of a prophet before extracting his soul. Abraham, for example, had asked God that he should not die until he himself has requested death; when his predestined time came—after an extraordinarily long life, Azrael disguised himself as a feeble old man and pretended to be attempting to feed a donkey by sticking fodder into its eye, ear, etc.; upon witnessing these dehumanizing effects of senility, Abraham asked God for death.[426] In the case of Moses, not only did he escape death by putting out one of Azrael's eyes, but also God offered to extend his life span by as many years as the number of ox's hairs that he (Moses) can cover with the palm of his hand.[427] Also with reference to Mohammad, it is believed that when God commanded Azrael, the Angel of Death, to seize his soul, Azrael wept and was reluctant to carry out the order. He asked the Prophet for advice; he counseled Azrael to obey God's command and thus—according to some sources—,[428] he sanctioned the continuance of death for himself and, consequently, for mankind. Also, albeit the unequivocal Koranic assertion about death (Koran, 31:34), numerous saints and "saintly" persons were reported to have had foreknowledge of the time and/or place of their own death.[429]

---

[425] al-¿Idwî, *Mashâriq*, p. 20. Cf. n. 429, below.

Motifs: V233.3.3§, ‡"Angel of Death (Azrael) offers pious mortal (saint, prophet) respite;" V233.3.4§, ‡"Angel of Death gives mortal choice as to how (when) to die;" M341.0.5§, "Person knows time of own death."

For references to texts from popular literature incorporating these themes, see El-Shamy, *MITON*.

[426] al-Tha¿labî, *Qiṣaṣ*, p. 58. Motifs: F571.9.1§, ‡"Senility (*zamânah*): madness (diminished mental capacity) from old age;" J216.6.1§, ‡"Death before advent senility chosen."

Also cf. El-Shamy, *DOTTI*, Tale-types: 1199, "*The Lord's Prayer.* [Devil (Death) must wait];" and 1199B, "*The Long Song.* Respite from death gained by long-drawn-out song."

[427] al-Tha¿labî, *Qiṣaṣ*, p. 139. (Motif: D1857.4§, ‡"Longevity for as many years as the number of hairs that can be covered by palm of hand.") Also see n. 37.

[428] Motif: A1335.16§, ‡"God instated death for all mankind because prophet (culture-hero) chose dying rather than living (eternally)."

[429] See for an example, al-Nabhânî (*karâmât al-'awliyâ'*, Vol. 2, pp. 8, 9). He reports that a certain *shaikh* (saint) predicted his own death, bade his *murîds* (novices/aspirants) farewell, and died. Cf. saints' ability at "Foretelling some of the unknown/the unseen." (See No. 14, associated with n. 534.) Also see "The Death of *shaikhah* Shafîqah's Brother," in El-Shamy, *Tales Arab Women Tell*, No. 43, pp. 314–315.

A close parallel of this contemporary social legendary event is given by M. al-'Ibshîhî (ca 1388–1446) in his *al-Mustaṭraf* (Cairo: al-Ḥalabî, 1952), Vol. 1, p. 149, as an undertaker's personal labor reminiscence (i.e., a memorate). According to this fifteenth-century account,

> One day a "youth of beauty," who knew the time of his own death—which is a saintly trait—contracted the undertaker to prepare him for burial; the youth died the same day. The youth's sister, who resembled her brother greatly, kissed her dead brother and promised to join him soon. She asked the undertaker whether his wife could prepare her for burial as adroitly as he did her brother. Upon his return accompanied by his wife to the brother and sister's house, the sister declared that only the wife may enter. The undertaker's wife found the young woman facing the Qiblah (Mecca)

In situations where a living creature seems to be in the phase of *munâza¿àh* ([soul]-contending) and the extraction of the creature's soul is inevitable but the creature survives, it is then said: *'ìnkatàb-luh ¿ùmr gdîd* ("a new life span has been written for him," i.e., received another "lease on life"). An example of this belief comes from the Prophet's tradition accounting for *mùnjiyât* (soul-savers); it tells of a man whose soul was about to be seized by the Angel-of-Death, but "his dutifulness toward his parents came and turned the Angel-of-Death away from him."[430]

The soul remains near the body, especially immediately after death;[431] this belief constitutes the basis for an important Islamic ritual. At burial, the dead person is instructed by the officiating cleric about what to say to the two angels who will interrogate him/her inside the tomb. This practice is labeled *tàlqîn* (prompting, or instructing; see n. 164). A *tàlqîn* text recorded as a corpse of a deceased man was being lowered into the grave directs the deceased to identify himself to "the two angels [Nâkir and Nakîr] by stating,

> Truly God (Allah) is my God, truthfully Mohammad is my prophet [i.e., the prophet I follow], the Koran is my code, the *Ka¿bàh* is my *qiblàh* (the direction toward which I pray). Moslems are my brethren, and Abraham—the bosom-friend-of-God—is my father, and his faith is my faith. . . . [432]

Repeating this "declaration" to the two interrogating angels guarantees that they accept the deceased as a believer and treat him as such. One account by a theologian states that upon hearing this statement recited aloud by the imam or the officiating cleric, as the corpse is being lowered into the tomb, the two angels would conclude that the deceased had been "prompted" his *ḥùggàh* (i.e., *ḥùjjàh*, irrefutable proof, evidence), and, consequently, needs no grave trial; in such a case, God becomes the defender of the deceased against the two angels (if they were to bring up charges at the final trial on Judgment Day).[433]

Some peripheral folk beliefs concerning the soul at the time of burial seem to harken back to antiquity and are often expressed in minor or regional ritual practices. In some areas of Upper Egypt, bread, salt, and water are occasionally placed with the deceased inside the tomb so that "he"/"she" (i.e., the soul) may "eat bread and salt"

> and deceased. She performed the corpse washing on her, and "*'anzalathâ ¿alâ 'akhîhâ* (lowered her upon her brother [in his grave]).

[Thus, the brother and sister, who may be assumed to have lived alone together, were buried together in one grave.] (*Tales Arab Women Tell*, p. 314)

[430] Khalîfah, *al-Dâr al-barzakhiyyah*, p. 197. Also see n. 37.

Motif: V4.5.1§, ‡"Dutifulness toward parents as intercessor."

[431] Lane, *Modern Egyptians*, p. 525; Amîn, *Qâmûs*, p. 140.

[432] Motif: V66.0.1§, "Instructing the dead before burial as to how to answer interrogative angels (*talqîn*, 'prompting')."

Informant: An undertaker-cleric, name unknown, at a grave side in an upper Egyptian village near el-Minya town (recorded in winter 1970). A virtually identical text was given by Lane, *Modern Egyptians*, pp. 523–525. Cf. n. 164.

[433] Khalîfah, *al-Dâr al-barzakhiyyah*, p. 151.

with the two interrogating angels Nâkir and Nakîr and thus the bond of "bread-and-salt" (friendship or compassion) would be established between the deceased and his tomb judges.[434] A similarly un-Islamic practice is the placing of some coins, labeled "*mi;addiyyàh*" (lit: "ferryboat" [fee]), with the corpse in the belief that it would help the deceased with the "crossing" (i.e., passing) of the test administered by the two angels.[435] In ancient Egypt the dead had to be ferried across the Nile to the west where afterlife was believed to be located: a concept that ceased to exist but the ritual persists.[436] Other seemingly ancient practices include throwing out the water with which the corpse was washed before the deceased is taken out of the house, so that the soul may not take someone along with it (i.e., another family member would die); and having verses from the Koran recited over the clothes worn by the deceased in order to drive the soul of the dead person out of the house (either so as to quickly catch up with the body—as it is supposed to do, or to evict it so that it may not envy those who are still alive);[437] an akin practice is the squeezing of corpse (body) of the deceased in order to force the soul out of it completely.[438]

The connection between the soul, its body, and the abode of souls during the interval between death and Resurrection (or Judgment Day) is a disputed subject. The controversy revolves mainly around the abode of souls and the consequent types of interaction between the soul and the corpse. Thus, souls are sometimes reported to go either to hell or Paradise, to dwell in the tomb close to the body, or to dwell in the *Bàrzàkh* (Isthmus) where their existence is known as "*al-ḥayâh al-bàrzakhìyyàh* (isthmusian life, Purgatory)." (See Section I.F) Occasionally the soul is reported to dwell in a well in Jerusalem called *Bîr el-Qùds* (Jerusalem Well), or in the Well of Zàmzàm in the courtyard of the Great Mosque at Mecca in Hejaz.[439]

---

[434] Khalîfah, *al-dâr al-barzakhiyyah*, pp. 327–328.

Motif: cf. P321, "Salt of hospitality. Eating a man's salt creates mutual obligation." See also n. 456.

[435] Khalîfah, *al-dâr al-barzakhiyyah*, pp. 327–328.

Motifs: V67.6§, "Objects (money) buried with the dead for use by the soul;" P613, "Charon's fee: putting coin in dead person's mouth to pay for ferry across Styx."

On the matter of placing food with the deceased in ancient Egypt, see Ions, *Egyptian Mythology*, pp. 129, 133.

[436] Ions, *Egyptian Mythology*, p. 133.

[437] Informant: an elderly woman named Âmnah, 68, from el-Miyna (October 1968).

These practices are also cited by Khalîfah (*al-Dâr al-barzakhiyyah*, pp. 327–328) and are attributed to women, presumably as exercised in his hometown of Qinâ, southern Egypt. He characterizes the beliefs underlying the practices as *fàsidàh* (corrupt) and points out that angels do not eat or drink, nor is it possible to influence the execution of their assigned tasks. (On the nature of angels, see n. 137)

With reference to averting death, Khalîfah reasserts the basic formal Islamic belief that death is predestined and that no ritual can alter its course. See n. 67.

[438] Blackman reports this practice as occurring "in certain parts of Egypt" (*The Fellâhîn*, 1927, p. 109).

[439] Informants: group of men in Kafr el-Zaytûn (see n. 314).

Motifs: E755.0.4.4.2.1§, ‡"Souls of believers reside in sacred well (e.g., Zamzam-well, Jerusalem-well, etc.);" E755.0.4.4.2.2§, ‡"Souls of disbelievers confined in torturous (condemned, bottomless, etc.) well (e.g., Barahût)."

Khalîfah, refers to these folk beliefs and adds that some say that the souls of unbelievers dwell in

Descriptions of the isthmusian life reveal social stratification of souls in accordance with their religious performance in worldly life.[440] The highest strata are those of God's messengers, prophets, martyrs, and saints. Thus, this structure of the community of souls mirrors that of the community of inhabitants of Paradise as well as that of living humans in the here-and-now, but within a religious, supernatural context (see Section III.A). This description of the isthmusian community is incongruent with the formal religious dogma according to which prophets, martyrs, the insane, and innocent children, among others, are admitted to heaven without *ḥisâb* (trial)[441] and dwell in Paradise immediately upon their death. Sometimes, it is reported that the souls of martyrs would be in Paradise in the form of (or inside) green birds.[442] It is also reported that after death, a soul joins its likes: souls of fornicators would be together in an oven, souls of "*ribâ*-eaters" (i.e., usurers) would be together in a river of blood, etc.[443]

When the soul is distant from the body, these two constituents of a living creature remain in touch through a mystical bond described as "a ray-like line of light;" the soul visits the corpse on special occasions, especially religious ones.[444] The customs of visiting graveyards and of talking to the dead are congruent with this belief,[445] and are likely to harken back to ancient Egyptian religious rituals. In spite of religious interdiction,[446] many modern Egyptians, like their ancient predecessors, spend

---

"Barahût Well" [??] (*al-Dâr al-barzakhiyyah*, pp. 264–265). He, however, judges these beliefs as "the most corrupt," and "contradictory to valid sunnah." Also see n. 241.

[440]See Ibn al-Sharîf, *al-Ḥayâh al-barzakhiyyah*, p. 67; and Khalîfah, *al-Dâr al-barzakhiyyah*, p. 240.

[441]Motif: Q172.0.5§, "Admission to Paradise without judgment (for prophets, martyrs, children, the insane, etc.)."

Numerous categories of people are believed to have gained admittance into Paradise before or at their death. These include God's messengers, saints, martyrs, children including abortions regardless of the religion of their parents etc. (See Khalîfah, *al-Dâr al-barzakhiyyah*, pp. 205–207)

[442]al-Digwî, in: *Nûr al-Islâm*, Vol. 3, No. 4, 1932, p. 265; and Khalîfah, *al-Dâr al-barzakhiyyah*, pp. 205–207; Ibn al-Sharîf, *al-Ḥayâh al-barzakhiyyah*, p. 67. Also see Burton *Arabian Nights*, Vol. 1, p. 171, n. 1.

[443]al-Digwî, in: *Nûr al-Islâm*, Vol. 3, No. 4, pp. 269–270. Cf. "The Man Who Didn't Perform His Prayers," in El-Shamy, *Folktales of Egypt*, No. 19, pp. 123–125; and "The Twelfth Month," No. 32, especially p. 157.

With reference to associating fornication and "oven," cf. Motif: Z186.8.2.1§, ‡"Symbolism: oven (furnace)—vagina womb." Also cf. Tale-types 1425, *Putting the Devil into Hell.* Obscene trick used to seduce woman; and 1425A§, *Seduction: Roasting the Ear of Corn in the Oven.*

[444]*al-Azhar*, Vol. 2, pp. 263–271; Gätje, *Koran und Koranexegese*, pp. 230–241.

Motifs: E722.4.1§, ‡"Soul connected with its dead body (corpse) via invisible light-like beam;" cf. E765.1.3, ‡"Life-lights in lower world. Each light mystically connected with the life of a person. When light is extinguished, person dies."

[445]Lane (*Modern Egyptians*, pp. 479–480) describes some of the activities that take place at cemeteries; these include use of palm branches, food at grave, with dancers and reciters of heroic *sîrah* of Abu-Zaid performing near-by. Also see, "*qarâfah*" (cemetery) in Amîn, *Qâmûs*, p. 322. Cf. App. 10.

Khalîfah (*al-Dâr al-barzakhiyyah*, pp. 310–311) states that the legitimacy of placing of green palm-leaves on tombs is subject to dispute; he concludes that the more weighty view (*al-'arjaḥ*) is that the practice is permissible (*mujawwaz*).

[446]Koran, 102:1. See Khalîfah, *al-Dâr al-barzakhiyyah*, pp. 295–297.

The formal religious stand on "visiting graves" is that it is permissible only for learning lessons from

religious holidays at cemeteries (*yìṭlàʿ el-qarâfàh*) among their dead relatives where they cook, eat, converse, and entertain one another—though in a solemn manner—in a picnic-like atmosphere.[447]

In traditional folk practices, only the living talk directly to the dead, and the dead may only listen and become informed. This occurs without any middle agent or ritual mediumistic intervention for, it is believed, the soul is in contact with the entombed body. The soul of a deceased person *may visit* the living in a dream and dyadic communication may be established.[448] In rare instances, a dead person—or, perhaps the soul—may provide tangible proof of having been in touch with a certain living person; such occurrences are usually reported in saints' legends as a matter of fact, especially when a concrete proof is required by a community in order to act on the saint's wish.[449]

Before burial it is believed that a deceased person (or the soul) can make his/her wishes known in a number of ways: the corpse may become immovable, or the bier carrying the corpse may become unmanageable, making it impossible for those carrying it (pole bearers) to stay on their intended route or direction; in this latter situation, the bier is thought to be "flying." The people in the funerary procession do whatever they think the deceased wanted to be done; normal conditions would be restored only when the actual wishes of the deceased have been met, presumably through trial and error.[450]

---

witnessing the inevitability of death and its effects; it is allowed only for men, or for an old woman in whom a man would have no [sexual] interest [due to the hazard-prone environment in cemeteries]. However, if visiting the dead is done "in the belief that the deceased pious-ones administer actualization of granting and depriving (denying)," then such visits are "unanimously judged by Moslem [theologians] as not permissible (*lâ yajûz bi 'igmâʿ al-muslimîn*".) See: 'A. al-Jazîrî, in: *al-Azhar*, Vol. 12, No. 10 (1941), pp. 583–586. Also cf. n. 569.

For a description of death rituals, such as erecting cenotaphs, slaughtering animals, lavish Koran reciting, food offerings, and the like, see Khalîfah, *al-Dâr al-barzakhiyyah*, pp. 312–324. He states that such folk customs are "*madhmûmàh*" (censured, i.e., inadvisable, or near tabu; cf. Motif C3§, ‡"*al-makrûh* ('the disfavored,' 'the disliked' [by God]): almost-tabu, merely tolerated—not the preferred way (for Moslems).") Also cf. n. 307.

[447] Motifs: V65.7§, "Visiting the dead;" V65.7.1§, "Holiday(s) spent in cemetery with deceased relatives;" V65.7.2§, "Feasting at cemetery (cookout in graveyard)."

See: Ions *Ancient Egyptian Mythology*, 137; Rosalie A. David. *The Ancient Egyptians: Religious Beliefs and Practices*. (Portland, OR: Sussex Academic Press, 1997), pp. 48, 78–79; Amîn, *Qâmûs*, 322; Lane, *Modern Egyptians*, pp. 479, 487, 527–528, 547.

[448] See Abu al-Naṣr, *al-Bukhârî*, Vol. 4, p. 327; see Lane, *Modern Egyptians*, pp. 214–216.

[449] Motifs: F1068, "Realistic dream;" F1068.1, "Tokens from a dream. Man brings objects received during a dream."

al-Nabhânî (*karâmât al-'awliyâ'*, Vol. 1, pp. 282–283) cites a saint's *karâmàh* in which a "saint," before his death, had a pact of no remarriage with his wife (Motif: M135.3§, "Spouse no-remarriage pact: each of husband and wife vows never to remarry if the other dies first"). However, her family tried to coerce her into marrying. The deceased husband visited his wife in dream to lend her support, and gave her a garment as a token proving his visit.

[450] Motifs: E406.1§, ‡"Corpse can be moved only when certain thing happens (condition met);" E405§, "Uncontrollable corpse ('flying bier'): bearers compelled as to speed and route."

For contemporary examples, see "The Grave That Wouldn't Dig," in El-Shamy, *Folktales of Egypt*,

Another facet of this belief complex dealing with the corpse is that a deceased and/or entombed person may be transferred by angels or some other supernatural power to different location that is more fitting to his actual fate and deeds.[451] Thus, a person not predestined to die in the holy-land (Hejaz), for example, but manages some how to be buried there would be evicted to the place of his predestined burial. Similarly, a hypocrite who is presumed to adhere to one faith but secretly commits sins tabued by his faith during his lifetime may be evicted from his tomb in the cemetery of his faith-group to the cemetery of another faith.[452]

On the "Day of Resurrection (*bà¿th*)," the soul will seek, locate, and then enter the body that it had inhabited during the here-and-now. Each corpse that was cremated, dismembered, and buried in separate places, devoured by fish or beasts will reconstitute or reassemble itself for the soul to reinhabit and animate it again.[453] Thus, the dead person is brought back to life. This process will occur once and for all creatures that are required to observe religious precepts beginning with Adam and concluding with the last man or jinni that is still alive at the time. Errors or mistaken identities as to the matching of a soul to its body are considered impossible. Thus, the Day of Resurrection that has arrived will be followed by the Day of Judgment.

Animals also have souls; yet, the soul of an animal is not believed to live after the death of the animal but vanishes (*tatalâshâ*) by disintegration or decomposition.[454] This concept is congruent with the belief that animals, unlike humans and jinn, are not *mùkallafîn* (i.e., obliged to observe the precepts of religion) and that they will not be resurrected. Rare exceptions to this rule are animals associated positively with prophets and major religious events. Such is the case with the she-camel (*nâqàh*) of Prophet Ṣâlìḥ (whose exact identity is uncertain), and the dog of *'Ahl al-Kàhf* (The People of the Cave). (See n. 185)

No. 38, pp. 166–167, p. 283; and "The Death of *shaikhah* Shafîqah's Brother" *Tales Arab Women Tell* No. 43, pp. 313–315, by the same author.

Also see Amîn, *Qâmûs*, p. 192. Compare the analogy Romer gives in his *Ancient Lives*, pp. 100–105, (see n. 241).

[451] Motifs: Q101, "Reward fitting to deed;" Q580, "Punishment fitted to crime."

[452] Motif E407.1§, ‡"Corpse mystically moved from one cemetery (burial site, land) to another. (Usually, by angels, God's Will or the like)." For an example, see App. 14.

Khalîfah (*al-Dâr al-barzakhiyyah*, p. 350) judges reports that certain deeds may cause a corpse to be transported from one burial place to another (e.g., angels transport corpses from Christian to Moslem cemeteries or vice versa) as baseless. Cf. n. 476.

[453] See: Khalîfah, *al-Dâr al-barzakhiyyah*, pp. 170–171, 344–346.

[454] Khalîfah reports a contrary viewpoint by a colleague (named Seḥaimî/Suḥaymî). Seḥaimî, who based his opinion on information he heard from his tradition-bound students, argued that except for angels and humans, the souls of all other creatures perish; but at Resurrection, God will reconstitute these perished souls and return them to the bodies (creatures) they originally occupied during life, and that—in accordance with the principle of 'Divine Justice'—animals will undergo trial and will subsequently be turned into dust (presumably, without continuing into the hereafter).

However, Khalîfah states that since he has not seen reliable religious texts to that effect, he "cannot judge" the merits of the claim (*al-Dâr al-barzakhiyyah*, p. 271).

II.E.1. *¿àfrît* (Ghost, Cf. Spook/Revenant)

If a person dies unnatural death, it is believed that an entity—referred to as that person's *¿àfrît* (ghost; cf. spook, revenant)—comes into being. This entity is to be differentiated from the category of jinn labeled Afrits (*¿àfàrît*, sing.: Afrit/*¿àfrît*/*¿ìfrît*). According to some accounts the ghost "issues out of the blood" of the victim.[455] Thus, death caused by murder, suicide, fire, poison, auto accidents, or the like produces a ghost.[456] The ghost, unlike the soul, is perceived as a masculine entity; even when the ghost belongs to a female, it is referred to as "the *¿àfrît* of a woman." Thus, the appearance of the feminine form of the word (i.e., *¿àfrîtàh*), typically signifies a mischievous female jinn, and not a female ghost. Yet, some researchers tend to view the soul and the ghost as two facets of the same entity. For the individual adherer, the main criterion that determines whether that entity is labeled *roaḥ* (soul) or *¿àfrît* (ghost) seems to be the role it plays vis-a-vis the living. If the role is benevolent, or if it is that of typical social interactional nature, such as instructing or inquiring, it is labeled a "soul," but if the role is malevolent—and particularly of a fear-evoking nature, it is labeled *¿àfrît* (i.e., ghost). Some suggest that the term "soul" is used to refer to that entity before the burial of the body to which it belonged, while the term *¿àfrît* refers to the same entity after the burial. This viewpoint, however, does not seem to be based on cited recurrent occurrences or field reports.

A *¿àfrît* (ghost) haunts the spot or the immediate vicinity where the victim of violent unnatural death lost his or her life; attempts to drive the ghost away or "lay the ghost," may be made. Hornblower gives a description of such a ritual in which a clay figure representing the ghost is made to wither.[457] In this respect, the *¿àfrît* is similar to the *sarûkh* and to the *hâmàh*, but is not cognitively associated with them. As such, the *¿àfrît* (ghost) is totally unrelated to the member of the jinn category also labeled *¿àfrît* (Koran, 27:39);[458] both entities exist side by side bearing the same label but each belonging to different cognitive subsystems.

The unnatural death of an animal is usually not perceived as a ghost-producing event. The absence of reports on ghosts of animals seems to correspond with folk beliefs that souls of animals vanish by disintegration or decomposition upon death due to the fact animals are not *mùkallafîn* (obliged to observe the precepts of religion)

---

[455] Khalîfah (*al-Dâr al-barzakhiyyah*, p. 326) reports the folk belief that the soul of a murdered person becomes a *¿àfrît* (i.e., ghost) after three days. He, however, judges such a belief as "corrupt" and sinful.

[456] Lane (*Modern Egyptians*, p. 226), observed that "The term *'efreet* is commonly applied rather to an evil ginnee than any other being; but the ghosts of dead persons are also called by this name; [. . .]; and great are the fears they inspire." (Cf. n. 417) Similarly, A.H. Sayce (*Folk-Lore*, Vol. 11, No. 4, pp. 388–389) associated the word *afrît* (ghost), with a murdered person, and reports some haunts of such supernatural beings, including the pyramids. Sayce also states that laying bread and salt functions as a spell against ghosts. (See n. 434)

[457] G.D. Hornblower ("The Laying of a Ghost in Egypt," In: *Man*, Vol. 31 (August 1931), p. 164) describes a ritual performed for dismissing a ghost (*¿âfrît*) of a man who died a violent death. In this regard, a clay figure representing the person/ghost is made and caused to wither away.

[458] This is the sole occurrence in Koran of the word "¿ifrît" (afrit). Cf. Lane, *Modern Egyptians*, p. 226, cited in n. 456.

and will not be resurrected.[459] Reports of a ghost of an animal that had suffered a violent death are, however, rarely reported; one such case was cited by Blackman.[460] This occurrence *may* be due to the belief that if a "jinni" through self-transformation or shape shifting assumes the form of an animal—such as a "viper, lion, ox, dog, donkey, etc."—and dies, he remains in the newly assumed form.[461]

II.E.2. Summoning the Soul (Seance, "Ouija Board")

As was pointed out, a living person may contact the soul of a dead relative or close friend during sleep or by simply visiting the grave site. Only during a sleeper's vision can the soul converse with a living person. However, there are traditional practices that seek to summon the soul and communicate with it under what is believed to be a situation of controlled conditions. A number of traditional techniques are used for this purpose. One such technique was reported by Lane[462] during the first half of the nineteenth century; Lane stated that a "magician" with the help of " . . . the magic mirror of ink which, like some other performances of a similar nature, is here termed '*ḍarb el-mendel*'" offered to put Lane in touch with "any person who was absent or dead." The "magician" accomplished his task through a boy who served as a medium; the boy conveyed the instructions of the "magician" to the jinn, who, in turn, caused the "images" of these persons to be formed on the surface of the "magic mirror." The communication between Lane (i.e., the client) and the *màndàl*-operator (whom he labelled "magician") on the one hand, and the jinn who caused the "images" to be formed on the other, took place via the medium. The projected images of persons Lane specified included that of the deceased English Admiral Lord Nelson and appeared as reflections on a mirror surface (i.e., with the mirror effect: right side of person to the left of image and left side to the right). Lane characterized the image the medium portrayed of Lord Nelson as "faultless." Portrayals of other persons proved to be "imperfect, though not all together incorrect."[463] (See Section II.B.2a, and App. 19)

It is not clear from Lane's account whether the "images" that the boy (the medium) described were in any way related to the souls of these persons. Currently, more than a century and one-half later, the practice of using the *màndàl* to cause jinn to constitute the image of a *living* person on a shiny surface is still practiced, but summoning the soul of a deceased person through the *màndàl* has not been reported in more recent times. The *màndàl*-opening clearly belongs to the category of rituals that attempt to seek information from jinn themselves (see Section II.B.2a). By contrast the practice of *tàḥḍîr el-'arwâḥ* (to cause souls to be present) or *'ìstid;â' el-'arwâḥ* (the summoning

---

459 Khalîfah, *al-Dâr al-barzakhiyyah*, p. 271. See n. 185.

460 *The Fellâḥîn*, 1968, p. 237.

461 Ḥusayn, *al-Ginn*, p. 56 (see also Section II.D); on jinn's shape-shifting, see al-Gindi, *al-Ginn*, Vol. 2, pp. 98–104.

462 Lane, *Modern Egyptians*, pp. 268–275.

463 Lane, *Modern Egyptians*, 273.

of souls, or "seance") uses a different technique and does not involve jinn in any instrumental manner.

Only recently has it become popular in urban centers to summon the soul of a dead person through a medium and communicate with it. The source of this basic departure from traditional learned (formal) and folk beliefs concerning the dead may be attributed to a series of articles in which M.F. Wagdî, the editor of the official journal of al-Azhar, and a leading theologian, sought to prove to "agnostics" and "materialists" the universality of the belief in the "soul," by showing his readers that technologically advanced Europeans also believed in the existence of the soul and communicate scientifically with souls through a certain practice. In 1937 Wagdî reported on "the summoning of souls in Europe" through a medium, as undertaken by "psychologists" and "experimental physical scientists."[464] His objective was to lend additional support to the Islamic beliefs in the independent existence of the soul and in that "fact" that souls continue to live eternally after the death of persons to whom they belonged. These beliefs, and the European "scientific," "experimental" practices associated with them were easily acceptable to both the Egyptian Moslem and Copt, for they were congruent with the basic tenets as to how the "soul" is perceived among members of both religious denominations. A few years after Wagdî published his reports, the soul-summoning procedure was propagated through popular weekly magazines[465] and spread rapidly among members of the literate middle and upper classes, especially in urban centers and provincial towns. Clubs, such as "*Gam¿ìyyàt al-Ahrâm ar-Rûḥiyyàh* (Pyramids' Spiritual Club, i.e., Pyramids' Club for Soul-Summoning)" became active. A number of literate groups sought to put the procedure to practical use. A theologian remarked that such clubs applied the imported practice in the treatment of incurable diseases with visible success in some cases, and that ". . . the late Sheik Ṭanṭâwî Gawharî was the pioneer [of this applied craft] in Egypt."[466]

On a lesser scale of significance, students also put the newly found "science" to practical—though dishonest—use through a simple procedure called "[soul-summoning by] the basket." Students sought to acquire knowledge of examination questions after becoming sure that the examination has already been formulated, printed, and kept under lock and key. The soul of a deceased person who had the reputation for honesty would be summoned and asked to look at the examinations and report on the questions, or at least on the main topics that the examination covers. "The basket" technique calls for a string to be tied to the handle of a basket (woven of thin bamboo stripes), a pencil to be attached to the basket bottom with its point barely touching a blank sheet of paper, and a *ṭâhìr* (immaculate, ritually clean) person holding the string (or, the string would be attached to the ceiling of the room where the ritual is taking place). The soul is believed to move the basket and cause the pen to write what the soul wishes to say.

[464] M.F. Wagdî, "'istiḥḍâr al-'arwâḥfi Orubbah (The Summoning of Souls in Europe)." In: *al-Azhar*, Vol. 8, pp. 105–114. Also see n. 398.

[465] Especially a weekly titled *Ṣabâḥ el-Khair* (Good Morning), aimed mainly at youthful readers.

[466] Khalîfah, *al-Dâr al-barzakhiyyah*, pp. 256–257.

While still in high school during the early 1950s, this writer along with two or three friends held such a soul-summoning session, as described in the weekly magazine mentioned above (see n. 465). After deciphering what the pencil (or the soul) had scribbled on the paper we were certain that we knew which topics are covered and which were not included on the test. However, the results were nearly disastrous: almost none of the topics and textbook chapters we dwelt on were included, and the ones we merely glossed over constituted the bulk of the test. So pervasive was the belief in the efficacy of the soul-summoning procedure that a distinguished Egyptian historian and dean of the faculty of arts states that he tried the procedure with reference to an illness that he had. He, however, adds that "it did not work."[467]

A noted case of soul summoning, touching on matters of national security, was reported in a leading newspaper. The seance, held before the 1973 war, involved a group of Egyptian top army generals, leading cabinet ministers, and other politicians. They "summoned" the soul of the late President Gamâl ¿Abd-en-Nâṣṣir to ask him how and when the Arab–Israeli conflict will end. The answer was that it would be solved soon with peaceful means.[468] Clearly, the information the "soul" gave proved to be quite different from subsequent events.[469]

Among the rest of folk groups—urban lower classes, fellahin, Bedouins, Siwans, and Nubians—the practice of summoning the soul, especially in their home communities, is virtually unknown. Considering the fact that the practice has been gaining grounds in cities, and has received qualified acceptance from some religious authorities, it is likely to spread to new regions.

Theologians and formal religious institutions, Islamic[470] as well as Coptic (as represented in the views of Pope Shenoudah III),[471] object to the practice of summoning the soul, but do not dispute the principle on which it is based. The main reasons for the objections are that the practice disturbs the tranquillity of the souls, and that the summoned "spirit" is often a satan, jinn, or demon who is trying to deceive those who are attempting to establish contact with the soul of a specific deceased person.

---

[467]The logical explanation for the basket attempt mentioned above is that the ever-present vibrations cause the string, the basket, or the pencil to scribble some letters on the paper. The reader projects his/her interpretations on these figures.

For Amîn's accounts, see his *Qâmûs,* pp. 35–36.

[468]Moḥammad Ḥasanayn Haykal, "taḥḍîr al-'arwâḥ," *Al-Ahram,* June 4, 1971, pp. 1, 3.

[469]Amîn (*Qâmûs,* p. 36) also reports a prediction made during the mid-1900s that WW III would break out "next November." It is obvious that the prediction by "soul" did not materialize.

[470]Ḥasan ¿Abdul-Wahhâb, "bid¿at 'istiḥḍâr al-'arwâḥ (The Deviant Innovation/Fad of Soul Summoning)." In *al-Azhar,* Vol. 31, pp. 1158–1159; and Khalîfah, *al-Dâr al-barzakhiyyàh,* p. 257.

[471]Pope Shenoudah the III, "Al-rûḥ fi al-masîḥiyyah (Soul in Christianity." In *al-Hilâl* Dec., 1971, pp. 152–153.

CHAPTER III

Al-'ince (Humans)

A human being per se is not viewed as a supernatural entity. As a phenomenon, however, humans are perceived within the context of the supernatural belief system, especially as a product of the act of original Creation (*al-khàlq al-'àwwàl*, i.e., Genesis) and as Adamites, the offspring of Adam and Eve. Numerous contemporary beliefs and practices associated with how a social group is perceived seem to stem directly from these original concepts.

Humans are typically referred to as *el-khàlq* (the [human] creatures), or *banî 'Âdam* (Adam's progeny, children of Adam); a number of vernacular derivatives of these two appellations are also used frequently: *'âdamìyy* ("Adamite"), and *el-khàlq, el-màkhâlîq, el-khalâyìq* ([human] creatures, or beings).[472] The word *'ìnce* (human beings) is applied to refer to mankind particularly in contexts that involve other categories of God's creatures, especially jinn;[473] the singular form, *'ìnsân*, is normally used as an adjective to indicate that a person has refined and compassionate qualities that are thought to be characteristic of a truly fine human being (i.e., "*mensch*").

Man was the last being to arrive on the scene of life. God created Adam of the crust of Earth (*'adîm al-'àrḍ*)[474] fetched by Azrael, the Angel of Death. Literary traditions,

---

[472]These plural forms occur mostly in vernacular, whereas *makhlûqât* is typically used in literary works.

[473]The word *'ince* occurs in Koran eighteen times all of which are in association with jinn (see for examples, Koran, 6:112, 6:128, 7:38, 41:29, 55:33, 72:5).

In folk narratives, the word occurs only in the formulaic question: "Are you *'ince* or gìnn?" The plural form, *'unûs* (humans), occurs only in vernacular. It is interesting to note here that al-Tha¿labî, *Qiṣaṣ*, p. 166, uses the word in its folk context (Tale-type 930F§, *The Predestined Fornication* (The phoenix's foster daughter is reached and impregnated), a further indication of the "folksy" nature of his source for the narrative; cf. the use of the word *ḍaw'*, n. 108. See El-Shamy, "Vom Fisch geboren (AaTh 705)", as in n. 175.

[474]al-Tha¿labî, *Qiṣaṣ*, pp. 16–17.

which are also known in folk circles though not fully narrated orally,[475] state that the first human being was called "'Âdam" after the substance from which he was made: the crust of the Earth. That is also why Azrael is the angel who is assigned the task of retrieving life out of humans by extracting their souls out of their bodies when the time of their death comes. The Islamic practice of burying corpses in "earth crust" (without a casket) is implicitly related to this belief.[476] At burial the dead person is instructed that God had stated: "Thereof [Earth] We created you, and thereinto We return you, and thence We bring you forth a second time [at Resurrection]."[477] The belief that man, like pottery, was created of clay is also found in ancient Egyptian sacred belief systems. The deity "Khnum, whose name meant 'to create' [. . .] was the creator of the gods and of men, which he fashioned from clay on a potter's wheel."[478]

Koran (96:2) also states that God created man from "*¿alàq* (a blood-clot, or congealed blood)." Other verses (Koran, 22:5, 23:14, and 40:67), however, specify that this substance was a later development in the creation process and that it is only a developmental stage within pregnancy.[479] Although in daily life human beings are typically referred to as "composed of flesh and blood," neither substance is believed to have entered into the original creation of Adam, the first man. The Earth from which Adam was constituted was of various colors and consistencies: red, black, and white; beautiful and ugly; mellow, firm, and hard.[480] The various sorts of clay account for the different race appearances and temperaments of man; this belief is common in both learned and folk traditions, and is usually cited to prove the strict equality of racial groups. Some literary sources state that only prophets were created of the white heart of Earth, fetched by the Archangel Gabriel—rather than Azrael, and later converted in heaven into light and mixed with the clay from which Adam was to be formed (created).[481] This view, that seems to have little currency in oral folk traditions, casts prophets into a different "race," so to speak. Yet, it does not carry any racial connotations but simply signifies the absolute natural purity of *all* of God's messengers and prophets. The belief that all humans were created from one and the same type of clay underlies the folk expression that would characterize a person as being "[constituted] of clay other than the clay (*mìn ṭînàh ghair eṭ-ṭînàh*);"

---

[475] In other words, born by passive bearers of traditions. On the differences in psychological processes involved in "active" and "passive" bearing of traditions, see n. 12.

[476] Cf. "Why the Copts Were Called 'Blue Bone,'" in El-Shamy, *Folktales of Egypt*, No. 25, pp. 139–140. Cf. n. 451.

[477] A "*tàlqîn*" performance recorded at a graveside in an upper Egyptian village. See n. 164 and 432.

[478] Motif: A1242§, ‡"Deity fashions man on potter's wheel—(Khnum)". See Ions, *Egyptian Mythology*, pp. 108–109; and cf. Maspero/El-Shamy, *Ancient Egypt*, No. 1, p. 12 note 1; No. 2, p. 39.

[479] See al-Tha¿labî, *Qiṣaṣ*, p. 16; and Ibrâhîm al-'Azraqî, *Tashîl al-manâfi¿ fi al-ṭibb wa al-ḥikmah* (The Facilitation of Benefits in Medicine and Wisdom), Cairo, 1963, pp. 226–227.

[480] al-Tha¿labî, *Qiṣaṣ*, p. 16.

Motifs: A1241.5, "Man made from earth brought from four different places;" A1241.5.1§, "Physical and personality attributes (temperament) are determined by characteristics of the earth from which the first man was created." Cf. n. 575.

[481] al-Tha¿labî, *Qiṣaṣ*, p. 16. Motif: A1241.6§, "Prophets made from more pure class of clay (heart of earth) brought by Gabriel." (Cf. n. 400)

this proverbial hyperbole signifies that the person so depicted is totally and utterly different from the rest of humanity.

A companion idea concerning Earth in relationship to a person distinguishes prophets further from other ordinary humans. A strongly held belief asserts that God made it sinful for Earth to "eat" (i.e., corrode, cause decomposition) the corpse of a prophet.[482] Consequently, corpses of prophets are believed to have suffered no decay during the centuries and millennia. The formal religious stand on this matter, which rests on a Prophet's tradition of disputable authenticity, is to uphold its validity and consider those who doubt it "ignorant."[483] Outside the formal religious circles, this belief is extended to include saints' corpses as well. Reports of saints' corpses found intact years after their death are frequently encountered.[484] Occasionally, an unearthed corpse that is found in preserved condition by natural means, would entitle the person to whom it belonged to some claim on sainthood.[485] However, this consideration is not extended to ancient deliberately mummified corpses.

Before God breathed life into the pottery-like figure of Adam, which was of transcontinental size, the figure lay on the ground (of heaven) for forty years. According to some literary sources, Eblis, then an angel, used to frolic with Adam's "hollow" figure by entering through its mouth and exiting via its anus, declaring: "It is hollow; I am solid;" and pledged: "If God favored this [thing] over us [angels], I will disobey Him, and if I am preferred over it, I will lead it to destruction."[486] (See Section I.D) God created *Ḥawwâ'* (Eve) out of Adam's rib, hence her name *ḥawwâ'*—which is interpreted to mean, "that which comes out of something *ḥàyy* (a living thing)."[487] The rib that was used in the making of Eve was—inevitably—crooked (*'a¿wàg*); therefore, Eve's nature and the nature and conduct of her female

---

[482]al-Tha¿labî, *Qiṣaṣ*, p. 221 (*passim*). Motifs: C908.1.1§, ‡"Tabu imposed on earth (of Earth);" C908.1.1.1§, ‡"Earth forbidden to corrode ('devour') corpse of prophet (saint);" E183§ "Body of a prophet does not decay after his death: earth may not corrode it."

It may be noted here that the word *gùththàh* (corpse) is not used to refer to the body of a deceased prophet, probably due to the fact that it implies lifelessness or being without a soul. Typically, the words *gùthmân* (body, usually of a martyr or an eminent person), *gasàd*, or *gism* (body) are used in this respect.

[483]Under the title "Question: Does Earth Corrode Prophets's Corpses?" a concerned reader wrote:

> What we believe, and is believed by every true monotheist, is that God has made it sinful for [i.e., prohibited] Earth to eat [i.e., corrode (decompose)] corpses of prophets. But now we find in *al-Manâr* magazine that its owner [editor] says that corpses of prophets do [indeed corrode], and he labors at *taḍ¿îf al-ḥdîth* (downgrading the authenticity of the Prophet's saying) [that affirms this validity of this belief].

Answer: An authority gave the formal stand of Islam on this issue, which is as follows:

> "The editor of *al-Manâr* is ignorant, and what is establish is that Prophets's corpses do not corrode (decompose)." (See: Y. al-Digwî, *Nûr al-Islâm*, Vol. 3, No. 6 (1932), pp. 397–407).

[484]For examples, see al-Nabhânî, *karâmât al-'awliyâ'*, Vol. 1, p. 267; Vol. 2, pp. 20, 39, and 375.

[485]Newspapers reports; personal reading by present writer during the 1950s.

[486]al-Ṭabarî, *Târîkh*, Vol. 1, p. 93; al-Tha¿labî, *Qiṣaṣ*, p. 17.

[487]al-Tha¿labî, *Qiṣaṣ*, p. 18. Morphologically, the "w" and the "y" are interchangeable.

descendants constituting womankind is viewed as crooked. A female is often referred to euphemistically as "*ḍil¿ 'a¿wag*" (crooked rib);[488] as such, it is often argued that forceful attempts to "straighten out" a female would result in destroying her just like attempts to straighten a curved bone (rib).[489]

Having been cast out of heaven for refusing God's command and desiring to mislead Adam and Eve, Eblis tried to enter Paradise but its angel keepers prevented him. Upon the advice of the peacock, Eblis resorted to the *ḥàyyàh* (viper),[490] who agreed to smuggle him past the guardian angel, Ruḍwân, into Paradise. Eblis transformed himself into "wind" (see Section II.E) and hid inside the viper's mouth between her fangs and thus gained entry. He instigated Adam and Eve to eat from the forbidden tree (fruit); Eve succumbed first, then enticed Adam to follow suit. Some variants of this account add that Eve succeeded only after getting Adam drunk.[491]

God cast the new sinners—Adam and Eve, the viper, and the peacock—out of Paradise and as further punishment inflicted certain negative qualities on each. The viper, which used to have legs, lost *her* pedal locomotion, was doomed to creeping on her belly, and killing her became legitimate for man even during prayers and pilgrimage.[492] God plagued Adam with social and emotional characteristics common to all mankind, particularly the males: enmity and warfare among his descendants, suffering worldly life and natural disaster, suffering defamation and disrepute, and failure and unhappiness.[493] Meanwhile, Eve suffered additional psychological and

---

[488] al-Tha¿labî, *Qiṣaṣ*, p. 18.

Motifs: A1371.5§, "Deviant women from Adam's 'crooked rib;'" A1275.1, "Creation of first woman from man's rib [Adam's rib];" W256.6.3.1§, ‡"Women's character: 'crooked [like a] rib.'"

[489] al-Tha¿labî, *Qiṣaṣ*, p. 18.

[490] al-Tha¿labî, *Qiṣaṣ*, p. 19; al-Kisâ'î, *Qiṣaṣ*, p. 37. The latter adds that Eblis swore by God falsely before he could persuade the viper (and the peacock) to help him reach his goal.

[491] al-Tha¿labî, *Qiṣaṣ*, p. 19.

al-Kisâ'î attributes Adam's submission to Eves temptation to predestination. Thus, "Adam had nothing to do with ordering this matter, nor with preventing [it], nor any will [in any form at all]" (*Qiṣaṣ*, pp. 39–40).

Motifs: A1332.9.1.1§, ‡"Eve makes Adam drunk in Paradise by giving him liquor;" A2532.1.1§, ‡"Why viper's venom potent. (Satan sat between her fangs when she smuggled him into paradise);" A1332.4.2§, ‡"Wheat as the forbidden fruit in paradise;" A1332.1§, ‡"Violation of food taboo in paradise results in need to defecate (assimilation of forbidden food is incomplete);" N100.2§, ‡"Predestined sinning (fornication, theft, killing, or the like)."

See also n. 580.

[492] al-Tha¿labî, *Qiṣaṣ*, pp. 20–21.

Motifs: A2236.2.1.1§ "Viper smuggles devil into paradise in her mouth: she is cursed;" A2236.2.1.1.1§, ‡"Punishment of viper: loss of wings (ability to fly);" A2236.2.1.1.2§, ‡"Punishment of viper: loss of legs (must creep on stomach);" A2236.2.1.1.3§, ‡"Punishment of viper: nakedness;" A2236.2.1.1.4§, ‡"Punishment of viper: split tongue;" A2236.2.1.1.5§, ‡"Punishment of viper: enmity (hate, fear) of people;" A2236.2.1.1.5.1§, ‡"Punishment of viper: may be killed inside sacred shrines and during holy periods (or prayers);" A2236.2.1.1.6§, ‡"Punishment of viper: being unjust (aggressor)."

[493] Motifs: A1650.5.1.1§, ‡"Punishment of Adam: God's reconciliatory reprimand (*¿itâb*);" A1650.5.1.2§, ‡"Punishment of Adam: infamy, disgrace;" A1650.5.1.3§, ‡"Punishment of Adam: thin skin;" A1650.5.1.4§, ‡"Punishment of Adam: banishment from God's realm;" A1650.5.1.5§, ‡"Punishment of Adam: long separation from wife Eve (100 years);" A1650.5.1.6§, ‡"Punishment of

emotional traits peculiar to women only, such as menstruation, pain of pregnancy and delivery, weakness, lack of religiosity, she never can become a ruler (sovereign), and interestingly enough, she will always be "under the male."[494] This latter trait was taken figuratively to signify the eternal superiority of the male over the female, and literally to mean that during sexual intercourse a woman may not be on top of a male.[495] The same opinion on this nuptial posture is expressed in some older books on traditional Arab "medicine;" however, these medical sources cite "physiological" and "anatomical" reasons pertaining to hygiene, susceptibility to conception, and the influencing of the sex of the fetus for the prohibition.[496]

The religious account that holds Eve responsible for Adam's sin is usually cited in folk and other traditionary circles to justify some of the negative attitudes toward women and the stereotypes these attitudes generate: "Had it not been for Eve, mankind would not have had to suffer by living on Earth;" "A woman is weaker than a man;" "Women are followers of Eblis;" and the like. The fact that the Islamic account is largely in agreement with the biblical tradition is often used to reinforce the truthfulness of these stereotypes and related practices. This attitude stands in sharp

---

Adam: strife (enmity toward one another);" A1650.5.1.7§, ‡"Punishment of Adam: branded as rebellious;" A1650.5.1.8§, ‡"Punishment of Adam: setting enemy against his descendants (becoming prey);" A1650.5.1.9§, ‡"Punishment of Adam: being earth-bound (prisoner in *ad-dunyâ*), and suffering the elements;" A1650.5.1.10§, ‡"Punishment of Adam: toiling and misery, the first to have his brow sweat from labor fatigue."

[494]al-Tha¿labî, *Qiṣaṣ*, pp. 20–21. (See n. 400 above)

Motifs: A1650.5.2§ "God's (fifteen) additional afflictions on women ('Eve and her daughters');" A1650.5.2.0.1§, ‡"Eve blamed for Adamites' troubles on earth (due to eviction from paradise). Usually blame extended to 'her daughters;'" A1650.5.2.1§, ‡"Punishment of Eve: menstruation;" A1650.5.2.1.1§, ‡"Tree in paradise bleeds: avenges self on Eve;" A1650.5.2.2§, ‡"Punishment of Eve: heaviness of pregnancy;" A1650.5.2.3§, ‡"Punishment of Eve: labor pains and childbirth pains;" A1650.5.2.3.1§, ‡"Punishment of Eve: craving during pregnancy;" A1650.5.2.4§, ‡"Punishment of Eve: deficiency in religion (faith);" A1650.5.2.4.1§, ‡"Menstruous women may not perform certain required religious services (e.g., fasting, prayers), and thus deficient in religion;" A1650.5.2.5§, ‡"Punishment of Eve: deficiency in reason (mind);" A1650.5.2.5.1§, ‡"Woman's testimony is worth half of man's, and thus deficient in reason;" A1650.5.2.6§, ‡"Punishment of Eve: inheriting half of a man's share;" A1650.5.2.7§, ‡"Punishment of Eve: imposition of *¿iddah* (waiting period before remarriage) on women only;" A1650.5.2.8§, ‡"Punishment of Eve: being 'under' men's hands;" A1650.5.2.8.1§, ‡"Punishment of Eve: female being 'below' male during coition;" A1650.5.2.9§, ‡"Punishment of Eve: having no right (power) to divorce spouse;" A1650.5.2.10§, ‡"Punishment of Eve: being exempt from partaking in *jihâd* (holy wars, struggles);" A1650.5.2.11§, ‡"Punishment of Eve: no prophet chosen from among women (Eve's female descendants);" A1650.5.2.12§, ‡"Punishment of Eve: no sultan nor ruler from among women (Eve's female descendants);" A1650.5.2.13§, ‡"Punishment of Eve: woman may not travel except when accompanied by a *maḥram* (sacrosanct, unmarriageable male, usually a close-relative);" A1650.5.2.14§, ‡"Punishment of Eve: Friday prayer-service (at mosque) may not be held with only women (*lâ tan¿aqid bihinna*—i.e., they would not constitute a legitimate congregation);" A1650.5.2.15§, ‡"Punishment of Eve: women may not to be greeted [with the typical] 'peace-be-upon' greeting (*lâ yusallamu ¿alayhin*);" A1650.5.2.16§, ‡"Punishment of eve: suffering defloration pains."

[495]al-Mas¿ûdî, *'Akhbâr*, p. 74. (Motif: A1352.4§, "Why a woman may not 'top' a man (in government, coition): punishment for sin (rebellion) of Adam's first mate."

Notably, al-Tha¿labî does not explicitly mention this taboo (interdiction) in his *Qiṣaṣ*.

[496]al-'Azraqî, *Tashîl al-manâfi¿*, pp. 115, 221–222.

variance with Koranic pronouncements where blame is set on Adam and Eve evenly, or more on Adam alone.[497] A first wife for Adam before Eve, a common belief in Jewish and Christian traditions, is rarely reported in earlier Islamic writings,[498] but seems to be totally absent among folk groups.

Once on Earth, Archangel Gabriel taught Adam and Eve the necessary crafts, such as agriculture, and brought them some seeds and animals essential to their survival in their new hostile environment. Eve bore twins regularly; each male married his non-twin sister. In one recurrent account, Qâbîl (Cain), who became a farmer, killed Hâbîl (Abel), who became a shepherd, because Cain wanted to keep his twin sister for himself.[499] This theme of marriage between primordial brothers and sisters is basic to ancient Egyptian religious systems; it is also found in contemporary folk beliefs and related practices about the jinn (see Section II.C; also compare with Section IV.D.2).[500] Adam's children and their descendants multiplied until all but a few were drowned by the deluge. According to written religious tradition, only Sâm (Sem), Ḥâm (Hem), and Yâfeth (Japhet), each representing a race, survived.[501] The Koranic account of the deluge, however, mentions only one son for Noah; that son opposed his father's faith, resorted to the top of a mountain that he thought would protect him, and was subsequently drowned by the deluge (Koran, 11:43).

God preferred man to all other creatures and endowed him with the faculty of thinking or intelligence (*fikr, ¿àql*).[502] Some literary sources cite the Koranic

---

[497] In this regard, the present writer observed:

> In spite of the fact that Qur'ân assigns responsibility for the commission of the sin to both Adam and Eve (Qur'ân 7:20–23) or even to Adam alone (20:117, 120–21), the prevailing view places much of the blame on Eve as the instigator and establishes a link between her and Satan (Eblis). (El-Shamy, *Tales Arab Women Tell*, p. 11)

[498] For examples, see Hanauer, *Holy Land*, p. 19; El-Shamy, "Belief Characters . . . ," p. 22.

[499] al-Tha¿labî, *Qiṣaṣ*, pp. 26–27; Ibn Kathîr, *al-Bidâyah wa al-nihâyah*, pp. 101–102. Also see El-Shamy, "Arab Psychiatry," p. 320; "Belief Characters . . . ," p. 22.

[500] Like contemporary Semitic believers, early Moslems were loath to accept this sinful practice as God's way; they introduced alternate explanations that exclude any possibility of incest. Currently, some modern western Christian writers conclude that biblical and other texts do not provide sufficient information as to the times, places, and circumstances of these first human marriages. However, they also declare,

> If we now work totally from Scripture, without any personal prejudices or other extra-biblical ideas, then back at the beginning, when there was only the first generation, brothers would have had to have married sisters or there would be no more generations! We are not told when Cain married or any of the details of other marriages and children, but we can say for certain that some brothers had to marry their sisters at the beginning of human history.

(See: Christian Answers Network:www.christiananswers.net/q-aig/aig-c004.html) Also see El-Shamy, "Sister and Brother, Motif: P253." In: *Archetype and Motifs*, Garry and El-Shamy, eds., pp. 349–361.

[501] Motifs: A1613§, ‡"Origin of the three races: Caucasoid (white), Negroid (black), and Mongoloid;" A1613.1§, ‡"Caucasoids, Negroids, and Mongoloids are descendants of Noah's three sons: Shem, Ham, and Japheth." Cf. Tale-type 758D§, *The Three Sons of Noah*. Origin of races (physical and social class characteristics). See El-Shamy, *DOTTI*.

[502] Motifs: A1210.1§, ‡"Creation of the human brain (intellect, mind, reason, etc.) by creator;" A1210.2§, ‡"Human brain as God's favorite creation."

account according to which God ordered all angels to prostrate themselves (*yasjudû*) before Adam as acknowledgment that God preferred man even to angels. During Adam's period all animals could talk; only man, however, was selected by God to continue to maintain this capability.[503] Residuals of this religious theme still recur in contemporary folktales. In accordance with the teachings associated with the establishment of life on Earth for Adam and Eve, humans may use animals and birds *only* for ends legitimized by God such as nourishment and as beasts of burden. Using animals for cruel pleasure, such as bullfights and the like, or as heathen sacrifice to jinni or devil, is deemed sinful. Since God ordained the superiority of man over animals, God's name must be mentioned at the slaughtering of an animal or bird to be used as nourishment or other legitimate purposes. Typically, the person who is performing the slaughtering must be a Moslem and must declare, "In the name of God, The Merciful, The Compassionate." This initiatory religious utterance—labeled *bàsmalàh* (i.e., *b-ìsm-i-llâh*, in [the] name-of-God)—is often extended to include a message to, or a prayer on behalf of the animal that states "May God give you patience over [i.e., to abide by] what He has doomed you to (*'Allâhùmma yiṣabbaràk ¿alâ mâ balâk*)."[504] Failure to observe this rule renders the meat of the animal or the fowl profane and thus sinful for a Moslem to eat.[505] Hunters, who must shoot their prey in a hurry and fear and may forget to utter the prayer, often have it engraved (inscribed) and fastened to the weapons or the traps they use.

III.A. Social Stratification in *'ìnce* Society

In its original Koranic form Islam is staunchly egalitarian, especially with reference to race and social class; differentiation among members of the Moslem community may be made only according to piety (*tàqwâ*) and similar religious considerations. Contrary to formal Islamic doctrine, however, folk cultures portray human society in a clearly stratified manner. Piety is usually but not exclusively, the basis upon which stratification is justified.[506] Legal innovations developing at later stages of Islamic jurisprudence, such as the doctrine of *kafâ'àh* (i.e., that marriage may be annulled if one spouse, especially a husband, proved to be inferior in social status or wealth to the

---

For a mythical account of the process involved in the themes of these motifs, see al-Kisâ'î, *Qiṣaṣ*, pp. 10–11; see App. 2.

503 al-Tha¿labî, *Qiṣaṣ*, pp. 17–18.

Cf. Motif: Z10.1.2§, ‡"Beginning formula: reversal of nature in former age (e.g., 'When animals could talk,' 'When the rocks were still soft,' etc.)."

504 Lane (*Modern Egyptians*, p. 95), praises the practice and states: "If the sentiment which first dictated this prayer were always felt, it would present a beautiful trait in the character of the people who use it." On mercy (*raḥmah*), see Abu al-Naṣr, *al-Bukhârî*, Vol. 4, p. 153.

Sengers (*Women and Demons*, p. 91) also mentions the practice in the *zâr* context. However, it should be noted here that mentioning God's name ("*allahu akbar*," [i.e., Allâhu . . .]) in the process of slaughtering an animal as part of a true *zâr* ritual is taboo. Ideally, true *zâr* avoids sacred entities and may not be held during holy days such as the fast month of Ramaḍân. (See Section II.C.2a, pt. 4, p. 105, and n. 308)

505 Lane, *Modern Egyptians*, p. 144, 224 note 2.

506 Motif: W4§, ‡"Religiosity (piety): most favorable trait of character."

other) promoted the nonegalitarian perspective.[507] Thus, human society is perceived in the same differential terms, which characterize the communities of angels, jinn, and human souls in the isthmian life. Folk groups recognize "old power" and "old aristocracy" as belonging to the uppermost strata of the society. Thus, it is prestigious to possess power (*gâh*) and property (*mâl*) after one's own father who himself had to have acquired these assets from own father (*'abàn ¿an gàdd*). Social stratification as perceived in Egyptian folk culture contains the same rungs, which were formed in western societies;[508] in Moslem communities; however, religiosity plays a critical role in determining class status. An utterance (tradition) by Prophet Mohammad, often quoted in folk circles, states that "People are equal just like the teeth of a comb." Yet, recurrent folk proverbial utterances justify differentiation and stratification in human society on basis of human physical qualities; such proverbial utterances state, "The fingers of your hand are not identical" and "The eye does not top the eyebrow."[509]

The view of a hierarchically stratified community is also countervailed by the egalitarian (in an ideal sense) philosophy that "all of us are the children of Eve and Adam." This doctrine of common ancestry nullifies racial differences and helps in reducing the intensity of religious and nationalistic conflict of interest.[510]

Following formal Islamic teachings, folk groups view humans as comprising three strata: first, Moslems—who are also referred to as "the nation of 'There is no god but Allah,'" or as "the Mohammadan Nation;" second, "Christians and Jews"—who are also referred to as "people of the Book (i.e., those who have had one of God's Books,

---

[507] Motifs: P530§, "Legal *kafâ'ah*: marriage is to be between persons of equal social class (status compatibility required);" P530.1§, "Marriage annulled (betrothal voided) upon discovering that groom comes from low class (non-*kafâ'ah*)."

See Amîn, *Qâmûs*, pp. 150–152; also see Farahat J. Ziyadeh, "Equality (Kafa'ah) in Muslim Law of Marriage." In: *The American Journal of Comparative Law*, Vol. 6, No. 4 (Autmn, 1957), pp. 503–517. Cf. Motif: P529.4§, "*muḥallil*-marriage: legal device for reinstating thrice-divorced wife." See also "*mustaḥall*" in Lane, *Modern Egyptians*, pp. 180–181; and "Sultan Hasan" in El-Shamy, *Folktales of Egypt*, No. 15, pp. 101–107, 264–265.

Tale-type 855B§, *Interim (Substitute) Groom Proves to be the Better Man.* Husband for a night is kept.

Motifs: T156.0.1§, ‡"Interim (substitute) groom proves to be the better man: husband for a night is kept;" V4.2§, "Being bearer of God's words outweighs worldly assets of wealth and high status."

[508] For a similar setting of social stratification, cf. the western system described in Allison Davis, et al., *Deep South: a Social Anthropological Study of Caste and Class* (Chicago, IL: University of Chicago Press, 1941) . See Hisham Sharabi, *Neopatriarchy* (New York: Oxford University Press, 1988); and Halim Barakat, *The Arab World: Society, Culture, and State.* (Berkeley, CA: University of California Press, 1993)

[509] Motifs: P750.0.1§, "Basis for social differentiation and stratification;" P750.0.1.0.1§, ‡"Natural (prevailing) social order: high is high and low is low;" P750.0.1.1§, "'An eye does not top an eyebrow;'" P750.0.1.2§, "'One's fingers are not alike.'"

Cf. Tale-types: 758, *The Various Children of Eve* [the hidden child receives no blessings: hence inequality among peoples]; 758B§, *Origin of Human Traits of Character*: animal characteristics for children of Noah (Eve); 758C§, *Origin of Sibling Rivalry*: conflict between siblings of the same sex began when one was favored over the other; 758D§, *The Three Sons of Noah.* Origin of races (physical and social class characteristics). See n. 351.

[510] Motifs: P750.0.3§, "Basis for social equality;" P750.0.3.1§, "'We all are children of Eve and Adam,'" P750.0.3.2§, "'We all are children of nine [month of pregnancy].'"

or Scriptures)" or as *dhimmiyyîn* or *'àhl adh-dhimmàh* (people of the Pact);[511] third, those who worship a god other than God (*mùshrikîn*), and idolaters (*wathàniyyîn*) who adhere to none of the three aforementioned religions. More commonly, especially in verbal lore, the latter non-Moslem groups are referred to as unbelievers (*kùffàr*). For Moslems, Islam is held to be the only correct religion at the present time, while Judaism (until the appearance of Christ) and Christianity (until the appearance of Mohammad) were the correct and true religions (usually all three systems of faith are spoken of as *one* religion: The Abrahamic Faith). It is believed that the original teachings of Prophets Mûsa (Moses) and ¿Îsâ (Jesus) were altered by Jewish and Christian scribes and clerics. Islam puts the two religions in their correct perspective and completes their teachings, and is the final revelation from God. Currently, it is believed that only true Moslems will enter Paradise, except for Christians who lived before Islam, Jews who lived before Christianity, and all pious people who lived before God's prophets and messengers conveyed His Word to man. In some accounts, all pious people who have not heard of Islam will also enter Paradise; the sin for their "ignorance" rests with Moslems for failing to spread God's Word.[512] This belief played an important role in generating the zeal with which Islam was spread. The language spoken in Paradise is Arabic.[513] An inhabitant of Paradise can acquire perfect Arabic, or whatsoever he or she may desire, merely by thinking about it: the thought is realized instantly. (See Section I.B.1)

III.B. Specific Classes

In addition to the general view of a stratified society composed of all past and present human beings, three classes (*ṭabaqât*, sing.: *ṭabaqàh*) each constituted of limited groups of individuals with supernatural powers are perceived. These are: God's messengers and other prophets; the companions of Prophet Mohammad and their companions, and saints.

III.B.1. *rusùl* ([God's] Messengers) and "*anbiyâ*" (Prophets)

At the peak of the hierarchy is the class (*ṭabaqàh*) of prophets that itself is stratified. Two grades or strata may be designated within this class: *rùsùl* (apostles/messengers of God) and *'anbiyâ* (prophets). The *rùsùl* (God's messengers) are prophets who received the Gospel. They are Moses, Jesus, and Mohammad; their gospels are represented by *at-Tàwrâh* (the Tora, Old Testament), *al-'Ingîl* (the Bible, the New Testament) and *al-Qùr'ân* (Koran), respectively. The *'anbiyâ* are the prophets who preached

---

511 Motifs: V371§, "Moslem traditions about *al-kitâbiyyîn* (Jews and Christians);" cf. W37.8§, ‡"*dhimmah*: economic, political, governmental, conscientiousness, and honesty."

512 See: Ṣâdiq Amîn, *al-Da¿wah al-Islâmiyyah farîḍah shar¿iyyah wa-ḍarûrah bashariyyah* (*The Summons to Islam is a Required Duty and a Human Necessity*), ¿Ammân: Jam¿iyyat ¿Ummâl al-Maṭâbi¿ al-Ta¿âwuniyyah, 1982.

513 Motifs: A1482.2§, "Arabic as language of heaven;" cf. A1482.1, "Hebrew as language of heaven." See n. 81.

the righteous message to people, especially about monotheism, without receiving a scripture or direct gospel from God. These include the following prophets who appear with varying degrees of frequency in contemporary oral traditions: Nûḥ (Noah), Ibrahîm (Abraham, "father of the prophets" and "God's bosom friend"), and 'Ismâ¿îl (Ishmael, father of the Arabs), 'Isḥâq (Isaac, "father of the Hebrews"), Lûṭ (Lot), 'Ayyûb-*el-mùbtalâ* (Job—"the afflicted"), Yûsìf (i.e., Yûsùf/Joseph), Selimân (i.e., Sulaymân/Solomon), and Dâwûd (David). Literary religious sources cite other Prophets mainly in agreement with biblical literature.[514] In common and folk usages a *rasûl* (sing.: of *rùsùl*, i.e., a messenger of God) may also be called a *nabî* (prophet), but a *nabî* is not referred to as a *rasûl*. A prophet or a messenger of God is typically titled *sayyìdnâ* (i.e., our lord/master), this label is also used to refer to cardinal angels (e.g., *sayyìdnâ* Gibrîl, *sayyìdnâ* ¿Aizrâ'îl, etc.); in the singular form (i.e., *sîdî*) the label signifies *a saint* (see n. 150). Associated with the concept of prophecy is that of *mù¿gizàh* (miracle). All of God's messengers and prophets were endowed with *mù¿gizât* (miracles) suited to the arts of their times as proof of the validity of their prophethood: Moses' miracles were magic like in order to refute the craft of Pharaoh's magicians, Christ's were medical like in order to refute the Greco-Roman medical feats of his era, and Mohammad's were linguistic (al-Qùr'ân) in order to nonplus the eloquence of pre-Islamic Arabs. In current folk culture, however, miracles associated with prophets are virtually boundless, and are not restricted to any single type. God granted his prophets the privilege of *shàfâ¿àh* (intercession) on behalf of sinners—as in the case, for example, of Prophet Idrîs (Henoch) interceding on behalf of the two fallen angels Hârût and Mârût. Only Prophet Mohammad has the right to *ash-shafâ¿àh al-¿ùẓmâ* (the great-intercession with God on behalf of his entire nation on the Day of Judgment). Thus, according to this doctrine, all Moslems, it is believed, will enter Paradise; even Moslem sinners will eventually be admitted.[515]

In Arab folk cultures, especially as expressed in belief narratives, Moses appears primarily as *kalîmu-Allâh* (the One-who-Spoke-with-God). The act of his addressing God and receiving God's response is referred to as *munâgâh* (affectionate-exchange, mystical "romancing," or "love-talk"). In many folk stories, important questions are answered when God himself replies to Moses' inquiries on behalf of other humans.[516] Similarly, Christ's appearance in Moslem folk cultures revolves around the events of Virgin Mary's miraculous conception, the Second Coming, and his power to resurrect the dead and secure an eyewitness report of ancient historical events. Such an account was received by Christ from Hâm (Hem), son of Noah, regarding the

---

[514] For example, al-Tha¿labî, *Qiṣaṣ*, al-Kisâ'î, *Qiṣaṣ*. See App. 37.

[515] Motif: Q174.0.1§, "*'ash-shafâ¿ah al-¿uẓmâ*: God grants person (prophet, saint) the boon of releasing souls from hell."

See Ibrahîm al-Gibbûsly/al-Gibâlî [??], "al-shafâ¿ah." In: *Nûr El-Islam Review*, Vol. 1, No. 10 (1931), pp. 771–779. See also n. 561.

[516] Motifs: A182.3.0.1, "God speaks to Moses from bush;" A182.3.0.1.2§, ‡"God speaks from heaven to Moses (at the bush)." See n. 52. Also see El-Shamy, *Folktales of Egypt*, p. 259.

Also see El-Shamy's *DOTTI*, Tale-types 460 A, *Journey to God to Receive Reward.*

exact characteristics of the ark and the *ṭûfân* (deluge).[517] Prophet Solomon had command over the Jinn and the wind, and understood the language of animals. He is a cardinal figure in para-religious practices dealing with jinn (often labeled "magical"). Solomon's oath, seal, and mere name are believed to have the utmost power over the jinn, especially the infidel ones.[518] There is some evidence in oral traditions to suggest that a number of wise functions of the ancient Egyptian god Toth, especially mollifying the Evil Eye, have been assigned to Prophet Solomon in oral traditions. (See Section VIII.C)

Alexander the Great (al-Iskandàr *al-'akbàr*) is a curious historical figure who appears in Moslem religious traditions as a prophet; he is usually nicknamed "*dhu-l-Qarnàyn* (i.e., the dual-horned)." Early Moslem writers give numerous "reasons" for ascribing this unusual physical characteristic to Alexander; their explanations, however, seem to be only symbolic interpretations of being named "the dual-horned."[519] Alexander appears in folk tradition as the main figure in religious legend cycle revolving around his "horns;" his quest for immortality and conquests. Portions of this legend cycle can be traced to the Gilgamesh epic; Alexander plays the role of the Babylonian hero-god Gilgamesh in seeking immorality, but fails to attain it.[520]

III.B.2. *ṣaḥâbàh* (The Prophet's Companions)

The *ṣaḥâbàh* (the "Companions" of Prophet Mohammad) are viewed as the next class (stratum) in the hierarchy; the adjective *saḥâbî* (or, *min eṣ-ṣaḥâbàh*) designates a person belonging to this group of extraordinary but venerated personages. Four companions served as *khulafâ'* (caliphs, i.e., successors to the Prophet) in leading the Moslem nation, and thus each became the head of the state in which religious and temporal matters were inseparable. This period is termed, *¿aṣr al-khulafâ' ar-râshidîn* (the Era of the Rightly Guided Successors), and is commonly referred to, in contemporary lore, as the "Days of the Companions." Three of the companions who succeeded the Prophet, i.e., Abu-Bakr (632–634 AD), ¿Umar (Omar, 634–644 AD), and ¿Uthmân (644–656 AD), appear only sporadically in oral folk traditions. In folk

---

[517] See al-Ṭabarî, *Târîkh*, Vol. 1, p. 181.

Tale-type: 792§, *Resuscitation in Order to Learn Truth* (*Get Information about Past Events*). The tell-tale corpse (mummy). Motifs: E177.1§, "Resuscitated man relates eyewitness account of past event(s);" E177.2§, ‡"Resuscitated person relates own experience (life-history) when alive;" E190.2§, ‡"Decomposed corpse (in forms of dirt, dust, smoke, gas, etc.) reconstitutes (reassembles) self;" E190.5§, ‡"Resuscitated person cannot remain alive because his predestined livelihood had already been consumed (during his normal lifetime);" J1151.3§, ‡"Posthumous witness: testimony acquired or given by deceased person."

[518] For graphic illustrations of such icons, see Ḥasan, Sulymân Maḥmûd, *al-Rumûz al-tashkîliyyah fî al-siḥr al-sha¿bî* (*Material Cultural Symbols in Folk Magic*; Cairo: Hay'at Quṣûr al-Thaqâfah, 1999).

[519] Motifs: F511.3, "Person with horns;" F511.3.2§, "Alexander, 'the dual-horned;'" cf. A131.6, "Horned god."

For an example, see al-Tha¿labî, *Qiṣaṣ*, p. 200. Also see Ions, *Egyptian Mythology*, p. 96; cf. n. 117.

[520] Heidel, *The Gilgamesh Epic*, pp. 80–88. See "How el-Khidr Gained Immortality," in H. El-Shamy, *Folktales of Egypt*, No. 23, pp. 271–272.

circles, Abu-Bakr is more often cited together with the Prophet, especially as his road-companion during the flight from Mecca to Medina to escape persecution; Omar is the most recurrent as an independent personage. A belief narrative cycle about Omar typically portrays him as the embodiment of piety, justice, humility, austerity, and self-abnegation—qualities, which the majority of Moslems believe must characterize the conduct of their rulers. The opulent lifestyle of contemporary heads of Islamic states is constantly evaluated and contrasted with Omar's life, with the inevitable result that modern rulers are found to be extravagant, ostentatious, and impious.[521] Only ¿Alî Ibn 'Abî-Ṭâlib, the Prophet's parallel paternal cousin, son-in-law, and fourth Caliph, has acquired among folk groups wide currency and special appeal beyond his historical roles. In Egyptian lore, ¿Alî has been transformed into a culture-hero of near divine proportions and solar mythological characteristics.[522] The veneration of ¿Alî in folk culture is opposed by formal Sunni orthodox religious institutions; the orthodox view ¿Alî only as a favorite companion of Prophet Mohammad, with no supernatural qualities, save those accorded saints. ¿Alî's cult has been institutionalized and in many cases formalized in the Shiite sect in Islam, which is virtually nonexistent in Egypt.

Additional substrata, such as *tâbi¿în* (lit.: followers, i.e., successors of the companions) and *tâbi¿î et-tâbi¿în* (successors of the successors of the companions), are specified in literary traditions.[523] Characters in these substrata, however, have little or no circulation among folk groups and do not seem to appear in contemporary oral lore.

III.B.3. Saints: Moslem *'awliyâ* ("God's Favorites") and Coptic *shuhadâ* ("Martyrs")

Saints and the concept of sainthood are pivotal forces in the lives of traditionary groups in Egypt. In daily life saints are typically referred to by the imprecise generic title of *mashâyìkh* (sing.: *shaikh*), a word that may also denote elders, head of a profession or craft, clerics, as well as shamans and magicians; or, less often, as *'awaliyâ'* [u-Allâh] (sing.: *walìyy*[-of God]). Towns, city quarters, villages, hamlets, and even desert roads, are strewn with thousands of simple shrines as well as intricate cenotaphs lavishly built for deceased individuals believed to possess saintly qualities.[524] In the minds of their own followers saints are organized into hierarchies, according to the pattern of

---

[521] Motif. W35.4.1§, ‡"'Justice of Omar ([Ibn al-Khaṭṭâb]).'"

Cf. Tale-type 919§, *Exemplary Justice.* Stories about ideal application (by king, judge, etc.) of law. (See El-Shamy, *MITON.*)

[522] See Goldziher, *Vorlesungen über den Islam*, A. and R. Hamori, trs., pp. 227–229.

[523] This phenomenon is also reflected in al-Nabhânî's classification of his collection where he designates two separate categories of saints; one is labeled "the Companions, who are 54 in number" (*karâmât al-'awliyâ'*, Vol. 1, pp. 13–164); the other is that of "Those named Muhammad" (Vol. 1, pp. 164–384); the rest of the saints are not labeled and are listed alphabetically from "*'Alif* to *Yâ'* (A to Y [i.e., A to Z])."

[524] Lane, *Modern Egyptians*, pp. 236, 240. The official view concerning burial in mosque is that it is not permissible (*lâ yagûz*): see *al-Azhar*, Vol. 8, No. 11 (1940) p. 502; and Khalîfah, *al-Dâr al-barzakhiyyah*, pp. 321–324.

distribution of other saints in the region and the saint's own perceived potency and sphere of his/her specialization. No community whose members consider it of proper size and status can afford to remain for long without a saint as one of its religious institutions (see App. 38). Consequently, some saints have national constituency while the majority are hardly known beyond the confines of the immediate community in which they lived prior to their death. Saints—like ancient local deities—are believed to protect the community and endow it with their *barakàh* (blessedness, grace);[525] they are called on in daily life to assist with every imaginable task, and situation.

In daily usage, a Moslem saint is referred to as *shaikh* (sheik) so-and-so, or as *sîdî* (my lord/master) so-and-so; occasionally, a saint may be further characterized as *sayyìdî-wa-sayyìdùk* (my lord and yours). As noted earlier,[526] the adjective *sayyìdnâ* (lit.: our lord or our master), when accompanied by a specific name, is used to designate only a prophet or an angel. A more specialized title used to designate a saint is *waliyy* (pl.: *'awliyâ'*). The word *waliyy* denotes a person who is a protege or a favorite of God. Meanwhile, saints in general are typically labeled as *el-mashâyìkh* (sheiks), *el-'awliyâ* ([God's] proteges or favorites), *rigâl-i-llâh* (i.e., *rigâlu Allâh*, men of God), and *en-nâs bitû¿ rabbìnâ* (people who belong to our Lord). A female Moslem saint is typically titled *shaikhàh* (female sheik), or *es-sayyidàh* (lady, a word that may also designate a female descendant of the Prophet, the masculine form of *sàyyid*); notably, the word *sìttî* (my lady, my chieftainess, or mistress—the feminine form of *sîdî*) does not seem to be commonly used by Moslems in this regard.

Also associated with sainthood is the concept of holiness (*al-qùdsìyyàh*), persistently assigned to Moslem "saints" in academic literature. It should be indicated here that although believers may in effect hold a saint as a "holy" person, this English adjective does not correspond to how saints are cognitively characterized by their own followers. A Moslem saint is never labeled *muqàddàs* (holy); only rarely are objects or traces belonging to such a saint characterized, perhaps hyperbolically, as "holy."[527]

Among Copts, a saint is typically referred to as *shahîd* (martyr; pl.: *shùhadâ*), or as *qiddîs* (lit.: one made holy, i.e., a [Christian] saint). Clergymen who had held formal ecclesiastical church ranks and are believed to be saints are referred to by their official titles, e.g., "*al-'ànbâ* Brâm" (Abba Brâm).[528] A female saint is referred to as *sìt* (lady, chieftainess, or mistress), *qiddîsàh* (i.e., female saint—with holy implications, saintess) or by the borrowed word *sànta* (i.e., female saint).

Members of each denomination characteristically use the title assigned to a saint by members of the faith to which the saint belongs. Thus, a Moslem, like a Christian,

---

[525] Lane, *Modern Egyptians*, p. 226.

Motifs: D1706§, ‡"A person's *barakah* (*mabrûk*-person, blessed person);" V220.0.5.2§, ‡"Saints are endowed with blessedness (*barakah*)."

Cf. the belief in reptiles as protectors: n. 197 and 367.

[526] Burton translates *sayyidnâ* correctly as "Our Lord." See n. 197.

[527] For reference to rare occurrences of the concept of holiness, see n. 25. Yet, in accordance with academic literature (Thompson's *Motif-Index*), a saint is occasionally referred to in newly developed motifs as "holy man" (e.g., Motif: F415.1§).

[528] *'Anbâ*: defined as "a high, ecclesiastic title of the Coptic church, preceding the names of metropolitan, bishops, patriarchs, and saints." (Hans Wehr, *A Dictionary of Modern Written Arabic*)

would refer to Mâr Girgìs as "*mâri* Girgìs," and to Saint Theresa as "*sànta* Traizàh;" while a Copt, like a Moslem, would refer to Abu-l-Ḥaggâg (in Luxor) as "*sîdî* Abu-l-Ḥaggâg," and to *shaikhàh* Shafîqàh (in Salamoan, Daqahliyyah) as "*shaikhàh*." (See App. 39)

The state of *wilâyàh* (sainthood) is closely associated with the concept of *khawârìq* (i.e., the breaking of the natural order of things and, therefore, generating "the supernatural"). The act of producing supernatural occurrences (*al-'ìtyân bi-l-khawâriq*) includes the solicitation and production of deeds by humans that violate the laws of nature. These deeds may be sacred or antisacred; a saint is believed to be capable of generating either type. A saint's supernatural deed is labeled *karâmàh*, a word that suggests that the feat constituting a violation of the natural order is an act of generosity (*karàm*) or benevolence from God toward the "saint" (thaumaturgic gift). Such a feat may also be called *bùrhân* (proof, evidence). A *karâmàh*, therefore, is *not* a miracle but a miracle-like manifestation of God's boon by a person who is not a God's prophet.

Generally speaking, there is no practical (typological) difference between a saint's *karâmàh* (miracle-like manifestation) and a prophet's *mù¿gizàh* (miracle). Generating miracles is the function of God's messenger or prophet; they are always accompanied by a *dà¿wàh* ("call for" a new religion, or proclamation of being a God's prophet); whereas generating a *karâmàh* is the function of a saint, and is not accompanied by such a call or proclamation. The occurrence of supernatural manifestations (*khawârìq*) is constantly reported in both learned and folk traditions, in both religious and nonreligious contexts. Consequently, ulama (religious scholars) differentiate between two basic types of supernatural manifestations.[529] The first is supernatural deeds generated at the hands of humans obedient to God; while the second is supernatural deeds brought about by *sìḥr* (magic) and "obedience to Satan," thus constituting acts of disobedience to God (see Sections II.B.2 and II.B.3). They maintain that both types exist side by side and endorse the first but censure or condemn the second.

In addition to these two types of the supernatural, a third may be designated as essentially nonsacred: it occurs neither through the agency of humans obedient to God nor humans obedient to Satan. Although this sort of the supernatural occurs, like everything else, only within God's Will, the connection between its taking place and the forces that trigger it may best be characterized as mechanical (see Section VIII).

The first type of supernatural occurrences due to obedience to God includes a prophet's *mù¿gizât* (miracles; see Section III.B.1) and saint's *karâmât* (miracle-like manifestations). The second type designates supernatural feats generated by unbelievers and is called *'ìstìdrâg* (i.e., leading on). The word *'ìstìdrâg* suggests that God allows practitioner of the sacrilege, whom He empowered to generate supernatural feats through the help of Satan and other sacrilegious forces, to perform these

[529] For ulama's views, see al-Nabhânî, *karâmât al-'awliyâ'*, Vol. 1, pp. 14–16.

supernatural deeds so that they may make the case against themselves through their persistence in refusing to see the right way. Thus, they are permitted this power as a rope by which "to hang themselves"—so to speak.[530] The word *karâmàh*, on the other hand, denotes that something is within the power of a human being because he/she is favored by God. Protagonists of the belief in the actuality of sainthood—such as al-Nabhânî—cite four types of "evidence" to support the reality of saints' *karâmât* (miracle-like manifestations). These are: (a) the Koran; (b) the Prophet's *ḥadîth*, or Tradition; (c) precedents in the lives of pious people who were not prophets or messengers of God; and (d) "rationality." For theologians, as well as for *all* good believers, "rationality" is a function of the first three: the Koran, tradition, and precedents, the truthfulness of which is always taken literally. Rationality and, consequently, credibility, are also functions of the source, i.e., the person who reports the account. Contemporary commentators on the supernatural in religious literature (i.e., the miraculous) typically state that had it not been for the sources to which the reports are attributed, all of whom are truthful and irreproachable, it would have been hard to believe these occurrences.[531]

In his encyclopedic index on saint's miracle-like manifestation, Yûsuf al-Nabhânî lists approximately 1400 saints whom he had located in printed sources,[532] or identified in oral traditions known to him. A preliminary survey reveals that approximately 3 percent of those saints are females. The supernatural feats of those saints span some fourteen centuries beginning with the period of the companions of Prophet Mohammad and to modern times. The number of saints specified by al-Nabhânî is relatively small considering that the presence of an enshrined saint is considered a necessary institution for every village, district, or town, and is indicative of its status. The manifestations that al-Nabhânî cited are, in his words, "no less then ten thousand." He outlines twenty-five major types of saints' manifestations, ranging from the ability to resuscitate the dead to the capacity to consume huge amounts of food.[533] A great many of the saints' manifestations have also been attributed to prophets as miracles. Quoting al-Tâg al-Subkî (d. 1370 AD), al-Nabhânî outlines twenty-five out of "more than one hundred types"[534] of saints' miracle-like manifestations and cites precedents to substantiate the realness of each type. These types are

---

[530]Koran, 7:172, 68:44. See al-Thaᶜlabî, *Qiṣaṣ*, p. 108.

Motif: A102.16.1§, "*'istidrâj* ('leading on'): God allows disbelievers powers so that they may have no excuse for their disbelief."

[531]Motif: U90§, "Credibility depends on characteristics of source."

[532]See al-Nabhânî, *karâmât al-'awliyâ'*, Vol. 1, pp. 9–11.

[533]Motifs: F632, "Mighty eater. Eats whole ox at time, or the like;" F632.0.1§, ‡"ways of mighty eaters: gluttonous eating."

See Littmann, "Aḥmed il-Bedawî, ein Lied auf den ägyptischen Nationalheiligen." In: *Akademie der Wissenschaft und der Literatur; Geistes und Sozialwissenschaftlichen Klasse*, (Wiesbaden: 1950, No. 3), pp. 50–123, esp. pp. 61–62; El-Shamy, "The Story of El-Sayyid Aḥmad El-Badawi with Fâṭma Bint-Birry: part I", pp. 152–153.

[534]al-Nabhânî, *karâmât al-'awliyâ'*, Vol. 1, pp. 48–60.

1. Bringing the dead back to life (resuscitation).[535]
2. Conversing with the dead.[536]
3. The sea parts becomes dry for them; and walking on water.[537]
4. Matter's "self-transformation" into another matter for them (i.e., wine becomes honey [for their sake]).[538]
5. Earth (i.e., distance) shrinks for them.[539]
6. Communicating with inanimate objects and with animals (cf. No. 8).
7. Curing disease and body defects (see App. 49).[540]
8. The obedience of animals and inanimate objects to them (cf. No. 6).

9–10. Folding time (i.e., making a long time period very short), and extending time (i.e., making a short time period long).[541]

11. God grants their requests.
12. The holding of the tongue (i.e., they become silent) and releasing the tongue.
13. Drawing together hearts that were in conflict (i.e., causing true reconciliation).
14. Foretelling some of the unknown/the unseen.
15. Abstaining from food and drink for a long time.
16. Solving problems (e.g., rain followed a saint wherever he went, while another sold rain for money).
17. Being able to consume huge amounts of food.[542]
18. Being protected against eating sinful (tabu) food.[543]
19. Being able to see, from behind veils (i.e., sight barriers [cf. X-ray sight]).[544]
20. The awe-inspiring appearance (*hàybàh*) that some of the saints possess (such awe may cause some to die instantly or to confess their sins).[545]
21. Being protected by God against the evil of those who wish to harm them; the evil turns out to be good.

---

[535] Motifs: E121.4, "Resuscitation by saint;" cf. E30, "Resuscitation by arrangement of members." See Maspero/El-Shamy, *Ancient Egypt*, No. 2, p. 34.

[536] Motif: E545.7, "Holy man converses with entombed dead."

[537] Motifs: D1551, "Waters magically divide and close. [Parting of the sea];" V228.5.1§, "Saint walks upon water." For an ancient occurrence of this motif, see: Maspero/El-Shamy, *Ancient Egypt*, No. 2 p. 29.

[538] Motifs: F1074.1.1§, ‡"Illicit (sinful) food becomes licit (legitimate);" D477.0.1.2, ‡"Wine becomes honey;" F1074.1.1.3§, ‡"Liquor (wine) becomes sweet punch, water, or the like."

[539] Motifs: D2121.4, "Magic journey by making distance vanishes. The road is contracted or the earth folded up;" cf. V225, "Saint in several places at once. [*min'ahl-al-khuṭwah, min al-'abdâl*]."

[540] Motifs: V221, "Miraculous healing by saints;" D2161.5.1, "Cure by holy man [(person)]."

[541] Motifs: D1858§, ‡"Time prolonged or shortened supernaturally (days become years, years become moments, or the like)."

[542] See n. 533.

[543] Motifs: V223.2.1§, "Saint detects unclean (tabu) food;" cf. V228.0.1§, "Infallibility (*¿iṣmah*: immunity from errancy) of *imâms* and certain saints."

[544] Motif: F642.3, ‡"Person can see through opaque objects. [(X-ray sight)]."

[545] Motifs: F580§, "Person of awe-inspiring appearance;" V206.1§, ‡"Awe-inspiring sacred person."

22. Being able to assume different form.[546]
23. Knowing the valuable contents of the earth (i.e., water, treasurers, etc.).
24. Great accomplishments in a short time and against overwhelming odds (such as carrying on with teaching, counseling, worshiping, and thinking while suffering from as many as thirty illnesses; or composing a great number of books).
25. Being immune to poison.[547]

Numerous other "types" of *karâmât,* such as solving a difficult riddle,[548] siring a child when at a very advanced age, and other aspects of "spiritual" and physical prowess recur throughout al-Nabhânî's collection as well as oral traditions. Some saints were described as having *karâmât* confined to harming others (*'adhâ*).[549] Thus, it may be concluded that although *karâmàh* is perceived as an act of benevolence (boon) by God toward a human being (i.e., saint), the application by that human of that gift to other humans or creatures need not necessarily be benevolent. A great number of the saints' manifestations are attributed, characteristically, to prophets as miracles (e.g., Moses' parting of the sea, and Christ's walking on water and resuscitating the dead). These two themes of the supernatural associated with sainthood on the one hand and with prophethood on the other are viewed as mutually complementary. Thus, al-Nabhânî states: "Whatsoever was a *karâmàh* for a saint, is a *mù¿gizàh* for His [(God's)] Prophet,"[550] and that "sainthood is a less specific type of prophethood."[551] Therefore, all prophets are considered *'awliyâ* (saints) as well. Among the broader folk groups, however, a prophet is viewed as *waliyy* of (i.e., a protege of) God, without being considered a member of a specific category of saints.

For the majority of traditionary groups, saints are further grouped and stratified in an all-inclusive system. As in the case of lesser angels and jinn, this system is known and maintained mainly through written sources and "specialists" within Sufi (mystic) organizations. One informant who used to regularly attend *ḥalqât dàrs* (instructional circles) in his village's mosque stated,

> We hear from our *mashâyìkh* (religion teachers, or preachers) that all *'àhl-i-llâh* (God's people, [i.e., saints]) are [classified into] *ṭabaqât* (strata, classes). First: there are the *'aqṭâb* (Axes, [sing.: *qùṭb*]); there can be only one Axis during a given *zamân* (era).[552] Second: there are the *'a'immàh* (imams, leaders of an entire community of believers); there are

[546] Motif: D631.1.5§, "Saint as shape-shifter (changes shape at will)."

[547] Motifs: D1840.1.2, "Saint invulnerable to poison;" V223.3, "Saint can perceive thoughts of another man and reveal hidden sins."

[548] See al-Nabhânî, *karâmât al-'awliyâ'*, Vol. 2, p. 58. (Motif: V223, "Saints have miraculous knowledge.")

[549] Motif: V220.0.8.2§, ‡"Harmful saint: uses his supernatural powers to cause mischief."
One such case is cited in al-Nabhânî, *karâmât al-'awliyâ'*, Vol. 2, p. 20.

[550] al-Nabhânî, *karâmât al-'awliyâ'*, Vol. 1, p. 11.

[551] al-Nabhânî, *karâmât al-'awliyâ'*, Vol. 1, p. 86.

[552] Mot. V220.0.1.2§, ‡"Limited number of cardinal saints may exist at one time or era: one, four, seven, forty, or the like, e.g., four *'aqṭâb* (Axes), four *'awtâd* (Pegs), seven *'abdâl* (Substitutes), etc."

only two imams during every era. Thirdly: there are the *'awtâd* (pegs, wedges); there are four of them during each era; each one of them is [situated] in one corner of [the planet] Earth. Fourth: there are the *'abdâl* (substitutes), each one of them is in a region of the seven regions of the Earth; there can be only seven *'abdâl* at one era; they were called *'abdâl* because God granted each one of them the ability to go to a distant location and leave in his own place a[nother] person—who looks exactly like himself. . . . Fifth: there are the *nuqbâ'* (deputies or marshals)—there are twelve of them during a given era. . . . These [deputies] are followed [in rank] by those who are called *er-Ragabiyyîn* ("Ragabites");[553] they are men of God ... but the condition of sainthood comes to them with the coming of the [Islamic lunar] month of Ragàb and leaves them with the departure of that month. Then there are *'àhl el-khaṭwàh* (people of the step) [who can be in more than one place at the same time].[554] Then, there are *el-malâmâtiyyàh* (those who blame themselves [excessively]), and *es-suwwâḥ* (those who tour [throughout the world], i.e., wanderers, travelers, tourists),[555] *al-fuqrâ'* (the poor), *al-mubtalîn* (the afflicted). There are also others, such as *rigâl el-fatḥ* (men of the opening or conquest). . . . In all, there are seventy-seven of these *ṭabaqât* (classes). But—("Glory be to Him Who never [commits an] oversight")—I cannot recall the rest.[556]

Another informant was able to name sixteen different groups corresponding to a considerable extent to those cited above; he, however, added two major facets.

There are *awliyâ* (saints) who take [i.e., derive their state of sainthood] from one of God's prophets. It is [thus] stated that they are on the heart of our lord Adam, may peace be upon him, or our lord Ibrahîm *al-khalîl* (Abraham: God's bosom friend). . . . That means that the group of saints all put together have been granted [by God] as much *¿ilm* (knowledge) and *'îmân* (faith) as our lord Adam or our lord Moses [Abraham]. . . . There are forty *waliyys* (saints) "on the heart of" our lord Noah, and seven [saints] "on the heart of" our lord Adam. . . . There is also one *khìtm el-'awlyâ'* (seal of saints); he ... [will be] the last saint—just like our lord Mohammad is "the seal of prophets"—he is our lord ¿Îsâ-'Ibnu-Maryàm (Jesus, son of Mary), he is a prophet and a saint at the same time. He will return [from Heaven] to Earth as *al-Masîḥ al-mùntaẓàr* (the awaited or anticipated Christ, [i.e., the Messiah])—after corruption and sin have prevailed everywhere. He will also be the last *waliyy*. After that, the Day of *Qiyâmàh* (End of World) would commence.[557]

Evidently, the *khìtm* of sainthood is another appellation for *al-Masîḥ al-mùntaẓàr* (the anticipated Christ, or the Messiah), who will come after *al-Masîḥ ad-dàggâl*, or *al-Masîkh* (the impostor Christ, i.e., Antichrist). It is worth noting here that

[553]Motif: D1719.9.3§, "Saintly power only during a certain month yearly (*'er-Ragabiyyîn'*)."

[554]Motif: V225, "Saint in several places at once. [*min 'ahl-al-khuṭwah, min al-'abdâl*];" V225.1§, ‡"Saint as *'abdâl*: leaves a replica of himself in his place and wanders away."

[555]Motif: P426.2.3§, ‡"Wanderer (*'sawwâḥ'*), usually due to mystical urges or disappointments especially in love."

[556]Informant: hajji Draihem, male, middle aged, from a village in middle Nile Delta; went on pilgrimage seven times (see n. 191).

Motif: V220.0.2§, ‡"Classes of sacred persons (prophets, saints) according to amount and source of gnosis (knowledge) they possess."

[557]Informant: S. Ghunaim, a 54-year-old policeman of Bedouin origin from Fayyûm Province, in November 1969.

according to formal Islamic beliefs, Christ was not crucified, but he was elevated to heaven and a substitute that looked like him was crucified in his place (Koran, 4:157); according to some accounts, the look-alike substitute was an angel in human form sent by God for that purpose. Christ will not die until he has fulfilled his mission after his second appearance.

These two oral traditional accounts seem to be partial recollections from an intricate, multiplex, and clearly esoteric system of classification maintained by institutionalized para-religious Sufi organizations. A detailed presentation of this system—where eighty-eight classes are specified—is given in al-Nabhânî's collection of saints' miracle-like manifestations.[558] Like the folk system, al-Nabhânî starts with a single "Axis" at the peak of the pyramid, and angles out at the base to include all the true believers. Thus, at least in principle, all good God-fearing men and women may be viewed as saints.

Among Copts, the beliefs and related practices concerning saints are not markedly different from those embraced by Moslems. Both religious systems (faiths, denominations) in Egypt recognize the principle of sainthood as God's boon to a particular person. However, Coptic informants state that a saint possesses the power of *shafâ;àh* (i.e., performing miracles). In this respect, the use by Copts of the word *shafâ;àh* (intercession) seems to denote the same concept involved in the word *karâmàh* as used by Moslems, in addition to the privilege to intercede with God or Christ on behalf of sinners. Copts also believe very strongly in Virgin Mary's right to *shafâ;àh* in the hereafter and vehemently oppose what they see as the denial by Protestants of this important doctrine.[559] By contrast, the majority of Muslims reserve the right of intercession to Prophet Mohammad on the Day of Judgment. Believers in certain powerful saints, and members of Sufi-brotherhoods claim this privilege also for the saints they venerate and for the heads of Sufi-brotherhoods. In this context, the followers are labeled *maḥâsîb* (proteges) of such-and-such saint. A person perceived in this manner is typically thought of as a member of a mystically privileged or favored social group: *mìn maḥâsîb* ... (i.e., of the proteges of ...).[560]

Belief in the effectiveness of numerous saints who belong to Islam, Christianity, and Judaism seems to be shared by significant numbers of members of each faith.[561]

---

[558]al-Nabhânî, *karâmât al-'awliyâ'*, Vol. 1, pp. 69–96.

[559]As expressed by Ibrâhîm Ḥ., 64, Copt, public scribe (main informant, July, 1970, Col. H. El-Shamy); other sources include: Gamâl B.B., engineer, from southern Egypt; and Fakhrî ??, janitor at a western college in Cairo, from southern Egypt. (See n. 304)

[560]Motif: V521.2.2.1§, ‡"Saint favors his (her) proteges (*maḥâsîb*)."

The concept may also be applied to a person who seems to be lax in exercising religious duties so as to signify that the person concerned still is a true believer and that his/her sins will be nullified by the intercession of the protecting saint or saintess, e.g., see: Nagîb Maḥfûẓ, *al-Sukkariyyah* (Cairo, 1960), p. 93, where a sister applies the privilege of being "*mìn maḥâsîb sayyidnâ* al-Ḥusain" to her brother who was being twitted for his negligence of performing prayers. (See also n. 515 and 569)

For *Mu;tazilàh*'s rejection of the principle of *shafâ;àh*, see: A. Schimmel, "Shafâ'a". In: *EI*, Vol. 9, pp. 177–79; and Goldziher, *Vorlesungen über den Islam*, A. and R. Hamori, trs., pp. 90–91.

[561]With reference to saints, Lane (*Modern Egyptians*, pp. 234–235) commented: "... Muslims, Christians and Jews, adopt each others superstitions, while they abhor the leading doctrines of each others faith." Similarly, discussing "Axes, Saints, and Culture Heroes," El-Shamy noted,

The tomb of "*sîdî* Abu-Ḥaṣîrah," located near Damanhûr city of Egypt, and the tomb of "*shaikh* el-Kabbûsî," on the outskirts of the district of el-Ma¿âdî (Maadi, a southern suburb of Cairo), are Jewish; the latter is particularly attractive to infertile women. Meanwhile, "*sànta* Traizàh" (i.e., "Sainte Teresa"), whose cathedral is located in Shobrâ, a district of Cairo, and "*Mâri* Girgìs" (i.e., Saint George), whose churches are in Old Cairo and in Mît Damsîs in the Nile Delta, are Christian; their shrines contain thousands of marble and brass plaques expressing the gratitude of Moslem as well as Christian believers who were benefited from the powers of their sainthood. Numerous Moslems credit Mâr Girgìs with ridding them of the evil spirits that had possessed them by slaying these demons.[562] In this respect, local folk cults hold sway over established formal religions.

Formal Sunni religious institutions recognize the validity of the principles of sainthood and miracle-like manifestations.[563] However, these institutions condemn the development of a cult (*¿ibâdàh*) around the person of a saint and equate such cultism (cult beliefs) and ritualistic practices with idolatry.[564] Nonetheless, the veneration of saints is not only as powerful as ever but is also spreading both vertically to upper classes and horizontally to more communities.

III.B.3a. *Ṣûfî* brotherhoods and other religious organizations

From a social organizational perspective, the nonformal belief subsystem concerning sainthood gives rise to one of the few voluntary associations found in traditional Arab societies: the *ṭarîqàh* (religious brotherhood, "path"), especially in the Sufi context.[565] In contradistinction to Christianity, Moslems see their faith as based on a direct relationship between a person and God, without any intermediary of formal or informal priesthood. Sunni Islamic clergy makes no use of the formal bureaucratic

---

> In a number of cases, belief in the powers of a national saint cuts across religious lines; Saint Theresa and Mar Girgis, for example, are two Christian saints who are also revered by Muslims. (*Folktales of Egypt*, p. 149)

More recently, Sengers (*Women and Demons*, 48 note 14.) reported:

> Every Sunday morning Muslim and Christian women stream into a well-known church in old Cairo to consult a priest that works there about magic.

See also Amîn, *Qâmûs*, p. 246, and n. 245, above.

[562] See El-Shamy, *Folktales of Egypt*, pp. 158–159.

[563] See: Y. al-Digwî's fatwa on "karâmât al-'awliyâ' (Saints' miracle-like manifestations)" In: *Nûr al-Islâm*, Vol. 1, No. 10 (1931), pp. 764–770.

[564] *al-Azhar*, Vol. 11, No. 6, pp. 342–343. Also see Goldziher, *Vorlesungen über den Islam*, A. and R. Hamori, trs., pp. 238–240 (No. 6). It is worth noting that M.Y. Mûsâ et al., the translators and editors of the Arabic edition (under the title *al-¿Aqîdah wa al-sharî¿ah fî al-Islâm*), recognize the validity of intercession and sainthood, and argue that "it is not as much of a threat as [. . . Goldziher] portrays it" (p. 261 /eds.' note).

Cf. al-Azhar's stand on the cult of *zâr* as *kùfr* (sacrilege), n. 331–333.

[565] See M. Gilsenan, *Saint and Sufi in Modern Egypt: An Essay in the Sociology of Religion* (Oxford: Oxford University Press, 1973).

hierarchy found in the Christian church especially Catholicism. However, there are formal offices such as *qâḍî al-quḍâh* (chief justice), and the *mùftî* (mufti, consulting ecclesiastical authority on sharia). Yet, the cults of sainthood and religious brotherhoods, its twin companion, project within their respective organizations patterns of strict stratification that enjoy remarkable pervasiveness and stability. A number of beliefs contribute directly to the strength of Sufi religious organizations, cohesion among their members, and, consequently, give heads of Sufi-brotherhoods controlling influence over followers.

A Sufi organization has a pyramidal hierarchical structure similar to that of saints especially at the peak. A *khalîfàh* (assistant-*shaikh*) in a northern Egyptian village[566] described this hierarchy, starting at the bottom of the pyramid.

1) *murîd* (lit.: "aspirant," i.e., candidate, novice)
2) *darwîsh* (dervish), whose main function is to participate in *zìkr* performances
3) *wakîl* (deputy)
4) *naqîb* (marshall)
5) *khalîfàh* (lit.: successor; i.e., assistant-*shaikh*), the main Sufi "official" appointed to represent the *shaikh* in a district; when a district is too large to be served by one "assistant-*shaikh*," a *khalîfàt al-khulafâ* (head assistant-*shaikh*) is appointed
6) *shaikh siggâdàh* (sheik of the [prayer]-rug)[567]
7) *shaikh el-mashâyìkh* (sheik over the sheiks, i.e., the uppermost sheik). Due to its critical role among the masses and its far-reaching political implications, the holder of the office of "Sheik over the sheiks of Sufi-brotherhoods" has, since the middle of the 1950s, been a presidential appointee.

A powerful sense of belonging and an esprit de corps exist among members of a given brotherhood within the broader, but seemingly impersonal, "nation of Islam." A member of a Sufi-brotherhood characteristically refers to himself in relationship to other members as "We all are *'awlâd ṭarîqàh* (lit.: children of the [same] path, i.e., Sufi-brotherhood);" "we are *'awlâd madàd* (children of the same [mystical] source for reinforcements and support);" and that in all the 366 paths that exist, "the sheik-of-the-path [in each brotherhood] is a 'father' to all its 'sons.'"[568] In daily life, heads of religious clubs instruct eagerly receptive followers on such matters as marriage, business enterprises and partnerships, employment, travel, personal relations, and even on how to perform conjugal functions and meet religious duties concerning coition and the family. Their political influence is also far reaching. Sufi sheiks define for their followers whether a ruler or a government is legitimate or illegitimate, and

[566]Informant: as given by *shaikh* Abu-¿Abdàh in April 1969, Kafr-Zaytûn. Motif: V455§, "Hierarchy within religious orders."

Also see "darweeshes" in Lane, *Modern Egyptians*, pp. 240–246; and Amîn, *Qâmûs*, p. 199.

[567]Described as "the spiritual throne." See Amîn, *Qâmûs*, p. 199.

[568]Informants: Yâsîn 'A., from the village of "Wilâd ¿Inân," Suhâj Governorate, nonliterate (Monday, May 5, 1986), works as *nâṭûr* (night-guard) in the state of Qatar; hajji Draihem, (as in n. 191); and others.

instruct them to act in certain political manners by supporting or opposing that government.

On matters of salvation, they are believed, as mentioned earlier, to protect their followers from Satan's instigation (see n. 172). Furthermore, the patronage by the Sufi-*shaikh* over his followers is not restricted to worldly life but is believed to extend to the hereafter. Sufis cite a verse from Koran (Koran, 17:71) in which it is stated, "One day We shall call together all human beings with their (respective) Imams" as irrefutable proof that a "*shaikh*" of a brotherhood (i.e., an imam) will advocate his followers' cases from the moment their souls depart their bodies up to and including the final trial on the Day of Judgment, and that God bestowed upon him the privilege of *shafâ¿àh* (intercession) on behalf of sinners within the ranks of his own followers. Thus, some Sufi laymen and women—it is believed—will be admitted to Paradise without trial while others will have their sins forgiven merely on the strength of an imam's testimony or pleading on their behalf. This Sufi view is often syllogistically extended to the four imams who founded the four *madhâhìb* (Islamic Schools of Jurisprudence).[569]

Consequently, membership in a Sufi-brotherhood is a lifelong commitment. A brotherhood guards its membership jealously; switching from one "path" to another is not permitted and is viewed as a form of apostasy. "Children" of each organization are expected to strictly observe the hierarchy and chain of command within their own organization as well as the spheres of influence of other brotherhoods. Thus, attempting to persuade a member of another brotherhood to join one's own, or to seek help from the head of a different "path"—even from a saint—would constitute a violation of the proper rules of "brotherhood" conduct.[570]

---

[569] al-Azhar's formal stand on the practice of "pleading with the deceased pious persons (*al-tawassul bi al-mawtâ al-ṣâliḥîn*)" is that it is disputed and remains unsettled (*maḥàll khilâf*). However, commoners have crossed over the boundaries and treat such persons as idols (*'awthân*); such treatment is unanimously judged as sinful (*muḥarrm bi 'igmâ¿ al-muslimîn*). See *al-Azhar*, Vol. 12, No. 10 (1941), pp. 583–586. Also see n. 446.

al-¿Idwî (*Mashâriq*, p. 265) poses the following rhetorical question:

> If the sheiks of the Sufis assist their followers/aspirants (*murîds*) in all affairs and situations of hardship (*shadâ'id*)—[both] in the here-and-now and in the hereafter, how, then, could this not be the case with the Four Imams of the Schools of Jurisprudence (*madhâhìb*)—who are the pegs (*'awtâd*) of Earth, and the Legislator's [i.e., God's] guardians over His Nation.

Cf. intercedence, n. 515 and 560.

On the four schools of Islamic Jurisprudence, see n. 215.

[570] al-Nabhânî (*karâmât al-'awliyâ'*) reports cases illustrating the spheres of influence among saints:

1) According to one account (Vol. 1, p. 267), the wife of a *shaikh* got ill; she called on [the arch-saint] el-Sayyid el-Badawî for help. He appeared to her [in vision] and said, reprimandingly

> "Don't you know that you are in the protection of a man ([husband]) of the 'majors/seniors' (*ḥimâyàt ragùl min al-kibâr*) [. . .] and we do not like him who calls on us while he is 'under the protection of one of the [major] men' (*fî mawḍi¿ ¿aḥad al-rigâl*)."

2) In another case (Vol. 1, p. 547):

In spite of their numerousness, doctrinal and ritualistic differences, and inter-group rivalries, Sufi-brotherhoods have enjoyed considerable longevity and success in maintaining group cohesion and the allegiance of their individual members. This accomplishment often serves as a model for individuals and other social organizations to emulate. A folk proverb stated, "Every sheik has his own *ṭarîqàh* (i.e., path, or [equally acceptable] 'way of doing things')." This saying is typically applied in situations in which uniformity, or *'ijmâ¿* (unanimity)—ideally preferred or required in Islamic political ideology,[571] is unattainable; the proverb also indicates that differences are to be expected and should be tolerated. Secular political parties in Egypt, it has been noted, copied the general pattern of membership developed by Sufi-brotherhoods so as to attain the same level of commitment from their partisans.[572]

III.C. *en-nâs* (People), and Folk Theories of Personality

The bulk of people are also perceived in a highly stratified manner according to a number of criteria that include religiosity and piety, blessedness and being a *sàyyìd* or a *sharîf* (feminine: *sharîfàh*) through claimed kinship to the Prophet (i.e., being of the *'ashrâf,* also called *sâdàh*, which literally means "the Honorable," and "the Masters," respectively). The attribute and consequent social status of *al-sharîf* is inherited from the mother, even the father is not a *shrîf.*[573] Frequently, ordinary persons who have been subjected—in spite of their piety—to God's trials through misfortune, pain,

---

As a head of Sufi brotherhood (shaikh *tarîqah*) tried to initiate an aspirant (*mubâya¿at tâlib*) according to the Shâdhlî-Brotherhood manner, the wall of the room where the action was taking place split open and another *shaik* came out of it and declared: "This is my aspirant (*murîd*)." Al-Khiḍr reconciled the two of them. Motif: D1932.1§, ‡"Wall opens to let in a being with supernatural power (afrit, ogre, magician, etc.) and then closes after he exits." Typically this theme appears in fantasy tales (*ḥawâdît*, i.e., *Märchen*); cf. Tale-type 894, *The Ghoulish Schoolmaster and the Stone of Pity.* (See El-Shamy, *MITON*, pp. 3 n. 17, 14 87, 60)

3) In a third case (Vol. 1, p. 551),

A sheik's heart appears as cock and preys on the heart of sheik al-Ḥummuṣânî (Heart = gnosis). The latter "was deprived of all his saintly assets (*suliba gamî¿ ḥâlih*)."

The theme of a person transforming himself into a cock appears in Tale-types 325, *The Magician and his Pupil.* [Apprentice overcomes evil master's magical arts]; and 325A§, *Contest in Magic between Two Master Magicians* (see "The *Maghrabi's Apprentice*," in El-Shamy, *Folktales of Egypt*, No. 6, p. 38, 45–46). Motifs: cf. B766.6.4.1§, ‡"Aggressive cock," F401.3.7.5.1§, "The 'rooster of the jinn;'" Z194.3.1.2§, ‡"Cock: quarrelsomeness."

[571] It has been argued that *'ijmâ¿*, as an aspect of religion, has led to "political quietism." (Motif: P501.2§, "Political indifference (quietism)"). See M. Berger, *The Arab World Today*, (New York, 1964) pp. 15, 39, 157. Also see L. Carl Brown, *Religion and State: The Moslem Approach to Politics* (New York, 2000), esp. pp. 68–75.

[572] Amîn, *Qâmûs*, p. 293. Also cf. Lane, *Modern Egyptians*, p. 243. For literary portrayal of *¿ahg*-giving, see M. Ḥusayn Haykal's *Zaynab*, pp. 256–264.

[573] al-¿Idwî, *Mashâriq*, pp. 159, 160.

Motifs: P70§, "Sherifs: Descendants of Prophet Mohammed (*'ashrâf, sâdah*);" P71§, ‡"Rights (privileges) of *'asharâf*;" P72§, ‡"Restrictions on personal conduct in interacting with a *sharîf* (Hashemite)."

See El-Shamy, *GMC*; and *MITON*. Also cf. n. 233 and 585.

and severe illness are viewed as constituting a special category of saints, or simply as favored by God; they are labeled *al-mùbtalîn* or *'aṣḥâb el-balâwî* (the afflicted) and are usually viewed as constituting a distinct "realm" labeled "*dawlàt al-mùbtalîn* (the 'nation' of the afflicted)."[574] Prophet Job (*sayyìdnâ* 'Ayyûb) is considered the major figure in this group. Also, the weak, the poor, the persecuted, the oppressed, and the afflicted are held to be special classes of people favored by God and to be "God's chosen people."

Another traditional subschema for grouping humans is essentially natural (or positivistic, if one wills) but instrumental to supernatural applications; it seeks to distinguish various *'anwâ¿* ("types," sorts) of people without necessarily establishing a hierarchical structure among the categories constituted by the individuals included within each "type." In the view of shaman-*mashâyìkh* (healing practitioners) who follow literary traditions, the bulk of humans may be grouped into three major types according to their *ṭibâ¿* (propensity, temperament, or character); a person can be either *hawâ'î* (lit.: aerial, i.e., whimsical and easily influenced), or *tùrâbî* (lit.: dirt/dust prone, or earth prone, i.e., one who is melancholic), or *nârî* (lit.: fiery; i.e., one who is explosive, temperamental, or aggressive); some sources add a fourth type *mâ'î* (lit.: aquatic, "watery").[575] This classification is of particular relevance to practitioners who seek to harness the jinn and lesser angels, or exercise similar "magical" activities. In rituals that require using a human medium to act as a conduit between the practitioner and the supernatural entities to be contacted (such as *fàtḥ/ḍarb el-màndàl*),[576] the practitioner specifies that the medium must be of the "aerial" (*hawâ'î*) type of character (evidently, because the aerial person would be more receptive to the shaman's suggestions and less likely to assert his or her own viewpoints and conclusions). (See Section II.B.2a; also see App. 19)

Physical attributes and the behavior of a person are usually correlated, mainly in congruence with cognitive components of the belief system. The majority of these components have supernatural qualities; others are not directly interconnected with the supernatural realm. As a traditional field of knowledge ("ethnoscience"), this process of judging character is labeled *firâsàh* (pḥysiognomy), and has been responsible for generating and/or maintaining highly stereotypical characters, with

---

[574]Nagîb Maḥfûẓ applies this concept to interpersonal attitudes among members of a middle-class Cairene family. In the third stage of his Trilogy, he describes how an "afflicted" sister who lost her husband and sons to an epidemic was reluctant to bestow upon her stepbrother a notable position in the "state of the afflicted," since he lost only one infant son who died before reaching the age of a full year. (See: *al-Sukkariyyah*, p. 28)

[575]Motifs: W250.1§, ‡"Basic types of personality (character) reckoned according to the elements;" W250.1.1§, ‡"Personality type: *hawâ'î* ('aerial,' whimsical, impressionable);" W250.1.2§, ‡"Personality type: *turâbî* ('earth-prone,' melancholic, passive);" W250.1.3§, ‡"Personality type: *nârî* ('fiery,' explosive-aggressive);" W250.1.4§, ‡"Personality type: *mâ'î* (Aquarius, aquatic, 'watery')." Cf. n. 480. See also El-Shamy, *MITON*.

It should be pointed out that these folk classifications overlap only in part with astrologers' planetary system.

[576]al-Bûnî, *Manba¿*, p. 308.

distinct ascribed social roles (behavioral expectations).[577] Some sources suggest that a person's external features (i.e., being handsome, ugly, etc.) probably correspond to the appearance of that person's soul; this conclusion is reached deductively on the premise that since this is the case with the angels and jinn both of whom are thought to be incorporeal (etherial), the same principle should also apply to a human soul for it is incorporeal as well.[578]

The religious account of the creation of Adam from various types of clay (see Section I.D) and the creation of Eve out of Adam's rib provide yet another system that explains the distinct and varying nature of various peoples and individuals. The broadest and most pervasive of such correlations is that of being a male and strength, on the one hand, and being a female and weakness on the other; a companion theme is that of correlating maleness and candor, as opposed to femaleness and *kàyd* (wiliness, deception, snare-setting).[579] The frequency and level of intensity with which these themes are typically expressed in folk cultures are more in agreement with para-religious literature than with formal religious dogma exemplified by the account of the expulsion of Adam and Eve from Paradise.[580] Similarly, age, gender, and the visible effects of aging, are also physical attributes correlated with behavioral patterns. Almost invariably an old man is angelic, while an old woman is satanic.[581]

A man with a clearly visible *¿ìrq hâshimî* (a Hashemite [blood] vein) in the temple would be viewed as highly emotional, yet good-hearted and compassionate; if excited, he may throw a temper tantrum. Lore portrays these physical and behavioral qualities as attributes of Imam ¿Alî Ibn Abî-Ṭâlib, of the Hâshim lineage, a companion, cousin, and son-in-law of Prophet Mohammad. Therefore, such behavior emanating from an ordinary person with similar physical traits should be accommodated. No instances of this quality have so far been reported with reference to a woman.

---

[577] Motif: W251.1§, "Physiognomy (*firâsah*): the judging of character."

On the concept of "role," see: El-Shamy, "Folkloric Behavior," p. 65.

[578] Khalîfah, *al-Dâr al-barzakhiyyah*, p. 240.

[579] It may be pointed out that the Koranic sentence (12:28) is: "Truly, mighty is your [*present women's*] snare," not: "Truly, mighty is *women's* snares." The statement is uttered by a high official of pharaoh's court at his wife and her friends concerning their false accusation of Joseph; meanwhile, the statement ". . . feeble in deed is the cunning of Satan" (4:76) is a mere assertion of Satan's evil powers. Juxtaposing the two assertions is illogical (italics added).

Motifs: G303.9.0.1.1§, ‡"'Truly the wiles of Satan are weak' (when compared to women's powers)—[Male's interpretation of scripture];" V384§, ‡"Extreme interpretations of holy text;" V384.1§, ‡"Extreme religious interpretations of religious dogmas concerning females (as social category)."

On extreme interpretations of sacred dogma cf. n. 579. The theme is subject to a cycle of narratives revolving around the question as to whose wiles (*kàyd*) are more potent: men's or women's? See *DOTTI*, Tale-type 1406A§, *Youth (Man) Learns about the Wiles of Women.*

Motifs: H1376.10§, "Quest: learning women's wiles;" H1597§, "Contest of the sexes: match between man and woman to settle claim as to whose wiles are more potent;" H1597.3§, "Sage declares his inability to deal with women's wiles;" H1598.2.1§, "Contest between old-woman and Satan in trouble-making."

[580] See El-Shamy, *Tales Arab Women Tell*, pp. 11–12. Also see n. 491.

[581] See Motifs: G303.10.5, "Where devil can't reach, he sends an old woman;" N1.8§, ‡"Betting between man and supernatural being (jinni, devil, ogre, etc.)." Also see Tale-type: 1353, *Old Woman as Trouble Maker* beats the devil.

Other physical qualities appear frequently in association with character traits: being excessively tall or short, for example, is linked to being moron-like or crafty respectively; a folk truism states: "*kùllu ṭawîlen habîl, wa-kùllu qsîren makîr* (every tall person is moronic, and every short person is crafty)." A child with lines on palm of hand that read "17" or "71" is assumed to be "innocent" and would be suitable as a medium in certain rituals.[582] A person with a *¿ain qawiyyàh* ("strong" or "blunt-eye," i.e., who stares and does not shy away or be stared down) is considered *qalîl el-ḥayâ* (lacking in sensitiveness, i.e., brazen, shameless, unblushing), and is more likely to be perceived as having an evil eye; this is also the case with persons who are cross-eyed or, less frequently, blue eyed—especially females needy in the area represented by the object being stared at (such as a child, a handsome face, being healthy or successful, a precious piece of jewelry, or the like).

A person's line of descent, the character of a person's kinsmen and their social rank are, likewise, important factors in judging that person's character. A girl, for example, is more commonly believed to "*tiṭla¿-li* (grow up to be like, i.e., take after)" her own mother and/or her own paternal aunt (*¿ammàh*, father's sister); a boy is believed to take after his maternal uncle (*khâl*, mother's brother) and only rarely after his own father or his father's brother (the boy's paternal uncle).[583] The concept of *makhwàl* (maternal – "unclehood") is critical in assigning the character of a man as well as that of an entire kinship group. A related concept is that of the legitimacy of one's birth; an *'ibn-ḥarâm* (child of sin, i.e., a mulatto, bastard) is typically assumed to have a bad character. The expression: being *'ibn-ḥalâl* (i.e., to be of legitimate birth) is used idiomatically to mean that a person has a good character: honest, kind, and compassionate. The expression to be an *'ibn-ḥarâm* may also indicate that a person is too individualistic, too competitive, and lacks kindness and compassion.[584] An alternate appellation for the latter pair of contrasting character attributes, as determined by one's descent, is *'aṣîl* (noble, or of good origins), and *khasîs* (vile, or of bad origins).[585]

The ability of a person to solicit God's help is also linked to kinship ties, especially to being a parent. In this respect, a parent's *dà¿wàh-li* (i.e., *dù¿â'*: a prayer for, a supplication on behalf of), or *dà¿wàh ¿alâ* (i.e., a curse, lit.: a prayer [aimed] against)

---

[582] Amîn, *Qâmûs*, pp. 381–382, (based on Lane's account). Cf. See Lane, *Modern Egyptians*, pp. 268–275 (cited in n. 240).

[583] See al-'Azraqî, *Tashîl al-manâfi¿*, p. 226.

Motifs: W251.2.1§, "*makhwal* ('maternal-unclehood') as basis for judging character;" P293.2.1.1§, "Boys take after their maternal-uncles;" cf. P294.0.1.1§, "Girls take after their paternal-aunts."

Also see El-Shamy, *Brother and Sister, Type 872∗*, pp. 48, 61 notes 54, 73, 77; and El-Shamy, "*Traditional Structure of Sentiments in Maḥfûẓ's Trilogy*," p. 64.

[584] See Tale-types: 655, *The Wise Brothers*. The king [(judge)] is bastard; and 655B§, *Which of the Three Brothers May Not Inherit?* See also: "Which Muhammad?" in El-Shamy, *Folktales of Egypt*, No. 16, pp. 108–114, 266–267 (cited as Tale-type 655A, *The Strayed Camel and the Clever Deductions*).

[585] Motif: W3.0.1§, ‡"Conduct (behavior, traits) of person of noble character."

See El-Shamy "'Noble and Vile' or 'Genuine and False,'" "Erwiderung." In *Fabula* 24:3–4 (Berlin/New York, 1983), pp. 341–346. Also see Tale-type: 920G§, *Deeds Betray Ancestry (Origins)*. Cf. n. 575.

For a contrast between *'aṣl/sharaf* (honor, nobility), on the one hand and "power," on the other in anthropological literature, see el-Aswad, *Religion and Folk Cosmology*, p. 55 note 21.

his or her own child is believed to be particularly effective, regardless of the parent's own standing with God. Thus, when uttering such a plea, a mother usually speaks for herself and for God by stating, "My heart and my God are content with you," or "My heart and my God are angry at you." Therefore, parents' approval of the conduct of their child is considered crucial for that individual's well being; it is a *barakàh* (blessedness, grace). A person is allowed to disobey his/her parents only if they ask for what would "anger God" (i.e., a cardinal sin). The success of a person may be typically attributed to parents' prayers, while constant failure may be attributed to parents' curse, or simply, their discontent with their son or daughter.[586]

Other categories of kinship ties are manifested less frequently, and the rationale for the link between the quality of the tie and its effects is not clear. For example, some shamanistic practices require a medium, usually a boy whose maternal uncle and paternal uncle are one and the same person, or a boy who is the seventh male child of a seventh male child.[587]

A mystical bond is assumed to exist among blood relatives. This bond is also believed to be responsible for the yearning among closely related family members for one another. Thus, father and daughter, father and son, mother and son, mother and daughter, brother and brother, sister and sister, as well as brother and sister—who do not know of the existence of this kinship tie between themselves—will be attracted to, and will yearn for each other unwittingly, especially when they accidentally meet. This assumption is expressed in the recurrent truism: "*ed-dàm yeḥìn* (lit.: blood feels affectionate toward, i.e., blood yearns, or longs for . . .)." Conversely, this blood bond is also believed to repulse incestuous desires, especially between brother and sister, or—though less frequently—between parent and child.[588] It is believed that in a situation where incest is about to be committed "*ed-dàm yìz¿aq*" (blood [will] howl) or, "*ed-dàm yùnfùr*" (blood [will] revolt or bolt away, i.e., will experience revulsion, or turning away in disgust). Consequently, sleeping arrangements, especially in large families with limited living space, do not necessarily separate male and female siblings. Although

[586]Motifs: M411.1, "Curse by parent;" P245§, "Parent's prayer (blessing or curse) always answered;" M511.1.1§, ‡"Supplication: blessed be the womb and the loins that brought person into being."

[587]Motifs: D2161.5.7, "Cure by seventh son of seventh daughter;" N207§, ‡"Person (animal, bird) with certain qualities fated to perform task;" N207.1§, ‡"Task can be performed only by person with certain social qualities (e.g., kinship ties, name, or the like);" N207.2§, ‡"Task can be accomplished only by person with certain physical qualities (e.g., lines on palm of hand form certain figures);" L111.5.1§, "Child born of brother-sister incest as hero: 'Son of own maternal-uncle.'" (Also see n. 305)

[588]Hasan El-Shamy, "The Brother-Sister Syndrome in Arab Family Life," p. 319; and El-Shamy, *Tales Arab Women Tell* Nos. 39, pp. 300, 43, 314.

This theme appears in a variety of additional folk narrative situations across the Arab world and among various religious groups. See El-Shamy, *DOTTI*: Tale-types 674A§, *Incest Averted: Talking Bed* (or another bedroom item) gives warning—(brother about to marry his sister); and 674B§, *Incest Averted: Identifying Token Discovered.* (Usually, brother and sister are involved.) Also cf. n. 322, where a sister succeeds in deceiving her brother into committing incest with her.

Motifs: H175.7§, "Blood-relative mystically recognized: 'Blood's yearning,' 'Blood's howling;'" N681.3.0.5§, "Incest believed impossible. Mystically repulsive: 'Blood's howling,' 'Flesh repels [same] flesh;'" T405.3.0.2§, "Groom experiences mystical paralysis at defloration of bride: they prove to be brother and sister."

fear of *el-ghalàṭ* ("the-erring") and the Devil's instigation that would lead toward the temptation of committing incest are present, the belief that such a horrendous act *cannot* take place (as a matter of natural human order) alleviates the effects of these concerns.[589]

The broad field of such folk beliefs of correlating physiological and other personal attributes to patterns of behavior may be called "implicit personality theory," or folk theory of personality and character.[590] These beliefs play an important role in setting traditional individualistic and social behavioral patterns on all levels of social interaction. In certain respects they constitute patterns of culturally sanctioned stereotyping.

---

[589]Numerous female informants placed their trust in the principle expressed in this belief and live accordingly. For example, Faṭima I. ¿A. (see "The Possessed Husband and His *Zar*," in El-Shamy *Folktales of Egypt*, No. 41, p. 175) described a case of brother–sister incest, which had taken place in her community:

> A girl got pregnant by her brother. The family claimed that she was only "ill" and, subsequently, said that she died. The brother was still walking around as if he had done nothing [wrong].

When asked about the sleeping arrangements for her own children (two brothers and one sister), Faṭima reported that they—like the majority of members of the population in Egypt and in other Arab countries—had shared the same bed till they were in their late teens or early twenties. Faṭima emphatically expressed her confidence that such "a thing" (i.e., incest) *could not* have happened because "flesh will not be (sexually) attracted to the same flesh." See El-Shamy, "The Brother–Sister Syndrome . . . ," pp. 319–320 (Motif: P605§, "Living (sleeping) arrangements within the household").

For a detailed description of typical sleeping arrangements in a low-income Egyptian family's home, see "Living Quarters" in: El-Shamy, *Tales Arab Women Tell*, pp. 34–35.

Also see Hasan El-Shamy, "Sibling in the Arabian Nights." In: *Marvels & Tales: Journal of Fairy-Tale Studies*, special issue: *The Arabian Nights: Past and Present*, U. Marzolph, guest ed. (Wayne University Press), Vol. 18, No. 2 (2004) pp. 170–186, especially, "Tales Illustrating the Brother–Sister Relationship," pp. 179–181; "Tales Illustrating the Brother–Sister-Like Relations," pp. 183–185. Cf. H. El-Shamy, *Brother and Sister: Type 872**.

[590]Motifs: W251§, "Beliefs (theories) about composition of character (personality). Implicit (folk) Personality Theory." W256§, "Stereotyping: generalization of a trait of character, from person to group (and vice versa)," which is further analyzed into following subdivisions: W256.1§, "Stereotyping: ethnic and national traits;" W256.2§, "Stereotyping: social class;" W256.5§, "Stereotyping: racial traits;" W256.6§, "Stereotyping: gender (sex) traits;" W256.8§, "Stereotyping: physical traits and appearance—general," etc.

CHAPTER IV

Deified Humans

THE ARCH-SAINTS

A number of historical religious figures seem to have acquired a new status and additional characteristics within the broader religious belief systems in Egypt. These new attributes transcend the "historical" roles these figures had played during the periods when they were actually alive. The title: *'ashkhâṣ mù'aṣnamûn* (idolized individuals, or "deified persons")—though bound to be repulsive to those who adhere to the beliefs—indicates that the new powers bestowed by folk groups on these figures seem to duplicate those of ancient deities and are incongruent with basic Islamic teachings.

IV.A. *el-'arbaȩah el-'aqṭâb* (The Four Axes [of the World])

Beside the single Axis (*qùṭb*, arch-saint) who exists during every period or era (see Section III.B.3, and n. 131), four such persons seem to have acquired cultural institutionalization. They are believed to continue to exist as "culture-heroes"[591] with powers that are more superior and diverse than those of average saints. These four are labeled *al-'aqṭâb* (the Axes); thus, they have been designated as arch-saints. Each one of the four has his own domain in the universe, powers, and fixed position within the hierarchy. Sometimes these axes are described as *ḥawwâshîn* ("those who shield," or "preventer" [of disaster]), *'àhl el-ghàwth* (those who bring relief at times of crisis), or *el-mùddàrrakîn* or *el-mudàrrakîn* (i.e., those each of whom has been assigned a

[591] Motif: A500, "Demigods and culture-heroes."

daràk, a precinct, or a domain of responsibility and power).[592] They are also viewed as those who "support" or carry the planet Earth. In the words of one informant, each one of the four is carrying Earth from *¿arqûb* (an ankle [as in a cow's]),[593] an image that suggest direct descent from ancient Egyptian cosmology. In the ancient sacred account (myth), four gods supported the legs of Nut (sky in the form of cow).[594]

The usual order of the arch-saints hierarchy is: *es-sayyìd* el-Badawî (d. 1276 AD), Aḥmad er-Rifâ¿î (d. 1175 AD), Ibrâhîm ed-Disûqî (d. 1298 AD), and ¿Abd al-Qâdir al-Jîlâni—typically mispronounced, "el-Kilâni" (d. 1166 AD).[595] All were actual historical figures and contemporaneous with the eras of the Mongol conquest and the Crusades, periods marked by high social and cultural tensions and upheavals. Of these four only ed-Disûqi is indigenous Egyptian by birth. Informants state that each one of the axes has one half of the power of his immediate superior. In this respect, el-Badawî is the undisputed chieftain.[596] Similarly, each axis (arch-saint) has its own abode. The most salient and recurrent of these areas of residence is *er-rùb¿ el-kharâb* (the Ruined Quarter [of Earth]), where—according to some accounts—all reptiles and scorpions are believed to emanate and reside; it is also the abode of er-Rifâ¿î, who is believed to have power over these creatures. That power and the craft of being able to ferret out snakes, be immune to their poison, and the ability to heal scorpion stings and viper bites are institutionalized and passed on to members of a Sufi-brotherhood called er-Rifâ¿iyyàh (i.e., those who pertain to arch-saint er-Rifâ¿î); a professional snake-trapper is labeled a "*rifâ¿î.*"[597]

---

[592]The word "mudàrrakîn" is often mistaken, even by native speakers of Arabic, for "*mudrikîn,*" i.e., "catching-up with" or "supporting" Earth. See Lane, *Modern Egyptians*, p. 232. Also see El-Shamy *Folktales of Egypt*, p. 149, and n. 131.

[593]Informant: "Abu ¿Abbâs," 70-year-old male, Cairene (recorded in January 1970).

In *Folktales of Egypt* (p. 141), I translated inaccurately the theme of the four arch-saints carrying/supporting the world by each holding a *¿arqûb*, as "each one of them is staying in his isthmus, *carrying the world at its four ends*" [emphasis added]; see "The Supreme Saints Cycle," pp. 149–153, especially Nos. 29–30. The translation given here of the word *¿arqûb* is more accurate. Also see Amîn, *Qâmûs*, p. 183.

[594]Ions (*Egyptian Mythology*, p. 50) describes the mythical event as follows:

> As she rose higher and higher, Nut began to tremble, so a god was appointed to steady each of her four legs, those chosen being Horus, Set, Thoth and Sopdu, representing the four quarters of the earth.

Motif: A665.2.1.1.1§, ‡"Horus, Set, Thoth, and Sopdu stabilize the legs of Nut (sky)."

Associated with this ancient concept is the current Motif A841.5§, "*al-'aqṭâb*: four Arch-saints at world-quarters support (carry) planet Earth: (el-Badawî, er-Rifâ¿î, al-Jîlanî/'el-Kilânî', ed-Disûqî)," cf. A501.2§, ‡"Four demigods."

See Lane (*Modern Egyptians*, pp. 229–230), where it is argued that belief in four *kuṭbs* is "a vulgar error."

[595]The name "el-Kilânî" (i.e., al-Kîlânî) is recurrent in Egyptian lore and is likely to be associated with the profession of "measuring"-grain; the root *kyl/kâla* signifies: to measure.

[596]See "When the Arch-Saints Exchanged jobs," in El-Shamy, *Folktales of Egypt*, No. 29, pp. 150–151, 277–278; and El-Shamy, "The Story of El-Sayyid Aḥmad El-Badawî with Faṭma Bint Berry," pt. II, pp. 145–146. Cf. Amîn, *Qâmûs*, p. 37.

[597]See Lane, *Modern Egyptians*, pp. 229–234. Amîn (*Qâmûs*, p. 199) assigns the capability of charming snakes to the "Sà¿diyyàh" brotherhood of dervishes.

Many of the current beliefs associated with axes are also found in ancient Egyptian belief systems about deities. As mentioned above, the contemporary belief in four deity-like arch-saints supporting the Earth, each holding "her/it from an ankle," has an ancient Egyptian counterpart.[598] The four arch-saints also participate in the *diwân* (Council [of Saints]) that preside over the affairs of the world (see Section IV.D.2, and n. 636). Infrequently, a major figure or a powerful local saint may replace one of the four axes; whenever this occurs, the displaced axis is one of the latter two. Such is the case with the Imam esh-Shâfi¿î (d. 820 AD), who was reported by a few informants as an axis. Esh-Shâfi¿î, whose school of sharia (religious jurisprudence) is the most widely adopted in Egypt, seems to have retained his role as a supreme judge until today; numerous Egyptians write letters addressed to him soliciting his justice. A study shows that esh-Shâfi¿i has become associated in the minds of numerous social categories of modern Egyptians with the same functions, which ancient Egyptians assigned to Osiris, the judge of the dead in the hereafter.[599] However, esh-Shâfi¿i is not normally viewed as one of "the Four Axes," or a supporter-bearer of the world.

IV.B. *el-Khiḍr* (The Green-One), St. George, Elijah

Another supernatural human character is el-Khiḍr (whose name suggests: the Green-one). Unlike the other arch-saints whose occurrences in social life are documented, el-Khirḍ's historical origins are ambiguous and shrouded in associations with heathen, Jewish, or Christian characters.[600] Legends present him as the companion and relative (usually the *'ibn khâlàh*, son of the maternal aunt/maternal cousin) of Alexander "the Dual-horned." According to one account, el-Khiḍr was merely a companion of Alexander on his quest for the "Fountain of [Eternal] Life," which is located in "the Dark Quarter" (*er-rùb¿ eẓ-ẓalâm*) of Earth. But it was el-Khiḍr who accidentally stumbled into the fountain and drank from its water, thus gaining immortality.[601] Although el-Khirḍ's name does not appear in the Koran, some traditions identify him as the "pious" man (sage, seer) implied in the Koranic events associated with Prophet Moses (Koran, 66:83). A number of informants explain: "el-Khiḍr was

---

[598] See Section IV.D.2, and n. 594.

[599] E.F. Wente, "The Contendings of Horus and Seth." In *The Literature of Ancient Egypt*, W.K. Simpson, ed. (New Haven, 1972), p. 123/145. Motif: E545.19.3§, "Addressing the dead by means of letter (written message)."

See S. ¿Uways, *Ẓâhirat 'irsâl al-rasa'il 'ilâ ḍarih al-'Imam al-Shâfi¿î* (*The Phenomenon of Letter-Sending to the Shrine of Imam al Shafi¿î*), Cairo, 1965. Also see "Letter to the 'Justice of Legislation,'" in El-Shamy, *Folktales of Egypt*, No. 36, pp. 162–164, 281–282; cf. App. 40.

[600] Motif: F440.3§, "al-Khiḍr (the Green-one): benevolent spirit associated with vegetation and water."

For the role of al-Khiḍr in Muslim belief systems, see A.J. Wensinck (1927). Also see El-Shamy, *Folktales of Egypt*, p. 271, notes to Tale No. 23. Cf. data related to n. 52 and 117.

[601] Motifs: H1376.7, "Quest for immortality;" H1376.7.1§, ‡"Failure on quest to gain immortality (e.g., Gilgamesh, Alexander, etc.)."

Tale-type: 774R§, *Why a Certain Mortal is Immortal.* Account of how immortality was gained by person or animal.

See: "How el-Khidr Gained Immortality," in El-Shamy, *Folktales of Egypt*, No. 23, pp. 137–138, 271–272; al-Tha¿labî, *Qiṣaṣ*, pp. 122–124, 127–128; and Lane, *Modern Egyptians*, pp. 231–232, note 1.

the son of the sister of our lord Moses. He traveled with our lord Moses to learn from him."[602] Other literary traditions identify el-Khiḍr as "Elyâs" (Elijah); in parts of Iraq both names are combined into "Khiḍr-Elyâs."[603]

El-Khiḍr is not one of the axes but has many of their capabilities, especially omnipresence. As one Nubian informant put it: "He is like them, but he is alone,"[604] a viewpoint also reported by Lane.[605] Unlike the four Axes, el-Khiḍr appears frequently in *ḥawadît* (*Märchen*, i.e., fantasy tales) as the hero's helper. This phenomenon suggests that his persona is more widely spread than the personas of the four axes and perhaps antedates them.[606]

Among the Copts of Egypt, el-Khiḍr is viewed as the Moslem variant of Mâr Girgìs (St. George); he is also an enshrined Coptic saint. However, in the central and eastern parts of the Arab world, each of the Moslem el-Khiḍr and the Jewish Elijah is separately regarded as a saint. His (or "their") shrines can be found in several locations.[607] No shrine for el-Khiḍr has been reported to exist in Egypt.

IV.C. *'Imâm* ¿Alî

Imam ¿Alî Ibn Abi-Ṭâlib is Prophet Mohammad's parallel paternal cousin and son-in-law; he married the Prophet's daughter, Faṭimah. ¿Alî was also the fourth Caliph (656–661 AD) and was assassinated by the rebel Kharijites in the year 661 AD. In Egyptian folk culture, Imam ¿Alî plays two completely distinct roles: a formal historical role as a religious and political figure, and a folkloric role as a saint with a cult typical of a culture-hero or demigod; frequently the two roles overlap. Although ¿Alî's two sons, el-Ḥasan and el-Ḥusain—also labeled: "al-Ḥasanain" (the two Ḥasans),[608]

---

[602] Informant: Ḥesain Abu-Aḥmad/Abu-¿Âdel (see n. 263).

[603] G. Ḥabîb, "Khiḍr Ilyâs" In: *al-Turâth*, Vol. 1, No. 11 (1969), pp. 32–35.

[604] Informant: ¿Abd al-Raḥîm I., Kunûzî Nubian, 63 (New Nubia 1969).

[605] Lane, *Modern Egyptians*, p. 231, note 1.

[606] Motif: N815.3§, "al-Khiḍr as helper". See El-Shamy, *MITON*.

In his *Qiṣaṣ*, al-Tha¿labî (p. 124–127), augments the legend and states that al-Khiḍr's name was Benyâmîn (Benjamin) and traces his genealogy to the son of Sâm (Sem) son of Noah, and adds that he ran away from home because his father wanted him to marry; to please his father, he married after telling his bride-to-be of his continence (celibacy) and giving her the choice to marry him on that condition or refuse him.

Motifs: F1040.7.1§, ‡"Aversion to sexual intercourse;" P529.6§, "Nuptial prohibition (nonsexual marriage): legal device by which sexual intercourse between 'married couple' is prohibited."

For instance where al-Khiḍr appears as helper, see R. Basset, *Mille et un contes, récites & légendes arabes*, 3 vols. (Paris, 1924–1926) Vol. 3, pp. 300–302, No. 180; p. 312, No. 187; El-Shamy, *Folktales of Egypt*, No. 1, p. 7; and "The Three Robbers and el-Khidr," No. 21, pp. 128–132. Also cf. M.C. Lyons, *The Arabian Epic: Heroic and Oral Story-telling*, 3 vols. (Cambridge, England, and New York, NY: Cambridge University Press, 1995), p. 296. Cf. n. 52 and 603.

[607] Hanauer, *Holy Land* pp. 51–61; see also K. Voller, "Chidhr," In: *Archive für Religions Wissenschaft*, Vol. 12 (1909), pp. 234-284; and Brannon M. Wheeler, "Moses or Alexander? Early Islamic Exegesis of Quran 18:60–65." In: *Journal of Near Eastern Studies*, Vol. 57, No. 3 (July 1998), pp. 191–215.

[608] Lane, *Modern Egyptians*, p. 236; Littmann, "Aḥmed il-Bedawî, . . . ," p. 73, note 24 (as in n. 533). Also reported in Ammar, *Growing*, p. 222, as the "Prophet's cousins;" clearly this is an oversight—they are the Prophet's grandchildren: the children of ¿Alî, the Prophet's paternal-cousin and son-in-law.

and his daughter, Zàynàb (typically referred to or addressed as *es-sayyidàh* Zainàb)—have also been assigned the status of sainthood, they constitute a triad with a cult fundamentally different from that of their father, Imam ¿Alî. Neither the father on the one hand, nor the children on the other, play a direct or significant role in the folk legend cycle of the other. Each party seems to belong to a separate cognitive system and is characterized by a distinct set of affective (psychological) qualities that distinguished it from the other.[609]

Imam ¿Alî is depicted as pious, knowledgeable, humble, austere, and generous. The folk legend cycle that revolves around his character is predominantly heroic, chivalrous, and military like; it reflects the same Olympian psychological pattern as that of *es-sayyìd* el-Badawî. Accompaniments of ¿Alî's image in Egyptian lore include his warhorse, al-Màymûn, and his sword, dhu-l-Fiqâr (see Section II.D.2). Some Shiites—outside Egypt—believe that thunder is the Imam's laughter or voice, and lightning is the glow of his sword (or the sword of al-¿Abbâs, another major Shiite figure).[610] This belief is also found sporadically among some Sunni folk groups in Egypt. A heroic epic-like account titled Râs el-Ghûl (The Ogre's Head) accredits Imam ¿Alî with fighting jinn and converting them to Islam.[611] Meanwhile, the children of the Imam appear in Egyptian folk traditions mostly in domestic, nonheroic, and nonmilitant roles. Unlike their father, they are addressed in hymns pleading for their help in curing emotional afflictions, including those chanted in the public *zâr* rituals (see App. 28, cf. App. 31). The nature of their roles is exemplified in the *diwân* or Divan (see Section IV.D.2).

IV.D. Organization among Arch-Saints

The belief in the powers of saints (*mashâyìkh*, *'awliyâ*) and their ability to mediate with God on behalf of man influence every aspect of daily life in Egypt. Certain saints tend to be associated with specific functions in which they are believed to be particularly effective.[612]

Saints are stratified in a hierarchical structure according to their powers and national eminence. At the top of their crowded community is a special class called *'aqṭâb* (sing.: *qùṭb*), which literally means "axis" or "pole" [of the earth]. Reflecting the same

---

[609] See "'Imamu ¿Ali's Narrative Cycle" in El-Shamy, *Folktales of Egypt*, pp. 149–158. On the difference between ¿Ali's Olympian (military) feats as compared to the nonheroic (nonmilitary) deeds of his children, it has been stated,

> From a psychological standpoint, ¿Ali's deeds contrast sharply with the nonmilitary, mainly domestic deeds of his children Zainab and al-Husain. The father on one hand and the children on the other represent different cognitive and emotional systems, which rarely overlap. (p. 154)

[610] See Goldziher, *Vorlesungen über den Islam*, A. and R. Hamori, trs., p. 227.

[611] An episode from a semiliterary *sîrah* titled *Râs el-Ghûl* (The Ogre's Head). Information cited here is derived from an oral rendition by ¿A. I. Ḥasan; see informant n. 78.

[612] Motifs: V220.0.1§, "Hierarchy (stratification) of saints;" V220.0.10§, ‡"Saint with specific responsibility (e.g., saintly ability to find the lost, aid with physical labor, etc.)" e.g., V220.0.10.1§, ‡"Saint with supernatural ability to locate (guide) the lost," or the like.

structure of power within the community of saints as do the four cardinal angels in the community of angels, these human persona may be labeled as "arch-saints." They are superior to all the rest in power but possess differing amounts of it. From an ideal viewpoint, there are only four arch-saints, one for each of the four quarters (sometimes called corners) of the Earth. (See Section I.D, and n. 131)

IV.D.1. The Concept of Power and the Right to Rule: The Parallel Government

The religion of Islam is held to be *¿aqîdàh wa sharî¿àh* (a religion and a legal code). Historically, Islam has been a political ideology in addition to being a religion and a social system; its tenets, as pointed out earlier, encompasses all facets of life of an individual as well as a social group. Thus, political, civic, and moral obligations—as perceived in a secular state—are subsumed under Islamic religious obligations.[613] Prophet Mohammad founded a monotheistic faith and headed a political state based on the precepts of that faith. After his death the office of the *khalîfàh* (Caliph), which literally means "successor [to the Prophet]," was founded. The Caliphate required that its holder lead the Moslem nation in all aspects of life, particularly the religious and the political spheres.[614] Early caliphs, labeled *al-râshidîn* ("the [four] Rightly Guided Successors") are perceived to have fulfilled both the sacred and the seemingly secular functions of their office. Ensuing caliphs, starting with the Omayyad Mu¿âwiyah (661–680 AD), are believed to have deviated from the righteous path and disregarded the prerogatives of the office they held. Thus, for the bulk of Moslems a caliph who had no right to the office, or who sinned—by drinking liquor, committing injustices, for example—is a ruler who ceased to be the head of the Nation (State) even though he continued to hold the political offices; such a ruler had only secular overt power, but lacked the sacred covert power.

Currently, among folk and other traditionary groups, the right of a person to rule is judged in terms of their conception of the caliphate as combining both religious and secular powers, and the capacity of that person to embody and enforce that principle of fusion between the sacred and the secular. Consequently, folk groups divide power into *ẓâhìr* (lit.: overt, external, or apparent), which is secular or nonreligious, and *bâṭìn* (lit.: internal or covert). Also two types of *ḥùkm* (rule or government) are specified: *ḥùkm eẓ-ẓâhìr* (overt rule), which is a secular nonreligious system of government, and the *ḥùkm el-bâṭìn* (covert rule), which is the religious system of government. The *bâṭìn* rule is held to be the legitimate real power, whereas *ẓâhìr* rule is a deviation from the legitimate way and, consequently, it is only a facade.[615]

A ruler may command power only in the *ẓâhìr* without possessing *bâṭìn* power; this is the case with kings, presidents, prime ministers, and other officials of a secular

[613] Islam is typically characterized as "*¿aqîdàh wa shrî¿àh*" (religious faith and political law).

[614] See *EI*², Vol. 5, p. 7; also see Goldziher, *Vorlesungen über den Islam*, A. and R. Hamori, trs., pp. 182–186.

[615] To be differentiated from the *bâṭiniyyàh* school of interpretation. On this school, see Ronart and Ronart, *CEAC*, Vol. 1, pp. 86, 573–574.

government. On the other hand, a religious figure may muster the *bâṭin* power without having any secular authority. Only a few truly pious caliphs were imbued with both types of powers. These were the early caliphs: Abu-Bakr, ¿Umar, ¿Uthmân, ¿Alî, and his son, al-Ḥasan; two of the Omayyads: Mu¿âwiyah Ibn ¿Abd-ul-¿Azîz (d. 683 AD), and ¿Umar Ibn ¿Abd-ul-¿Azîz (717–720 AD); and one Abbasid: al-Mutawakkil (847–861 AD).[616] The rest of Moslem rulers are perceived as having possessed only secular power. *bâṭin* power is, therefore, the sacred right to rule over what is referred to as "*el-màmlakàh er-ràbbâniyyàh* (the Divine Kingdom, i.e., the Moslem Nation and State)." Thus, *bâṭin* (covert) power is in effect a "parallel government."

Contemporary upheavals represented by "Islamic fundamentalism," are social movements seeking to restore the original state/government that combines the sacred and the secular, with the latter being totally derived from, and legitimized by, the former. For many tradition-bound groups on all social levels of society, the time has come for the appearance of *al-màhdî al-mùntaẓàr* (the anticipated Messiah). News of providential conceptions and fetuses that recite holy verses in their mothers' wombs surface periodically. One such case was reported during the early fifties and received considerable newspaper coverage, until the government intervened and censored any mention of it. It proved to be a hoax.[617]

In January 1985 a clique of Egyptian culture elite professionals (including medical doctors, engineers, and others of similar occupational status), all of whom received degrees from secular universities, formed a *gamâ¿àh Islâmiyyàh* (Moslem [worship] organization). They held a meeting, with the exact time and place known only to members of its inner circle, in order to discuss whether *'Âyàtù-Allâh* al-Khumaynî (Khumaini) is the Messiah. According to one of its members, they reached the conclusion that he was not.

IV.D.2. *ed-Dîwân* (the Divan/Council), and the Cult of Martyrdom

Associated with this concept of *bâṭin* power is the folk belief in the existence of the *dîwân* (pronounced: *dewân*, i.e., divan or council), which is a supernatural office representing bureaucratic organization of saints. The council administers the *bâṭin* religion-based sacred power in a nation (Egypt) that is governed by *ẓâhir* secularly based power dispensed by kings, presidents, and prime ministers, rather than the ulama and other clerics.

Three sets of religious figures constitute the Divan: first, a troika of two brothers and their sister; second, the Four Axes (Arch-saints); and third, all the lesser saints. The siblings are el-Ḥasan, el-Ḥusain, and their sister Zàynàb ('Zainàb, in vernacular); they are the children of Imam ¿Alî ibn Abî-Ṭâlib and Fâṭimah *al-zàhrâ'*, Prophet Mohammad's daughter.[618] Thus, they are also the maternal grandchildren of Prophet Mohammad. Not all of Imam ¿Alî's children, it should be pointed out, are included

---

[616] al-Nabhânî, *karâmât al-'awliyâ'*, Vol. 1, p. 69.

[617] Personal reading in newspapers from the 1950s till the present time.

[618] Of Fâṭimah's titles, Burton (Vol. 8, pp. 251–252, note 1) states:

in this power organization; another daughter, 'Um-Kulthûm, for example, is never included in the Divan or even thought of actively in saintly terms in folk practiced in Egyptian daily life. The exclusion of 'Um-Kulthûm is possibly due to apparent historical conflict between her and her older sister, Zàynàb.[619] A folk praise song (hymn) addressed at Zàynàb illustrates the network of ties within the family of Imam ¿Alî:

yâ sayyidàh, yâ sayyidàh,
O sayyidàh [Zainab], O sayyidàh [Zainab]
yâ Ommû esh-shimû¿ el-qâyidàh
You, the one with lighted candles
yâ 'ukht el-Ḥasan
You, who is the sister of al-Ḥasan
wa akhûkî el-Ḥusain
And el-Ḥusain is your brother
yâ bint akràm wâlidah
O you, daughter of the most noble of mothers.[620]

Only four members of Ali's family are included in the hymn; the father, Imam ¿Ali, is not one of them. The inclusion of el-Ḥasan, the older brother, is evidently honorary and mostly due to his kinship position and his early unsuccessful claim to the caliphate. Unlike el-Ḥusain and Zàynàb whose names recur daily on the lips of millions of Sunni Egyptians, el-Ḥasan hardly ever appears or pleaded with *independently* in oral folk traditions.

Available data indicate that the Divan is not known outside communities of the Nile Valley area of Egypt. It seems to be unknown to Egyptian Copts. One learned Copt stated,

> "We [Copts] do not have the idea of a *diwân* of saints; but we have stratification in the ranks of angels and *qiddîsîn* (saints)."[621]

Her titles are Zahrâ and Batûl [. . .] both signifying virgin. Burckhardt translates Zahrâ by "bright blooming" (the etymological sense): it denotes literally a girl who has not menstruated, in which state of purity the Prophet's daughter is said to have lived and died. "Batûl" has the sense of a "clean maid" and is the title given by Eastern Christians to the Virgin Mary. The perpetual virginity of Fatimah even after motherhood (Hasan and Husayn) is a point of orthodoxy in Al-Islam as Juno's with the Romans and Umâ's with the Hindû worshippers of Shiva. ([Note: In Burton's transliteration system, an à=â, ù=û]).

Motifs: A511.1.3, "Culture-hero incarnated through birth from virgin;" T547, "Birth from virgin." Cf. the ancient theme of how Isis conceived Horus from her dead husband Osiris (cf. Motif: A511.1.3.3, "Immaculate conception of culture-hero"). See Budge, *Gods*, Vol. 2, pp. 192–193; and Ions, *Egyptian Mythology*, p. 59. Also see n. 628.

[619] See ¿Â'ishah ¿Abd al-Raḥmân, *al-Sayyidah Zaynab baṭalat Karbalâ'* (Cairo, 1966) pp. 40–43.

[620] El-Shamy, "Dr. Hasan El-Shamy Clarifies", in *al-Qabas* (Kuwait) 12/9/1987, No. 5594, p. 28.

[621] Informant: Mr. Lewîs: see n. 268 (Sat. June 24, 1972).

Moslem informants agree that "el-Ḥusain is the Head of the Divine Kingdom." Sometimes he is euphemistically described as "a kingdom;" "el-Ḥasan is a sultan;" "*as-sayyidàh* Zàynàb is *ra'îsìt ed-diwân* (the head of the Divan)." She is also "*ṣâḥbàt esh-shûrâ*" (the chancellor, or the sole guide [in deliberations]).[622] The Four Axes (arch-saints) report the affairs of the kingdom to the three siblings, take part in the decision-making process, and administer the execution of the judgments passed in the Divan. The lesser saints function as guards and wardens—each in his own *daràk* (precinct, domain)—and as agents who execute the judgments of the Divan. The regular session of the Divan takes place routinely on the "night of Sunday (i.e., Saturday night)." This evening is also called "the eve of *sayyidàh* Zainàb."[623]

The sibling triad and the Divan had their counterpart in ancient Egyptian religious beliefs: a triad composed of two gods and one goddess, and the ennead, a council of nine gods, which was "often regarded as a triad of triads."[624] The modern Islamic trio seems to be the modern version of the ancient Osiris-Isis-Horus triad: a sister, brother, and their son. This viewpoint may be further supported by other functions of *sayyidàh* Zàynàb, which parallel those performed by the ancient Egyptian Isis. Beside being perceived as "*es-sìt et-ṭâhràh*" (the pure or immaculate Lady),[625] *sayyidàh*-Zàynàb is commonly referred to as *'Omm-el-¿awâgìz* (mother of, or the protector of, the disabled and sometimes, more specifically, the blind).[626] She is also reported as "having raised many an orphan." The reference here is obviously to her nephew, ¿Alî Zayn-al-¿Âbidîn, the only male survivor of her entire Hashemite lineage, the son of her "martyr" brother, el-Ḥusain.[627]

Apparently ¿Alî Zayn-el-¿Âbidîn has been equated—only in this context—with the Osirian Horus.[628] After the murder of Osiris at the hands of his brother Seth, Isis, his wife (who was also his sister), protected and raised Horus, their child. Similarly, Zàynàb protected and raised her brother's orphaned son ¿Alî Zayn-el-¿Âbidîn.

In Egypt, only el-Ḥusain, the younger of the two brothers, and his sister Zàynàb are enshrined. Their mosque-tombs are located in Cairo in two adjacent city quarters

---

[622] See "An Arch-Saint's Attempt to Punish Sinners," in El-Shamy, *Folktales of Egypt*, No. 30, p. 152.

[623] Yet, as Lane (*Modern Egyptians*, pp. 466–468) reports, "her moolid [(saint's day celebration)] is always on the eve of Wednesday." Amîn (*Qâmûs*, p. 388) comments that the festivity is ancient Egyptian, continued by Egypt's Copts, and adopted by Moslems who colored it with Islamic traits.

[624] See Ions, *Egyptian Mythology*, p. 65.

Motifs: A167.1, "Council of the gods;" A167.2§, "*dîwân*: council of deified humans (arch-saints, culture-heroes);" A169.1, ‡"Judge and tribunal of the gods. [Ennead]."

[625] Sharon Kelly Heyob, *The Cult of Isis Among Women in the Graeco-Roman World* (Leiden: Brill, 1975). On Isis and Virgin Mary, see Budge, *Gods*, Vol. 2, pp. 220–221.

[626] Yaḥyâ Ḥaqqî, *Qindîl 'Omm-Hâshim* (The Lantern of . . . [i.e., *al-sayyidah* Zaynab]) [A novel] (Cairo, 1954). 'Omm-Hâshim being a nickname for *sàyyidàh* Zaynab of the Hashemite lineage. See also App. 27A, where the title "*'Omm-el-¿awâgìz*" occurs.

[627] Anthony Nutting, *The Arabs* (New York, 1965) pp. 71–73.

[628] For the ancient account, see Budge, *Gods*, Vol. 1, p. 114. For the parallelism between the Islamic trio and the ancient Egyptian triad, see "An Arch-Saint's Attempt to Punish Sinners," in El-Shamy, *Folktales of Egypt*, No. 30, pp. 151–153, 278, p. 151. Cf. n. 623 above.

named after them, yet their bodies lie elsewhere. El-Ḥusain is referred to as "The Martyr," unlike his brother el-Ḥasan, who is reported to have been poisoned by his wife after having given up his struggle for the caliphate against the Omayyads and having retired to Hejaz.[629] The "martyrdom" of el-Ḥusain is formalized in the Moslem Shiite sect that views the failure of its members to support him as the main reason for his murder and the "usurping" of the caliphate by others, especially the Omayyads. The day of his death, *¿Âshûrâ'*, the tenth of the lunar month of Muḥarram, is commemorated among the Shiia Moslems by collective wailing, lamenting, and self-punitive expressions.[630] Among Shiites the act of murdering el-Ḥusain is reenacted dramatically annually accompanied by self-punishment and guilt-bound expressions; this reenactment represents the only "true" folk theater in Islamic cultures.[631] This practice has not been reported from any part of Egypt. Among the Sunni Moslems, the occasion is observed by the acts of piety such as performing optional fast and prayers during the day of ¿Âshûra. The majority, however, commemorate the event by preparing a special sweet delicacy of wheat pudding—also called *¿ashûrâ*—and exchanging with friends and neighbors ornate dishes of it garnished with nuts and sweets. Thus, this solemn event is associated—at least among children, who are likely to retain some of their childhood sentiments when they become adults—with some pleasant festive mood (see n. 630).

The el-Ḥusain cult in Egypt, and the Shiite formal religious (ecclesiastical) format elsewhere especially in Iraq and Iran, is the closest parallel in Islam to the Christian guilt-generating ethos (to be differentiated from "sin")[632] of "Jesus died for you." In the folk culture of Sunni Egypt, the guilt experience is minimal and is represented only by deep feelings of compassion and belief in the sainthood of el-Ḥusain and his two siblings. However, it seems that the emotional foundation for the attitude toward this sacred trio is their kinship relationship to Prophet Mohammad, combined with the tragedy of martyrdom. This argument can be substantiated further by pointing out that 'Um-Kulthûm, the younger sister of Zàynàb, is virtually unheard of in folk traditions; she shared the honor and prestige of their descent with her sister Zàynàb, but not the involvement in the tragedy. Zàynàb accompanied her brother el-Ḥusain to Karbalâ, witnessed his death, and saved his son from certain death at the hands of the Ommayads; conversely, 'Um-Kulthûm played no active role in that fateful event.

---

[629] Nutting, *The Arabs*, p. 69.

[630] Motifs: cf. V1.1.3.3§, ‡"Experiencing guilt as effect (result) of martyrdom-based religious faith;" V1.1.3.3.1§, ‡"Self-torture (self-punishment) as atonement for martyred sacred person (prophet, saint)."

On customs of ¿Âshûrâ in Egypt see, Lane, *Modern Egyptians*, p. 251, 428–433; and Walker-Ismâ¿îl, *Folk Medicine*, p. 104, where ¿Âshûrâ is presented as a Moslem (voluntary) fast day, along with a special charm. (Motif: V65.0.5.1§, "*¿Âshûrâ*: commemoration of martyrdom;" cf. V4.4§, ‡"Extra-religious exercise (prayers, fasting, etc.) undertaken for extra-religious credit.")

Also, see n. 55 and 693.

[631] Arthur R. Wollaston, ed., *The Miracle Play of Hasan and Husain*, Collected from Oral Tradition by Colonel Sir Lewis Pelly (Westmead, UK, 1970).

[632] On Guilt vs. sin/shame, see n. 176.

Sunni orthodox Islam evidently is based on affective foundations that are different from those characteristic of Shiite Islam (and Christianity). In its Sunni context, Islam promotes no such guilt feelings toward any of its major figures. It is to this guilt-free, nonmartyrdom of the patriarchal figure[633] that official Islam and the cults of the mighty and invincible Imam ¿Alî and *es-sayyìd* el-Badawî belong. Evidently, among the folk of Egypt, the cult of el-Ḥusain countervails the Olympian Sunni orthodox Islam. At the time Islam was being introduced into Egypt both the psychological (affective) and the cognitive foundations for the cult of martyrdom were already deeply rooted in Egyptiàn culture and psyche. The Osirian and the Christian "tragedies" were emotionally identical with the one that the Moslem troika suffered. Among the masses, the new Islamic figures of a sister and her two brothers seem to have simply replaced the older "pagan" Isis, her brother Osiris, and their son Horus. Martyrdom in Coptic (Christian) Egypt proved compatible with martyrdom of al-Ḥusain and its emotional consequences.

IV.E. *jihâd*: Righteous-Struggle and Greater Martyrdom

As a concept, *jihâd* (or as it is commonly pronounced: *gihâd*) is "a struggle, an effort, a striving." It is a struggle against injustice (*ẓùlm*) and infidelity (*kùfr*, considered a form of injustice). In formal Islam, *jihâd* is not one of the five "pillars" of Islam, but it is required when the nation is in peril. In such a case it is labeled "*jihâd fî sabîl 'Allâh* (righteous struggle in the cause of God). *Ṣûfîs* speak of two classes of jihâd "the greater jihâd," which is against one's own sinful desires and lusts; and "the lesser jihâd," which is against infidels.

In oral folk traditions, "lesser" jihâd, or holy war, is cited almost exclusively in religious legends revolving around the emergence of Islam and in a specialized cycle of heroic religious epic-like *siyàr* (i.e., life histories of heroes, sing.: *sîràh*) portraying the wars mostly between Moslems and European Christians.[634]

A companion concept of *jihâd* is that of martyrdom. The Arabic word for "martyr" is *shahîd* and the word for martyrdom is *shahâdah* or *'istìshhâd*, which also denotes being present as a witness (see n. 646). Learned informants point out that a "perfect martyr," is one who has either given his life in a righteous religious war "in the path of God (*fî sabîl-Illâh*)," or one who had his life taken away (killed, executed) unjustly. The death of the perfect martyr is believed to be purifying; thus the perfect martyr may be buried without the rituals of washing-of-the-dead, changing of clothes, and replacing them with shrouds required in ordinary deaths. In Islam, the concept of martyrdom encompasses much more than the status of those who give their lives in

[633] On the issue of patricide, see S. Freud, *Moses and Monotheism* (New York: A.A. Knopf, 1939). Also see Jan Assman, *Moses the Egyptian: The Memory of Egypt in Western Monotheism* (Cambridge, Harvard University Press, 1997).

[634] See: Hasan El-Shamy, "The Story of El-Sayyid Aḥmad El-Badawî . . . ," Part I, An Introduction," pp. 1–13; Lyons, *The Arabian Epic* (Cambridge, 1995).

Motif: V357§, ‡"Holy war (crusade, jihâd-*muqaddas*, etc.)." Also see n. 56.

defense of the faith.[635] Beside the rank of the "perfect *shahîd*," martyrdom is also bestowed on all those who die in a manner that would elicit pity and compassion in other human beings, such as a mother's death during childbirth, or a chaste lover's death from love, or death by drowning, fire or at the hands of a robber or a thief, or from a malignant disease, or in the process of acquiring knowledge or seeking legitimate employment (making a living), or while being a stranger in foreign lands, or during helping a person in need. Such persons are entitled to the rank of martyr, but not to the higher honor of being buried without the required washing and purification restricted to perfect martyrdom. Thus, special blessing is promised to those who die "on God's path" (*jihâd*), a path that includes diverse activities, albeit the seeming restriction to holy wars. They are to be counted as not dead but alive in heaven (Koran, 3: 163).[636]

Koran acknowledges Christian martyrs as such (Koran, 85: 4–11). One of the salient cases is that of "'Aṣḥâb al-'Ukhdûd" ("People of the Trench") where thousands of Christians in pre-Islamic Arabia were killed for refusing to convert to Judaism.[637]

---

[635] Burton observed,

> "Shuhada," highly respected by Moslems as by other religionists; although their principal if not only merit seems as a rule to have been intense obstinacy and devotion to one idea for which they were ready to sacrifice even life. The Martyrs-category is extensive including those killed by falling walls; victims to the plague, pleurisy, and pregnancy, travelers drowned or otherwise lost when journeying honestly, and chaste lovers who die of "broken hearts," i.e. impaired digestion. Their souls are at once stowed away in the crops of green birds where they remain till Resurrection Day, "eating of the fruits and drinking of the streams of Paradise," a place however, whose topography is wholly uncertain. (*Arabian Nights*, Vol. 1 p. 171, note 1. (Cf. n. 421)

Motifs: V463, "Religious martyrdom;" V463.0.2§, ‡"Hierarchy (stratification) of martyrs;" V463.7§, ‡"Occurrences (and deeds) that entitle a person to the rank of martyrdom;" V463.7.1§, ‡"Martyrdom: giving own life for a religious cause ('for the sake of God');" V463.7.1.1§, ‡"Martyrdom: giving own life for a national (patriotic) cause;" V463.7.1.2§, ‡"Martyrdom: giving own life for justice;" V463.7.2§, ‡"Martyrdom: having one's life taken away ('sacrificed') to save lives of many;" V463.7.3§, ‡"Martyrdom: being unjustly killed (executed);" V463.7.4§, ‡"Martyrdom: dying from (for) love;" V463.7.5§, ‡"Martyrdom: dying accidental, unnatural (violent) death (e.g., drowning, burning, etc.);" V463.7.5.1§, ‡"Martyrdom: to be killed (devoured) by sacred animal;" V463.7.5.2§, ‡"Martyrdom: to die during childbirth."

See also "Ancient Egyptian Analogues," in W. Blackman, *Fellahin*, p. 315.

[636] Motif: V463.0.1§, ‡"Martyrs are alive (in heavens)." See Basset, *Mille*, Vol. 3 No. 196, pp. 325–326.

[637] Christian martyrs of Najrân, a city and region in the Najd, (today in Saudi Arabia) who by order of the Himyarite king Dhû-Nuwâs were burnt alive in a ditch which they had to dig themselves (523 AD).

Dhû-Nuwâs, a fanatical convert to Judaism, suspected the Najrân Christians of conspiring against him with the Abyssinians, also Christians, took the city after a heavy fight and offered the inhabitants the choice between Judaism or death. Most of them—according to Oriental martyrologists some 20,000—remained true to their religion and were killed.

The Oriental churches commemorate the martyrdom of the *aṣḥâb al-'ukhdûd* on different days in the month of October.

Similarly, literary Moslem traditions assign the rank of "lord and leader of all martyrs on Day of Judgment" to John the Baptist.[638]

The concept of martyrdom and consequent rewards in life to come are not new to the religious systems of the region. Martyrdom has its parallel (and, perhaps, roots) in the ancient belief in honorific death by drowning: this is how the evil god Seth (Typhon) murdered his good brother Osiris.[639]

---

[638]al-Tha¿lâbî, *Qiṣaṣ*, p. 213.

Motifs: V463.2.0.1§, ‡"First martyr;" V463.2, ‡"First martyr: John the Baptist;" V463.2.1§, ‡"John the Baptist: lord and leader of all martyrs on Day of Judgment."

Al-Tha¿labî (*Qiṣaṣ*, p. 28) assigns the rank of first martyr also to "Abel son of Adam" who was unjustly murdered by his brother—Motif: V463.2.0.1.1§, ‡"First martyr: Abel son of Adam murdered by his brother (Cain)."

[639]In this respect Maspero writes,

> The term *hasi*, the praiser, the singer of the god, is applied to the dead in a manner that is almost constant from the time of the second Theban empire: *To praise Râ* is a euphemism for the act of dying, more especially that of dying by drowning. In the Ptolemaic period *hasi* means *drowned*, and it is much used for Osiris, whose body Typhon had thrown into the Nile [. . .]. Thus, *he was praising Râ* is here equivalent to *he was drowning*. (Maspero, *Ancient Egypt* (1967), p. 130, note 2.)

Motifs: V1.1.3.1§, ‡"Spiritually advantageous death;" V1.1.3.2§, ‡"The cult of martyrdom (*al-'istishhâd, al-shahâdah*);" V1.1.3.2.1§, ‡"Veneration of martyred mortal (prophet, saint, e.g., ¿Îsâ,/Jesus, al-Ḥusayn, etc.)." Also see n. 635.

CHAPTER V

Powers and Abstracts

This segment of the supernatural beliefs system and related practices is distinguishable from that of characters and their functions (Section I.A) since its components are typically perceived as forces existing independently of specific characters. Although some of the forces and abstract entities can ultimately be attributed to a "character," they are viewed in daily life as independent *sui generis*.

V.A. Sacred Powers

This segment incorporates two major constituents: God's power, and knowledge as a "power" in and for itself.

V.A.1. God's Power

God's *mashî'àh* (will), *qùdràh* (omnipotence), and *'îrâdàh* (volition)—all of which are different facets of the same entity—are responsible for the existence and control of the entire universe. God's power suspends planets in heavens and makes the sun rise and set; it causes a person to perform well and be pious or to err and commit sin; it also causes plants to grow, conception to happen, birth to take place, planes to fly, and chemical reactions to occur. In short, absolutely nothing occurs outside God's Will. The raison d'être for any and every happening, whatsoever, is God's command and the obedient response of the object or the creature that receives the command. This doctrine is expressed in a self-validating quote from the Koran, "'*kùn!' fa-yakûn* ([God commands]: 'Be!' It becomes;" Koran, 2:117; 3:47, 19:35, and 36:82). Even among the secularly educated, recognition of "natural laws" is always mediated by attributing these laws to God's Will and God's volition over nature and the universe as a whole;

recently there have been urgent calls to integrate this doctrine in science curricula taught at secular schools and colleges. *'in-shâ'a 'Allâh* (If God wills)—or a similar statement—is a necessary declaration that must precede any plan for the future, i.e., plans succeed or fail only "If God wills." Failure to observe this rule is considered a sign of unbelief and arrogance—which is equated with ignorance—or, at least, ill manners; see n. 153). Past events are also explained in terms of: this is what "*rabbinâ shâ'* (our Lord willed)." "*mâ shâ'a 'Allâh* (whatsoever God willed)" is a truism applied by virtually all members of the society regardless of religion, profession, social class, or level of education. It is uttered aloud to bless or express nonthreatening admiration for a noteworthy quality such as beauty, health, success, strength, or the like; it is also seen painted on vehicles, or written in amulets, or hung in decorative styles on walls in offices, businesses, and homes, or engraved in gold or silver and worn as ornaments as well as protection against unforeseen dangers such as the evil eye or road accidents.

A curious entity (or character) called *ṣàyrafiyy al-qùdràh* (the bursar of [God's] omnipotence) appears occasionally in folk religious legends. The belief accounts for the reported ability of certain individuals, especially saints, to produce money by merely stretching their hands toward heavens or "into a solid wall."[640]

V.B. *al-¿ìlm* (Gnosis, Knowledge)

Knowledge was created *a priori* (see Section I.B.1). Moslem theologians, as well as laymen, differentiate between two types of knowledge: "natural" (gnosis), and "induced."[641] Natural knowledge is bestowed in various amounts on creatures (animals, humans, jinn, and angels) as part of creation or at a later stage of the creature's life as a result of divine revelation. Such is the case concerning the instinctual homing capabilities of pigeons or fish, the ability of birds to build nests, bees to construct honey combs, and the like. This type of knowledge is labeled "*hidâyàh*," a word that signifies "leading to the correct path by divine or mystical power." Additional means of acquiring natural knowledge and truth are through visions (dreams) and meditations by the pious, especially prophets, or by means of induced dissociative and similar states of altered consciousness such as *zìkr* and public-*zâr* rituals. During these activities the individual can nullify the shackling effects of the mind and body, thus setting the soul free to join the rest of the spiritual moiety (side) of the universe. In Sufi parlance the process of reaching such a state through meditations is called *shàṭḥ* (i.e., to go into the Beyond [of human limitations of knowledge]).[642] The soul then

---

[640] al-Nabhânî, *karâmât al-'awliyâ'*, Vol. 1, pp. 267, 304.

Motifs: A473.0.3§, "'Bursar of [God's] Omnipotence'—dispenses money that seems to be acquired mysteriously;" D2179§, "Money supernaturally produced (by saint)."

[641] Motif: J1§, ‡"Capacity to know (knowledge) from instinct: (innate, 'from God,' *'ilhâm, hidâyah*)."

For cases of *ḥidâyàh*, see: al-Jâḥiẓ, *al-Ḥayawân* (The Book of Animal[s]), Vol. 2, pp. 147–148, 155–156/a (infant), 156–158/b (pigeons); Vol. 3 pp. 187–188.

[642] Motifs: V462.8.0.2§, "*shaṭḥ*: philosophical unorthodoxy due to ascetic immersion;" cf. V462.8.0.3.1§, ‡"Epileptic ecstasy (convulsions)."

comes into the presence of God (*galâlah, ḥaḍrah*), for the barrier-to-gnosis affects only the body, not the soul. (See Section I.E) All these ways of acquiring knowledge have sacred connotations and are instrumental in foretelling the future by means of "reading" it directly on the tablet-of-destiny safeguarded in heavens, acquiring it intuitively because it already exists, or by being instructed by an angel—if God wills. Such information and accompanying feelings are labeled *¿ìlm ladùnnî* (lit.: knowledge that is from His [Domain] i.e., Divine Knowledge). At all times the individual must not be a sinner, otherwise this knowledge could be *'ìstìdrâg* by God (leading on so as to condemn oneself; see Sections II.B.3.2 and III.B.3), or misleading and erroneous information generated by Satan.

Induced means of acquiring knowledge include *'ìgtihâd* (to be diligent in applying one's own brains in a *rational manner*, i.e., thinking) in order to establish general rules governing the relations among things, or *qiyâs* (to infer new rules based on older established cases, i.e., judging by analogy, or syllogism).[643] Even in this respect, success or failure is believed to be determined by God's Will. Expressions such as *rabbìnâ fatàḥ ¿alaih* (God opened [His door] for him) mean that a person was successful in acquiring knowledge or performing a task simply because God willed his success and removed whatever obstacles that may have impaired that person's vision, logic, or abilities. All correct knowledge is viewed as *min nûr-i-llâh* (of God's light). *al-¿ìlm nûr* (knowledge is light, i.e., is illumination) is a truism that is taken both literally as well as allegorically.[644] These induced means of acquiring knowledge may also be used to foretell the future, but on a strictly deductive basis. Astrology, geomancy, omen interpretation, and similar specialized professional (shamanistic) "sciences" and simple folk practices exercised by nonprofessionals may be used to predict the future by means of inference and according to the vaguely—but constantly—perceived doctrine of the unity of the universe (*wiḥdìt ek-koan/al-wugûd*, i.e., *wiḥdàt al-kàwn/al-wujûd*).[645]

The possessing of knowledge, especially the sacred (gnosis)—held by the masses until relatively recently to be the only true and respectable *¿ìlm* ("science")—is believed

---

This phenomenon was reported from ancient Egypt, see Maspero/El-Shamy, *Ancient Egypt*, No. 15, p. 208, note 1.

Rosenthal translates *shàṭḥ* as "ecstatic utterances" (see Ibn Khaldûn/Rosenthal, *The Muqddimah*, Vol. 3, pp. 100–103).

In his commentaries on Bukhârî's *ṣaḥîḥ*, Abu al-Naṣr (*al-Bukhârî*, Vol. 4, p. 220.) points out that Abû-Ḥâmid Muḥammad al-Ghazzâlî (1058–1111 AD) states that Sufis introduced the idea of two types of *¿ishq 'Allâh* (enamorment with God): "unintelligible words, often emanating from confusion in the mind, and disorientation of the self/soul (*ḥayrah fî an-nafs*)." He adds that these practices are among the widespread deviant fads/innovations (*bidà¿*) causing great harm.

643 For a succinct description, see "Qiyâs," in Stephan and Nandy Ronart, *Concise Encyclopaedia of Arabic Civilization*, Vol. 1, p. 440. For a folk application of the concept of "*qiyâs*," see App. 41.

644 See Ibn Khaldûn/Rosenthal, *The Muqddimah*, Vol. 3, pp. 111ff. Tawfîq al-Ṭawîl, *al-Tanabbu' bi al-ghayb ¿inda mufakkirî al-'Islâm* (*Foretelling the Future in the [Philosophy of] Islam's Thinkers)* Cairo, 1945.

645 In scholastic Sufi philosophy the concept is typically attributed to the Andalusian philosopher Muḥyî-al-Din Ibn ¿Arabî (1165–1240). In his "Terminal Essay" to the *Arabian Nights*, Burton (*Arabian Nights*, Vol. 10, p. 64) observes:

to be proportionate to a person's position within the stratification of humans. For example, a *qùṭb* (Axis) is regarded as a "tumultuous sea of knowledge," for he is the closest to God when compared to all other saints in the lower ranks. Meanwhile, two categories of saints, *ṣiddîqîn* (instantaneous true-believers, sing.: *ṣiddîq*) and *shùhadâ* or "*'àhl esh-shahâdàh*" (people-of-the-testimony that "there is no god but God and Mohammad is His Prophet," sing.: *shahîd*—to be differentiated from *shahîd/shùhadâ*, i.e., martyr/s), are both equally close to God's knowledge (i.e., God's light). However, these two groups may be differentiated on the basis of the "completeness" of their share of that light. An instantaneous believer's (*ṣiddîq*'s) light is more complete than that of a witness (*shahîd*) because the former's adherence to the principle of the oneness of God—or more generally, to religious precepts—stems from belief rather than from knowledge; "he is [therefore] below the instantaneous believer (*ṣiddîq*) in the rank of belief and above the *ṣiddîq* in the rank of knowledge."[646]

V.B.1. Sources of Knowledge and Truth

The vague concept of *ḥâgàh* or "*shai'*" (i.e., *shày'* something, "presentiment") that leads the individual to know or act, may be viewed as a parallel to the secular concept of "intuition;"[647] thus, *ḥâgàh 'ilâhî* or *ḥâgàh rabbânî* (lit.: something godly, i.e., from God) designates a concept that may be called sacred or divine intuition. Often that "something" is perceived in personified manner in the form of a *hâtìf* (a [supernatural] caller or voice)[648] stemming from an invisible source that becomes audible to the individual concerned.[649] If the source of the "thing" or the *hâtìf* is sacred, it may be viewed as *'ìlhâm* ([minor] revelation from God); in the case of prophets this *'ìlhâm* becomes of sufficient intensity to warrant calling it *wàḥy* (revelation [from God]), usually through the Archangel Gabriel. Only prophets and immediate family members, such as a prophet's mother, experience *wàḥy*, while all good humans may receive *'ìlhâm* or become inspired through some other divine source. It is also believed that God may send an angel—usually a lesser one—in the form of a human being, to instruct a pious person, or show that person how things ought to be done by setting an example for handling a problem.[650]

Considered in a higher phase, the mediaeval Moslem mind displays, like the ancient Egyptian, a most exalted moral idea, the deepest reverence for all things connected with his religion and a sublime conception of the Unity and Omnipotence of the Deity.

[646] al-Nabhânî, *karâmât al-'awliyâ'*, Vol. 1, 87.

[647] Motifs: D1812.4, "Future revealed by presentiment: 'knowledge within;'" D1812.4.2§, ‡"The unknown revealed by presentiment: 'knowledge within.'" Cf. Burton's use of "my heart presageth," (see El-Shamy, MITON)

[648] The word "telephone" has been Arabized as "*hâtìf.*"

[649] Motifs: A182.3.5.2§, ‡"God's proclamation (instruction) perceived as supernatural voice—(*munâdî, hâtif*);" F966, "Voices from heaven (or from the air). [*hâtif/'munâdî*];" cf. F1046§, ‡"Hallucination: false perception without adequate stimuli."

[650] See for examples Motifs: A1591.1.1§, "Ravens (crows) show Cain how to bury Abel;" and J216.6.1§, ‡"Death before advent senility chosen."

V.B.2. Instructive Dreams (Sleeper's Vision, *manâm*)

Dreams are held to be a source of truth and instruction especially concerning the unknown and the future. It is believed that during sleep the soul is temporarily freed from the body (see: Soul, in Section II); then the soul is in touch with the rest of the universe, especially the transparent side within the other side of the Veil. What the sleeper "sees" (i.e., dreams of), is usually held to be the truth expressed directly, or as the case is often, indirectly under symbolic guise (acts are typically interpreted as the opposite of the manifest ones seen in the dream). Manuals for interpreting dreams have existed for millennia.[651]

The word *ḥìlm* (dream) denotes a broad concept that incorporates two major categories of experiences:

> First, a "*ḥìlm*" (dream) sper se may be viewed as fiction and is thus contrasted to reality experienced cognitively when one is awake; during an incredibly unique experience a person usually will wonder by voicing the rhetorical question, "*'anâ f-ḥìlm wàlla f-¿ìlm*?" ("Am I in a dream or reality?") A *ḥìlm* may also be viewed as nonsense caused by certain physical conditions such as overeating or getting cold because of being improperly covered during sleep. A *ḥìlm* may also be thought of as generated by Satan or the jinn, and can, therefore, be a trap—often referred to by the literary term *'adghâthu 'àḥlâm*.[652] A threatening, or bad, *ḥìlm* is labeled *kâbûs* (nightmare), a word that literally means "a stifler" or "a compressor."

In the latter, Abraham had asked God to not order his soul seized until he himself requests death. However, Abraham reached the age of senility without asking for dying. Azrael assumed the form o. a feeble old man trying to feed a donkey by putting morsels in its eye, ear, etc. (al-Tha¿labî, *Qiṣaṣ*, p. 58). See El-Shamy, *DOTTI*, Tale-type 1199, *The Lord's Prayer*. [Devil (Death) must wait].

For another case where an angel appearing in the form of an old man shows a woman how to act, see "Who will Enter Paradise First?" in El-Shamy, *Tales Arab Women Tell*, No. 18, pp. 178–182. (Tale-type 756D§, *The Most Devout Will Enter Paradise First: Obedient Wife*).

[651] Maspero states,

> Dreams played a decisive part in the lives of the sovereign and distinguished personages, whether they were caused by the voluntary intervention of a god, or whether they were sought by sleeping for a night in certain temples.[...] The belief in signs reigned everywhere supreme, [...]. So many people had received these mysterious warnings that no one would be inclined to dispute their probability when they met with them in a romance. (Maspero, *Ancient Egypt*, pp. xlix–l, 1967)

Also see John Romer, *Ancient Lives*, pp. 68–72; and Amîn, *Qâmûs*, p. 176. In this respect, Muḥammad Ibn Sîrîn (d. 728 or 729 AD) is regarded as the foremost of Arab dream interpreters; see his *Tafsîr al-'aḥlâm al-kabîr* (The Greater Interpretation of Dreams). Cairo: Ṣubaih, 1963.

Motifs: D1812.3.3, "Future revealed in dream. [Divination through interpretation of dreams];" D1812.3.3.3, "Prophetic dream induced by incantation;" M302.0.3§, "*'istikhârah*: prophesying by asking God to indicate right choice (through: dream, opening Holy Book, rosary);" M302.7, "Prophesy through dreams;" D1812.3.3.10, "Dream interpreted by opposites." Cf. n. 656.

[652] Koran, 12:44, 21:5. See also Abu al-Naṣr, *al-Bukhârî*, Vol. 4, p. 322, No. 3.

> Motifs: J1798§, ‡"Which is real and which is illusory? (The actual is mistaken for imaginary (dream-like)—or the imaginary is mistaken for actual;" J157.8§, ‡"Dream as source of misleading information (misinformation) (*'dghâthu 'aḥlâm*);" J157.8.1§, ‡"Satan misleads in dreams (and similar experiences, such as communication with the dead);" J157.8.2§, ‡"Physiological state of sleeper

Second, a *rù'yàh* ("sleeper's vision," pl.: *rù'â*, or—occasionally—*marâ'î*), also called *manâm* (pl.: *manâmât*), is a dream that is truthful and instructive of past, present, or future events. Learned sources state that *rù'yâ* are perceptions by the soul of the sleeper, received by means of other than the five senses; they are perceived by *al-baṣîrah* (insight) or in logicians's jargon "*al-ḥawâs al-bâṭinah*" (internal, or inner, senses).[653] The truthfulness of a *rù'yàh/manâm* is considered one of forty-six "indicators of prophethood (*dalâ'il al-nùbuwwàh*)."[654] Also, the significance and validity of a *ru'yàh/manâm* increase if it occurs repeatedly. Thus, when a person "sees" the same dream three times (or seven), he/she feels obliged to act on it. A prophet's *ru'yàh/manâm*, regardless of its contents, is held to be a divine command because his (prophet's) soul is permanently in contact with God, never with Satan. Such was the case of Prophet Abraham who "saw in a *manâm*" that he was slaughtering his son Ishmael. He informed his son who agreed with his father that God's command must be obeyed (Koran, 37:102); consequently, God sent a ram from Paradise to be sacrificed as a ransom of the son. Likewise, the sleeper's vision of a pious person or a

---

as cause of misleading dream (e.g., full stomach, being cold, or the like)." (Also see El-Shamy, *MITON*)

[653]In his commentaries on the Prophet's Traditions, Abu el-Naṣr presents résumés of five types of *ru'â* as designate by a certain Dihlawiyy [??]:

1. *bushrâ* (herald of good news)—is from God. Its true nature is that if the *nàfs* (self, soul) becomes crystalline (pure) and abandoned the shackles of the body, it becomes ready to receive the divine abundance [of gifts]. Such a *rù'yâ* is divine instructions; visions by prophets and the pious belong to this category. It is through these visions that true sciences are addressed to them.
2. *rù'yâ malakìyyah*, [i.e., of the *malkât* (faculties, propensities)]—from man's faculties, good and ugly. It shows man his merits and demerits in an ideal image.
3. *takhwîf* (fear-evoking)—emanating from Satan [is comparable to nightmare]; it is the experiencing bewilderment or fear from such a thing as a disturbing animal—like a monkey, an elephant, or a biting dog. The one who experiences should *yataʿawwdh bi-Allâh* (state that he seeks refuge in God), spit thrice to his left, and turn over on his other side.
4. *ḥadîth al-nàfs*—what a sleeper experiences of what was retained in his capacity to imagine/visualize (*mukhayyilah*) when he awakens, due to his being concerned with it or accustomed to it.
5. *al-khayâlât al-ṭabaʿiyyah* (images due to one's nature)—occurs when self (*nàfs*) becomes aware of its harm to/within body (*badàn*).

See Abu-el-Naṣr, *Bukhârî*, Vol. 4, pp. 321–323. Also see Lane's statement on "faith in dreams," *Modern Egyptians*, p. 261 note.

Tale-types: 725, "*The Dream*. [Youth persecuted for not relating his dream of future greatness: it is fulfilled];" and 725A§, "*Prophecy of Becoming the Sole Ruler*. Prophecy (vision, dream) realized." Motifs: V515, "Allegorical visions;" N385.5§, "Person refuses to tell dream because listener did not say, 'Good, if God wills;'" C53.5.1§, "Tabu: planning for the future without saying, ''*in-shâ'-Allâh* (If God wills);'" C53.5.2§, "Tabu: dealing with omens (dreams) without saying, 'Good, if God wills;'" V517§, "Instructive sleeper's-vision or dream (*ru'yàh, manâm*)."

[654]al-Thaʿlabî, *Qiṣaṣ*, p. 72; Khalîfah, *al-Dâr al-barzakhiyyah*, p. 185.

Motif: V513.0.3§, "Visions (*ru'â*) are one of forty-six signs of being a prophet (sent by God)."

saint is held to be a command from God.[655] Some forms of *'istikhârah* (asking God's counsel on an important affair that requires making a choice) include requesting a *ru'yah* or *manâm*.[656] According to this ritual, before going to sleep, a person would perform the ritual ablution, recite certain verses from the Koran that include God's phrases, i.e., "We show," "We reveal," or the like, and ask God to show him/her the right path or choice. The "sleeper's vision" that the person experiences is thought to be God's choice (see Section VI.C). Although this practice may be exercised by any person in good standing with God at the time, it is typically undertaken on behalf of an interested party by a pious person who has acquired a reputation for having truthful "sleeper's visions" due to his/her piety and purity of soul.

"Sleeper's visions" are believed to be also means by which the dead can communicate with the alive. A living person may dream of a deceased relative or friend and receive verbal instructions concerning a given matter from that relative (friend); or the deceased may "appear" in a certain affective (emotional) state, such as being unhappy, angry, or in pain, that is visible to the sleeper. In the latter cases, the reasons suspected for causing these feelings are sought and addressed. Recurrent examples for the dead to be seen as unhappy revolve around being ignored or forgotten, failure to pay a debt that the deceased owed, or disregarding instructions or counsel given by the deceased on certain matters such as marriage, partnership, travel, or the like.

In such cases the encounter is considered a visit by the deceased to the living and is typically reported as follows: "I saw my father last night in the *manâm* . . . ," or "Sheik so-and-so came to me in the *manâm* and said to me. . . . " Also, a living person may request to be visited by a dead person; the visit occurs during a *manâm*. Failure of the petitioner to "see" the dead person is usually considered a sign of anger on the part of the deceased. (See App. 38, 48; also see Section VI.C)

The manner by which the dead are believed to communicate with the living is a common means for neglected saints to declare their desire for attention, enshrinement, or even demand communal recognition of their sainthood. Perhaps the earliest recorded incident of the occurrence of such communication took place in ancient Egypt some 3400 ago. The details are inscribed on a red granite tablet (known as the "dream stella") found between the paws of the Sphinx. Prince Thutmosis went out hunting and sought refuge from the burning sun in the shade of the head of the Sphinx, which was buried up to its neck in sand. In a vision, the Sphinx spoke to him stating "My son, I am your father Ra Harmakhis . . . ," and asked that sand should be cleared away from around his body. The Sphinx, being a god, promised to ensure that the price would attain greatness and kingship over both Upper and Lower

---

[655] Khalîfah, *al-Dâr al-barzakhiyyah*, p. 200 (Motif: V513.0.1§, "A prophet's vision (dream) is a command from God.")

The present writer read in a daily newspaper (*Al-Ahram*) in the early 1970s that in Algeria, an old man slaughters his son because he had a vision (dream) instructing him to do so. His rationale was that Abraham acted in the same manner. The outcome of the trial is unknown to the writer.

[656] Lane, *Modern Egyptians*, pp. 261–262; cf. Amîn, *Qâmûs*, p. 38.

See: El-Shamy in Maspero/El-Shamy, *Popular Stories of Ancient Egypt*, No. 10 p. 174; and cf. No. 9 p. 171, and No. 22 p. 286 (by prayer and sacrifice). For motifs associated with this theme, see n. 651.

Egypt. Thutmosis undertook the task of freeing the Sphinx from the encroachments of the desert and time. The Sphinx kept his promise and the prince became Pharaoh Thutmosis IV and had the entire event recorded on the "dream Stella."[657]

V.C. Concepts and Abstract Forces

Another category of the supernatural deals with abstract concepts and related circumstances all of which are derived from the doctrine of God's a priori creation of the past, the present, and the future. Yet the actual perception of these forces, as they influence an individual's daily activities, often bestows upon them concrete, corporal-like qualities, thus minimizing their abstract conceptual nature: in other words these concepts are typically personified. *el-maktûb* (that which is written, i.e., predestined), *el-wà¿d* (that which has been promised [by fate]), *el-qaḍâ* (divine resolution or verdict), *el-qadàr* (destiny), *el-muqaddàr* (that which has been preordained or predestined),[658] *el-qismàh* (*kismet*, that which is one's "share/lot" in life, or portion in the division of livelihood), and *en-naṣîb* (that which is one's due) are concepts of predestination and the inevitability of the preordained. These concepts are central in the belief–practice system and in shaping how the world is viewed on all levels of society—folk as well as elite. They constitute self-sufficient raison d'être for any occurrence; for example, a mechanic trying to explain why a part of a new car's engine wore out too quickly stated authoritatively: "*naṣîbùh kidàh*" (its [predestined] share/*kismet* is such!); similarly, the death of a generally healthy person during a routine surgical operation is explained: "Such is his *naṣîb*!" and "*'agalùh kidàh*" (such is his [predestined] life-span).[659]

---

[657] See "The Prince and the Sphinx," in Roger Lancelyn Green, *Tales of Ancient Egypt* (New York: Henry Walack, 1967) [No. 6], pp. 60–64. Designated as new Tale-type 760B§, *Restless Soul*: Deceased cannot rest because of worldly concerns; his soul contacts the living to make his wishes known. Motifs: D1610.18.1.1§, ‡"Sphinx speaks;" V113.0.1.1§, ‡"Shrine built (repaired) at demand of (dead) saint." (See App. 38)

[658] For a discussion on *qaḍâ'* as differentiated from *qadàr*, see Abu-el-Naṣr, *al-Bukhârî*, Vol. 4, pp. 276–286.

[659] Motif: V318.1§, ‡"Submission to fate (God's prejudgment: *qaḍâ'*, *qadar*) a mark of true faith." As examples from the present writer's own personal experiences, the following may be offered:

> While in Cairo in 1981–1982, a member of my family purchased a new European car; the contract called for the car to be serviced by the Agency after 3,000 kilometers. The mechanic in charge discovered that a certain steel part of the steering mechanism was worn out "as if the [sic] it was several years old." He, however, concluded that a new (costly) replacement is due at no charge.
>
> When asked, "Why would a steel part such as this wear out so quickly?" he readily responded: "that is his/its *naṣîb* (lot in life)."
>
> The writer's own conclusion is that the part (which is in great demand, but hard to find on the open market) had been replaced by a dishonest service station worker where that car had received some routine work earlier.

Similarly,

> During a visit to Egypt, I was informed of the death of Shâkir, a retired shaman-*shaikh*, and source of valuable information, as he underwent a minor surgical operation (appendectomy). When I expressed surprise and the view that no one dies from such a simple surgery, the person that told me

As operative social forces, these concepts minimize the effect of an individual's sense of personal responsibility in whatever takes place in actual life and thus provide strong defensive mechanisms. (Compare with "Luck," in Section VI.B)

V.C.1. *barakàh* (Blessing/Grace/Benediction)

The concept of *barakàh* is general and all encompassing.[660] Some anthropologically oriented writers have equated *barakàh* with the animistic force-labeled "*mana*,"[661] while others define it as "holiness," "magical power,"[662] or the like. However useful as these definitions may be, *barakàh* may be described as supernatural [positive] power residing in an object, act, or person. It is similar to a saint's miracle-like manifestation (*karâmàh*) but is not identified with it. Occasionally it may be associated with the concept of *khair* (goodness). *barakàh* is an attribute that God may bestow on a person, an object (including such intangibles as a specific idea, or a certain letter of the alphabet), or an act; it may refer to dexterity in performing an act, the personal appeal or attractiveness of a person, the religiosity and piety of an individual, the auspiciousness of a certain hour, day, or year, or the positive and desirable characteristics of a plant, animal, or object—such as a phrase, word, or letter. Sometimes the blessedness of a particular time or an object seems to derive from an historical religious context. Thus, certain hours, days, and years are viewed as *'awqât mubârakàh* (blessed times): all days of Ramaḍân, the fasting month, especially *Lailìt el-Qàdr* (the Eve of [Divine] Power),[663] Prophet Mohammad's birthday, a saint's

---

of the death seemed troubled by my statement. He later confided in one of my former colleagues that he was quite concerned about my spiritual wellbeing since I seemed to be questioning God's judgment (in his estimation). The possibility that Shâkir died due to negligence or malpractice—both of which are quite common in hospitals—was never entertained as a possibility.

[660] Motifs: D1705§, "*barakah* (blessedness): supernatural [positive] power residing in object, act, or person;" D1752§, "*barakah* (blessedness) passes from body to body."

G.S. Collin, defines *barakah* as "Beneficent force, of divine origin, which causes superabundance in the physical sphere and prosperity and happiness in the psychic order" (*EI*, Vol. 1, 1986, p. 1032). Also see: Blackman, *Fellâhîn*, pp. 33, 65, 99; Ammar, *Growing*, p. 73; Gilsenan *Saint and Sufi*, pp. 33–34; el-Aswad, *Religion and Folk Cosmology*, p. 120; and Sengers, *Women and Demons*, esp. p. 144.

For an example of *barakah* residing in an object, see "The Three Robbers and el-Khidr," in El-Shamy *Folktales of Egypt*, No. 21, esp. p. 130. (Motifs: D1707§, ‡"Blessed objects;" D1707.6§, ‡"Blessed coin (money).")

[661] E.g., Joseph Harold Greenberg, *The Influence of Islam on a Sudanese Religion*, (New York, 1946), p. 2, note 4; J.H. Bousquet, "La baraka, le mana et le dunamis de Jesus." In: *Revue africaine* Vol. 91 (1947), pp. 166–170.

[662] Kriss & Kriss-Heinrich *Volksglaube in Bereich des Islams*. Vol. 2, pp. 4–6. They write that *barakah* is a sort of magical power, which is transferred from the saint to his children and grandchildren.

[663] Motif: A798§, "Origin of *ṭâqat al-qadr* ('[Light-]Halo of Power');" D1761.3.1§, "Wishing by *ṭâqat al-qadr* ('[Light-] Halo of Power')."

See "Famous *layâlî*," in Amîn, *Qâmûs*, p. 349; and "Night of Power, or of the Divine decree," in Lane, *Modern Egyptians*, pp. 478–479.

A succinct description of the supernatural beliefs and practices associated with this night, and

day,[664] etc., are considered recurring blessed times by virtue of the religious event that took place during that period. A recurrent belief associated with the Eve-of-*Qàdr* is that of *ṭàqìt-el-qàdr* (halo-of-power). According to this belief, a halo of light may appear to some fortunate individual on that blessed evening; if the person were to make a wish before the halo vanishes, the wish most certainly will be realized because the doors of heaven would be wide open.[665] Similarly, certain directions (e.g., east–west, north–south, right–left, etc.) are considered to be endowed with *barakàh*. Invariably, the right side or limb of a person's body is viewed as blessed; an oft-quoted utterance (tradition) attributed to the Prophet—"Opt for the right [side] whenever you can (*tayàmànû ma 'istaṭ¿ṭùm*)"—provides powerful rationale for the belief in the blessedness of the right side. Thus getting out of bed with one's left side first, or putting on pants or footwear beginning with the left leg or foot is considered near-tabu (*màkrûh*).[666] Likewise, certain directions (orientation) are thought of as endowed with *barakàh*; one such direction is facing the Qìblàh (in Mecca)—which will vary according to the perceiver's geographic location.[667]

Although other directions may be viewed as desirable or friendly no *barakàh* is assigned to them. Such is the case in Egypt with the north (*baḥàrî*, lit.: sea-wise, i.e., northerly) and the west (*qìblî*, sunset-wise, westerly, or southerly); the north is the source of cool sea breeze coming from the Mediterranean Sea that provides welcome relief from summer heat and helps Nile ships sail against the mighty river's water flowing from south to north into the sea. Native lore takes advantage of stable qualities of these two directions. In traditional architecture, a good site for a house

---

cross-cultural parallels, is given by Burton:

> On the Night of Power the Koran was sent down from the Preserved Tablet by Allah's throne, to the first or lunar Heaven whence Gabriel brought it for opportunest revelation to the Apostle (Koran xcvii). Also during this night all Divine Decrees for the ensuing year are taken from the Tablet and are given to the angels for execution whilst, the gates of Heaven being open, prayer [. . .] is sure of success. (*Arabian Nights*, Vol. 6, p. 180 n. 2)

[664] Unlike the Prophet's birthday, the celebrating of a saint's day—though called *mûlìd* (i.e., *màwlìd*, birth)—is typically reckoned according to the date of the saint's *death*. This practice seems to be due to the fact that until relatively recently no official birth records were kept, and that people date such an event in relationship to another significant one (e.g., "the year of" such and such).

Motif: P781§, "Local history reckoned in relation to a person's past disgraceful act."

[665] This belief is commonly cited to account for a person's seemingly mysterious financial good fortunes that appear suddenly, rather than the belief in "magic-ring," or "magic-lamp." See n. 204.

For a depiction of this belief in a humorous context, see Tale-type: 555, *The Fisher and his Wife*. [Wishes granted: wasted (used foolishly).] (El-Shamy, *DOTTI*)

[666] Motif: C3§, ‡"*al-makrûh* ('the disfavored,' 'the disliked' [by God]): almost-taboo, merely tolerated—not the preferred way (for Moslems)."

[667] For example, in the ritual burial of the dead in Lower Egypt, the corpse is laid in the grave its right side facing south, the Qiblah (Ka¿bah), while the head is oriented toward the west. See el-Aswad, 1987, "Death rituals in rural Egyptian society: A symbolic study." In: *Urban Anthropology and Studies of Cultural Systems and World Economic Development*, Vol. 16: 205–241; and "The Cosmological Belief System of Egyptian Peasants." In: *Anthropos*, Vol. 89 (1994): 359–377.

should provide northerly windows for summer breeze and westerly exposure to the sun's warming rays in the winter. A recurrent image in love songs is having a heart that is "*màftûh ¿-al-bàḥàrî*" for the sweetheart (i.e., open in the widest possible way). Nonetheless, no blessedness is assigned to these directions within these contexts.

Certain times—as well as objects, locations, or individuals—perceived as imbued with "blessedness" are thought to have acquired special *ḥàq* ("right," i.e., privilege). Consequently, pleading with God may typically evoke that "right." Pleadings such as: "By the right of this [blessed] day (*bi-ḥàq hâdhâ al-yoam*)," and "By the right of this [blessed] place (*bi-ḥàq hâdhâ al-makân*)" are believed to strengthen one's case and ensure an answered prayer. With reference to a blessed person, the "right" may be assigned to the *gâh* ([social] power, or influence) that individual has with God; in this case, the supplication would be: "By the right of the power of so-and-so" (*bi-ḥàq gâh* so-and-so, e.g., by the right of power/influence of our lord Mohammad).

Similarly, the hoopoe bird is thought to be full of *barakàh* because it was the bird that led Prophet Solomon to the Queen of Sheba, whereas the crow (raven) in toto, at least on the cognitive level, is thought to be devoid of any *barakàh* (probably because of its negative role in Noah's search for dry land after the deluge) and the strong negative status ascribed to it. Some local traditions attribute the knowledge of the whereabouts of Noah's ark to the crow and maintain that every crow's nest contains a piece of wood from that ark. True to its nature lacking in blessedness, the crow deviously harbors "his" knowledge and refuses to lead people to that blessed object (see n. 371).

Saints are typically described as *kùlluhùm barakàh* ("are sheer blessedness") and are perceived as capable of bestowing that quality or state on other persons, places, plants, animals, and so forth. A recitation or reading from the Koran and the utterance of similar sacred phrases bring *barakàh* to households and businesses.[668]

Another aspect in which *barakàh* manifests its effects may be described as sufficiency, especially with reference to food. Failing to say "In the name of God" before beginning to eat is believed to invite Satan to the meal and thus reducing its blessedness: the food will be exhausted before eaters have eaten their fill. Similarly, certain recipes for preparing food are thought of as lacking in *barakàh*. A mother trying to feed a large family on a limited amount of meat, for example, would assert that frying or baking the meet "*yiqill bàràkìt-hâ* (reduces its blessedness)," whereas cooking it as stew with added tomato sauce and vegetables would not have that *barakàh*-robbing effect of frying or baking (which does away with the meat's juices and produces a meal reduced in volume when compared to the size of original ingredient).

Although *barakàh* is described as "from God" and that He grants it to true believers, they are not the only ones who may possess it. According to Islamic practices *barakàh* may be perceived as localized in parts of the body, such as the hand or the tongue. Thus a Christian or a Jewish surgeon, for example, may be thought of as having a blessed hand (*'îdùh mabrûkùh*). Winifred Blackman, a British anthropologist who worked

---

[668] Amîn, *Qâmûs*, pp. 124–125; Ammar, *Silwa*, p. 73, 74. Cf. "'Blow for Blow,'" in El-Shamy, *Folktales of Egypt*, No. 27, pp. 143–145.

in southern Egypt during the early part of the twentieth century, was regarded by her peasant women friends and acquaintances not only to be in possession of objects imbued with *barakàh* but as having *barakàh* herself.[669] This is also the case with the shrines of Christian and Jewish saints revered by Moslems and vice versa (see Section III.B.3). Thus, *barakàh* normally resides with persons and objects of God's choice but the person involved may not be evil or sacrilegious (such as a practitioner of "nether-magic"), for blessedness signifies God's contentment with (*riḍâ ¿àn*) that person.

Thus, *barakàh* is a sacred entity, constituted of both efficiency and God's help, which is diffusible from its owner to other persons, objects, and acts. In a number of cases the blessedness of a living *shaikh* (i.e., a person with saintly qualities) was perceived as having been diffused to that *shaikh*'s son, in spite of the fact that the son was regarded as reckless, and even as sinner. Naturally, it was expected that the son's behavior would be modified so as to live up to the prestige assigned to the newly acquired state. In such a case the diffusing or transferring *barakàh* to another person may *not* be viewed as due to heredity (*wirâthàh*); it is simply an act, by a human source, of bestowing his/her *barakàh* on another, and does not necessarily include *all* the heirs of the *shaikh*. In this respect, a truism states: "He (God) may bring forth a corrupt descendant from the loins of a pious predecessor—(and vice versa)."[670]

Frequently the practical and utilitarian aspects of *barakàh*, and similar good abstract entities, are referred to as *fâ'idàh* (benefit or usefulness, a word that may also suggest "profit"). Such deeds are frequently perceived in concrete personifications; a good deed is presumed to take the form of a tangible entity, usually a human-like being or that of another benevolent creature. The personified deed will interact with, or act on behalf of, the doer in accordance with *barakàh* (blessedness, grace), *khair* (goodness), or *fâ'idàh* (benefit, i.e., blessedness), which is incorporated in the deed or act concerned. Expressions such as "her prayers came and said to her . . . ," "his fasting appeared and advised him . . . ," or the like, are typical ways in which deeds are personified (see App. 52).[671]

V.C.2. *la¿nàh, ghaḍàb/sùkhṭ, niqmàh* ([God's] Curse, Anger/Wrath, Vengeance)

God's anger or wrath may befall a sinner in a most effective manner. Yet, this type of discontent and subsequent punishment may be seen as an attribute of a person (or other creature). In this respect, God's wrath or curse may be viewed as an

---

[669] Blackman, *Fellâhîn*, pp. 97–99, and 100, respectively.

[670] Field data indicate that *barakàh* is not *necessarily* hereditary. In numerous instances a saint's son turned out to be a sinner or an outlaw with no blessedness assigned to him. Such situations are expressed in recurrent folk truisms: Motifs: U5.3.1§, ‡"'He (God) may bring forth a corrupt descendant from the loins of a pious predecessor'—(and vice versa);" and U5.2§, "'Fire begets ashes.'"

[671] Motif: Z129§, "Religious exercise personified: 'benefit of' alms giving, prayers, fasting, pilgrimage, etc." Cf. Z125.1§, ‡"*ma¿rûf* (benevolence, kindness, chivalry, etc.) personified (usually as an angel named Ma¿rûf, '*shaikh* Ma¿rûf', or the like)." Also cf. *mùnjiyât*, [soul]-rescuers/savers, n. 37.

entity antithetical to that of *barakàh* (blessedness) and *riḍâ* (God's contentment with a person). Thus, a certain individual may be characterized as *¿alaih ghaḍàb-Allâh,* or *¿alaih ghaḍàb-rabbinâ* (God's anger is on him, or Our Lord's anger is on him). Such a person is perceived as incapable of doing anything correctly, and is expected to be followed by mishaps. In addition to this unhappy state being "natural" and permanent, it can also be "wished on," a person through a verbal pleading with God (i.e., a curse). The curse of parents, particularly that of a mother against her child, is believed to be readily answered.[672] This is also true of the curses of the disabled, the weak, and the oppressed; if a woman removes her head-scarf thus becoming bareheaded, and aims her eyes toward heavens and utters a curse at a specific time (e.g., dawn or midday), her appeal is believed to be infallible. A typical beginning statement for such a curse is *dà¿wìt wilyyàh sâ¿ìt ḍùhriyyàh* (a woman's plea at the hour of midday).

God's *sùkhṭ* (extreme anger, or wrath; Koran, 3:162; cf. 5:80) may result in severe punishment for an individual or an entire nation or race. It is believed that monkeys (Koran, 2:65, 5:60, and 7:166) and pigs (Koran, 5:60), for example, used to be normal people but God caused them to be debased, or—perhaps—become "devolved" (*sakhaṭhùm*) into their present form of low life (lesser creatures). It is not always clear whether all monkeys or just certain monkey groups are a product of *sàkhṭ* (the act of rendering into a debased form of life; also labeled as *màskh*). A folk legend states that the baboon was once a woman who, while too busy at baking, used a hot loaf of bread to wipe feces from the rear of her infant: God "debased" her into a baboon "with a red [burnt, inflamed] posterior."[673] Another race (or races) that is occasionally thought of as having suffered a similar degenerative fate in the relatively recent past (i.e., period of Alexander the Great) is "Gog and Magog." (See Section II.D.1) Their new lower form is that of demonic creatures rather than of monkeys or pigs. A creature that is perceived as having undergone such a degenerative punishment is labeled *màskhûṭ* (pl.: *masâkhiṭ*—a word also used as either an adjective or a noun to designate an adult who acts childishly, as if having undergone similar degeneration. This folk concept refers to behavioral phenomena designated under the psychoanalytic term "regression."[674]

In vernacular Egyptian Arabic, the word *sùkhṭ* is hardly ever encountered in daily life outside learned religious circles. The word that is typically applied to indicate extreme anger is "*ghaḍàb*." Yet, the word *sàkhṭ* (rendering into a debased form of life) and the concept it designates are in active usage.

---

[672] Amîn, *Qâmûs,* p. 210.

[673] Motifs: A1737§, "*sakhṭ, maskh* (devolution): creation of animals through degeneration to present forms;" A2362.1.1§, "Why monkey (baboon) got red posterior (rear)—punishment: was woman who abused bread (wiping child's feces with it)." On the *màskh,* see al-Gindi, *al-Ginn,* Vol. 2 pp. 71–74

The theme is used as a ruse for seduction or similar acts of deception; cf. Tale-type 1515, *The Weeping Bitch.* [Said to be transformed woman who rejected lover: trick to frighten virtuous woman.]

[674] Motif: W199§, "Self-deception (rationalization, regression, projection, etc.)." A belief legend portraying this pattern has been designated as Tale-type: 1394§, *Old Wife Acts Too Youthful or Childish: Rebuked*).

A concept similar to the *la¿nàh* ("curse") is *nàḥs* (bad omen—often deliberately mispronounced "*nà¿s*" so as to avert the evil effects of the *word* or the state of being inauspicious); it is also labeled *shù'm* (or *shûm* in vernacular).[675] A person (or creature) who is *mànḥûs* or *màsh'ûm* is a person who has been implicitly cursed by God. In this context *nàḥs*, like *barakàh*, is thought of as diffusible to others; the person, animal, or object perceived as *mànḥûs* is believed to be the harbinger of disaster, and is to be avoided. Such is the case, for example, with a one-eyed person, especially if the bad eye happened to be the left eye. A humorous anecdote tells of a king who punished a one-eyed man repeatedly for being in his way by mere chance, and explained, "You are a bad omen!" The hapless man counter argued: "You met me several times and nothing evil came to you; I met you just as many times and was beaten each time and prevented from gaining my livelihood. Now, which one of the two of us is the 'bad omen!?'"[676]

As a concept, *nàḥs* may also be designated as a nonsacred personified entity. A person visited by *nàḥs* is, simply, a person who is hapless or luckless (see Section VI.B).

Formal Islam condemns *taṭayyùr* (belief in omens). A religious authority states that belief in omens is sinful, whereas belief in "*'ìstikhâràh shàr¿iyyàh*" (religiously endorsed asking God for His counsel . . .) is legitimate.[677] (See Section V.C)

---

[675] Labeled *taṭáyyùr* in classical Arabic.

Motifs: N120.1.1§, ‡"Entity (animal, human, object, time-period, etc.) associated with certain events becomes harbinger of omen;" cf. D1812.5, "Future learned through omens."

[676] Amîn, *Qâmûs*, p. 36; Lane, *Modern Egyptians*, pp. 261–262 (especially left-eye).

Motifs: N134.2.1§, "One-eyed person brings bad luck;" N134.2.1.1.1§, ‡"Person with bad left eye surely brings bad luck."

See Tale-type: 1874D1§, *Who Should Be Ashamed: Cruel (Insensitive) Ruler or Person with Physical Handicap?*

[677] Abu el-Naṣr, *al-Bukhârî*, Vol. 4, p. 131; Lane, *Modern Egyptians*, pp. 260–261. Also see n. 686.

CHAPTER VI

Nonsacred Forces and Concepts

VI.A. Temporal Forces, Quasi Powers of Fate: *ez-zamàn/ez-zamân* (Time), *ed-dàhr* (Time-Epochs), *el-'ayyâm* (Days), *el-¿îshàh* (Life), ed-dùnyâ/dìnya (World, Life)

Another category of the supernatural may be described as essentially nonsacred without being necessarily secular. *ez-zamàn/ez-zamân* (time), *dàhr* (time-epochs), *el-'ayyâm* (days, i.e., passage of time), *el-¿îshàh* (life), *ed-dùnyâ/ed-dìnyâ* (the world, or life)—are concepts designating entities that are associated with supernatural powers. These concepts involve predestination only implicitly and are often viewed as causes for gradual, but inevitable, reversal of fortunes from better to worse; their impact on existing things (including human lives, and other animate and inanimate objects) parallels the effects of the preordained. These "time"-bound concepts may be residuals or survivals of earlier counter-religious arguments by a school of atheistic thought known in formal religious literature as *ad-dàhriyyàh* (i.e., those who attribute issues of life and death to the effects of *ed-dàhr*, i.e., time-epochs) rather than to God's Will and powers of creation and predestination.[678]

---

[678] Koran, 45:24. The use of the concept in Koran—where it occurs in connection with the infidels or the ungodly erring and blinded—appears to have had a decisive influence on its semantic evolution, which has given it a philosophical meaning far removed from its original sense. These ungodly men said: "There is nothing save our life in this world; we die and we live, and only a period of time (or: the course of time, *dahr*) makes us perish." See W.L. Schrameier, *Über den Fatalismus der vorislamischen Araber* (Bonn, 1881), pp. 12–22.

VI.B. Chance: *ḥaẓẓ/bàkht* (Luck), zàhr (Dice), *el-yâ-naṣîb/lutariyyah* (Lottery), *ṣùdfah* (Accident, Chance), *ṭâlì¿* (One's Place in the Horoscope)

Another subgroup of the nonsacred forces and concepts involve *ḥaẓẓ* or *bàkht* (luck),[679] *zàhr* (dice)[680] and to a lesser extent *el-yânaṣîb/lùtariyyàh* (the "O what a due share," i.e., lottery),[681] *ṣùdfàh* (accident or chance), and *ṭâlì¿* (one's place in the horoscope).[682] All of these entities may involve an element of predestination but not as an active component of the immediate situation of which they are a part.

VI.C. Learning of the Unknown: *el-kàff* ([Reading] the Palm of the Hand); *el-f ìngân* ([Reading the Residuals in a Coffee] Cup); Divination through *er-ràml* ("[Cutting] Sand"); *el-wadà¿* (Sea Shells); *eṭ-ṭâli¿* (One's Horoscope)

Certain practices of foretelling the future by divination rest on similar assumptions. These are *el-kàf* ([reading] the palm of the hand) where the lines are believed to represent one's future, *el-fingân* (or *fingâl*, reading the residuals in a ["Turkish"] coffee cup),[683] divination through *ḍarb er-ràml* ("striking/cutting sand")[684] and *el-wadà¿* ([casting] sea shells),[685] and the horoscope. All these activities rely on the mechanical, nonsacred relationship among different components of the universe, all of which are, however, ultimately controlled by God's Will and permission.

VI.C.a. Soliciting God's Choice (*'ìstikhâràh*), and Bibliomancy (*fàtḥ el-kitâb*)

By contrast to the mechanical relations cited above, *'ìstikhâràh*, asking God to show His choice through the petitioner's use of the *sibḥah* (*misbaḥàh*, rosary), *rù'yàh/manâm* (requesting an instructive dream), or *fàtḥ el-kitâb* (lit.: "opening the

---

[679] A.R. Ṣâliḥ, *al-'adab*, Vol. 1, p. 109; Amîn, *Qâmûs*, p.171. (See App. 5, where the force of *Dàhr* and its [malevolent] deeds are cited.)

[680] For a literary description of this concept, see M. Ḥusayn Haykal's *Zainab*, pp. 79–80. Also see App. 53.

[681] Amîn, *Qâmûs*, p. 419. The title seems to be derived from street cries by peddlers' of lottery tickets.

[682] Amîn, *Qâmûs*, pp. 275–276; Lane, *Modern Egyptians*, pp. 259–260. (The practice appears in older folk narratives as an alternative to sand-cutting.)

[683] Amîn, *Qâmûs*, p. 311.

The traditional way of preparing coffee is to add powdered coffee beans to hot water, which must not be brought to a boil. The amount of coffee-powder must be sufficient to form a thick mixture. The mixture must be sipped away (drunk) before the powdery contents sink to the bottom of the cup. Residuals left in the cup form various patterns that can be visually examined and interpreted as foretelling the future in the same manner as the technique of "cutting sand."

[684] Amîn, *Qâmûs*, pp. 268–269. Burton, gives a succinct description of the technique of "Zarb al-Raml" (strike of sand . . .). He points out (p. 170) that mixing it with geomancy often complicates it. See: *Arabian Nights*, Vol. 3., pp. 269–70, note 2.

[685] Walker-Ismâ¿îl, *Folk Medicine*, pp. 35–36.

[Holy] Book," i.e., bibliomancy)[686] have direct sacred supernatural connotations and are endorsed by formal religious institutions (see App. 17 and 18). The concerned person himself performs all these processes (as "individualistic cult institutions;" see n. 225). However, typically the petitioner (supplicant) is a cleric or a pious person acting on behalf of another person who holds himself/herself less capable of performing the task or less favored by God. The petitioner must be ritually clean (through ablution), and should recite certain holy passages believed to assist in the process of "revealing" or "showing" (e.g., Koran, 1:17, 23:20, 75:6, etc.). Typically, the truism, "*al-khîrah fîmâ 'ikhtârahu Allâh* (The [ideal] choice is in what has chosen)," follows the process involved, and signals acceptance of the course of action inferred.

VI.D. Risks and Gambles: *miqàysàh/muqâyasah* (Risk-Taking, Venturing), *muqâmarah* (Gambling, or Taking a Gamble), *'istibyâ¿* (Venturing Everything Out of Desperation)

Similarly, the *miqàysàh* (i.e., *mùqâyasàh*: risk-taking, venturing) constitutes another nonsacred concept that may lead to a practice comparable to, but not necessarily identical with, *mùqâmaràh* (gambling, or taking a gamble—typically referred to in folk parlance as *'ìstibyâ¿*: venturing everything out of desperation. A person who acts in such a desperate manner is described as *mìstàbya¿* or *bâyì¿ ¿umrûh*, i.e., "has sold his life"). The *miqàysàh* and *'ìstìbyâ¿* differ from relying on God (*el-'ìttikâl ¿alâ 'Allâh*, usually cited in the abbreviated vernacular form: *¿ala-Allâ*) in that the result of the first two may be viewed as a random outcome of events, whereas the outcome of the latter is an effect caused by God's Will and permission. Relying on God is the religiously recommended practice; risk-taking is simply tolerated, but taking a gamble and venturing all out of desperation are viewed as sinful (or, at least, bordering on the sinful) regardless of the outcome.

---

[686]Lane, *Modern Egyptians*, pp. 260–261; Walker-Ismâ¿îl, *Folk Medicine*, p. 36; Blackman, *Fellâhîn*, p. 196.

Burton argues that these practices are survivals from pre-Islamic era, thus he notes,

> . . . praying for direction by omens of the rosary, opening the Koran and reading the first verse sighted, etc., etc. At Al-Medinah it is called Khirah [i.e., *khîràh*] and I have suggested . . . that it is a relic of the Azlam or Kidah [i.e., *'azlâm* or *qidâḥ*] (divining arrows) of paganism. (*Arabian Nights*, Vol. 5, p. 44, note 1)

On instructive dreams, see n. 656.

CHAPTER VII

Anti-Sacred Forces

VII.A. *shàrr* (Evil), *khair* (Goodness)

An important aspect of the belief–practice system is the concept of *shàrr* (evil), which is typically contrasted in daily life with *khair* (i.e., *khàyr*, goodness). The issues of whether evil was created by God a priori, and whether evil and harm are of man's own choice or a matter of predestination, have been subject for intense and protracted debates among various theological and philosophical schools.[687]

In Koran, the word *khàyr* recurs but is infrequently contrasted to the word *shàrr*, which occurs far less frequently.[688] Numerous Koranic passages affirm man's responsibility for evil acts (sin, injustice, etc.); one such statement asserts that whatever good (*ḥasanàh*) a human may receive is from God, while whatever sin/evil (*sayyi'àh*) may befall man is from man himself (Koran, 4:79); another maintains that "Whatever misfortune Happens to you, is because of the things your hands Have wrought. . . . "[689]

Yet, in ordinary daily living, and among tradition-bound groups, good is invariably attributed to God, whereas evil may be viewed as either from God or Satan. If an evil (harmful) occurrence is viewed as from God, then it is perceived as a "necessary evil" that has been preordained by God "for a *ḥikmàh* ([wisdom], pl.: *ḥikàm*) known only to Him;" in such a case the harm is assumed to be a part of the trials and tribulations with which God puts individuals and groups to the test. An inscrutable and inexplicable but unavoidable occurrence is often reacted to by the expression: "*ḥikàm*!" ("[Incidents of God's] wisdom!"); such an occurrence may range from

---

687 On the concept of predetermination (compulsion), see *qadar*, "Qadarites," and "*Jabrîya*" in Goldziher, *Vorlesungen über den Islam*, A. and R. Hamori, trs., pp. 82–91.

688 Examples of such a contrast may be found in the following: Koran, 2:216, 10:11, 17:11, and 41:49.

689 Koran, 42:30—as translated by Abdallah Y. Ali; see n. 25. Cf. Koran, 10:44.

reflecting on "Why do earthquakes have to take place," to "Why an idiot seems to be successful and prosperous," and "Why an evil person seems to be healthy and enjoying a long life."[690] Only rarely do individuals and groups assume direct responsibility for an evil act. In the first case, where a disaster or a malady befalls a believer, it is usually interpreted as a test of the strength of a person's faith in God. In such a case the harm is not viewed as evil (*shàrr*) but merely an affliction (*'ìbtilâ'*). An oft-quoted truism states: "*el-mu'mìn muṣâb* (the true believer is [always] afflicted)."

A peripheral folk belief, associated with the arch-saints, states that God sends four *maṣâyìb* (i.e., *maṣâ'ìb*; sing.: *muṣîbàh*, i.e., affliction, disaster, calamity) to Earth with every sunrise. Arch-saints, in their capacity as *ḥawwâshîn* (i.e., "Preventers" [of disaster]) absorb most of these calamitous events on behalf of mankind; only a fraction of the original mishaps arrive on Earth and are responsible for all wars, suicides, murders, thefts, and the like.[691] In such a sacred context calamitous events are—at least on a conceptual level—not equated with *shàrr* (evil) but occur as a matter of course and enactment of God's Will.

VII.B. Eblis (Satan), Other "Satans." Cf. *shàrr* (Evil)

The concept of actual or real *shàrr* (evil) is invariably perceived to be a product of Eblis (Satan) and his agents who severed their ties with the godly ways and followed those of Satan and other devils. Eblis' agents and allies may be other satans, humans, or jinn. The occurrence of evil, especially through the agency of a human, is believed to be due to the *waswasàh* (egging on, temptation) of Eblis. The main objective of Eblis is to mislead Adam's children (i.e., mankind) as he had declared even before Adam was endowed with a soul, and upon his eviction from Paradise. When a human feels that he is being tempted to commit evil (i.e., to sin), he should utter God's name, verses from the Koran, or the phrase, "*'Allâhu-mma 'ikhzîk yâ sheṭân* (May God dishonor you [by making you fail], O Satan!)." Such utterances are believed to drive away Satan and foil his attempt to cause a person to go astray.[692] The actual realization of evil in this context requires following antisacred forces and the adoption or the committing of antisacred acts.

Occasionally, however, good and evil are perceived as anthropomorphic independent entities. The most frequent occurrence of "Good" and "Evil" as such is associated with a peripheral belief expressed in the truism "*el-khair w-esh-shàrr 'ikhwât*! (Good and Evil are brothers)!" This concept also appears in folksongs and a belief narrative (belief legend) stating that these two brothers had a dispute and asked people to act as umpires. People ruled in favor of Evil and deemed that he should stay while Good

---

690 Motif: N190§, ‡"Fate's inexplicable inequalities (injustices)."

691 Amîn, *Qâmûs*, p. 183. See "When the Arch-Saints Exchanged Jobs," in El-Shamy, *Folktales of Egypt*, No. 29, pp. 150–151, 278. Also see Section I.B.1.b, n. 78, where the creation of the *'âfàh* (pestilence) is presented.

692 Motif: V90§, "Miraculous effects of invoking God's attributes (*basmalah*, *ḥasbanah*, *ḥawqalah*, etc.)." For folk literary examples, see El-Shamy, *MITON*.

must depart.[693] Evidently, this narrative and the underlying concepts have been part of the supernatural belief–practice scene of the Egyptian scene for millennia. Its core theme harkens back to the ancient Egyptian sacred account of the struggle between Horus (Good) and the evil Seth who was Horus' paternal as well as maternal uncle.[694]

As abstract forces within the folk cognitive systems, Good and Evil, seem not to be clearly delineated independently of concrete or personified entities. Each is typically attached to another entity or force and perceived as one of its functions. (See "Satan and other fallen angels," in Section II.A.2, and "Sorcery or folk para-religious ritual?" in Section II.B.3a. Also compare the concept of *nàḥs*, i.e., bad omen, the state of being inauspicious, Section V.C.2.)

---

[693]Tale-type 613A§, "*Who May Remain in Town: Truth or Falsehood?*" Umpires decide in favor of Falsehood (Evil). See "Truth and Falsehood," in El-Shamy, "Tales Arab Women Tell," Résumé No. 11, pp. 46–47. For details, see El-Shamy, *DOTTI.*

[694]For a description of the conflict between Horus and his paternal/maternal uncle, see "The Noble and the Vile," in El-Shamy, *Folktales of Egypt*, No. 14, pp. 96–101, 261–262. Also see the following Tale-types in El-Shamy, *DOTTI*: 613B§, *Council of Judges (Gods) Rules in Error (The Judgment of the Ennead: The Lost or Damaged Item)*; 613B1§, *Judging in Error: The Bull Gave Birth to a Calf*; 613B2§, *Judging in Error as to Who Is the Legitimate Heir: The Son of the Deceased or a 'Stranger'?*

CHAPTER VIII

Mechanical Associations within the Supernatural

Tradition-bound individuals and groups clearly perceive the cause–effect relationship between one component of the system and another, and the instrumentality of certain forces and agents in the actualizing of that effect. A prayer to God for success will cause God to bring about success; appeal to a saint for help will get the saint (with God's permission, or through the saint's appeal to God) to cause help to take place; touching a revered object or a person endowed with *barakàh* (blessedness, grace) will cause the effects of that *barakàh* to diffuse to the individual who touched it. Also in practices seeking to harness jinn and minor angels, any person may ward off the jinn by simply uttering sacred words that will drive these beings away or will shield that person against their powers. Even with reference to works (*¿amalât*) by shaman-*shaikh*s (professional practitioners), the average layman recognizes the relationship between the work and its compelling effects on the supernatural, yet he will only be vaguely cognizant of the specific roles played by the intervening supernatural beings and forces. Clearly, not all the perceived relationships between presumed causes and effects are objective or logical, but the instrumentality of one on bringing about of the other through the agency of an intermediary (jinni-aid, angel-assistant, etc.) is thought to exist.

Another category of beliefs and related practices seems to manifest a different pattern of instrumentality or lack thereof; they also appear not to be organically related to the broader system. Although these beliefs still incorporate a cause-and-effect relationship, there seems to be no intermediate agent—such as jinn or angels that would link the two. Components of this category may range from the simplex (i.e., systems with a few components) to the intricate and multiplex (i.e., systems with numerous components); it includes: *khuzà¿balât* (superstitions), *mushâhràh* (causing barrenness or infertility in a female), *el-¿ain* (the [Evil] Eye), *and el-kìlmàh* ("the word").

VIII.A. *khuzà¿balât* (Superstitions)

This term occurs almost exclusively in its plural form; the singular, *khuzà¿balàh*, seems not to be in active usage. It is loosely applied to designate all "false" beliefs, especially those that are not derived from or cognitively related to a major formal religion. Such beliefs are also referred to more generally as *khùrâfât* (myths, or false beliefs that are held by "others" to be true). Unlike the term *mù¿taqàd* ("belief"), which bears no value judgment as to its correctness or incorrectness, the term "superstition" is an exoteric one, involving a value judgment applied mostly by the "learned" to characterize the folk beliefs that they judge as false or incorrect. In folk communities and parlance, such cognitive elements are simply unlabeled beliefs, typically expressed in the form of truisms: "[If you stack] one brick on top of another, [this] will cause a quarrel to continue (*ṭûbàh ¿ala ṭûbàh tikhalli-l-¿arkàh manṣûbàh*);" "A turned-over slipper will bring grief (*esh-shìbshìb el-maqlûb yigîb en-nakàd*);" "If your eye throbs [lit.: flutters, twitches], then something [important] will occur (*làw ¿ainàk trìff, yibqâ ḥâgàh ḥa-tìḥṣàl*);" or "Sweeping the floor by night brings about unhappiness (*el-kàns bi-l-lail yigîb en-nakàd*)."

Superstitions are essentially simplex (single) cognitions involving a single cause and effect. They are cognitive isolates; each one of these beliefs does not seem to be related to an intricate multiplex cognitive system where congruence and interconnectedness among components of the larger system are evident. Crossing over a fishing rod will cause it fail; standing with the fingers of one hand fitted into the fingers of the other hand and with palms of hands rested on one's head is a bad omen; breaking a water jug behind an unwanted guest after he/she has departed will cause that guest not to return; if a bird makes droppings on your clothes you will be receiving new ones from somebody—all are examples of this simplex belief category. Apart from the external sociological and psychological connotations, the relationship between cause and effect are supposed to be "mechanically" connected without the instrumental intervention of other agents such as jinn, angels, blessedness, curse/God's anger, etc. Some of these beliefs are congruent with the larger belief system, without necessarily being directly or cognitively related to it. For example, the cawing of a crow (raven) is always taken as a bad omen, and the hooting of an owl is indicative of an approaching disaster. These beliefs represent a cause-and-effect relationship that are congruent with the roles both birds played in the broader religious belief system, where they had mischievous roles.[695] Yet, the crow and the owl are not usually associated in a cognitive manner with these specific roles in the context of the "superstitions" (see Section II.D.4).

[695] al-Tha¿labî, *Qiṣaṣ*, p. 35; Amîn, *Qâmûs*, p. 298. On the owl's negative role, see Motif: A2231.15.1.2§, ‡"Owl opposes predestination: punished with blindness during daytime." Also see El-Shamy, "Vom Fisch geboren (AaTh 705)", as in n. 175.

VIII.B. *mushâhràh, kàbsàh,* or *sàkt* (Induced Loss of Fecundity, Barrenness, Infertility)

Being fertile and giving birth to numerous children, especially male offspring, is the most important criterion by which a married woman is judged in her husband's household. Also, a central asset in a woman's concept of herself and her self-esteem is being a mother and having the potential to continue to give birth.[696] A woman who has reached menopause is labeled "*qat¿àh el-khlàf* (ceased to beget)" or "*ma-bi-tiḍnîsh* (she does not bring forth beloved ones)."[697] Significantly, in learned circle menopause is termed "*sìnn el-yà's* (lit.: the age of despair or hopelessness)," a phrase adopted by psychologists and other social scientists as a term designating "the age of... loss of capacity for birth-giving."[698] Being a mother, especially of a boy, entitles a wife to certain "privileges," or more accurately, enables her to exact the treatment due for a full member of the household, which is typically patriarchal, patrilineal, and patrilocal.[699]

Usually, considerable matriarchal influence is present and mitigates the absolute dominance of the patriarch. This system of social power is evident also among members of the ever-expanding middle class where new patterns of family organization have developed. Patriarchal authority, especially with reference to decision-making has been lessened by a wife's (mother's) newly acquired greater share of *overt* economic and status power. Factors contributing to the increase of a woman's influence include the establishment of a new household for the newly weds (neolocal residence) instead of living with husband's parents, spread of the new practice of allowing the newly weds to dwell for extended periods that may last for years with the parents of the *bride* due to the severe housing shortage, and general acceptance of the economically self-sufficient working female. These changes have given a wife more freedom at *her own* home. Yet, the desire, especially of the wife, to have children as soon as possible is largely unchanged. Fear of barrenness, or even temporary infecundity (that a wife may *ti¿awwàq*, i.e., *tu¿awwàq*, suffering undesirable delay in becoming pregnant not due to infertility per se but due to other factors affecting her capacity to conceive), and consequent divorce or abandonment constitute major concerns for newly wed, young women in Egypt (and all other Arab countries) regardless of their social status or class.[700] The reasons cited for a female barrenness, or infecundity, are multiple and

[696]Motifs: P231.0.1§, "Mother of a son more valuable;" W164.1§, "Promoters of self-esteem;" W164.1.10§, ‡"Fertility (fecundity) as promoter of self-esteem."

[697]Literally, the word *ḍanâ* means arduous labor; it is typically used by females to indicate the fact that a child is so dear and precious, being the outcome of intense physical and emotional toil.

[698]Alhefnee, *Encyclopedia of Psychology & Psycho-Analysis*, p. 469.

[699]See Raphael Patai, Golden River to Golden Road: Society Culture and Change in the Middle East (Philadelphia, 1969), pp. 412–419, 435–436, 469–470. Also see Halim Barakat, *The Arab World: Society, Culture, and State* (Berkeley, 1993).

[700]In discussing infertility, Amîn (*Qâmûs*, p. 286.) points out the necessity of bearing children to a woman, and states that "women surrender their honor" for the sake of becoming pregnant.

An example of the drastic measures a childless woman would take to secure an offspring can be cited from the present writer's boyhood experiences. "Having grown in a town close to an ancient Egyptian

varied; for the most part they are perceived as supernatural in origin, rather than as the effects of a *maràḍ* or *¿ayâ* (i.e., organic illness).[701]

The presumed reasons for infertility may include the typical effects of a harmful *¿amàl* ("fix," charm) done against the bride, and the mischief of jinn, especially the *Qàrînàh* (Counter-spirit, Spouse, Correlative) and the *'Ukht* (supernatural sister; see Section II.C.1a, and App. 17). Additionally, another subcategory of supernaturally induced infertility is labeled *mushâhràh*, an appellation apparently derived from the arabic word *shàhr* (month).[702] *mushâhràh* is a process triggered by specific persons, objects, or acts that appear within specific contexts. It is also called *kàbsàh* or *sàkt* (lit.: "compression" or "silencing"/"rendering still," respectively); the latter names suggest that a female's procreative organs have been compressed or stilled and, therefore, have become unproductive.[703]

The most common form of *mushâhràh* occurs as an inevitable outcome when a person with certain personal attributes enters the room where a woman in a specific physiological condition is located. The physiological state is closely linked to marriage and parturition, and is in existence during postnuptial and postpartum intervals. This encounter is usually referred to as *yùkhùshsh/yùdkhùl ¿alâ* ("to enter upon") someone. The process may be described as an encounter between a stationary female in one of these two physiological conditions and (1) another female in a similar physiological condition; (2) a recently wed woman—usually having been married for a period *under* forty days—"entering upon" another recently married woman—having been married for a period *over* forty days; or (3) a menstruous woman "entering upon" another female who has recently given birth. In addition, a woman's infertility will

---

site called Tàll Baṣṭah (Bubastis), I along with a group of boys used to visit that site as a recreation (hiking), especially during winter school break. A certain ancient stone statue of a human standing in a regal posture, but without any facial features, seemed to have a great deal of potsherds scattered around it. No one of us was able to find out the reason. Finally, an older boy from the neighborhood explained that the reason was that women desiring to bear a child visit the site when no one would be watching, rub their genitals against the stone statue (presumed to be of the mighty disbeliever '*fara¿oan*'/Pharaoh) and would implore: "*ḥàbbìlnî yâ fara¿oan*! *ḥàbbìlnî yâ fara¿oan*! . . . ! (O Pharaoh, impregnate me! O Pharaoh, impregnate me! . . . !)" Upon completing this ritual they would break an earthenware water pitcher (with a spout) if they were wishing for a boy, or a water bottle if wishing for a girl. I remember that during these trips, we occasionally saw *baldî* (country, low-class) women in the vicinity, but never witnessed the ritual being performed."

Motifs: T591.5§, "Pregnancy induced by abnormal means (magic, philtre, potion, etc.);" Z139.9.3.2§, ‡"Water jug (jar, bottle, inkwell, etc.)—female, vagina, womb (or body orifice);" Z186.5§, "Symbolism: pitcher's spout—penis."

Also see Blackman, *Fellâhîn*, pp. 97–99; M.C. Inhorn, *Quest for Conception. Gender, Infertility, and Egyptian Medical Traditions* (Philadelphia: University of Pennsylvania Press, 1994). Cf. n. 244 and 245.

[701]Walker, in Walker-Ismâ¿îl, *Folk Medicine*, p. 47, note 2. The same observation was made by I. Rushdi, "Maraḍ al-iklimbsia" (eclampsia)", pp. 293–294. Also see n. 297.

[702]Ammar, *Silwa*, pp. 103, 123; John G. Kennedy, "Nubian Zar Ceremonies as Psychotherapy." In: *Human Organization*, Vol. 26 (1967), pp. 185–194; Fawziyyah Diyâb, *al-Qiyam wa al-¿âdât al-'igtimâ¿iyyah* (*Social Values and Customs [in Egypt]*), Cairo, Dâr al-Kitâb al-¿Arabî, n.d., pp. 302–303; Inhorn, *Quest for Conception*, pp. 114–120.

[703]Informant: Nabawiyyah Y. (Oct. 20, 1969). See n. 212.

be brought about by another person with a specific mannerism "entering upon" her; such a person may be a man or a youth who has just had a haircut; a person carrying certain objects such as fresh meat or eggplant,[704] and a woman dressed in black, or wearing heavy gold jewelry. These objects are thought of as catalysts for the *mushâhràh* process; the mere presence of the object without the other personal and interpersonal components would not in itself trigger the incapacitating injurious result. Other catalysts are less frequently encountered; one such agent is *nîlàh* (indigo), which was reported at the end of the nineteenth century as instrumental in causing barrenness in a human female.[705]

Field reports from the southernmost regions of Egypt, especially Nubia,[706] indicate that the time of the month when the encounter takes place is also instrumental in the *mushâhràh* process. In broader context of practices associated with the weaning and subsequent circumcision of children, the time frame in which these events take place is believed to significantly influence the child's fertility (or fecundity) during adulthood. Consequently, the time for applying the practice is reckoned according to the position of the moon: if child weaning or circumcision is done after the appearance of the new moon (i.e., *shàhr*/month), "the child is liable to be 'tied up' (mushahir) [(i.e., *mishshâhr*)], the consequence of which may be that the wound might not heal quickly, or the child might eventually be sterile."[707]

In the *mushâhràh* process, the acts of "entering upon"—or performing weaning or circumcision on a child at the wrong time of the lunar month—on the one hand, and the consequent infertility on the other, are mechanically associated. Unlike barrenness induced through *¿amàl* ("fix" belonging to para-religious or "magical" practices), neither jinn nor minor angels are the agents through which infertility is brought about. Yet, one case in which the jinn may be involved in the *mushâhràh* was reported to the present writer, which is as follows:

> When a virgin is being deflowered, if a drop of the defloration blood falls on earth [i.e., the ground, floor], the *mùlûk* ("kings," i.e., jinn) will *yishâhrûha* (cause her to become barren).[708]

---

[704]Eggplant is typically perceived as black in color. See: Amîn, *Qâmûs*, p. 79; Walker-Ismâ¿îl, *Folk Medicine*, pp. 45–46. See also n. 715.

[705]Walker-Ismâ¿îl, *Folk Medicine*, p. 45.

[706]Informant: Faniyyah G., Kunûzi Nubian, widow, aged 44, from Dahmit, lives in Cairo, and Mr. ¿U. ¿U. Kidr (March 22, 1969; col. El-Shamy). See also J.G. Kennedy, "Nubian Zar Ceremonies . . . ," 1967.

[707]Ammar, *Silwa*, p. 123. (See also n. 700 and 719)

With reference to this phenomenon of vulnerability at certain times, Ammar states that "one might be led to infer that the moon must have been connected with fertility rites in some period of Egyptian history." He suggests (p. 103) that an association may exist between the ancient Egyptian god Seth, who was also God of barrenness, and the moon on one hand, and *mushâràh* or the appearance of the new moon (month) on the other. Ammar, however, concludes that more research is needed before the existence of this link can be assumed.

[708]Informants: 'Asmâ Ḥ., from the southern city of el-Minya, age 68 (October 20, 1969); Nabawiyyah Y., a native Cairene woman, agreed with the report (see n. 212).

Even in this situation, the jinn seem to merely act in human-like manner; they simply replace the human being initiating the encounter with the vulnerable human female susceptible to *mushâhràh*; the resulting sterility still occurs mechanically.

The undoing of the *mushâhràh* may be very simple or quite elaborate. Women may take protective measures against that danger by wearing a special object referred to as *el-mushâhràh*, *ḥagàr el-kàbbâs* (the compression stone), and *ḥagàr eṭ-ṭàrafàh* (the abrasion stone).[709] Such an object may function as a preventive amulet (charm), or as a cure.[710] Usually it is made of amber or similar semiprecious stones and strung along with other artifacts of lesser size; some of these items are labeled *masâkhîḥ* (devolved beings—creatures reverted to a lesser form of life usually as punishment). Another more elaborate procedure requires that the afflicted female cause the same type of harm to another woman, thus ridding herself of the effect of *mushâhràh*. This procedure is known as "unloading" an affliction by transferring it to a third innocent party.[711] Unless the jinn are a party to the *mushâhràh*, as in the case of the dripping of blood on the ground during defloration, counter-jinn rituals are not employed.

Barrenness induced in such a mechanical manner is not restricted to human females; *mushâhràh* may also affect certain plants. One notable case is the eggplant—an infertility-inducing agent itself. A number of females from various parts of Egypt gave information confirming the continued existence of the belief. In the words of a Bedouin woman living in a settled community on the eastern outskirts of Cairo,

> If a menstruous woman were to step into an eggplant field, the plants would die; there is no remedy for it; its owner will have to pull the shrubs out [and start anew].

The informant explained,

> This is because eggplant is *sharîf* (pure, honorable) and cannot withstand *nagâsàh* (defilement).[712]

A companion aspect of this belief seems to have had a commercial dimension. Ismâ¿îl reported that all that is required to cure infertility due to *mushâhràh* by

[709]The word *ṭarfah* is usually used to refer to an accidental abrasive touch to the eye that causes some pain and eye irritation. Its appearance in the context of supernatural healing suggests that the stone is meant to treat a bodily abrasion or a scuff. There may be a noncognitive association between harm to the "eye" and harm to a woman's reproductive organ (vagina) usually likened to an eye; cf. Motif: Z186.9.2.1§, "Symbolism: 'the red eye'—vagina, anus."

[710]Walker-Ismâ¿îl, *Folk Medicine*, p. 22; Amîn, *Qâmûs*, p. 155; cf. Blackman's "*ḥagar eṭ-ṭarfâ* (Stone of the Tamarisk)," *The Fellâhîn*, p. 203.

[711]Motifs: D1500.3.1, ‡"Charm shifts diseases to another person;" cf. D2177.5§, "Exorcism by transferring spirit to another person (or to an animal)."

[712]Informant: 'Omm Shindî, see n. 312 (Cairo, 1969).

Motifs: C141.1, "Tabu: menstruous woman not to go near any cultivated field or crop will be ruined. [*mushâhrah*];" C1.1.1§, ‡"The profane (*najiss/najass/'nagâsah'*): the opposite of the pure/immaculate (*ṭâhir/ṭuhr*)."

black eggplant is that the victim "has only to visit a field of egg-plants." He further noted that keepers of gardens in urban centers set aside portions for eggplants, "because they make a lot of money from the visitation of [... *mushâhràh*-afflicted] women to them."[713] Cucumber (*khiyâr*) is another plant also susceptible to "withering," or sustaining considerable damage if trespassed on by a menstruous woman.

Reasons for the development of such cognitive clusters correlating blood of menstruation and "*'adhâ*" (harm, hurt) may be readily found in religious edicts that advise "avoiding" coition with a menstruous woman (*maḥîḍ*)[714] due to its harmful effects (Koran, 2:222). With reference to plants, presently available data seem to indicate that items susceptible to *mushâhràh* are among those that bear fruit that may symbolically be associated with male genitalia. According to a number of informants, the word *bedìngân* (i.e., *bâdhìngân*—eggplant) is derived from the phrase *baiḍ el-gân* (lit.: "eggs of the jinn" [i.e., jinn's testicles]).[715] Similarly, a cucumber and a phallus are often cognitively correlated. One Cairene female informant who cited cucumbers as an agent causing *mushâhràh* also narrated a tale in which a girl masking as man added on a masculine physical disguise:

> She went and got two *doam* (fruits of doam palm) [... which resemble testicles] and something like that which men have (say: a *cucumber*, a carrot...! Any thing in that form) [i.e., which looks like a phallus], and she tied them to herself [thus giving the appearance of having the organs of a male].[716]

With reference to other agents of *mushâhràh*, the relationship may be less readily discernible; in cases where indigo is a barrenness-generating agent, a symbolic association may be argued to exist—thus forming a cognitive cluster—between indigo as an "inauspicious" substance on the one hand, and sexual activities and genitalia in general on the other. In females' parlance (or "women's talks"),[717] reference to male genitalia and sexual intercourse is often made through the euphemisms *nîlàh*

---

[713]Walker-Ismâ¿îl, *Folk Medicine*, pp. 45–46.

[714]Motifs: cf. C142, "Tabu: sexual intercourse during menses;" C3§, ‡"*al-makrûh* ('the disfavored,' 'the disliked' [by God]): almost-tabu, merely tolerated—not the preferred way (for Moslems)."

[715]This case of folk etymology was reported to the present writer by Mr. Ṣâber el-¿. (in Cairo, 1969–1970), a university graduate, Material Culture specialist.

There are two varieties of eggplant: *¿arûs* (straight and slender—black or white, suitable for stuffing) and *'alâgah* (large, pear shaped—mainly for stewing or frying), the reference here is to the second type. See also n. 704.

Motifs: Z105§, ‡"Shape (form, color) symbolism: association based on similarities of visually perceived properties of object;" T511.1.3.3§, "Conception from eating eggplant;" Z166.3.2.3§, ‡"Eggplant-testicles. ('*bedingân'/bâdhingân* = *baiḍ el-gân*: lit.: 'eggs of the jinn' [i.e., jinn's testicles]);" D1367.1.1§, ‡"Insanity (idiocy, lunacy, etc.) from eating eggplant."

For the association between eggplant and eccentric behavior, see Burton, *Arabian Nights*, Vol. 5, p. 4, note 1.

[716]El-Shamy, *Tales Arab Women Tell*, No. 9, p. 121, 372, note 200. Also see: "Oral Traditional Tales and the Thousand Nights and a Night: The Demographic Factor," p. 80.

[717]Motif: W202.1.1.1§, ‡"Indicator of femininity: women's speech-tone (soft, low-key)."

(lit.: indigo, or blue-black, i.e., ominous thing, a mess), and *sùkhâm* (i.e., disgusting thing, a mess). Nubian informants who had cited black and blue clothes as agents of *mushâhràh* narrate a tale that accounts for the experiences of a husband who severed his own phallus so as to demonstrate to his "dying" wife that he will not remarry after her death. However, the wife recovered and reproached him for "being without a 'thing.'" He fled to a distant land, and was selected by lot to become king and marry a princess.

> He told her [i.e., his bride] the story. He said to her, "I was very much in love with some woman, and married her. When she was dying she said to me, 'You will remarry after I am gone.' She made me cut it off!" She [the bride] replied, "Is it only with that *nîlàh* and *sùkhâm* [mess and sad stuff; i.e., sex] that people can live! Does this mean that one cannot live without it [i.e., of course one can do without]!"[718]

Clearly, barrenness caused by the mechanical associations characteristic of *mushâhràh* is typologically different from that induced through the agency of jinn evoked by *¿amàl* ("fix," "magic" charm), or by the jinn as components of the self (e.g., *Qarînàh*, *'Omm-eṣ-Ṣùbyân*, etc.; Cf. respectively, Section II.B.2, and App. 34; Sections II.C–II.C.1a; and App. 17 and 18).

Meanwhile, as pointed out (see Section II.B.3), "tying" (*ràbṭ*) is a procedure that seeks to affect adversely the potency of a male. It is comparable in this respect, to *mushâhràh*. The effects of *ràbṭ* are the generating of phallic depression or impotency in a man. The goal of "tying," as described by one informant, is to render that target man "to be just like a woman." Unlike *mushâhràh*, causing phallic depression is never accidental and the cause–effect relationship is not mechanical. The ritual must be carefully constructed and executed by a professional (or some other practitioner, or a layman with sufficient knowledge of the ritual). The victim, usually during the wedding procession, must be told: "You are *màrbûḥ* (tied)!," or at least he must be made to believe in some way that he is under a phallic depression spell.[719] Cases in which the victim was not informed are occasionally reported under the label "tying." In these situations, however, impotency was to be induced by a typical *¿amàl* (fix, work), placed by a wife against her own husband, and formulated so as to be effective only if he were to interact erotically with *another* woman (i.e., in situations of marital

---

[718] For the full text see El-Shamy, *Tales Arab Women Tell*, No. 24, p. 208.

Lexicographers Badawî and Hinds, *A Dictionary of Egyptian Arabic*, write: "'sukhâm' = male sexual organ, 'sakhkham' = 'fucking'" (p. 403). Similarly, they identify "'nîla' = lousy, rotten; 'nayyil' = 'to fuck'" (p. 895).

[719] A possible exception here is H. Ammar's unspecific general report concerning the effect of weaning and circumcising on children, which he labeled "'tied up' (mushahir [i.e., 'mitshâhir'])," (Ammar, *Silwa*, p. 123; also see n. 707, above). However, in this context the label *mushahir* seems to be used in a broader sense involving the long-lasting effects of *mushâhrah* as delineated above. In this respect, it may be presumed that the child will grow up as an impotent, and, consequently, the motivation for "tying," or initiating *mushâhrah*—to use Ammar's term—would be nonexistent, and the ritual irrelevant.

infidelity, or pondering taking another wife).[720] As in the case of undoing *mushâhràh* (barrenness that occurs through mechanical association), nullifying the effects of *rabḥ* requires an elaborate process involving identifying the affliction, the persons involved, the supernatural *agents* at work, and the supernatural *forces* used in the formulation of the "work" and responsible for its continued efficacy. Once these elements have been identified, the practitioner may use countermeasures to revoke their effect.[721] Unlike *mushâhràh*, *rabṭ* cannot be undone by simply "unloading it" on someone else.

VIII.C. *el-ḥasàd* ([Malicious] Envy) and *el-¿Ain* (The [Evil] Eye)

Another category of beliefs where the link between a certain act and its effects may be seen as mechanically actualized (without the jinn, angels, etc. being involved as agents or catalysts) is that concerned with *el-ḥasàd* ([malicious] envy) and *el-¿ain* (i.e., *al-¿àyn*: the [Evil] Eye). Reports that cite jinn as the agents causing harm are inaccurate or, perhaps, were produced by a scholar's zeal to have informants' account for aspects of traditional culture that exist as unarticulated or vague premises. One such case is that given by Edward Westermarck who reported that in Morocco, when the [evil] glance leaves the eye, it is joined by a jinni who accompanies that glance to the envied object and causes it harm.[722]

Belief in the malice of envy and the Evil Eye is universal and plays a central role in forming the foundations of how social groups view their world. In folk parlance the two words and their derivatives occur in a broad spectrum of simple and idiomatic usages, without *necessarily* involving supernatural powers. For example, speaking of *el-'a¿âdî* (the enemies), *el-'akhṣâm* (the adversaries), *el-¿awâzìl* (those who censure, or reproach), and *el-ḥussâd* (the envious ones, those who envy) is commonplace, especially in lyric songs.[723] Yet, no supernatural powers are assumed to be invoked. Similarly, one may speak of the act of someone *yibùṣṣ li* (to glance at), *yibàḥlàq* (stare), *yirâ¿î* (to have an extended look at), *yishûf* (to see [may also mean: "I'll pay you," or "I'll take care of you later"), *yigàḥawàr ¿inaih* (give an insolent, challenging, glaring, stern stare), *yìẓghùr* (to give an angry warning or threatening stare), etc., without necessarily involving the Evil Eye. As a belief with supernatural implications, envy (*ḥasàd*) is based on the premise that certain individuals possess the power to inflict harm by simply desiring the malicious effect (i.e., by wishing it on someone or something). Thus, some formal religious literature views envy as caused by a spiritual

---

[720]Motifs: T591.0.2§, "*rabṭ*: supernaturally induced impotence;" T591, "Barrenness or impotence induced by magic."

See "The Only Murder in Girshah," in El-Shamy, *Folktales of Egypt*, No. 42, pp. 178–179, 285; and App. 36. Also see a wife's comment on this ritual in "The Love Sick Husband," in El-Shamy, *Tales Arab Women Tell*, No. 29, p. 234. Cf. Sengers, *Women and Demons*, p. 158.

[721]Amîn, *Qâmûs*, p. 209. (See App. 35)

[722]Edward Westermarck, *Ritual and Belief in Morocco*, 2 vols. (London, 1926).

[723]Motif: W199.3.3§, ‡"Blaming 'The other'—('people/society,' 'adversaries/enemies,' 'blamers,' 'censurers,' 'the envious,' etc.)."

effect of the *nàfs* (i.e., the psyche) and not necessarily by the "eye."[724] The unleashing of this power of ill will may be either intentional or accidental; in either case the resulting harm occurs mechanically. The effects of envy may also be generated by malicious intent or caused unintentionally. In the first case, where malice is involved,

(a) there is an unspoken desire that evil may befall a person; thus an envious person thinking of an enviable personal attribute, such as health, or a piece of property such as an automobile, will bring about harm to the envied individual vis-à-vis that attribute or that property;

(b) there can be a voiced declaration that harm will or ought to befall a person, such as "What a beautiful healthy child!" or "What a shiny car!" In this respect envy comes very close to the belief in "curse" (*dà¿wàh ¿alâ*), but without pleading with God—or other supernatural beings such as jinn or angels—to inflict the damage desired.

Similarly, envy due to benign intent occurs unintentionally by thinking of good aspects of a person thus inviting envy; or by unintentionally speaking out and enumerating individual's good assets.

Envy emanating from benign intent may afflict the person who is thinking or speaking of his own enviable qualities. It is considered "bad manners" as well as "dangerous" for one to enumerate or dwell on his or her personal good fortunes. A traditional saying states, "*ma-yeḥsìdsh el-mâl 'illâ-ṣḥâbùh*" (property is envied only [i.e., mostly] by those to whom it belongs). The voiced or verbalized means of affecting envy (*ḥasàd*) is typically referred to as *qàrr*, or *nàqq* (envy-inviting praise, talk that would invite envy and its destructive effects); a proverbial saying warns those who talk too much about an object, "*yâ nâs yâ shàrr, baṭṭalû qàrr*" (O you evil people, cease [your] envy-inviting comments!).[725] This aspect of belief constitutes a hazard for scholars doing fieldwork, interviewing individuals about their children's diet, clothing, health, etc. Such inquisitiveness can easily be perceived as envy-inviting *nàqq* or *qàrr*.

A person who is envious (*ḥassâd*; female: *ḥassâdàh*) is assumed to be driven by a malicious desire to cause harm, or more accurately, to cause the loss of a positive asset or quality that another individual possesses. Thus, although envy is mostly willful and deliberate, it may also be brought about accidentally through negligence or inattentiveness through praising or admiring saliently but failing to use "protective" prayers.[726] The envious person is also assumed to have an Evil Eye. Yet, a blind person may be envious, as well. A person who has an Evil Eye need not be willfully envious; such a person, therefore, is not necessarily malicious. This aspect of the belief complex

---

[724] *al-Azhar*, Vol. 12, No. 3 (1941), pp. 161–162.

[725] Amîn, *Qâmûs*, p. 319. See El-Shamy, "'Noble and Vile' or 'Genuine and False'? Some Linguistic and Typological Comments on *Folktales of Egypt*." In: *Fabula*, Vol. 24 (1983) Nos. 3–4, pp. 341–346.

[726] Motifs: D2071.1, "Averting Evil Eye;" D2073§, "Bewitching by means of a spoken word (*naqq, qarr*);" D2071.1.4.0.2§, ‡"Holy verse (text) guards against Evil Eye (*raqwah*);" Z13.9.1§, ‡"Speaker wards off evil effects of own speech (words);" V90§, "Miraculous effects of invoking God's attributes (*basmalah, ḥasbanah, ḥawqalah*, etc.)."

is congruent with other beliefs that a certain organ of the body, such as the hand or tongue, may act independently of its owner.[727]

Envy and the Evil Eye may also affect animals and objects. However, when nonhuman subjects are the targets for envy, it is almost exclusively in their quality of being an extension of (i.e., property of or being especially meaningful to) a human being. A person may harmlessly "envy" birds for their ability to fly, lions for their strength and courage, flowers for their beauty without wishing they lose the merits envied. However, if a person envies another person's bird (e.g., falcon) because it hunts so well, a circus trainer's lion for its dexterity and strength, or someone's flowers because they are exceptionally pretty, these beings and objects, it is believed, would be susceptible to developing serious illnesses or defects as a result of envy and "the Eye."

Envy (*ḥasàd*) and the evil generated by an envious person are explicitly cited in the Koran as a fact of social life. The evil of envy is equated but not identified with that of magic (Koran, 113:5). In most literary traditions envy is differentiated from *ghibṭàh*, which is a person's desire to have the good asset that another individual possesses without wishing that the other would lose it. Both *ghibṭàh* and *ḥasàd*, as pointed out earlier, are typically perceived to be an effect of the *nàfs* (psyche) and not necessarily generated by "the Eye."[728] From a religious standpoint, *ghibṭàh* is sanctioned, but *ḥasàd* (envy) is condemned.

VIII.C.1. *el-¿ain* (The Eye)

The belief complex concerning the eye may be considered a more specific and concrete aspect of envy. Generally, the eye is viewed as a source of supernatural power that in certain cases may be benevolent and comparable to *barakàh* (blessedness), or malevolent, and thus a part of the mechanism of envy. The eye—or more accurately—*en-naẓràh* (i.e., the glance, the look from the eye)—of a prophet, a saint, or a blessed person is believed to cause desirable effects such as healing, giving strength, or bestowing blessedness.[729] In formal Islamic dogma, the Evil Eye is reported only in the Prophet's tradition.

The belief in the Evil Eye can be shown to harken back to the Heliopolitan "cosmogony" of ancient Egypt; the two deities, Shu and Tefnut, were lost and the god Atum sent his eye to search for them. During its absence Atum replaced it with another. The eye was enraged and became destructive. In another variant the eye

---

[727] Motif: F1042§, "Mania: compulsion—uncontrollable (involuntary) behavior." See: "The Man Who Didn't Perform His Prayers," in El-Shamy, *Folktales of Egypt*, No. 19, p. 123, 269.

This was also the case with the two angels Ḥârût and Mârût; their wings refused to obey them after they sinned. (See al-Tha¿labî, *Qiṣaṣ*, p. 31, and Section II.A.2a) Cf. Motif E709.1§, ‡"Conflict between soul and body" (Khalîfah, *al-Dâr al-barzakhiyyah*, p. 211).

[728] Yûsuf al-Digwî, "al-ḥasad wa al-ruqyah minh" (Envy and [how to] confront it through [Religious] incantation). In: *al-Azhar*, Vol. 12, No. 8 (1941), pp. 161–162.

Motif: D1273.0.6§, "'*raqwah*'/*ruqwah*: charm containing sacred words renders invulnerable (protects)." (See n. 306)

[729] Motif: V221.0.1.4§, ‡"Glance (*naẓrah*) from saint's eye heals (bestows power)."

belonged to the deity Ra; Thoth, the moon god, was sent to fetch and mollify it.[730] In "modern" folk rituals against the [Evil] Eye, Thoth's role is usually assigned to Prophet Sulaymân (Solomon).[731]

In contemporary culture, the Evil Eye is presumed to be "ḥâmyàh (burning-hot, or fiery);" it can cause widespread destruction including burning crops and residential areas. A defensive prayer against the fiery Evil Eye is for the person glancing at an enviable object or quality to state "May He [God] render my eye cool on you!"

Although Satan is believed to have been cast out of heavens because of his jealousy/envy of God's preference for Adam over him,[732] he does not seem to be directly associated with this vice. Envy is only implicitly understood to be a sinful desire instigated by Satan, who compels a person to be envious. Meanwhile, the Evil Eye is only rarely perceived as a product of satanic functions.[733] Statements and exclamations such as *mànẓûr* (glanced at), *ṣàybâh ¿ain* (stricken by an Eye), *naẓràh we-ṣâbìt* (a glance that proved to accurately hit its target) may indirectly indicate Satan's instrumentality in the process.

However, the modern Evil Eye, like ancient eye of Atum, seems to be autonomous of both the body and the will of the person of whom it is a part. The Eye may act independently, and even against the person's wishes. Thus, as precaution, a person with such an Eye may wear a patch over it to prevent it from unleashing its powers on others. The Eye may also act in accordance with its owner's wishes. In the former case, Islamic jurisprudence did not hold a person responsible for the action of his/her own Evil Eye. Ibn Khaldûn stated: "A person who kills with his Eye may not be executed, for the deed is involuntary,"[734] and would be treated as "involuntary manslaughter" according to Islamic jurisprudence. Thus perceived, fear of envy and the Evil Eye are ever present among groups pertaining to all social levels, ages, genders, and religious affiliations. The Evil Eye cult, however, seems to be more pronounced among females. The centrality of the belief rests on, among other things, the fact that it manifestly

---

730 Ions, *Egyptian Mythology*, p. 27, 41.

Motif: A128.2.1.1§, "Eye of deity becomes vengeful and evil (the Evil Eye)." See introductory note to "The Stone in Bed," in El-Shamy, *Folktales of Egypt*, No. 45, p. 286 (App. 47).

731 Cf. Walker-Ismâ¿îl, *Folk Medicine*, p. 96, note 3.

One such incantation verse is given in Fawziyyah Diyâb, *al-Qiyam wa al-¿âdât al-'igtimâ¿iyyah* (Social Values and Customs [in Egypt]), p. 324 (App. 44). Cf. a shamaness' threats to place the eye in a copper cucurbit (*qumqum*); see A.R. Ṣâliḥ, *al-Adab*, Vol. 1, pp. 121–122.

732 In para-religious literature, Eblis is reported to have said,

> I've been worshiping God for so many thousands of years and He has not admitted me in Paradise, while this [Adam] is a creature that God has just created now and admitted into Paradise. (Tha¿labî, *Qiṣaṣ*, p. 19)

Cf. Motif: W195.0.2§, ‡"Angels envious (jealous) of Adam for being favored by God (being His exquisite creation, successor on Earth, etc.)."

733 For example, Abu-Ṭâlib al-Mufaḍḍal Ibn ¿Âṣim, a ninth century Moslem writer, attributes the cause of the Evil Eye to Satan. See Ibn-¿Âṣim, *al-Fâkhir* (Cairo, 1960), No. 320, p. 198.

734 Ibn Khaldûn/Rosenthal, *The Muqddimah*, Vol. 3, p. 171.

makes every individual, no matter how poor, weak, sickly, unattractive, etc., the *sole* possessor of at least one precious and enviable quality beyond the reach of others. Being the owner of something distinctive is a basic requirement for promoting one's self-esteem, and attaining a "mentally healthy" self-concept. Under the Evil Eye belief no person is ever lacking in positive assets.[735]

Devices against envy and the Eye may be seen as either preventive or therapeutic. For prevention, an individual may hide his or her good assets, make them appear less attractive (such as soiling the face of a child after having given it a bath),[736] wearing protective amulet or object believed to ward off the Evil Eye (e.g., the hand, the blue bead, a *mashàllàh* [i.e., a piece of jewelry with the inscription "*mâ-shâ'a-'Allâh*, What God has willed [will take place]"), a verse from the Koran, especially *sûràt* (chapter) "Yâ-Sîn," (Koran, 36), "al-Falàq," (Koran, 113), or "al-'Ikhlâṣ" (Koran, 112; also known as "eṣ-Ṣamadiyyàh"). There are also dozens of truisms, epithets, and drawings that are attached to or sketched on objects believed to be inviting targets for envy: a truck may bear the statement, "*al-ḥasûd lâ yasûd* (an envious person does not prevail [socially])," or "*ma-tbùṣṣlîsh bi ¿ain radiyyàh, bùṣṣ li-lli màdfû¿ fiyyàh* (Do not glance at me with a sinister eye, [but] look at what was paid for acquiring me [i.e., look at the troubles and expense sustained by owner in order to purchase me])." Some truisms assume that the continued good fortune (i.e., not being involved in a wreck, or having a breakdown) is due to the fact that being stricken by an Evil Eye is inevitable, but due to divine mercy the envied item has been spared from the damage—thus it states, "*¿ain we ṣâbìt, wi rabb-el-¿àrsh naggânî* (An Eye struck me, [but] the Lord of the Throne safeguarded me)!" It is also considered good etiquette for a speaker who will be referring to an attractive person, or other enviable object, to state: "May God's name protect him/her;" "May the Prophet's name, protect him," or "*¿ainî ¿alaih bârdàh* (May my eye be cool on him)!" Another way for preventing the Evil Eye from bring about its damage is to frighten the suspect glancer while in the act of casting his/her Evil Eye (i.e., glance) by stating: "*ḥayyàh warâk*! (A viper is behind you!)," thus causing the glancer to direct his/her attention to another object and divert the harmful glance away from the intended target; a similar verbal formula: "*tiff mìn buqqàk* (spit [it] out of your mouth," i.e., 'Bite your tongue') would produce a similar result by cleansing the mouth of the harmful effects of the envious words spoken. (See Section VIII.C.2)

Therapeutic practices (countermeasures) to cure the effects of envy or the Evil Eye may range from do-it-yourself rituals to elaborate measures requiring professionals. These may be religious, such as reciting passages from the Holy Book, or to resort to clerics or shaman-*mashâyìkh* (practitioners of faith healing, magicians) in order to identify the person inflicting the damage and to deal with the affliction accordingly. (See App. 45)

---

[735]Motifs: W164.1.1§, "Belief that one is target for Evil Eye promotes self-esteem;" cf. W195.0.1§, ‡"'Everyone that has been blessed (endowed) with an asset is envied.'"

See "The Stone in Bed," in El-Shamy, *Folktales of Egypt*, No. 45, p. 182 (App. 47).

[736]Lane, *Modern Egyptians*, p. 57.

VIII.C.2. *el-kelmàh* (The Word)

Believing that the word (as it is pronounced in classical: *al-kalimàh*), spoken or written, as an active entity, is based on the tendency to perceive inanimate objects and abstracts in anthropomorphic terms. It is also grounded in the sacred belief that letters, words, holy phrases, etc. were created by God, and consequently, assigned the status of "creatures" (see Section I.B.1)

Apart from the direct links among names, their referents, and the jinn and angel servants of these names (see Science of Letters, Section II.B.2), the spoken word is believed to embody its own cause–effect mechanisms. As a result, words with affective aspects such as being "good" or "bad," "harmful" or "beneficial," "auspicious" or "inauspicious," etc. are perceived to also have effects that parallel those of the supernatural. A folk truism states "Poison [resides] in the tongue (*es-sìmm fe-l-lisân* [of the speaker])." Consequently, names of dangerous things (animal, disease, murder, disaster, etc.) are not to be "spoken at" a person without the use of precautionary measures. These protective devices include the uttering of the following: "*el-bi¿îd/el-'ab¿ad* (Distant-one/More distant-one)," "*bi¿îd ¿annàk* (Away from you)," "*fàssarnâ bi-r-Raḥmân* (We've reckoned [this matter in terms of] The Compassionate—i.e., God)", or similar protective aphorisms.[737]

Upon addressing a word or a statement that has harmful or evil implications at a person, if the speaker fails to apply a precautionary measure, the addressee will feel that he has become the target for the ill-effects of the word, and will try to rectify the situation by uttering or performing the precaution himself. In this latter situation, God's name or one of His attributes may also be applied in expressions such as "*'Allâhu 'akbàr*" (God is greater),[738] *yâ Ḥafîẓ* (O You Guardian, Protector), or simply "'Allâh!"

It is also believed that the speaker's spitting could avert the potential harm of a spoken evil word; thus the addressee may order the speaker "*tiff mìn buqqàk* (spit [it] out of your mouth)!" The rationale for the presumed efficacy of this practice is that the evil attributes of the word are spit out and thus cast "away from" a target. For example, the word "*khaṭàr* (danger)" is often required to be placed in hazardous location or on dangerous objects such as flammable or explosive matters. Truck drivers whose vehicles have exposed gas tanks typically display the warning word (usually in red) but seek to transform its meaning by using it in the common phrase: "*khaṭàr ¿alâ bâlî* (occurred to my mind)."

Other supernatural functions are assigned to letters, words, and phrases in congruence with the contexts in which they appear in sacred dogma.[739] The letter-cluster

---

[737]These are designated as Motifs: C433, "Tabu [Taboo]: uttering name of malevolent creature (Eumenides, [(the gracious)]). To avoid the evil results of naming these creatures other names are substituted;" C434§, "Names of dangerous things (animal, disease, murder, etc.) are not to be uttered at a person without use of precautionary measures (e.g., 'Distant one,' 'Away from you')."

See El-Shamy, *Folktales of Egypt*, pp. liv–lv.

[738]Western literature reports this shibboleth as "God is great!" However, the accurate translation would be "God is greater! [than . . . injustice, evil, tyranny, etc.]."

[739]This perception is a function of cognitive association (clustering).

Motifs: Z108§, ‡"Sound (name) symbolism: association based on sound similarities (homophony);"

"K-H-Y-¿-Ṣ" (pronounced: "kâ-hâ-yâ-¿ain-ṣâd") is believed to aid memory and to help a person in the process of recall (remembering).[740] It is in this function that this letter-cluster appears in Koran (Koran,19:1), paired with God's "*dhìkr* (thinking of/mentioning/remembering)" his Servant Zakarìyyâ (Zachariah). Similarly, Christ's names appear in the context of healing just as Christ's miracles included healing and resuscitating the dead,[741] while Moses' and his staff appear in practices aimed at countering the effects of magic, just as Moses' staff did vis-a-vis Pharaoh's magicians.[742] Likewise, God's name "[Al]-Ẓâhir ([The] Manifest)" appears in contexts of "having hidden matters manifested to him" and unearthing hidden treasures; similarly, an angel named "Nûryâ'îl (Light-yâ'îl)" appears in contexts of restoring "light" to blind eyes and treating other eye ailments.[743]

In all the cases given above (superstition, *mushâhràh*, the [Evil] Eye, and "the word") the relationship between a cause and its effect is an association or link triggered in a manner that may be characterized as mechanical. No agency of jinn, angels, "magic," saint's *karâmah*, etc. is involved.

Z95§, Puns (homophony); Z97§, ‡Alliteration (simple, plain); Z139.9.4§, ‡Dry container (box, chest, trunk, bag, pocket, etc.)—anal or vaginal orifice (see App. 34).

[740] al-Bûnî, *Manba¿*, pp. 164–169.

Motif: D1766.1.9.1§, ‡"Sacred formula (from scripture) aids memory (e.g., '*Ka-Ha-Ya-¿Ain-Ṣâd*')."

[741] al-Bûnî, *Shams*, Pt. 1, pp. 49–51.

[742] al-Bûnî, *Manba¿*, pp. 154–156.

Motifs: D1693, "Magic rod swallows other rods;" D1693.3§, "Moses's staff becomes serpent and swallows magicians' rods (snakes)."

[743] al-Bûnî, *Shams*, pt. 2, p. 46; and *Manba¿* p. 244, respectively (cf. p. 46 where God's name Al-Nûr (The Light) is applied to enlighten/brighten the heart and remove dimness from the eye).

CHAPTER IX

Appendixes

God/Allâh and Creation

Appendix 1: The Ninety-Nine Names of God

The following is a list of God's names as perceived by the learned. Some of the names (e.g., al-Muntaqim and al-Mumît) do not appear as personal names associated with ¿Abd-al-. . . . Variations on the name may appear in daily usages such as zikr (dhìkr) *rituals.*

1. Allâh	God
2. Aḥad (Al-)	The One
3. Âkhir (Al-)	The Last
4. Awwal (Al-)	The First
5. Badî¿ (Al-)	The Exquisite
6. Bâqî (Al-)	The Enduring
7. Bâri' (Al-)	The Maker
8. Barr (Al-)	The Benefactor
9. Baṣîr (Al-)	The Seer
10. Bâsiṭ (Al-)	The Expander
11. Bâṭin (Al-)	The Hidden
12. Bâ¿ith (Al-)	The Resurrector
13. Ḍârr (Aḍ-)	The Distresser
14. Fattâḥ (Al-)	The Opener
15. Ghaffâr (Al-)	The Forgiver
16. Ghafûr (Al-)	The Forgiving
17. Ghanî (Al-)	The Self-Sufficient
18. Ḥakam (Al-)	The Judge
19. Ḥakîm (Al-)	The Wise
20. Ḥalîm (Al-)	The Gentle
21. Ḥamîd (Al-)	The Praiseworthy
22. Ḥaqq (Al-)	The Truth
23. Ḥasîb (Al-)	The Reckoner
24. Ḥayy (Al-)	The Living
25. Hâdî (Al-)	The Guide
26. Hâfiẓ (Al-)	The Guardian
27. Jabbâr (Al-)	The Repairer
28. Jalîl (Al-)	The Majestic
29. Jâmi¿ (Al-)	The Gatherer
30. Kabîr (Al-)	The Great
31. Karîm (Al-)	The Generous
32. Khabîr (Al-)	The Aware
33. Khâfiḍ (Al-)	The Humbler
34. Khâliq (Al-)	The Creator

35. Laṭîf (Al-)	The Subtle	66. Qahhâr (Al-)	The Vanquisher
36. Mailk (Al-)	The King	67. Qawî (Al-)	The Mighty
37. Majîd (Al-)	The Glorious	68. Qayyûm (Al-)	The Self-Subsistent
38. Mâjid (Al-)	The Noble	69. Quddûs (Al-)	The Holy
39. Mâni¿ (Al-)	The Preventer	70. Ra'ûf (Ar-)	The Pardoner
40. Matîn (Al-)	The Firm	71. Râfi¿ (Ar-)	The Exalter
41. Mu'akhkhir (Al-)	The Deferrer	72. Raḥîm (Ar-)	The Compassionate
		73. Raḥmân (Ar-)	The Merciful
42. Mu'min (Al-)	The One with Faith	74. Raqîb (Ar-)	The Watcher
		75. Rashîd (Ar-)	The Rightly Guided
43. Mubdi¿ (Al-)	The Originator	76. Razzâq (Ar-)	The Provider
44. Mudhil (Al-)	The Disgracer	77. Ṣabûr (Aṣ-)	The Patient
45. Mughnî (Al-)	The Enricher	78. Ṣamad (As-)	The Eternal
46. Muḥṣî (Al-)	The Counter	79. Salâm (As-)	The Peace
47. Muḥyî (Al-)	The Life-Giver	80. Samî¿ (As-)	The Hearer
48. Muhaymin (Al-)	The Protector	81. Shahîd (Ash-)	The Witness
49. Mujîb (Al-)	The Responder	82. Shakûr (Ash-)	The Grateful
50. Mumît (Al-)	The Death-Giver	83. Tawwâb (At-)	The Acceptor of Repentance
51. Muntaqim (Al-)	The Avenger		
52. Mun¿im (Al-)	The Grace-Bestower	84. Wadûd (Al-)	The Affectionate
		85. Wahhâb (Al-)	The Bestower
53. Muqaddim (Al-)	The Expediter	86. Wâjid (Al-)	The Finder
54. Muqît (Al-)	The Nourisher	87. Wakîl (Al-)	The Trustee
55. Muqsiṭ (Al-)	The Equitable	88. Wâlî (Al-)	The Governor
56. Muqtadir (At-)	The Capable	89. Waliyy (Al-)	The Friend
57. Muṣawwir (Al-)	The Fashioner	90. Wârith (Al-)	The Inheritor
58. Mutakabbir (Al-)	The Imperious	91. Wâṣi¿(Al-)	The Englober
		92. Ẓâhir (Aẓ-)	The Manifester
59. Muta¿âlî (Al-)	The Exalted	93. ¿Adl (Al-)	The Just
60. Mu¿îd (At-)	The Restorer	94. ¿Afwu (Al-)	The Pardoner
61. Mu¿izz (Al-)	The Honorer	95. ¿Âlîm (Al-)	The Knower
62. Nâfi¿ (An-)	The Benefactor	96. ¿Aliyy (Al-)	The Lofty
63. Nûr (An-)	The Light	97. ¿Aẓîm (Al-)	The Eminent
64. Qâbiḍ (Al-)	The Contractr	98. ¿Azîz (Al-)	The Precious
65. Qâdir (Al-)	The Able	99. Hû (*Huwa*)	He

Appendix 2: Reasons for Creation

The following literary account elaborates on a Koranic passage stating that God created humans and jinn solely to worship Him (Koran, 51:56). The elaboration involves events and concepts that are not part of Koran.

Ulama (religious savants) say that God created the universe so as to declare (publish, inform of) His existence. Had He not created [the universe], His existence would not have been known. He created in order to manifest the completeness of His knowledge and power through His perfectly exquisite accomplishments (creations), which could not have come except from an Omnipotent, Omniscient (wise) [being].

[Another reason for creation by God is for Him] to be worshipped, for He likes the worshipping by worshippers and He rewards them for it in the amount of His benevolence, not in the amount of the worth of their deeds [that constitute worship]. Yet, He has no need to be venerated by his creation: the obedience of the obedient adds not to His Sovereignty (Kingship), nor does the disobedience of the disobedient subtract from His Sovereignty.

God created both humans and jinn in order to worship Him, so that He may manifest his benevolence because He is benevolent. He brought them into being in order to be benevolent to them, to be generous to them and treat some with justice, some with generosity.

He created true believers especially for mercy.

[. . .]

It is told that when Adam (¿.s.) was created and shown his [predestined future] progeny, he found them to include the healthy along with the sick, the handsome along with the ugly, the black along with the white.

Adam pleaded with God, "O my Lord, would You make all of them equally alike!?"

God replied, "[No! for] I like to be thanked [for giving an advantage to some]."

[One savant] said: God created angels to show Omnipotence; He created things [for people] to learn from; He created livelihoods to test by ordeal [of scarcity].

Other savants said, "He creates to manifest Omnipotence; He grants livelihoods to manifest generosity; He makes the living die to manifest Overwhelming-Compulsion (*qàhr*) and Absolute-Might (*jabarût*), He then resurrects to manifest Justice, Generosity, and Reward-and-Punishment."

Others said, "All of creation was for the sake of Mohammad (ṣ.A.¿.s.)."

Appendix 3: The Tablet and the Pen (Reed) of Destiny

Predestination is often expressed in the concrete terms of a pen and a tablet. These were the common writing implements at the presumed time when these accounts were developed. A Preserved Tablet is mentioned in the Koran once (22:85) with reference to alQur'ân.

The first thing God created was the Preserved Tablet (*al-lawḥ al-maḥfûẓ*), on which all that has been and ever shall be until the Day of Resurrection was recorded. Only God (t.) knows what is [recorded] on it. It is made of white pearl.

Then, from a gem God created the Pen, the length of which would take five hundred years to traverse. The end of it is cloven, and from it light flows in the same manner that ink flows from [reed] pens used by people of this world. The Pen was called upon (*nûdiya*): "Write!" The Pen trembled due to the awesomeness of the command (call) until it began to reverberate in exaltation [of God], just like thunder reverberates. The Pen flowed across the Tablet writing what God has determined to exist until the Day of Resurrection.

The Tablet was filled and the Pen ran dry, and consequently whosoever was [predestined] to be fortunate became so, and whosoever was to be wretched became so.

Appendix 4: Creation of Earth and the Mountains

The following literary report elaborates on Koranic passages about creation and the function of mountains.

When God willed to create the dry land, He commanded the wind to churn up the water. When the water became turbulent and foamy, its waves went up and gave off rising steam. Then God commanded the foam to solidify, and it became dry. In two days He created the dry land on the surface of the waters, as He [God] has said: "Say: Is it that ye Deny Him Who created The [E]arth in two days?" (Koran, 41:9).

Then He commanded these waves [to be still], and they did—thus forming the mountains, which He used as stabilizers (pegs) to hold down the earth, as He has said: "And we have set on the [E]arth Mountains standing firm, Lest it should shake with them [. . .]" (Koran, 21:31).

Were it not for the mountains, the earth would not have been stable enough for its inhabitants. The veins of these mountains are connected with the veins of Mount Qâf, which is the range that encircles the earth.

Appendix 5: Resuscitation in Answer to Prayer: Image of the Universe

The following is an excerpt from a folk ballad that tells a love story between a young man and a young woman from two enemy families. The youth invited his beloved to come clandestinely to his home for dinner. She agreed, and the two met in the youth's room. The youth's father learned of the visit; he confronted his son and slapped him on the face for associating with a "whore." The girl died of shame. She was smuggled back to her home, placed in her own bed, declared dead, and buried. The young man bribed the cemetery attendant, borrowed the girl's corpse, and took it to his home. There, he prayed to God to bring the young woman back to life. His prayer got answered. They married with their parents' blessings. (The author–performer concludes his presentation by reiterating the truthfulness of his account.)

The grieving lover's plea (stanza 36) portrays a vivid and typical image of how God and His creation are perceived in common daily activities.

36. He carried the lass on the [back of the] colt and returned to his home.
He laid her on the bedding and kept lamenting over his state
And wailed earnestly [in the hope that] his state would straighten out
He said: "O Lass, how come your roses have become withered
"Where has your beauty gone, and where are your dreamy eyes?
"Where has the day—when you woke me up from my sleep—gone?
It was not my expectation, O lass, that "Days" would deal us [such] perfidy!
"I grieve over the lass, [and] what has become of her
"O Creator-of-[All]-Beings, and Who-is-All-Knowing of their [secrets].

"O Creator-of-Heavens: seven layers, [with] the moon and the stars in them,
[Along with] the Tablet, the Chair, and the angels: kneeling and prostrating themselves in them
"O Creator-of-Paradise, O my Lord, and the pious [residing] in it
"O Creator-of-Earth: seven layers, and You are All-Knowing of what is in it
"O Creator-of-mountains, O Lord, [as] stabilizers of Earth
"Creator-of-the-seas, You who cause ships to sail on them
"You are the All-Able Lord
"You are the All-Able Lord. You make [all] creatures die, [then] resurrect them
With your Omnipotence, O Lord-of-the-Throne, resuscitate her."
The girl sneezed, and her soul returned into her:
With the permission of Him, who-Knows its [i.e, the soul's] mystery and unknowns!

[Short musical interlude]

37. He placed his hand on her heart; he found it beating, as well
He exclaimed, "I wonder, O Sa¿d, [whether] this matter is falsehood or truth!?"
(You, all, who are present, my talk is truthful.)
(The Lord-of-[All]-Beings, just as He created us, is capable of making us die and resurrect[ing] us. And He is [The]-Truth.)
The lass said, "I attest that my Lord is [The]-Truth,
"And [that] Moḥammad, His Prophet, is the Messenger of the truth.
"But, O Sa¿d, [it seems to me] I was in a slumber! [What have you done to me?]
"Where have my dresses gone!? And, [in addition] you've brought me shrouds!
"My father's words, that you are of our enemies, proved [correct]!"
He said to her, "Beloved-of-the-heart, everything is with us.
"'Time' (*ez-Zamàn*) had been too unjust, it entered the house with us:
"After drudgery and suffering The Lord-of-the-Throne gave us contentment."
He called and said, "Come on, O father, O father, O father
"Come on to me, O father, O father, O father, O father
"By the Prophet [I swear that you should come], O father, come to me father *'âh, 'âh, 'âh*, come to me father. . . . etc.

Appendix 6: Tour of Sky-Worlds

The following is an excerpt from a ballad based on a widely spread folk saint's legend. It tells of some of the karâmât *(miracle-like feats) of the Egyptian arch-saint Ibrâhîm ad-Disûqî (i.e., Abraham of Disûq); also nicknamed Abû-el-¿Aynain.*[744] *The story presents the saint as a prodigious child who offended his mother with a minor misdeed and seeks to regain her contentment (*riḍâ*) with him. Yet, the mother makes bizarre demands, but her saintly son fulfills them all. One of these demands is a tour of Paradise and Hell. The ballad depicts these two supernatural sites in a manner typical of how they are commonly*

[744]According to belief legend, the arch-saints were playing Hide and Go seek; ed-Disûqî's hiding place could not be found. He informed the others that he was hiding in [the celestial space] "between the eyes of the Messenger [(i.e., Prophet Mohammad)]." Hence, the nickname.

Motifs: Z183.0.1§, "Meaning of a name," F969.8.2§, ‡"Hiding in mystical location between Earth and the sky; e.g., in an arch-saint's domain, the Isthmus (*al-barzakh*), or the like)."

perceived, especially with reference to locations and contents. In the worldview of an Egyptian villager, Paradise is a walled garden attended by a guard or keeper.
[His mother said]:

"Oh Abraham, I wouldn't be content with you
nor would my heart forgive you
until you have carried me between your hands
[so as to] show me Rudwan's Paradise."
Abraham took her and flew
("Two thousand blessings upon the Selected-one")
He reached, along with her, in full view:
going with her over to Rudwân's Paradise.
He said to her, "O mother, I long for
showing you the Tablet, along with the Chair.
Look, and your heart will settle
to Him who elevated the Sky, and set up the Balance."
He knocked at the door of Paradise
and called, "Ye people who have received [God's] coveted-reward,
he who follows the path of the *sunnah*, and
would, for so doing, get into Rudân's Paradise."
"Who are you, and who is that with you,
you who knocked at the door of Bliss?"
He answered, "Open, it is I: Abraham.
After me, 'The Foremost Authority in Islam,' did quote."
"Who are you, and who is that with you?
Sire, tell me, for sure.
Only be patient, under the Generous,
Patience, is a mark of recognition [of God's Graces]."

"The one with me is my mother,
[since] the day of delivery, she has looked after me.
Open, so that I may show my mother.
Otherwise, I might climb, along with her, over the walls [fence]!"
Rudwân opened the door of Paradise,
and said to her, "Mother, get in.
Look at the fruits of Paradise,
('And the roses blossomed for The-¿Adnân [Prophet]).'"
"Amuse yourself, and see with your eye[s]:
the fruits of Paradise would please you;
the houris are before you
testifying to the oneness of The King, The Rewarder!"
"Amuse yourself, and look at the field,
whoever enters it would not suffer 'concern' (*maiṭ* [??]).
In it, trees have born fruit, out of [solid] wall
And the plums are on the branches."
"Mother, look at the birds,
and look at these palaces.

and look at the houris, inside of them.
All, with no exception, bless the ¿Adnân [Prophet]."
"But, mother, be content with me.
And let your conscience be clear [i.e., bear no grudge]."
She replied, "O you who are the light of my eyes,
Still, my heart is angry at you!"
"O Abraham, I would not be content with you
Nor would my heart forgive you
until you have carried me between your hands
and shown me the Fires [of Hell].
Abraham took her and flew
("Two thousand blessings upon the Selected-one.")
He came with her openly publicly [??];
until he reached the Fires [i.e., Hell].
There he would find Sultan Mâlik:
sitting at the door of Hell: in charge
(Oh Lord, save us from the pitfalls,
that dispatch [one] to the Fires.)
He said to him, "Open for your brother, Abraham:
the one who knocked at the door (gate) of the Inferno
For we are among the children of [God's] Graces.
And let us witness the Light of The Compassionate.
"Open, so that I may show my mother
[who] carried me for nine month [of pregnancy].
O Mâlik, open, and don't be stubborn with me!
Otherwise, I will shut the doors of Hell [in spite of you]!"
Mâlik opened for her the first door,
and the second, and the third door,
and the fourth, and the fifth door,
and the sixth door, and the seventh: All fires
She asked, "O my son—'Abu-l-¿Aynayn' [i.e. Abraham],
tell me, for whom is this fire [intended]?"
He answered her, "For the sinners
who cheat with the scales [in the marketplace]."
She asked, "O my son—Abu-l-¿Aynayn,
tell me, again, for whom is this fire?"
He answered her, "For the one lacking in faith,
who would eat up the property of orphans."
She asked, "O my son—Abu el-¿Aynayn,
tell me, again, for whom is this fire?"
He answered her, "For the one lacking in faith,
who would bear false witness and false testimony."
She asked, "O my son—Abu el-¿Aynayn,
tell me, again, for whom is this fire?"
He answered her, "For the one lacking in faith
who would say, '[She] So-and-so, and [He]-So-and-so' [i.e., backbite]"
She asked, "O my son—Abu el-¿Aynayn,
tell me, again, for whom is this fire?"

He answered her, "For the one lacking in faith
who would fail to fast for even one day of Ramadan."
She asked, "O my son—Abu el-¿Aynayn,
tell me, again, for whom is this fire?"
He answered her, "For the one lacking in faith
who has abandoned prayers to The Rewarder."
She asked, "O my son—Abu el-¿Aynayn,
tell me, again, for whom is this fire?"
He answered her, "For the one who disobeys parents:
his mother, along with his father as well."
She asked, "O my son—Abu el-¿Aynayn,
tell me, again, for whom is this fire?"
He answered her, "For the one lacking in faith
who slanders/insults women."
She asked, "O my son—Abu el-¿Aynayn,
tell me, again, for whom is this fire?"
He answered her, "For the one lacking in faith:
who robs a person of the fruits of his labor."
She asked, "O my son—Abu el-¿Aynayn,
tell me, again, for whom is this fire?"
He answered her, "For the one lacking in faith,
who dwells on the affairs of the 'inattentive'"
She asked, "O my son—Abu el-¿Aynayn,
tell me, again, for whom is this fire?"
He answered her, "For the ones lacking in faith,
the negligent along with the drunkard."
"But, mother, be content with me
for, here are all your demands, met!"
She replied, "A-a-a-ah, O you the light of my eye,
still, my heart is angry at you!"
"O Abraham, I would not be content with you,
O my son, [I swear] by your eyes,
until you have carried me between your hands
and returned me to Ruḍwân's Paradise."
"Take me to the gate of Paradise
[so that] I may die there and enjoy the bliss
('May the Lord predestine us all for Paradise,'
me, and the listeners, for meeting with The Compassionate)."
Abraham took her between his hands and flew,
(two thousand blessings to the Selected-one),
and reached with her to above the *'aghâr* [??],
and immediately he entered with her the "Paradise of Eden"
After [all] that: "Mother, be content with me,
in this Prophet-bound court [presence]."
She replied, "O you who are the light of my eyes,
I, still, my heart is angry at you!"
"This Paradise of yours would not satisfy me.

And this life [-style] of yours, would not suffice me.
Bring your father here to me, to comfort me,
to amuse me in Ruḍwân's Paradise."
With vision, he reached out with his hand
and fetched his father, along with the mat [on which he was asleep].
And said to her, "This [mat] is his bed.
Here, I have brought my father, he is still asleep."
The old man woke up from his sleep
to find Paradise in front of him.
He sat upright and adjusted his waist band,
and looked around like a person in a daze.
He lifted his face toward The Lord-of-Omnipotence,
"O Disûq [village], you have for ever been barren!"
Not a single tree is in you.
From where do these tree-branches would have come to us!?"
He turned around and said, "Oh my son, honest-one,
at this very hour, where are we, son?"
"Oh son, O you Abu-al-¿Aynain
Where is the village [Disûq], and drinking at [its] tavern!"
He replied,"Father, what village!
You with the glory, what tavern!
You are in the Paradise of Grace
And the one who brought you here is the-sulṭân [i.e., me]."
"But, mother, be content with me,
and let your conscience bear no grudge."
She replied, "O you who are the light of my eyes,
still, my heart is angry at you!"
"Oh Abraham, I wouldn't be content with you,
nor would my heart forgive you,
until you have carried me between your hands,
and shown me the lands of the Blacks!"
[. . . , etc.]

Angels

Appendix 7: Love Song for a Dead Sweetheart

Allusion to Nâkir and Nakîr, the two angels believed to interrogate the deceased inside the grave, is made in this brief dirge. The poem illustrates a woman's protective love for her beloved.

The dirge was chanted by two adult women, probably in their thirties or forties, in a village near El-Minya city in middle southern Egypt (winter 1970).
[Singing in unison, in a moaning tone]:

'asmar ¿alîl esh-shafâyiff, 'âhi ma-aṭûlu
'âhi ma-aṭûlu:

'akhushi-lu ṭurbitu w-atmadd-i-fî ṭûlu
'atmadd-i-fî ṭûlu:
tîgi-l-malâyka teḥasbu, 'ana-rudd mas'ûlu.
(A tan-one, with faint [soft] lips: oh! If I were to reach him!
Oh! If I were to reach him!:
I would enter for him into his grave, and lay myself in his figure [lit.: height/length]
I would lay myself in his figure:
[When] angels come to interrogate him, I would answer on his behalf).

Appendix 8: A Turk Is Introduced to the Two Angels

This humorous anecdote is based on the belief in the angel-keepers of a person. It alludes to the formal prayer ritual of uttering the greeting to the right and left upon concluding the performance of a prayer ritual.

The Turk is stereotyped as bombastic and unfamiliar with religious rituals. The assumption is that the Turk is in Egypt. The story was recorded in March 1969, in Cairo, from Mr. S.S., fifty-five, a businessman and craftsman.

Once a Turk went to the mosque to perform prayers. After he was finished, he noted that all worshippers would turn their heads to the right and say, "Peace be upon you, and God's mercy . . . ," then to the left and say, "Peace be upon you, [. . .]" [without receiving an audible answer to their greetings]. He became puzzled [and wondered]: "To whom are these people speaking!?"

He looked around and found an aged man (may be the imam, or someone who looked like he should know). So he went [to that man] and asked: "Why is everyone turning his head this way [to his right] and saying 'Peace be upon you,' then that way [to his left] and saying, 'Peace be upon you'?"

The man answered: "They are greeting the two angels: the Angel of the Right, and the Angel of the Left." This is a sunnah ("Tradition" after Prophet Mohammad, a recommended act).

The Turk looked at the man's shoulders and said, "I see no angels!" Then he felt his own shoulders and said [in a distrustful tone], "There are no angels!"

The man answered, "One doesn't see angels, but they are there all the time; everyone has them."

The Turk asked, "What do they do?"

The man answered, "The Right-side Angel records your good deeds; the Left-side Angel records your sinful acts. All [they record] will be reported to God [on the Day of Judgment], and He will judge you according to what they report."

Our friend (the Turk) *râḥ nâtish-luh rak¿itain* (went ahead and "snatched for himself a-two-genuflections-[prayer];" i.e., "did a quicky" of a prayer). When he was done with the *taḥiyyât* ["Greetings," the concluding part], he turned his head to the right and said [softly, in broken Arabic and in "Turkish"], "Angel-right! *¿afârim* (presumed to be Turkish for 'Bravo,' or 'Good for you!')" Then he turned his head to the left and said [in a reprimanding tone and with a grimace], "Angel-left! *kharîs*! (presumed to be a Turkish expression denoting: 'Louse!,' 'You are the pits!,' 'Fink!')! *'itfû-û-û* (onomatopoeic denoting: 'I spit on your conduct')!"

Appendix 9: Chain of Command among Archangels

This humorous anecdote was told by Shaikh M.Ḥ., a cleric-teacher in his sixties, as a recollection of "something" he had read in an old book. Clearly, the anecdote has its roots in literary traditions.

A poor man, a beggar, saw one of those palaces of rich people. He went to that palace and knocked at the gate several times. Finally, someone came to the door and said, "What do you want?" The beggar answered, "Something, for God's sake!"

The doorkeeper went away and after a while came back and said, "Wait until they ask my master, the owner of the palace, for he is upstairs."

After a while the beggar heard [the owner's] voice shouting:

—"O Morgan, tell Mabrûk, to tell Mas¿ûd, to tell Sa¿îd the doorkeeper, to tell him [the beggar]: '*yiḥannin*!' (May He [God] make [the heart of someone else] kind toward[s] you)!"

The poor beggar was vexed. [He raised his face and hands toward heavens and] prayed:

— "O Lord, tell Gabriel, to tell Michael, to tell Israfîl, to tell Azrael to seize his [the rich owner's] soul!"

Appendix 10: Crumbs as Fee for Admission into Paradise

This joke mocks graveside performers of death rituals (fu'ahâ). It was told by a boy from the city of Zagazig; he was about fourteen to fifteen years of age. The present writer had heard the joke during his boyhood in the 1950s.

A lady went to the cemetery carrying *qaraqîsh er-raḥmah* (mercy-crackers), in order to visit her [deceased] husband and distribute the crackers [to the poor]. There she read the "*Fâtḥah*" [*Fâtiḥah*, the opening chapter in the Koran] *¿alâ roaḥoh* (over his soul), and gave away (as a credit on his behalf) all the crackers. As she was about to leave, a blind *fiqî* (member of lower clergy, beggar-like Koran recitalists) came and said: "Lady, I'll recite a chapter or two [from the Koran] over your husband's soul." She answered, "I have nothing left to give you." But as she looked into her basket, she found some crumbs. So she said to him, "I have nothing left except some cracker crumbs!"

He replied [despondently], "They will have to do!"

He took the crumbs, packed them in his handkerchief, and crouched down [on the ground] and began reciting: "Seize, ye [angels of Hell/zabâniyàh], him. And bind, ye, him. And burn, ye, him in the Blazing-Fire [!!!]" (Koran, 69:30–31).

The woman cried out [in horror]: "Hold it! 'Seize, ye, him' what! 'Bind, ye, him' what! 'And burn, ye, him in the Blazing-Fire' what! Do you want God to *yirḥamuh walla yighimuh* (to have 'mercy,' on him, or to 'burn him in Hell')!?"

He replied [in disbelief]: "You don't expect 'Gardens of Eden beneath which rivers flow' [(Koran, 2:25; 3:136; 3:198, etc.)] for only some cracker-crumbs!!!"

Jinn and Familiars

Appendix 11: How Shâkir Became a Shaman-*Shaikh*: "Working from the Books"

*The personal history of the development of a Shaman's interest in the para-religious supernatural is outlined in the following personal account. Shâkir is a retired shaman-*shaikh *in his forties. He worked mainly from "the book;" and sought to control the lesser supernatural beings via the power of the written word within the religious context; although he admits that for a brief period he was engaged in the sacrilegious* sùflî *("nether" magic), he may not be labeled* saḥḥâr *(i.e., magician/sorcerer). Also, Shâkir stated that he did not derive his power through* mikhawiyya *("bebrothering").*

However, Shâkir's friends suspect, contrary to his assertion, that he was indeed mikhâwi *(has a jinni foster-sister) and cite as proof the fact that he remained a bachelor until the late age of forty-one (he married for the first time in 1968, only four years prior to this recording). They also consider his reluctance to talk about "Whether he is or he is not" as further evidence of having a female jinni foster-sister, especially since the human party in such a relationship is required to never divulge the secret. Both Shâkir and his friends, however, agree that if he were indeed* mikhâwi, *his relationship with his jinni foster-sister was strictly personal and that he did not use it for professional purposes. They also state that his belated marriage could not have happened without the permission of his jinni foster-sister.*

Date:	Saturday, June 24, 1972.
Time:	4:00 p.m., after government office business hours (8:00 a.m.–2:00 p.m.).
Place:	The Folklore Center on the fourth floor of an office building in the centre of the business district in Cairo.
Persons:	Beside El-Shamy (the interviewer), three informants are involved.

1. Shâkir ¿A., the shaman-*shaikh*, (45 years old, formerly a faith healer, magician, etc.)
2. Ḥesain (Ḥusain) also called "Abu-Aḥmad/Abu-¿Âdil" (46-year-old janitor, married)
3. Moḥammad A. (35 years old)

Both Shâkir and Ḥesain Abu-Aḥmad are friends, and hail from the same village in el-Fashn Region in middle southern Egypt. Moḥammad hails from a village (Yazmul) in Sharqiyya Governorate in northeastern Egypt; Shâkir, our main informant, and Moḥammad were meeting for the first time; all three informants are recent migrants to Cairo, and work as janitors in governmental offices.

Setting: I had arranged with Shâkir, who was employed at another government office, to meet me after work hours at the Folklore Center (in downtown Cairo). Muḥammad and a younger companion (Manṣûr, twenty years old)—both of whom work for a commercial office located on an upper floor in the same building—were going down the staircase on their way home; evidently, they overheard the conversation, were intrigued by it, wandered in, and joined the discussion (which was being tape-recorded). While Shâkir is a retired professional shaman, neither Abu-Aḥmad nor Moḥammad had had any previous experience in professional shamanism or faith healing; yet, both have shown considerable familiarity with the various aspects of the craft's rituals.[745]

El-Shamy: I would like you to tell us about how you got started on your *kâr* (craft, profession). How did you learn these things? Did you learn the craft in a *kuttâb*?[746]

Shâkir: When I first went to school—education [in the village] did not take place in schools, but in a *kuttâb*. I went to the *kuttâb* to learn Koran, but I did not complete [the normal course that requires a child to memorize, then to recite the Koran in full, three times. I learned [recited/*samma¿t*] it only once [but did not "repeat," nor "conclude"].

Ḥesain: [Questioning the accuracy of Shâkir's claim] A-â-â-h! Did you [really get that far]!?

Shâkir: [Emphatically] I, by God, did memorize it at *Shaikh* Maḥmûd's [*kuttâb*]. After that, negligence occurred. That negligence was [as follows]: my father took me out of the *kuttâb* and put me to work in the field. I forgot the Koran. I was about thirteen years old then.

El-Shamy: Do you have brothers?

Shâkir: I have two brothers, one older than I am, the other younger.

El-Shamy: And sisters?

Shâkir: Only one who is older than I am.

I had an aspiration; that aspiration was to learn "magical" things out of books. So, I looked through "books" often. There was a man in our village named *Shaikh* ¿Alî el-Badrî [who owned books]. I used to look through his books.

---

[745]This format for presenting fieldwork data was introduced in 1967 by the present writer in his "Folkloric Behavior." It is meant to provide some aspects of the context, or "the intermediary stimuli" that may affect the participants.

[746]Religious, traditional, elementary school for children, where basic skills in reading, writing, and arithmetic are taught as secondary curriculum to memorizing the contents of the scripture (Koran, or Bible). Typically, such a school consists of one room, has one low-ranking cleric as teacher and owner—sometimes assisted by another male or female instructor—and is occasionally annexed to a mosque or church.

Fees were paid mostly in kind (food, clothes, etc.), at intervals corresponding to a pupil's completion of a segment of the curriculum. Graduation followed a three-fold memorization process: *khatam, we-¿âd, we-samma¿* (i.e., memorizing [every chapter in the Holy Book], relearning or repeating, and reciting all from memory). For more information on the *kuttâb* and its instructors in oral traditons, see El-Shamy, *Tales Arab Women Tell,* No. 13, p. 143.

El-Shamy: Why did you want to learn "magical" things?

Shâkir: Here, I am telling you. When I was young I wished to "write" ["fixes"] aimed at girls [to cause them to fall in love with me]. I, myself, wanted to "write" at certain girls. Some man named ¿Abd-el-¿Azîm Abu-Zahrân had tricked me and ruined me financially in [the course of] "writing" [works aimed] at two girls. He kept on demanding: "Give me five cigarettes!" "Give me twenty-five piasters!" All of this was in order to teach me how—(as if [he himself knew how])! Another man in the village named Zaki Abu-Hdiyya also duped me; he used to charge me a *riyâl* [(twenty piasters)], or twenty-five piasters [per service] in order to "write" for me [a 'fix"] aimed at a girl named Ḥalawiyyâyah (Piece-of-Candy). [Evidently, these "fixes" did not produce the desired results]. Finally, I said to myself: "Instead of being duped like this, why don't I learn and do these things for myself. I am educated and can read and write; I [also] can read the Koran!"

El-Shamy: Were these girls maidens or married?

Shâkir: They were maidens. The writing was in order to have them fall in love with me.

El-Shamy: Did that "writing" work?

Shâkir: When I began "writing" for myself, God caused me to become chaste toward[s] those things [i.e., I lost my interest in women]. God caused me to be chaste toward[s] everything. I did my "fixes" for other people and not for myself. People hounded me constantly in order to have me write to cause love to happen on their behalf. [. . .]

El-Shamy: Did ¿Abd-el-¿Azîm Abu-Zahrân let you take his book to your home?

Shâkir: No! The book remained at his house. I kept after him until one day he and his wife were very needy. He said to me, "We want six *kaila*s of wheat."[747] I asked for the book. He gave me the book. I took the book home and kept on going through it, but I did not comprehend a thing in it. I also used to go to a *shaikh* in the village—a *¿âlim* [i.e., of the ulama]—his name was ¿Alî el-Badrî; he used to give religious lessons [i.e., sermons] in the mosque—so that he may teach me. He died [before I could learn]. I used to take things, such as cigarettes, tea, and sugar, from our home—behind the back of my late father—and give them to him [as a fee] so that he may teach me. I was about seventeen or eighteen years of age then. I acquired *¿ilm* (religious science); he taught me some things. After he died I resorted to his brother because he was an acquaintance of mine. His brother, Moḥammad el-Badrî, was a butcher. . . . He allowed me to examine the books that [his late brother] sheikh ¿Alî, left behind. I retained the books that contained a benefit for me and left those that had no benefit. Meanwhile, Moḥammad had been drawing from the grocer's shop on credit, and I kept on paying his bills. When I found out that the books I got were beneficial I was very pleased; I began "writing." [At first] when someone came to me for something such as [an incantation for] a sick child, I "wrote" without charging any fees. The child would recover. Things went well and I acquired fame. At that time I had a paternal uncle

[747] *kaila/kailah* = a dry cereal measure = 16.721.

living in the village named ¿Abd-eṣ-Ṣamad; he was a *shaikh ghafàr* ("chief of village guards"). He instructed me: "O Shâkir, do not sell cheaply. Don't [over]-extend yourself!" I began charging a fee. I started handling the heavy operations such as *rabṭ* ("tying," i.e., inducing impotence) and *ḥàll* (untying, i.e., restoring sexual potency). In the beginning, if there was someone who wanted to tie another [man], I did it for free, but I charged for untying. Later, I became "like a saw; it eats [i.e., cuts] as it goes up and eats as it comes down" [i.e., I charged for both [the] operations].

El-Shamy: Did you charge more for *khair* (generating benevolent effects) or *shàrr* (generating malevolent effects)?

Shâkir: [I charged more] for *shàrr*! [However I] practiced *shàrr* reluctantly. I used to write the paper and stand between the hands of God and say: "God, the command is Your command. The secret is Your secret. There is no God except You: [You are] The King, The Truth, The Rẹvealer." I was afraid of God's punishment to the extent that when I performed *shàrr* (evil), I did it in a wrong way; I simply wrote up words [other than those specified in the book; or not in the right order] on a piece of paper. But, by God, such "works" still worked [and generated the desired effect]!

El-Shamy: How did you "write?"

Shâkir: Every door has its own key; if you apply the wrong key to a lock, it will not work [I got the key from the book, ...].

El-Shamy: Are you *mikhâwi* (i.e., have you established a foster-brother relationship with a jinni woman who helps you as a "sister-familiar")?

Shâkir: No! I worked according to what was before me [i.e., what the books prescribed]. I am not *mikhâwî*; but every problem has its own prescribed approach for solving it . . . whether a "magical" [i.e., evil] or benevolent problem. If it is a benevolent issue, you consult the book; from the book, you locate [the client's] *ṭawâli¿* (signs of the zodiac [sing.: ṭâli¿]), and the *'a¿wân* (supernatural helpers) assigned to the *ḥurûf* (letters of the alphabet found in the client's name, and in related objects). After you have done so, you formulate the *¿amàl* ("fix") according to what is prescribed in the book. Any and everything I did, I took from the book [. . .].

Due to the large amount of "writing" I undertook, I acquired [steady] *'a¿wân*. The *'a¿wân* perform the tasks assigned to them [begrudgingly]. One night, while I was asleep, they (the *'a¿wân*) came to me that night. I was asleep but awake [i.e., in shallow sleep]. I found out that the *'aryâḥ* ["winds," i.e., wind-like jinn]—whom I have put to compulsory labor by the powers of the "oaths" (incantations) I held over their heads—were coming at me [in a rebellious menacing mood]. I was asleep on the [flat top of] [mud] oven, in the oven room (bakehouse); they were inside the oven. There was only about a four meter [distance] between them and me. They hummed in a deafening volume, "Hae. Hae. Hae." They wanted to get into my body.

El-Shamy: What did they look like?

Shâkir: They were [each], in the form of a human being but with a different image. Their heads were squarish; they had hoofs like those of goats, but iron hoofs.

They were about to enter into me. [To stop them] I recited, "*Qul huwa Allahu 'aḥad,* . . . " ("Say: He is Allah, the One and only . . . ;" Koran, 112), but it did not stop them! I recited "*Qùl 'a¿ûdhu bi-rabbi el-falaq*" ("Say: I seek refuge in the Lord of Dawn . . . ;" Koran, 113), but it did not stop them. I began to apply to them [the "fixes"] in the *Suryânî* (Syriac) tongue: "*halhalat la¿lalat* . . . " and other verses from the *at-Tawrâh* (Torah) and *al-Ingîl* (New Testament, the Bible. . . . [these "verses" evidently stopped them].[748] My brother came running into the room to my aid; he found me shivering and soaked wet [from sweat]. But the *'a¿wân* were gone. They wanted to harm me because I harm them and put them to forced labor. [. . .]

El-Shamy: What is *suflî* (nether) magic?

Shâkir: To perform magic via nether means one must get Satan and the infidel *gìnn* (jinn) to work for him. They will perform tasks that no other *'a¿wân*—due to their fear of God's punishment—would perform.

El-Shamy: How does one get Satan and infidel jinn to work for him?

Shâkir: By desecrating holy things and by committing *kabâ'ir* (cardinal, or major, sins). The one who performs nether magic becomes a *kâfir* (infidel). When Satan sees that he [i.e., the practitioner] is doing things that evoke God's anger, he [Satan] becomes very pleased and places himself in the service of that nether-magician. Such things as placing the Koran or another of God's books ([i.e., Bible etc.]) in the latrine; using milk for ablution. [Here, members of the audiences expressed their abhorrence at the idea exclaiming: "We resort to God [for protection against Satan!!!"]

El-Shamy: Can nether magic be used to generate benevolent effects?

Shâkir: Whether one generates benevolent or malevolent things does not matter; they are all *shàrr* (evil or malevolent). Once one has committed such *kabâ'ir* (cardinal sins), everything you generate is malevolent [even though it might benefit someone].

El-Shamy: Did you work with *suflî* (nether, i.e., sacrilegious magic)?

Shâkir: No!

Ḥesain: [to Shâkir, in disagreement: Yes, you did!] You once swore, in writing, that you repent; you did so due to the sickness that befell you.

El-Shamy: [to Ḥesain/Abu-Aḥmad] Did he [Shâkir] become sick?

Ḥesain: Oh yes! For a brief period, he worked with the *suflî* (nether [magic]). God punished him by making him sick. He swore not to practice it again. After he repented, he remained for a while without having even as much as one piaster in his pocket [due to lack of clients]. A woman came to him seeking to conceive through *siḥr* (i.e., sorcery, magic). He (Shâkir) exclaimed [addressing God]: "O God! I had foresworn practicing [*suflî*]-magic! [But you are not allowing me to carry out my promise]." The woman gave him one fourth of a pound [i.e., a twenty-five piaster bill] or maybe fifty piasters and said to

[748] The sample Shâkir gave of these "incantations" was clearly nonsensical utterances. However, he seemed to sincerely believe that they were in these languages of which he knew nothing. Sengers (p. 106 note 9) reports this phenomenon and cites a number of its ocurrences in the works of others.

him, "write" for me a paper so that I may become pregnant. He replied to her [sarcastically]: "Am I the one . . . who is going to impregnate you!?" He wrote for her on a piece of paper [i.e., an amulet, that is not to be opened]:

> "Go! If you will become pregnant, you will become pregnant; if you will not, you will not! (i.e., 'Whatsoever may happen will happen!')" [Laughter from all participants in the session].

It was he [(Shâkir)] that told us about this event.

Shâkir: [Disagrees with the details of the account given by Ḥesain/Abu-Aḥmad, and explains]

"That woman had come to a person other than me; she had come to see a shaman-*shaikhàh* (woman practitioner) in our village but did not find her. [So] she came to me. She had brought a few things with her including some bread and a pullet. She wanted to have a *¿àqd* (contract) made for her 'on' the blood of that pullet [i.e., she did not seek nether magical ritual]. . . . We [she and I] discovered that the pullet had died. I noticed that she became sad and subdued. I said to her, 'Lady, do not be sad.' I went to the butcher shop and got her some blood from the animal that he had slaughtered. I wrote a *ḥigâb* (amulet) for her, and performed a *raqwah* (protective oral incantation) using the name of God. I said to her, 'On your way home put a little lump of mud within its ([the amulet's]) folds [for fertility, as if a field to be planted]. Before you sleep with your husband, go around it seven times, then sleep [with him].' About ten months later she appeared unexpectedly, hauling a large billy goat behind her; she had meanwhile begotten a child [and intended to give me the goat as a reward]. I told her, 'I have no right to get this goat. It belongs to God . . . ; it is He that lifted me up [after I had fallen by using nether magic]. Go give a *zìkr* ('mentioning' God's name) ceremony for God's sake [and use the goat's meat to feed the participants]. I did not labor or have to work hard at it [i.e., at solving your infertility problem].' Instead, the woman gave me two and one-half pounds [which is a very substantial fee at that time period]."

[Thus, Shâkir continued to practice his para-religious rituals and never resorted to nether, sacrilegious magic again. Yet, he did use his craft to perform "shàrr" (evil, harmful) service. Such an evil service led to his departure from his village]. (See App. 35)

Appendix 12: How Shamaness-*Shaikhah* 'Âmnah Acquired Her Supernatural Powers: Working with a Jinni-Familiar

Working with a nazîl *(a familiar who is also a "bebrothered" jinni) is described in this exchange with a shamaness. She dwells and practices in the environs of Aghûr, a village in Qalyûbiyyah Governorate, in the Nile Delta. Initially, our informant was reluctant to mention her actual name or age, stating, "Everyone knows me as* el-ḥaggàh *(Pilgrimess)." Her assistant provided the answers on her behalf (summer, 1969).*

El-Shamy:	O *ḥaggàh* [(pilgrimess/she-hajji)], would you tell us your name?
'Âmnah:	I am "your servant" 'Âmnah. . . . [(She is about fifty or fifty-five years of age).]
Assistant:	People call her "*El-ḥaggàh* 'Âmnah."
El-Shamy:	Did you go on a pilgrimage?
'Âmnah:	By the heart [i.e., soul/spirit] only.
El-Shamy:	Why do people call you *ḥaggàh*?
'Âmnah:	Just due to their generosity [as courtesy]. You are "all sight/vision" [i.e., you are a perceptive person and can see for yourself that my appearance and manners are those that should characterize a hajji].
El-Shamy:	How did you become a *shaikhàh* [i.e., a practicing female shaman, healer . . . etc.]?
'Âmnah:	"God's command" [i.e., because God willed it to be so].
El-Shamy:	Surely, everything happens only by God's command. I just want to know how? Were you born . . . ?
'Âmnah [interrupting]:	No one comes out of his mother's belly [i.e., womb] educated. It was a little before the [1967] War. We were returning from a funeral in Barshoom. We—I and a number of other women from our village—were returning home from Barshoom. We were at a funeral. ("May long life be yours"), one of *nasayibnâ* (our in-laws, relatives by marriage) had died and we went to extend our condolences. We stayed there overnight and as we were returning [on foot] I felt my feet getting heavier. I couldn't walk and fell behind. So I sat down on the ground to catch my breath. It was after *¿ishâ*-prayers time [i.e., about 9:00 or 10:00 p.m.], and all the buses and [commuter] taxis had stopped. The women who were with me asked, "Why did you sit down?" I answered them, "Only a little fatigue. You go ahead, I will catch up with you in a little while." When I tried to walk I felt as if my feet were sinking into *laḥm* (meat, flesh); I was walking on heaps of raw meat. They [the jinn] appeared to me. I could see them just [as clearly] as I see you now. I screamed and (away from you) I fell down. The women who were with me splashed water on my face. My family came and carried me home. I remained for a week, seven days along with seven nights, between life and death. Finally, when God willed and I came to, I couldn't speak, I couldn't move; my tongue was *ma¿qûd* (knotted, [i.e., I couldn't utter a sound]) and my hands and feet were twisted. I could neither talk, nor move, nor eat, nor drink. Abu-Aḥmad [my husband] brought the doctors to me. They gave one medicine after another, and prescriptions—each prescription bigger than the other, but nothing helped. I remained in this condition (away from you) for three months or four. Finally, they took me to [shaman]-*shaikh* Ḥ., *'Allâh yirḥamùh* ("May God be merciful to him"). He made *'illi ¿alayya—yig¿al kalâmnâ khafîf ¿alaihum* (those who are on me, i.e., the possessing jinn—may God render our words light on them [and cause them to take no offence]) speak out. And that is all.
El-Shamy:	What did they [the jinn] say?
'Âmnah:	One, only *¿âriḍ* (intruding spirit). They were only one [male jinni].

El-Shamy:	What did he say?
'Âmnah:	I wasn't conscious. But . . .
Assistant [interrupts to explain]:	*¿ishiqhâ* (He fell in [erotic] love with her). That is due to [the fact that] she is *simḥa* (pleasant-faced and kind), *liwnah* ("of good-color," physically attractive), and *ṭâhrah* (ritually pure).
El-Shamy [to 'Âmnah]:	How did shaman-*shaikh* Ḥ. oust [expel] the one who was "on you?"
Assistant:	He [the possessing jinni] is the one who now "tells" her [i.e., helps her in her craft].
El-Shamy:	*khâwetîh*? (Did you "bebrother" him, [establish a foster-sister relationship with him])?
'Âmnah:	. . . . [No reply].
El-Shamy:	Some people say that this [type of relationship] is *mikhawiyyah* ("bebrothering").
'Âmnah:	You said it, not I.
Assistant:	She can't say . . . , if she spoke about it [i.e., her relationship with the jinni foster-brother], he would cause her harm.
El-Shamy:	When does he come to you?
'Âmnah:	He is with me all the time.
Assistant:	He is *minhâ fîhâ* ("from her and within her"). He is with her all the time, but he becomes present and speaks [only] when she asks him to do so.
El-Shamy:	How does he become "present?"
Assistant:	He wears her [like a person would wear a gown] and speaks through her tongue, exactly as you have seen for yourself.

Appendix 13: How Was the Temperamental Father Handled: A Psychodrama

In personal familial life, it is believed that jinn can cause sickness; a jinni may possess a person by, literally, entering that person's body and dwelling in it. As indicated in actual field cases, the sex/gender of the possessing spirit is invariably the opposite of that of the possessed person. In such a context, the spirit is, or becomes, what we may label here as a "personality spirit (i.e., a component of the individual's personality, or self)." Frequently, more than one jinni will possess a person. In such cases, the possessing spirits are related to one another. One of them, usually not the main spirit, may be of the same sex as the person afflicted.

One case of possession reveals the close association between the actual social conditions under which a person lives and the qualities of a possessing jinni.[749] *The social realities of this case are as follows:*

[749](n. 10 of the orig.). For a number of years the present writer witnessed the unfolding of the various chapters in the lives of the members of this family. Three accounts of the present incident were recorded: one by the father, another by Abdu himself, and a third by Abdu's mother. The three reports are very

Abdu is a handsome, blondish young man in his middle twenties; he comes from a fairly well-to-do family of farmers. He is married and—at the time—had two children but both had died before reaching the age of two.

As the customary rules of the village require, Abdu, his wife (and their children) resided in his father's house;[750] they occupied one room on the second floor. Meanwhile Abdu's father, mother, and younger brothers and sisters—who ranged in age from three to eighteen—occupied the rest of the house. Abdu went to the village school and was "the top of his class;" he even received a trophy for being "the best" while his competitor Ṭâha, did not.

Being the eldest son, Abdu's father took him out of school when he was about fourteen and assigned him the task of tilling the land. Abdu carried out the arduous assignment with some help from the father and younger brothers. The father—then in his forties—withdrew gradually from the actual farming chores and maintained only a supervisory role; he kept all financial matters and major farming decisions in his grip. The father led a leisurely life that a farmer of his social rank, success, and number of sons, expects to enjoy at that age. He dressed neatly, traveled often, enjoyed the company of his friends and had a good deal of prestige in the community; he was viewed as religious (pious), honest, firm, and temperamental.

The father became enamored with Hejaz; he used considerable amount of family's income to go on pilgrimage to Mecca. Although pilgrimage is required of a Moslem, who can afford it, only once in a lifetime, he went several times. The family resented this extravagance, especially since they themselves received very little monetary rewards and had to live austerely. The family, however, could not openly challenge the "right" of its head to spend his money on such a "noble" cause.

Abdu himself was totally dependent on his father in financial matters; he received only pocket money, while the father provided the entire household with food, clothes, medicine, and even luxury items (such as perfumes) as gifts for the son's wife on special occasions. Furthermore Abdu had to submit to the will of his father in social and family affairs; the father rebuked him repeatedly in front of his wife, which led her to taunt him for carrying no weight in the household. Another event made matters worse for Abdu; Ṭâha, his competitor at school had completed his education, become a teacher, taught abroad, and returned to the village for a visit. Ṭâha had his own car, a Mercedes, that he had bought with his savings.

The climax of Abdu's psychological condition came one summer day in 1956. As Abdu slept under a guava tree in the field, he woke up abruptly; he was in a state of shock and was shivering. His neighbors and younger brothers carried him home. For days Abdu was ill; he could not even stand up. His father thought it was "fright" and invited the official sheiks of the mosque to recite the Holy Book, but their treatment did not work. The father took Abdu to a number of medical doctors in Cairo where he

similar except in one respect: the father in his report places far less blame on himself and more on Abdu's wife.

[750](n. 11 in the orig.). Residence in Egyptian villages is patrilocal; the newlyweds reside with the groom's father. See Hamed Ammar, *Growing Up in an Egyptian Village* (New York: Octagon, 1966), pp. 42–50.

received shots, pills, and other medicines; this treatment had only limited short-lived success. Abdu became more and more withdrawn; he ate very little and could not work. Occasionally he threw tantrum fits, he shouted insults, and his body shook violently to the extent that "ten men could not make his arms still."

Neighbors told Abdu's mother that her son was possessed and suggested that they invite *mashâyikh* (faith healers, shamans) to exorcise the possessing spirit; however, the father refused adamantly to believe this "nonsense."[751] The mother took her son behind the father's back to faith healers in neighboring areas, but they failed to cure him. Finally, neighbors prevailed over the father and extracted his consent to invite the neighborhood *shaikh* (shaman); the father, however, insisted that he himself would not attend.

In the presence of all the family and neighbors, "men and women," the shaman and his assistant arrived into Abdu's room. Only the father was missing; he sat in the guestroom downstairs. The *shaikh* diagnosed Abdu's illness as possession; one of the jinn had entered his body and was responsible for his sickness and improper actions and words, especially toward his father. After the necessary rituals were conducted the *shaikh* managed to establish contact with the spirit: a female jinni. Then the healer said. "Call his father!" From his own perspective, the father gave an account of the affair and his dialogue with the possessing jinni spirit:[752]

People came to me and said, "Come, see!" I said, "No!" They said, "Just come so that you can hear and see for yourself."

[When I finally went upstairs], I found that the boy [i.e., Abdu] was talking [in a feminine voice]. She finally spoke; she spoke [to me] through his tongue, but he himself was in a state of unconsciousness. I was amazed and exclaimed, "May God help us!" She said [to me, in reference to the medical treatment],

> "You have been driving hypodermic syringes into me. And you did to me such and such. I am [a female jinni] from Mecca. I am Moslem, of the best Moslems . . . He [i.e., Abdu] was lying under a guava tree . . . he was feeling unhappy with his wife because she was playing hard to get. I came to him so that he would marry me; he has a *ṭâhir* [i.e., pure, unprofaned] body and I like a pure body. [When he refused to marry me], I became angry with him. I had intended to drown him in a well or a river, but *for your own sake*, I changed my mind."

[I said to her] "Lady, why all this!? We are peaceful people and we mind our own business." She said, "By God, I was kind to him only *for your own sake*." She wanted him to wear silk clothes and perfumes and to do no work [on the farm]. I said to

---

751(n. 12 in the orig.). The pattern of the reactions of the puritanical father to this ritual, which lies outside formal religious practices, is typical: "ridiculing disbelief, reluctant tolerance, participation, then total acceptance."

See Hasan El-Shamy, "Mental Health in Traditional Culture: A Study of Preventive and Therapeutic Folk Practices." *Psychiatry and the State*. Mark C. Kennedy, (ed.). A special issue of *Catalyst* (Fall, 1972, Petersborough, Ontario), pp. 13–28.

752(n. 13 in the orig.). Tape recorded on October 29, 1971.

her, "Lady, he is a *ḥayy* ([bashful], decent) person and has pride. How could you force him to wear flagrant colors and to wear perfumes? People will ridicule him and may even think that he is a queer! . . . You say, 'I was kind to him only for your own sake [i.e., the father's],' and you say that you are from Mecca. Mecca is the place for pilgrimage [i.e., such things are not allowed there] . . . We are fellahin and [from well-known] families; each one has his own traditions. No, [I can't consent] to these demands.'"

She said, "Alright [no colorful or silk clothes; no perfumes], but he must not be made unhappy."

I said to her, "That is even worse! Lady, since you are 'a Moslem, and of the best Moslems,' [you should know] that the [occasional] feeling of being unhappy is a part of the nature of human beings. How can a person avoid it? This can't be!"

She said, "*You* should not make him unhappy."

I said, "I will try not to make him unhappy. However, if unhappiness is unavoidable this would be something that is out of our control and [happens] in spite of us. [For] if he did not become unhappy with his father, he may become unhappy with his wife or his mother. Sometimes a person becomes unhappy even with himself; however, I will try."

She said, "Alright, but he must not work [on the farm]."

I said, "This is a difficult [condition], but can be managed. His younger brother can take his place. If he did wish to help his [younger] brother, let it be; if he didn't, let it be."

[She said], "He must wear only clean, neat clothes."

I said, "Let it be, but regular clothes: No [flagrant] colors." (He did not ask for these things! *It was she* who did not want him to work. She wanted him to remain neat, clean, and attractive). We agreed to these conditions. . . .

Neighbors, men and women, were all around. It was something *embarrassing*.

Now it was time for her to get out [of his body]. She wanted to get out through his eye [but the *shaikh* insisted she get out through a wound to be made in his little toe]. . . . [At first she refused.] The *shaikh* said, "I will take my complaint against you to your king! What brought you here! Why are you causing harm to innocent people! You will be put in prison [. . .] Do you think that the Kingdom [from which you came] is loose! I'll take you to your king."

She said [imploringly], "Please, let us not harm each other. I will come out [through the toe]."

As soon as she got out, he [Abdu] went like this: "A-A-A-h-h-h-h . . . [i.e., became completely relaxed]." He looked terribly embarrassed; [for] it was just like acting in the movies . . . But, had I not seen it with my own eyes, I would not have believed it."

Abdu's troubles were lessened; he gained some independence and more considerate treatment from his father, especially in the presence of others. He did not have to work in the fields, nor wear the shabby working clothes, nor carry unattractive agricultural implements. Eventually, he even moved with his wife and children in a next-door house, which his father owned.

However friction between Abdu and his father did recur, but on a subdued level. Under the terms of the agreement with the possessing jinni, the temperamental father had to control his anger and not lean heavily on his son.

Occasionally, minor relapses in Abdu's condition occurred; these relapses were always interpreted as signs of the return of the jinni-woman, because the father broke or was about to break the contract. Meanwhile, Abdu was gradually asserting his newly found independence. He started to make small business deals on his own and earn some money; as the father saw it, Abdu "began to spend on himself, his wife, and his children in slight excess." Abdu finally moved to Cairo, against his father's wishes, but his wife and children remained in the village. He and his father were not on speaking terms, but there were no confrontations. Perhaps, it was not purely coincidental that Abdu's job in the city was that of a guard in a movie theater. His father had thought that the affair of possession was "Just like acting in the movies."

The father died in 1971 while on his ninth pilgrimage; to die in Hejaz was his most cherished hope. Subsequently, his wife (Abdu's mother) managed to keep the farm largely intact [. . .] (see App. 48). Abdu assisted her during his frequent visits to the village. The spirit, which had possessed Abdu never returned.

In this case, the social problems of a young man led him into a state of emotional disorder. The intruding psychological realities were expressed symbolically in the person of a possessing spirit. Apart from its general qualities as a jinni, the exact nature of the possessing spirit was not fixed a priori; her characteristics emerged as a result of a dynamic encounter and exchange among the father, his son, the shaman, and last—but not the least—all the [relatives and] neighbors who witnessed the entire event. The presence of the neighbors generates a sense of shame,[753] which is an essential agent for social control in traditional communities.

Considering the father's religiosity, and his passion for Mecca, it was no accident that the possessing spirit turned out to be a good Moslem, from Mecca and to be enamored with the unprofaned body of the handsome and virtuous son. It was also not coincidental that she was not a royalty and that she had respect for the father, and did things for his sake, just like other members of his social group did. The demands made by the possessing spirit are also a part of her perceived entity; they were public pronouncements of what the son lacked. The spirit is, therefore, an anthropomorphic representation of the son's social grievances and of the emotional state they generated in him. The healer adroitly created a psychodrama,[754] in which the son plays the role of the possessing jinni-woman, while the father retains his normal role; they publicly negotiated their differences without either party losing face; the blame was placed on the possessing jinni. Thus, the healer induced a situation in which the oppressive social system could be *reorganized in order to accommodate the afflicted party.* This traditional technique is possible only when all parties share the cognitions, sentiments, and action tendencies involved in a belief.

---

[753](n. 15 in the orig.). For a discussion on the differences between "shame" and "guilt" as agents for social control, see El-Shamy, "Mental Health," pp. 24–27.

[754](n. 16 in the orig.). See Lewis Yablonsky, *Psychodrama: Resolving Emotional Problems through Role-Playing* (New York: Basic Books, 1976).

Appendix 14: The Value of Dying in the Holy Land

This account is a sequel to Appendix 13, above. The father (Hajji M . . .) died in Hejaz in 1971. Under Islamic laws of inheritance, the land of the deceased father had to be divided among all the heirs: his sons, daughters, and wife. The mother (the deceased's wife), however, managed to keep the farm largely intact by managing it.

The following is a folk belief narrative (religious legend) told by a member of the family of the deceased father. The story clearly indicated the family's lingering resentment of his frequent pilgrimage expenditures and casted doubts on their usefulness. During a belated visit to extend his condolences, the present writer was received by the widow of the deceased (S . . .) and her silfah *(sister-in-law, the wife of her husband's brother), whose own husband had already been dead for a number of years. Although the two temperamental brothers (husbands) were not on speaking terms with each other, their widows became good friends after the death of their husbands. When the present writer mentioned the belief that "It is sinful for Hell to touch [with its flames] the body of a person who performed pilgrimage seven times," the sister-in-law, almost compulsively, narrated a story that may be summarized as follows:*

The Servant of the Holy Shrine (*al-Masjid al-Ḥarâm*) in Mecca noticed that a certain man came every year. He asked him about the reason for these yearly visits. The pilgrim answered that he wished to die and be buried there, and that he and his family endured financial hardships so that he may accomplish his goal. Upon hearing that, the Servant asked him to sleep in a certain corner of the shrine one afternoon and to tell him of any dreamer's visions (*manâmat*) he may have.

The man "saw in a dreamer's vision" biers flying into the Shrine from far away places, and biers flying out of the Shrine to distant lands. The Servant explained: "The first ones carried bodies of people who died away from the shrine but were predestined to be buried nearby; meanwhile, the others carried the bodies of people who died inside the Shrine but were *not* predestined to be buried there [in the Holy Lands]."

The narrator concluded that one could die in a distant land and still, supernaturally, be buried in Mecca or Medina.

Abdu's mother (the wife of the deceased) fully agreed. (See also App. 48)

Appendix 15: Why It Is Preferable to Seek Reconciliation with the Jinn

*In the following account Shâkir (see introduction to App. 11) explains some of the rules governing the interaction between jinn and the shaman-*shaikh *(practitioner) who seeks to control them*: tarâḍî *or* ṣulḥ *(reaching accommodation, reconciliation, peace-making, etc.) is preferred to confrontation and open conflict. A practitioner who applies the powers available to him through* ta¿âzîm *(verbal incantations, conjuring) in excess of what is required is guilty of the mishandling of these dark powers. The retaliation by the jinn is, therefore, understandable.*

Jinn are believed to be particularly active after dark, and in oven-rooms. The dream of "being stuck in a heap of meat" is recurrent and is typically considered a cause of supernatural illness. (See Appendix 12, where a shaman-shaikhàh reports a similar dream)

A jinni has relatives; if you were to kill a jinni his children will pursue you, or pursue your children, or pursue the children of [your] children.[755] In the book [manual] it is stated: "Do not aggress against the jinn; for if you do, they will pursue you." My grandfather, on my mother's side, had treated them violently; they pursued [i.e., stalked] him until they caused his death. My father was from one village and my mother from another. My mother's father was a religious *'usatâdh* [(i.e., learned cleric)] and a Koran reciter, his name was sheikh ¿Adàl; he actually had a *kuttâb*-school.[756]

One time he pursued a jinni-woman. She hid from him inside a palm tree; he imprisoned her inside the tree. She kept on begging him: "Set me free! Set me free!" He answered, "Never!" and condemned her to die. So they [i.e., her relatives] pursued him.

When they pursued him they wanted to kill him because he aggressed against them. They got to [i.e., possessed] a female client of his. He [trapped one of them] and ordered him, "Get out! Do you want to get out?" [The jinni] would say, "Yes! But I will get out via her eye [i.e., the eye should be pierced out]." My grandfather would say, "No! You get out via the little toe of her left foot!" [When the jinni refused] my grandfather tortured him with fire; fire caused by the fact that my grandfather recited [powerful] *ta¿âzîm* (verbal incantations). Finally, the jinni came out and said, "Peace be upon you." He got out via her toe: her toe burst.

My grandfather had hurt them; . . . they killed him through another way [i.e., not in an open confrontation between him and them].

The means they followed was . . . (you know the oven in the countryside—[typically located in a separate building, away from sleeping quarters])—[as my grandfather was getting out of the oven-room one day while it was dark] they caused heaps of [raw] meat to be in my grandfather's path: heaps of cut up meat [to be in his path]. As he stepped out of the oven-room—like this [informant enacts the situation by pretending to step out of a place]—he set his foot down to find that it was landing and sinking into flesh. He would [scream], "O girl, ¿Aishah!" (He was calling my maternal aunt, the sister of my mother), "O, ¿Aishah!" [but no one heard his cries for help]. As he was moving like this [i.e., trying to pull his feet out of the heaps of flesh], he fell flat on his face. [During an encounter with jinn] the moment a human falls [to the ground, he becomes helpless], the jinni takes away whatever health [i.e., strength] is in him, but as long as the human is standing upon his own feet and remains alert, the jinni can't touch him; [that is so] because the earth (i.e., the ground) belongs [totally] to them [while the earth surface belongs to humans and jinn].

My grandfather fell on top of that flesh in the late evening; (away from you) in the morning, he was being taken out to the cemetery (by his family).

That is why I, *always*, first seek reconciliation [with the jinn].

---

[755] See the story of "The Merchant and the Afrit [Jinni]." In: *Alf laylah wa laylah*, Vol. 1, pp. 8–14; resumé in Chauvin, *Bibliographie*, Vol. 6, p. 22, No. 194. Also see Duncan B. Macdonald's commentary titled: "From the Arabian Nights to Spirit." In: *The Moslem World*, IX (3), July 1919, pp. 336–348.

[756] A one-room school for teaching children the Koran, reading, writing, and basic arithmetics; see n. 746.

Appendix 16: Pregnancy via Artificial Insemination

The following report was given in the summer of 1982 by Miss Hodâ S. and Miss Sumayyah M., both in their early twenties, university students, in Cairo. The account was told with reference to the pregnancy of a housemaid in the service of one of the two.[757]

We have a servant-woman named Badî¿ah. . . . She has been married for a number of years but never became pregnant. She tried several *waṣfât* (recommended concoctions) for pregnancy, especially those a person gets at *¿aṭṭârîn* (spice-vendors, herbalists), but to no avail. We told her that we would take her to our gynecologist—I mean the one our family uses—but she did not accept. She was afraid that her husband would find out and divorce her or something [like that]. He was always demanding that she became pregnant, and told her he is thinking of "marrying [another] over her."

A woman neighbor told her about one of those shaman-*shaikh*s who treat these things by "magic." She went to him along with that woman neighbor. After two or three visits he gave her something they call *ṣûfah* to wear inside her (see n. 230). A few weeks later she found out that she had become pregnant.

We [the two of us], were writing a term paper about these old customs for a sociology class. We asked Badî¿ah (the maid) to get us a *ṣûfah* from that shaman-*shaikh* and gave her money for herself and for the *shaikh*'s fee.

We gave the *ṣûfah* to T . . . [a relative of ours studying medicine] to analyze. When he examined that *ṣûfah* under the microscope he discovered that it contains human semen. Most likely, the semen is the *shaikh*'s!

Appendix 17: How Shâkir Cured a Case the Medical Doctor Couldn't

The following account may be seen as contrasting the one-sided approach of the academic medical doctor to the multifaceted art of the native folk healer.

In effect, the healer here acts as a social worker. He relies on the shared communal beliefs and on involving a broad social group in the treatment in order to alleviate the pressures placed on a young wife suffering the consequences of intense and protracted "role-strain." The strain is generated by her obligations to her father and the sensitiveness of her proud but less than well-to-do husband. The familial setting is slightly unusual: the husband is living with his wife at her father's home (uxorilocal residence); the more common practice is that the wife joins her husband at his father's home (patrilocal residence). In pressuring the husband to change his ways through nonconfrontational technique (mild-coercion), the practitioner is careful not to cause him public embarrassment; such an act may result in the husband resorting to assuming a defensive stance and refusing to cooperate.

Informants: See App. 11.

Shâkir: A man named Hajji ¿Abd-esh-Shâfi was in the employ of M. . . . Bey [a rich and powerful landlord]. Hajji ¿Abd-esh-Shâfi had a daughter named

[757] For an elaborate account of a parallel situation in literary folk culture, see: "The Rogueries of Dalilah the Crafty and Her Daughter Zaynab the Coney-Catcher," in Burton, *Arabian Nights*, Vol. 7, pp. 144–172, esp. 147.

Ḥamîda; she was married to a man named Shulgâmi [i.e., Shulqâmi]. They had no children. They all lived in her father's house. The father's wife [(Ḥamîda's mother)] had died. Ḥamîda looked after all of them.

Ḥamîda became ill. She suffered from headache [fits] that attacked her periodically. She also had periodic swelling in her legs; her legs would swell—swell—swell!; then they would deflate back to normal. Since her father worked for *nâs 'akâbìr* [(lit.: grandees, "big-shots"—a family with power, money, and fame, i.e., more than just notables; cf. aristocrats)], he was in touch with famous doctors [through his employer]. Her father became very concerned about her condition, more than her husband was. So her father took her to a [medical] doctor in el-Fashn [city]. The doctor prescribed pills. They used to get the pills from the city using the private automobile of the Bey [the father's employer]; his chauffeur would have the prescription filled [and bring the drug back to the village]. This was done for the sake of the Bey's [fore]man [i.e., Hajji ¿Abd-esh-Shâfi]. The pills helped her for a short while but the condition recurred. They kept on going to the doctor [in the city] and coming back [to the village] until the doctor told Hajji ¿Abd-esh-Shâfi, "Listen, I can keep on treating your daughter and on taking your money. However, the illness of your daughter is not my specialty; her cure is not in my domain. Take her to someone who 'Opens the Book'" [i.e., a shaman-*shaikh*, faith healer].

Ḥamîda's husband had a brother named Ḥusainî. He was the one who came to me and asked me to "open the Book" for her; he was a very dear friend of mine. So, I went to her home with him and did what was necessary. God cured her.

El-Shamy: How? What type of illness did she have?

Shâkir: She was suffering from her *'Ukht* [supernatural Sister].

El-Shamy: Did she have a sister in real life?

Shâkir: No, only an older brother; he, his wife, and their children were living in a far away place.

El-Shamy: Then how come she had a [supernatural] Sister?

Shâkir: They say that it is the *Tâbi¿ah* (She-Follower), that is also called *'Ukht* (Sister), the *Qarînah* (Spouse/Counter-spirit/Correlative), and also *'Omm-eṣ-Ṣobyân* (Mother of male-children). They afflict women.

El-Shamy: What exactly was her problem?

Shâkir: Her husband was staying with her father [i.e., they were living at her father's home]. Her father's income was greater [than that of her husband]. Her father bought things [that her husband could not afford]. Her husband accused her of favoring her father over him. He kept on nagging at her about that. She thought constantly about her situation and became sad [i.e., feeling melancholic and depressed]. She was always crying. She could not have good luck with her husband, nor could she give up her father.

Ḥesain [one of the audience]: Her father was not aware of any of that. She wanted neither to remiss [in her duties] toward her husband nor toward her father.

Shâkir: One day her husband started shouting at her, "You give your father [more]! And you do [more] for your father!" She answered, "Now! Why are you mad? My father buys two kilograms of sugar at a time, plus tea [i.e., plenty, more than most people are capable of doing]. You—who happens to be my husband—eat and drink from my father's earnings!!"

[Thus, the husband, Shulgâmî, was humiliated].

Due to such confrontations, *dammahâ inḥabàs* (her "blood was arrested," i.e., "clogged-up"); sadness loomed over her; her *'Ukht* [supernatural Sister] struck her, and she became ill.

I did what was necessary and God cured her.

El-Shamy: What did you do? Did you say to Shulgâmî, her husband, "Listen, you. . . . "

Shâkir [interrupts]: Oh, no! When I say something, everyone hears it [so, I have to be careful].

Ḥesain [explains]: The custom is that all those who hold the patient dear to themselves would attend [the healing session], i.e., the patient herself, her father, her husband, and all the friends and relatives. They would be in the room, or just outside the room.

El-Shamy: Did you address your talk to the husband?

Shâkir: No! What I would say would [be addressed at no particular person, and would] be like this:

"The patient is a virtuous and perfect [mannered] woman. She was crying, as she sat beside the *kanûn* [fire pit], she was crying. The *Qarînah* struck her with some dust over her head; thus resulting in her sickness."

We will have to arrange for a *ṣulḥ* (reconciliation) with the *Qarînah*.

I will write the beginning of the *Raḥmân* chapter [from the Koran: 55], the ending of the *'A¿râf* chapter [Koran: 7]. The writing will be done on the inside of a pure vessel; the vessel should be filled with pure water and she should bathe with this water.

Thus they will have known, and become surely cognizant that her sickness is caused by her being sad and feeling. . . . "

El-Shamy [interrupts]: Would you say, "Sadness caused by her husband?"

Shâkir [emphatically]: No! I would say, "Sadness brought about by some of the closest people to her. They accuse her of something of which she is innocent."

Naturally, her husband will think. Her father will think. . . . She will think. . . . All of them will talk about the matter among themselves; each will try to identify what had been done or said and caused the problem. The problem will get solved.

Ḥesain: The people who would be present would hear what was said and, naturally, they know [the real issue].

El-Shamy: Would her husband ask you: "What should I do?"

Shâkir: [No, but] I would take him aside and talk to him in a low voice, *but loudly enough so that the rest of the people could hear*: "By God, brother Shulqâmi, you got angry at her; and maybe—just maybe—you accused her of something she did not commit. Disagreements happen all the time [in all families], but they are [amicably] solved."

El-Shamy: Did you tell them not to do certain things?

Shâkir: I would not say, "You must do this or that!" The party involved might [publicly] say, "No!" [thus committing themselves to a certain course of action that would be hard to change due to pride]. But I would say, "If she were forced to do such and such [a] thing, or if she were to be made sad again or accused falsely, they [jinn] would hurt her more and she would certainly die."
I also added: "Do not believe in me personally; I can neither help nor hurt. Believe only in God. I can help or hurt only if God wills it!"

[And thus, by getting the husband to be less critical of his wife's attention to her father (and reorganizing other elements of the social system to accommodate the afflicted), Shâkir was able to heal a woman whom the medical doctor could not cure.]

Appendix 18: Miscarriage: A Problem of a Young Bride Addressed

*Shâkir, a retired shaman-*shaikh *(see App. 11), gave the following account of a case he had handled in his village. It involves a young wife, her husband and his sister, and the wife's supernatural "Sister."*

*In this case, the family problems of a recently wed young woman, evidently, generated a great deal of emotional stress for her. She also suffered a number of miscarriages. Since the woman involved proved to be capable of normal pregnancy and delivery, it may be assumed that the miscarriages were a psychosomatic symptom of her emotional condition. The healer knows the community very well; he perceives the social situation in which a husband's sister—who may also be addressed as "sister" by the young afflicted wife—fosters the conditions that lead to the young wife's stressful situation, and consequently, to her physiological malfunction. Without accusing the husband's sister of mischief, the shaman-*shaikh *intuits that the supernatural "Sister" is the source of affliction. The supernatural being is presented in anthropomorphic terms that parallel those of the husband's human sister. Consequently, the husband's human sister realizes her culpability as the reason for the miscarriages.*

A girl named Fayda—she was the daughter of . . . got married to Sa¿d, son of. . . . When she moved to her husband's house [actually the house of her husband's father] things did not go right for her. After a week or so, they said to her, "Come and bake," "come and cook," "come and do the landry," and things like that. Actually the mother of Sa¿d was a decent and good-hearted woman; so was his father, but the one that caused her [i.e., Fayda] the troubles was Sa¿d's sister. He actually had two sisters, Fâṭma and Si¿da; Si¿da, was too young [to cause trouble], but the trouble came from Fâṭma . . . This is the nature of things. She did not want him to marry Fayda and used to say, "She is not fit for him" and things like that.

The crux of the matter is that Fayda ended up doing the whole workload for the household. In addition, Sa¿d's sister was constantly setting traps for her; if something got broken, she would say, "Fayda [did it]!" If something got lost, she would say, "Fayda took it to her father's house," and things like that. The girl [i.e., Fayda] lived in constant distress especially because her husband did not curb his sister.

Fayda got pregnant and miscarriage took place three times in a row. She never passed her sixth month [of pregnancy]. . . . Her husband's family said, "She can't bear children." Actually, she was of slight build and never gained weight.

They finally sent a messenger to call me [to their house]. . . . They told me [via messenger], "Things are such and such." I had known about this problem already. [. . .] I went and did the necessary things. . . . When I "opened the book" I found out that her [supernatural]-"sister" has been antagonistic to her. So, I told them about what I saw:

> "This woman was sitting alone beside the oven; she was crying and feeling unhappy because the people who are the closest to her accuse her of things of which she is innocent. They also lean on her too heavily. She receives no support, not even from those who are the closest to her. The accursed *'Ukht* (Sister) struck her and caused her to become ill and to lose her child [i.e., fetus], because of jealousy and hatred. That accursed *Qarînàh* [i.e., female Counter-spirit] would suffocate the infant before it was born.
>
> "This woman is a virtuous one: she does not commit what may anger God; she does not steal or lie. She came from an honorable household to another like it in honor. The accursed 'sister' is seeking her destruction, but I—with the aid of 'The Seven Pledges' [that] Prophet Solomon [secured from] the 'Mother-of-male-children' (*'Omm-eṣ-Ṣubyân*) . . . will burn the accursed 'Sister' if she returns. 'It is against the unjust-ones that things turn out to be.' This woman needs comforting and reassuring."

I made a "Seven Pledges" amulet for her to wear around her waist and [and instructed her to] never take it off. [I declared aloud that] "this amulet would burn any aggressor."

According to the shaman-*shaikh*, Fayda was spared most of the friction, especially with her husband's sister, and she soon conceived. With the complete consent of her husband and his parents, Fayda went to her parents' home to "complete her last six months of pregnancy." Her husband's family visited her daily and showed her great affection. Fayda gave birth to a baby boy and returned to her husband. Shortly after her return, Fâṭma, the sister-in-law, got married and moved away to her husband's home.

When the preset writer pointed out to the healer that he first mentioned the supernatural "Sister" then switched to the "Counter-spirit," he readily explained: "What is the difference! They are all the same." Thus, his first choice, the "Sister," was highly congruent with the specifics of the case he was handling in that instance.

The shared belief that the amulet "would burn any aggressor" generated the sentiment of fear in the husband's sister; she acted according to this new feeling. Her actions, but perhaps not her sentiments, toward the wife changed and the wife was spared most of the stress-generating friction.

Appendix 19: Detective-Divination by *màndàl*: A Successful Case

The ritual described below for detecting a thief seems to date back to Egyptian antiquity. In ancient Egypt the ritual was conducted through the power of a deity-king to look into men's hearts, whereas in contemporary Egypt, it is done through a jinni-king's ability to observe clandestine deeds. (See data associated with n. 240 and 241)

Introduction

The present writer comes from a middle-class family; his father, a Cairene, worked for the Ministry of Justice. After a number of appointments in a few towns, the father headed an administrative department in the civil court in the town of ez-Zaqazîq, capital of Sharqiyyah "Province" (currently, "Governorate"), northeast of Cairo.

Until moving back to Cairo in 1955 to enter the university, the writer had spent practically all of his childhood and adolescent years as a resident of a subdivision of a suburb of that provincial town. The apartment building where he lived was situated between two quarters of the same region of that town. One quarter, labeled *es-Sarayât* (the palaces), stretched along a riverfront and was inhabited mostly by civil servants of relatively high rank (e.g., the chief of police, and his second-in-command, the head of the civil court, etc.) practically all of whom hailed from other parts of Egypt. Families who, literally, were in-between the higher and lower social classes inhabited the in-between section. The apartment building where the present writer lived had six apartments occupied by the families of the secretary of the kindergarten ("*er-roaḍah*"), the head of the municipal public library, a retired civil servant (with two daughters working as nurses), the daughter of the landlady and her family, and a son of the landlady and his family. The other section, away from the river, with boundaries blending with rural regions, and inhabited mostly by relatively poorer and largely unschooled, *baladî*-groups ("country-folks," e.g., craftsmen, shopkeepers, low-rank unskilled civil employees, etc.), who until a few decades earlier were the indigenous inhabitants of both sites that were still rural areas.

Most apartment buildings in the first quarter were owned by a few financially successful individuals from the third and second sections, who seem to have "developed" the area so as to provide adequate urban housing for the expanding middle class of white-collar civil servants coming from other regions of Egypt due to central governmental appointments and transfers of employees. Adults from these two demographically distinct urban quarters did not interact on social bases, except at the *zâwyah* (lit.: "corner" or "nook," i.e., neighborhood's small and simple mosque). Yet, children attended—according to gender—the same schools post the kindergarten stage; they also, usually against "upper-class" and "middle-class" parents' wishes, intermingled and formed friendships and play-groups (including both genders for some games); these groups were often interrupted by a member of the lower class taken out by a parent and injected into the labor force as a full-time worker at an early age (8–13), or the member of the higher class moving away to attend college, or due to routine transfer of a parent to a new governmental post in another city. Naturally, there were exceptions to this pattern of class-educational level (many lower-class boys continued their education and received college degrees).

Within this context and apart from social class position, socially visible families on both sides of the hazy "class" divide were assigned certain tradition-bound attributes: *ibn-'uṣûl* (of good-origins, person with honor or good-conduct), *ṭîbah* ("being good-hearted/helpfulness," *tadàyyùn* ("religiosity"), *barakàh* ("blessedness"), etc. on the one hand, or *¿adîm el-'aṣl/¿adîm esh-sharàf* (lit.: "origin-less" or "honor-less," i.e., of bad origins, rootless, vile, without honor), "hardness of heart," "immorality," "lack of religiosity," "quarrelsomeness," etc. on the other. These attributes gave rise to another type of social ranking, or stratification. (See implicit personality theory, Section III.C) For example, one older widow from the poorer quarter acquired the reputation of being *ṭayyibah* (good-hearted) and of having *'îd mabrûkah* ("blessed hand"), and, hence, of *khair* (goodness) being with her; she was titled and addressed only as *el-ḥaggah* (the pilgrimess—the she-hajji/pilgrim) in spite of the fact that she had not performed the pilgrimage ritual (nor did she claim to have done so). Many expecting mothers on both sides of class-divide (neighborhoods) requested that she, as a personal favor, assist them in giving birth; she did not accept payment for her services, but would accept *zakâh* (alms-tax, tithe) or gifts on religious occasions from only a few out of the many grateful households.[758] Thus, in spite of the existence of *mustàwṣàf* (free, government-provided gynecological and pediatric services), *el-ḥaggah* became the preferred proficient, but nonprofessional midwife for both communities. However, she was known to decline entering homes "wanting in religiosity, or honor (morality)." Consequently, she was assigned a "high" social status. By contrast, the assistant chief of police was known as a conceited man, with "a roving eye" (for women); thus—in spite of his acknowledged authority and power—he was assigned a "low" social rank; consequently, members of his family came to be viewed as "coming from a house wanting" in religiosity, honor, and goodness.

In Arab social life, parents are typically nicknamed after their firstborn child as "father/mother of so-and-so;" children are identified as "son/daughter of so-and-so."[759] As a rule, parents are held responsible for the conduct of their offspring, even when the "child" is an adult. This fact is represented by the oft-cited folk truism: "A "shit-kid" [i.e., bad/troublesome child] brings curse upon his parents." Thus, recurrent curses state "May the Lord damn the father of the belly [i.e., womb, the mother] that carried you," or "May the Lord damn the father of him/her who had raised you," etc. Also common is the holding of the parents of a person who *yitshaddid li* (supports, backs-up, defends) another responsible for the support by that person.

---

[758] Cf. Inhorn, *Quest for Conception*, p. 102.

[759] In one case, for example, a boy named Amîn proved to be unknown to the grocer, who asked: "Who are you?" The boy answered: "Amîn el-. . . . " Unable to relate the boy to a family, the grocer still inquired, "Whose son are you?" The boy answered, "Papa is el- . . . effendi,. . . . Head of the Land-survey Department at. . . . !" Still the grocer could not identify the boy. A woman shopper volunteered an identification: "Amîn *ibn* 'Omm-Amîn" ([This is] Amîn, the son of Amîn's Mother!"). The grocer made the identification.

The event

The following experience took place around 1950; I was about twelve years of age then, in my second year of high school.[760] Beside myself, the main persons involved were another young boy (¿A., but will be referred to here by the pseudonym "Ḥâmid") and his mother: 'Omm-¿A (who will be referred to here as 'Omm-Ḥâmid).

One evening during early autumn, 'Omm-Ḥâmid showed up unexpectedly for the first time at our apartment. She was a resident of the poor neighborhood, wife of a semi-literate, low-ranking "policeman," and mother of five boys; her eldest son, Ḥâmid, was a member of the play-group composed of the sons of middle-class families including myself. The purpose of her visit was to ask my mother to allow her to borrow for a short time one of the elder two children (preferably the eldest daughter, who was then about thirteen) to act as medium in a *màndàl*-opening operation. The ritual was for the purpose of locating missing household money (food-money); she explained that she needed a person who is *ṭâhìr* (pure, sinless), and that the "house of esh-Shâmî effendi" was known for its *ṭîbah* ("good-heartedness") and *ṭùhr* (purity). But my mother exclaimed: *Yâ khabàr!* (i.e., "What a [shocking] piece of news [this would be]!"), and refused the request on the ground that family conventions do not accept such a [superstitious] practice, and its mores would not allow for the placement of a girl in such a [vulgar] situation. Subsequently, 'Omm-Ḥâmid asked for me. My mother stated that there were numerous households that are *'ahl-kamâl* (of perfect-character or righteousness) in the neighborhood; but 'Omm-Ḥâmid quickly retorted by pointing out faults with the heads of many of these households, thus disqualifying the families named: "Whose!?" She rhetorically asked, "M. effendi's [the assistant-chief of police], the man with the roving-eye [for women]!? Or N.'s effendi's: "the one with-the-[liquor]-glass" (i.e., who drinks liquor)! Or Sh. effendi, whose powdered and painted wife pretends to be dusting off one thing or another out of her [ground floor apartment] window—while still in her nightgown—whenever [Mr.] Nagâtî [a handsome and rich owner of an industrial flour mill located at the edge of the neighborhood] just happens to be driving by in his [huge private] automobile!? Or. . . . "

My mother interrupted this "sinful backbiting" by saying: "The children can hear! [so, stop]. This is only "people's talk" [i.e., hearsay]!" But 'Omm-Ḥâmid quickly replied, in too friendly a manner: "Wake up, *yâ rôḥî* (lit.: 'my soul,' i.e., sweetheart)! Wake up! 'Is there smoke without fire!?' Why haven't people said 'Omm-L. [i.e., 'you'] did [such things]!' or, 'Omm-Ḥâmid [i.e., 'I'] did [such things]!"

In reaction to having been addressed by a woman she barley knew as "sweetheart," my mother aimed an icy glance in my direction (meaning: "see what trouble you have brought upon us!"). However, apparently out of concern that by continued refusal she might jeopardize the family's good reputation, or engender the ire of this tactless and

---

760 The secular school system then was as follows: "elementary" stage, starting at the age of six: 4 years; "secondary" (or high) stage: 5 years, leading to two diplomas after passing national examinations: "General Culture" (*al-Thaqâfah*), after the fourth year, and "Pre-college" or "the Directional" (*al-Tawgîhiyyah*), after the fifth.

shalaq ("verbally aggressive and potentially abusive") woman, and—perhaps—also motivated by the flattering characterization, my mother relented. She set the condition that I must be returned home "soon," and "before night becomes too advanced."

I left with 'Omm-Ḥâmid for her house, situated next door to that of the kindly *el-ḥaggah*, in the other neighborhood, located only a few narrow streets away from where we lived. We entered a small room on the second floor of the modest rural-style house ("without running water or electricity," and with a mud-oven room on the ground floor—where the family bread was baked biweekly). A crowd of people of all ages filled up the room, the doorway, the narrow corridor outside and spilled onto the upper steps of the staircase. The tiny jam-packed room, being lit by a small "No. 10" kerosene lamp, was fairly dim and stuffy; the odor of the burnt kerosene was quite noticeable. In a small opening in the middle of the crowd sat a figure of a man dressed in a *galabiyyah* (ankle length street-shirt) and a skullcap; he was the *màndàl*-operator; he was addressed as "*shaikh*" (though he was not dressed in a cleric's vestments); before him were a small *manqàd* (brazier, a portable pottery fire-pan with a short pedestal seat), a handless small coffee-cup full of liquid, and a heavy bath-towel of white color.

I was presented by 'Omm-Ḥâmid to the shaman-*shaikh*—presumably as the person who meets the specifications required in a *màndàl*-medium, particularly of being "pure" and "innocent": "Here he is!" The operator examined me for a few seconds with a keen eye, and asked me my name. Since I spoke with a lisp then, I timidly answered: "Ḥa*th*an" (this childhood speech defect must have added to the aura of "innocence"). He signaled his approval and asked me to sit in the vacant spot before him. I sat down, cross-legged, on the floor on a coarse mat. The shaman-*shaikh* carefully handed me the cup and asked me to hold it and be careful not to spill its contents; he then placed the towel around my neck. Before starting, he tested the flickering embers in the brazier by throwing some incense on them: a muffled sound of a little explosion was heard, it was accompanied by gusts of bellowing smoke arching up toward the low ceiling, and brought tears to my eyes. He also had to ask the spectators a number of times to move back so as not to interfere with the operation. After a few minutes, that seemed much longer, he draped my head and shoulders with the towel, and the actual divination ritual began. There was a total silence.

For a few minutes, the shaman-*shaikh* murmured something in a recitational tone and style of delivery characteristic of religious sermons (see n. 239–240); the sounds of muffled little explosions were coming from the direction of the fire-pan at even intervals; the heavily fragrant smoke was seeping underneath the towel draping me: my eyes became more tearful; since both my hands were holding the cup, I was unable to wipe my eyes dry. Then the operator commanded me to repeat after him:

"*yâ sukkân el-makân! yâ mulûk el-gân!*"

"..."

"*'iḥḍarû, we ¿alaikum el-'amân!*"

(O you inhabitants of the place! O you kings of jinn!)

(...)

(Be present, and safety is upon you!)

This command was repeated several times (probably seven); each time it was accompanied by the same sound of a muffled little explosion in the brazier and by more smoke. Then, the shaman-*shaikh* asked me:

—What do you see?

—Nothing!

—Look carefully. What do you see?

—Nothing!

—Nothing at all!?

—Nothing at all!

The shaman-*shaikh* repeated the recitation calling on the jinn "to be present," and that their safety is "assured" and "re-assured;" he then readdressed to me the same question. Still, I saw nothing. The eerie silence that had prevailed began to crack; I could hear numerous murmurs and comments made by the spectators. With a hint of impatience in his voice, the shaman-*shaikh* once more repeated the recitation and asked:

—What do you see!?

—Nothing!

This time, there were no follow-up questions nor instructions to be observant, but absolute silence. A heavy period (probably only a few moments) that seemed like a long time hovered and dwelt over the place; a sense of failure, disappointment, and discomfort loomed over the place and seemed to have everyone, especially me, in its grips. I felt the texture of the floor mat to be sharper and more invasive; my legs were becoming numb and stiff from sitting cross-legged for such a long time; I felt an urge to wipe off my eyes, and to get up and move about or do something (after all, I was "infamous" for the "inability to be still even for one full minute"); the kerosene odor became more piercing, and the perfumed smoke much thicker: breathing while under the towel was getting much harder.

Out of that foreboding silence, a female spectator's faint whisper reached my ears, and certainly everyone else's:

"*yimkin ma-huwwâsh ṭâhìr!* (Maybe he is not 'pure' [or innocent]!)"

For me, this "innocent" casual comment was like an exploding bombshell or an earthquake for it carried truly menacing ramifications. The most immediate of the many crises that were to await me would have been: How am I going to explain to my very propriety-conscious mother the charge that her eleven-year-old son (the "son-of-the-daughter-of an Azhar-professor of sharia (jurisprudence)," "the child-of-the-house-of- . . . ," etc.) is not "pure to an extent that the judicious kings of the jinn refuse to even acknowledge his presence? Under the circumstances, such a charge would have been irrefutable: guilt has already been established. Driven by an acute need to eschew the impending disaster (and inevitable admissions to having disobeyed several of my parents' instructions and prohibitions), I gazed harder and harder through wet and burning eyes at the glimmering surface of the liquid in the cup. At that moment, I discovered my quivering hands. They were still clenched around the cup. I tried to clear the tears away by tightly clenching my eyelids together; with every eyelid movement, a new visual pattern was formed on the surface of the liquid in the cup. Suddenly—and genuinely—I "*saw*" something; or, perhaps, the "things" I had seen earlier but could not comprehend began to be meaningful. These were *no* longer the twinkling dots and lines of broken rays of faint light radiating lazily from the kerosene lamp and filtering through the towel placed over my head, nor were they from the oscillating little "tongues of pure flame" in the brazier, as I had previously thought! These were something else! Out of a dry mouth and through a wavering voice, words pleading for a second chance eked out:

—"I, . . . , see . . . , something."

Promptly, the shaman-*shaikh* declared, "Oh! Thank God!"
(I also must have wholeheartedly thanked God for that second opportunity.)
Silence returned to the room; then the shaman-*shaikh* asked me:

—"What do you see?"

—. . . . (Silence; for I could not describe what I "saw.")

—"Is what you see big, or is it small?"

—"Small!" I answered promptly.

—"How small? Very small?"

—"Very small!"

—"Does what you see look like a man or a woman?"

—"A man!"

—"What is he wearing?"

—. . . . (Silence; for the only memorable jinni I had "seen" was the one in the American movie "The Thief of Baghdad," who wore a next to nothing G-string-like underpants: attire unsuitable to be that of a king of the jinn.)

The shaman-*shaikh* broke the silence:

—"Is he wearing a *za¿bûṭ* [(a sort of country-style mantle)]?—[(but I had never seen one in real life)].

—"Does he have a *ṭarṭûr* (high conical cap, 'fool's cap') on his head?"

—"Yes: *za¿bût* and *ṭarṭûr* [are what he is wearing]!"

—"Say to him: 'May peace be upon you, and upon those who are present with you'"

—"May peace be upon you, and upon those who are present with you!" (I addressed that character whose image was in the cup.)

—"What did he say (i.e., what was his answer)?"

—"And upon you may peace be!" [was his answer].

—"Say to him, 'Are you the king or the servant?'"

—"Are you the king or the servant?"

—. . . .

—"He says, 'I'm the servant.'"

—"Say to him, 'Sweep the place!'"

—"Sweep the place!"

—"Say to him, 'Spray the place [with water, so as to cool it, and settle the dust down].'"

—"Spray the place [with water, as is customary for people who plan to have a social getting together]!"

—"Has he swept and sprayed?"

—"Yes!"

—"Say to him, 'Set up the chairs, and prepare the divan [i.e., court for the king].'"

—"Set up the chairs, and prepare the divan!"

—"Say to him, 'Are you done?'"

—"Are you done!?". . . . He says, "Yes!"

—"Say to him, Call the king and say to him, 'O King, hold the court!'"

—. . . .

—. . . .

At the end of this phase of the ritual, I could visually "see" a row of—perhaps eleven—tiny men, seated on miniature chairs, inside a pavilion, with their king wearing a high conical cap and sitting in their midst; also I was able to "communicate" with the king by asking questions and receiving answers, and to "ascertain" that all the judges were present, and that all were pious, trustworthy believers.

Once the court was in full session, the shaman-*shaikh* presented the case via addressing me:

> The lady 'Omm-Ḥâmid had placed the sum of three pounds—*mâl ḥalâl* (legitimate money) earned by her husband as part of his monthly salary—inside a box, that she concealed under some items of [folded] clothes on the top shelf of the wardrobe in the bedroom. Now, the money that was to be used to feed the family for the rest of the month, was gone; the family cannot wait until the next monthly payday; Moḥammad Abu-Gh., and hajji el-B. [each being owner of a grocery shops in the neighborhood], have both refused to let the family buy on credit [because they have been unable to pay back previous debts]. Also missing was one of a twenty-one karat gold pair of earrings.

After presenting the case, the *shaik* ordered me:

—"Ask him, 'Who stole the money and the earring?'"

Having conveyed the crucial question to the head of the court, "the King of jinn" (of this location), I sensed that the "entire world" was breathlessly awaiting the answer. (I do not remember what deliberating steps the jinn's court took, or who spoke on its behalf.) The answer (verdict) came to me in a flash of insight (bypassing all possible thinking, reasoning, and rationalizing processes) in one word:

-Ḥâmid! [The eldest son of 'Omm-Ḥâmid.]

The search for the thief, abruptly and unexpectedly, came to an end when 'Omm-Ḥâmid grabbed her eldest son, Ḥâmid, and yelled: "*'inta! ya ¿irsît baitàk*" (You! Ichneumon/mongoose [i.e., thief] of your own home!). Equally abruptly, but perhaps not totally unexpectedly, Ḥâmid confessed to stealing the money, but not the earring. He swore his innocence and offered to take an oath on *el-khìtmàh* (i.e., the Koran) that he did not steal the earring. His mother retorted: "They said to the thief 'Swear [to your innocence].' He thought: 'Relief has come'" (i.e., a thief's oath is worthless—a proverbial saying).

With that confession my own tribulation, or test of worth by ordeal, came to a safe ending. The reward to my family was that its "goodness" has been reaffirmed—or, perhaps more accurately, not doubted; the shaman-*shaikh* attributed my initial "failure" at winning the trust of the jinn to my being afraid and inexperienced at such matters. As for me, escaping being interrogated by my mother, and the inevitable fact-finding inspection that would have ensued—had that initial failure persisted—was great enough a reward. (These facts would have included such infractions as: having a crush on a girl from our neighborhood and timing of my departure for school and my return home to coincide with hers; getting involved in some gambling games, borrowing money from friends, swimming in the river, occasionally skipping school and going to the cinema, keeping company with objectionable friends—including Ḥâmid, etc.)

I do not remember when or how that court of the jinn (though its work was actually only detective work) was dismissed. However, I remember that the shaman-*shaikh* accepted Ḥâmid's claim of innocence with reference to the missing earring, on the grounds that it was implausible that a *¿àyyìl* (young boy, kid) would have been able to fence stolen jewelry. As a result, the procedure of *màndàll b-el-qùllàh* (divination/detecting via a pottery water-bottle) was begun: that ritual was performed by the *shaman-shaikh* himself, and proved to be someone else's ordeal (see App. 20).

Appendix 20: Detective-Divination via Pottery Water-Bottle: A Failure

The following account is a sequel to App. 19.

After reciting the necessary incantations required for enlisting the help of the jinn (see n. 239) the shaman-*shaikh* balanced a "*qullàh ghashîmah*" (lit.: "clumsy/inept . . . ," i.e., new unused pottery/earthenware water-bottle) on the palm of his hand, and moved in the direction in which the bottle seemed to lean or drift (or rather in the direction in which the jinn were believed to caused it to drift). The crowd of spectators, including me, followed. Moving through narrow dark lanes past numerous houses, the bottle finally seemed to plunge toward the door of a small one-room building used as a workshop and belonged to a man named Abu-Ṣâbir

(Father-of-Ṣâbir). That man lived in a corner house across the street from the workshop; he made his living mainly by extracting flower essences, and then bottling and whole-selling rose water. He also undertook other small recycling operations such as removing solder from old kerosene lanterns, sold by the British army as scrap metal; this was accomplished by burning them in an open fire set in the middle of the small square in front of his workshop, sifting the ashes for the melted solder droppings, and then dumping the scorched metal into the nearby river. This latter practice was thought of as harmful to people who used the river for water drawing, fishing, clothes washing, and bathing (many a wounded foot was blamed on sharp metal produced by this practice by Abu-Ṣâbir); it was also believed to be offensive to the river's own supernatural inhabitants ("*gìnnìyyât,*" female water spirits, and other water spirits). Abu-Ṣâbir was assisted full-time by his son, Ṣâbir, a boy of about twelve years of age, who was taken out of school to join his father's trade, and was not allowed to play or mix with boys of his age group.

Both the shop and the house were in total darkness. 'Omm-Ḥâmid, with the flickering light of the lamp in her hand casting oscillating shadows over her angry face, looked quite menacing and frightful—for although she had pretty facial features, she had a bad eye with a "white cloud" that caused her to have to turn her head sharply in order to see in the direction of the side of the bad eye; also she was "tall and thin" [i.e., slender—(an undesirable feature in a woman by local beauty standards)]. She and a few others behind her began to pound on the door and windows of the residence while shouting accusations of thievery, and of pretence of innocence by feigning being asleep. The man—Abu-Ṣâbir—and his family, so rudely and unexpectedly awakened, emerged from their home in total bewilderment. In disbelief, he vehemently denied the charge. He accused 'Omm-Ḥâmid of madness, and the crowd of childishness, and of violating the sanctity of a home in a manner that would be a sin if inflicted even on an infidel (*ma-tgozsh ḥattâ ¿alâ al-kâfir*), let alone a believer (Moslem); and threatened to take the matter to the police. The man's wife, 'Omm-Ṣabir, accused 'Omm-Ḥâmid of coming to their home at night just "like a *sala¿awwah* (ogress-like creature), without *'iḥim, walâ 'dastûr!*" (i.e., without pretending to be clearing her throat so as to let the residents of the house know of the presence of a stranger, nor seeking permission by saying, "Permission!" as if entering upon a jinni's place of residence). A sharp verbal squabble and exchange of insults ensued, but neither side seemed to prevail.

At this point my elder sister, having been dispatched along with mother's instructions to bring me home, arrived on the scene and gave me the message; under the circumstances, this order had to be—uncharacteristically—promptly heeded. Yet, I received a relatively light reprimand: "*yâmâ gâb el-ghurâb l'-ommuh* (Many a thing has the crow brought back to his mother [i.e., 'A troublesome child drags in nothing but trouble,' or 'See what the cat dragged in']);" I was also reminded that a good child stays at home studying or helping, and that had I—in total disregard of innumerable times of counsel—not be *dâyir yitnaṭṭa¿*... (a cruiser-sticker in "streets and back-allies,"' i.e., a loiterer) mixing with objectionable characters, my family (especially mother and elder sister) would not have been placed in this presumptive and embarrassing situation.

I learned of the outcome of the squabble from my friends at school the following day: both parties went to the police station, where Ḥâmid's father worked; an "official report of theft" was made. (Later the case was dismissed.)

Addendum: the rationale

Although I am convinced that I visually "saw" nothing on the surface of that liquid in the cup, I am equally convinced that I experienced perceiving the panel of jinn judges in the manner described above; their collective image has been etched in my memory until today, almost forty years later. Yet, until the present time (1970s)[761] I cannot find an explanation as to why the jinn I "saw" were tiny; in fantasy tales and legends I had heard or read, they were either of human-like size or gigantic. Also, the jinn I "saw" sat on chairs that looked like those in *qâ¿at el-galsât* ("trials hall") in the courthouse where my father worked; I had seen these judge's chairs when I was a little boy during the times I visited my father at his office in the courthouse, wandered about the building and occasionally found the huge "trials hall" empty; yet that real court in the courthouse had only three judge's chairs in the middle of the platform (judge's bench), and a fourth—on the side—for the district attorney; the rest were regular seats or benches.

The explanation for this "old" experience came some seventeen years later (in 1967–1968) while reading through literature on "the psychology of perception," when I taught a course on social psychology. As for the "seeing" of supernatural beings (i.e., jinn constituting a court of law), an explanation of this experience was provided by a psychological experiment that indicated the cause–effect link between frustration of wants and fantasizing as a response.[762]

Intuition

In a flash of insight, the following affective and mentalistic facts—in addition to others, mostly noncognitive—are perceived:

Ḥamîda was the eldest of five brothers (Ḥâmid, Fikry, [. . .], [. . .], and the youngest—known to us only by his nickname "Shîtah" [i.e., Tarzan's chimpanzee "Chita"]; in spite of being only in his early teens (perhaps thirteen or fourteen), he was already shaving his beard, and considerably taller and stronger than any boy in our group; he had numerous tiny hairless spots on his head (presumably from an early scalp infection). Ḥâmid used his strength to bully and intimidate; in retaliation, he was occasionally taunted of being the "Son-of-a-nobody," and that an ibis-bird must has pecked holes in his scalp.

Moreover, he was a habitual fibber, especially concerning his imaginary erotic-love adventures; worst of all, he was notorious for his brazen heckling of girls (even,

761 This segment of the book was written in 1973.

762 See a résumé of the experiment and related literature under the heading "Wants, Blocks and Distorted Cognitive Organizations," in Krech et al., *Individual in Society*, pp. 35–37.

women) on city streets, and even in our own neighborhood. One time he was picked out of a lineup of all our high-school classes (first through fifth grades), by a girl who had just been harassed (probably pinched, or poked in the chest with the shoulder) while on her way to the girl's high school, located a few blocks down the street from ours. The severe punishment he received—paddled on the bottom of his feet and buttocks in front of the entire student and teacher body—was administered by the owner-headmaster of the school in person, and was meant to be a lesson for others. By contrast, almost every member of our group harbored a secret love for a girl (typically "a friend's sister"), and would work hard at being "accidentally" in her route to or from school, or at acquiring and displaying the latest study-guides, magazines, or novels, hoping that his "girl" would find it interesting enough (and defensible at home) to borrow. With the exception of exchanging class notes, study-guides, and directly related materials, our parents frowned upon such "love" activities; in their views they were "manifestations of lack in good-manners," "showing the effects of inadequate upbringing at home," and constituting "the first step toward the immoral."

Although Ḥâmid's father was known to be a "good man," he was also thought of as deferring to his domineering wife, who could see no fault with her sons, especially the eldest. Thus, whenever Ḥâmid's parents were informed of his deviant conduct, his mother would defend and shield him; in the case of the serious sex-harassment of the school girl, Ḥâmid's mother was reported to have stated, "He is only a harmless kid!" and euphemistically explained: "Even his 'thing' would not [be large enough so as] to apply kohl to an eye" [i.e., it is smaller than a woman's mascara eye-liner applicator, and, consequently, he is harmless].

Prior to the discovery of the theft, Ḥâmid seemed to have more spending money than ever before: he spent "extravagantly," and purchased "expensive" items at the school's buffet and town's stationery stores (he had costly pastel-colored and perfumed letter-writing pad and envelops set of the "Ashly"-brand, which he claimed to be love letters from several girls to him); he also had skipped classes to go to movie matinees: "From [A.M.] ten to one [P.M.]."

In short, not only did Ḥâmid appear to be the most appropriate candidate for being the thief but also he indiscreetly flaunted the fruits of the theft. Thus, arriving at this conclusion by someone in possession of the above-cited pieces of evidentiary information—inaccessible and unknown to adults—is quite human. The supernatural (jinn-court) merely provided a catalyst for the transfer of the evidence from the circle of youngsters to that of adults, or, plainly stated: to act as *fattân* (tattle-tale). The security provided by getting the information from a jinni parallels the legal practice of providing protection to a vulnerable witness, or granting a witness "immunity from prosecution." Ḥâmid did not seek to punish me later.

Appendix 21: A Case of Missing Jewelry

Recorded from Mrs. Z.Ḥ., a middle-aged mother and homemaker. She is literate. Narrator's father, Sheik Ḥ. . . , was of the ulama—a holder of al-¿Âlimiyyah *degree (the formal Degree of*"¿Âlim"), *a professor of jurisprudence at al-Azhar University (in Cairo), and a prominent figure in his home village where he owned some land. A cleric of his rank would be addressed as* ṣâḥib al-faḍîlah *(lit.: man-of-virtue, i.e., "His Eminence," "Reverend," or the like). She married at an early age; both she and her husband lived in Cairo, but had strong family ties (and some land holdings) in the village, which they visited occasionally.* (For more information on the *shaman*-shaikh, see App. 22.)

Mrs. Z.Ḥ. reported,

When I was still a bride [i.e., newly wed]—only a teenage girl [i.e., unacquainted with the wiles of in-laws], the daughters of the sisters of my husband came for a visit. I had my *sîghàh* (i.e., *maṣûghât*, gold[-jewelry]) packed in a handkerchief that I placed on the dining-room table. Later, I discovered that the kerchief with its contents disappeared—I mean someone, deliberately, "lifted" it.

Their [the visitors'] maternal-uncle [i.e., my husband] refused to ask them about it; he said, "This is a question that may not be asked!" When I innocently asked them [my husband's nieces], "Has anyone seen my gold-jewelry?" they replied [in anger], "We are not thieves! We don't stay where our honesty is suspect[ed]." And they left in a huff-and-puff. Still, we looked everywhere, but did not find the missing things.

When we traveled to the village; we went to [shaman-] *shaikh* Ḥaggâg [at his home]. He is *râgil màbrûk* (a blessed man, i.e., has *barakàh*). We sat in the entrance-hall awaiting admittance [into his room], without telling anyone who we were. When he was ready to see us, he told his assistant [who was his younger brother], "Call in The [. . .]" [citing our family name]. Without having been told a word about what we had intended to ask, he stated:

> "O you daughter of *ṣâhib al-faḍîlah* (his Eminence) *Shaikh* Ḥ . . . , you have come in connection with the gold-jewelry. But it is gone and will not be recovered. The person or persons who lifted it are not strangers to you. You should say: 'May God compensate [us for this unfair loss]!' ([i.e., proceed from the perspective that it is lost permanently])."

Surely, I never saw again my "engagement gold": two pairs of bracelets, a five-tier necklace, and a lady's [gold]-watch.

This event marked the *qaṭî¿ah* (boycott, antipathy) between my husband's sisters and me.

Appendix 22: A Jinni-Woman Pays an *'încî*/Human Friend a Visit

*Reported by Mrs. Z.Ḥ. (see App. 21). In this account, the shaman-*shaik's *familiar, who is the female-jinn cited in App. 21, visits the informant (an* 'inciyyah*; i.e., female human) She does so in the form of a sickly kitten. For the informant the event is a personal experience narrative (memorate).*

[Shaman]-*shaikh* Ḥaggâg was very famous and his reputation had traveled throughout all of Egypt. They say that the wife of [Moṣṭafâ] el-Naḥḥâs Pasha [a former prime minister] came in a private chauffeured car to see [consult] him. This is something that is known to the young and the old [in the village].

He was *mikhâwî waḥda minhum* (he had bebrothered "one of them" [i.e., a female jinni] as foster-"sister"). Whenever he would wish to consult her over some matter or problem, he would cover himself with his *¿abâyah* (mantle); then she would *tilbisuh* (wear him, get into him); his body would shake and quiver, then her voice would come through [his tongue]: the voice of a woman—without a doubt or equivocation (*bilâ shàkk wa-bilâ làbs*) a woman's voice. She would say [in a gentle manner, in correct, classical Arabic], "*'as-salâmu ¿alàykum* (Peace be upon you)!" Then one would ask whatever one would wish, then receive the answer from her, through him [i.e., his tongue]. Her answers always proved to be correct.

When things [in a consultation session] were over; she would exit his body in the same manner in which she had entered it, i.e., his body would shake and quiver, she would say, "Peace be upon you," and would exit. He, *yâ ¿ainî* ("poor thing") would be so pale, and sweat would be pouring out of his forehead. Most often he would not remember what she [his familiar jinn-"sister"] had said [concerning the issue under consideration].

She promised to visit us for a little while in Zaqazîq [the town in which we were residing]. A few years later, the children brought home a *birrâwiyya* (feral, not house-broken) she-kitten, [it was sick and emaciated]. [At first] I refused to let them keep it; but they pleaded, "O Mama, 'by the Prophet' (i.e., for the Prophet's sake)! We will take care of her [it], and clean after her." [So, I relented.] After a few days, the kitten [that was suffering from diarrhea] made a mess on the baby's crib. Everyone of the children would say, "Yack-ck-ck! I cant' clean that!" I said, "She must go! I can hardly keep up with your own messes!" The children cried, and pleaded again, "O Mama, 'by the Prophet!'" but this time I insisted. They took her [the kitten] out, but she ran away from them at the front door [of the apartment (located on third story)] on the staircase. They looked for her everywhere [within the apartment building] and outside, but [even] a trace of her was not to be found anywhere.

Then I realized that the kitten was [the spirit] *'illî mikhawiyyah esh-shaikh* Ḥaggâg (the one [jinn-woman] who has "bebrothered" sheik Ḥaggâg (i.e., his foster-sibling, familiar-sister). As she had promised, she came to us [in the form of a kitten] for a brief visit. The sickness, and the rest [of her characteristics] were a ruse so that she would not have to stay [i.e., be kept] for longer than she wished.

She had said she would visit us for a brief period, and [indeed] she did.

Illness

Appendix 23: The Thigh of the Duck

Reported in March 1971 by 55-year-old "Uncle" ¿Abdu, a shoemaker from Cairo. ¿Abdu is married and has a number of children. I paid a business visit to ¿Abdu's workshop, which lies directly across the street from his apartment; his fourteen-year-old daughter came to see him. He noted that she had not been feeling well lately and reminisced about her previous illness, then told me this story.

In our present account the shaman receives advice from a female jinni with whom he has developed a friendly brother-sister relationship; she is called his "sister." This type of bond is typical of the category of healers who use their supernatural aids to diagnose and prescribe a treatment. In this respect, the healer is unlike the magician, who claims to have the power to control and coerce the jinn.

About seven, maybe five, years ago when my daughter Loula—whom you have seen here in the workshop before—was about ten years old, something wondrous happened to her. One day, it was a *moosim* day [seasonal celebration], we had a male duck slaughtered. As my daughter was going into the bathroom, she saw a great big she-cat holding the thigh of that male duck and eating it. Loula took (do not blame me) the wooden clog off her foot and threw it forcefully at the cat. It hit the cat in the stomach. The cat howled, "Awwwuuu . . . ," left the thigh, and attacked Loula and bit her big toe (this one, the right toe). She fell ill. I took her to all doctors until I grew dizzy [from going around], but to no avail.

Finally, a friend of mine (a good man like yourself) told me about a man called Sheik Muhammad in Monoufiyyah province, in a village called Megiryeh, or something like that, and said, "This is the one who will cure her."

I said to myself, "Let us see; maybe God will cause recovery at his hands."

On Sunday [because of business requirements, several shops close on Sunday instead of Friday, the Moslim sabbath] that friend of mine and I, and our wives, who came along, took the bus. We got there right before the time of afternoon prayers. We asked, "Where is Sheik Muhammad's house?" They showed us his house. As soon as we knocked at the door, it was ajar, and the sheik called from inside, "Come in, haji [i.e., honorable] ¿Abdu!" (By God, it happened just as I am telling you right now. How did he know my name? I don't know.) He was sitting on a mat, leaning against one of those stiff rectangular cushions used in the countryside. We sat next to him. He said to me, "Open that door over there." I opened it. I found there a pitcher of water. My! What water! Sweet, cool, and fragrant! As I was drinking, I looked around and found neither a window nor a hole in the wall. I took the pitcher for the others to drink. He asked us, "How are you?" and things like that. A short while later, maybe five or ten minutes later, he said to me, "Haji ¿Abdu, open that door again." I opened the door. I found there one of those large round trays full of all God's gifts. I ate soup that tasted like no soup I have ever had before; bread, rice, meat, fowl, everything! We were hungry, so we ate "until we thanked God." After we drank tea, as we were drinking it, Sheik Muhammad said, "That duck's thigh, was it absolutely necessary?"

When I heard that, I was astonished! How did he know? How did he know my name! From where did that food come? How did he know about the duck's thigh! I answered, "A mistake! She is only a little girl; she doesn't know [any better]."

He said, "Was it that necessary? Why! Why!"

The girl's mother said to him, "By God, master sheik, ask them to forgive her." She gave him one [of Loula's] handkerchiefs, which she had brought along.

He said to us, "Spend the night here," but I said to him, "We must return to Cairo, for I have to open my shop on Monday; customers and things, you know."

He said to us, "Well, peace be with you, but come back 'like today' [i.e., a week from today]."

Next Sunday I went alone. He had consulted the lady whom he had "bebrothered." She told him, he said to me, "Listen, I want you to buy three young ducks of the highest quality. Slaughter them as you mention God's name this time. If they [the jinn] are Moslims, they will take them, if they wish to do so. [The implication here is that if they were not Moslims, he would have to repeat the procedure without using God's name.] Fry them in pure clarified butter, put them in one large plastic bag, and go to Maadi near Sheik—" I forgot his name—"and bury them in the hills. Don't let anybody see you. Then go back the following day and see what happened. If they are gone, then they [the jinn] have accepted our offering. If not, God forbid, come back to me."

I did exactly as he told me to do. The following day I went back. I had marked the spot with a few bricks. When I dug the sack out, by God, the ducks had become nothing but dry bones. Every speck of meat and fat was gone. Not a single bone was out of place. I swear by God, it happened just as I am telling you. When I returned home I found Loula recovered and better than ever.

Appendix 24: "Mari" Girgis, The Devil Slayer

Reported in the winter of 1971 by Mr. Gamâl B.B., about twenty-five years of age, from Asyout. He is unwed and holds a degree of Engineer. He heard the account from numerous Moslems and Copts. He adds "I know the person involved as an neighbor."

We have someone in our town who got very ill. His illness was not physical but was in his soul (*er-roaḥ*). His name was Maḥmûd. . . . [i.e., a Moslem], and was married and had many children. He was a farmer who was educated to some extent and had a good amount of [agricultural] land, but he lived here in Cairo with one of his grown-up children, in Roaḍ el-Farag district [where many Copts reside].

All of a sudden he got sick: his body would shake from head to foot; then he would become very violent. He broke up things: dishes, furniture, and things like that; they say that he even broke the bicycle that his son used to get to work. After such violent happenings, he would calm down and would not be able to remember any of the [destructive] things that he had done.

He went to doctors (i.e., physicians) and [Moslem] *shaikhs* but no one was able to cure him. He finally went to a famous priest who deals with *el-'umûr er-rûḥiyyah* (matters of the soul, spiritual affairs). The priest told him that he was possessed by Satan (*esh-sheṭân dakhaluh*), and that the only one [i.e., power] that can help him is the Martyr Mâr Girgis.

He traveled to Meet Damsees, near Kafr El-Shaikh city [(a town in the Nile Delta)], during the annual mass service performed at the Mar Girgis church. There were many people—men, women, and children, all dressed in white and praying for healing through the *shafâ¿ah* of the Martyr. Then the Martyr appears on his horse in the form of a flash of light with his spear in his hand, and makes the "killing," then vanishes into the air.

After this, a spot of blood appeared on the white garment he was wearing. It was in the shape of a crescent: meaning that he was a Moslem. No one there knew beforehand that he was not Coptic, except that man himself. Now he is completely healed.

Zâr

Appendix 25: *Zâr 'asyâd*: A Pantheon (I, II, III)

The following lists of Zâr 'asyâd *provided by various students of the zâr illustrate familial ties as they occur within the context of the ritual. As will be observed, the brother–sister tie dominates in these select lists.*

I. Littmann's list No. 1[763]

1. The big master (*es-sîd el-kibîr*) Mâmma al-hudâ
2. Yûsaih—the son of "Mâmma"
3. Mustaghîta [(the One-Who-Is-Crying-Out-for-Help)]," Mâmma's sister
4. Sister of Yâsaih—[unnamed]
5. Sayyid, [the] Egyptian
6. [Sayyid's] sister [unnamed]
7. Mamûna
8. Rûm-Nagdî
9. Sister of Rûm-Nagdî [unnamed]
10. The Sudanese, one of the mawâlî
11. Yâwrî Bey
12. el-Hawânim 'awlâd el-ḥabash—Abyssnian ladies
13. Safîna, sister of the Sultan Mariner
14. Wallâg—slave of Safîna
15. Mother of Wallâg
16. Lady Sâlkîna, inhabitant of Bornu
17. ¿Arab el-¿Orbân—the pride of the Hilâlite Arabs
18. Shagar al-ghulâm—sister of ¿Urbân
19. Sîd Nagd (Master of Nagd)
20. ¿Awaisha [el-maghrabiyya, (Little ¿Aisha-from-the-Maghreb)]
21. Maghrabî: Si Ladyâ ¿Abd el-Qâdir

[763]In his *Geisterbeschwörungen*, pt. 41, pp. 35–36 (Arabic orignial pp. 93–94). With reference to the neglible interest this invauable work had no scholars, see n. 15.

II. Shumays's/Fawwâz's List[764]

1. Sultan Mamma
2. His sister, Mustaghîta [i.e., the One-Who-Is-Crying-Out-for-Help] [. . .]
3. Yûsaih *el-middalà¿* (the-Spoiled) son of Mamma
4. Um-Ghulâm [Mother-of-the-Lad]—his sister
5. Dair Balâla—Mamma's vizier/minister[765]
6. Sister of Dair Balâla [unnamed]
7. *sîd maṣrî* (an Egyptian spirit)
8. Um-el-Warâyid-Wardî, sister of the Egyptian spirit
9. Mammûna, sister of Sayyid
10. Rûm Nagd (dressed in his sword, greeting his guest)
11. Marûma, sister of Rûm Nagd (see App. 27)
12. el-Sûdânî (the Sudanese)
13. Safîna (Ship), sister of Sulṭân Baḥriyyah
14. Sulṭân Bahariyyah (Sultan of Mariner)
15. Wallâg—Safîna's slave
16. el-Dallûkah—*fâris among 'ikhwâtuh* (a horseman/knight/champion among his brethen or sisters)
17. Dingah [cited under Wallâg]
18. Omm Wallâg—from Bornu
19. Tarngah Omm-Walâg's son (mother of Wallâg)
20. ¿Arab el-¿Urbân (of the Hilali Tribe)
21. Dalîla—sister of ¿Arab el-¿Urbân
22. Salîma—sister of ¿Arab el-¿Urbân
23. Wazîra—sister of ¿Arab el-¿Urbân
25. Shagar el-¿Urbân—sister of ¿Arab el-¿Urbân
26. ¿Uwaisha el-maghrabiyyah (from-the-Maghreb)
27. el-Maghrabî ¿Abd-el-Qâdir.

III. El-Shamy's list[766]

1. Sultan Mummah
2. Mustaghîta [the One-Who-Is-Crying-Out-for-Help], his sister

---

[764] ¿A. Shumays, "al-zâr masraḥ ghinâ'î lam yataṭawwar (The Zar: a lyric drama that did not evolve)." The primary data given by Shumays is derived from Zaynab Fawwâz's 1893 pioneering study (see n. 319). The numbers are provided by the present writer.

[765] It is cited here (p. 87) that Mustgheetha is Mamma's mother (rather than sister).

[766] See: El-Shamy, "Belief Characters," p. 27; also see App. 26.

3. Yûsaih-the-Spoiled," the son of Mamma Um-Ghulâm [Mother-of-the-Lad], Yûsaih's sister
4. Mârî-Mariyyâ
5. *el-Qassîs* (the Priest), her brother
6. Rînâ [a female Christian spirit]
7. Wazîr (the Minister)
8. Abu-l-Ghaiṭ (The-One-with-the-Field/Farm) Wraida (Little-Rose), his sister
9. Rûm-Nagdî
10. Marûma (The Sought After), his sister
11. Ṣulṭân-Baḥariyyah (Sultan-of-the-Mariners)
12. Safîna (Ship), his sister (also cited as sister of el-Ghawwâṣ)
13. el-Ghawwâṣ (the Diver)
14. Safîna (Ship), his sister (also cited as sister of Ṣulṭân-Baḥariyyah)
15. ¿Arab el-¿Urbân/el-¿ârbah (The-Arab-of-the-Arabs/Bedouins)
16. Galîla, his sister
17. Wallâg (Inserter, the One-who-Enters/Penetrates) is Galîla's slave
18. ¿Uwaisha el-Maghrabiyya (Little-¿Aisha from Maghreb) Sister of the el-Maghrabî
19. el-Maghrabî (the man from Maghreb) [brother of ¿Uwaisha]
20. Yâwree Bey
21. Omm-Mamûn (Mamûn's mother), his sister
22. Manzûh (Dandy-life [??])
23. Manzûhah, his sister

    Groups of spirits that K. mentioned include:
24. *el-maṣârwah* (the Egyptians/the Cairene)
25. *salâṭîn ed-dair* (Sultans-of-the-Monastery that are included in the Egyptian group)
26. *el-sûdâniyya* (the Sudanese)
27. *el-ḥabash* (the Abyssnians)
28. *el-badw* (the Bedouins/Nomads)

Appendix 26: How the *Zâr*-Ritual Solved a Childless Woman's Problem

This true life experience is reported as a personal experience by Mrs. K.S. (See her list of 'asyâd, *App. 22, pt. III). She is a middle-aged, very attractive, well-to-do, Cairene woman.*[767] *She has one full brother and two half brothers and one half sister from the mother. Although she married a number of times, she did not bear any children and yearned for a child. K. was quite attached to her full brother—he also displayed a great deal of affection toward her. They lived in two separate but close districts of Cairo. To the chagrin of his wife (K.'s sister-in-law), K.'s full brother agreed to let her raise his*

[767] Recorded in September 1968; K. was about fifty-five years of age then.

first son. She kept the son with her for about fourteen years, called him "my son," and assigned him a new nickname. The son "visited" his actual parents on special occasions, only accompanied by K., his foster-mother. The animosity between K. and her brother's wife (the boy's mother) was exceptionally acute; the two women, however, had to control the public display of their feelings toward each other. The brother's wife (the boy's mother) complained: "When she was not feuding with me, she treated me as if I did not exist!"

Mrs. K. reported:

"I [personally] was possessed by the big Sultan, 'Sultan Mamma' [. . .]." [She] cited twenty-four individual zar spirits; only four relationships: Mamma and Yousaih's, Rena, the minister, and Galîla and Wallâg's were not perceived as that of brother and sister. It is significant to observe here that Mamma has a sister; he also has a son, but he has no wife. Also Yosaih has a sister, but she is not perceived as Mamma's daughter. Evidently, the brother and sister relationship in this context overrides that of the daughter and father.

In another list containing *zar* spirits published by the distinguished orientalist–folklorist Enno Littmann, the brother and sister association also dominates.[768] That list names twenty-one characters. Two of these represent ethnic identities rather than particular personal characteristics: they are "the White Slaves" and "the [Abyssinian]/Ethiopian Ladies." Of the remaining nineteen, twelve are given in pairs of brother and sister, two are presented as father and son, and two (slaves) are portrayed in son–mother relationships. The rest are individual "spirits" with no kinship relations.

K.'s perception of the pattern of organization of the zar spirits is congruent with other aspects of the belief system, especially those concerning the affectionate bond between a supernatural Sister and her human brother. This organization is also highly indicative of K.'s own social and psychological real conditions. At the time when the state of her "possession" was at its peak, some twenty years earlier, K. had one full brother and two half brothers and one half sister from the mother. Although she married a number of times, she did not bear any children and yearned for a child. K. was quite attached to her full brother, he also displayed a great deal of affection toward her. To the chagrin of his wife, K.'s full brother agreed to let her raise his first son. She kept the son with her for about fourteen years, called him "my son," and assigned him a new nickname. The son "visited" his actual parents on special occasions, only accompanied by K. The animosity between K. and her brother's wife (the boy's mother) was exceptionally acute; the two women, however, had to control the public display of their feelings toward each other. "When she was not feuding with me, she treated me as if I did not exist," said the brother's wife.

The belief state that K. adopted from the *zar* characters is a duplicate of her own psychosocial conditions. Mamma, the spirit that possessed K., had a sister and a son, but no wife of his is mentioned; K. herself had a brother but no son. Thus when K. took over her brother's son and viewed him as her own, she was playing the role of Mamma's sister "Mùstaghîtah (the-One-Who-Is-Crying-Out-for-Help)."

Indeed, K. was crying out for help in a symbolic guise, which is to be understood only within the context of the systemic relations of the zar characters in which she believed.

[768] See n. 15, 208, and 316.

Appendix 27: Marûma's *nidâ*

Marûma is the sister of Rûm Nagd. The brother was presented in a preceding nidâ *as an Arab chieftain from Najd (in Arabia), "wearing his sword and greeting his guest." The text also instructed him:* "'ishṭaḥ wi 'itmâyil *(run wild or unruly, and sway to and fro)."* (On *shaṭḥ*, see n. 642)

rummânik yâ Marûma, yâ hooh!
(O Marûma, your pomegranates, o wow!)
korsikî fi-l-ginainah naṣabûh.
(Your chair has been erected in the garden.)
'akhûkî Rûm Nagd nadahûh.
(Your brother, Rûm Nagd, has been called.)
rummânik, yâ Marûma ṭâb.
(O Marûma, your pomegranates became ripe.)
wi-kalû minnu el-'aḥbâb.
(And the loved-ones ate of them.)
kabshik/kibâshik kibîr dabaḥûh.
(Your [sacrificial] ram/s is/are big, it/hey got slaughtered.)
sham¿ik 'âhum qâdûh.
(Your candles, they have lit them.)
wi 'ismik 'âhum nadahûh.
(And your name they have called.)

The symbolic implications that may be inferred from this Marûma's *nidâ* duplicates a situation depicted in a cluster of songs presented in El-Shamy's study titled *Brother and Sister. Type 872** [. . .]. Thus, the study reported

A song sung by an adolescent girl states:
O palace, you whose windows are overlooking those oases;
inside you is the handsome-one who entangled us [with love] and left.
O, who would bring me my sweetheart, so that he may stay comfortably;
[to] eat from the peaches and roll over the roses.
O, who will bring me my sweetheart on the bed at night;
so that he may eat from the peaches and roll over the roses.[...]

Taken within its broader sequence of songs, the palace of the above-cited song is of particular interest to our present inquiry. The song was sandwiched between two others; it was directly preceded by a song in which the same adolescent female singer insisted that she will *not* marry anyone except a "person with a governmental job and high rank;" then the second song cited above blends with a third song about "the [. . .] victory of my brother [. . .] which made the government happy." Briefly stated, the girl's message, expressed in three consecutive songs, is: I will marry only a person with a high governmental rank; I want my sweetheart to enjoy me inside a palace; my brother is the one with the high governmental rank. Thus, these three successive songs, though seemingly independent, clarify one another, represent an integrated emotional continuum, and express an attitude toward the brother, the overt expression of which is socially unsafe.[...]

A similar "unsafe" message may be inferred from this Marûmâ-Rûm Nagdî text(s), especially with reference to the symbolic significance of entering Marûma's garden and eating of her ripe pomegranates.

Appendix 27A: Safînah's *nidâ*

Recorded in April 1969, from Husain in the village of Kafr el-Zaytoun. It should be noticed that the word "God" does not occur in this daqqàh/nidâ *(call).*

Leader:	*ya safîna fi-l-baḥr ¿awwâma* (O Safinâ, in the sea [you are a] swimmer)
Chorus:	*ya safîna fi-l-baḥr ¿awwâma*
Leader:	*baḥarriyya fi-l-mayya ¿awwâma* (mariners are swimmers in the water)
Chorus:	*ya safîna fi-l-baḥr ¿awwâma*
Leader:	*we-mlûk el-mayya fi-l-baḥr ¿awwâma* (the water kings [i.e., jinn] are swimmers in the sea)
Chorus:	*ya safîna fi-l-baḥr ¿awwâma*
Leader:	*baḥarriyya fi-l-mayya ¿awwâma* (mariners are swimmers in the water)
Chorus:	*ya safîna fi-l-baḥr ¿awwâma*
Leader:	*we-um el-¿awâgiz fel-mayya ¿awwâma* (And the Mother-of-the-Disabled [i.e., Sayyidah Zaynab] is a swimmers in the water)
Chorus:	*ya safîna fi-l-baḥr ¿awwâma*
Leader:	*baḥarriyya fi-l-mayya ¿awwâma* (mariners are swimmers in the water)
Chorus:	*ya safîna fi-l-baḥr ¿awwâma*
Leader:	*we-mlûk el-mayya fi-l-baḥr ¿awwâma* (the water kings [i.e., jinn] are swimmers in the sea)
Chorus:	*ya safîna fi-l-baḥr ¿awwâma*
Leader:	*baḥarriyya fi-l-mayya ¿awwâma* (mariners are swimmers in the water)
Chorus:	*ya safîna fi-l-baḥr ¿awwâma*
Leader:	*we-um el-¿awâgiz fi-l-mayya ¿awwâma* (And the Mother-of-the-Disabled is a swimmer in the water)
Chorus:	*ya safîna fi-l-baḥr ¿awwâma.*

Appendix 28: Saints in *Zâr*-Like Ritual ("The Love for el-Ḥasan and al-Ḥusain")

Recorded during a live performance of a local "Tuesday zikr" (i.e., "public zâr") in the village of Kafr el-Zaytoun, April 1969 and May 1982. (See n. 336)

Leader: *ḥobb el-Ḥasan wa-l-Ḥusain*
(The love for el-Ḥasan and al-Ḥusain)

Leader: *ḥobb el-Ḥasan wa-l-Ḥusain fi muhgatî sakin*
(The love of el-Ḥasan resides in my inner-soul/heart)
lakîn ḥobb en-nabî, guwwa-l-ḥigâb hâgi¿
(But the Prophet's love is settled inside my chest [??])

Chorus: *ḥobb el-Ḥasan wa-l-Ḥusain fi muhgatî sakin*
lakîn ḥobb en-nabî, guwwa-l-ḥigâb hâgi¿

Leader: *ḥobb el-Ḥasan wa-l-Ḥusain fi muhgatî sakin*
lakîn ḥobb en-nabî, guwwa-l-ḥigâb hâgi¿

Chorus: *ḥobb el-Ḥasan wa-l-Ḥusain fi muhgatî sakin*
lakîn ḥobb en-nabî, guwwa-l-ḥigâb hâgi¿

Leader: *'âh arûḥ azûr en-nabî, we-¿al-ḥram sâkin*
(Oh, I would go to visit the prophet, and become settled in the Shrine)
wa-'aẓur ḥamâm el-ḥimâ, guwwa-l-ḥaram hâgi¿
(and visit the doves of the protected domain: inside the Shrine they've come to rest)

Chorus: *ḥobb el-Ḥasan wa-l-Ḥusain fi muhgatî sakin*
lakîn ḥobb en-nabî, guwwa-l-ḥigâb hâgi¿

Leader: *'âni, yâ muṣṭafâ, min ghrâmak ma-banâm el-lail*
(O Chosen-one, due to infatuation with you, I don't sleep nights)
ta¿âla, 'anâ gait baitak, 'anâ ba-mdaḥak yâ zain
(I have set out, come to your house, [and] I am praising you, O handsome-one)

Chorus: *ḥobb el-Ḥasan wa-l-Ḥusain fi muhgatî sakin*
lakîn ḥobb en-nabî, guwwa-l-ḥigâb hâgi¿

Leader: *'âa ya bakht min raḥ wi zârak yâ kaḥîl al-¿ain*
(O-o-o, lucky, is he who went and visited you, O with kohl-colored eyes)
el-qalb farḥân wa-nâ [. . .] hâgi¿
(the heart is thrilled, while I am [. . . .] settled

Chorus: *ḥobb el-Ḥasan wa-l-Ḥusain fi muhgatî sakin*
lakîn ḥobb en-nabî, guwwa-l-ḥigâb hâgi¿
[Change in tempo: faster beat; chorus stops]

Leader: *sayyidna el-Ḥusain, we-râ¿îna, we-nnabî*
(O our lord el-Ḥusain, cast a [blessed] regard on us)
sayyidna el-Ḥusain, we-râ¿îna, we-nnabî
(O our lord el-Ḥusain, cast a [blessed] regard on us)

Leader: *'âh yâ nabî,*
(O, Prophet!)

'âh yâ nabî,
(O, Prophet!)
'âh yâ nabî,
(O, Prophet!)

Leader: *ya-khî maddaḥ en-nabî, we-râ¿îna, we-nnabî*
(O brother, praise the Prophet, and by the Prophet, cast a [blessed] regard on us)
'âh yâ nabî,
'âh yâ nabî,
'âh yâ nabî,

Leader: *ya-um ed-dalâl, we-râ¿îna we-nabî*
(O you one-with cool and coquetry (i.e., sayyidah Zainab), cast a [blessed] regard on us)
ya-um ed-dalâl, we-râ¿îna we-nabî
(O you one with cool and coquetry (i.e., sayyidah Zainab), cast a [blessed] regard on us)
'âh yâ nabî,
'âh yâ nabî,

Leader: *ya-khî maddaḥ en-nabî, we-râ¿îna, we-nnabî*
'âh yâ nabî,
'âh yâ nabî, 'âh yâ nabî, 'âh yâ nabî,
[etc.]

Appendix 29: The Possessed Husband and His *Zâr*

Recorded on July 9, 1972 from 45-year-old Fatma I. ¿. She is a widow and the mother of two grown-up sons and a daughter. She lives in the rural part of Manyal, a district of southern Cairo. After the death of her husband, about fifteen years earlier, she had to go to work in order to support herself and her children. She works as a door-to-door vendor, selling primarily eggs. She can neither read nor write.

Our account illustrates some sources of conflict between husband and wife; it also shows how an emotionally disturbed person—who is, among other things, a transvestite, is treated through belief in jinn. This report on the experience of a close relative is one step removed from a memorate; it is also not quite a local legend, for this report per se does not circulate within the community. Such a report may be termed a "postmemorate" or a "prelegend."

Haji D., the owner of the district butcher shop, is the husband of my sister Karam. My sister married him while he was, I swear by God, working only for seven piasters per day. When my sister entered his life, she entered accompanied by good fortunes. He used to work [for a small contractor] beside the Nile before the building of the Nile Boulevard. We used to plant [the strip of land] between the river and the bank. We always planted watermelons. Those who worked around there used to stroll by. He saw my sister Karam. She was very beautiful, very, very beautiful. He said, "I'll marry this girl." Then my mother said to him, "You are a Cairene, and we are *fellahin*. If you marry her, you will not be able to live [the way you are used to]." He said, "No, I will marry her." Circumstances deemed it so, and he took her for a wife.

When he took her, his daily wage was very little, seven piasters [the equivalent of seventy cents]. My mother never let them rough it on their own. She always took [foods and other stuff] to them. He was able to stand on his own feet, little by little, and became rich—for she [Karam] came to him along with good fortune. He bought a piece of land and built a house, and [they] stayed in it. She first had Ibrahim [a boy], then ¿Ali, [another boy]; then she slapped [her husband] with five girls in a row [this apparently depressed him].

When my mother went to visit, during the height of his wealthy period, he would say to my sister, "Listen, I will make you swear on the Koran not to take anything [from my house] and give it to your mother. If your mother comes, feed her and make her tea, and make her comfortable, but she should not take out anything from my house. If your head scarf wears out, show it to me [before you give it to her]." That was the husband of the daughter talking about the mother-in-law who supported him when he was in the midst of poverty! Now he was saying [to his wife], "If your slip wears out, show it to me before you give it to your mother."

Now, when the distant one [i.e., the husband] became rich and stood on his [own] feet and "carried and put down" [i.e., went through much interaction], you might say his body became possessed. He remained at home for about three years without opening his shop or selling. He would lock behind him (in his home) a door like this one [in the editor's home] and not open it at all. He asked for neither food nor drink, nor tea, nor tobacco, nor anything. Did he last long [in this mood]?—For about six months. They tested his "trace" [something that belonged to him] and said he was "visited" [(*minzâr*)] and needed a "beat."

They went ahead, invited men and women [a team of *zar* exorcists]. They got candles and said to him (don't blame me), "You need a ram and six pairs of pigeons [three to be slaughtered and offered to the possessing spirit; the blood would be used to rub the body of the possessed person]. He got all that, and God alleviated his affliction. Before, when my sister would enter his room, just as soon as she got to the doorstep, he would say to her, "God's line [separates] between you and me. Stay out!"

That one who was from underneath the earth [a female jinni] had put a barrier between him and his wife. He wouldn't talk to her for three years. When they made the "beat" and quieted down the one who possessed him, things were better and are better now, thank God.

They found that she [the possessing one] was an Arab [i.e., Bedouin]. She laid down her conditions (don't blame me), that he should wear rings and wear clothes that she liked. When he responds to the "beat" [by doing the ritual dance climaxing in dissociation], he must wear an Arab woman's garb (don't blame me); he should hide his face with a red veil, wear an ankle bracelet, wear [female] rings, silver arm bracelets—those thick silver ones—and some chain necklaces. He does the dance until he is exhausted and hits the ground. After that he takes this costume off [and leads a normal life until the next ceremony].

He was very much interested in marrying someone else in addition to my sister, but the one who possessed him wouldn't let him. She could bear neither the old [wife] nor the new [prospective wife]. So she seized him and arrested him [i.e., his power]. He has to do the "beat" three times yearly, just to get some comfort. For "the distant one" [that is, the narrator's brother-in-law] has no comfort; he can't sleep or even "catch a glimpse" of sleep [without the zar].

Appendix 30: Moslem Woman Possessed by Christian *Zâr*-Spirit

Reported in 1971 by Omm-Ṣalâḥ, a former tenant of an apartment in the buildings owned by Omm-Ḥasan Sr. The narrator attributes her own son's troubles with his final national high school examinations to the noise and sleeplessness the zâr *rituals caused.*

'Omm-Ḥasan S . . . *el-kibîrah* (Sr.)—("may God have mercy on her [soul]"), who owned the two apartment buildings, was a widow (*'armalah*). Her husband had died and left her four sons and one daughter, named Ḥaayât, but every one knew her [the daughter] as *Omm*-Ḥasan *eṣ-ṣughayyarah* (Jr.). This daughter is married to hajji M., and has only one son; his name is ¿Abd-es-Salâm, but they call him Ḥasan, and nickname him Semsem (Sesame). She ['Omm-Ḥasan Sr.] lived on the ground floor of one building [consisting of two apartments made into one], with her two younger sons, . . . , their wives and their children. Her two elder sons lived in apartments in the other building. She was the chieftainess of them all.

One of the tenants was Nagîb effendi, who was—as they said—an engineer with the power company. He was tall, light complected (*'abyaḍânî*), with a moustache [and handsome]. He and his family (for he was married and had children) lived on the top floor in the same building as she did.

They say (away from you) *¿alaihâ* (she has on her [i.e., possessed by]) one of the *'asyâd* [possessing *zâr*-spirits] who was *nuṣrânî* (Nazarene, i.e., Christian). She would have a *zâr* [ceremonial ritual] in which she would wear the garb of a Christian priest, put on a large chain with a large silver cross around her neck, wear lots of Christian gold [ornaments with Coptic icons], and *tifaqqàr* (do the ritual dance). Crowds of women attended her *zâr* [ceremonies], which would last for days. They say she never offered [a sacrificial animal] less than a ram or a young calf. She also used to get living *qarâmîṭ* (catfishes), place them in a large basin and play with them as if she were a girl-child. Then, these catfishes would be slaughtered and she would be smeared with their blood.

Inhabitants of the district became fed up with the noise; some went to the police and complained because they had sons and daughters in schools and could not study for their exams [but their complaints were unheeded]. Since she was a *kebîret ¿ailah* (the chieftainess of a family) and well-to-do, she spent lavishly.

After the *zâr*, she would be tranquil for a few days. But she would revert to her intimidating and bombastic ways a short while later. She was (away from you) a frightening woman.

Zikr and Worship

Appendix 31: *dhikr* Worship: "O Moḥammad, You Are My Beloved"

Recorded after late evening prayers with chant-leader/(munshid) *and about a twelve* zakkîrs. *It should be noted that the leader did not allow the worshippers to get into the faster, more emotionally involved tempo that leads to a state of dissociation. When he noted that the control of ritual was getting out of hand, he terminated it.*

Leader:	*Yâ Muhammad 'anta badru al-tamâmû* (O Mohammad, you are the perfection of the full moon)
Leader:	*'anta ḥabîbî wa-sandun lî ya-Muḥammadd* (You are my beloved and my support, O Mohammad)
Group:	*Allââh*
Leader:	*'anta ḥabîbî wa-sandun lî ya-Muḥammadd* (You are my beloved and my support, O Mohammad)
Group:	*Allââh*
Leader:	*wa-'anta li-l-'anbiyâ khitâmu* (And for Prophets, you are seal)
Group:	*Allââh*
Leader:	*wa-'anta li-l-'anbiyâ khitâmu* (And for Prophets, you are seal)
Group:	*Allââh*
Leader:	*kânu jamî¿an, yâ ḥbîbî, ghàlli (or, ḍalli)* (All of them, O beloved, were shackled, or misguided)
Group:	*Allââh*
Leader:	*'imḍî [binâ] sarî¿an 'ilâ nabîna* (Take us quickly [O guide], to our Prophet)
Group:	*Allââh*
Leader:	*kânu gamî¿an man darâ qadr en-nabî* (All of them were of those who comprehended the stature of the Prophet)
Group:	*Allââh*
Leader:	*fa kun shafî¿an lahum, nabîna* (Be the Interceder on their behalf, O Prophet of ours)
Group:	*Allââh ḥayy* (Allââh is Alive)
Group:	*Allââh ḥayy*
Group:	*Allââh ḥayy*
Group:	*Allââh ḥayy*
Leader:	*madad! madad! madad!* ([Give us] support! Support! Support!)
Group:	*Allââh ḥayy*
Leader:	*madad-madad! madad-madad!*
Group:	*Allââh ḥayy*
Leader:	*madad-madad! madad-madad! yâ rasûl Allââh, madad!* ([Give us] Support! Support! Support! O God's Messenger, Support!)
Group:	*Allââh ḥayy*

Leader:	*madad-madad! madad-madad!* *madad-madad! madad-madad!* *madad-madad! madad-madad!* *madad-madad! madad-madad!*
Leader:	*madad-madad! madad-madad! yâ rasûl Allââh, madad!* ([Give us] Support! Support! Support! O God's Messenger!)
Leader:	*madad-madad! madad-madad! yâ rasûl Allââh, madad!* Leader concludes by slowing down tempo to a close.

Martyrdom: Advantageous Death

Appendix 32: "In Order Not to Gain Martyrdom"

Narrator is an adult, works as servant. He told the account at the request of his young mistress who was collecting narratives as class assignment. Also see n. 635.

They say that a man cursed Eblis one thousand times daily. One day while he was asleep [next to a wall], a stranger came and awoke him saying, "Get away: the wall is falling!"

The man asked, "Who are you so as to have shown me that [great] kindness?" The stranger replied, "I am Eblis!" The man wondered, "How could this be! I curse you a thousand times every day!" Eblis answered, "This is due to the fact that once I realized [how great] a status [reward] God accords martyrs, I feared that you might become one of them [by dying in an accident] and, thus, receive [the great rewards] they receive."

Suffering

Appendix 33: The Blind Man and Satan

Informant: see App. 32.

The following narrative may be seen as an exemplum. It promotes the religious virtue of charity and illustrates the belief that a benevolent act by one person can result in divine forgiveness of others.

There was an old man who used to do his prayers at the mosque. No matter how cold or hot it might be, he still went to the mosque at dawn for dawn "group-prayer" [for which one receives more credit]. He would get up very early, do his ablution, and head for the *zawyàh* (small neighborhood mosque); on his way he would praise God and mention His Name. This old man grew older and became—(away from you)—blind; it was not easy for him any longer to walk by himself: darkness, [street] potholes, trash piles, and the like. So, a friend of his, as good a man as he is, would pass by, call on him, and would lead him by the hand to the mosque. After prayers, he would escort him back to his home.

Now, who was watching all this, for all those years—fifty or sixty, may be more years? Satan! Satan was very upset to see this man do his prayers—and *gamâ¿àh* (in group [which is the preferred way]), at the mosque! He kept on instigating him to skip even once; but he [Satan] did not succeed.

One day, after that man had become blind, his friend got ill and could not come to escort him. The old man waited but his friend did not come. Still, he went alone, feeling his way in the dark [narrator imitates the hand movements]. When Satan saw that, he assumed the form of that man's [friend] and pretended to catch up with him. At midway, there was a ditch—one of those ditches where women dump dirty water, trash, and the like: all sorts of *nagâsàh* (defiling substances). So, Satan pushed the blind man into it and disappeared. Naturally, the man couldn't go to the mosque with his ablution violated (*mànqûḍ*). He endured [the hardships], until he went back to his home; of course he had to bathe and do his ablution anew. This was the first time that he did his dawn prayer *qaḍâ* (past-dew), and not in "group" [-prayer]; Satan was very pleased with himself, for he finally succeeded.

The following day, at dawn, the same thing happened. But—(as you know: "He who fears the Afrit . . . , [will be encountered by him"])—that [blind] man feared falling into that dirt-ditch of yesterday. This time he, without being aware of it [the ditch] and by trying very hard to avoid it, found himself on its edge. As he was about to fall in, he felt a hand getting hold of him and setting him away from the ditch and in the direction of the mosque.

The blind man said [to the helper], "*yâ fâ¿il el-khair* (O good-deed doer), may God reward you."

The one who helped him answered, "It was not for God's sake that I helped you."

The man recognized the voice; it was the voice he had heard the time before, [so he exclaimed]: "Who are you? Why did you push me in yesterday, and why did you keep me from falling in today?"

The voice answered, "When I pushed you into [the ditch] yesterday, Our Lord forgave half the sins of all human beings for your sake. Now I am helping you so that He would not forgive the other half of their sins. I am Satan!"

The man replied, "May God dishonor you [by making you fail], O Satan!"

And with this [prayer], Satan was burnt [to a cinder].

Nether-Magic

Appendix 34: How Za¿zû¿ Can Be Summoned to Perform a Task: A Case of Nether-Magic

The following is a step-by-step description of how a powerful jinni named Za¿zû¿ can be summoned and coerced into performing a task.

In order to test Shâkir's (see App. 11) knowledge, Moḥammad brought up the subject of summoning this jinni, provided a few details, and left the rest for Shâkir to "fill-in the spaces." Occasionally, Moḥammad interrupted by providing details that seemed to him to be missing in Shâkir's description. The complete agreement between the two informants—who had never met or known each other before then, one hailing from Northeastern Egypt, while the other (Shâkir) from middle Upper Egypt—indicates the high degree of stability that seems to characterize the ritual in folk communities.

The kanûn, *cited in this account as an instrument, may be described as a brick cooking-stand or enclosure; it is a three-sided or semicircular hearth, usually built of adobe or brick and plastered with mud (clay). The cooking pot would be placed on its open top, resting on the rim of its walls, with fire built underneath the pot, within the hearth.*

The underlying erotic nature of the process is represented by the social situation that Shâkir gives as an example for the need to summon Za¿zû¿: "forcing a woman back to her husband or back to her sweetheart." This sexual disposition is also expressed symbolically via a number of objects and acts that include the kanûn (or fire enclosure, or pit), riding the fire-pit while naked, oscillating on the fire-pit, placing the brick inside the box. The physical posture assumed is identical with the one typically used in baladî *(native) latrines for both defecation and urination;*[769] *western-style toilets, requiring contact between body and toilet seat, or standing up at a urinary, are considered unclean and potentially violators of ritual cleanliness. Additionally, the verbal aspect of this ritual involves words with syllabic structures, which, when uttered, suggest sex organs.*[770] *The identification of the targets for the ritual is done through their maternal descent.*

Date, time, place, persons, setting are the same as in App. 11. Moḥammad is abbreviated as Moḥ., and El-Shamy as Shamy.

Moḥ.:	[addressing Shâkir]: Have you ever performed the *kanûn*-operation?
Shamy:	What is "the *kanûn*?"
Moḥ.:	It is real fire. They get *en-nâr lammâ tṣàfṣàf* ("fire wood after it has burned down to its purest form," i.e., become blazing embers with no smoke or tongues of fire); . . . they put it underneath a cooking pot and summon [a jinni].
Shâkir:	Its name [title] is *shàbshàbìt*-Za¿zû¿.
Shamy:	*shàbshabàh*!? [The word suggests the use of a slipper (footwear).] (See Section II.B.3)
Shâkir:	Yes, *shàbshabàh*! It is used for different purposes, [such as] forcing a woman back to her husband or back to her sweetheart. [It is done as follows:]

---

769 This is the position assumed when using *baladî* (country-style) latrine. Motif: P717.2§, ‡"Tribal characteristics (private)—latrine functions (defecation and urination, attending call of nature)."

770 The sign ":" here indicates syllabic structure. Examples of this facet are the words "*kùss:baràh* (courlander)" and "*kùss:b* (cake made of residuals of pressed cotton seed, used as animal fodder), the first and more salient syllable is "kùss:" is the common appellation for the female genital organ. (Cf. The occurrence of a jinni named "Sindâs" in Walker-Ismâ¿îl, *Folk Medicine*, pp. 96–98.)

In a broader context, the symbolism involved in the occurrence of fire pits/ovens etc. is further illustrated by recurrent tale types known to the informants and their social groups; these include AT Type: 1425, *Putting the Devil into Hell*, (characterized by S. Thompson as "Obscene Trick used to seduce woman;" Type 1425A§, *Seduction: Roasting the Ear of Corn in the Oven*; and Type: 1425B§, *Seduction: Putting the Bird (or Animal) in its Natural Habitat.*

In these texts, "Devil," "Ear of Corn," "Animal" (mule, stallion, etc., "Bird" (Cock, "Pigeon") represent phallus. Also see n. 739.

One goes on a Friday—while holding his tongue [(i.e., without uttering a word, observing total silence)]—to a cemetery, and enters [it] with his back [by walking backward]. He fetches a brick from it and commands it: "Be Za¿zû¿!" Then, he returns to his home.

Moḥ.: Doesn't the cemetery from which you would bring that thing have to be abandoned [i.e., not in use]?

Shâkir: Yes! Abandoned! That person should get the brick and go out via the same spot [where he had entered]. He should also take along a piece of shroud, and wash the brick with it. [(Moḥammad agrees.)] He should place the brick inside the *kanûn* [i.e., within the fire itself]; then he should mount the *kanûn* [i.e., squat, with his feet resting on top of the *kanûn* walls as if a cooking pot]. He must be stark naked, bareheaded. [Now!], what should he have ready in front of the *kanûn*? [He should have] incense ready! When [smoke from] the incense rises he should say:

> "I have released the *kùss:b* (cotton-seed cake) and *kammûn* (cumin); in addition to the *gâwi* (benzoin) that is *maqrûn* (coupled with [??] . . .). I have made an oath that you, Za¿zû¿, O you who are Abu-ez-Za¿âzî¿ (father of all the Za¿zû¿s, i.e., boss of all . . .)."

(I used to have [in memory] the whole "oath/incantation" [but I forgot it]; I never performed this operation.)

He [the practitioner] should keep on reciting the oath and on releasing the smoke of the incense into the air until he finds himself [feeling]-like the scale beam [i.e., almost afloat, oscillating but in balance]. One side of the *kanûn* will drop [on one side] while the other will rise [that is], he will find one of his feet going down while the other goes up. He will feel like he is about to fall off the *kanûn*. When he realizes that all these things have happened, he should rest for one hour; he should also remove the brick from the spot where he had placed it, deposit in a box, and lock it.

Ḥesain [in amazement]: He would take it out of the fire!?

Shâkir: [No!] The fire is only for the incense. Then he should lock up the box with a padlock, because if he [Za¿zû¿] got loose, he would *yi¿àfratùh* (bedevil, torment) him. . . .

Moḥ.: That is, while the brick is locked up [in the box].

Shâkir: [ignoring Moḥmmad's augmentation continues]: . . . and would release more incense. He should do so three times. He will find that the brick begins to cry and say (sobbingly): "Return Za¿zû¿ to his mother!" Then he [the practitioner] should say:

> "We will do so! But [only] after you have brought she-so-and-so, daughter of she-so-and-so, back to he-so-and-so, son of she-so-and-so, and after you have [also] 'wrapped her sleeve on his,' ([i.e., tied her to him]) and caused her to follow him [while she is] disheveling (messing up) her hair, slapping her face, and screaming '[I feel like I am on] Fire! Fire!'"

After he has said the above to Za¿zû¿, he should rest for a while, then repeat [the command]. At the third time Za¿zû¿ will say: "I have already brought her back to him!" If this proves to be true, you let him go. If not, repeat.
This is a *¿amàl* ("work," charm) [that harnesses Za¿zû¿ the jinni].

[Moḥ. agrees that this is how this ritual is done, and signals that he gives Shâkir a passing grade.]

Appendix 35: How Shâkir Was Pressured into Leaving His Village and Giving Up His Craft

The following account of a segment of Shâkir's life history, a memorate, *illustrates the centrality of the practitioner in the domestic life in the village, and by extension in this situation, in the city. The community as a whole sanctions the conduct of the shaman-*shaikh *and of his clients and exercises considerable control over their acts. The community as whole, represented by its notables, punishes incidents of malpractice; the severity of punishment depends on the seriousness of the offense.*

El-Shamy: What is the *¿amàl* ("fix") that you say you undertook and caused a crisis in the village?

Shâkir: When the news spread in the village that I perform *shàrr* ("evil") to "tie" and "untie" (i.e., cause impotence, and restore virility), cause hatred and the like (but—[I swear] by God!—I performed "benevolent" things much more than "malevolent" ones), people sought me [. . . But events developed in an adverse manner]. I finally had to swear on the Koran to give it [my practice] up.
The reason was:
There was that woman [. . .], her husband's name was ¿Âshûr [. . .]. He had died. [Thus] she was a widow, in good shape [she was attractive and fairly well-to-do]. A man named ¿Ukâsha—he is her husband now—used to court her by going to her house. Before him, there was another man named Fawzî [. . .]; he used to visit her [(i.e., call on her courting)]. He spent quite a bit [of money] on her. That ¿Ukâsha came along and married her. Fawzî got mad.

Fawzî came to me and said, "I want you to 'write' (i.e., prepare a 'fix') against ¿Ukâsha because he cut in on me. 'Write' to achieve hatred and separation."

For the money [fee: a pound and one half, then a substantial sum] I said, "I'll write." My intention was to pacify him so that he would not go outside [the village for another practitioner]. Also it would be possible for me to undo the "fix" whenever the undoing became needed. Surely! I wrote a *¿amàl* ("fix") [composed of two parts]; one was to be placed in the cemetery with the dead, and the second to be buried underneath the threshhold of the front door of the target [i.e., the couple—¿Ukâshah and his wife].

Moḥ.: [A listener, anticipating the occurrence of the crisis, interrupts]: "Why did you not write the *¿amàl* on the head of a catfish [and then release it back in the river, so that it could not be found or traced back to the source]?"

Shâkir [curtly]: "It wouldn't have worked!"

The *¿amàl* malfunctioned; it reversed itself into *rabṭ* (impotence) [i.e., ¿Ukâsha became impotent].

Meanwhile, Fawzî (who had asked me to do the "fix") visited someone in the village and said, "I have done such and such, to so-and-so, at Shâkir's." He revealed the secret![771]

The lady of the house, to whom he had spoken, carried his words to the target [person], that is, to ¿Ukâsha. He, his family, and friends went to the cemetery and found the *¿amàl* exactly where it had been placed. They also dug underneath the threshhold and unearthed the other part that I had written.

They went to the notables of the village: the mayor, *sheikh-el-balad*, and all those who are outstanding. They held a *maglis* (council). They summoned the parties involved. [The evidence concerning Fawzî's involvement was in writing], the "fix" read:

> ". . . that she-so-and-so, the woman, should abandon her husband, he-so-and-so, and that she should fall in love with Fawzî [. . .]."

There was no way for him to deny his involvement.

The council sentenced Fawzî to pay a fine of one hundred pounds: twenty for [the expenses of] the council and eighty [as compensation] for the victim. Fawzî and the heads of his family argued back and appealed to the council [on the basis that they were poor]. The council reduced the fine to ten pounds; they took an "IOU" receipt from Fawzî and his relatives.

Afterward, they turned their attention to Shâkir [i.e., to me]. They told me, "Why did you do that?"

I answered them frankly, "I did it. I agreed to do it so that he would not have had to resort to someone else from outside the village, and so that the whole operation [including the undoing] would remain within our reach."

They said: "No! This is not good enough a reason."

They made threats, verbally, and said, "We must burn your books [i.e., the 'magic' manuals]."

I [defiantly] answered, "Burn them!"

One [member of the council] named Saif, told them, "What is the use of burning the books [he can replace them]; instead, we should have him swear on God's Book [i.e., The Koran] that he never engages in what is *shàrr* [harmful, malevolent 'works'/'fixes']."

I said, "I cannot swear to that!" [For] I was afraid I might err; it is a grave (weighty) oath. But I said, "I will not 'write' *shàrr* (malevolent 'fixes') [for those living] within the village, but I will do so [for those from] outside."

They said, "No! You swear on all—inside the village and outside the village. We will let you undertake benevolent things: [generate] amity, cure an ailment, save an animal, . . . ! But, that is all!!"

I finally consented and swore to that.

[771] The sequence of these two events seems to be the reverse of how they are presented here: 'Ukâsha's "impotence" seems to have occurred as a result of having been informed of Fawzî's claim of the existence of the "fix" against him.

[However, Shâkir found out that his clients paid handsomely only for harmful "fixes." He was unable to make a living from his practice by performing only "benevolent" works.]

Shâkir: After the oath, a circumstance occurred and I came here [to Cairo]. It is as follows:

There was a big (important) man in the village, [named] H.G.A. He sent me a messenger saying, "You must come to Cairo with me for an important matter." I asked, "What [is it]?"

He said that he had a friend there who was "ill," and "You should 'write' for him or against his wife, because she is separated from him!"

That man had divorced his wife; [but] he still loved her and wanted to remarry her but she refused. He tried every means possible but she still refused; that made him ill for he still "wanted" her back. He spoke to H.G.A. and he said: "I want her back. I want someone to 'write' for me." H.G.A. told him: "I have someone named Shâkir [who can do that for you]."

I agreed to try to get his wife back to him. [I came to Cairo.] As I talked with the man I found that he and his wife had quarreled constantly. They were not meant for each other; they had different natures. I also noticed that he was ill, I mean he was in [physical] pain. The woman hated him. He wanted her back ["just to get even with her," for spite].[772]

I told him we can make her come back, but it would be better to first make him feel well. One night he told me, "All right, I don't want her back [right now]. Just cure me." She had a *¿amàl* ("fix") written that caused him to have *wùswâs*—[*waswasàh*, constant suspicions, jealousy, and feelings of inadequacy]—and to have buzzing, like that of wasps, in his head. He also had constant backache and his bones were tired [(i.e., suffered from debilitating fatigue)]. (See obsessive-compulsive neurosis in n. 170)

I read his *ṭâli¿* (horoscope, signs of Zodiac). I also brought cod liver oil, camphor oil, and other [medicinal] things. I told him to have his body rubbed with it [as a massage]. Meanwhile, I also "wrote" for him. I did what was necessary. God cured him. He gave up on his wife; he realized that even if she were brought back to him, it would not work and that she would not be what he wanted her to be.

[Mr.] H.G.A. rewarded me; he got me a new set (outfit) of clothes, and told me, "When [i.e., if] you return to the village, I know you will go back to practicing 'malevolent' works. A big crisis is bound to happen."

I replied, "No. I have sworn [not to perform evil works]."

He said, "No! Now you have become 'my man' [(i.e., one of my proteges)]. I will find you a job; you should remain here [in Cairo]."

I agreed and said, "But it will have to be . . . [an easy job]; I am not used to arduous labor!"

---

[772]This statement was offered by Shâkir at a later time. The theme is recurrent in folk literature. For examples, see: El-Shamy, *Tales Arab Women Tell*, No. 15, p. 160; and No. 28, p. 229; cf. No. 50, p. 358, where a husband abandons his wife and refuses to divorce her so that she would remain "suspended" by being unable to remarry.

[And so it was.]
That was in 1960 [and I have been living in Cairo, and working as janitor since then. It has been twelve years].

Appendix 36: Magic Fix Written on a Catfish

*Reported in May 1982 by Mr. Amîn A. . . . , a school teacher from a village in the Nile Delta. Amîn, among others including the present writer, witnessed the public part of the event in 1956 (or 1957) when the afflicted person arrived seeking help from its shaman-*shaikh. *Amîn still remembered that the "bewitched" came to the village dressed in a silken greenish shirt that was mostly unbuttoned almost to his lower chest and that he was driving a sports car (a convertible Triumph).* Also see n. 720.

I forgot the name of that man who came here [in 1956 or 1957], but he was from a small town. He was tall and smart looking. I remember his story as he told it to *shaikh* Ḥaggâg. He had left his town and gone to Cairo, and studied in the college of engineering. He was also sent to Germany to be trained for he was working for the new Iron and Steel Mill that a German company was building in Helwan.

When he returned from abroad, he engaged a girl from his paternal uncle's household. The marriage took place quickly, and on the night of the *dùkhlah* (consummation) as he and his bride were being led to their bridal chamber [in his father's home], someone whispered something in his ear. He could neither tell who did the whispering, nor what was exactly said; but he could hear: "You are tied." He did not understand what these words meant. To the rest of his family and friends everything seemed to be going well.

He and his bride moved to Helwan [near Cairo], for his job was there. For the length of the entire year he (the afflicted) would not touch his wife or have marital intercourse with her. They went to many medical doctors, but no medicine proved useful. He said he even used hashish; still it did not help. About a year later he heard of *shaikh* Ḥaggâg from some of his friends. One told him, "The solution to your problem would be in the hands of this man." But he did not believe in such superstitions. Finally, he came to the village to see *shaikh* Ḥaggâg.

Shaikh Ḥaggâg found out that someone had written a *¿amal-bi-er-rabṭ* (a tying-fix) with him (the afflicted) as its target. That fix was written on the belly of a catfish, and then released back into the water: either in a well or a river. The only thing he (the afflicted) could do was to pray that this catfish gets caught by a fisherman and sold and cooked, or someone or something else would eat it: "If it dies, the 'fix' would be undone."

We never heard about how things turned out.

Prophets and Saints

Appendix 37: God's Messengers (Apostles)

With the exception of Hûd, Luqmân, Ṣâliḥ, and—possibly—Alexander, all God's Prophets according to Islam are Judaeo-Christian. Prophet Moḥammad is perceived as the Seal (i.e., last) of God's Messengers.

1. Âdam	Adam	15. Luqmân	—-
2. Alyasa¿	Elisha	16. Lûṭ	Lot
3. Ayyûb	Job	17. Mûsâ	Moses
4. Dâwûd	David	18. Nûḥ	Noah
5. Dhu-l-Kifl	Exekiel (Ezekiel)	19. Ṣâliḥ	——
6. Dhu-l-Qarnayn	The Dual-horned (Alexander the Great)	20. Shu¿ayb	Jethro
7. Hârûmn	Aaron	21. Sulaymân	Solomon
8. Hûd	——	22. ¿Azâr	Ezra
9. Ibrâhîm	Abraham	23. Yaḥyâ	John the Baptist
10. Idrîs	Henoch/Enoch	24. Ya¿qûb	Jacob
11. Ilyâs	Elijah	25. Yûnus	Jonah
12. ¿Îsâ	Jesus	26. Yûsuf	Joseph
13. Isḥâq	Isaac	27. Zakariyyâ	Zechariah
14. Ismâ¿îl	Ishmael		

Appendix 38: The Generating of a Saint for a "Saint-Less" Community: A Dead Person Demands Recognition

Reported by Yaḥyâ . . . , a middle-aged man, then a janitor in a governmental office. He had served as an enlisted man in the Egyptian Army during the 1948 Arab–Israeli war and sustained battle injury that was classified as causing him loss of a certain percentage of his ability to move. Consequently, he received preferential treatment at work; his duties were few and confined to nonphysical type of labor. He had received medical treatment in government hospitals and veterans' medical centers for several years. In 1969, he was still suffering from "impaired movement." Thus, Yaḥyâ reported that he has been making use of the zâr*-like rituals held every Tuesday night in his home village of Kafr el-Zaytoun (Gharbiyyah Governorate). According to Yaḥyâ, the ritual dance* (tafqîr) *allows him to move all his limbs without pain.*

It was upon Yaḥyâ's suggestions and through his contacts that a small group of researchers visited his village so as to interview its shaikh *(named Abu-¿Abdah) and his son who substituted for him frequently. The aged but still quite active shaman-*shaikh *was said to be "ill." He passed away shortly afterward. About one year later Yaḥyâ reported the following:*

Did you know that *shaikh* Abu-¿Abdah *bayyin karâmàh* (has shown a miracle-like manifestation (thaumaturgic gift): during his funeral, some thieves from [the neighboring larger town of] Simbu came to attend his funeral. When everybody was busy with the burial, they tried to steal the riding-animals of the people who were there. But the *shaikh* made them freeze; they got hold of [. . .] the riding animals but they froze and could not move from their places. This is one of the *shaikh*'s *karâmât*.

Upon revisiting the same village for a follow-up study in May 1982, thirteen years later, Yaḥyâ reported:

Shaikh Abu-¿Abdah came repeatedly to [certain] people in the village [in visions] and told them [reprimandingly]: "Where is my *maqâm* (shrine)!?" He told them that he is [i.e., was] *za¿lân* (offended, unhappy, disappointed) that nothing has been done on his behalf [in this respect]. Village people are now collecting money in order to build him a *qùbbàh* ("dome," [i.e., shrine]).

Appendix 39: The Death of *Shaikhah* Shafîqah's Brother

Reported in May 1982, by Miss Sanâ' W., aged nineteen, a university student, from Salamoan, near the city of Manṣûrah, Daqahliyyah Governorate, Egypt. She had heard this "true event" from other girls in high school, as a "miracle-like manifestation (karâmah)" *by the woman saint. "This [manifestation] was also written about in newspapers and magazines," the narrator added.*

The account indicates the strength of the mystical bond between brother and sister.

We have, in Salamoan, a lady saint. Her name is *esh-shaikhah* Shafîqah; there are some people who call her [by the nick-name of] 'Omm-¿Ali (Mother-of-Ali). This lady saint was married [and living with her husband] in a town—that might have been Faqqûs, or Esh-Shoabak in Sharqiyyah [Governorate]. She was married to someone who was rich, i.e., a man of means. During her youth, she was very beautiful; they say she was the most beautiful one in our town and her father married her off to that man from Sharqiyyah [Governorate] and she went with him [to live in his hometown].

God willed that her brother should die. She had only one brother and two sisters. Her brother died—she was the immediate younger. When they were about to entomb him, he [i.e., the corpse] adamantly refused to be buried. They kept on placing him on the bier and taking him to the cemetery, but whenever they would look for him, they would find the bier empty. They would return home and look [only] to find him laid [on his back] in his room. People kept wondering: "Why is he refusing to be buried? He was neither indebted nor did he owe or was owed; also, he did all the [required] fasting and praying."

It happened that his sister Shafîqah had not arrived [for the funeral]—that was before she entered the ranks of saints (*qabl ma-titmashyakh*) [by becoming a recluse with diminished mental faculties, but with enhanced spiritual capacities]. She arrived . . . ! She entered upon him and cried silently over him.

They [the undertaker and bier bearers] came back, placed him on the bier anew, and went to the cemetery; they placed him down, buried him, and returned. [This time he remained in his grave.]

His sister entered his room and—(we appeal to the Merciful, i.e., God: *fassarnâ bi-r-Raḥmân*). She suffered some mild diminished mental capacities (*luṭf*).[...] She remained naked; she would not allow a piece of clothing to touch her body. She would not eat, nor drink, nor speak, nor . . . , nor. . . . She remained in this condition for a long while—say six or seven months. [It happened] that she was still a bride—one full year had not gone by [since her marriage]. She had given birth to a baby boy from that husband of hers. He tried many a time to get her to return with him [but did not succeed, for] she had become [i.e., entered] in[to] another world (*¿âlam tânî*)!!

They force-fed her; they pushed food down her throat. She remained in her room with whatever garment that happened to cover her; she adopted the dervish ways (*'iddarwishit*), and the saints' way (*'itmashyakhit*). She said nothing without it turning out to be true. Many miracle-like manifestations (*karâmât*) appeared at her hands. Some people say, "The Veil[-of-gnosis] has been lifted off her [i.e., she became clairvoyant, can see the Divine sphere]." Many a person did she heal! And many a [sinful] person foreswore sin due to her.

Appendix 40: The Shaman-*Shaikh*'s *Barakàh* Produces the Lost Wallet

The following is an account of a personal experience of the present writer. It took place in early 1950s when he was twelve or thirteen years old. The account sheds light on the "mystical" power of beliefs. On the efficacy of the perceived power of the saint, see "Letter to the 'Justice of Legislation,'" in H. El-Shamy, Folktales of Egypt, *No. 36, pp. 162–164, 281–282; also see n. 599.*

During summer-break, I was spending a few weeks in the village at my maternal grandfather's country house; one of my maternal cousins (*ibn-khâl*) named ¿A. was my companion. Lacking anything interesting to do, we thought we would earn some money by substituting for hirelings doing manual farm labor. We presented the proposition to Mr. M. (the writer's eldest maternal uncle and father of ¿A.), who agreed to let us haul twenty-seven loads of farm dirt into the animal's *zariba*—to be converted by the farm animals into "organic fertilizer" (*sibâkh*); we were to receive twenty-five piasters (a quarter pound) each for our labor.

Being city schoolboys, we had no idea as to the immensity of the intensive labor required for accomplishing the task. After completing seven or eight hauls it became clear to the two of us that it was impossible to complete the terms of the contract. We explained the matter to Mr. M., he grinned and made some comment on our naivete concerning farm work—(I do not remember now his exact words). We asked that we be paid for the amount of work actually completed, on prorated basis. But to our surprise and dismay, he declared that the agreement was on all-or-nothing basis, and insisted on his interpretation. We received no pay. We felt cheated.

A few days later, we found a leather wallet on the ground in the house courtyard, between the residential quarters and the storage and animal quarters. Clearly, someone had dropped it. The wallet contained two one-pound bills, and a few small coins. My cousin recognized the wallet as "belonging to Mr. M." (his father, and the writer's maternal uncle). We kept the matter secret and intended to keep the money for ourselves for, after all, we thought that a significant portion of it should have been paid to us. A short while later, Mr. M. began inquiring as to whether anyone had seen a wallet; all answered that they had not. When asked, my cousin and I denied having seen it.

After some time, it became evident to all that the wallet was not simply misplaced, but indeed lost. There were numerous debates as to what could be done.

Then a visitor (Mr. N., who is also a relative, a member of the extended family and a teacher like Mr. M.) suggested that shaman-*shaikh* Ḥaggâg would certainly be able to locate it through his *barakàh* (blessedness) and [jinni-woman] familiar.

Once the two of us knew this idea, a feeling of total defeat coupled with a sense of looming infamy and disgrace gripped us. Images of the shaman-*shaikh* revealing the truth:

> "It is these two boys [Ḥasan and ¿A.]! They found the wallet in the yard but decided not to return it. They have it hidden in the hay storeroom, in such and such a place."

Of course, we thought, Mr. M. will first refuse to believe that his own son and sister's son can do such a thing, but the shaman-*shaikh* will assure him that this is the truth. This notion alone was sufficient to persuade us that to save ourselves from inevitable shame and disgrace, the wallet had to be surrendered to its rightful, but unfair, owner.

The visitor noticed our confusion and silence. He was able to see signs of guilt written all over our faces. However, he looked closely into our eyes, but made no accusations.

Quietly, we placed the wallet close to where we had found it. It was soon spotted by a member of the family and returned to Mr. M. There were some doubts about the spot where it was found, since that location had already been searched and nothing was found. However, all agreed that the credit for finding the wallet goes to shaman-*shaikh* Ḥaggâg's *barakàh*: the mere intent to seek his help produced this happy result almost instantly.

The two of us, and perhaps the visitor, knew that this conclusion was true, but only in part. Our own belief in the inevitability of being exposed played a role more cardinal than the shaman-*shaikh*'s "familiar" or "blessedness" could ever have.

Appendix 41: Can a Woman Be More Beautiful than the Moon? Ibrâhîm ed-Disûqî and the Ulama

Tape-recorded in Doha, Qaṭar on Monday, May 5, 1986 from Mr. Yâsîn ¿I. . . , of Wilâd ¿Inân, Suhâj, Upper Egypt. He is nonliterate and works as guard in Doha, Qatar. Two other persons (Dr. Gamâl el-Ṣ. . . , M.D., and Dr. Aḥmad R. . . , university professor) attended the session that took place in the present writer's hotel room in Doha.

The frequency with which divorce oaths are cast by men on all social levels of society constitutes a major issue in Islamic jurisprudence, especially with reference to whether it was in earnest or in jest or frivolity (see n. 507). The perceived time-period for the occurrence of the divorce oath, and the supposed resorting to the Saint in Disûq are incompatible for they are separated by six or seven centuries.

A man—at the time of the "Companions [of the Prophet]" and the pious-ones—looked at his wife while she was adorned. He [was fascinated, and admiringly] said to her, "Oh my! May you be divorced [from me] if you are not more beautiful than the moon!"

When he recovered from his fascination-spell, he went to the ulama and asked them, "I made a divorce-oath that my wife is more beautiful than the moon, [would the oath be binding?]"

They answered him, "Your oath has taken effect [i.e., it became binding, and you have indeed divorced your wife]. How could it be that your wife is more beautiful than the moon, that lights up [all other] beings!"

Everyone of the ulama to whom he went would tell him, "Your oath has been fulfilled."

That man, as you might say, made his wife sinful [to himself]. He heard that *sîdî* Ibrâhîm ed-Disûgi* had excelled [over other ulama] and is learned. He went to him and said, "O *sîdî* Ibrâhîm, I [. . .]"

[Before the man could state his case] ed-Disûqî said to him, "And I, from within [i.e., sincerely], tell you that your oath is not binding, and that your wife is prettier than the moon and is more preferred than the moon. As for those ulama who told you that your oath is biding, go and bring them to me."

—[With relief and pleasure] "Is that so!" [replied the man].

—Yes! your wife is [. . . .]

The man went out dazed; he went and brought the ulama and said to them, "I got a *fatwâ* (fatwa, religious edict), someone named Ibrâhîm ed-Disûqî said to me, 'Your oath is non-binding.'" The ulama gathered together and headed for Ibrâhîm ed-Disûqî. On their way, they were saying, "Ibrâhîm ed-Disûqî what! This is a kid,. . . . " They backbit him.

sîdî Ibrâhîm ed-Disûqî [being aware of their slanders] came to a wall at the entrance of the city of Disûq, [stood on its top], lifted his clothes off as they were passing by and (don't blame me) urinated on the ulama. [Laughter by narrator and listeners.]

They said [in disgust], "Boy, may the Lord punish you for this. What is this that you have done. You *naggistinâ* (defiled/polluted us)."

He answered, "A dead person [has no] urine, therefore my urine is *ṭâhir*: [God says of those who speak ill of (backbite) one behind one's back], 'Would any of you like to eat the flesh of his dead brother? Nay, ye would abhor it [. . .]'" (Koran, 49:12). [Since you were backbiting me, I, therefore, am dead].

[. . .]

He took them as his guests into his house. He called his *naqîb* (marshall), and said to him, "Make coffee [for them]."

[He served] coffee, after coffee, after coffee, until it was noon time.

They leaned toward one another [whispering]: they've become hungry.

He told his *naqîb* these fellows' brains are still [sealed like] a talisman; go collect some watermelon rinds off the [grounds] of Disûq's *sûq* (marketplace) and feed them. He (no offense) gathered watermelon rinds [that had been cast away], placed them in a large soft basket. *sîdî* Ibrâhîm washed them with his own hands, then placed them in a cauldron (*"gazân"/qadhân*) in front of him, and he kept on turning the watermelon rinds around [in the pot].

The ulama [wondered]: "How could that be! We are knowledgeable individuals, and cultured/refined (*muthaqqafîn*) ulama!" They leaned toward one another, and kept on *yilâghû ba¿d bi-l-¿ilm* (communicating in [the jargon] of science).

[They said emphatically], "O you Ibrâhîm, O you the-Disûqi, [the Lord says] '*lâ yukallifu Allâhu nafsan 'illâ wis¿ahâ* (On no soul [i.e., person] doth God place a burden greater than it can bear).'" (Koran, 286, cf. 2:233)

He answered them, "Order [whatsoever food you may wish for]."

Some of them asked for chicken. He [. . .] said: "By the right (i.e., power) of the [letter] 'K', and [the letter] 'N' [be] chicken! 'And if the Lord wills it, it becomes'" (Koran, 2:117; 3:47, 19:35, and 36:82).

[He asked his *naqîb* to serve.] The *naqîb* would say, "In the name of God the Merciful, the Compassionate," and would dish out [food]; the one [of the ulama] who had said: "chicken," he dished out chicken for him; the one that said *kunâfah* (a pastry, desert), he dished out *kunâfah* for him.

In short, he fed them dinner, and made them coffee after dinner. Then, he asked them, "That man [who had sought your *fatwâ*: what have you told him?]"

They answered [in a reprimanding tone]: "O you Ibrâhîm, O you-the-Disûqi! The Moon with which [all] beings have been lit: How can it be that a man's wife—a person not worth [much]—be preferred and more beautiful [than the moon]!"

He replied, "Alright, Our Lord says 'Take from Koran what you wish for what you wish (i.e., need).' Let one of you let me hear [i.e., recite some] verses from 'The *Wise-Dhìkr*' (i.e., Koran)."

They replied, "You recite. You are young and we wish to hear your voice [in reciting]."

. . . .

He immediately—([narrator addresses his benefactor] O Dr. ¿Alî . . .)—sat cross-legged and began reciting:

"By the fig, and by the olive./ And by the Mount of Sinai./ And this city of security./ We have indeed created '*al-qamara* (the Moon)' in the best of moulds." (cf. Koran, 95:1–4).

They shouted [in horror]: "Oh! Oh! You have erred with the Koran!"

He asked [innocently], "[In] what?"

They replied, "Our Lord did not say: 'We have indeed created the *Moon* . . . !'"

He asked [in pretended innocence], "What, then, did our Lord God say?"

They replied, "Our Lord said: 'We have indeed created the *al-'insâna* (the human being) [in the best of moulds].'"

He said to them, "Isn't that man's wife [also] of *banî-l-'insân* (mankind). [. . .]!?"

They said to him [in total resignation], "*shihidnâ-lak* (We acknowledge your [preeminence], O *shaikh* Ibrâhîm)."

Appendix 42: Arch-Saint as Deity: ed-Disûqî's Power Display

Informant: See informant data for App. 41.

The following is a part of a much longer religious ballad (cf. epic) in which each of the four arch-saints boasts of his power and miracle-like deeds. shàṭḥ *(philosophical unorthodoxy) is clearly illustrated. In ordinary contexts, the statements climaxing with the declaration: "I am Allah" would be seen as sheer blasphemy. See n. 55; also cf. App. 6)*

The belief that the saint materialized before he was conceived or born by his mother has its counterpart, and perhaps roots, in the ancient beliefs about the Egyptian deity Horus. (See Maspero/El-Shamy, *Ancient Egypt*, No. 10, p. 174)

Informant: With reference to that [incident of Wife as Moon], he [ed-Disûqî] said to es-Sayyid el-Badawî:

"When I grew up, and became of age: the masters of *¿ilm* (Gnosis) did not measure up to me [..]."

'ana illi kawânî zamânî mitain we-'alfaian kayyah
'ana illi kawânî zamânî mitain we-'alfaian kayyah
'ana illi dawâwîn/dawâwîr el-hawâ naṣabit ¿alayyah
'ana illi marâkib ~~eas~~ eṣ-ṣabr ḥallat ¿alayyah
'ana illî ḥamait ommî we-hiyya bunayyah
w-'ana ḥadîs el-¿aish fî ḍahr 'abûyâ mâ'an gariyyâ*
(Informant explains: [. . .] see translation below)
we-lamma kibirt w-bâḥ sinnî, mashâyìkh el-¿ilm ma-gidrûsh ¿alayya.
(*w—ṣâr yaṣiff*):
'ana-ed-Disûqî, 'ana-ess-sâqî, ana-l-khammâr
'ana, w-anâ fi-l-ghaib, ḥaḍart en-nabî w-Abu-Bakr yoam dukhûl el-ghâr.
we-lailet esh-shafâ¿ah ma-sabaqit li-n-nabî el-mukhtâr
(Informant explains: that he [alone would have the right to "intercession"])
'ana nisidd bâb el-gaḥîm bi-khams . . .
(and say to our Lord, "Stop! Dont' weigh good deeds and bad-deeds.")
'ana nisidd bâb el-gaḥîm bi-khams, we-nbaṭṭàl el-mîzân
'ana el-loaḥ, 'ana-l-¿arsh, 'ana el-qalamm. 'ana-Allâh!
[El-Sayyid] *gâllu: "bàss, bàss, bàss!"*
I'm [the one], whose Time branded him with fire, two hundred and two thousand brandings [i.e., 200,000]
I'm [the one], on whose top the "wind-mills" (or the divans of love, or whirlwinds) were set up
I'm [the one], for whom the boats-of-patience arrived (or, are due)
I'm [the one], who protected my mother while she was [yet] a lass
while I was [still] new to life: [still] running water in my father's loins
*(Informant explains: a band of some people [criminals] had surprised his mother, wanting to fornicate with her. He, while still in the world-of-the-unknown, prevented the *wabâ* (disease/malaise) from reaching his mother, and protected her from rape.)
And when I grew up and my age became discernible, the heads of gnosis (knowledge) couldn't overcome me.
(And he went on describing)
I'm ed-Disûqî! I'm the liquor-server, I'm the liquor-maker
I, while still in the unknown (i.e., future), was present [with] the Prophet and Abu-Bakr [during] the day-of-entering the Cave [to escape infidel pursuers].[773]

[773] Allusion here is made to a sacred event associated with the Flight of Prophet Moḥammad and his companion Abu-Bakr from Mecca to Medina.

And [during the time when] "intercession" was given *a priori* to the Chosen-Prophet
(. . .)
I would close the door of Hell with five [acts??]. . . .
(and say to our Lord, "Stop! Don't weigh good deeds and bad deeds.")
I would close the door of Hell with five, and stop the Balance
I am the Tablet! I am the Throne! I am the Pen. *I'm Allâh (God)*!
[Es-Sayyid] said to him [in astonishment]: "Enough! Enough! Enough!"

Appendix 43: Bes, El-Badawî, and St. Nicholas: From Ancient Egyptian Deity to Moslem *waliyy*, to Christian Saint

The following is an excerpt from a study by the present writer titled "The Story of El-Sayyid Aḥmad El-Badawî with Fâṭma Bint-Birrî." The transition from Bes to El-Badawî to St. Nicholas represents a case of syncretism in which the ancient is redefined in terms of the new.

El-Sayyid Aḥmad el-Badawî (1200?–1276 AD) is one of the most powerful saints in Egypt, with a cult that comprises large segments of the Egyptian population as well as people outside Egypt.[. . .] This cult derives much of its power from Sufi (mystic) philosophy and rituals, which lead to ecstatic experiences and rhetorical poetic expressions.

Syncretism: a case of transformation of character

Scholars of various persuasions agree that saints' cults in Egypt date back to ancient times.[774] The transition from an ancient polytheistic religion to Christianity and subsequently to Islam did not radically alter the basic religious beliefs and practices of the native Egyptians, especially the peasantry. The present versified story of El-Sayyid Aḥmad el-Badawî provides strong evidence for this argument.

The majority of Egyptians, especially in rural areas, live according to three separate temporal systems. The oldest of these is the ancient solar system known as the *taqwîm qibṭî* (Coptic Calendar), which is used exclusively in agricultural and related activities.[775] The second is the more recent lunar system, which begins with the year

---

Tale-type: 967 (formerly 967*), *The Man Saved by a Spider Web.* [Pursuers conclude that cave in which fugitive is hiding has not been disturbed.]

Motifs: B523.1, "Spider-web over hole saves fugitive;" B523.1.1§, ‡"Bird-nest—(usually dove's)—at entrance of cave saves fugitive."

[774](n. 9 in the orig.) See Aḥmad Amîn, *A Dictionary of Egyptian Customs, Traditions and Expressions* (Arabic), Cairo: 1953, p. 388; Enno Littmann, *Aḥmed il-Bedawi: Ein Lied auf den agyptischen Nationalheiligen.*" Publications of Akademie der Wissenschaften und der Literatur, Abhandlungen der Geistes- und Socialwissenschaftichen Klasse, (Jahrgang 1950) Nr. 3, p. 55. See also Ignaz Goldziher's discussion on "Die Heiligenverehrung in Islam," in his *Muhammedanische Studien*, vol. 2 (Hildesheim: Olms, 1961), especially pp. 336–343; and Vollers, p. 194.

[775](n. 10 in the orig.) See Edward W. Lane's *An Account of the Manners and Customs of the Modern Egyptians*, written in Egypt during the years 1832–1835 (London, England: Ward, Lock and Co., 1902), pp. 198–200.

of prophet Mohammad's Hegira (flight) from Mecca to Medina in the year 622 AD; it was introduced with Islam during the first half of the seventh century anno Domini (AD), first century anno Hegirae (AH), and is labeled *taqwîm hijrî*. The third and most recent system is the European solar calendar, which was introduced only during the French conquest of Egypt (1798–1801); it is labeled *taqwîm 'afrangî* (European), or *taqwîm mîlâdî* (according to the year of the birth of Christ). Currently, Egyptian folk groups reckon major agricultural occasions according to the Coptic, Islamic religious occasions according to the Islamic, and governmental formal occasions according to the European system. It has been observed that celebrating Aḥmad's birthday (*mûlid*) is linked *only* to the agricultural calendar.[776] Aḥmad's festivals are generally held *around* the first half of October (after the cotton harvest) and *around* April (after the wheat and bean harvest); a third and lesser festival is held on January 17 or 18 but seems to have diminished.

A number of scholars consider a belief in supernatural powers associated with trees, wells, and animals to be a survival from ancient religious systems.[777] The effect of ancient religious beliefs, however, seems to have been much greater than merely isolated concepts, practices, and calendar festivals. We may propose here that in Ṭandata the cult of Aḥmad El-Badawî was transformed from that of a Sufi fakir to a cult of an ancient Egyptian deity—or, perhaps the metamorphoses of the ancient deity's cult into the form of a folk one with Islamic features. This transformation involved Aḥmad's physical appearance and functions, as well as his overall character.

Early "historical" sources describe Aḥmad as follows:

> He was thick legged, long armed, large faced, black eyed, tall, wheat colored [i.e., with copper-tone skin]. There were three smallpox marks on his face, one on his right cheek and two on the left. His nose was aquiline. It had two moles on it—one on each side; each [mole] was smaller than a lentil seed. Between his eyes was a razor-blade wound caused by the son of his brother al-Ḥasan . . . while he was in Mecca and still young . . .[778]

Another source describes Aḥmad as having "thin skin, straight slender flesh and a lean body."[779]

These sources also indicate that in the manner of the austere Sufis, Aḥmad ate very little. He spent a great deal of his Sufi life on the top of the house in a trance, just staring at the heavens. He spoke sparingly, laughed or frolicked rarely, and certainly did not participate in either one of the two major wars that were being waged by conquering armies during that period: by the Mongols in the east, and by the crusaders in Egypt itself.

With the exception of the alleged battle with Bint-Birrî (which is reported by historical sources to have taken place before his actual sainthood), early accounts agree on these general characteristics. According to folk belief, however, Aḥmad

[776] (n. 11 in the orig.) Lane, p. 220; Littmann, "Aḥmed . . . ," p. 55; Vollers, p. 194; ¿-shûr, pp. 275–276.

[777] (n. 12 in the orig.) See Lane, pp. 222–223 and p. 225; see also Winifred S. Blackman's "Sacred Trees in Modern Egypt." In: *Journal of Egyptian Archaeology*, Vol. II (London, 1925), pp. 56–57.

[778] (n. 13 in the orig.) Z. ¿Aabd al-Ṣamad, *al-Jawâhir*, pp. 14–15; see also Vollers, p. 193.

[779] (n. 14 in the orig.) Al-Khafâgi, *al-nafaḥât*, p. 233.

combines a number of roles found in ancient Egyptian religion. As one of the four "Axes," he is believed to carry the world. A counterpart for this belief is found in the ancient Egyptian belief in four gods, the sons of Horus, supporting the legs and arms of Nut, the heavens.[780]

Aḥmad's physical characteristics are depicted in oral lore as follows: a dwarf with a huge mouth and belly, a scabby head usually covered with a long conical cap, a joker, a military warlord, a helper, and an avenger. None of these traits (except the last two, which are normally assigned to any saint) are congruent with Aḥmad's image portrayed in historical reports.

> He is usually depicted in the form of a dwarf with a huge bearded head, protruding tongue . . . long but thick arms and bowed legs . . . on his head he wears a tiara of feathers . . . [he is] a god of music and the dance; he is a god of war and slaughter, and . . . a destroying force of nature . . .[781]

This is not a description of Aḥmad as he appears in our text, but of the ancient Egyptian god Bes, also of foreign descent. Budge states that " . . . Bes is certainly African."[782] In other folk accounts of Aḥmad, he is said, among other things, to control the wind and help in childbirth. These functions were also assigned to Bes in Ancient Egypt.

Veronica Ions wrote that Bes

> . . . was enthusiastically adopted by the common people and became one of the most popular deities. . . . Though sometimes portrayed in military dress as slayer of his worshippers' enemies, he was primarily a god of good humor and of merrymaking.[783]

Similarly, E.A. Wallis Budge wondered:

> It is difficult to understand the change of view on the part of the Egyptians which turned the god of mirth, and laughter, and pleasure into an avenging deity, but it may be explained by assuming that he only exhibited his terror and ferocity to the wicked, while to the good in the underworld he was a true friend and merry companion.[784]

Today, we may ask the same question about Aḥmad El-Badawi, who underwent a similar process of transformation in his physical appearance, roles, and character. The answer maybe found in the political and psychological conditions of Aḥmad's era.

[. . .].

---

[780] (n. 15 in the orig.) Ernest A.W. Budge, *The Gods of the Egyptians*, (London, England: Methuen, 1904) Vol. 2, p. 106; Veronica Ions, *Egyptian Mythology* (Middlesex, England: Hamlyn, 1968), p. 46.

[781] (n. 16 in the orig.) Budge, *Gods*, vol. 2, p. 284.

[782] (n. 17 in the orig.) Budge, *Gods*, vol. 2, p. 288.

[783] (n. 18 in the orig.) Ions, *Egyptian Mythology*, p. 111.

[784] (n. 19 in the orig.) Budge, *Gods*, vol. 2, p. 287.

Littmann points out the similarities between the cult of "Aḥmed il-Bedawi" and its Christian European counterparts.[785] He draws attention to the fact that Aḥmad's first festival was held during the 17th and 18th of January contemporaneously with the Christian Epiphany. Littmann finds strong similarities between Aḥmad's life history and that of Saint Nikolaus Pregrinus, as outlined in Heinrich Günter's *Die Christliche Legende des Abandlandes* (1910) and suggests that in a number of spots the Christian Hellenistic concepts were substituted for those associated with Aḥmad. (If this indeed is the case, then the Christian Santa Claus, i.e., Saint Nicholas, is a descendant of Bes, the ancient Egyptian deity.)

The Evil Eye

Appendix 44: *el-¿Ain* (The Eye): Incantation (*ràqwàh*)

This incantation was acquired from a female practitioner. It appears in print in a sociology book. Solomon is cited as an effective power against the Evil Eye, a role played by the deity Thoth in ancient Egypt. See n. 730–731.

el-'awwila bi-sm-Illâ
(The first is: In the name of God)
w-et-tâniyâ bi-sm-Illâ
(The second is: In the name of God)
w-et-tâlitâ bi-sm-Illâ
(The third is: In the name of God)
w-er-râbi¿â bi-sm-Illâ
(The fourth is: In the name of God)
w-el-khâmisâ bi-sm-Illâ
(The fifth is: In the name of God)
w-essâtitâ bi-sm-Illâ
(The sixth is: In the name of God)
w-essâbi¿â bi-sm-Illâ
(The seventh is: In the name of God)
Allâhu 'akbar, wa-lâ-ḥawla walâ qùwwata illâ bi-Illâh
(God is greater, and there is no ability or power except by God)
raqaitak w-estarqaitak
(I have shielded you with an incantation, and asked others to shield you)
zayy ma-raq'â Mḥammad naqtû, min gmâ¿tû
(as Mḥammad placed an incantation on his she-camel, against his fellows)
ḥaṭṭ-i-lhâ el-¿alîq: madâqitûsh
(He placed the fodder for her [but] she did not [even] taste it)
we-gâb-lahâ ṣaghirhâ: maraḍḍa¿itûsh
(And he brought her young to her, but she did not suckle him)

---

785 (n. 34 in the orig.) Littmann, "Aḥmed . . . ," p. 58. See also Frederic C. Tubach, *Index Exemplorum: A Handbook of Medieval Religious Tales*. Folklore Fellows Communications, Vol. 86, no. 204 (Helsinki, 1969), p. 270, nos. 3468–3473.

kânit ¿asîr we-ṣabaḥit yasîr
(Things were hard [but] became easy)
bi-'izn-Illâh el-¿Aliyy el-Qadîr
(With the permission of God the Lofty, the All-Capable)
b-ism-Illâh 'a¿ûz minnik, yâ ¿ain
(In the name of God, I seek protection from you, O Eye)
yâ ¿ain, yâ qawiwwah; yâ khaynah yâ radiyyah:
(You Eye, who are strong, O you who are treacherous, O you who is sinister)
tikhrugî mi [So-and-so], bi-qudrit-Illâh el-qawiwwah
(You [must] exit out of [so-and-so], with God's mighty power)
bi-ḥaq 'Âdam we-Nûḥ, we-Ṭâhâ en-nabî el-mamdûḥ:
(By the right of Adam and Noah, and Ṭâhâ, the praised Prophet)
takhdi-en-enafas bi-¿akas we-trûh[i]
(Take the breath reverse-wise and go away)
'Allâhu 'akbar ¿alaiki yâ ¿ain! 'Allâhu 'akbar!
(God is greater: against you, O Eye! God is greater)
liqîhâ sayyinâ Selimân tâyhah bain el-gibâl
(Our Lord Solomon found her lost in the mountains)
qâl-lahâ, "râyḥâ fain, yâ la¿înah
(He said to her "To where are you going, O cursed-one")
yâ-llî ma-lkîsh ¿andinâ qîmah?"
(You, who has no value for us)
qâlit-luh, "'anâ rayḥah li-l-walad el-fâliḥ 'aghummuh
(She answered him, "I am going to the thriving lad in order to depress him)
w-'âkhud el-laban min biz 'Ommuh!"
(and take away the milk from his mother's breast")
qal-lahâ, "Ḥâs! Ḥâs!: l-akhtim ¿alaiki b-er-ruṣâs
(He said to her: Woe to you! Woe to you! Indeed, II'll [impression] you under a lead seal)
w-arayyaḥ min 'azâki en-nâs!"
(And relieve people from your harm)
[. . . .]
ḥaṣṣantuka bi-l-Ḥayy el-Qayyûm,
(I have shielded you by the Ever-living, the Self-subsistent)
ad-Dâ'imi al-lazî lâ yamût
(The Ever-lasting, who does not die)
wa-dafa¿utu ¿anka al-¿ayna 'alfa 'alfa marrah!
(And drove away the Eye from you a thousand thousand times!)
[. . . .]
el-'awwila bi-sm-Illâ
(The first is: In the name of God)
etc.

Appendix 45: The Source of Illness Was the Eye

Reported by 'Omm-Ṣalâḥ concerning her daughter Firyâl. She dwelt on the ground floor in the same apartment building as the present writer's family. The event took place some twenty years earlier when Firyâl was a girl of ten or eleven years of age.

Firyâl my eldest daughter got very sick. [. . .] 'Omm-Bahîg [a dear friend of the family] came for a visit, and said, "She [Firyâl, my daughter], has been inflicted by an [Evil] Eye." She helped us remedy the [effects of the Evil] Eye. She got *shabbah* (alum, one of the compounds of Alumina), *fasûkhah* (sweet-smelling pine-risen), and *libân gâwî* (Javanese frankincense); then she burnt them on the *manqad* (brazier, earthenware fire-pan, used mostly indoors). She waited until all was melted and burnt down. A [human] face could be seen clearly in the burnt incense.

'Omm-Bahîg said the burnt ashes formed a shape that was the faces of those two nurses—¿Aliyya and her sister 'Iḥsân [who are our neighbors, and are still unmarried]. The faces had circles around the eyes and were of different colors; these two women were the only ones [women] in the neighborhood who wore eyeglasses (spectacles); they also had blue eyes, "wore red and white" (i.e, cosmetics, paint), and tight dresses.

She ['Omm-Bahîg] *raqìt* (performed a prayer-ritual incantation on) Firyâl, and got a needle and drove it several times into the eyes [of those figures]. A few days later, God healed her [Firyâl], and her health returned to her again.

We heard later that these two sisters had to replace their eyeglasses [presumably due to the effect of the piercing of the figures representing them with the needle].

The "[Evil] Eye" is a matter [whose validity] no one can dispute.

Appendix 46: The New Car

I overheard this narrative in December 1970, while waiting in a medical doctor's reception room in Cairo. Two adult males, about 35–40 years of age, were involved in a conversation. One of the men told this account of the Evil Eye event to the other. From titles used in the conversation, it was evident that both men were graduates of an engineering college.

The following account demonstrates the potency of the belief in the Evil Eye as a defensive mechanism. The person who parked the car without applying the emergency brakes did not consider himself to be at fault. It was the "Eye" of the envious friend that caused the accident, not the negligence of the owner.

A friend of mine from college days had his brother, who is in Spain, send him a car. He took his wife and his forty-day-old son for the first ride in the car. He met another fellow from work and said to him, "Come with us."

The whole time they were driving, that friend of his did not take his eyes off the car. He kept on saying, "How beautiful! How neat!" How this! How that!

My friend did not pay much attention to what he was saying. After they finished their ride, his friend stepped out, and he drove the car to the garage.

The following day when he went to the garage, he found that the car had rolled down a steep slope and crashed against the wall. He immediately remembered what his friend had been saying the night before and how he had eyed the car. He said, "Thanks to God that it was not my child or my wife that his eye hit!"

Appendix 47: The Stone in Bed

Recorded in October 1969 from Nabawiyya M. Y., about 45, from the Geeza district in southern Cairo. Nabawiyya was looking for a job as a housemaid when I met her. A 68-year-old woman who may be called a service-broker was introducing her to a prospective employer. Both women wore amulets against the Evil Eye.

The belief in the power of the Evil Eye is universal in all parts of Egypt as well as all other Arab countries. Practices associated with the prevention of the Evil Eye are visible in all walks of life. The belief in the Evil Eye has an extremely important psychological function. Among other things, it makes every individual the sole owner of something unique and very valuable, which is unobtainable by others. Thus, a person's self-concept is never lacking in positive assets. See n. 735.

There is a woman in our neighborhood who has got an eye that is evil. No one or thing she looks at escapes the harm [her eye causes]. One time one of my neighbors gave birth; her baby boy was very big. Of course, we neighbors and friends went to visit. I wasn't there, but I heard from the others. While they were sitting around her, for she was still in bed, they told her "So-and-so," meaning that woman, "is coming." Immediately she said, "Her eye is evil!"

Of course her son who had just been born was beside her, covered with a bedcover. She said, "Take the boy to the other room, and get me the stone from beside the front door."

It was a big piece of limestone to sit on. She put the stone beside her in bed and covered it with the bedcover. That woman walked in, looked at the baby and said, "My! Your son is big. He is as big as a calf." After a short while she left.

When that woman, the mother of the boy, took the cover off the stone, it was split in two!

Instructive Dreams and Other Visions

Appendix 48: A Widow's Dream—Sayyidah's Dream

Reported by Mrs. Sayyidah D. as a sequel to data given in App. 13.

In this personal experience account, a wife expresses her conflicting feelings toward her deceased husband. She perceives her late husband to be angry at her in spite of all she has done in his behalf. Her account also reveals her own inhibited rage at him. The violent destruction with a farming hoe of the radio he treasured may be seen as symbolically directed at the "ungrateful" husband himself.

He (my husband) had a radio that Dr. Ḥ. [a relative of ours] had sent to him [as a present]. Right after he [(my husband)] left for Hejaz, the radio broke down. I was about to go crazy. I kept on wondering: "*yâ kharâbî*! (O, what ruinous affair for me!)" What is he going to do to me when he returns? [And I wondered:] how come the radio would not break down except when he leaves!? I sent the radio to ¿A.-Ḥ. [our son] in Cairo in order to have it repaired. It came back to us the day after we received the notification [of his death in Hejaz].

Do you think that I wept!? No! I did not weep! He did not like such things [as wailing . . .]. I stood up and took the hoe to the radio [and destroyed it]. ¿A. kept on saying: "Mother! Is there anyone that would do such a thing? Is there anyone who would ruin own property with own hand?" I replied, "Yes! [I would], out of may *qàhr* (sense of being vanquished)!"

I served him. I served him all lifelong: "*¿a-s-sintiyân*" [??] ([probably, to the most minute wish]). I made him needing nothing whatsoever. Now, see! He comes [in dreams] and visits everyone, except me. The other day I saw him in a dream. See, he was standing right here (as you know this was his room). I ran after him saying, "Talk to me!" But he turned his back at me, and never said a word to me. Yes, by God, he never said a word to me. He came to all people [in the village], except me!

The [mechanical] water pump that is in the field broke down. We got tired begging ¿A-F. (my younger son) to take it to Cairo to be repaired. [But] he did not agree (obey). But his father came to him in the *manâm* (sleeper's vision) and told him [to do it]. The following day he went to Cairo, got in touch with [his brother ¿A.-H.] at work. They bought a new pump. For [my elder son ¿A.-Ḥ.] refused to have it fixed and decided to buy a new one.

But he [my deceased husband] would not talk to me.

Appendix 49: El-Sayyid el-Badawî Cures a Case of Heart-ailment

In December 1981, the present writer and his family accompanied friends from the United States on a visit to Luxor and Aswan. On the tourist "floating-hotel," he met an Egyptian engineer (probably in his late thirties), owner-director of "E . . . " (a corporation marketing and servicing heavy earth-moving equipment). The engineer was accompanied by his wife, infant son, mother, and a young girl (probably twelve or thirteen) serving as the infant's attendant.

The engineer asked the present writer about his profession; he replied: "I study folklore." He then inquired as to what does one who deals with "folklore" do. During the conversation, the subject of "beliefs" came up, and he asked: "Do you believe in el-gamâ¿ah el-mashâyìkh wi el-karâmât *(i.e., the 'family' or 'clique' of saints and their miracle-like manifestations)?" Upon receiving the answer, which he apparently considered unsatisfactory, he declared, "For me, these things [(i.e., the manifestations)] do happen and they are true (i.e., real)."* Then, he reported,

Ṣalâḥ esh-Shâhid, who was Director of [former President] ¿Abd-en-Nâṣṣir's office, was very ill. On many occasions he was "between life and death." He quit his job and remained at home in bed. One night es-Sayyid el-Badawî came to him in a *manâm* (vision) and commanded him, "O Ṣalâḥ, get up and go to work. You are well!" But he, [Ṣalâḥ], could not move. This happened a number of times, and each time he would feel too weak to even move.

[Informant switches to direct speech ("I"-style)] Ṣalâḥ said: "One night he came to me and said [emphatically], 'You: O Ṣalâḥ, O Shâhid, get out of bed!' And he got hold of me and dragged me out of bed. I woke up only to find myself on the floor. I stood up, went to the bathroom, did ablution (*itwaḍḍait*), and did two genuflections (*ṣallait rakʿitain*) [i.e., prayed to God, as thanks]."

[Speaker switches to indirect speech ("He"-style)] He kept on improving, and got his health back. He retired from politics, commerce, and everything else; he became one of el-Badawî's *maḥâsîb* [i.e., dedicated follower, and consequently, a "protegee" of the saint]. He never misses a year without going to Ṭanṭâ-[city] for es-Sayyid's *mûlid* (saint's day celebration).

Appendix 50: A Utopia and Mental Illness

The typical Egyptian, Moslem, or Christian, believes that Heaven is a place, that God exists in Heaven, and that Paradise and Hell are two locations within heavens. Holy scriptures outline these beliefs that evoke a feeling of holiness; believers act accordingly.

Another place that is believed by some to actually exist is a hidden land of ideal life, a utopia. Descriptions of this utopian community appear in the oral lore of various groups, especially as a folk narrative. The story was narrated by an adult male businessman from Cairo, the full text of this narrative may be found in H. El-Shamy, Egypt, No. 12, pp. 86–93. *It may be summarized as follows:*

A poor man became tired of his life so he decided to go to the desert hoping that a beast may kill him and thus he may finally rest. He walked into a cave and found himself in front of nine men slapping their faces and shouting in unison, "It serves me right!" The poor man joined in their strange ritual. Soon the men discovered his presence and told him that he did not belong to them. They cast him into the cave. He found himself in a strange country and among strange people. There, he learned that he had come to a community where money, greed, dishonesty, and interference in the affairs of others (that plague modern life) did not exist. Every member of the community calculated the number of blessings (from God) that he earned and spent within the limits of his income.

At first the poor man lived according to the code of honor, but soon he was overcome by his "worldly life" vices. He became greedy and acquired things to which his actually earned blessings did not entitle him. His acquisitions included marrying the king's daughter, but on the condition that he was not to interfere in or inquire about things that were not of his concern. After a brief period of happy married life, he became discontented and decided to leave the palace and wander about. He saw three incidents that aroused his curiosity to such an extent that he could not resist interfering and asking "why?" The incidents were: an old man harvesting ripe and unripe watermelons; a man bailing water out of a river only to pour it back into the very stream from where it had just been drawn; and two groups of people standing opposite to each other on the banks of a river pulling a beautiful house-boat, each group was trying to pull it toward itself. The first two times, the poor man was forgiven for having broken the contract not to interfere, but the third time he was told that he had to go. The three incidents that he had seen were explained to him as follows: The first was the angel of death; he takes away the souls of the young and the old alike. The second was the "stream of livelihood;" God grants different people varying amounts but no one retains anything and all reverts to the main stream. The third was "worldly life;" each person tries to pull it toward himself but to no avail.

After hearing these simple facts of life, the poor man was cast out. He found himself in the cave with the others. He joined in their repentful, self-punishment and shouting: "It serves me right!"

For the majority of Egyptians this narrative does not involve a belief in the actuality of its contents. For a few, however, it is a belief narrative to the extent that it can radically alter a person's actions. The altered pattern of behavior is manifested in the actual acts of a Sufi (mystic), dressed in rags who continuously roams the streets of his town in total bewilderment. He has a small rock in his hand with which he beats on his chest shouting, "It serves me right! It serves me right!" Three cases of this severe emotional disturbance were reported from the Nile Delta, Cairo city, and Middle Southern Egypt [. . .].[786] In all three, people who were close to the disturbed Sufi cited the story about the utopia and explained, "He was there."

The social reality, as seen by mystics, is that human nature drives a person to greed that generates dishonesty and intrusion into the affairs of others; contemporary human societies are plagued by these vices. A utopian community where these social ills are not found is believed to exist. This utopia is described in terms of the actions of its human-like beings; the ideals, values, and symbols expressed in the story are highly anthropomorphic.

For the three (mentally disturbed) Egyptian mystics, the utopia described in the story was real; they not only believed in its existence, but also experienced being "there." The psychological reality is determined by the perceptions—real or hallucinatory[787]—of the existence of this "belief community" and their subsequent experience that seems to be identical with those of the "hero" of the story.

Academic psychiatrists routinely characterize such phenomena as "exotic syndromes."

Appendix 51: Unfulfilled *nàdhr* (Pledge) to Saint

The following report is an affirmation of the power of a saint. Reported by Aḥmad Yusrî M. Fahmî, pupil, age 13, from Zagazig City in Northern Egypt.

My paternal cousin,. . . . , had made a *nàdr* (pledge) to [saint] es-Sayyid el-Badawî: "If I were to pass the [school] examination this year, I will visit you, O Sayyid." It happened that the examination proved to be very difficult and the percentage of success was very low, but still my paternal cousin passed. They gave out the *ḥalâwah* (gratuities for the happy event) and people [who participated] drank the punch.

A month passed and my paternal cousin did not visit es-Sayyid. Another month passed, and another, and he forgot about his pledge. Then, the following year the same

---

786 (n. 7 in the orig.) These locations indicate that the phenomenon is very widespread.

787 (n. 8 in the orig.) Hallucination is "a false perception which has a compulsive sense of the reality of objects, although relevant and adequate stimuli for such perceiving are lacking." See Horace B. English and Ava C. English, *A Comprehensive Dictionary of Psychological and Psychoanalytical Terms* (New York: David McKay, 1966).

thing happened: he made the pledge, passed the examination, and then forgot to visit es-Sayyid. The year that followed, he made the pledge, prepared for the examination, and went to sleep. This time es-Sayyid came to him in a *manâm* (vision) and yelled at him: "Every year you say 'O Sayyid! [Help!]' and I will visit you, and do such and such [for your namesake], but you do not!" Then es-Sayyid raised his arm high and slapped him on the cheek. My paternal cousin woke up in horror; he realized that it was only a dream (for he thought it was real). In the morning, he traveled to Tanta [city] and visited es-Sayyid's shrine there and *wàffâ en-nadr* (fulfilled the pledge).

Appendix 52: The Benefit of Friday

This folktale, an exemplum, portrays a wife's fortitude and a husband's weakness. It was narrated in a mosque by a female preacher in her fifties. She narrates religious and moralistic tales regularly to women worshippers after formal prayer service.

Once there was a lady who was a believer in God. She always celebrated Friday, did nothing [of the household chores], and would *tisàbbàḥ* ([serenely] praise God).

One Friday as she was seated, Satan came to her in the form of a man and told her, "Give me a dress of yours."

She replied to him, "You are a man, while I am a lady! How could it be that you would take a dress of mine!"

He said, "Then give something of your husband's."

She replied, "I cannot. These are his things. I may not dispense of it. You go to him at such-and-such place and ask him for what you want."

Satan went and met her husband; he [the husband] was not a true believer as she. Satan told him, "Every Friday, your wife prays and praises God! Is a woman's prayer acceptable! [i.e., of course not]. You must go and take provisions, [and claim] that guests are coming. If she refuses [to cook], take a knife and slit her belly. When her blood is spilled [on the ground], a treasure—hidden at home for you for years—will 'open up' for you."

The husband went home and took with him vegetables, meat, and other things; he gave them to his wife so that she would cook them for the guests.

At that moment Our Lord sent her a revelation, and led her to the path (*rabbinâ 'alhàmhâ w-hadâhâ*). She said, "Alright."

After he had gone out, she kept on thinking: How could she cook on Friday while she has sworn not to do anything [i.e., chores] on Friday!

Suddenly, she looked only to see the wall split open, and a maiden of utmost beauty stepped out of it.

She [the girl] said to her, "Never mind. You stay where you are and I'll do everything [that needs to be done] in the house."

The lady was astonished and asked her, "Who are you?"

The girl answered, "I am the Friday that you celebrate. I've come to help you and rescue you from the dilemma in which you are!"

In a blink of an eye, everything was neatly done; and the lady was very happy. Before the girl departed, she told her that the man who had come to her at her home was Satan [and that after he had left went to her husband].

Before departing, the girl got hold of the believing-lady's finger and pricked it with a pin; one drop of blood fell on the ground: the treasure opened up for her. When her husband returned, he was astonished because he found the food prepared, and the treasure present in front of his wife.

When she told him the story, he was more astonished; he kissed her hand and asked her forgiveness. He begged his Lord's (God's) forgiveness and became a believer.

Luck

Appendix 53: Luck: Playing with Dice

Excerpt from an Upper Egyptian folksong sung to the tunes of a rabâbàh *(rebec). Performer is an adult male.*

¿ayyân ya ṭabîb:
ma-ḥadd jâ-nî w-gâl, "¿awâ-fi-î-h."
sab¿ el-jibâl 'intasal (imtathal), kalb el-balad ¿awâ fîh
ṣajarr ej-janâyinn nishiff, we-ṣâr w-ahû-¿awâ-fi[-h]
O doctor, I am ailing:
no one came to me and said, "[I wish you] health."
The Lion of the mountains capitulated, the village dog howled at him
Trees of the gardens withered, became something else, and [they are being] howled in.
[. . . .]
qa¿adt 'al¿àb ez-zàhr, qa¿adt 'al¿àb ez-zàhr,
waga¿ min yaddi-yy—el-yamîn—fard:
¿awazlî kisbum: w-ana illî 'it'akhkhàrt ¿an jîlî
I kept on playing the dice, I kept on playing the dice;
out of my hand—the right [hand], dropped out a single [dice]:
my foes won, while I am the one who lagged behind my generation.

Notes to Appendixes

1. The Ninety-Nine Names of God
Based on V. Danner, *The Islamic Tradition*, pp. 245–247.

Motifs: A102.0.1§, God's names (99 attributes); A102.0.1.1§, ‡Opposite attributes of God (e.g., forgiver–vengeful, honorer–abaser, etc.); Z0071.6, ‡Formulistic number: nine (99, 900, 999, 99,999, etc.).

2. Reasons for Creation
Given in al-Thaʿlabî, *Qiṣaṣ*, p. 15.

Motifs: A5, ‡Reason for creation; A100.1§, ‡Monotheism: belief in one God; A100.1.1§, ‡The One-God, no other deity but He—(Allah); A102.1, Omniscient God. [All-knowing God]; A102.4, Omnipotent God. [Almighty God]; A5.1§, ‡God created the universe so as to declare (publish, inform of) His existence; A102.0.2§, ‡God likes to be worshipped (venerated); A1618, ‡Origin of inequalities among men; A1618.1§, ‡Inequalities among social groups established at creation; A1618.1.1§, ‡Inequalities among social groups (nations) from deity's act favoring a certain group (segment of population); A0102.0.3§, ‡God likes to be thanked; N190.0.1§, ‡Inexplicable inequality in possessions (wealth, power, etc.); N190.0.1.1§,_cf. ‡"God grants whomsoever He pleases without limit;" A5.5§, ‡Creation of the universe for the sake of a certain (sacred) person—(e.g., Abraham, Mohammed, Zoroaster/Zardusht); A5.5.1§, ‡Creation of the universe for the sake of Prophet Mohammed.

3. The Tablet and the Pen of Destiny
Given in al-Kisâ'î, *Qiṣaṣ*, p. 06.

Motifs: A1142.10§, Thunder from trembling of clouds due to fearing God; A604.3§, *maktûb, muqaddar, qismah* (written, predestined, kismet)—one's fated lot; A182.3.5.2§, ‡God's proclamation (instruction) perceived as supernatural voice—(*munâdî, hâtif*); A604.1.0.1§, ‡Attributes of the Tablet of destiny (size, substance from which it is made, etc.); A604.1.1§, ‡Tablet of destiny filled after fate has been determined at creation; A604.2.1§, ‡Pen of destiny runs dry after fate has been determined at creation; N101.0.1§,_cf. ‡"The pen has [already] run with His judgment;" A1618.1§, ‡Inequalities among social groups established at creation.

4. Creation of Earth and the Mountains
Given in al-Kisâ'î, *Qiṣaṣ*, pp. 8–9.

Motifs: A834§, ‡Earth created from fumes of boiling water; A857.4§, ‡God steadies earth with mountain(s); A965.5.2§, ‡Mountains stabilize earth; A965.0.1§, ‡All mountains and mountain chains are connected by underground "veins."

5. Resuscitation in Answer to Prayer
From the ballad of "Sa¿d [Felicity] and Farag-Illâh." See: *CMC-A*, No. II.2 _23_.
Tale-type: AT 885A (formerly 885*), *The Seemingly Dead [Princess]*. [She is suscitated by her sweetheart.]

Motifs: A102.4, Omnipotent God; A101.1, ‡Supreme God as creator [to the exclusion of other gods]; A102.4.3§, ‡Life-giving, death-giving God; A650.0.1§, ‡God's Power (Will, Volition, etc.) supports the universe (and regulates its functions); E63, Resuscitation by prayer; E128§, Resuscitation by sweetheart; E165.4§, Resuscitated sweetheart (girl) still in shroud: suspicious of lover's intentions; E175, Death thought sleep; F1041.1.13.3§, ‡Girl dies of *¿âr/khizy* (excessive shame, dishonor, disgrace) at being discovered in man's room; K303.2.3.1§, ‡Corpse (cadaver) stolen or borrowed.

6. Tour of Sky-Worlds
From a folk booklet (16-pager) titled "qiṣṣat al-¿ulamâ' ma¿a sayyidî Ibrâhîm" (The Story of the Ulama with Saint Ibrâhîm), in: *qiṣṣat sayyidî Ibrâhîm ed-Disûqî wa-mâ garâ [lahu] min al-¿agâ'ib wa-al-gharâ'ib wa-al-karâmât*. Versified by *shaikh* Ṭâher ibn Ya¿qûb. [Pamphlet] (Cairo: Maktabat al-Jumhûriyyah al-¿Arabiyyah, c. 1950?), pp. 7–10. (See GMC: App. III, No. VI.C.II.1 _59_)
Tale-types: 806§, *Tour of Sky-Worlds* and 806A§ (formerly 806§), *Mortal Taken to Paradise and Hell for a Visit, and is Brought Back to Earth*.

Motifs: A664.1§, ‡Paradise is located in the sky; A664.1.1§, ‡Paradise is located beyond Hell, in the sky; A671.0.1.1.1§, Hell is located in the sky; A671.1.1§, Archangel Mâlik: Porter (guardian) of Hell; A661.0.1.3.1§, Archangel Ruḍwân as porter of Heaven; A671.2.4.14§,_cf., Seven strata of Hell's fires; A595.3§, Arch-saint threatens to render Heaven and Hell inoperative; F69.1§, Saint takes person (mother) on tour of Paradise and Hell; P240.3§, Mother's spiraling demands: price for her heart's contentment; F516.5§, Person (saint) with transcontinental reach; Q172.4.1§, Palace in Heaven (Paradise) assigned to person as reward; F499.2, Nymphs of Paradise (houris [*ḥûriyyât*]); Q560, Punishments in Hell; A671.2.4.14§,_cf. Seven strata of Hell's fires; A671.2.4.14.1§, ‡Seven chambers (compartments) of Hell's fires.

7. Love Song for a Dead Sweetheart
Motifs: P681.1.1.1§, Mourning: verbal expressions (wailing, dirge, elegy, *¿adîd, nadb*); T39.1§, ‡Lover protects (defends) the beloved; T39.1.1§, ‡Girl would enter dead sweetheart's corpse (in grave) so that she my answer interrogative angels (correctly) on his behalf; V67.6.1§, Protecting the deceased by answering correctly for him; A679§, Interrogative angels (Nâkir and Nakîr, Munkir and Nakrân, etc.) question the dead at the time of burial.

8. A Turk Is Introduced to the Two Angels
Tale-type: 1718§, *Foolish Attempt to Punish Higher Powers*—(god, angel, fate, etc.).

Motifs: A189.8.1§, Angel-keepers (*ḥafaẓah*) of a mortal. They also act as accountants of deeds; A189.8.1.1§, "Angel of the Right" registers mortal's good deeds, "Angel of the Left" registers mortal's sins; J1738, Ignorance of religious matters; J1738.9§, Ignorance of religious service (ritual); J1740§, Foolish attempt to punish (reprimand) the higher powers (god, the angels, fate, etc.); J1742.6.1§, Religious rituals misunderstood; V4.3§, ‡*al-sunnah*: the preferred way for Moslems, as set by the Prophet; P727.1§, ‡Characteristic behavior of Turks (Sarkassians, etc.); W256.1§, Stereotyping: ethnic and national traits; J1704§, Stupid ethnic group (or race); X600, Humor concerning races or nations; Q471, ‡Spitting in face as punishment.

9. Chain of Command among Archangels
Tale-type: 1871B§, *Beggar Turned Down through Chain of Command in a Miser's Palace.* He evokes a divine chain of command to punish the miser: God, Gabriel, Michael, . . . , Azrael (Death).

Motifs: J1335§, Beggar turned down through chain of command in a miser's palace. He evokes a divine chain of command to punish the miser: God, Gabriel, Michael, . . . , Azrael (Death); V247.1.2§, Chain of command among angels; M411.2, Beggar's curse.

10. Crumbs as Fee for Admission into Paradise
Tale-type: 1872§, *Jokes on Sale of Redemption (Admission to Heaven, Forgiveness).* Sold by beggars, clerics, undertakers, etc.

Motifs: V4.5§, ‡*munjiyât/'munaggiyât'* (soul-savers): deeds that serve as "intercessors" to spare person from Hell; V65.8§, ‡Deeds done (at grave-side) on behalf of the deceased—("mercy-soliciting" deeds); V65.8.1§, ‡Holy text recited "over the soul of deceased," V65.8.2§, ‡Food given to the needy "over the soul of deceased" ("mercy-crackers," or the like); V65.8.3§, ‡Money given the poor "over the soul of deceased;" X420.3§, Jokes on *fu'ahâ*'s abuse of religious services (sale of benefices); X420.3.1§, ‡Fee (alms) given insufficient for receiving redemption (admittance to Paradise); A671.1.5§, *zabâniyah*: Hell's angels—they administer punishments (torture); Z1.1.2§, ‡Clerical speech (parlance): formulas that are formal, archaic, grammatically conscious (but not necessarily correct).

11. How Shâkir Became a Shaman-*Shaikh*
Tale-type: 1641B1§, *Haphazard Healing at Hands of Faith-Healer (Exorciser, Magician).*

Motifs: F302.0.3§, Jinn-"*mikhawiyyah*" ("bebrothering"): jinniyyah (fairy, jinn-woman) as a man's foster-sister; Q551.6, cf. Magic sickness as punishment; F300.0.1§, ‡Secrecy required for keeping marriage or liaison with fairy; D1266.1, Magic writings (gramerye [gramarye], runes); N649.1§, ‡Amulet containing irrelevant materials (or nonsensical phrase) given to patient: yet patient is healed; P465§, Faith-healer, or exorciser; U240.1§, ‡Beliefs may heal or cause sickness; V1.2.2.1§, *siḥr shayṭânî/bi-es-suflî* rituals as veneration (worship) of devil; G303.22.5.1§, Desecration of holy objects so as to please devil (*siḥr-suflî*); D1766, Magic results produced by religious ceremony. [*siḥr nûrânî, ¿ulwî* (upper magic)]; F230, Appearance of fairies [jinn]; F230.1.1§, ‡Shape of jinni's head; F230.1.1.1§, ‡Jinni has square head; F499.3.5.2§, Jinn dwell with humans (in such odd places as bathroom, oven room, under staircase); G303.4.5.10§,_cf. ‡Devil (afrit, ogre) has goat's (ass') hooves' (legs); N649.1§, ‡Amulet containing irrelevant materials (or nonsensical phrase) given to patient: yet patient is healed; Q551.6.8§, ‡Supernatural (magic) sickness as punishment for practicing witchcraft (sorcery, nether magic); U240, Power of mind over body.

12. How Shamaness-*Shaikhah* 'Âmnah Acquired Her Supernatural Powers
Motifs: F403.2.1, Acquisition of familiar spirit; F302.0.4§, Jinni as woman's foster-brother; F403.2.3.6, Spirit gives counsel; F1069.1§, cf., "Insanity" from a vision (story); D1032.5§, Meat produced (generated) supernaturally (in dream) by jinn causes magic illness; C645§, The

one forbidden thing: revealing secret of being married to fairy (jinniyyah, jinni); F300.0.1§, ‡Secrecy required for keeping marriage or liaison with fairy.

13. How the Temperamental Father Was Handled: a Psychodrama
Excerpt from El-Shamy, "Belief Characters as Anthropomorphic Psychosocial Realities," pp. 13–21.

Motifs: F415.1§, Invisible spirit negotiates terms of departure with healer (shaman, exorcist, holy man, etc.): healing psychodrama; F405.14.1§, ‡Possessing spirit leaves body of possessed person via wound (made by exorciser); P526.3.1§, ‡Conditions that render a person not responsible for consequences of own actions (e.g., being a minor, insanity, drunkenness, etc.); F362.4.1§, ‡Spirit possessing person refuses to exit (depart) except via wound; F252.1.0.1.1§ (formerly-F0252.1.0.1§), King of the jinn; W205.0.1§, ‡Authoritarian person's pride; P788.2§, ‡Social control by shaming (publicly) into compliance (conformity); W206§, Authoritarian person's (father's) "love."

14. The Value of Dying in the Holy Land
Excerpt from El-Shamy, "Belief Characters as Anthropomorphic Psychosocial Realities," pp. 32–33 n. 14. Also see App. 14 and 48.

Motifs: J157, Wisdom (knowledge) from dream [instructive dream]; V85.5.1.1§, ‡Desiring death (and burial) in "Holy Land;" E754.3, Burial in certain ground assures going to heaven; D1812.3.3.2.1§, ‡Truest dream induced by sleeping in certain place (position); V85.5.2§, ‡Burial in holy land; V85.5.2.1§, ‡Burial near the Prophet; Q28.1§, ‡Repeated pilgrimage saves from Hell fires (entitles to eternal salvation); E407.1§, ‡Corpse mystically moved from one cemetery (burial site, land) to another (usually, by angels, God's Will, or the like).

15. Why Is It Preferable to Seek Reconciliation with the Jinn

Motifs: F361.8, Fairy takes revenge for slaying of his relatives; F415.1§, Invisible spirit negotiates terms of departure with healer (shaman, exorcist, holy man, etc.): healing psychodrama; F361.0.1§, ‡Vengeful fairy (jinni); F386.1, ‡Fairy imprisoned in tree; F386.5, Fairy imprisoned as punishment; D1032.5§, Meat produced (generated) supernaturally (in dream) by jinn causes magic illness; F405.14.1§, ‡Possessing spirit leaves body of possessed person via wound (made by exorciser); F362.4.1§, ‡Spirit possessing person refuses to exit (depart) except via wound; F380.1.2§, ‡Falling on ground renders person vulnerable to jinn's malice (because underground belongs to jinn).

16. Pregnancy via Artificial Insemination

Motifs: P230.0.1§, Childlessness; T531.2§, Conception from "wearing" semen-stained clothing item; T591.5.1.1§, ‡"*ṣûfah*": inseminating agent placed on ball of wool (cotton or the like) and "worn" by woman (i.e., placed in vagina as love-philtre). Typically, it contains human semen.

17. How Shâkir Cured a Case the Medical Doctor Couldn't

Tape-recorded in June 1972 (see App. 11)

Motifs: P261.1§, ‡Father-in-law and son-in-law; P261.3§, ‡Husband jealous of his wife's father; P7.1§, ‡Role strain (role conflict): effects of difficult choices between conflicting obligations; P201, Inherent enmity between members of a family; P243.0.2§, ‡Father-love for daughter; T109.3§, cf., Matrilocal residence: groom moves to home of bride's family; M302.8.1§, Prophesying by opening holy book (Bibliomancy: *fatḥ al-kitâb*); E724.3.5.1§, ‡Counter-spirit harms human counterpart; E724.3.0.1§, ‡Counter-spirit forces its human-counterpart to express (act) its will (person acts involuntarily, and is not responsible for own actions); W181, Jealousy; P788.2§, ‡Social control by shaming (publicly) into compliance (conformity).

18. Miscarriage: A Problem of a Young Bride Addressed

Excerpt from El-Shamy, "Belief Characters as Anthropomorphic Psychosocial Realities," pp. 23–26.

Motifs: T109.1§, Patrilocal residence: bride moves to home of groom's family; T109.1.1§, Bride's troubles at in-laws' home; T109.1.1.1§, Wife put to hard work by her in-laws; T109.1.1.2§, ‡Wife kept out of husband's family matters (or she is overlooked); P264.1§, Bad relations between wife and husband's sister; T572.5§, Miscarriage (or stillbirth); E724§, A person's counter-spirits (Qarînah, Qarîn, 'Ukht, 'Akhkh, 'Omm-eṣ-Ṣubyân, etc.); E724.3.5.2.1§, ‡Counter-spirit causes death to human children; D1745.4§, ‡Use of sacred "objects" (God's name, holy verse) nullifies magic power; F382.3, Use of God's name nullifies fairies' powers; F382.3.1§, ‡Use of prophet's name (or insignia, emblem) nullifies fairies' powers.

19. Detective-Divination by *màndàl*: A Successful Case

Tale-type: 926M§, *Mysterious Crime (Murder) Solved through Induced Confession.* (From culprit, confederate, witness).

Motifs: D1810.0.4.1.1§, *mandal* ("magic liquid-mirror"): knowledge from jinn shown on surface of ink (or oil) in cup; D1817.5§, Detection of crime through "magic liquid-mirror" (*mandal*); W250.1.1§, ‡Personality type: *hawâ'î* ("aerial," whimsical, impressionable); D1714.0.1§, Medium in benevolent magic ritual must be person without sin; D1421.1.7, cf. ‡Magic incense (when burned) summons genie; P788.2§, ‡Social control by shaming (publicly) into compliance (conformity); M109.1§, ‡They said the thief, "Swear [to your innocence]?" He thought, "Relief (escape) has come [in spite of guilt]!"; N619.1§ (formerly-N619§), Lucky (haphazard) guess; P193.3§, ‡Curious crowd of people; U248.0.3§, ‡Wants affect perception (cognitions); U248.2§, Fear affects perception.

20. Detective-Divination via Pottery Water-Bottle: A Failure

Motifs: D1311.15.3§, ‡Magic oracular vessel (jar, bottle, or the like used for divination); A182.1.1.1§, cf. ‡Deity's replica (statue, insignia, or the like) used as divination rod; D1536.1§, ‡Jinni (fairy) enters oracular object and animates it; V1.2.5§, cf. ‡Demon (devil, jinni, afrit, etc.) enters into idol and animates it; Z139.9.3.2§, ‡Water jug (jar, bottle, inkwell, etc.)—female vagina, womb, (or body orifice).

21. A Case of Missing Jewelry

Motifs: D1705§, *barakah* (blessedness): supernatural [positive] power residing in object, act, or person; D1706§, ‡A person's *barakah* (*mabrûk*-person, blessed person); D1817.0.1.6, Wizard detects thief by a trance; F403.2.3.6, Spirit gives counsel; P264.1§, Bad relations between wife and husband's sister; F404.3§, ‡Spirit must be asked to enter shaman's body (so as to be able to speak through him).

22. A Jinni-Woman Pays a Human Friend a Visit

Motifs: F401.3.6.1§, Spirit (afrit, jinni) in the form of cat; D1420.4.1§, cf. ‡Supernatural being summoned by mere mentioning of his name; F404.3§, ‡Spirit must be asked to enter shaman's body (so as to be able to speak through him); F302.0.3§, Jinn-"*mikhawiyyah*" ("be-brothering"): jinniyyah (fairy, jinn-woman) as a man's foster-sister; F404.3.0.1§, ‡Spirit's entry into a human body causes convulsions (contortions, fits) in the human; Z13.9.1§, ‡Speaker wards off evil effects of own speech (words).

23. The Thigh of the Duck

From H. El-Shamy, *Folktales of Egypt*, No. 40, pp. 173–175, 284.

Motifs: F401.3.6.1§, Spirit (afrit, jinni) in the form of cat; F362.0.1§, ‡Fairies (jinn) cause sickness (illness); F362.0.1.1§, ‡Jinni (fairy) in animal form bites person and makes him sick, causes sickness; F406, Spirit propitiated; F406.2, Food left out for spirit at night; F385.2§, Jinni (fairy) placated; F332.1§, cf., ‡Spirit grateful for offering (gift: food, drink).

24. "Mari" Girgis, the Devil Slayer

Motifs: G303.9.8.13.3§, ‡Satan (The Devil) possesses person (animal); G303.16.14, The devil exorcised; D2176.3.3, Evil spirit exorcised by saint; D2176.3.4, Devil cast out of possessed man's body; A583§, ‡Culture-hero as demon slayer (he kills devil, dragon, evil spirit, and the like).

25. Zâr *'asyâd*: A Pantheon

Motifs: F200.7.3§, ‡Family of jinn; F200.7.3.0.1§, ‡Clique of jinn. Usually labeled: line (*ṣaff*), household, a number of jinn and their servant or slave); F200.7.3.1§, ‡Pairs of blood related *zâr*-jinn (brother and sister, parent and child); F252.1.0.3§, Sultan of *asyâd ez-zâr* (possessing-jinn); Z112.3.1§, ‡Possessing spirits ("'asyâd-ez-zâr", jinn, etc.) personified.

26. How the *Zâr*-Ritual Solved a Childless Woman's Problem

Excerpt from El-Shamy, "Belief Characters as Anthropomorphic Psychosocial Realities," pp. 20–29.

Motifs: P230.0.1§, Childlessness; T670, Adoption of children; P465.1§, *zâr*-priestess (*kodyah*); F252.1.0.3§, Sultan of *asyâd ez-zâr* (possessing-jinn); F385.2.1§, Possessing-jinn placated by supplications (song, dance); F385.2.2§, Possessing *zâr*-jinn (*asyâd*) placated by sacrifice; P253, Sister and brother; P264.1§, Bad relations between wife and husband's sister; P275, Foster son; P294.0.1§, Paternal-aunt (*¿ammah*); P294.1.3.1§, ‡Sister (*¿ammah*) adopts her brother's child; T415.8§, cf. Sister who desires a son sired by her brother achieves her goal: the unsuspecting brother.

27. Marûma's *nidâ*

The text is given in Shumays "al-zâr masraḥ" p. 78 (presumably as it appeared in Z. Fawwâz's 1893 pioneering study).

Motifs: Z197.3.1§, ‡Knife, sword, dagger, saw, etc.—penis (male); F575.1.5.5.1§, ‡Pomegranate-like breast; Z166.1.1§, Symbolism: pomegranate (apple, orange)—breast; Z186.8§, ‡Symbolism: building (palace, house, inn, etc.)—female; Z170.0.1§, ‡Symbolism: eating (swallowing, chewing)—sexual activity.

27a. Safînah's *nidâ*

Motifs: F420, Water-spirits; F420.0.2§, ‡Jinn live under water; V250.0.1§, *as-sayyidah* Zaynab: supreme saint (culture-heroine, "The Lady," "The Chieftainess," etc.); Z183.0.1§, Meaning of a name; Z183.6§, "Mother-of-_" (*'Omm/'Umm-_*); V220.0.7.1§, ‡Pleading to saint (holy man) for a [blessed] "Glance!" Z187§, ‡Symbolism: vessel (boat, ship, etc.)—female.

28. Saints in *Zâr*-Like Ritual

Motifs: M119.8.6§, cf. ‡Swearing by love; V220.0.7§, Pleading to a saint for help; V220.0.7.1§, ‡Pleading to saint (holy man) for a [blessed] "Glance!" V219.1§, ‡Pleading to prophet (messenger of God) for help; V52, Miraculous power of prayer; V90.0.1§, cf., ‡Miraculous power of uttering (mentioning) God's name; V90.0.3§, ‡Miraculous power of uttering name of sacred person (prophet, saint); D1707.2.3.1.1§, ‡Glance from eye of sacred person bestows blessedness.

29. The Possessed Husband and His *Zâr*

From H. El-Shamy, *Folktales of Egypt*, No. 41, pp. 175–176, 284–285.

Motifs: F569.9§, ‡Lifestyles in conflict (rural–urban, nomadic–settler, modern–conventional/traditional, etc.)—each is unusual for the other(s); W154, Ingratitude; P262.5§, ‡Mother-in-law and her daughter's husband (son-in-law); P215.5.1§, ‡Husband suspects (accuses) his wife of stealing from him; T339§, Husband averse to conjugal relations; E728, Evil spirit possesses person; D2176, Exorcising by magic; T339.3§, ‡Aversion to conjugal relations motivated by desire to marry someone else (dislike for present spouse); F385.2.5§, ‡Possessed person placates possessing spirit (*zâr*-jinni) by adopting the spirit's lifestyle (e.g., racial, ethnic and religious identity, gender, clothing, speech, jewelry, etc.) Psychodramatic role-playing; F956.7.2.1§, ‡Curative effects of strenuous physical activity (till exhaustion).

30. Moslem Woman Possessed by Christian *Zâr*-Spirit

Motifs: F381.0.1§, Fairy (jinni, spirit) possesses man; V331.8.1§, ‡Christian jinni (fairy); F385.2.2§, Possessing *zâr*-jinn (*asyâd*) placated by sacrifice; Z186.4.4§, cf., ‡Catfish (eel)—penis.

31. *dhikr* Worship

Motifs: P350§, Sufi brotherhood (religious order); F689.1§, ‡Ecstacy from immersion in music (song); V462.8.0.3§, cf. *'ingidhâb*: madness (dissociation) from ascetic immersion; V93.1§, Ecstasy (trance) through religious dancing (*dhikr*, '*zikr*'); F956.7.2.1§, cf. ‡Curative effects of strenuous physical activity (till exhaustion).

32. "In Order Not to Gain Martyrdom"

Archives: AUC 15, No. 9.

Tale-type: 824B§, *Devil (Satan) Helps Person In Order To Prevent Him from Gaining Credit for Good Deed.*

Motif: V463.0.2.1§, ‡Highest ranks of martyrs are situated closest to God; G303.3.1, The devil in human form; V463.7.5§, ‡Martyrdom: dying accidental, unnatural (violent) death (e.g., drowning, burning, etc.); J1281.1§, cf. "In order not to gain martyrdom": that is why the tyrant ruler was saved from drowning; V4.4.4.1§, ‡Cursing Eblis (Satan) earns extra religious credit; G303.22.15§, "So that God would not credit you for a good deed." That is why Satan helped the disabled man.

33. The Blind Man and Satan

Archives: AUC, 15, No. 9.

0824A§, cf. *Devil (Satan) Leads Astray, Exposes, Then Disavows and Absolves Himself.*

Motifs: V8.9.2.0.1§, ‡Communal (group, *jamâ¿ah*) exercising of religious service favored—(e.g., prayers, pilgrimage); V4.4.1§, ‡Religious exercise performed in spite of disability receives more religious credit; G303.9.9, ‡Pranks played by the devil; G303.22.15§, "So that God would not credit you for a good deed." That is why Satan helped the disabled man; V4.4.4.1§, ‡Cursing Eblis (Satan) earns extra religious credit; V463.7.5§, ‡Martyrdom: dying accidental, unnatural (violent) death (e.g., drowning, burning, etc.); V545.2§, ‡Person performs an act of benevolence: God forgives sins of sinners for the sake of that act; V90.0.1§, cf. ‡Miraculous power of uttering God's name; V90.1§, Unintentional curse: accidental calling on God's name destroys tyrant (devil etc.).

34. How Za¿zû¿ Can Be Summoned to Perform a Task

Motifs: D1§, ‡*siḥr* (magic, sorcery): controlling (coercing, harnessing) the supernatural and the natural by means of supernatural agents other than God and His powers; D1783.7.1§,

‡Magic ritual requires entering cemetery (grave) backward. ("Summoning Za¿zû¿"); D1787.1§, ‡Magic results from contact with fire; D1787.1.1§, ‡Jinni (demon) summoned by contact with fire (fire-place, fire-pit, furnace, etc.); D2177, Imprisoning by magic; D2063.1, ‡Tormenting by magic; F387.1§, ‡Supernatural being (fairy, jinni, etc.) enslaved; E478§, cf. ‡Living person's traffic with the dead; C60.3§, ‡Ritual polluter: contact with unclean substance or object (urine, blood, liquor, etc.); D1779§, ‡Magic results from performing toilet functions (urinating, defecating); C677.1§, ‡Compulsion: silence during magic-ritual (is required); C677.3§, ‡Compulsion: ritual impurity during performing nether magic-ritual (is required); T149.1§, Mother's name required for supernatural (magic, religious) ritual; D1278.3§, ‡Sorcerer uses brick from grave; Z108§, ‡Sound (name) symbolism: association based on sound similarities (homophony).

35. How Shâkir Was Pressured into Leaving His Village and Giving Up His Craft

Motifs: C10.2§, ‡Tabu: nether magic (sorcery, witchcraft, black-magic); Q225.5§, ‡Practice of nether magic (sorcery, witchcraft) punished as *kufr* (disbelief); G303.22.0.1§, ‡Devil (demon) serves man so that man may serve him; P145.1§, *majlis*: arbitration-council by notables; P535, Éric fines (imposed for personal injury, etc.); T127.2§, ‡Husband and wife as contrasts: in temperament; T100.0.9.3§, ‡Marriage to gain control over wife; Q94, Reward for cure.

36. Magic Fix Written on a Catfish

Motifs: T591.0.2§, *rabṭ*: supernaturally induced impotence; T357§, ‡Groom does not touch his bride due to prohibition by third party (or tabu); D2077§, ‡Bewitching by means of concealed incantation ("fix"). Magic formula hidden in (on) animal (fish, bird); K1872.3.5§, ‡Magical incantation ("fix") written on catfish, which is released back into water.

37. God's Messengers (Apostles)

Based on V. Danner, *The Islamic Tradition*, pp. 248–249.

Motifs: A165.2, Messenger of the gods; V210, Religious founders. [Messengers of God]; V211.0.4, Christ as prophet [(founder)]; V213§, Abraham as prophet (founder): God's bosom-friend; V214§, Moses as prophet (founder); V215§, Mohammed as prophet (founder).

38. The Generating of a Saint for a "Saint-Less" Community

Tale-Type: 760B§, *Restless Soul*: Deceased cannot rest because of worldly concerns—his soul contacts the living to make his wishes known. (Cf. Maspero, *Ancient Egypt* [No. 20], "Fragments of a Ghost Story.")

Motifs: E721.1.0.1§, The dead "come to" (communicate with) the living in dreams (visions); V68, Preparations for burial; V113, Shrines; V113.0.1.1§, ‡Shrine built (repaired) at demand of (dead) saint; V220.0.8.2.0.1§, ‡Saint causes mischief to enforce demand; V510.3.1§, ‡Sacred person (prophet, saint) speaks in vision to mortal; E419.1, cf. ‡Soul wanders and demands that a temple be built for him; V113.0.1.1§, ‡Shrine built (repaired) at demand of (dead) saint; V220.0.8.2.0.1§, ‡Saint causes mischief to enforce demand; D2072.3, Magic paralysis caused by saint.

39. The Death of *Shaikhah* Shafîqah's Brother

From H. El-Shamy, *Tales Arab Women Tell*, No. 43, pp. 313–315, 450.

Tale-type: 971C§, *Insanity (Death) from Death of Beloved Sibling (Brother, Sister)*. Cf. 751H§, *Only One Garment (Shirt) in the Household: To Be Worn Alternately*.

Motifs: V220.0.4§, "Woman saint (*shaikhah/waliyyah/qiddîsah* 'saintess');" Z183.6§, "Mother-of-_" (*'Omm/'Umm-_*); F1041.8.2, "Madness from grief;" E405.1§, "Vanishing (elusive) corpse;" P253.3.1§, "Sister favors brother over her husband;" P253.9.1§, "Sister becomes insane due to death of brother;" T405.3§, "Sister's nakedness or exposure;" N384.0.2§, "Insanity (loss of senses) due to calamity or fright."

40. The Shaman-*Shaikh*'s *barakàh* Produces the Lost Wallet

Motifs: D1705§, *barakah* (blessedness): supernatural positive power residing in object, act, or person; D1706§, ‡A person's *barakah* (*mabrûk*-person); Q496§, Shame and disgrace as punishment; W163§, ‡Infamy (notoriety); P788.1§, ‡Excessive shame (dishonor, disgrace: *¿âr, khizy*) from violation of mores; K2054.3§, ‡Thief returns stolen goods so as to avert further search for culprit: he thinks he is about to be discovered; N276§, ‡Culprit thinks he is about to be discovered: he remedies the situation by undoing what he has done (e.g., secretly replace stolen goods, correct the forgery, etc.).

41. Can a Woman Be More Beautiful than the Moon?

Tale-type: 918§, *Wise (Learned) Judicial Decisions*. Legal defenses based on knowledge of the law. (See GMC: App. III, No. VI-C-II.1 _60_)

Motifs: M147§, Conditional "divorce-vow": oath that divorce will have occurred unless certain matter is brought to pass; P529.2.3§, ‡Wife (unintentionally) divorced because of "divorce-vow" (divorce-oath) by husband; V223.3, Saint can perceive thoughts of another man and reveal hidden sins; J1178.1§, ‡Inducing correct answer (judgment) by misquoting: judge (adversary) cites the correct quotation thus nonplussed (confounding self); P526.0.3.1§, ‡Judging by legal precedent (*qiyâs*); P522.0.2.2§, ‡*fatwâ*: rendering religiously binding opinion on a case (situation) that had not been heretofore legislated for; D1810.0.3.3§, Prodigious child has supernatural knowledge—(Horus, ed-Disûqî, etc.); P426.0.4§, ‡Ignorant cleric; D2105.9§, Watermelon rind transformed into different foods (through power of saint); D1273.6.1.1§, ‡The power of the letter "Kâf" (k) and the letter "Nûn" (n), i.e., "Kon" ("Be"); J1261, cf. ‡Repartee based on levity toward sacred persons and things; Z10.8.1§, ‡Emphasis: character addressed by full name, each component separately (e.g., "O you Zayd, O you Son of ¿Amr!" "Yâ Sindibâd, yâ Baḥarî!," etc.); Z159.3.1§, ‡Symbolism: moon—beauty.

42. Arch-Saint as Deity: ed-Disûqî's Power Display

Tale-type: allusion to 967—(formerly-967*), *The Man Saved by a Spider Web*. [Pursuers conclude that cave in which fugitive is hiding has not been disturbed.]

Motifs: B523.1, Spider-web over hole saves fugitive; B523.1.1§, ‡Bird-nest—(usually dove's)—at entrance of cave saves fugitive; A595.1§, Arch-saint proclaims himself a divinity: "I am God;" A595.1.1§, Arch-saint proclaims his fusion (immersion) with the divine: "I am the throne, the tablet, the pen, [etc.];" A595.3§, Arch-saint threatens to render heaven and hell inoperative; A595.3.1§, ‡Arch-saint threatens to suspend "the balance" (scales of Judgment Day); P426.2.1.1§, ‡Unreasonable mystic (sufi)—seems to speak nonsense; V462.8.0.2§, *shaṭḥ*: philosophical unorthodoxy due to ascetic immersion; V229.27.0.1§, ‡Saint (holy man, etc.) materializes before birth; T579.5, Saint performs miracles while yet unborn; Q174.0.1§, *'ash-shafâ¿ah al-¿uẓmâ*: God grants person (prophet, saint) the boon of releasing souls from Hell; V521.1.1§, Prophet Mohammed as the Intercessor (*ash-shafî¿*).

43. Bes, El-Badawî, and St. Nicholas

Excerpt from El-Shamy, "The Story of El-Sayyid Aḥmad El-Badawî with Fâṭma Bint-Birrî: An Introduction." In: *Folklore Forum*, Vol. 10, No. 1, pp. 1, 3–4, 6.

Motifs: V462.8.0.2§, *shaṭḥ*: philosophical unorthodoxy due to ascetic immersion; P350§, Sufi brotherhood (religious order); P991.1§, Saint's day festival (*mawlid*, '*mûlid*'); N793.1§, ‡Mystic (spiritual) experience while in cave (in mountain); M302.7, Prophesy through dreams; J157, Wisdom (knowledge) from dream. [Instructive dream]; F898.0.1§, ‡Lunar calendar:

time reckoned according to moon (nonseasonal); F898.0.2§, ‡Solar calendar time reckoned according to sun (seasonal); P951§, ‡Lunar calendar celebrations (formal religious: Jewish, Islamic, etc.); P952§, ‡Solar calendar celebrations (Coptic, agricultural, *'ifrinjî, mîlâdî*, etc.); F632, Mighty eater. Eats whole ox at a time, or the like; V462.7, Ascetic cleric never smiles; F591, ‡Person who never laughs; A485.0.2§, ‡Bes as god of war; A489.4.1§, ‡Bes as god of good humor and merriment.

44. *el-¿Ain* (The Eye): Incantation (*ràqwàh*)
From Fawziyyah Diyâb, *al-Qiyam wa al-¿âdât al-'igtimâ¿iyyah*, p. 342.
Motifs: D2071.1.4.0.2§, ‡Holy verse (text) guards against Evil Eye (*raqwah*); D1711.1.1, Solomon as master of magicians; D2071.1.4.5§, ‡Prophet's name (emblem) as guard against Evil Eye; D2071.1.8.1§, ‡Evil Eye imprisoned.

45. The Source of Illness Was the Eye
Motifs: D2071.3§, ‡Death (illness) from Evil Eye; D2071.1.5.1§, ‡Image of eye pierced by arrow (bullet) as counter measure against Evil Eye; D1782, Sympathetic magic. Magic results obtained by imitating desired action; D1273.0.6§, "*raqwah*"/*ruqwah*: charm containing sacred words renders invulnerable (protects).

46. The New Car
From H. El-Shamy, *Folktales of Egypt*, No. 46, pp. 183, 287.
Motifs: J1063.0.1§, Projection: attributing to others one's own shortcomings (defects); W0199§, Self-deception (rationalization, regression, projection, etc.); D2073§, Bewitching by means of a spoken word (*naqq, qarr*).

47. The Stone in Bed
From H. El-Shamy, *Folktales of Egypt*, No. 46, pp. 182, 286–287.
Motifs: D2071, Evil eye; D2071.1.3.1.2§, ‡Child hidden so as to avert Evil Eye; D2071.2.2§, ‡Person breaks (destroys) solid objects with glance of Evil Eye; W164.1.1§, Belief that one is target for Evil Eye promotes self-esteem.

48. A Widow's Dream—Sayyidah's Dream
Motif: E721.1.0.1§, The dead "come to" (communicate with) the living in dreams (visions); P233.10.1§, ‡Father in vision reproves son for neglecting duties; F956.7.7§, ‡Venting anger or frustration (*fashsh el-ghill*). Dissipation of negative emotions through strenuous behavior (acts); C762.2, Tabu: too much weeping for dead; C898.1.1§, Tabu: wailing for the dead [(as indignity to corpse)]; F956.7.7.1.2§, cf. ‡Venting anger (stress) by beating on doll (dummy).

49. El-Sayyid el-Badawî Cures a Case of Heart-Ailment
Motifs: J157, Wisdom (knowledge) from dream. [Instructive dream]; V517§, Instructive sleeper's vision or dream (*ru'yah, manâm*); V221, Miraculous healing by saint; V229.27§, Saint mystically appears and aids person in distress; V510.1.1§, cf. ‡Image of deity speaks in vision to devotee; Z10.8.1§, ‡Emphasis: character addressed by full name, each component separately (e.g., "O you Zayd, O you Son of ¿Amr!" "Yâ Sindibâd, yâ Baḥarî!," etc.); V521.2.2§, ‡Saint's followers as spiritual (social) club.

50. A Utopia and Mental Illness
Excerpt from El-Shamy, "Belief Characters as Anthropomorphic Psychosocial Realities," pp. 10–11.
Tale-type: 470C§, *Man in Utopian Otherworld Cannot Resist Interfering: Meddler Expelled* ("It Serves me Right!").

Motifs: P192.10§, *magdhûb*: half-wit, "village-idiot;" S110.0.2§, Suicide intended (attempted); C411.1, Tabu: asking for reason of an unusual action; C816§, Tabu: interfering (meddling); C952, Immediate return to other world because of broken tabu; F9§, Utopian otherworld; F111, Journey to earthly paradise; F171.0.1, Enigmatic happenings in otherworld that are later explained; F171.6.0.1§, Futile behavior (efforts) in otherworld; F179§, Piety (religious exercise) as a system of earnings (economic) in utopian otherworld; H591, Extraordinary actions explained; H614, Explanation of enigmatic phenomenon; J155.4, cf. ‡Wife as [wise] adviser; J679§, Defences by avoiding meddling (interfering) in the affairs of others; J1144.3§, Owner takes notice of missing food: intruder detected; P776.4§, cf. ‡Living beyond one's means (on borrowed funds); Q340, Meddling punished; Q432.0.1§, Divorce as punishment; Q522.0.1§, cf. ‡Self-punishment as penance; F956.7.7.2§, ‡Venting frustration (expressing sorrow) by causing pain to oneself (hitting own head, slapping own face, biting own finger, or the like).

51. Unfulfilled *nadhr* (Pledge) to Saint

Motifs: M117.0.1§, *nadhr*/"*nadr*": conditional vow, i.e., pledge to perform certain (good) act if prayer is answered (request is granted); P775.2.1.1§, ‡Gratuity given (demanded) at occurrence of happy event ("*ḥalâwah*/*ḥulwân* of" graduation, safe return, birth of child, etc.); V220.0.8§, Vengeful saint; M209.1§, Dream as reminder of unfulfilled vow.

52. The Benefit of Friday

Archives: AUC, 15, No. 4.

Tale-type: 561D§, *Opening of Treasure by the Shedding (Sprinkling) of Blood.* Intended (sacrificial) victim escapes death.

Motifs: D2101.0.1§, Blood opens treasure; Z129§, Religious exercise personified: "Benefit of" almsgiving, prayers, fasting, pilgrimage, etc.; G303.9.4.0.4§, ‡Quarrels (domestic) instigated by Satan (devil); H492.1.1§, Wife refuses to murder her husband for high honors; husband agrees to murder wife; S263.7§, ‡Husband is to kill his wife so as to use her blood in magic ritual to open treasure; T127.4§, ‡Husband and wife as contrasts: in morality (honesty, gratitude, dutifulness, etc.); D1932.1§, ‡Wall opens to let in a being with supernatural power (afrit, ogre, magician, etc.) and then closes after he exits; V9§, Religious faith conquers adversity (sickness, despair, poverty, etc.).

53. Luck: Playing with Dice

Motifs: N100.0.1§, "Luck" as nonsacred entity: e.g., *bakht, ḥaẓẓ* (luck), *zahr* (dice), *zaman* (Time); M414.0.1§, cf., Luck ("Time," dice, etc.) cursed; W172.5.1.1§, ‡Self-pity song (poem): *mawwâl 'aḥmar* ("red-*mawwâl*"), *ghurbah*-song ("song of strangerhood," "being a stranger") i.e., "the blues;" U22.3§, ‡Injustice: Suffering more than other members of one's own generation (group).

Register of Tale-Types

0217,	*The Cat and the Candle.* [Trained cat drops lighted candle to chase mouse.]	114 n. 389
0310A§,	*The Maiden in the Tower: Louliyyah.* Youth cursed to fall in love with ogre's (ogress, witch) daughter: elopement, transformation (separation), and disenchantment (reunion).	105 n. 344
0325,	*The Magician and His Pupil.* [Apprentice overcomes evil master's magical arts.]	53 n. 169
0325A§,	*Contest in Magic between Two Master Magicians.*	154–155 n. 570
0327,	*The Children and the Ogre.*	104 n. 343
0361,	*Bear-Skin.* [Bargain with the devil.]	19 n. 49
0363A§,	*Husband Discovers that His Wife Is a Ghoul (Witch).*	104 n. 343
0425L,	*The Padlock on the Enchanted Husband.* [Human wife cast out for discovering supernatural husband's secret: forgiven.]	63 n. 210
0450,	*Little Brother and Little Sister.* [They flee from home; brother transformed into deer, sister nearly murdered by jealous rivals.]	98 n. 322
0460A,	*Journey to God to Receive Reward.*	142 n. 516
0465,	*The Man Persecuted because of His Beautiful Wife.* [Supernatural wife helps husband perform impossible tasks.].	63 n. 209
0470C§,	*Man in Utopian Otherworld Cannot Resist Interfering: Meddler Expelled.* ("It Serves me Right!")	38 n. 121, 306 n. 50
0470E§,	*Man in Utopian Otherworld Punished for His Desire To Marry Foster-Sister(s).*	63 n. 207
0555,	*The Fisher and His Wife.* [Wishes granted: wasted (used foolishly).]	184 n. 665

0560,	*The Magic Ring.* [Lost, but recovered by grateful cat, dog, and mouse.]	61 n. 204
0561,	*Aladdin.* [Magic wishing lamp (ring) from treasure-trove stolen and subsequently recovered by means of another magic object.]	61 n. 204
0561D§,	*Opening of Treasure by the Shedding (Sprinkling) of Blood.* Intended (sacrificial) victim escapes death.	307 n. 52
0613B§,	*Council of Judges (Gods) Rules in Error (The Judgment of the Ennead: The Lost or Damaged Item)*	195 n. 694
0613B1§,	*Judging in Error: The Bull Gave Birth to a Calf.*	195 n. 694
0613B2§,	*Judging in Error as to Who is the Legitimate Heir: The Son of the Deceased or a "Stranger"?*	195 n. 694
0655,	*The Wise Brothers.* The king [(judge)] is bastard.	158 n. 584
0655A,	*The Strayed Camel and the Clever Deductions.*	158 n. 584
0655B§,	*Which of the Three Brothers May Not Inherit?*	158 n. 584
0705,	*Born from a Fish.*	54 n. 175
0725,	*The Dream.* [Youth persecuted for not relating his dream of future greatness: it is fulfilled.]	180 n. 653
0725A§,	*Prophecy of Becoming the Sole Ruler.* Prophecy (vision, dream) realized.	180 n. 653
0751H§, cf.	*Only One Garment (Shirt) in the Household: To Be Worn Alternately.*	304 n. 39
0756C,	*The Greater Sinner.* [One more cardinal sin (murder) brings redemption.]	16 n. 37
0756C1§,	*Forgiveness Indicated by the Blooming of a Dry Rod (Staff).* For a full text, see "The Killer of Ninety-Nine."	16 n. 37
0756D§,	*The Most Devout Will Enter Paradise First: Obedient Wife.*	178 n. 650
0758,	*The Various Children of Eve.* [The hidden child receives no blessings: hence inequality among peoples.]	140 n. 509
0758B§,	*Origin of Human Traits of Character.* (Animal characteristics for children of Noah (Eve))	140 n. 509
0758C§,	*Origin of Sibling Rivalry.* (Conflict between siblings of the same sex began when one was favored over the other.)	30 n. 90, 140 n. 509
0758D§,	*The Three Sons of Noah.* (Origin of races, physical and social class characteristics.)	30 n. 90, 138 n. 501
0759,	*God's Justice Vindicated.* (The Angel and the Hermit.)	20 n. 52
0760B§,	*Restless Soul.* (Deceased cannot rest because of worldly concerns; his soul contacts the living to make his wishes known.)	182 n. 657, 304 n. 38
0774M2§,	*Why One Group (Nation) Is Poor while Another Is Rich: Bad or Careless Messenger.*	31 n. 91
0774R§,	*Why a Certain Mortal is Immortal.* (Account of how immortality was gained by person or animal.)	163 n. 601
0792§,	*Resuscitation in Order to Learn Truth (Get Information about Past Events).* The telltale corpse (mummy).	143 n. 517

0802A*, *His Faith in the Balance.* 9 n. 21

0806§, *Tour of Sky-Worlds.* 298 n. 6

0806A§ (formerly 0806§), *Mortal Taken to Paradise and Hell for a Visit, and Is Brought Back to Earth.* 298 n. 6

0809§, *One Act of Charity Redeems All Sins.* 15 n. 36

0809*, *Rich Man Allowed to Stay in Heaven for Single Deed of Charity.* 15 n. 36

0809X§, *One Uncharitable Act Erases All Benevolent Deeds.* 15 n. 36

0816A§, *Devil as a Skillful Cook, then Physician: Corrupts Just King.* 110 n. 365

0824B§, *Devil (Satan) Helps Person In Order To Prevent Him from Gaining Credit for Good Deed.* 303 n. 32

0827C§, *No Place Secret Enough for Sin* (God is all-seeing, omnipresent). 18 n. 46

0830C, *If God Wills.* [Successive misfortunes because of forgetting to say, "If God wills."] 9 n. 22, 49 n. 153

0855B§, *Interim (Substitute) Groom Proves to be the Better Man.* Husband for a night is kept. 140 n. 507

0872*, *Brother and Sister.* [Brother's wife calumniates his sister]. 2 n. 2, 2 n. 4, 86 n. 286, 262 n. 27, 583 n. 158, 589 n. 160

0885A (formerly 885*), *The Seemingly Dead [Princess].* [She is suscitated by her sweetheart.] 298 n. 5

0894, *The Ghoulish Schoolmaster and the Stone of Pity.* [A maiden's long sufferings caused by her accidental learning of teacher's secret.] 104 n. 343

0909§, *Taming the Disgruntled (Shrewish) Husband Is Like Taming a Lion with Patience and Tenderness (Appeasement).* 89 n. 296

0918§, *Wise (Learned) Judicial Decisions.* Legal defenses based on knowledge of the law. 305 n. 41

0919§, *Exemplary Justice.* Stories about ideal application (by king, judge, etc.) of law. 144 n. 521

0920G§, *Deeds Betray Ancestry (Origins).* 158 n. 585

0926M§, *Mysterious Crime (Murder) Solved through Induced Confession.* (From culprit, confederate, witness.) 301 n. 19

0930F§, *The Predestined Fornication* (The phoenix's foster daughter is reached and impregnated.) 112 n. 376, 133 n. 473

0932§, 933, *Brother–sister Incest: the Sethian Complex (Syndrome).* 98 n. 322

0932A§ (formerly-932§), *The Sister Who Desires a Son Sired by Her Brother Achieves Her Goal: The Unsuspecting Brother.* 98 n. 322

0932B§, *A Mother's Own Daughter as Her Daughter-in-law; Bride Behaves as a Daughter-in-law.* Brother–sister marriage (sister as wife). 98 n. 322

0967 (formerly-967*), *The Man Saved by a Spider Web.* [Pursuers conclude that cave in which fugitive is hiding has not been disturbed.] 283 n. 773

0971C§, *Insanity (Death) from Death of Beloved Sibling (Brother, Sister).* 304 n. 39

0985,	*Brother Chosen Rather than Husband or Son.* [A woman (a sister) may save only one from death.]	110 n. 365
1199,	*The Lord's Prayer.* [Devil (Death) must wait.]	123 n. 426, 183 n. 660
1199B,	*The Long Song.* Respite from death gained by long-drawn-out song.	123 n. 426
1353,	*Old Woman as Trouble Maker.* Beats the devil.	157 n. 581
1366§,	*Groom Traumatized by His Maniac Bride.* (Insane wife terrorizes husband.)	34 n. 104
136A*,	*Confession of Animals.* [The unjust (thieving) partner swears falsely: fails trial.]	32 n. 96
1394§,	*Old Wife Acts Too Youthful or Childish: Rebuked.*	187 n. 674
1406A§,	*Youth (Man) Learns about the Wiles of Women.*	157 n. 579
1424,	*Friar Adds Missing Nose* (fingers [added to fetus]). [Gullible woman thus seduced.]	75 n. 245
1424A§,	*Seduction by Pretending to Show (Instruct, Teach) Husband How it Is Done.*	75 n. 245
1424B§,	*Seduction by Other Tricks.* Sexual intercourse under pretence of strengthening, increasing eyesight, (or the like).	75 n. 245
1425,	*Putting the Devil into Hell.* Obscene trick used to seduce woman.	126 n. 443
1425A§,	*Seduction: Roasting the Ear of Corn in the Oven.*	126 n. 443
1515,	*The Weeping Bitch.* [Said to be transformed woman who rejected lover: trick to frighten virtuous woman.]	187 n. 673
1641B1§,	*Haphazard Healing at Hands of Faith-healer (Exorciser, Magician).*	299 n. 11
1718§,	*Foolish Attempt to Punish Higher Powers* (God, angel, fate, etc.).	298 n. 8
1871B§,	*Beggar Turned Down Through Chain of Command in a Miser's Palace.* He evokes a divine chain of command to punish the miser: God, Gabriel, Michael, . . . , Azrael (Death).	299 n. 9
1872§,	*Jokes on Sale of Redemption (Admission to Heaven, Forgiveness).* Sold by beggars, clerics, undertakers, etc.	15 n. 36, 31 n. 93, 299 n. 10
1874D1§,	*Who should be Ashamed: Cruel (Insensitive) Ruler or Person with Physical Handicap?*	188 n. 676

Register of Motifs

A. Mythological [and Related Belief] Motifs

A0005,	‡Reason for creation.	297 n. 2
A0005.1§,	‡God created the universe so as to declare (publish, inform of) His Existence.	297 n. 2
A0005.5§,	‡Creation of the universe for the sake of a certain (sacred) person (e.g., Abraham, Mohammed, Zoroaster/Zardusht).	297 n. 2
A0005.5.1§,	‡Creation of the universe for the sake of Prophet Mohammed.	297 n. 2
A0053.1§,	Astronomical size of angels.	50 n. 156
A0054.3.1.1§,	Eblis refuses to prostrate himself before Adam.	28 n. 79
A0100.1§,	‡Monotheism: Belief in one God.	297 n. 2
A0100.1.1§,	‡The One God, no other deity but He—(Allah).	297 n. 2
A0101.1,	‡Supreme God as creator [to the exclusion of other gods].	298 n. 5
A0102.0.1§,	God's names (99 attributes).	297 n. 1
A0102.0.1.1§,	‡Opposite attributes of God (e.g., forgiver–vengeful, honorer–abaser, etc.).	297 n. 1
A0102.0.2§,	‡God likes to be worshipped (venerated).	297 n. 2
A0102.0.3§,	‡God likes to be thanked.	297 n. 2
A0102.1,	Omniscient God. [All-knowing God.]	297 n. 2
A0102.2,	All-seeing God.	18 n. 46
A0102.4,	Omnipotent God. [Almighty God].	297 n. 2, 298 n. 5
A0102.4.3§,	‡Life-giving, death-giving God.	298 n. 5

A0102.5,	Omnipresent God.	18 n. 46
A0102.16.1§,	*'istidrâj* ("leading on"): God allows disbelievers powers so that they may have no excuse for their disbelief.	147 n. 530
A0128.2.1.1§,	Eye of deity becomes vengeful and evil (the Evil Eye).	208 n. 730
A0131.3.0.1§,	‡Deity in the form of cat ("cat-goddess").	115 n. 392
A0131.3.1.1§,	Bast: Goddess with cat's head.	115 n. 392
A0131.6,	Horned God.	143 n. 519
A0132.1.2§,	‡Deity in form of snake (serpent, viper).	110 n. 367
A0151.7.1,	‡Deity resides in tree.	42 n. 133
A0156.7.4.1§,	‡Cock (rooster) as God's bird (animal).	111 n. 374
A0157.8§,	‡Shooting star (*shahâb*) as god's weapon.	37 n. 113
A0157.8.1§,	‡Shooting star destroys Satan (devil, demon) flying near (spying on) heavens.	37 n. 113
A0165.2,	Messenger of the gods.	304 n. 37
A0165.2.3.1.1§,	‡Archangel Gibrîl (Gabriel) as the "spirit trusted by God" (*al-rûḥ al-'amîn*).	47 n. 145
A0167.1,	Council of the gods.	169 n. 624
A0167.2§,	*dîwân*: Council of deified humans (arch-saints, culture-heroes).	169 n. 624
A0169.1,	‡Judge and tribunal of the gods. [Ennead.]	169 n. 624
A0170.1§,	‡Miracle. Supernatural deed or manifestation by God.	4 n. 16
A0182.1.1.1§, cf.	‡Deity's replica (statue, insignia, or the like) used as divination rod.	301 n. 20
A0182.3.0.1,	God speaks to Moses from bush.	142 n. 516
A0182.3.0.1.2§,	‡God speaks from Heaven to Moses (at the bush).	142 n. 516
A0182.3.5.2§,	‡God's proclamation (instruction) perceived as supernatural voice—(*munâdî, hâtif*).	297 n. 3, 178 n. 649
A0189.8.1§,	Angel-keepers (*ḥafaẓah*) of a mortal. They also act as accountants of deeds.	298 n. 8, 51 n. 160
A0189.8.1.0.1§,	‡Angel-keepers abandon mortal during commission of sin.	51 n. 163
A0189.8.1.1§,	"Angel of the Right" registers mortal's good deeds, "Angel of the Left" registers mortal's sins.	298 n. 8, 51 n. 161
A0194.2.1§,	"God may give respite, but never neglect."	20 n. 52
A0412,	‡City-gods.	110 n. 367
A0416.1§,	‡*mudarrak*-axis: Arch-saint with assigned *darak* ("precinct," post—also referred to as *barzakh*).	41 n. 131
A0416.2§,	‡Patron saint of city or district (guardian–genius, or agathodaemon).	60 n. 197
A0462.3§,	‡God is beautiful and likes beauty.	13 n. 27

A0464.5§,	"The balance" of Judgment Day: For weighing religious exercise (soul, heart, etc.).	33 n. 98
A0473.0.3§,	"Bursar of [God's] Omnipotence"—dispenses money that seems to be acquired mysteriously.	176 n. 640
A0485.0.2§,	‡Bes as God of war.	305 n. 43
A0487,	God of death.	46 n. 141
A0487.2§,	Azrael (¿Izrâ'îl, '¿Azrâ'îl,' '¿Uzrâ'în', etc.): Angel of death.	46 n. 141
A0489.4.1§,	‡Bes as God of good humor and merriment.	305 n. 43
A0500,	Demigods and culture-heroes.	161 n. 591
A0501.2§,	‡Four demigods.	162 n. 594
A0511.1.3,	Culture-hero incarnated through birth from virgin.	167 n. 618, 302 n. 24
A0511.1.3.3,	Immaculate conception of culture-hero.	167 n. 618
A583§,	‡Culture-hero as demon slayer. (He kills devil, dragon, evil spirit, and the like.)	302 n. 24
A0595.1§,	Arch-saint proclaims himself a divinity: "I am God."	21 n. 55, 305 n. 42
A0595.1.1§,	Arch-saint proclaims his fusion (immersion) with the divine: "I am the Throne, the Tablet, the Pen, [etc.]."	305 n. 42
A0595.3§,	Arch-saint threatens to render Heaven and Hell inoperative.	298 n. 6, 305 n. 42
A0595.3.1§,	‡Arch-saint threatens to suspend "the balance" (scales of Judgement Day).	305 n. 42
A0604§,	Creation of destiny (*al-qadar, al-'aqdâr*: determination of fate).	25 n. 67
A0604.1§,	Tablet of destiny (fate).	25 n. 67
A0604.1.0.1§,	‡Attributes of the Tablet of destiny (size, substance from which it is made, etc.).	25 n. 67, 297 n. 3
A0604.1.1§,	‡Tablet of destiny "filled" after fate has been determined at creation.	25 n. 67, 297 n. 3
A0604.2§,	‡The Pen of destiny.	25 n. 67
A0604.2.0.1§,	‡Attributes of the Pen of destiny (size, substance from which it is made, etc.).	25 n. 67
A0604.2.1§,	‡Pen of destiny runs dry after fate has been determined at creation.	297 n. 3
A0604.3§,	*maktûb, muqaddar, qismah* (written, predestined, *kismet*)—one's fated lot.	297 n. 3
A0608§,	‡Determination of *al-ḥalâl* (the licit, legitimate), and of *al-ḥarâm* (the illicit, sinful) for man.	14 n. 31
A0625.2.1.1§,	‡Heaven and earth originally layers of one mass: ripped (peeled) apart by deity.	27 n. 76

A0650.0.1§,	‡God's Power (Will, Volition, etc.) supports the universe (and regulates its functions).	298 n. 5
A0650.1.1§,	‡The world is suspended within the universe by the movement of a celestial animal (whale, serpent).	26 n. 74
A0651,	Hierarchy of worlds. [Cosmological stratification.]	49 n. 155
A0651.1.4,	Seven heavens.	49 n. 155
A0651.3.1,	Seven worlds above and below. An angel upholds the Seven Worlds on his shoulders. Under him in turn are: rock, bull, fish [(whale)], vast sea, air, fire, and serpent.	26 n. 74
A0652,	World-tree. Tree extending from lowest to highest world.	43 n. 135
A0652.3,	Tree in upper world.	43 n. 135
A0652.3.0.1§,	‡"Tree of Heaven." Its fruits are the foods of the gods and give them immortality.	43 n. 135
A0652.3.1§,	*Sidrat-al-Muntahâ*: the Lote-tree of the Extremity of the universe. (Zizyphus lotus.)	43 n. 135
A0652.3.2§,	Tree of life-spans in upper world. (Has as many leaves as there are living persons, when a leaf falls the corresponding person dies.)	43 n. 135
A0661.0.1.3.1§,	Archangel Ruḍwân as porter of heaven.	298 n. 6
A0661.0.5.1,	Soul-bridge: easy for righteous to cross, more difficult for others.	32 n. 97
A0661.0.5.2§,	Soul-path (*aṣ-ṣirâṭ al-mustaqîm*): Sharper than razor's edge, thinner than a hair.	32 n. 96
A0661.0.5.2.1§,	‡Soul-path spans over Hell and leads to Paradise: Sinners will fall off before reaching Paradise.	32 n. 96
A0661.0.5.2.2§,	‡Traversing the Soul-path (*ṣirâṭ*) requires 3000 years descending, 1000 years ascending, and 1000 years of leveled travel.	32 n. 96
A0664.1§,	‡Paradise is located in the sky.	298 n. 6
A0664.1.1§,	‡Paradise is located beyond Hell, in the sky.	298 n. 6
A0665.2.1.1.1§,	‡Horus, Set, Thoth, and Sopdu stabilize the legs of Nut (sky).	162 n. 594
A0671.0.1.1.1§,	Hell is located in the sky.	29 n. 82, 298 no. 6
A0671.0.1.1.3§,	Hell is located in the seventh earth.	29 n. 82
A0671.0.2,	‡Creation of Hell.	35 n. 106
A0671.0.5,	Size and arrangements of hell.	35 n. 106
A0671.0.5.1§,	Hell has seven doors (gates).	35 n. 106
A0671.1.1§,	Archangel Mâlik: Porter (guardian) of Hell.	31 n. 94, 47 n. 148, 298 n. 6
A0671.1.5§,	*zabâniyah*: Hell's angels; they administer punishments (torture).	31 n. 93, 299 n. 10

A0671.2.4.11,	‡Fiery columns in Hell.	35 n. 106
A0671.2.4.14§,	Seven strata of Hell's fires.	35 n. 106, 298 n. 6
A0671.2.4.14.1§,	‡Seven chambers (compartments) of Hell's fires.	298 n. 6
A0679§,	Interrogative angels (Nâkir and Nakîr, Munkir and Nakrân, etc.) question the dead at time of burial.	52 n. 164, 298 n. 7
A0691§,	*al-barzakh* (Isthmus): Intermediate world between heavens and earth.	41 n. 126
A0698.6.1.1§,	‡The highest strata in Paradise are those closest to God.	35 n. 105
A0704§,	Seven strata of sky ("seven skies").	49 n. 155
A0726.0.1§,	‡Sun drawn (pulled) across sky by supernatural beings (angels, deities, etc.).	36 n. 111
A0726.3.1§,	‡Sun drawn across sky seated on wheel.	36 n. 112
A0737.1.2§,	‡Eclipse of moon due capture (imprisonment) by supernatural being.	30 n. 88
A0737.1.2.1§,	‡Houris (nymphs of Paradise) capture moon, thus causing eclipse.	30 n. 88
A0755.8.1§,	Creation of night by making moon dim: Archangel Gabriel wipes moon with his wing.	36 n. 109
A0755.8.2§,	Sun puts out an eye of her brother moon: made dim.	36 n. 110
A0785§,	‡"Residence" (location) of major planets within the seven skies.	37 n. 114
A0785.1§,	‡Saturn (Zuḥal) resides in the Seventh Sky.	37 n. 114
A0785.2§,	‡Jupiter (al-Mushtarî/Mushturâ) resides in the Sixth Sky.	37 n. 114
A0785.3§,	‡Mars (al-Marrîkh/Mirrîkh) resides in the Fifth Sky.	37 n. 114
A0785.4§,	‡Sun (al-Shams) resides in the Fourth Sky.	37 n. 114
A0785.5§,	‡Venus (al-Zahrah) resides in the Third Sky.	37 n. 114
A0785.6§,	‡Mercury (¿Uṭârid) resides in the Second Sky.	37 n. 114
A0785.7§,	‡Moon (al-Qamar) resides in the First Sky.	37 n. 114
A0787,	Relation of planets to human life.	37 n. 114
A0787.5§,	‡Character (nature) of twelve signs of the Zodiac.	37 n. 114
A0787.5.1§,	‡Three signs correspond to (four) personality types.	37 n. 114
A0789.2.1§,	‡Certain day controls certain planet.	28 n. 80, 37 n. 114
A0789.2.1.1§,	‡Sun controlled ("owned") by Sunday.	37 n. 114
A0798§,	Origin of *ṭâqat al-qadr* ("[Light-] Halo of Power").	183 n. 663
A0834§,	‡Earth created from fumes of boiling water.	298 n. 4
A0841.5§,	*al-'aqṭâb*: Four Arch-saints at world-quarters support (carry) planet earth: (el-Badawî, er-Rifâ¿î, al-Jîlanî/'el-Kilânî', ed-Disûqî).	162 n. 594
A0857.4§,	‡God steadies earth with mountain(s).	298 n. 4
A0871.4§,	‡Four corners of earth.	37 n. 115

A0876,	Midgard Serpent. A serpent surrounds the earth.	26 n. 71
A0965.0.1§,	‡All mountains and mountain chains are connected by underground "veins."	298 n. 4
A0965.5.2§,	‡Mountains stabilize earth.	298 n. 4
A1002.0.1§,	‡Doomsday: Day of End of World ("*Qiyâmah*"—to be followed by Resurrection Day, and then Judgment Day).	26 n. 74
A1002.2,	Signs before the Day of Judgment.	39 n. 122
A1002.2.0.1§,	‡Latter Days (*'Âkhir al-Zamân*).	39 n. 122
A1002.2.4,	‡Unusual migration of birds as sign of Doomsday.	39 n. 122
A1002.2.4.0.1§,	‡Change in habitual behavior of animals (birds, insects) as sign of Doomsday.	39 n. 122
A1002.2.4.1§,	‡Extinction (disappearance) of creature as sign of Doomsday.	39 n. 122
A1002.2.4.1.1§,	‡Failure of locusts to appear as sign of Doomsday.	39 n. 122
A1002.2.4.3§,	‡Talking animal as sign of Doomsday.	39 n. 122
A1002.2.6§,	‡Abandonment of "God's ways" (violation of sacred tabus) as sign of Doomsday.	39 n. 122
A1002.2.7§,	‡Coming of the "Seal of Prophets" as sign of Doomsday.	39 n. 122
A1002.2.7.1§,	‡Appearance of the False-Messiah (Antichrist, "al-Masîkh," *al-Daggâl*) as sign of Doomsday.	39 n. 122
A1002.2.7.2§,	‡Return to Earth of the Messiah (al-Mahdî) as sign of Doomsday.	39 n. 122
A1002.2.8§,	‡Excessive adornment of Earth (high civilization, luxurious development) as sign of Doomsday.	39 n. 122
A1063,	Extraordinary wind at end of the world.	39 n. 122
A1070.2§,	Speaking-monster ('*dâbbat al-'arḍ*') as sign at end of the world.	39 n. 122, 108 n. 362
A1080,	Battle at the end of the world. Armageddon.	39 n. 123
A1082.3.2§,	End of the world comes when Leviathan (Whale) encircling the world catches its tail. (Its movement stops.)	26 n. 74
A1088§,	Black ("Abyssinians") and white races kill each other at end of the world.	39 n. 123
A1093,	End of the world announced by trumpet.	46 n. 138
A1093.1§,	‡Archangel Isrâfîl will blow the trumpet, announcing commencement of End of the World.	46 n. 138
A1142.10§,	Thunder from trembling of clouds due to fearing God.	297 n. 3
A1145.5§,	Earthquakes from movements of Qâf Mountains.	38 n. 118
A1210.1§,	‡Creation of the human brain (intellect, mind, reason, etc.) by creator.	138 n. 502
A1210.2§,	‡Human brain as God's favorite creation.	138 n. 502

A1228§,	‡Man remodeled to provide for terrestrial (earthly) life needs.	30 n. 90
A1228.1§,	‡Adam remodeled: Body orifices (for urination and defecation) added.	30 n. 90
A1241.0.1§,	‡Adam made from clay brought from earth crust (*'adîm al-'arḍ*).	53 n. 167
A1241.5,	Man made from earth brought from four different places.	134 n. 480
A1241.5.1§,	Physical and personality attributes (temperament) are determined by characteristics of the earth from which the first man was created.	134 n. 480
A1241.6§,	Prophets made from more pure class of clay (heart of earth) brought by Gabriel.	34 n. 481
A1242§,	‡Deity fashions man on potter's wheel—(Khnum).	134 n. 478
A1275.1,	Creation of first woman from man's rib [Adam's rib].	136 n. 488
A1278.1.2§,	‡Remodeled angel given physical and emotional attributes suited for life as member of mankind (on Earth).	30 n. 90
A1278.1.2.1§,	‡Remodeled houri: Given physical and emotional attributes of human female.	30 n. 90
A1278.1.2.1.1§,	‡Abel given remodeled houri (from paradise) as wife—(favoring treatment).	30 n. 90
A1303.2§,	‡Gog and Magog as giant races.	106 n. 351
A1332.1§,	‡Violation of food tabu in paradise results in need to defecate (assimilation of forbidden food is incomplete).	136 n. 491
A1332.4.2§,	‡Wheat as the forbidden fruit in Paradise.	136 n. 491
A1332.9.1.1§,	‡Eve makes Adam drunk in Paradise by giving him liquor.	136 n. 491
A1335.16§,	‡God instated death for all mankind because prophet (culture-hero) chose dying rather than living (eternally).	123 n. 428
A1352.4§,	Why a woman may not "top" a man (in government, coition): Punishment for sin (rebellion) of Adam's first mate.	137 n. 495
A1371.5§,	Deviant women from Adam's "crooked rib."	136 n. 488
A1388.2§,	Hatred begins when a daughter of Adam and Eve (¿Unâq, Lilith) discovers that she cannot marry because she has no twin brother to exchange for a husband with other brother–sister twins.	85 n. 279
A1443.0.1.1§,	‡Cock as first domesticated creature.	111 n. 374
A1482.1,	Hebrew as language of Heaven.	141 n. 513
A1482.2§,	Arabic as language of Heaven.	141 n. 513
A1541.8.1§,	‡Why Friday is the "chieftainess" of the days [of the week].	26 n. 72
A1591.1.1§,	Ravens (crows) show Cain how to bury Abel.	178 n. 650

A1599.10.1§,	Origin of witchcraft due to hatred: ¿Unâq (Lilith) as the first witch.	85 n. 280
A1613§,	‡Origin of the three races: Caucasoid (white), Negroid (black), and Mongoloid.	138 n. 501
A1613.1§,	‡Caucasoids, Negroids, and Mongoloids are descendants of Noah's three sons: Shem, Ham, and Japheth.	138 n. 501
A1618,	‡Origin of inequalities among men.	297 n. 2
A1618.1§,	‡Inequalities among social groups established at creation.	297 n. 23
A1618.1.1§,	‡Inequalities among social groups (nations) from deity's act favoring a certain group (segment of population).	297 n. 2
A1650.5.1.1§,	‡Punishment of Adam: God's reconciliatory-reprimand (*¿itâb*).	136 n. 493
A1650.5.1.2§,	‡Punishment of Adam: infamy, disgrace.	136 n. 493
A1650.5.1.3§,	‡Punishment of Adam: thin skin.	136 n. 493
A1650.5.1.4§,	‡Punishment of Adam: banishment from God's realm.	136 n. 493
A1650.5.1.5§,	‡Punishment of Adam: long separation from wife Eve (100 years).	136 n. 493
A1650.5.1.6§,	‡Punishment of Adam: strife (enmity toward one another).	136 n. 493
A1650.5.1.7§,	‡Punishment of Adam: branded as rebellious.	136 n. 493
A1650.5.1.8§,	‡Punishment of Adam: setting enemy against his descendants (becoming prey).	136 n. 493
A1650.5.1.9§,	‡Punishment of Adam: being earth-bound (prisoner in *ad-dunyâ*), and suffering the elements.	136 n. 493
A1650.5.1.10§,	‡Punishment of Adam: toiling and misery, the first to have his brow sweat from labor fatigue.	136 n. 493
A1650.5.2§,	God's (fifteen) additional afflictions on women ("Eve and her daughters").	137 n. 494
A1650.5.2.0.1§,	‡Eve blamed for Adamites's troubles on earth—(due to eviction from Paradise). Usually blame extended to "her daughters."	137 n. 494
A1650.5.2.1§,	‡Punishment of Eve: menstruation.	137 n. 494
A1650.5.2.1.1§,	‡Tree in Paradise bleeds: avenges self on Eve.	137 n. 494
A1650.5.2.2§,	‡Punishment of Eve: heaviness of pregnancy.	137, 494
A1650.5.2.3§,	‡Punishment of Eve: labor pains and childbirth pains.	137 n. 494
A1650.5.2.3.1§,	‡Punishment of Eve: craving during pregnancy.	137 n. 494
A1650.5.2.4§,	‡Punishment of Eve: deficiency in religion (faith).	137 n. 494
A1650.5.2.4.1§,	‡Menstruous women may not perform certain required religious services (e.g., fasting, prayers), and thus deficient in religion.	137 n. 494
A1650.5.2.5§,	‡Punishment of Eve: deficiency in reason (mind).	137 n. 494

A1650.5.2.5.1§,	‡Woman's testimony is worth half of man's, and thus deficient in reason.	137 n. 494
A1650.5.2.6§,	‡Punishment of Eve: inheriting half of a man's share.	137 n. 494
A1650.5.2.7§,	‡Punishment of Eve: imposition of *¿iddah* (waiting period before remarriage) on women only.	137 n. 494
A1650.5.2.8§,	‡Punishment of Eve: being "under" men's hands.	137 n. 494
A1650.5.2.8.1§,	‡Punishment of Eve: female being "below" male during coition.	137 n. 494
A1650.5.2.9§,	‡Punishment of Eve: having no right (power) to divorce spouse.	137 n. 494
A1650.5.2.10§,	‡Punishment of Eve: being exempt from partaking in holy-wars (struggles).	137 n. 494
A1650.5.2.11§,	‡Punishment of Eve: no prophet chosen from among women (Eve's female descendants).	137 n. 494
A1650.5.2.12§,	‡Punishment of Eve: no sultan nor ruler from among women (Eve's female descendants).	137 n. 494
A1650.5.2.13§,	‡Punishment of Eve: woman may not travel except when accompanied by a *maḥram* (sacrosanct, unmarriageable male, usually a close relative).	137 n. 494
A1650.5.2.14§,	‡Punishment of Eve: Friday Prayer-service (at mosque) may not be held with only women (*lâ tan¿aqid bihinna*—i.e., they would not constitute a legitimate congregation).	137 n. 494
A1650.5.2.15§,	‡Punishment of Eve: women may not be greeted [with the typical] "peace-be-upon" greeting (*lâ yusallamu ¿alayhin*).	137 n. 494
A1650.5.2.16§,	‡Punishment of Eve: suffering defloration pains.	137 n. 494
A1689.11.3§,	Disbelievers more powerful (rich) than believers since former have the here-and-now, but not the hereafter.	31 n. 91
A1737§,	"sakhṭ, maskh (devolution): creation of animals through degeneration to present forms."	187 n. 673
A1811.2,	Creation of cat: Sneezed from lion's nostrils.	114 n. 389
A1871.0.2§,	Creation of pig (hog): discharged from elephant's anus.	114 n. 389
A2221.7,	Dove returns to ark in obedience to Noah: receives sheen of raven [as reward].	111 n. 371
A2228.1§,	‡Cock (chanticleer) from heaven: God sent as timing-device so as to help Adam mark prayer times.	111 n. 374
A2228.1.1§,	‡Cock crows when he sees an angel.	111 n. 374
A2231.15.1.2§,	‡Owl opposes predestination: Punished with blindness during daytime.	198 n. 695
A2236.2.1.1§,	Viper smuggles devil into Paradise in her mouth: She is cursed.	136 n. 492
A2236.2.1.1.1§,	‡Punishment of viper: loss of wings (ability to fly).	136 n. 492

A2236.2.1.1.2§,	‡Punishment of viper: loss of legs (must creep on stomach).	136 n. 492
A2236.2.1.1.3§,	‡Punishment of viper: nakedness.	136 n. 492
A2236.2.1.1.4§,	‡Punishment of viper: split tongue.	136 n. 492
A2236.2.1.1.5§,	‡Punishment of viper: enmity (hate, fear) of people.	136 n. 492
A2236.2.1.1.5.1§,	‡Punishment of viper: may be killed inside sacred shrines and during holy periods (or prayers).	136 n. 492
A2236.2.1.1.6§,	‡Punishment of viper: being unjust (aggressor).	136 n. 492
A2362.1.1§,	Why monkey (baboon) got red posterior (rear)—punishment: was woman who abused bread (wiping child's feces with it).	187 n. 673
A2489.2§,	‡Cock (chanticleer) as (dawn) prayer-crier.	111 n. 374
A2491.2.1§,	Why owl lives in the ruins and is not seen during daytime. Because of her shame over rejecting predestination.	111 n. 372
A2491.2.2§,	‡Owl hides during daylight to avoid the Evil Eye (being envied for her beauty).	111 n. 372
A2494.1.1,	Enmity between cat and mouse.	114 n. 389
A2494.1.1.1§,	‡Cat created to attack mice.	114 n. 389
A2532.1.1§,	‡Why viper's venom potent. (Satan sat between her fangs when she smuggled him into Paradise.)	136 n. 491
A2905.1§,	Jinn created from fire.	53 n. 167
A2909§,	Origin of jinn: generated by hallucination caused by sensory deprivation.	89 n. 296
A2924§,	‡Hermaphroditic Eblis (Satan) begets he-satans and she-satans.	54 n. 175

B. Animals

B0003§,	‡Viper (*ḥayyah*, female serpent) as animal central to supernatural beliefs (religious records).	26 n. 71
B0014.5§,	Ghoul (ogre) as hybrid of jinniyyah and hyena.	104 n. 339
B0015.7.17§,	‡"*dâbbat al-'arḍ*": hybrid animal with ox's head, pig's eyes, elephant's ears, stag's antlers, lion's chest, tiger's color, cat's waist, ram's tail, camel's legs—with twelve cubits between each two joints (*mifṣalayn*).	39 n. 122
B0031.1,	Roc. A giant bird, which carries off men in its claws.	112 n. 375
B0031.1.2,	Roc drops rock on ship. Rock is so large that it destroys ship.	112 n. 375
B0032,	Phoenix. [(al-¿Aanqâ').]	112 n. 377
B0039.5§,	Bird from hell (*'abâbîl*).	112 n. 380

B0041.3§,	‡*al-Burâq*: angel-horse.	106 n. 353
B0041.3.1§,	‡*al-Burâq* as riding-animal with the speed of lightening (*barq*).	106 n. 353
B0091.2,	Plumed serpent.	110 n. 369
B0099.2,	Mythical worm.	108 n. 362
B0128.3.1§,	‡Bird uses rock as tool (weapon).	112 n. 380
B0147.2.1.3§,	Hoopoe as bird of good omen.	111 n. 371
B0147.2.1.4§,	‡Dove (pigeon) as bird of good omen.	111 n. 371
B0147.2.2.1,	Crow as bird of ill omen.	111 n. 371
B0147.2.2.3,	Raven as bird of ill omen.	111 n. 371
B0147.2.2.4,	Owl as bird of ill omen.	111 n. 371
B0184.1.3.1.1§,	‡al-Maymûn: supernatural hybrid stallion whose movements are controlled by rider's thoughts (hoof lands where rider's eyesight aims).	107 n. 357
B0201.1§,	‡al-¿Anqâ': human-like bird. Giant female bird (falconiform) with human face, breasts, and speech.	112 n. 377
B0251.4.3§,	‡Cat prays when it purrs.	114 n. 390
B0256.5.1.1§,	‡Flock of birds attack saint's adversary (at saint's command).	120 n. 414
B0268.3,	War-elephants.	112 n. 380
B0433.3.1§,	‡Domesticated ichneumon ("*nimce*"—in Egypt) as snake killer.	114 n. 387
B0523.1,	Spider-web over hole saves fugitive.	283 n. 773
B0523.1.1§,	‡Bird-nest—(usually dove's)—at entrance of cave saves fugitive.	283 n. 773
B0766.6.4.1§,	‡Aggressive cock.	154 n. 570
B0784.5§,	*Ṣufar*: viper in man's stomach (intestines) causes hunger.	110 n. 370
B0811,	Sacred animals.	57 n. 185
B0811.3.5.1§,	Sacred she-camel (*nâqah*).	57 n. 185
B0843.1.1§,	Wings grow on serpent (viper) when it becomes aged.	110 n. 369
B0844.1§,	"Cat has seven souls (lives)."	114 n. 388

C. Tabu

C0001.1.1§,	‡The profane (*najiss/najass/'nagâsah'*): the opposite of the pure/immaculate (*ṭâhir/ṭuhr*).	14 n. 30, 202 n. 712
C0003§,	‡*al-makrûh* ("the disfavored," "the disliked" [by God]): almost-tabu, merely tolerated—not the preferred way (for Moslems).	126 n. 446, 184 n. 666, 203 n. 714

C0010.2§,	‡Tabu: nether magic (sorcery, witchcraft, black-magic).	304 n. 35
C0053.5.1§,	Tabu: planning for the future without saying, "*'in-shâ'-Allâh* (If God wills)."	180 n. 653
C0053.5.2§,	Tabu: dealing with omens (dreams) without saying, "Good, if God wills."	180 n. 653
C0060.3§,	‡Ritual polluter: contact with unclean substance or object (urine, blood, liquor, etc.).	303 n. 34
C0092.1.0.1,	"Tabu: killing animals for sacrifice."	93 n. 307
C0092.1.0.1.1§,	‡"Tabu slaughtering animal as offering for jinn."	93 n. 307
C0141.1,	Tabu: menstruous woman not to go near any cultivated field or crop will be ruined [*mushâhrah*].	202 n. 712
C0142,	Tabu: sexual intercourse during menses.	203 n. 713
C0222§,	‡Tabu: eating or drinking during Lent whatever comes from a creature-with-soul—(e.g., cow, chicken, fish, etc.)—("Christian's fasting").	73 n. 242
C0411.1,	Tabu: asking for reason of an unusual action.	306 n. 50
C0433,	Tabu: uttering name of malevolent creature (Eumenides, [(the gracious)]). To avoid the evil results of naming these creatures other names are substituted.	210 n. 737
C0434§,	Names of dangerous things (animal, disease, murder, etc.) are not to be uttered at a person without use of precautionary measures (e.g., "Distant one," "Away from you").	210 n. 737
C0645§,	The one forbidden thing: revealing secret of being married to fairy (jinniyyah, jinni).	299 n. 12
C0677§,	‡Compulsions during performing magic-ritual (is required).	74 n. 243
C0677.1§,	‡Compulsion: silence during magic-ritual (is required).	303 n. 34
C0677.2.1§,	‡"Abstinence from eating or drinking whatever comes from a creature-with-soul (e.g., milk, eggs, meats, etc.) during preparation for magic-ritual."	74 n. 243
C0677.3§,	‡Compulsion: ritual impurity during performing nether magic-ritual (is required).	303 n. 34
C0762.2,	Tabu: too much weeping for dead.	306 n. 48
C0816§,	Tabu: interfering (meddling).	306 n. 50
C0898.1§,	Tabu: indignities to corpse (beating, cremation, etc.).	38 n. 120
C0898.1.1§,	Tabu: wailing for the dead [(as indignity to corpse)].	306 n. 48
C0908.1.1§,	‡Tabu imposed on earth (of Earth).	135 n. 482
C0908.1.1.1§,	‡Earth forbidden to corrode ("devour") corpse of prophet (saint).	135 n. 482
C0910,	Permanent sign of disobedience for breaking tabu.	16 n. 39
C0952,	Immediate return to other world because of broken tabu.	306 n. 50

D. Magic

[And Similar Supernatural Occurrences]

D0001§,	‡*siḥr* (magic, sorcery): controlling (coercing, harnessing) the supernatural and the natural by means of supernatural agents other than God and His powers.	303 n. 34
D0477.0.1.2,	‡Wine becomes honey.	148 n. 538
D0631.1.5§,	Saint as shape-shifter (changes shape at will).	149 n. 546
D0631.3.3,	Sword large or small at will.	107 n. 358
D0631.3.3.1§,	‡Sword's strikes controlled by eyesight (thoughts) of striker.	107 n. 358
D0759.3.1§,	*ḥalb en-nugûm* (milking the stars): magic ritual performed by naked virgin at dawn.	75 n. 246
D1015.6§,	‡Magic animal placenta (afterbirth).	115 n. 391
D1015.6.1§,	‡Cat's placenta has supernatural effects.	115 n. 391
D1016.1§,	‡"Magic ritual requires slaughtering of certain animal (bird)."	93 n. 307
D1032.5§,	Meat produced (generated) supernaturally (in dream) by jinn causes magic illness.	299 n. 12, 300 n. 15
D1221,	‡Magic trumpet.	46 n. 138
D1266.1,	Magic writings (gramerye [gramarye] runes).	70 n. 230, 299 n. 11
D1273.0.6§,	"*raqwah*"/*ruqwah*: charm containing sacred words renders invulnerable (protects).	93 n. 306, 306 n. 45
D1273.6.1.1§,	‡The power of the letter "Kâf" (k) and the letter "Nûn" (n), i.e., "Kon" ("Be").	305 n. 41
D1278.3§,	‡Sorcerer uses brick from grave.	303 n. 34
D1279§,	‡Charm (amulet) of flesh. Made of human or animal flesh.	115 n. 391
D1311.15.3§,	‡Magic oracular vessel (jar, bottle, or the like used for divination).	301 n. 20
D1344.3,	Amulet renders invulnerable.	70 n. 231
D1355.3.0.1§,	Carnal love charm: made from human menstrual blood, pubic hair, milk, semen, etc.	76 n. 248
D1367.1.1§,	‡Insanity (idiocy, lunacy, etc.) from eating eggplant.	203 n. 715
D1420.4.1§,_cf.	‡Supernatural being summoned by mere mentioning of his name.	301 n. 22
D1421.1.7,_cf.	‡Magic incense (when burned) summons genie.	301 n. 19
D1500.3.1,	‡Charm shifts diseases to another person.	202 n. 711
D1536.1§,	‡Jinni (fairy) enters oracular object and animates it.	301 n. 20
D1551,	Waters magically divide and close. [Parting of the sea.]	148 n. 537
D1610.18.1.1§,	‡"Sphinx speaks."	182 n. 657

D1654.9.1,	Corpse cannot be moved.	73 n. 241
D1693,	Magic rod swallows other rods.	211 n. 742
D1693.3§,	Moses' staff becomes serpent and swallows magicians' rods (snakes).	211 n. 742
D1705§,	*barakah* (blessedness): supernatural positive power residing in object, act, or person.	18 n. 43, 183 n. 660, 301 n. 21, 305 n. 40
D1706§,	‡A person's *barakah* (*mabrûk*-person, blessed person).	145 n. 525, 301 n. 21, 305 n. 40
D1707§,	‡Blessed objects.	183 n. 660
D1707.1.5.1§,	‡Sacred words (from holy book) blessed.	93 n. 306
D1707.2.3.1.1§,	‡Glance from eye of sacred person bestows blessedness.	302 n. 28
D1707.6§,	‡Blessed coin (money).	183 n. 660
D1708.1§,	‡Use of right side blessed.	34 n. 102
D1711.1.1,	Solomon as master of magicians.	58 n. 190, 306 n. 44
D1714.0.1§,	Medium in benevolent magic ritual must be a person without sin.	301 n. 19
D1719.9.3§,	Saintly power only during a certain month yearly ("*er-Ragabiyyîn*").	150 n. 553
D1745.4§,	‡Use of sacred "objects" (God's name, holy verse) nullifies magic power.	301 n. 18
D1752§,	*barakah* (blessedness) passes from body to body.	183 n. 660
D1761.3.1§,	Wishing by *ṭâqat al-qadr* ("[Light-] Halo of Power").	183 n. 663, 61 n. 204
D1766,	Magic results produced by religious ceremony. [*siḥr nûrânî, ¿ulwî* (upper magic).]	71 n. 236, 299 n. 11
D1766.1.9.1§,	‡Sacred formula (from scripture) aids memory (e.g., "*Ka-Ha-Ya-¿Ain-Ṣâd*").	211 n. 740
D1779§,	‡Magic results from performing toilet functions (urinating, defecating).	303 n. 34
D1782,	Sympathetic magic. Magic results obtained by imitating desired action.	71 n. 232, 306 n. 45
D1782.0.1§,	Magic result from effigy in the likeness of target for magic ritual (Voodoo doll).	71 n. 232
D1783.7.1§,	‡Magic ritual requires entering cemetery (grave) backward. ("Summoning Za¿zû¿.")	303 n. 34
D1787.1§,	‡Magic results from contact with fire.	303 n. 34
D1787.1.1§,	‡Jinni (demon) summoned by contact with fire (fire-place, fire-pit, furnace, etc.).	303 n. 34
D1789§,	Contagious magic. Magic results obtained by contact or touch.	71 n. 232

D1789.0.1.1§,	"Trace-measuring:" magic diagnosis from a person's residuals.	71 n. 232
D1810.0.3.3§,	Prodigious child has supernatural knowledge—(Horus, ed-Disûqî, etc.).	305 n. 41
D1810.0.4.1.1§,	*mandal* ("magic liquid-mirror"): knowledge from jinn shown on surface of ink (or oil) in cup.	72 n. 240, 301 n. 19
D1812.3.3,	Future revealed in dream. [Divination through interpretation of dreams.]	179 n. 651
D1812.3.3.2.1§,	‡Truest dream induced by sleeping in certain place (position).	300 n. 14
D1812.3.3.3,	Prophetic dream induced by incantation [(*'istikhârah*)].	179 n. 651
D1812.3.3.10,	Dream interpreted by opposites.	179 n. 651
D1812.4,	Future revealed by presentiment: "knowledge within."	178 n. 647
D1812.4.2§,	‡The unknown revealed by presentiment: "knowledge within."	178 n. 647
D1812.5,	Future learned through omens.	188 n. 675
D1817.0.1.6,	Wizard detects thief by a trance.	301 n. 21
D1817.5§,	Detection of crime through "magic liquid-mirror" (*mandal*).	301 n. 19
D1840.1.2,	Saint invulnerable to poison.	149 n. 547
D1857.4§,	‡Longevity for as many years as the number of hairs that can be covered by palm of hand.	123 n. 427
D1858§,	‡Time prolonged or shortened supernaturally (days become years, years become moments, or the like).	148 n. 541
D1925,	Fecundity [(fertility)] magically induced.	75 n. 245
D1932.1§,	‡Wall opens to let in a being with supernatural power (*ifrīt* or afrit, ogre, magician, etc.) and then closes after he exits.	154 n. 570, 307 n. 52
D2063.1,	‡Tormenting by magic.	303 n. 34
D2071,	Evil eye.	306 n. 47
D2071.1,	Averting Evil Eye.	206 n. 726
D2071.1.3.1.2§,	‡Child hidden so as to avert Evil Eye.	306 n. 47
D2071.1.4.0.1§,	‡Amulet guards against Evil Eye.	70 n. 231
D2071.1.4.0.2§,	‡Holy verse (text) guards against Evil Eye (*raqwah*).	206 n. 726, 306 n. 44
D2071.1.4.1§,	Blue as guard against Evil Eye.	70 n. 231
D2071.1.4.5§,	‡Prophet's name (emblem) as guard against Evil Eye.	306 n. 44
D2071.1.5.1§,	‡Image of eye pierced by arrow (bullet) as countermeasure against Evil Eye.	306 n. 45
D2071.1.8.1§,	‡Evil Eye imprisoned.	306 n. 44

D2071.2.2§,	‡Person breaks (destroys) solid objects with glance of Evil Eye.	306 n. 47
D2071.3§,	‡Death (illness) from Evil Eye.	306 n. 45
D2072.3,	Magic paralysis caused by saint.	304 n. 38
D2073§,	Bewitching by means of a spoken word (*naqq*, *qarr*).	306 n. 46, 206 n. 726
D2077§,	‡Bewitching by means of concealed incantation ("fix"). Magic formula hidden in (on) animal (fish, bird).	304 n. 36
D2101.0.1§,	Blood opens treasure.	307 n. 52
D2105.9§,	Watermelon rind transformed into different foods (through power of saint).	305 n. 41
D2121.4,	Magic journey by making distance vanish. The road is contracted or the earth folded up.	148 n. 539
D2156.5.0.1§,	Saint has control over reptiles. ("er-Rifâ¿iyyah" Brotherhood).	37 n. 116
D2161.3.11,	Barrenness magically cured.	75 n. 245
D2161.5.1,	Cure by holy man [(person)].	148 n. 540
D2161.5.7,	Cure by seventh son of seventh daughter.	159 n. 587
D2176,	Exorcising by magic.	303 n. 29
D2176.3.3,	Evil spirit exorcised by saint.	302 n. 24
D2176.3.4,	Devil cast out of possessed man's body.	302 n. 24
D2177,	Imprisoning by magic.	303 n. 34
D2177.5§,	Exorcism by transferring spirit to another person (or to an animal).	202 n. 711
D2179§,	Money supernaturally produced (by saint).	176 n. 640

E. The Dead

E0030,	Resuscitation by arrangement of members.	148 n. 535
E0063,	Resuscitation by prayer.	298 n. 5
E0121.4,	Resuscitation by saint.	148 n. 535
E0128§,	Resuscitation by sweetheart.	298 n. 5
E0165.4§,	Resuscitated sweetheart (girl) still in shroud: suspicious of lover's intentions.	298 n. 5
E0175,	Death thought sleep.	298 n. 5
E0177.1§,	Resuscitated man relates eyewitness account of past event(s).	143 n. 517
E0177.2§,	‡Resuscitated person relates own experience (life-history) when alive.	143 n. 517
E0178.0.1§,	‡Resurrection at Judgment Day when horn (trumpet) is sounded.	46 n. 140

E0178.0.4§,	‡Resurrection at Judgment Day by water of life that flows from under God's Throne. ("mâ' al-ḥyawân.")	46 n. 140
E0183§,	Body of a prophet does not decay after his death: earth may not corrode it.	135 n. 482
E0190.2§,	‡Decomposed corpse (in forms of dirt, dust, smoke, gas, etc.) reconstitutes (reassembles) self.	143 n. 517
E0190.5§,	‡Resuscitated person cannot remain alive because his predestined livelihood had already been consumed (during his normal lifetime).	143 n. 517
E0230,	Return from dead to inflict punishment.	120 n. 413
E0405§,	Uncontrollable corpse ("flying bier"): bearers compelled as to speed and route.	73 n. 241, 127 n. 450
E0405.1§,	Vanishing (elusive) corpse.	304 n. 39
E0406.1§,	‡Corpse can be moved only when certain thing happens (condition met).	127 n. 450
E0407.1§,	‡Corpse mystically moved from one cemetery (burial site, land) to another. (Usually by angels, God's Will, or the like.)	128 n. 452, 300 n. 14
E0419.1,	‡Soul wanders and demands that a temple be built for him.	304 n. 38
E0451.9.1§,	‡*hâmah* ceases to appear when revenge is accomplished.	113 n. 386
E0473.1§,	‡*ṣadâ*: ghost of murdered person in bird-form that cries at the *hâmah* for revenge.	113 n. 386
E0473.2§,	‡*hâmah*: ghost of murdered person in owl-form that cries for revenge.	113 n. 386
E0478§,_cf.	‡Living person's traffic with the dead.	303 n. 34
E0545.1,	Conversation between the dead.	119 n. 408
E0545.19,	Addressing the dead.	119 n. 410
E0545.19.3§,	Addressing the dead by means of letter (written message).	163 n. 599
E0545.7,	Holy man converses with entombed dead.	148 n. 536
E0577.4§,	‡Dead person plays the game of draughts (checkers, or the like).	119 n. 411
E0577.4.1§,	‡Living person plays draughts with a dead person (mummy, ghost).	119 n. 411
E0702.1§,	The soul is etherial.	118 n. 403
E0709.1§,	‡Conflict between soul and body.	207 n. 727
E0721.1.0.1§	The dead "come to" (communicate with) the living in dreams (visions).	304 n. 38, 306 n. 48
E0722.0.1§,	‡Gasping (*shahqah*) accompanies soul's departure from body at death.	122 n. 423
E0722.0.2.1§,	‡Soul being extracted out of body emits scraping sound of excruciating pain—(*ḥashrajah*/*sakrât* al-mawt).	122 n. 423

E0722.1.4.1.1§,	‡Soul out of its body in the form of green bird.	121 n. 421
E0722.4.1§,	‡Soul connected with its dead body (corpse) via invisible light-like beam.	126 n. 444
E0723,	Wraith [guardian angel] of person separate from body.	51 n. 163
E0724§,	A person's counter-spirits (*Qarînah*, *Qarîn*, *'Ukht*, *'Akhkh*, *'Omm-eṣ-Ṣubyân*, etc.).	301 n. 18
E0724.0.1§,	‡The *Ka* as a person's counter-spirit ("Double").	80 n. 258
E0724.1.2.1§,	‡A poet's counter-spirit: inspires poetic creativity. Also labeled a poet's "satan," *tâbiʿ* ("follower"), etc.	83 n. 270
E0724.3.0.1§,	‡Counter-spirit forces its human-counterpart to express (act) its will—(person acts involuntarily, and is not responsible for own actions).	79 n. 256, 300 n. 17
E0724.3.1.1.1§,	‡*'Ukht* (Sister) protects her human brother.	86 n. 286, 300 n. 17
E0724.3.5.1§,	‡"Counter-spirit harms human counterpart."	82 n. 286, 300 n. 17
E0724.3.5.1.1§,	‡*'Ukht* (Sister) injures her human sister.	86 n. 286
E0724.3.5.2.1§,	‡Counter-spirit causes death to human children.	82 n. 268, 301 n. 18
E0724.3.5.2.1.1§,	‡"SIDS" (Sudden Infant Death Syndrome, "*khunnâq*" etc.) caused by suffocation by malevolent counter-spirit (*Qarînah*, *'Ukht*, etc.).	82 n. 268
E0728,	Evil spirit possesses person.	303 n. 29
E0732,	Soul in the form of bird.	80 n. 258, 121 n. 421
E0732.10§,	‡Soul in the form of owl.	113 n. 386
E0734.7,	Soul in the form of fly.	121 n. 421
E0734.7.1§,	Soul in the form of blue (green) fly.	121 n. 421
E0754.3,	Burial in certain ground assures going to heaven.	300 n. 14
E0755.0.4.4.2.1§,	‡Souls of believers reside in sacred well (e.g., Zamzam-well, Jerusalem-well, etc.).	125 n. 439
E0755.0.4.4.2.2§,	‡Souls of disbelievers confined in torturous (condemned, bottomless, etc.) well (e.g., Barahût).	125 n. 439
E0765.1.3,	‡Life-lights in lower world. Each light mystically connected with the life of a person. When light is extinguished, person dies.	126 n. 444
E0765.2.1§,	‡Person to live as long as a certain eagle lives: (Lubad, the seventh of seven eagles, or the third of three eagles).	114 n. 388

F. Marvels

F0009§,	Utopian otherworld.	38 n. 121, 306 n. 50
F0069.1§,	Saint takes person (mother) on tour of Paradise and Hell.	298 n. 6
F0111,	Journey to earthly paradise.	306 n. 50

F0171.0.1,	Enigmatic happenings in other world, which are later explained.	306 n. 50
F0171.6.0.1§,	Futile behavior (efforts) in other world.	306 n. 50
F0179§,	Piety (religious exercise) as a system of earnings (economic) in utopian other world.	306 n. 50
F0200.0.1§,	‡Solomon as supreme ruler of all jinn and similar beings (afrits, dwarfs, elves, etc.).	58 n. 190
F0200.7.3§,	‡Family of jinn.	302 n. 25
F0200.7.3.0.1§,	‡Clique of jinn. Usually labeled: line (*saff*), household, a number of jinn, and their servant or slave).	302 n. 25
F0200.7.3.1§,	‡Pairs of blood-related *zâr*-jinn (brother and sister, parent and child).	302 n. 25
F0230,	Appearance of fairies [jinn].	299 n. 11
F0230.1.1§,	‡Shape of jinni's head.	299 n. 11
F0230.1.1.1§,	‡Jinni has square head.	299 n. 11
F0233.0.1§,	Color of jinni (fairy) is one of its racial (ethnic) attributes.	57 n. 187
F0252,	Government of fairies [(jinn)].	62 n. 205
F0252.1.0.1.1§,	King of the jinn.	300 n. 13
F0252.1.0.3§,	Sultan of *asyâd ez-zâr* (possessing-jinn).	302 n. 26
F0300,	Marriage or liaison with fairy.	89 n. 298
F0300.0.1§,	‡Secrecy required for keeping marriage or liaison with fairy.	299 nos. 11, 12
F0300.0.2§,	‡Fairy (jinni) and human as rivals in love.	109 n. 364
F0302.0.3§,	Jinn-"*mikhawiyyah*" ("bebrothering"): *jinniyyah* (fairy, jinn-woman) as a man's foster-sister.	299 n. 11, 301 n. 22
F0302.0.4§,	Jinni as woman's foster-brother.	299 n. 12
F0332.1§,_cf.	‡Spirit grateful for offering (gift: food, drink).	302 n. 23
F0337.3§,	Fairy (in viper form) saved from pursuer (unwanted suitor): grateful.	59 n. 196, 100 n. 366
F0337.3.1§,	‡Jinni-maiden (woman) grateful for protection from sexual assault (recusing her sexual honor or modesty).	59 n. 196
F0361.0.1§,	‡Vengeful fairy (jinni).	300 n. 15
F0361.8,	Fairy takes revenge for slaying of his relatives.	300 n. 15
F0362.0.1§,	‡Fairies (jinn) cause sickness (illness).	302 n. 23
F0362.0.1.1§,	‡Jinni (fairy) in animal form bites person and makes him sick (causes sickness).	302 n. 23
F0362.4.1§,	‡Spirit-possessing person refuses to exit (depart) except via wound.	300 nos. 13, 15
F0380.1.2§,	‡Falling on ground renders person vulnerable to jinn's malice. (Because underground belongs to jinn.)	300 n. 15

F0381.0.1§,	Fairy (jinni, spirit) possesses man.	303 n. 30
F0381.0.5§,	‡Fairy (jinni, spirit) possesses by "riding" ("mounting," "wearing") victim.	87 n. 290
F0382.3,	Use of God's name nullifies fairies' powers.	301 n. 18
F0382.3.1§,	‡Use of prophet's name (or insignia, emblem) nullifies fairies' powers.	301 n. 18
F0384.3,	Iron powerful against fairies.	301 n. 18
F0384.3.1§,	‡Driving iron needle into shoulders of jinni (afrit) assuming form of animal nullifies his power.	107 n. 359
F0385.2§,	Jinni (fairy) placated.	302 n. 23
F0385.2.1§,	Possessing jinn placated by supplications (song, dance).	302 n. 26
F0385.2.2§,	Possessing *zâr*-jinn (*asyâd*) placated by sacrifice.	93 n. 307, 302 n. 26, 303 n. 30
F0385.2.5§,	‡Possessed person placates possessing spirit (*zâr*-jinni) by adopting the spirit's lifestyle (e.g., racial, ethnic and religious identity, gender, clothing, speech, jewelry, etc.). Psychodramatic role-playing.	303 n. 29
F0385.2.8.1§,	"Initiation sacrifice (for site): animal (bird) slaughtered as offering to jinn-dwellers (*¿ummâr*)."	93 n. 307
F0386.1,	‡Fairy imprisoned in tree.	300 n. 15
F0386.5,	Fairy imprisoned as punishment.	300 n. 15
F0387.1§,	‡Supernatural being (fairy, jinni, etc.) enslaved.	303 n. 34
F0401.0.1.1.1§,	‡Afrit (jinni) assumes form of wind or smoke.	118 n. 404
F0401.0.1.1.1.1§,	‡Jinni named "Whirlwind" ("*Zawba¿ah*").	83 n. 270
F0401.3.1.1§,	Spirit in the form of mule.	107 n. 359
F0401.3.6.1§,	Spirit (afrit, jinni) in the form of cat.	301 n. 22, 302 n. 23
F0401.3.7.5.1§,	The "rooster of the jinn."	154 n. 570
F0401.3.8,	Spirit in the form of snake.	120 n. 414
F0403.2.1,	Acquisition of familiar spirit.	299 n. 12
F0403.2.3.6,	Spirit gives counsel.	299 n. 12, 301 n. 21
F0404.3§,	‡Spirit must be asked to enter shaman's body (so as to be able to speak through him).	301 nos. 21, 22
F0404.3.0.1§,	‡Spirit's entry into a human body causes convulsions (contortions, fits) in the human.	301 n. 22
F0405.14.1§,	‡Possessing spirit leaves body of possessed person via wound (made by exorciser).	99 n. 325, 300 nos. 13, 15
F0405.15§,	Spirit leaves when exorciser threatens to resort to its government.	62 n. 205
F0406,	Spirit propitiated.	302 n. 23
F0406.2,	Food left out for spirit at night.	302 n. 23

F0411.1, Demon travels in whirlwind. 83 n. 270
F0415.1§, Invisible spirit negotiates terms of departure with healer (shaman, exorcist, holy man, etc.): healing psychodrama. 99 n. 325, 300 nos. 13, 15
F0420, Water-spirits. 302 n. 27A
F0420.0.2§, ‡Jinn live under water. 302 n. 27A
F0420.6.1, Marriage or liaison of mortals and water-spirits. 63 n. 210
F0440.3§, *al-Khiḍr* (the Green-one): Benevolent spirit associated with vegetation and water. 47 n. 149, 163 n. 600
F0499.2, Nymphs of Paradise (houris [*ḥûriyyât*]). 30 n. 88, 298 n. 6
F0499.3.5.2§, Jinn dwell with humans (in such odd places as bathroom, oven room, under staircase). 299 n. 11
F0499.4.1§, ‡Jinni (fairy) kills human. 109 n. 364
F0499.9.1§, ‡Serving-boys of Paradise (*wildân*). 30 n. 87
F0499.9.1.1§, ‡Beardless waiters of Paradise are for serving foods and drinks only. 30 n. 87
F0510.2§, Gog and Magog as monstrous races. 106 n. 351
F0511.2.5.1§, ‡"Lower ear as mat–upper ear as cover." 104 n. 341
F0511.3, Person with horns. 143 n. 519
F0511.3.2§, Alexander, "the dual-horned." 143 n. 519
F0516.5§, Person (saint) with transcontinental reach. 298 n. 6
F0531.1.5.1, Giantess (fairy, mountain woman, [ogress]) throws her breasts over her shoulders. 104 n. 341
F0545.3.3§, ‡Mole (*khâl, ḥasanah, shâmah*) on cheek. 16 n. 38
F0559.9.1.1.1§, ‡"Broken wind causes whirlwind on earth and smoke-trail in sky." 118 n. 404
F0559.9.1.2§, ‡Whirlwind is "afrit's fart." 83 n. 270, 118 n. 404
F0561.14§, ‡Social groups who live on weed-like greens (leek, radish, watercress, dandelion, etc.). 94 n. 310
F0569.9§, ‡Lifestyles in conflict (rural–urban, nomadic–settler, modern–conventional/traditional, etc.)—each is unusual for the other(s). 303 n. 29
F0571.9.1§, ‡Senility (*zamânah*): madness (diminished mental capacity) from old age. 123 n. 426
F0575.1.5.5.1§, ‡Pomegranate-like breast. 302 n. 27
F0580§, Person of awe-inspiring appearance. 148 n. 545
F0591, ‡Person who never laughs. 305 n. 43
F0632, Mighty eater. Eats whole ox at a time, or the like. 147 n. 533, 305 n. 43
F0632.0.1§, ‡Ways of mighty eaters: gluttonous eating. 147 n. 533

F0642.3,	‡Person can see through opaque objects. [(X-ray sight)]	148 n. 544
F0689.1§,	‡Ecstacy from immersion in music (song).	23 n. 64, 303 n. 31
F0689.1.1§,	‡Madness from listening to marvelous music or song (violent reactions: Ecstatic convulsions, clothes slit, self-injury, etc.).	23 n. 64
F0701.2,	Land of the blessed. Everything as it should be.	38 n. 121
F0709.5.3.1§,	‡The Ruined Quarter of Earth: faraway.	37 n. 116
F0709.5.3.3§,	‡The Dark Quarter of Earth: faraway.	37 n. 117
F0756.8§,	‡Valley of precious metals and stones.	37 n. 117
F0898.0.1§,	‡Lunar calendar: time reckoned according to moon (nonseasonal).	305 n. 43
F0898.0.2§,	‡Solar calendar: time reckoned according to sun (seasonal).	305 n. 43
F0950.0.1§,	Hallucinatory drugs (hashish, opium, etc.) used as cures.	98 n. 324
F0950.0.1.1§,	‡Hashish (opium, etc.) used to treat pain (distress).	98 n. 324
F0950.0.2§,	Hallucinatory drugs used to induce state of altered consciousness in exorcism rituals.	98 n. 324
F0950.0.2.1§,	‡Drug-induced illusion (hallucination).	98 n. 324
F0956.7.2.1§,	‡Curative effects of strenuous physical activity (till exhaustion).	23 n. 64, 303 nos. 29, 31
F0956.7.7§,	‡Venting anger or frustration (*fashsh el-ghill*). Dissipation of negative emotions through strenuous behavior (acts).	306 n. 48
F0956.7.7.1.2§,_cf.	‡Venting anger (stress) by beating on doll (dummy).	306 n. 48
F0956.7.7.2§,	‡Venting frustration (expressing sorrow) by causing pain to oneself (hitting own head, slapping own face, biting own finger, or the like).	306 n. 50
F0959.7§,	‡Music as therapy: marvelous cure (healing) by music.	23 n. 64
F0966,	Voices from heaven (or from the air). [*hâtif/‘munâdî’*]	178 n. 649
F0969.8.2§,	‡Hiding in mystical location between Earth and the sky; e.g., in an Arch-saint's domain, the Isthmus (*al-barzakh*), or the like).	217 n. 744
F1040.7.1§,	‡Aversion to sexual intercourse.	164 n. 606
F1041.1.13.3§,	‡Girl dies of *¿âr/khizy* (excessive shame, dishonor, disgrace) at being discovered in man's room.	298 n. 5
F1041.8.2,	Madness from grief.	304 n. 39
F1042§,	Mania: compulsion—uncontrollable (involuntary) behavior.	34 n. 104, 207 n. 727
F1043.1§,	Hallucinatory experiences from sensory deprivation.	89 n. 296
F1046§,	‡Hallucination: false perception without adequate stimuli.	178 n. 649
F1068,	Realistic dream.	127 n. 449
F1068.1,	Tokens from a dream. Man brings objects received during a dream.	127 n. 449

F1069.1§,_cf.	"Insanity" from a vision (story).	299 n. 12
F1074.1.1§,	‡Illicit (sinful) food becomes licit (legitimate).	148 n. 538
F1074.1.1.3§,	‡Liquor (wine) becomes sweet punch, water, or the like.	148 n. 538

G. Ogres [and Satan]

G0001§,	‡Origin of ogres. (Where ogres come from.)	104 n. 339
G0002.1§,	‡Hideous ogre (ogress).	104 n. 341
G0011.18,	Cannibal tribe.	106 n. 350
G0011.18.0.1§,	Namnam as cannibal tribe (race).	106 n. 350
G0225,	Witch's familiar spirit [(*tâbi¿*)].	83 n. 270
G0303.0.1§,	‡Other entities labeled "satan."	88 n. 292
G0303.10.5,	Where devil can't reach, he sends an old woman.	157 n. 581
G0303.16.14,	The devil exorcised.	302 n. 24
G0303.22.0.1§,	‡Devil (demon) serves man so that man may serve him.	304 n. 35
G0303.22.5.1§,	Desecration of holy objects so as to please devil (*siḥr-suflî*).	299 n. 11
G0303.22.5.2§,	*shabshabah*: sorceress beats own vulva with slipper so as to please devil.	75 n. 246
G0303.22.15§,	"So that God would not credit you for a good deed." That is why Satan helped the disabled man.	303 nos. 32, 33
G0303.3.1,	The devil in human form.	303 n. 32
G0303.4.5.10§,	‡Devil (afrit, ogre) has goat's (ass's) hooves (legs).	104 n. 341, 299 n. 11
G0303.9.0.1.1§,	‡"Truly the wiles of Satan are weak" (when compared to women's powers)—[Male's interpretation of scripture].	157 n. 579
G0303.9.4.0.4§,	‡Quarrels (domestic) instigated by Satan (devil).	307 n. 52
G0303.9.8.13.3§,	‡Satan (The Devil) possesses person (animal).	302 n. 24
G0303.9.9,	‡Pranks played by the devil.	303 n. 33
G0654.1§,	‡Indicator of ogress' contentment (peacefulness): disheveled appearance.	104 n. 341
G0654.2§,	‡Indicator of ogress' anger (foulness of mood): neat (groomed) appearance.	104 n. 341

H. Tests

H0175.7§,	Blood-relative mystically recognized: "Blood's yearning," "Blood's howling."	159 n. 588
H0220,	Ordeals. Guilt or innocence thus established.	32 n. 96
H0221.2.3§,	‡Ordeal by hot-iron placed on tongue of accused ("*al-bash¿ah*").	32 n. 96

H0492.1.1§,	Wife refuses to murder her husband for high honors; husband agrees to murder wife.	307 n. 52
H0591,	Extraordinary actions explained.	306 n. 50
H0614,	Explanation of enigmatic phenomenon.	306 n. 50
H1376.10§,	Quest: learning women's wiles.	157 n. 579
H1376.7,	Quest for immortality.	163 n. 601
H1376.7.1§,	‡Failure on quest to gain immortality—(e.g., Gilgamesh, Alexander, etc.).	163 n. 601
H1379.1§,	Fool's errand: quest for the "orphan chick."	92 n. 305
H1597§,	Contest of the sexes: match between man and woman to settle claim as to whose wiles are more potent.	157 n. 579
H1597.3§,	Sage declares his inability to deal with women's wiles.	157 n. 579
H1598.2.1§,	Contest between old woman and Satan in trouble-making.	157 n. 579

J. The Wise and the Foolish

J0001§,	‡‡Capacity to know (knowledge) from instinct: (innate, "from God," *'ilhâm, hidâyah*).	176 n. 641
J0006§,	‡"Ideal culture." (Learned ways and values for social living as they are supposed to be: good, bad, or neutral.)	3 n. 6
J0148.2.1§,	‡One word (phrase, sentence, idea) evokes another associated with it. ("Principle of polarity:" stability of syntax, word sequence, word order).	120 n. 416
J0155.4,_cf.	‡Wife as [wise] adviser.	306 n. 50
J0157,	Wisdom (knowledge) from dream. [Instructive dream.]	300 n. 14, 305 n. 43, 306 n. 49
J0157.8§,	‡Dream as source of misleading information (misinformation) (*'ḏghâthu 'aḥlâm*).	179 n. 652
J0157.8.1§,	‡Satan misleads in dreams (and similar experiences, such as communication with the dead).	179 n. 652
J0157.8.2§,	‡Physiological state of sleeper as cause of misleading dream (e.g., full stomach, being cold, or the like).	179 n. 652
J0216.6.1§,	‡Death before advent senility chosen.	123 n. 426, 178 n. 650
J0225.4,	Angel (Jesus) kills man. Done because man is plotting a murder.	20 n. 52
J0225.4.1§,	Hermit (al-Khiḍr) kills boy: predestined to cause grief to his pious parents.	20 n. 52
J0250§,	‡Choice between the supposed (presumed) in life and the actual ("ideal culture," and "real culture").	3 n. 6
J0675.0.1§,	Preemptive actions: anticipatory treachery countervailed by treacherous acts.	20 n. 52

J0679§,	Defences by avoiding meddling (interfering) in the affairs of others.	306 n. 50
J1063.0.1§,	Projection: attributing to others one's own shortcomings (defects). W0199§, Self-deception (rationalization, regression, projection, etc.).	306 n. 46
J1144.3§,	Owner takes notice of missing food: intruder detected.	306 n. 50
J1151.3§,	‡Posthumous witness: testimony acquired or given by deceased person.	143 n. 517
J1178.1§,	‡Inducing correct answer (judgment) by misquoting: judge (adversary) cites the correct quotation thus nonplussed (confounding self).	305 n. 41
J1261,_cf.	‡Repartee based on levity toward sacred persons and things.	305 n. 41
J1281.1§,_cf.	"In order not to gain martyrdom": that is why the tyrant ruler was saved from drowning.	303 n. 32
J1335§,	Beggar turned down through chain of command in a miser's palace. He evokes a divine chain of command to punish the miser: God, Gabriel, Michael, Azrael (Death).	299 n. 9
J1704§,	Stupid ethnic group (or race).	298 n. 8
J1738,	Ignorance of religious matters.	298 n. 8
J1738.9§,	Ignorance of religious service (ritual).	298 n. 8
J1740§,	Foolish attempt to punish (reprimand) the higher powers (God, the angels, fate, etc.).	298 n. 8
J1742.6.1§,	Religious rituals misunderstood.	298 n. 8
J1768.2.1.1§,	‡Youth thought to be a man's lover (actually his son).	13 n. 27
J1798§,	‡Which is real and which is illusory? (The actual is mistaken for imaginary (dream-like)—or the imaginary is mistaken for actual.)	179 n. 652
J2203.1§,	‡Sinful interest in a beautiful person rationalized: "God is beautiful and loves beauty."	13 n. 27
J2215.7.1§,	‡God created temptation but ordered worshippers not to give in.	13 n. 27

K. Deceptions

K0303.2.3.1§,	‡Corpse (cadaver) stolen or borrowed.	298 n. 5
K1339.6.1§,	Priest seduces woman (at confession).	75 n. 245
K1397.1§,	Seduction (rape) by threatening woman with defamation and causing scandal: woman fears for her reputation and surrenders.	75 n. 245
K1872.3.5§,	‡Magical incantation ("fix") written on catfish, which is released back into water.	304 n. 36

K2054.3§, ‡Thief returns stolen goods so as to avert further search for culprit: he thinks he is about to be discovered. 305 n. 40

L. Reversal of Fortune

L0111.5.1§, Child born of brother–sister incest as hero: “Son of own maternal-uncle.” 159 n. 587

M. Ordaining the Future

M0109.1§, ‡They said the thief, “Swear [to your innocence].” he thought, “Relief (escape) has come [in spite of guilt]!” 301 n. 19

M0117.0.1§, *nadhr*/“*nadr*”. Conditional vow: pledge to perform certain (good) act if prayer is answered (request is granted). 18 n. 47, 307 n. 51

M0119.8.6§,_cf. ‡Swearing by love. 302 n. 28

M0135.3§, Spouse no-remarriage pact: each of husband and wife vows never to remarry if the other dies first. 127 n. 449

M0147§, Conditional “divorce-vow:” oath that divorce will have occurred unless certain matter is brought to pass. 305 n. 41

M0209§, Reminder of unfulfilled (forgotten) vow: recipient must execute own part of pledge (bargain). 18 n. 47

M0209.1§, Dream as reminder of unfulfilled vow. 307 n. 51

M0210, Bargain with devil. 19 n. 49

M0302.0.3§, *'istikhârah*: prophesying by asking God to indicate right choice (through dream, opening Holy Book, rosary). 179 n. 651

M0302.7, Prophesy through dreams. 179 n. 651, 305 n. 43

M0302.8.1§, Prophesying by opening Holy Book. (Bibliomancy: *fatḥ al-kitâb*). 300 n. 17

M0341.0.5§, Person knows time of own death. 123 n. 425

M0411.1, Curse by parent. 18 n. 45, 159 n. 586

M0411.2, Beggar’s curse. 299 n. 9

M0412.4.1§, ‡Curse: A “Take!” B: “May you get taken by Azrael!” 46n 142

M0414.0.1§, cf. Luck (“Time,” dice, etc.) cursed. 307 n. 53

M0511.1.1§, ‡Supplication: blessed be the womb and the loins that brought person into being. 159 n. 586

N. Chance and Fate

N0001.8§, ‡Betting between man and supernatural being (jinni, devil, ogre, etc.). 157 n. 581

N0100.0.1§, “Luck” as nonsacred entity: e.g., *bakht, ḥaẓẓ* (luck), *zahr* (dice), *zaman* (Time). 307 n. 53

N0100.2§,	‡Predestined sinning (fornication, theft, killing, or the like).	136 n. 491
N0101.0.1§,_cf.	‡"The pen has [already] run with His judgment."	297 n. 3
N0101.0.2§,	‡"What is written on the forehead will [inevitably] be witnessed by the eye."	25 n. 68
N0101.5.1§,	‡"Caution does not prevent [(alter)] fate."	25 n. 68
N0120.1.1§,	‡Entity (animal, human, object, time-period, etc.) associated with certain events becomes harbinger of omen.	188 n. 675
N0127,	The auspicious (lucky) day (days).	28 n. 80
N0127.3,	Thursday as lucky day.	28 n. 80
N0134.2.1§,	One-eyed person brings bad luck.	188 n. 676
N0134.2.1.1.1§,	‡Person with bad left eye surely brings bad luck.	188 n. 676
N0182.2§,	Seemingly worthless objects (onion skin, garlic skin, etc.) turn into gold.	108 n. 360
N0190§,	‡Fate's inexplicable inequalities (injustices).	194 n. 690
N0190.0.1§,	‡Inexplicable inequality in possessions (wealth, power, etc.).	297 n. 2
N0190.0.1.1§,_cf.	‡"God grants whomsoever He pleases without limit."	297 n. 2
N0207§,	‡Person (animal, bird) with certain qualities fated to perform task.	159 n. 587
N0207.1§,	‡Task can be performed only by person with certain social qualities (e.g., kinship ties, name, or the like).	159 n. 587
N0207.2§,	‡Task can be accomplished only by person with certain physical qualities (e.g., lines on palm of hand form certain figures).	159 n. 587
N0207.4§,	‡Task can be performed only by using animal (bird) with certain physical qualities (e.g., color, size, age, etc.).	92 n. 305
N0276§,	‡Culprit thinks he is about to be discovered: he remedies the situation by undoing what he has done (e.g., secretly replace stolen goods, correct the forgery, etc.).	305 n. 40
N0384.0.2§,	"Insanity (loss of senses) due to calamity or fright."	304 n. 39
N0385.5§,	Person refuses to tell dream because listener did not say, "Good, if God wills."	180 n. 653
N0619.1§ (formerly-N619§),	Lucky (haphazard) guess.	301 n. 19
N0649.1§,	‡Amulet containing irrelevant materials (or nonsensical phrase) given to patient: yet patient is healed.	299 n. 11
N0681.3.0.5§,	Incest believed impossible. Mystically repulsive: "Blood's howling," "Flesh repels [same] flesh."	159 n. 588
N0793.1§,	‡Mystic (spiritual) experience while in cave (in mountain).	305 n. 43
N0812,	Giant or ogre as helper.	105 n. 345

N0812.2,	Giantess [(ogress)] as helper.	105 n. 345
N0815.3§,	al-Khiḍr as helper.	164 n. 606

P. Society

P0007.1§,	‡Role strain (role conflict): effects of difficult choices between conflicting obligations.	300 n. 17
P0070§,	Sherifs: descendants of Prophet Mohammed (*'ashrâf, sâdah*).	155 n. 573
P0071§,	‡Rights (privileges) of *'asharâf.*	155 n. 573
P0072§,	‡Restrictions on personal conduct in interacting with a *sharîf* (Hashemite).	155 n. 573
P0145.1§,	*majlis*: arbitration-council by notables.	304 n. 35
P0192.10§,	*magdhûb*: half-wit, "village-idiot."	306 n. 50
P0193.3§,	‡Curious crowd of people.	301 n. 19
P0201,	Inherent enmity between members of a family.	300 n. 17
P0215.5.1§,	‡Husband suspects (accuses) his wife of stealing from him.	303 n. 29
P0219§,	Aging wife's fears (anxiety).	96 n. 314
P0230.0.1§,	Childlessness.	300 n. 16, 302 n. 26
P0230.0.1.1§,	Misery of childlessness (person weeps).	75 n. 245
P0231.0.1§,	Mother of a son more valuable.	199 n. 696
P0233.10.1§,	‡Father in vision reproves son for neglecting duties.	306 n. 48
P0240.3§,	Mother's spiraling demands: price for her heart's contentment.	298 n. 6
P0243.0.2§,	‡Father-love for daughter.	300 n. 17
P0245§,	Parent's prayer (blessing or curse) always answered.	18 n. 45, 159 n. 586
P0253,	Sister and Brother.	138 n. 500, 302 n. 26
P0253.3.1§,	Sister favors brother over her husband.	304 n. 39
P0253.9.1§,	Sister becomes insane due to death of brother.	304 n. 39
P0261.1§,	‡Father-in-law and son-in-law.	300 n. 17
P0261.3§,	‡Husband jealous of his wife's father.	300 n. 17
P0262.5§,	‡Mother-in-law and her daughter's husband (son-in-law).	303 n. 29
P0264.1§,	Bad relations between wife and husband's sister.	301 nos. 18, 21, 302 n. 26
P0275,	Foster son.	302 no. 26
P0293.2.1.1§,	Boys take after their maternal-uncles.	158 n. 583
P0294.0.1§,	Paternal-aunt (*¿ammah*).	302 n. 26
P0294.0.1.1§,	Girls take after their paternal-aunts.	158 n. 583
P0294.1.3.1§,	‡Sister (*¿ammah*) adopts her brother's child.	302 n. 26

P0297.0.1§, "The maternal-uncle can swear, 'This is my sister's son, but a paternal-uncle, cannot swear 'This is my brother's child.'" 71 n. 234

P0321, Salt of hospitality. Eating a man's salt creates mutual obligation. 125 n. 434

P0350§, Sufi brotherhood (religious order). 303 n. 31, 305 n. 43

P0352.1.1§, "He who has no *shaikh* has Satan for a leader." 54 n. 172

P0426.0.4§, ‡Ignorant cleric. 305 n. 41

P0426.0.8§, ‡Immoral (corrupt) cleric (judge). 75 n. 245

P0426.2.1.1§, ‡Unreasonable mystic (sufi)—seems to speak nonsense. 305 n. 42

P0426.2.3§, ‡Wanderer ("*sawwâḥ*"). (Usually due to mystical urges or disappointments especially in love.) 150 n. 555

P0465§, Faith-healer, or exorciser. 299 n. 11

P0465.1§, *zâr*-priestess (*kodyah*). 302 n. 26

P0501.2§, Political indifference (quietism). 155 n. 571

P0522.0.2.2§, ‡*fatwâ*: rendering religiously binding opinion on a case (situation) that had not been heretofore legislated for. 305 n. 41

P0522.2§, Vendetta: a life for a life, of equal (or higher) social rank. 113 n. 386

P0526.0.3.1§, ‡Judging by legal precedent (*qiyâs*). 305 n. 41

P0526.3.1§, ‡Conditions that render a person not responsible for consequences of own actions (e.g., being a minor, insanity, drunkenness, etc.). 79 n. 256, 300 n. 13

P0528§, ‡Euthanasia: mercy killing. Person (animal, demon, etc.) put to death so as to relieve his suffering. 20 n. 52

P0529.2.3§, ‡Wife (unintentionally) divorced because of "divorce-vow" (divorce-oath) by husband. 305 n. 41

P0529.4§, *muḥallil*-marriage: legal device for reinstating thrice-divorced wife. 140 n. 507

P0529.6§, Nuptial prohibition (nonsexual marriage): legal device by which sexual intercourse between "married couple" is prohibted. 164 n. 606

P0530§, Legal *kafâ'ah*: marriage is to be between persons of equal social class (status compatibility required). 140 n. 507

P0530.1§, Marriage annulled (betrothal voided) upon discovering that groom comes from low class (non-*kafâ'ah*). 140 n. 507

P0535, Éric fines (imposed for personal injury etc.). 304 n. 35

P0553.3§, ‡Flying device (airplane, air-ship) as weapons. Air force. 112 n. 380

P0553.5.1§, ‡Elephant used as weapon. 112 n. 380

P0605§, Living (sleeping) arrangements within the household. 160 n. 589

P0613, Charon's fee: putting coin in dead person's mouth to pay for ferry across Styx. 125 n. 435

P0681.1.1.1§,	Mourning: verbal expressions (wailing, dirge, elegy, *¿adîd, nadb*).	298 n. 7
P0717.2§,	‡Tribal characteristics (private)—latrine functions (defecation and urination, attending call of nature).	271 n. 769
P0727.1§,	‡Characteristic behavior of Turks (Sarkassians, etc.).	298 n. 8
P0750.0.1§,	Basis for social differentiation and stratification.	140 n. 509
P0750.0.1.0.1§,	‡Natural (prevailing) social order: high is high and low is low.	140 n. 509
P0750.0.1.1§,	"An eye does not top an eyebrow."	140 n. 509
P0750.0.1.2§,	"One's fingers are not alike."	140 n. 509
P0750.0.3§,	Basis for social equality.	140 n. 510
P0750.0.3.1§,	"We all are children of Eve and Adam."	140 n. 510
P0750.0.3.2§,	"We all are children of nine [month of pregnancy]."	140 n. 510
P0775.2.0.2.1§,	‡"The veiled charity (*ḥasanah*) is [given] through buying-and-selling."	15 n. 34
P0775.2.1.1§,	‡Gratuity given (demanded) at occurrence of happy event ("*ḥalâwah*/*ḥulwân* of" graduation, safe return, birth of child, etc.).	307 n. 51
P0776.4§,_cf.	‡Living beyond one's means (on borrowed funds).	306 n. 50
P0781§,	Local history reckoned in relation to a person's past disgraceful act.	184 n. 664
P0788.1§,	‡Excessive shame (dishonor, disgrace: *¿âr, khizy*) from violation of mores.	305 n. 40
P0788.2§,	‡Social control by shaming (publicly) into compliance (conformity).	300 n. 17, 13, 301 n. 19
P0790.0.1§,	‡Need for interacting with others.	119 n. 408
P0790.0.1.2§,	‡Invitation to have "conversation."	119 n. 408
P0794.2.1§,	‡Murder committed (war waged) to ensure one's own survival.	20 n. 52
P0951§,	‡Lunar calendar celebrations (formal religious: Jewish, Islamic, etc.).	305 n. 43
P0991.1§,	Saint's day festival (*mawlid*, "*mûlid*").	305 n. 43
P952§,	‡Solar calendar celebrations (Coptic, agricultural, *'ifrinjî, mîlâdî*, etc.).	305 n. 43

Q. Rewards and Punishments

Q0028.1§,	‡Repeated pilgrimage saves from hell fires (entitles to eternal salvation).	300 n. 14
Q0094,	Reward for cure.	304 n. 35
Q0101,	Reward fitting to deed.	128 n. 451

Q0172.0.3§,	‡Reward in the hereafter (Heaven) preferred to that in the here-and-now.	35 n. 107
Q0172.0.4§,	Animal admitted to heaven.	57 n. 185
Q0172.0.5§,	Admission to Paradise without judgment (for prophets, martyrs, children, the insane, etc.).	126 n. 441
Q0172.4.1§,	Palace in heaven (Paradise) assigned to person as reward.	298 n. 6
Q0174.0.1§,	*'ash-shafâ¿ah al-¿uẓmâ*: God grants person (prophet, saint) the boon of releasing souls from hell.	142 n. 515, 305 n. 42
Q0221.3,	Blasphemy punished.	21 n. 55
Q0225.5§,	‡Practice of nether magic (sorcery, witchcraft) punished as *kufr* (disbelief).	304 n. 35
Q0331.3§,	‡Conceit (arrogance) punished.	48 n. 152
Q0340,	Meddling punished.	306 n. 50
Q0411.16§,	‡Death as punishment for blasphemy.	21 n. 55
Q0432.0.1§,	Divorce as punishment.	306 n. 50
Q0471,	‡Spitting in face as punishment.	298 n. 8
Q0496§,	Shame and disgrace as punishment.	305 n. 40
Q0501.2.4§,	Punishment of Hârût and Mârût. Hung upside down over pool, tongues cannot reach water.	55 n. 180
Q0522.0.1§,	‡Self-punishment as penance.	306 n. 50
Q0550,	Miraculous punishments.	87 n. 287
Q0550.0.3.1§,	‡"A killer will (inevitably) be killed [i.e., die by violence] even after a [long] while."	19 n. 51
Q0551.6.8§,	‡Supernatural (magic) sickness as punishment for practicing witchcraft (sorcery, nether magic).	299 n. 11
Q0552.2.3.2.6§,	‡Earth swallows arrogant (vain, proud) person.	48 n. 152
Q0560,	Punishments in Hell.	298 n. 6
Q0560.5§,	‡Eternal life in Hell for certain cardinal sins (e.g., disbelief, murder, etc.).	113 n. 386
Q0580,	Punishment fitted to crime.	128 n. 451

R. Captives and Fugitives

R0181.3§,	Demons (jinn) escape forced labor through accidental knowledge of captor's (Solomon's) death.	58 n. 190

S. Unnatural Cruelty

S0011.9§,	Runaway father (deserts family).	63 n. 210
S0110.0.2§,	Suicide intended (attempted).	306 n. 50

S0263.7§,	‡Husband is to kill his wife so as to use her blood in magic ritual to open treasure.	307 n. 52
S0481.3.1§,	‡Animal cruelly beaten for desecrating place of worship.	115 n. 394

T. Sex

T0039.1§,	‡Lover protects (defends) the beloved.	298 n. 7
T0039.1.1§,	‡Girl would enter dead sweetheart's corpse (in grave) so that she my answer interrogative angels (correctly) on his behalf.	298 n. 7
T0100.0.9.3§,	‡Marriage to gain control over wife.	304 n. 35
T0109.1§,	Patrilocal residence: bride moves to home of groom's family.	301 n. 18
T0109.1.1§,	Bride's troubles at in-laws' home.	301 n. 18
T0109.1.1.1§,	Wife put to hard work by her in-laws.	301 n. 18
T0109.1.1.2§,	‡Wife kept out of husband's family matters (or she is overlooked).	301 n. 18
T0109.3§,_cf.	Matrilocal residence: groom moves to home of bride's family.	300 n. 17
T0127.2§,	‡Husband and wife as contrasts: in temperament.	304 n. 35
T0127.4§,	‡Husband and wife as contrasts: In morality (honesty, gratitude, dutifulness, etc.).	307 n. 52
T0149.1.1§,	Maternity (childbirth) is indisputable, paternity (impregnation) is not.	71 n. 234
T0156.0.1§,	‡Interim (substitute) groom proves to be the better man: husband for a night is kept.	140 n. 507
T0198.3.4§,	‡Unhappy (angered) husband leaves marital home.	63 n. 210
T0331.4,	No place secret enough for fornication.	18 n. 210
T0339§,	Husband averse to conjugal relations.	303 n. 29
T0339.3§,	‡Aversion to conjugal relations motivated by desire to marry someone else (dislike for present spouse).	303 n. 29
T0357§,	‡Groom does not touch his bride due to prohibition by third party (or tabu).	304 n. 36
T0405.3§,	"Sister's nakedness or exposure."	304 n. 39
T0405.3.0.2§,	Groom experiences mystical paralysis at defloration of bride: they prove to be brother and sister.	159 n. 588
T0415.8§,_cf.	Sister who desires a son sired by her brother achieves her goal: the unsuspecting brother.	302 n. 26
T0429.1.1§,	‡Faith-healer (exorcist, etc.) seduces (seeks to seduce) client.	75 n. 245
T0481.0.2§,	‡Lustful regard—("fornication-with-eye").	13 n. 27

T0511.1.3.3§,	Conception from eating eggplant.	203 n. 715
T0512.6,	Conception from drinking sperm.	54 n. 175
T0531.2§,	Conception from "wearing" semen-stained clothing item.	70 n. 230, 300 n. 16
T0547,	Birth from virgin.	167 n. 618
T0570.2.1§,	‡Appearance of "*waḥmah*" (birth-mark) as result of mother's craving.	16 n. 38
T0572.5§,	Miscarriage (or stillbirth).	301 n. 18
T0579.5,	Saint performs miracles while yet unborn.	305 n. 42
T0591,	Barrenness or impotence induced by magic.	205 n. 720
T0591.0.2§,	*rabṭ*: supernaturally induced impotence.	205 n. 720, 304 n. 36
T0591.5§,	Pregnancy induced by abnormal means (magic, philtre, potion, etc.).	199 n. 700
T0591.5.1.1§,	‡"*ṣûfah*": inseminating agent placed on ball of wool (cotton or the like) and "worn" by woman (i.e., placed in vagina as love-philtre). Typically, it contains human semen.	70 n. 230, 300 n. 16
T0591.5.2.1§,	‡Barren (childless) woman sacrifices her honor to become pregnant.	75 n. 245
T0604.4.1.1§,	"Baby talk (by an adult)."	94 n. 311
T0670,	Adoption of children.	302 n. 26

U. The Nature of Life

U0001§,	‡Not every thing (practice, value) that one is instructed exists really exists as presumed.	3 n. 6
U0005.2§,	"Fire begets ashes."	186 n. 670
U0005.3.1§,	‡"He (God) may bring forth a corrupt descendant from the loins of a pious predecessor"—(and vice versa).	186 n. 670
U0022.3§,	‡Injustice: suffering more than other members of one's own generation (group).	307 n. 53
U0090§,	Credibility depends on characteristics of source.	147 n. 531
U0230.0.2§,	Cardinal sins (*kabâ'ir*), and minor sins (*ṣaghâ'ir*).	15 n. 33
U0230.0.2.1§,	‡Hierarchy of sins: great, greater, and greatest sin.	15 n. 33
U0240,	Power of mind over body.	299 n. 11
U0240.1§,	‡Beliefs may heal or cause sickness.	299 n. 11
U0248.0.3§,	‡Wants affect perception (cognitions).	301 n. 19
U0248.2§,	Fear affects perception.	301 n. 19
U0265.1§,	‡Prayer-times as timing devices (they mark times of day).	17 n. 42

U0300§, Relativity of perception: "Adaptation level" (judgment depends on circumstances, objects of comparison, frame of referece, or context.) 82 n. 264

U0303§, Relativity of perceiving physical attributes (size, shape, form, etc.). 89 n. 296

V. Religion [and Religious Services]

V0001.1.3.1§, ‡Spiritually advantageous death. 173 n. 639

V0001.1.3.2§, ‡The cult of martyrdom (*al-'istishhâd, al-shahâdah*). 173 n. 639

V0001.1.3.2.1§, ‡Veneration of martyred mortal (prophet, saint; e.g., ¿Îsâ,/Jesus, al-Ḥusayn, etc.). 173 n. 639

V0001.1.3.3§, ‡Experiencing guilt as effect (result) of martyrdom-based religious faith. 170 n. 630

V0001.1.3.3.1§, ‡Self-torture (self-punishment) as atonement for martyred sacred person (prophet, saint). 170 n. 630

V0001.2.2.1§, *siḥr shayṭânî/bi-es-suflî* rituals as veneration (worship) of devil. 299 n. 11

V0001.4.2, Worship of the sun. 111 n. 373

V0002.1§, Jinn and humans are required to worship God. 108 n. 360

V0003§, Required religious services ("pillars," corners, *'arkân, furûḍ*) and fundamental beliefs. 17 n. 42

V0003.3§, ‡Required alms-tax (*zakâh*, given out yearly—compare: *tithe*). 108 n. 360

V0004.2§, Being bearer of God's words outweighs worldly assets of wealth and high status. 140 n. 507

V0004.3§, ‡*al-sunnah*: the preferred way for Moslems, as set by the Prophet. 298 n. 8

V0004.4§, ‡Extrareligious exercise (prayers, fasting, etc.) undertaken for extrareligious credit. 170 n. 630

V0004.4.1§, ‡Religious exercise performed in spite of disability receives more religious credit. 303 n. 33

V0004.4.4.1§, ‡Cursing Eblis (Satan) earns extrareligious credit. 303 nos. 32, 33

V0004.5§, *munjiyât/"munaggiyât"* (soul-savers): deeds that serve as "intercessors" to spare person from Hell. 16 n. 37, 299 n. 10

V0004.5.1§, ‡Dutifulness toward parents as intercessor. 16 n. 37, 124 n. 430

V0004.5.2§, ‡Mentioning God as intercessor. 16 n. 37

V0004.5.3§, ‡Prayers (ritual) as intercessor. 16 n. 37

V0004.5.4§, ‡Ramadan-fasting as intercessor. 16 n. 37

V0004.5.5§, ‡Cleansing self of the effects of coition (by bathing) as intercessor. 16 n. 37

V0004.5.6§,	‡Pilgrimage and *¿umrah* as intercessor(s).	16 n. 37
V0004.5.7§,	‡Almsgiving as intercessor.	16 n. 37
V0004.5.8§,	‡Kindness to relatives (other than parents) as intercessor.	16 n. 37
V0004.5.9§,	‡Preaching the exercise of *ma¿rûf* (benevolence, kindness) and the avoidance of *munkar* (malevolence, the sinful) as intercessor.	16 n. 37
V0004.5.10§,	‡Being mild mannered as intercessor.	16 n. 37
V0004.5.11§,	‡Fearing God as intercessor.	16 n. 37
V0004.5.12§,	‡Deceased offspring (child) as intercessor.	16 n. 37
V0004.5.12.1§,	‡Pious (saintly) offspring as intercessor.	16 n. 37
V0004.5.13§,	‡Placing one's hope (faith) in God as intercessor.	16 n. 37
V0004.5.14§,	‡Shedding a tear due to experiencing awe toward God as intercessor.	16 n. 37
V0004.5.15§,	‡Assuming that God is compassionate as intercessor.	16 n. 37
V0004.5.16§,	‡Praying on behalf of the Prophet as intercessor.	16 n. 37
V0004.5.17§,	‡*tashahhud* (uttering the testimony that "There is no god but God") as intercessor.	16 n. 37
V0006§,	Expiatory-deed (*kaffârah*): negligence in religious exercise made-up for by additional good deeds.	15 n. 35
V0006.0.1§,	‡Minor good-deeds erase cardinal misdeeds (sins).	15 n. 35
V0007§,	Religious exercise (fasting, pilgrimage, prayers, etc.) performed by proxy (surrogate).	18 n. 44
V0008§,	‡Divine commandments (as prescribed in formal religious dogma).	18 n. 44
V0008.9.2.0.1§,	‡Communal (group, *jamâ¿ah*) exercising of religious service favored (e.g., prayers, pilgrimage).	303 n. 33
V0009§,	Religious faith conquers adversity (sickness, despair, poverty, etc.).	307 n. 52
V0052,	Miraculous power of prayer.	302 n. 28
V0052.16§,	‡Prayer (to God) for one's own death—"O God, take me away!" "O God, grant me death!" etc.	89 n. 294
V0061.8.2§,	Moslem buried into earth (in shroud) without coffin.	38 n. 120
V0061.8.2.1§,	‡Burial into earth returns man (Adamite) to place of origin (from where he had come: "Ashes to ashes, dust to dust").	38 n. 120
V0065.0.5.1§,	*¿Âshûrâ*: commemoration of martyrdom.	170 n. 630
V0065.7§,	Visiting the dead.	127 n. 447
V0065.7.1§,	Holiday(s) spent in cemetery with deceased relatives.	127 n. 447
V0065.7.2§,	Feasting at cemetery (cookout in graveyard).	127 n. 447
V0065.8§,	‡Deeds done (at grave-side) on behalf of the deceased—("mercy-soliciting" deeds).	299 n. 10

V0065.8.1§,	‡Holy text recited "over the soul of deceased."	299 n. 10
V0065.8.2§,	‡Food given to the needy "over the soul of deceased" ("mercy-crackers" or the like).	299 n. 10
V065.8.3§,	‡Money given the poor "over the soul of deceased."	299 n. 10
V0066.0.1§,	Instructing the dead before burial as to how to answer interrogative angels (*talqîn*, "prompting").	124 n. 432
V0067.6§,	Objects (money) buried with the dead for use by the soul.	125 n. 435
V0067.6.1§,	Protecting the deceased by answering correctly for him.	298 n. 7
V0068,	Preparations for burial.	304 n. 38
V0085.5.1.1§,	‡Desiring death (and burial) in "Holy Land."	300 n. 14
V0085.5.2§,	‡Burial in holy land.	300 n. 14
V0085.5.2.1§,	‡Burial near the Prophet.	300 n. 14
V0090§,	Miraculous effects of invoking God's attributes (*basmalah, ḥasbanah, ḥawqalah*, etc.).	17 n. 41, 194 n. 692, 206 n. 726
V0090.0.1§,_cf.	‡Miraculous power of uttering God's name.	302 n. 28, 303 n. 33
V0090.0.3§,	‡Miraculous power of uttering name of sacred person (prophet, saint).	302 n. 28
V0090.1§,	Unintentional curse: accidental calling on God's name destroys tyrant (devil, etc.).	17 n. 41, 303 n. 33
V0093.1§,	Ecstasy (trance) through religious dancing (*dhikr*, "*zikr*").	23 n. 64, 303 n. 31
V0093.2§,	‡Ecstasy (trance) through sacrilegious dancing (*zâr*-ritual).	98 n 324
V0113,	Shrines.	304 n. 38
V0113.0.1.1§,	‡Shrine built (repaired) at demand of (dead) saint.	178 n. 647, 304 n. 38
V0206.1§,	‡Awe-inspiring sacred person.	148 n. 545
V0210,	Religious founders. [Messengers of God.]	304 n. 37
V0211.0.4,	Christ as prophet [(founder)].	304 n. 37
V0213§,	Abraham as prophet (founder): God's bosom-friend.	304 n. 37
V0214§,	Moses as prophet (founder).	304 n. 37
V0215§,	Mohammed as prophet (founder).	304 n. 37
V0219.1§,	‡Pleading to prophet (messenger of God) for help.	302 n. 28
V0220.0.1§,	Hierarchy (stratification) of saints.	165 n. 612
V0220.0.1.2§,	‡Limited number of cardinal saints may exist at one time or era: one, four, seven, forty, or the like, e.g., four *'aqṭâb* (Axes), four *'awtâd* (Pegs), seven *'abdâl* (Substitutes), etc.	149 n. 552
V0220.0.2§,	‡Classes of sacred persons (prophets, saints) according to amount and source of gnosis (knowledge) they possess.	150 n. 556
V0220.0.4§,	Woman saint (*shaikhah/waliyyah/qiddîsah* "saintess").	304 n. 39
V0220.0.5.2§,	‡Saints are endowed with blessedness (*barakah*).	145 n. 525

V0220.0.6§,	Miracle-like manifestation by saint (*karâmah*).	4. n. 16
V0220.0.7§,	Pleading to a saint for help.	302 n. 28
V0220.0.7.1§,	‡Pleading to saint (holy man) for a [blessed] "Glance!"	302 n. 28
V0220.0.8§,	Vengeful saint.	120 n. 414, 307 n. 51
V0220.0.8.2§,	‡Harmful saint: uses his supernatural powers to cause mischief.	149 n. 549
V0220.0.8.2.0.1§,	‡Saint causes mischief to enforce demand.	304 n. 38
V0220.0.10§,	‡Saint with specific responsibility (e.g., saintly ability to find the lost aid with physical labor, etc.).	165 n. 612
V0220.0.10.1§,	‡Saint with supernatural ability to locate (guide) the lost.	165 n. 612
V0221,	Miraculous healing by saint.	148 n. 540, 306 n. 49
V0221.0.1.4§,	‡Glance (*naẓrah*) from saint's eye heals (bestows power).	207 n. 729
V0223,	Saints have miraculous knowledge.	149 n. 548
V0223.2.1§,	Saint detects unclean (tabu) food.	148 n. 543
V0223.3,	Saint can perceive thoughts of another man and reveal hidden sins.	149 n. 547, 305 n. 41
V0225,	Saint in several places at once. [*min 'ahl-al-khuṭwah, min al-'abdâl.*]	148 n. 539, 150 n. 554
V0228.0.1§,	Infallibility (*ʿiṣmah*: immunity from errancy) of *imâms* and certain saints.	148 n. 543
V0228.5.1§,	Saint walks upon water.	148 n. 537
V0229.27§,	Saint mystically appears and aids person in distress.	306 n. 49
V0229.27.0.1§,	‡Saint (holy man, etc.) materializes before birth.	305 n. 42
V0231,	Appearance of angel.	49 n. 154
V0231.1.0.1§,	Angel with bird face.	49 n. 154
V0231.7§,	Angel with animal-face.	49 n. 154
V0231.9.1§,	‡Angel in human form (shape)—general.	49 n. 154
V0233.0.1.1.2§,	‡Angel of death has multiple eyes).	46 n. 141
V0233.3.3§,	‡Angel of Death (Azrael) offers pious mortal (saint, prophet) respite.	123 n. 425
V0233.3.4§,	‡Angel of Death gives mortal choice as to how (when) to die.	123 n. 425
V0236.5§,	Hârût and Mârût as fallen angels.	55 n. 177
V0238,	Guardian angel.	51 n. 163
V0238.0.1§,	‡Guardian angel abandons mortal (under certain circumstances).	51 n. 163
V0247.1.2§,	Chain of command among angels.	48 n. 150, 299 n. 9
V0249.9§,	Angels with specific assignments: "Angel of such and such." Angel controls the elements, insects, disease, etc.	47 n. 146

V0250.0.1§,	*as-sayyidah* Zaynab: supreme saint (culture-heroine, "The Lady," "The Chieftainess," etc.).	302 n. 27A
V0301.1§,	‡"Deeds are [judged] according to intent (*niyyât*)."	17 n. 40
V0310.1§,	‡Religious universe (all of God's creation—animate and inanimate—worship).	117 n. 398
V0310.1.2§,	‡Objects praise or worship God.	117 n. 398
V0311.4.1.1§,	‡The tomb as a person's home ("everlasting house") till the hereafter.	80 n. 259
V0318.1§,	‡Submission to fate (God's prejudgment: *qaḍâ', qadar*) a mark of true faith.	182 n. 659
V0324§,	‡Heresy: rejecting (doubting) predestination.	112 n. 376
V0331.8.1§,	‡Christian jinni (fairy).	303 n. 30
V0334.1§,	‡Moslem jinni (fairy).	99 n. 325
V0357§,	‡Holy war (crusade, jihâd-*muqaddas*, etc.).	171 n. 634
V0371§,	Moslem traditions about *al-kitâbiyyîn* ("People-of-the-Book:" Jews and Christians).	141 n. 511
V0384§,	‡Extreme interpretations of holy text.	157 n. 579
V0384.1§,	‡Extreme religious interpretations of religious dogmas concerning females (as social category).	157 n. 579
V0455§,	Hierarchy within religious orders.	153 n. 566
V0462.7,	Ascetic cleric never smiles.	305 n. 43
V0462.8.0.2§,	*shaṭḥ*: philosophical unorthodoxy due to ascetic immersion.	23 n. 64, 176 n.642, 305 n. 42
V0462.8.0.3§,_cf.	*'ingidhâb*: madness (dissociation) from ascetic immersion.	303 n. 31
V0462.8.0.3.1§,	‡Epileptic ecstasy (convulsions).	176 n. 642
V0463,	Religious martyrdom.	172 n. 635
V0463.0.1§,	‡Martyrs are alive (in heavens).	172 n. 636
V0463.0.2§,	‡Hierarchy (stratification) of martyrs.	172 n. 635
V0463.0.2.1§,	‡Highest ranks of martyrs are situated closest to God.	303 n. 32
V0463.2,	‡First martyr: John the Baptist.	173 n. 638
V0463.2.0.1§,	‡First martyr.	173 n. 638
V0463.2.0.1.1§,	‡First martyr: Abel son of Adam murdered by his brother (Cain).	173 n. 638
V0463.2.1§,	‡John the Baptist: Lord and leader of all martyrs on Day of Judgment.	173 n. 638
V0463.7§,	‡Occurrences (and deeds) that entitle a person to the rank of martyrdom.	172 n. 635
V0463.7.1§,	‡Martyrdom: giving own life for a religious cause ("for the sake of God").	172 n. 635
V0463.7.1.1§,	‡Martyrdom: giving own life for a national (patriotic) cause.	172 n. 635

V0463.7.1.2§,	‡Martyrdom: giving own life for justice.	172 n. 635
V0463.7.2§,	‡Martyrdom: having one's life taken away ("sacrificed") to save lives of many.	172 n. 635
V0463.7.3§,	‡Martyrdom: being unjustly killed (executed).	172 n. 635
V0463.7.4§,	‡Martyrdom: dying from (for) love.	172 n. 635
V0463.7.5§,	‡Martyrdom: dying accidental, unnatural (violent) death (e.g., drowning, burning, etc.).	172 n. 635, 303 n. 32
V0463.7.5.1§,	‡Martyrdom: to be killed (devoured) by sacred animal.	172 n. 635
V0463.7.5.2§,	‡Martyrdom: to die during childbirth.	172 n. 635
V0510.1.1§,_cf.	‡Image of deity speaks in vision to devotee.	306 n. 49
V0510.3.1§,	‡Sacred person (prophet, saint) speaks in vision to mortal.	304 n. 38
V0513.0.1§,	A prophet's vision (dream) is a command from God.	181 n. 655
V0513.0.3§,	Visions (*ru'â*) are one of forty-six signs of being a prophet (sent by God).	180 n. 654
V0515,	Allegorical visions.	180 n. 653
V0517§,	Instructive sleeper's vision or dream (*ru'yàh, manâm*).	180 n. 653, 306 n. 49
V0521.1.1§,	Prophet Mohammed as the Intercessor (*ash-shafî¿*).	305 n. 42
V0521.2.2§,	‡Saint's followers as spiritual (social) club.	306 n. 49
V0521.2.2.1§,	‡Saint favors his (her) proteges (*maḥâsîb*).	151 n. 560
V0540.0.1§,	‡Providence (God's wisdom) is behind seemingly apparent injustice (i.e., "The Lord moves in mysterious ways").	19 n. 50, 20 n. 52
V0545.2§,	‡Person performs an act of benevolence: God forgives sins of sinners for the sake of that act.	303 n. 33

W. Traits of Character

W0003.0.1§,	‡Conduct (behavior, traits) of person of noble character.	158 n. 585
W0004§,	‡Religiosity (piety): most favorable trait of character.	139 n. 506
W0026.1§,	Job's patience.	87 n. 287
W0035.4.1§,	‡"Justice of Omar ([Ibn al-Khaṭṭâb])."	144 n. 521
W0037.8§,	‡*dhimmah*: economic, political, governmental, conscientiousness, and honesty.	141 n. 511
W0124.0.1§,	‡Moody person ("*bi-ghazâlah*").	121 n. 419
W0154,	Ingratitude.	303 n. 29
W0163§,	‡Infamy (notoriety).	305 n. 40
W0164.1§,	Promoters of self-esteem.	199 n. 696
W0164.1.1§,	Belief that one is target for Evil Eye promotes self-esteem.	209 n. 735, 306 n. 47

W0164.1.10§, ‡Fertility (fecundity) as promoter of self-esteem. 199 n. 696

W0172.5.1.1§, ‡Self-pity song (poem): *mawwâl 'aḥmar* ("red-*mawwâl*"), *ghurbah*-song ("song of strangerhood," "being a stranger") i.e., "the blues." 307 n. 53

W0180.1§, ‡"If I cannot have it (him, her, etc.), no one else will!" Useful thing (object, person, etc.) destroyed so that others may not benefit from it. 109 n. 364

W0181, Jealousy. 300 n. 17

W0195.0.1§, ‡"Everyone that has been blessed (endowed) with an asset is envied." 209 n. 735

W0195.0.2§, ‡Angels envious (jealous) of Adam for being favored by God (being His exquisite creation, successor on Earth, etc.). 208 n. 732

W0199§, Self-deception (rationalization, regression, projection, etc.). 187 n. 674

W0199.3.3§, ‡Blaming "the other" ("people/society," "adversaries/enemies," "blamers," "censurers," "the envious," etc.). 205 n. 723

W0202.1.1.1§, ‡Indicator of femininity: women's speech-tone (soft, low-key). 94 n. 311, 203 n. 717

W0205.0.1§, ‡Authoritarian person's pride. 300 n. 13

W0206§, Authoritarian person's (father's) "love." 300 n. 13

W0250.1§, ‡Basic types of personality (character) reckoned according to the elements. 156 n. 575, 301 n. 19

W0250.1.1§, ‡Personality type: *hawâ'î* ("aerial," whimsical, impressionable). 156 n. 575

W0250.1.2§, ‡Personality type: *turâbî* ("earth-prone," melancholic, passive). 156 n. 575

W0250.1.3§, ‡Personality type: *nârî* ("fiery," explosive–aggressive). 156 n. 575

W0250.1.4§, ‡Personality type: *mâ'î* (Aquarius, aquatic, "watery"). 156 n. 575

W0251§, Beliefs (theories) about composition of character (personality). Implicit (folk) Personality (theory). 160 n. 590

W0251.1§, Physiognomy (*firâsah*): the judging of character. 157 n. 577

W0251.2.1§, *makhwal* ("maternal-unclehood") as basis for judging character. 158 n.583

W0256§, Stereotyping: generalization of a trait of character, from person to group (and vice versa). 160 n. 590

W0256.1§, Stereotyping: ethnic and national traits. 160 n. 590, 298 n. 8

W0256.2§, Stereotyping: social class. 160 n. 590

W0256.5§, Stereotyping: racial traits. 160 n. 590

W0256.6§, Stereotyping: gender (sex) traits. 160 n. 590

W0256.6.3.1§, ‡Women's character: "crooked [like a] rib." 136 n. 488
W0256.8§, Stereotyping: physical traits and appearance—general. 160 n. 590

X. Humor

X0420.3§, Jokes on *fu'ahâ*'s abuse of religious services (sale of benefices). 299 n. 10
X0420.3.1§, ‡Fee (alms) given insufficient for receiving redemption (admittance to Paradise). 299 n. 10
X0600, Humor concerning races or nations. 298 n. 8

Z. Miscellaneous Groups of Motifs [and Symbolism]

Z0001.1.2§, ‡Clerical speech (parlance): formulas that are formal, archaic, grammatically conscious (but not necessarily correct). 299 n. 10
Z0010.1.2§, ‡Beginning formula: reversal of nature in former age (e.g., "When animals could talk," "When the rocks were still soft," etc.). 139 n. 503
Z0010.8.1§, ‡Emphasis: character addressed by full name, each component separately (e.g., "O you Zayd, O you Son of ¿Amr!" "Yâ Sindibâd, yâ Baḥarî!," etc.). 305 n. 41, 306 n. 49
Z0013.9.1§, ‡Speaker wards off evil effects of own speech (words). 301 n. 22, 206 n. 726
Z0013.11.1§, ‡Uncertainty about accuracy of truthful report: "And God knows best," "And God is Omniscient" (or the like). 42 n. 133
Z0066.4.1§, ‡Endearment: to be referred to (or addressed) in the diminutive. 94 n. 311
Z0071.6, ‡Formulistic number: nine (99, 900, 999, 99,999, etc.). 297 n. 1
Z0071.12, Formulistic number: forty. 46 n. 140
Z0084.1.1§, Insult: mention of mother's name. 71 n. 233
Z0092.2§, Formulas of astronomical (celestial) distances (thousands of years walk or flight). 50 n. 156
Z0095§, Puns (homophony). 210 n. 739
Z0097§, ‡Alliteration (simple, plain). 210 n. 739
Z0105§, ‡Shape (form, color) symbolism: association based on similarities of visually perceived properties of object. 203 n. 715
Z0108§, ‡Sound (name) symbolism: association based on sound similarities (homophony). 77 n. 251, 303 n. 34
Z0110, Personifications [of abstractions]. 100 n. 328
Z0111, Death personified. 43 n. 136

Z0112.3.1§,	‡Possessing spirits ("'asyâd-ez-zâr," jinn, etc.) personified.	302 n. 25
Z0113.1§,	Life (the world) personified as a beautiful young woman.	100 n. 329
Z0122.7.1§,	‡Temporal forces ("Time") responsible for man's misfortune (troubles).	100 n. 329
Z0125.1§,	‡*ma¿rûf* (benevolence, kindness, chivalry, etc.) personified. (Usually as an angel named Ma¿rûf, "*shaikh* Ma¿rûf," or the like.)	186 n. 671
Z0126.9.1.1§,	‡Sleep as "the lesser Death."	121 n. 420
Z0127,	"Sin personified."	35 n. 106
Z0129§,	Religious exercise personified: "Benefit of" alms giving, prayers, fasting, pilgrimage, etc.	34 n. 101
Z0129.9§,	‡Deeds (acts) personified—miscellaneous.	34 n. 104
Z0139.9.3.2§,	‡Water jug (jar, bottle, inkwell, etc.)—female, vagina, womb (or body orifice).	199 n. 700, 301 n. 20
Z0139.9.4§,	‡Dry container (box, chest, trunk, bag, pocket, etc.)—anal or vaginal orifice.	210 n. 739
Z0145.2§,	Green: auspicious color.	121 n. 421
Z0159.3.1§,	‡Symbolism: moon—beauty.	305 n. 41
Z0166.1.1§,	Symbolism: pomegranate (apple, orange)—breast.	302 n. 27
Z0166.3.2.3§,	‡Eggplant–testicles. ("*bedingân*"/*bâdhingân* = *baiḍel-gân*: literally, "eggs of the jinn" [i.e., jinn's testicles]).	203 n. 715
Z0167§,	Tree (plant) symbolism.	43 n. 136
Z0167.2.2.1§,	Symbolism: carob tree—decay.	58 n. 190
Z0170.0.1§,	‡Symbolism: eating (swallowing, chewing)—sexual activity.	302 n. 27
Z0179.1.2.1.1§,	‡Submission: kneeling.	28 n. 79
Z0179.1.2.1.1.1§,	‡Submission: kissing ground (before a certain person).	28 n. 79
Z0183.0.1§,	Meaning of a name.	302 n. 27A
Z0183.6§,	"Mother-of-_" (*'Omm/'Umm-_*).	302 n. 27A, 304 n. 39
Z0183.7§,	‡Personal names formed from one of God's names (deus-nymics)—e.g., ¿Abd-Allâh, ¿Abd-al-Karîm, 'Amatu-Allâh, etc.	13 n. 26
Z0186.4.3.1§,	Symbolism: wearing (slipping on, pounding "it" into, etc.) a shoe or garment—sexual intercourse.	87 n. 290
Z0186.4.3.4§,	‡Symbolism: spirit-possession (being "epileptic," worn or ridden by spirit)—sexual desire (lust).	89 n. 297
Z0186.4.4§_cf.,	‡Catfish (eel)—penis.	303 n. 30
Z0186.4.4§,	‡Catfish (eel)—penis.	303 n. 30
Z0186.5§,	Symbolism: pitcher's spout—penis.	199 n. 700
Z0186.8§,	‡Symbolism: building (palace, house, inn, etc.)—female.	302 n. 27

Z0186.8.2.1§,	‡Symbolism: oven (furnace)—vagina, womb.	126 n. 443
Z0186.9.2.1§,	Symbolism: "the red eye"—vagina, anus.	126 n. 443
Z0187§,	‡Symbolism: Vessel (boat, ship, etc.)—female.	302 n. 27A
Z0194.3.1.2§,	‡Cock: quarrelsomeness.	154 n. 570
Z0197.3.1§,	‡Knife, sword, dagger, saw, etc.—penis (male).	302 n. 27

Bibliography

¿Abd al-Mun¿im, Amîrah. "Educated Women Become Oriented Toward the zâr, while Non-literate Women Turn to Psychiatry". In *Al-Ahram*, Dec. 2, 1971, p. 3.

¿Abd-al-Laḥîf M. al-Barghûthî, *ḥikâyât jân min Banî-Zayd (Jinn-Tales from Bani-Zayd [Palestine])*. (Jerusalem, 1979)

¿Abd-al-Raḥmân, ¿Â'ishah. *al-sayyidah Zaynab baṭalat Karbalâ' (Sayyidah Zaynab: The Heroine of Karbala)*. Cairo, 1966.

¿Abd-al-Ṣamad, zay al-Dîn, *al-Jawahir al-saniyyah* (Cairo: 1860).

¿Abdul-Wahhâb, Ḥasan. "bid¿at istiḥḍâr al-'arwâḥ" (The Deviant Innovation of Soul Summoning). In: *Al-Azhar*, Vol. 31, pp. 1158–1159.

¿Idwî (al-) al-Ḥamzâwî, Ḥasan. *Mashâriq al-'anwâr fî fawz 'ahl al-'i¿tibâr (Daybreaks Concerning Salvation for Those Who Pay Heed [to Signs])* (Cairo, 1863).

¿Uthmân, ¿Abd-al-Raḥmân Mḥammad, ed. *Sunan al-Tirmidhî (Sunan* [according to] *al-Tirmidhî's)* Vol. 3. (Cairo: al-Madanî, 1964).

¿Uways, Sayyid. *Ẓâhirat 'irsâl al-rasa'il 'ilâ ḍarîh al-'Imam al-Shâfi¿î (The Phenomenon of Letter-Sending to the Shrine of Imam al-Shafi¿î)*, Cairo, 1965.

Abu al-Naṣr, ¿Abdul-Galîl ¿Îsa. *Ṣafwat ṣaḥîḥ al-Bukhârî* [The Choicest from Bukhari's Authenticated (Utterances of Prophet Muhammad)]. Cairo, 1953.

Ahram (-al). (Aug. 17, 1970). "The Mentally Ill Outside the Fences of el-¿Abbâsiyyah [Asylum]. For the First Time: Cairo Tries the Treatment of the Ill Mentally and Psychologically in Public Hospitals Amidst People and Society."

Ahram (-al). (Feb. 16, 1971). "Professional Women in *zâr* (University Graduates Constituted 8 Percent); Meanwhile, the Study Indicated that Nonliterate Women Were Beginning to Visit Psychiatries," p. 3.

Ahram (-al). (Dec. 2, 1971). "Educated Women Become Oriented Toward the *zâr*, While Non-Literate Women Turn to Psychiatry," p. 3.

Ahram (-al). No. 41833 (Jun. 19, 2001). "What *al-Naba'* [Newspaper] Published Is Injurious to the Church and Offends the Hollies of Christianity."

¿Alâ' (Abu-al) [al-Ma¿arrî]. *Luzûmiyyât*. Cambridge, Mass.: Harvard University, 1984.

Alhefnee, Abudlmunem. *Encyclopedia of Psychology & Psycho-Analysis.* 2 vols. Cairo: Madbouli, 1978.

Ali, Abdallah Yousuf, tr. *The Glorious Kur'an.* [Beirut], 1973.

Âlûcî (al-), Maḥmûd Shukrî. *Bulûgh al-'arab fi ma¿rifat aḥwâl al-¿Arab* (*The Attainment of Goal in Knowing of the Affairs of Arabs*). M.B. al-Atharî, ed. 3 vols. Cairo, [1964].

Amîn, Ṣâdiq. *al-Da¿wah al-Islâmiyyah farîḍah shar¿iyyah wa-ḍarûrah bashariyyah* (*The Summons to Islam is a Required Duty and a Human Necessity*). ¿Ammân: Jam¿iyyat ¿Ummâl al-Maṭâbi¿ al-Ta¿âwuniyyah, 1982.

Amîn, Aḥmad. *Qâmûs al-¿âdât wa al-taqâlîd wa al-ta¿âbîr al-miṣriyyah* (*Dictionary of Egyptian Customs, Traditions and Expressions*). Cairo, 1953.

Ammar, Hamed. *Growing Up in an Egyptian Village.* New York: Octagon, 1966.

Anonymous. "al-dhikr ¿ala 'awaa al-mûṣîqâ wa al-ghinâ' (*dhikr* to the Sounds of Music and Singing)". In: *Al-Azhar*, Vol. 31, p. 377.

Anonymous, "'ithbât al-rûḥ al'insâniyyah ḥissiyyan (Proving [the Existence]) of the Human Soul Tangibly." In: *Al-Azhar*, Vol. 12, No. 5 (1941), pp. 375–377, 433–437.

———. Qiṣṣat Sârrah wa al-Khalîl (The Story of Sarah and [God's] Bosom Friend). [Pamphlet, "16-pager"] Cairo, Maktabat al-Jumhûriyyah al-¿Arabiyyah, c. 1950?.

Arnold, Edwin. *Pearls of the Faith, or Islam's Rosary, Being the Ninety-Nine Beautiful Names of Allah (Asma-el-Husna), etc.* London: Trubner, 1883.

Assman, Jan. *Moses the Egyptian: the Memory of Egypt in Western Monotheism.* Cambridge: Harvard University Press, 1997.

Aswad (el-), El-Sayed. "Death Ritual in Rural Egyptian Society: A Symbolic Study." In: *Urban Anthropology and Studies of Cultural Systems and World Economic Development* Vol. 16 (1987), pp. 205–241.

———. "Aṣṣabr fi at-turath ash-sha'bî al-miṣ[r]î dirdsah anthropolojiyyah (The Concept of Patience in Egyptian Folklore)." Alexandria: Munsh'at al-Mar'âf [??], 1990.

———. "The Cosmological Belief System of Egyptian Peasants." In: *Anthropos*, Vol. 89 (1994), pp. 359–377.

———. *Religion and Folk Cosmology: Scenarios of the Visible and Invisible in Rural Egypt.* Westport, CT: Praeger, 2002.

AT/AaTh: See Antti Aarne and Stith Thompson.

AUC: The American University in Cairo Collections. Private Archives.

Azhar (*al-*), Vol. 2, pp. 263–271.

Azhar (*al-*). Vol. 12, No. 10 (1941), pp. 583–586.

Azhar (*al-*). Vol. 31 (1959–1960). "*God's Justice Vindicated.* (The Angel and the Hermit)—[apparent misdeeds explained]," the narrative belongs to Tale-type 759, p. 647.

Azhar (*al-*). (1981) al-Qahirah : Majma¿ al-Buhûth al-Islâmiyyah. Continues: Jami' al-Azhar. *Majallat al-Azhar.*

Aziz, Yassin M. "Personal Names of Address in Kuwaiti Arabic." In: *Anthropological Linguistics*, Vol. 20, No. 2 (1978), pp. 53–63.

Azraqî (al-), Ibrâhîm. *Tashîl al-manâfi¿ fî al-ṭibb wa al-ḥikmah* (*The Facilitation of Benefits in Medicine and Wisdom*), Cairo: Ṣubaiḥ, 1963.

Badawi, El-Said, and Martin Hinds. *A Dictionary of Egyptian Arabic: Arabic-English.* Beirut, 1986.

Bahjat, Aḥmad. *al-Burâq.* Madînat Naṣr, al-Qâhirah: al- Zahrâ', 1989.

Barakat, Halim. *The Arab World: Society, Culture, and State.* Berkeley, CA: University of California Press, 1993.

Barakât, M.K. *Al-¿Ilâj al-nafsî (Psychiatries)*. Cairo, n.d.

Barghûthî (al-), ¿Abd al-Laîf M. *ikâyât jân min Banî-Zayd (Jinn-Tales from Bani-Zayd* [Palestine]) Jerusalem, 1979.

Basset, René. *Mille et un contes, récites & légendes arabes*, 3 vols. Paris, 1924–1926.

Bausani, A. "Bahâ'ism". In: *Encyclopedia of Islam*, Vol. 1 (1986), pp. 915–918.

Berger, Morroe. *The Arab World Today.* New York: Doubleday, 1964.

Berlo, D.K. *The Process of Communication*. New York, 1961.

Blackman, Winifred S. "Sacred Trees in Modern Egypt." In: *Journal of Egyptian Archaeology*, Vol. II (London, 1925), pp. 56–57.

———. "The Karin and Karineh." In: *Journal of the Royal Anthropological Institute*, Vol. 56 (1926), pp. 163–169.

———. *The Fellâhîn of Upper Egypt*. London: Frank Cass, 1968.

Bousquet, J.H. "La baraka, le mana et le dunamis de Jesus." In: *Revue africaine* Vol. 91 (1947), pp. 166–170.

Brown, L. Carl. *Religion and State: The Moslem Approach to Politics.* New York: Colombia University Press, 2000.

Budge, Ernest A. Wallis. *Egyptian Ideas of Future Life.* New York: AMS Press, 1976.

———. *Egyptian Heaven and Hell*, Vol. III, p. 159. Chicago, IL: Open Court Publishing Company, 1974.

———. *Egyptian Tales and Romances: Pagan, Christian, and Muslim.* London, 1931.

———. *The Gods of the Egyptians, or Studies in Egyptian Mythology*. 2 vols. London: Methuen, 1904.

———. *The Mummy*, 2nd ed. New York, 1894, 1974.

Bûnî (al-), A. *Manba¿ 'uṣûl al-ḥikmah* (*The Source of the Foundation for Wisdom*). Cairo, 1965.

———. *Shams al-ma¿âarif al-Kubrâ* (*The Great Sun of Knowlege*). Cairo, n.d.

Burton, Richard F. *Arabian Nights: The Book of the Thousand Nights and a Night.* Vols 1–10. London, 1894.

Bûshî (el-), Muḥammad ¿Abd-al-Ḥamîd. "hal yantafi¿u al-mayyitu bi-¿amali al-ḥayy? (Would the Dead Benefit from the Deeds of the Living)." In: *Al-Azhar*, Vol. 31 (1959), pp. 707–715.

Bushnaq, Inea. ed., tr., *Arab Folktales.* New York, 1986.

Carapenzano, Vincent. *The Ḥamadsha: A Study in Moroccan Ethnotherapy.* Berkeley, CA, 1973.

Chauvin, Victor. *Bibliographie des ouvrages arabes ou relatifs aux arabes: publiés dans l'Europe chrétienne de 1810 à 1885*. 12 vols. Liège, 1892–1922.

Chejne, Anwar G. *The Arabic Language: Its Rôle in History.* Minneapolis, MN, 1969.

Christian Answers Network. www.christiananswers.net/q-aig/aig-c004.html.

Colin, G.S. "Baraka, Blessing". In: *Encyclopedia of Islam*, Vol. 1 (1986) p. 1032.

Coult, Lyman H. *An Annotated Bibliography of the Egyptian Fellah*. Coral Gables, FL: University of Miami Press, 1958.

Critchfield, Richard. "The Persistent Past: Passing the Buck to Demons," In: *The New Republic*, November 8, 1975, p. 15.

Ḍabbî (al-), al-Mufaḍḍal. See Ibn-¿Âṣim.

Damîrî (al-), Muḥammad ibn Mûsâ. *Ḥayât al-ḥayawân al-kubrâ*. wa bi-hâmishihi kitâb *¿ajâ'ib al-makhlûqât wa gharâ'ib al-mawjûdât*, by . . . Zakariyyâ ibn Muḥmmad al-Qazwînî (The Greater Life of Animals. On its Margins is the Book of *The Wondrous of the Creatures* . . .), 2 vols. Cairo: al-Maktabah al-Tugâriyyah al-Kubrâ, 1963.

Danner, Victor. *The Islamic Tradition: An Introduction*. New York, Amity House, 1988.

David, Rosalie A. *The Ancient Egyptians: Religious Beliefs and Practices*. 2nd rev. ed. Portland, OR: Sussex Academic Press, 1997.

Davis, Allison, Gardner, Burleigh, and Gardneret Mary R. *Deep South: A Social Anthropological Study of Caste and Class.* Chicago, IL: University of Chicago Press, 1941.

Digwî (al-), Yûsuf. "al-fatâwà wa al-'aḥkâm–karâmât al-'awliyâ' (Fatwas and Judgments—Saints' Miracle-Like Manifestations)" In: *Nûr al-Islâm*, Vol. 1, No. 10 (1931), pp. 764–770.

———. "'ayna maqarru al-'arwâḥ ba¿da al-mawt? (Where is the Abode of Souls After Death?)." In: *Naur al-Islam* 3 (1932), No. 4, pp. 263–271.

———. "al-ḥasad wa al-ruqyah minh (Envy and [How to] Confront it Through [Religious] Incantation)." In: *Al-Azhar*, Vol. 12, No. 8 (1941), pp. 161–162.

———. "ta¿allum al-siḥr wa al-ḥukm fîh (The Learning of Magic, and [How it is] Judged [in Islam])." In: *Al-Azhar*, Vol. 12, No. 8 (1941), pp. 490–491.

Diyâb, Fawziyyah. *al-Qiyam wa al-¿âdât al-'igtimâ¿iyyah* (*Social Values and Customs* [in Egypt]). Cairo: Dâr al-kitâb al-¿Arabî, n.d. [c. 1966].

DOTTI: See Hasan El-Shamy, *Types of the Folktale in the Arab World.*

EI, *Encyclopedia of Islam* (Leiden, the Netherlands, 1960–2004).

Elias's Modern Dictionary: English-Arabic, 6th ed. Cairo, 1969.

Elsarrag, M.E. "Psychiatry in the Northern Sudan: A Study in Comparative Psychiatry." In: *British Journal of Psychiatry*, Vol. 114 (1968), pp. 945–948.

English, Horace B. and Ava C. English. *A Comprehensive Dictionary of Psychological and Psycho-Analytical Terms.* New York: David McKay, 1966.

Faruqi (al-) Louis Ibsen. "Muwashshaḥ: A Vocal Form in Islamic Culture." In: *Ethnomusicology*, Vol. 19, No. 1 (January, 1975), pp. 1–29.

Faulkner, Dr. Raymond. *The Egyptian Book of the Dead: The Book of Going Forth by Day*. 2nd ed. With an introduction by Dr. Ogden Goelet, and a preface by Carol Andrews. San Francisco, CA: Chronicle Books, 1998.

Freud, S. *Mosesand Monotheism.* New York: Vintage Books, 1939.

Funûn (al-). *Al-Funûn Al-Sha¿biyyah* (*Folk Arts*). Cairo: Ministry of Culture, 1966–1971.

Gätje, H. *Koran und Koranexegese*. Zürich and Stuttgar: Artim, 1971.

Gawhary (al-), Mohamed M. "Die Gottesnamen im magischen Gebrauch in den al-Buni Zugeschriebenen Werken." Ph.D. Dissertation. Bonn, 1968.

———. "al-siḥr al-rasmî wa al-siṛ al-sha¿bî: naẓrah gadîdah . . . (Professional and Folk Magic, ...)" In: *The National Review of Social Sciences*, Vol. 7 (Cairo, 1970), No. 2, pp. 3–23 (English abstract, pp. 23–29).

———. "al-ginn fi al-mu¿taqad al-sha'bî (Jinn in the [Egyptian] Folk Beliefs)." In: *The National Review of Social Sciences*, Vol. 9, No. 1 (Cairo, 1972), pp. 95–131.

———. *¿ilm al-folklore.* (Cairo, 1980), Vol. 2, p. 431.

Gibbûsly (al-) [??], Ibrahîm. "al-Shafâ¿ah." In: *Nûr El-Islam Review*, Vol. 1, No. 10 (1931), pp. 771–779.

Gilsenan, M. *Saint and Sufi in Modern Egypt: An Essay in the Sociology of Religion.* Oxford: Oxford University Press, 1973.

Gindî (al-), A.S. *al-Ginn bayna al-haqâ'iq wa al-'asâṭîr* (*Jinn Between Facts and Legends*). 2 vols. Cairo: Maktabat al-Anglo, 1969–1970.

Goldziher, Ignác. *Madhâhib al-tafsîr al-'Islamî.* Translation of: *Die Richtungen der Islamischen Koranauslegung* (Leiden, the Netherlands: Brill 1920 and 1952); ¿Abd al-Ḥalim al-Naggâr tr. Cairo: al-Khângî, 1955.

———. "Die Heiligenverehrung in Islam." In: *Muhammedanische Studien*, Vol. 2 Hildesheim: Olms, 1961.

———. *al-¿Aqîdah wa al-sharî¿ah fî al-Islâm*, (translation of: *Vorlesungen über den Islam*: Heidelberg, 1910/1925) Moḥammad Y. Mûsâ, ¿Alî H. ¿Abd-al-Qâdir, ¿Abd-al-¿Azîz ¿Abd-al-Ḥaqq, trs., eds. Cairo: Dâr al-Kitâb al-Ḥadîth, and Baghdad: al-Muthannâ, 2nd ed., 1964.

———. *Vorlesungen über den Islam* (*Introduction to Islamic Theology and Law*), Andras and Ruth Hamori, trs.; with an introduction and additional notes by Bernard Lewis. Princeton, NJ: Princeton University Press, 1981.

GMC: see Hasan El-Shamy. *Folk Traditions of the Arab World.*

Green, Roger Lancelyn. *Tales of Ancient Egypt, Selected and Retold.* New York: Henry Walack, 1967/1968.

Greenberg, Joseph Harold. *The Influence of Islam on a Sudanese Religion.* Monograph of the American Ethnological Society, No. 10. New York, 1946.

Ḥabîb, ḥâhâ. In: *Nûr el-Islam Review*, Vol. 3, No. 3, p. 217.

Ḥabîb, G. "Khidr Ilyâs." In: *al-Turâth*, Vol. 1, No. 11 (1969), pp. 32–35.

ḥâliÃ-A.R. In: *al-'Adab*, Vol. 1, pp. 109, 121–122, 125. Lebanon.

Ḥaqqî, Yaḥyâ. *Qindîl 'Omm-Hâshim* (The Lantern of . . . [i.e., *sayyidah* Zaynab]). [A novel] Cairo, 1954.

Ḥasan, Sa¿îd Muḥammad. *Haqâ'iq al-Isrâ' wa-al-Mi¿râj* (The Facts About the *'Isrâ'* and the *Mi¿râj*). Cairo: 1977.

Ḥasan, Sulymân Maḥmûd. *al-Rumûz al-tashkîliyyah fî al-siḥr al-sha¿bî* (*Material Cultural Symbols in Folk Magic*). Cairo: Hay'at Quṣûr al-Thaqâfah, 1999, pp. 269–272/Gohar-bibl.

Ḥawwâs, ¿Aabd-el-Ḥamîd, and Ṣâbir El-¿Aadily. "Mulâḥaẓât ḥawla ba¿ḍ al-ẓawâhir al-folkloariyyah fî muḥâfaẓat al-Beḥairah (Observations on Some Folkloric Phenomena in Behairah Governorate)." In: *Al-Funûn*, No. 12 (Cairo, March 1970), pp. 62–83.

Haykal, Moḥammad Ḥasanayn. "taḥḍîr al-'arwâḥ." In: *Al-Ahram*, June 4, 1971, pp. 1, 3.

Hanauer, James E. *Folklore of the Holy Land: Moslem, Christian, and Jewish.* London, 1907.

Hartmann, Martin. "Über die Muwashshaḥ genannte Art der Strophengedichte bei den Arabern." In: *Actes der X congres international des Oreintalists.* (Geneva, 1894), Vol. 2, pt. 3, pp. 47–67. Ktaus reprints- Nendeln-Leichtenstein, 1972.

Haykal, Moammad Asanayn. "taḥḍîr al-'arwâḥ." In: *Al-Ahram*, June 4, 1971, p. 1, 3.

Haykal, Moḥammad Ḥusayn. *Zaynab: manâdhir wa 'akhlâq rîfiyyah* (*Zaynab: Rural Scenes and Morals*) (1914). Cairo: 3rd ed., 1967.

Heidel, Alexander. *The Gilgamesh Epic and Old Testament Parallels.* Chicago, IL: University of Chicaco Press, 1970.

Heyob, Sharon Kelly. *The Cult of Isis Among Women in the Graeco-Roman World.* Leiden, the Netherlands: Brill, 1975.

Ḥigâb, A.M.j. *al-¿Iẓah wa al-'i¿tibâr fî ḥayât al-Sayyid al-Badawî al-dunyawiyyah wa ḥayâtihi al-barzakhiyyah* (The Moral [Lesson] and Example in al-Sayyid al-Badawî's Worldly and Isthmusian Life). Cairo, 1966 or 1967. 8/17/1970.

Hornblower, G.D. "Traces of a Ka Belief in Modern Egypt and Old Arabia." In: *Islamic Culture* (1927), pp. 426–430.

———. "The Laying of a Ghost in Egypt." In: *Man*, Vol. 31: p. 167, August 1931, p. 164.

Ḥusayn, Sayyid ¿Abd-Allâh. *al-Ginn: fî dhikr gamî¿ 'ahwâl al-ginn* (*Jinn: Concering Mentioning all Ginn Affairs*). Cairo: al-Ḥalabî, n.d. [1970?].

Ibn al-Kalbî, Abu-al-Mundhir Hishâm. *Kitâb al-'aṣnâm* (*The Book of Idols*). Aḥmad Zakî, ed. Cairo: al-maktabah al-¿Aarabiyyah, 1960/1965.

Ibn Kathîr, Ismâ¿îl ¿Umar. *al-Bidâyah wa al-nihâyah fî al-târâkh* (*The Beginning and the End in History*). 14 vols. Cairo, Kurdstân Press, [1928 or 1929].

Ibn Khaldûn, ¿A. 1958. *The Muqaddimah*, Franz Rosenthal, ed., tr., 3 vols. New York: Pantheon, 1958.

Ibn al-Sharîf, Maḥmûd. *al-Ḥayâh al-barzakhiyyah* (*Isthmusian Life*). Cairo: al-Sha¿b, 1972.

Ibn Shuhyd, Abû ¿Âmir Aḥmad. *al-Tawâbi¿ wa al-zawâbi¿* (*The Treatise of Familiar Spirits and Demons*) James T. Monroe, tr. ed. Berkeley, CA: U. of Cal. Press, 1971.

Ibn Sîrîn, Muḥammad. *Tafsîr al-'aḥlâm al-kabîr* (*The Greater Interpretation of Dreams*). Cairo: Ṣubaih, 1963.

Ibn ¿Âṣim, Abu-Ṭâlib al-Mufaḍḍal. *al-Fâkhir*, ¿Abd-al-¿Alîm al-Ṭaḥâwî, ed. Cairo, 1960.

Ibshîhî (al-), Muḥammad 'ibn Ahmad. *al-Mustaṭraf fî kull fann mustaẓraf* (*The Quaint in Every Art that is Considered Cute*), 2 vols. Cairo: al-Ḥalabî, 1952.

ICAES: IX International Congress of Anthropological and Ethnological Sciences, held at Chicago, Illinois in September 1973. Abstract No. 0637, p. 61.

Idrîs, Yûsuf. *al-Naddâhah*. Cairo: Maktabat Gharîb, 1978.

Inhorn, Marcia C. *Quest for Conception. Gender, Infertility, and Egyptian Medical Traditions*. Philadelphia, PA: University of Pennsylvania Press, 1994.

Ions, Veronica. *Egyptian Mythology*. Middlesex: Paul Hamlyn, 1968.

Ismâ¿îl, ¿Abd al-Raḥmân (Efendî). *ṭibb al-rukka*. (Cairo, 1892–1894) or *Old Wives Medicine*. See Walker, John.

Jâḥiẓ (al-), Abu ¿Uthmân ¿Amr Ibn Baḥr. *kitâb al-Ḥayawân*. (*The Book of Animal*) 8 vols., ¿Abd-al-Salâm Muḥammad Hârûn, ed., 7 vols. Cairo: al-Ḥalabî, 1938–1945.

Jahn, Samja al-Azharia, ed., tr. *Arabische Volksmärchen*. Berlin: Akademie-Verlag, 1970.

Jazîrî (al-), ¿Abd al-Ramân. "ziyârat al-qubûr wa 'ittikhâdh sukkânihâ shufa¿â' ¿inda Allâh (The Visiting of Graves and Taking their Inhabitants as Intercessors with God)". In *Al-Azhar*, Vol. 12, No. 10 (1941–1942) pp. 583–586.

Karm (al-), 'Usâmah. *ḥiwâr ma¿a al-ginn. 'asra¿ ṭuruq ¿ilâg al-'amrâḍ al-musta¿ṣiyah bi al-Qur'ân* (*Discourse with Jinn. The Fastest Methods for Treating Incurable Illnesses with Koran*). Cairo: Madbûlî, 1990.

Kennedy, John G. "Nubian Zar Ceremonies as Psychotherapy." In: *Human Organization*, 26 (1967), pp. 185–194; also in: *Nubian Ceremonial Life*, (1978), pp. 203–223.

Kennedy, Mark C., ed., *Psychiatry and the State. Catalyst*. (Special isuue: Fall, 1972). Petersborough, Ontario: Trent University Press.

Khaldûn, Ibn. *The Muqaddimah*: *An Introduction to History*, tr. Franz Rosenthal. Vol. 3, pp. 171–182. New York: Pantheon Books, 1958.

Khalîfah, Muḥammad ¿Abd al-Ẓâhir. *Kitâb al-dâr al-barzakhiyyah, mina al-mawt ilâ al-ba¿th* (*The Book of Isthmusian-Abode: From Death till Resurrection*). Cairo, n.d. [1973?].

Kisâ'î (al-), Muḥammad ibn ¿Abdallâh. *Qiṣaṣ al-'anbiyâ'* (Vita Prophitorum), Isaac Eisenberg, ed. Leiden, the Netherlands: Brill, 1922.

"Kitâb as-siḥr al-ḥalâl fî naẓm al-mawwâl—wa bihi mawwâl Shilbâyah": ta'lîf I.S. el-Shaikh, ghinâ' Ḥusain ¿Abd-el-Salâm Khalîfah (*The Book of the Legitimate Witchcraft. . . .*). Cairo: Gumhûriyyah Bookshop, n.d. [pomphlet, "16-pager"]

Kline, Nathan S. "Psychiatry in Kuwait." In: *British Journal of Psychiatry*, Vol. 104 (1963), pp. 766–774.

Klunzinger, C.B. *Upper Egypt, its People and its Products.* London, 1878.
Kouly (al-), Fawqiyyah. "Islam Prohibits Magic and Contact with Jinn, and [Secular] Law Considers These Acts Crimes of Impostery." In: *Al-Ahram,* (Sep. 8, 1978) p. 11.
Krech, David, Richard S. Crutchfield, and Egerton L. Ballachey. *Individual in Society.* New York: McGraw Hill, 1962.
Kriss, R. and H. Kriss-Heinrich. *Volksglaube in Bereich des Islams.* 2 vols. Wiesbaden: Harrassowitz, 1960–1962.
Lane, Edward William. *An Account of the Manners and Customs of the Modern Egyptians.* New York: Dover, 1973.
Laoust, Emile. *Contes berbères du Maroco.* 2 vols. Paris, 1949–1950.
Liebert, Robert M. and Spiegler, Michael D. *Personality: An Introduction to Theory and Research.* Homewood, IL, 1970, pp. 80, 87–93.
Littmann, Enno. *Tales, Customs, Names, and Dirges of the Tigré Tribes. Publications of the Princeton Expedition to Abyssinia,* Vol. 2. Leiden, The Netherlands, 1910.
———. "Ahmed il-Bedawi, ein Lied auf den ägyptischen Nationalheiligen." In: *Akademie der Wissenschaft und der Literatur; Geistes und Sozialwissenschaftlichen Klasse* (Wiesbaden: 1950), No. 3, pp. 50–123.
———. *Arabische Geisterbeschwörungen aus Ägypten.* Leipzig: Otto Harrassowitz, 1950.
Loubignac, *Zaër,* Pt. I, 271–272, No. 22, Morocco.
Lyons, M.C. (Malcolm Cameron) *The Arabian Epic: Heroic and Oral Story-Telling,* 3 vols. Cambridge, England, and New York, NY: Cambridge University Press, 1995.
Macdonald, Duncan B. "From the Arabian Nights to Spirit." In: *The Moslem World,* Vol. 9, No. 3 (July 1919), pp. 336–348.
Maḥfouẓ, N. *al-Sukkariyyah.* Cairo, 3rd Printing, 1960.
Malinowski, Bronislaw. *Magic, Science, and Religion.* Garden City, NY: 1925.
Manâr (al-) Journal, volumes 1–34. Cairo, 1898–1934.
Maspero, Gaston C. *Popular Stories of Ancient Egypt,* A. Johns, tr. New York, 1967.
———. *Popular Stories of Ancient Egypt,* A. Johns, tr., Hasan El-Shamy, ed. Santa Barbara, CA, 2002 and Oxford, 2004.
Mas¿ûdî (al-), Abu al-Ḥasan ¿Ali. *'Akhbâr al-zamân* [*The Events of Time*]. Beirut: Dâr al-'Andalus, 1966.
MITON, See: El-Shamy.
Motif: See Stith Thompson, *Motif-Index of Folk Literature,* or Hasan M. El-Shamy, *Folk Traditions of the Arab World.*
Mûsâ, A., et al. "The Deforked Monk Usurped 400.000 Egyptian Pounds, and 4 Kilograms of Gold From Blackmailing Women." In: *Al-Ahram,* No. 41832 (Jun. 18, 2001), p. 30.
Nabhânî (al-), Yûsuf Ibn-Ismâ¿îl. *Gâmi¿ karâmât al-'awliyâ'* ([An Inclusive] Collection of Saints' [Miraculous] Manifestations). 2 vols. Cairo, 1962.
Nawfal, ¿A. *¿Âlam al-ginn wa al-malâ'ikah* (*The World of Jinn and Angels*). Cairo, 1968.
Nöldke, Theodor. "Die Schlange nach arabischen Volksglauben." In: *Zeitsch für Völkerpsychologie und Sprachwissenschaft.* (Berlin: Fred. Dümmler), Vol. 1 (1860), pp. 412–416.
Nûr al-Islâm (*The Light of Islam*)/(*Majallat Al-Azhar*). Cairo: Mashyakhat al-Azhar Jami¿ al-Azhar.
Nutting, A. *The Arabs: A Narrative History from Mohammed to the Present.* New York: Mentor Books, 1965.
Okasha, A. "A Cultural Psychiatric Study of El-Zar in U.A.R." In: *British Journal of Psychiatry,* Vol. 112 (1966): No. 493, pp. 1217–1221.

———. *Contemporary Medical Psychology* (in Arabic). Cairo: El-Anglo, 1969.

Osman, Ahmad I. "In Praise of the Prophet: A Structural Analysis of Sudanese Oral Religious Poetry." (Ph.D. Dissertation) Bloomington, IN: Indiana University: Brill, 1990.

Padwick, C.E. "Notes on the Jinn and Ghoul in the Peasant Mind of Lower Egypt." In: *Bulletin of School of Oriental and African Studies*, Vol. 3 (1923), pp. 421–446.

Patai, Raphael. *Golden River to Golden Road: Society Culture and Change in the Middle East.* Philadelphia, PA: University of Pennsylvania Press, 1969.

Pellat, C.H. "al-Jâḥiẓ". In: *Encyclopedia of Islam*, Vol. 2, pp. 385–387.

Peters, J.R.T.M. *God's Created Speech: A Study in the Speculative Theology of the Mu'azilî Qadi l-Gudât Abu-Ḥasan Abd Al-Jabbâr bn Ahmad Al-Hamadânî.* Leiden, the Netherlands, 1976.

Pope Shenoudah (the Third) III (Al-Baba Shenuda). "Al-rûḥ fi al-masîḥiyyah (Soul in Christianity)." In: *Al-Hilal*, Vol. 79. Cairo, December 1971.

Pritchart, James Bennett. Ed., *Ancient Near Eastern Texts Relating to the Old Testament.* Princeton, NJ: 1950, p. 29.

Prym, Eugene and Albert Socin, *Der neu-aramaeische Dialekt des ûr ¿Abdîn: Syrische Sagen und Märchen aus dem Volksmunde*, Vol. 2 (Göttingen, Germany, 1881).

Rhodokanakis, Nikolaus. *Der vulgärarabische Dialekt im Dofâr* [*Unknown Binding*]. Leipzig: Kaiserliche Akademie der Wissenschaften, Vol. 8, 1908.

Romer, John. *Ancient Lives: Daily Life in Egypt of the Pharoahs.* New York: Holt, 1984.

Ronart, Stephen and Nandy. *Concise Encyclopedia of Arabic Civilization* I. *The Arab East*; II. *The Arab West.* Djambatan: Amsterdam, 1966).

Rosenthal, F. See Ibn-Khaldun.

Rushdi, I. "maraḍ al-iklimbsia (Eclampsia)." In: *al-Muqtaṭaf*, Vol. 22 (April 1898), pp. 293–294.

Ṣâliḥ, Amad Rushdî, *al-'adab al-sh¿bî* (Folk Literature). Two vols. Cairo, 1954.

Ṣâliḥ, Ḥ.A. "al-'âthâr al-¿ulwiyyah fî al-mu¿taqdât al-¿arabiyyah (Heavenly [solar] Survivals in Arabic Beliefs)." In: *Al-Turâth* (Baghdad) Vol. 3 (1970), Nos. 5–6, pp. 37–56.

Sakr, Ahmad H. *Life, Death, and the Life After.* Lombard: Foundation for Islamic

Sayce, A.H., "Cairene and Upper Egyptian Folklore." *Folklore,* Vol. 11, No. 4 (London, 1900), pp. 351–395; and Vol. 31, No. 3 (1920), pp. 173–203.

Schimmel, Annmarie. "shafaa¿a". In: *Encyclopedia of Islam*, Vol. 9, pp. 177–179.

Schrameier, W.L. *Über den Fatalismus der vorislamischen Araber* (Bonn, Germany, 1881), pp. 12–22.

Sengers, Gerda. *Women and Demons: Cult Healing in Islamic Egypt.* Leiden, the Netherlands: Brill, 2003.

Shamy (el-), Hasan. "African World View and Religion." In: *Introduction to Africa.* P. Martin and P. O'Meara, Eds. (Indiana University Press, Bloomington, IN, 1977).

———. "Al-dîn wa al-thaqâfah: naẓrah anthropoalojiyyah (Religion and Culture: an Anthropological View)." In: Majallat al-khiṭâb al-thaqafî (*Journal of Cultural Discourse*). Vol. 1, No. 1 (Fall, 2006), pp. 1–24. (King Saûd University, Riyadh, Saudi Arabia).

———. *A Motif Index of The Thousand and One Nights.* Bloomington, IN: Indiana University Press, 2006.

———. "Belief Characters as Anthropomorphic Psychosocial Realities" (with a resumé in Arabic). In: *al-kitâb al-sanawî li-ᶜilm al-'igtimâᶜ* (Annual Review of Sociology), published by Department of Sociology, Cairo University, Vol. 3, (1982), pp. 7–36; Arabic Abstract, pp. 389–393.

———. "Belief and Non-Belief in Arab, Middle Eastern and Sub-Saharan Tales: the Religious-Non-Religious Continuum. A Case Study." In: *al-Ma'thûrât al-Sha'biyyah*, Vol. 3, No. 9 (Doha, January 1988), pp. 7–21.

———. *Brother and Sister. Type 872*: A Cognitive Behavioristic Text Analysis of a Middle Eastern Oikotype*. (Folklore Monograph Series, No. 8.) Bloomington, IN, 1979.

———. "The Brother-Sister Syndrome in Arab Culture: A Preliminary Report," IX ICAES, Supplement II, Abst. No. 1717. Chicago, IL, 1973.

———. "The Brother-Sister Syndrome in Arab Family Life. Socio-cultural Factors in Arab Psychiatry: A Critical Review." In: *International Journal of Sociology of the Family*, Special Issue, *The Family in the Middle East*, Mark C. Kennedy, ed., Vol. 11, No.2 (July–December 1981), pp. 313–323.

———. "Collective Unconsciousness and Folklore." In: *al-Majallah*, 126 (Cairo, June 1967), pp. 21–29.

———. "Emotionskomponente." In: *Enzyklopädie des Märchens* (Göttingen) Vol. 3, Nos. 4–5, pp. 1391–1395 (1981).

———. "Folkloric Behavior: A Theory [and Field Case Analysis] for the Study of the Dynamics of Traditional Culture." Doctoral dissertation, Indian University, Bloomington, IN, 1967, p. 74.

———. *Folk Traditions of the Arab World: A Guide to Motif Classification*, 2 vols. Bloomington, IN, 1995.

———. "Dr. Hasan El-Shamy Clarifies," In: *al-Qabas* (Daily Newspaper, Kuwait) 12/9/1987, No. 5594, p. 28.

———. *Folktales of Egypt: Collected, Translated and Annotated with Middle Eastern and African Parallels*. Chicago, IL: University of Chicago Press, 1980.

———. "Hermaphroditism," in *Archetypes and Motifs*, Garry and El-Shamy, eds., pp. 57–63.

———. "Mental Health in Traditional Culture: A Study of Preventive and Therapeutic Folk Practices in Egypt." In: *Psychiatry and the State*. Ed. M.C. Kennedy, a special issue of *Catalyst* (Fall 1972) Vol. 6, pp. 13–28. (Trent University, Ontario, Canada: 1972.)

———. "'Noble and Vile' or 'Genuine and False'? Some Linguistic and Typological Comments on *Folktales of Egypt*." In: *Fabula*, Vol. 24 (1983) Nos. 3–4, pp. 341–346.

———. "Oral Traditional Tales and the Thousand Nights and a Night: The Demographic Factor." In: *The Telling of Stories: Approaches to a Traditional Craft*. Morton Nøjgaard, et al., Eds. (Odense University Press, Odense, Denmark, 1990), pp. 63–117.

———. "A Response to Heda Jason's Review [of El-Shamy's *Folk Traditions of the Arab World*]: Issues Related to the Computerized Typology and Motif Classification." In: *Asian Folklore Studies*, LVII No. 2 (Nagoya, Japan, 1998), pp. 345–355.

———. "Sibling in *Alf laylah wa laylah*." In: *Marvels & Tales: Journal of Fairy-Tale Studies*. Special Issue: *The Arabian Nights: Past and Present*, U. Marzolph, Guest ed. (Wayne University Press, 2004) Vol. 18, No. 2, pp. 170–186.

———. "Sister and Brother, Motif P280." In: Jane Garry and Hasan El-Shamy, eds. *Archetypes and Motifs* (Armonk, New York, London: M.E. Sharpe, 2005), pp. 349–361.

———. "The Story of El-Sayyid Aḥmad El-Badawi with Fâṭma Bint-Birry: Part I, an Introduction." In: *Folklore Forum* (Indiana University) Vol. 10, No. 1 (1976), pp. 1–13.

———. "The Story of El-Sayyid Aḥmad El-Badawî with Faṭma Bint Berry: An Egyptian Folk Epic, part II, text and explanatory notes." In: *Folklore Forum*, Vol. 11, Nos. 3–4 (1976), pp. 140–163.

———. "The Supernatural Belief Practice System in the Contemporary Egyptian Folk Culture," Folklore Forum Monograph Series (Mimeographed). Bloomington, IN, 1973–1974.

———. "The Sure News is Up Ahead," "The Falcon's Daughter," "The Sparrow and the King," "The Cruel Mother-in-Law." [Tale texts, collected, translated, and annotated.] In: *Folktales Told Around the World*, R.M. Dorson, ed. (Chicago, IL, 1975), pp. 149–168.

———. *Tales Arab Women Tell: and the Behavioral Patterns They Portray*. Bloomington, IN: Indiana University Press, 1999.

———. "Towards A Demographically Oriented Type Index for Tales of the Arab World." In *La tradition au présent (Monde arabe)*. Ed., Praline Gay-Para, *Cahiers de Littérature Orale*, No. 23 (Paris, 1988), pp. 15–40.

———. "The Traditional Structure of Sentiments in Maḥfûẓ's Trilogy: A Behaviorist Text Analysis." *Al-ᶜArabiyya: Journal of the American Association of Teachers of Arabic* 9: l–2 (1976), pp. 53–74. Also in: *Critical Perspectives on Naguib Mahfouz*, Trevor Le Gassick, ed., pp. 51–70. Washington, DC: Three Continents Press, 1991.

———. *Types of the Folktale in the Arab World: A Demographically Oriented Approach*. Bloomington, IN, 2004.

———. "Vom Fisch Geboren (AaTh 705)." In *Enzyklopädie des Märchens* (Göttingen). Vol. 4 (1984), Nos. 4–5, pp. 1211–1218.

Shamy (el-), Hasan and Gregory Schrempp. "Union of Opposites, or Coniunctio Oppositorum." In: *Archetypes and Motifs in Folklore and Literature*, eds. Jane Garry and Hasan El-Shamy (M.E. Sharpe: Armonk, NY, 2005), pp. 481–488.

Sharabi, Hisham. *Neopatriarchy*. New York: Oxford University Press, 1988.

Shumays, ¿Abd al-Mun¿im. "al-Zâr masraḥ ghinâ'î lam yataṭawwar (The Zar [:] a Lyric Drama that Did Not Evolve)." In: *Al-Funûn al-Sha¿biyyah*, No. 17 (Cairo, 1971), pp. 72–83. (Based on an article by Zaynab Fawwâz, published in *Al-Nîl* newspaper, Cairo, 1893.)

———. *al-Ginn wa-al-¿afârît fî al-adab al-sha¿bî al-Miṣrî*. [Cairo]: al-Hay'ah al-Miṣriyyah al-¿Âmmah lil-Kitâb, 1976.

Shuqayrî (al-), M. ¿Abd-al-Salâm Khiḍr. *al-Sunan wa al-mubtada¿ât al-muta¿alliqah bi-al-adhkâr wa al-ṣalawât (Prophet's Traditions and Deviant Fads in Remembrances and Prayers)*. Cairo: maktabat al-Jumhûriyyah al-¿arabiyyah, 1969.

Simpson, William Kelly, ed. *The Literature of Ancient Egypt* (New Haven, CT: Yale University Press, 1972)

Ṭabarî (al-), Muḥammad ibn Jarîr. *Târîkh al-rusul wa al-mulûk* (*The History of Prophets and Kings*) 10 vols. Cairo: Al-Maarif 1960–1969.

Tawfîq, Riyâḍ, and Muṣṭafâ el-Ṭarâbîshî. "An Objective Pause Concerning the Innocent-[Verdict] for an Accused of Contact with *gân*." In: *Al-Ahram*, No. 34101 (Sunday, April, 24, 1980), p. 3.

Ṭawîl (al-), Tawfîq. *al-Tanabbu' bi al-gayb ¿inda mufakkirî al-'Islâm* (*Foretelling the Future in the [Philosophy of] Islam's Thinkers*). Cairo, 1945.

Te Velde, Herman. *Seth, God of Confusion*. Leiden, the Netherlands, 1967, pp. 13–26, 109–52.

Tha¿labî (al-), Aḥmad Ibn Muḥammad. *Kitâb qiṣaṣ al-'anbiyâ' al-musammâ bi al-¿arâ'is* (*The Book of Prophets's Stories*, Labelled: al-'arâ'is). Cairo, n. d.

Thompson, Stith. *Motif-Index of Folk Literature*, 6 vols. Bloomington, IN: Indiana University Press, 1955–1958.

Thompson, Stith, and Antti Aarne. *The Types of the Folktale*. FFC No. 184. Helsinki, Finland, 1961 and 1964.

Tubach, Frederic C. *Index Exemplorum, A Handbook of Medieval Religious Tales*. FFC No. 204. Helsinki, Finland, 1969.

Turâth (al-): *al-Turâth al-Sha¿bî* (Folk Legacy), monthly magazine journal issued by the Ministry of Culture and Information, Baghdad, Iraq, 1969ff. Voller, K. "Chidher." In *Archive für Religion Wissenschaft*, Vol. 12. Leipzig. (Krauss reprint) 1965.

Vuckovic, Brooke Olson. *Heavenly Journeys, Earthly Concerns: The Legacy of the mi¿raj in the Formation of Islam*. New York: Routledge, 2005.

Waardenburg, J.D.J. "Official and Popular Religion as a Problem in Islamic Studies." In: Peter Henrik Vrijhof & Jacques Waardeburg, eds. *Official and Popular Religion, Analysis of Themes for Religious Studies*. Religion and Society (The Hague/Paris: Mouton 1979) 19, pp. 340–386.

Wagdî, M.F. "'istiḥḍâr al-'arwâḥ fi Orubbah (The Summoning of Souls in Europe)." In: *Al-Azhar*, Vol. 8 (1937), pp. 105–114.

Walker, John, tr. and ed. *Folk Medicine in Modern Egypt*. Being the Relevant Parts of *ṭibb al-rukka*, or Old Wives Medicine, of ¿Abd al-Raḥmân Ismâ¿îl. London, 1934.

Wallace, Anthony F.C. *Religion: An Anthropological View*. New York: Random House, 1967.

Waugh, Earle H. *The Munshidîn of Egypt: Their World and Their Song*. Columbia, SC: U. of South Carolina Press, 1989.

Wehr, Hans. *A Dictionary of Modern Written Arabic*. Ithaca, NY, 1961.

Wensinck, A.J. 1927. "Hârût and Mârût." In: *Encyclopedia of Islam*, Vol. 2, pp. 272–273.

Wente, Edward F., "The Blinding of Truth by Falsehood." In: *The Literature of Ancient Egypt*. W.K. Simpson, Ed. (New Haven: Yale University Press, 1972), pp. 127–32.

Wente, E.F. Tr. "The Contendings of Horus and Seth." In *The Literature of Ancient Egypt*, W.K. Simpson, ed. New Haven, CT: Yale University Press, 1972, p. 123/145.

West, John Anthony. *Serpents in the Sky: The High Wisdom of Ancient Egypt*. New York: Harper, 1979.

Westermarck, Edward. *Ritual and Belief in Morocco*, 2 vols. London, 1926.

Wheeler, Brannon M. "Moses or Alexander? Early Islamic Exegesis of Quran 18: 60–65." In: *Journal of Near Eastern Studies*, Vol. 57, No. 3 (July 1998), pp. 191–215.

Wieland, Almut. *Studien zur Ginn-Vorstellung im modernen Ägypten*. Würzburg: Ergon, c1994.

Willmore, J. Seldon. *The Spoken Arabic of Egypt*. London, 1901.

Winkler, H. *Siegel und Charaktere in muhammedanische Zauberei*. In: *Studien zur Gesch. u. Kultur des islamischen Orient*. Berlin, 1930.

Winkler, Hans Alexander. *Die reitenden Geister der Toten*; eine studie über die besessenheit des 'Abd er-Râdi und über gespenster und dämonen, heilige und verzückte, totenkult und priestertum in einem oberägyptischen dorfe. Stuttgart: W. Kohlhammer, 1936.

Wollaston, Arthur R., ed. *The Miracle Play of Hasan and Husain*, Collected from Oral Tradition by Colonel Sir Lewis Pelly; rev. with explanatory notes by Colonel Sir Lewis Pelly Westmead, U. K., 1970.

Yablonsky, Lewis. *Psychodrama: Resolving Emotional Problems Through Role-Playing*. New York: Basic Books, 1976.

Yamanaka, Yuriko. "Alexander in the *Thousand and One Nights* and the Ghazâlî [i.e., Gazzâlî] Connection." In: *The Arabian Nights and Orientalism: Perspectives from East and West*, Yuriko Yamanaka and Tetsuo Nishio, eds., pp. 93–115. London: I.B. Tauris, 2006.

Ya¿qûb (ibn-), Ṭâhir, ed. "qiṣṣat al-¿ulamâ' ma¿a sayyidî Ibrâhîm" (*The Story of the Ulama with Saint Ibrâhîm*), in *qiṣṣat sayyidî Ibrâhîm ed-Disûqî wa-mâ garâ [lahu] min al-¿ajâ'ib, wa-al-gharâ'ib wa-al-karâmât*. Verified by *shaikh* Ṭ. ibn Ya¿qûb [pamphlet, "16-pager"]. Cairo: Maktabat al-Jumhûriyyah al-¿Arabiyyah, c. 1950.

Yûnus, ¿Abd al-Ḥamîd. *Mu¿gam al-fûlklûr* (*Dictionary of Folklore*). Beirut: Maktabat Lubnân, 1983.

Zbinden, Ernest. *Die Djinn des Islam und der altorientalische Geisterglaube*. Bern, Switzerland: P. Haupt, 1953.

Ziyadeh, Farahat J. "Equality (Kafa'ah) in Muslim Law of Marriage." In: *The American Journal of Comparative Law*, Vol. 6, No. 4 (Autumn 1957), pp. 503–517.

General Index

Abnormality: Illness as inclusive state of, 87; normal, 71–72
Abode: For souls during interval, 41, 125
Abraham: Abyssinian ruler (*Abrahàh*), 112–13; "father of the prophets" and "God's bosom friend", 142; death of, 123
Abraham's: *manâm* (dream/vision), 180
Abrahamic: Faith, 141
Abstention: from consuming whatsoever has soul, 73
Abstract: forces, 182–88; objects perceived in, anthropomorphic terms, 210; straight path as, 32
Abstracts: perceiving powers and, in anthropomorphic terms, 210; powers and, 175–88
Abu al-Naṣr, ¿A. ¿Î.: 139 n. 504, 179 n. 652
Abu-Bakr: Caliph, 167; in narrative lore, 143
Abu-Kaff: case of, 79 n. 256
Abu-l-Walîd: succeeded his father as king of jinn, 61
Abu-Rìgl-Màslûkhàh: (the One-with-a-skinned-leg/bogeyman), 105
'Abu-Ṣalâḥ: mantis (Father of Ṣalâḥ), 116 n. 397
Academic: confusion on nature of belief-characters, 82; works or "studies", 4 holiness assigned to Moslem "saints" in literature, 145; problems with some, studies on possessing agents, 87–89
Accommodation: granted by possessing spirit, 94
Accommodating: afflicted by *re*organized social system, 92; persons with certain physical attributes, 157
Accompaniment: music as, of *zâr*, 93, 95, 98; music as, of *zìkr*, 20
Accompaniments: of Adam's fall, 40; of ¿Alî's image, 165
Accountability: of angels and jinn before higher powers, 68
Acquiring: means of, natural knowledge, 176–77
Actions (deeds): are either legitimate or illegitimate, 14; lead either to Paradise or to Hell, 35
Active: bearer of tradition, 4 n. 12; folk beliefs, 94; and passive bearing of traditions, 134 n. 475
Adam: and Eve taught necessary crafts, 138; daughter of, *see* ¿Unâq; made from clay, 53 n. 167; made of Earth crust, 133; punishment of, 136; was of transcontinental size, 135

Adamites: and jinn will be resurrected, 46; offspring of Adam and Eve, 133
Adam's: accompaniments of, fall, 40; first wife for, before Eve, 138
Adversaries: (*el-'akhṣâm*), 205; soul and the body as, 34
Affect: feeling component, 2 n. 4
Affecting: abnormality, whole person, 80; factors, dreaming, 181; woman's capacity to conceive, 199
Affective: anthropomorphic representations of, and intellectual states, 100; bases for membership in cult of martyrdom, 171; component of belief, 2 n. 4
Affects: Barrier-to-gnosis, only the body, 177
Afflicted: nation of the, 156; sister (in novel), 156 n. 574; true-believer is always, 194; in community are accommodated, 102
Affliction: (*'ìbtilâ'*), 194; hymns pleading for saints' help with, 165
"*afrît*": (ghost) in *zâr* explained, 120
Agathodaemon: guardian-genius, 60 n. 197; in serpent form, 110
Age: stereotyped, 157
Aging: woman's concerns, 96 n. 314
'ahl al-kitâb (*kitabiyyîn*), *see* Book
Aids: helpers (*'à¿wân*), 61
al-Azhar: highest Islamic authority, 20; on saints, 154 n. 569
Alcohol: hashish and, in *zâr*, 98
Alexander: (the Great), 37 n. 117; plays role of hero-god Gilgamesh, 143; the Dual-horned legend cycle, 37; el-Khiḍr as companion of, 163; legend cycle about, 37–38; period of, 187
Ali, Abdallah Yousuf: (translation of *The Glorious Kur'ân*), 12 n. 25; translation, 72 n. 239
¿Alî Ibn 'Abî-Ṭâlib: Caliph, 167; culture-hero of near divine proportions, 144; plays two distinct roles, 164; Prophet's cousin and son-in-law, 163
¿Alî's: children are not part of his cult, 165; heroic cycle, 144; depiction of, characteristics, 165
Allegorical (*see also* Euphemism): Koran's, sense, 32 n. 95
Alms-tax: (*zakâh*), 15
'amîn: Gabriel labelled *al-* (the trustee), 47; Michael as, at "weighing" of deeds, 33
Amîn, Aḥmad, 18 n. 44, 20 n. 53, 60 n. 198, 66, 70 n. 230, 76 n. 248, 77 n. 249 and 250, 132 n. 469
Ammar, Hamed, 201 n. 707, 204 n. 719
Ammut: roles of, and Anubis in "Hall of Double Justice", 51 n. 161
Anatomy: houri's, 30
Angel: in human form instructs person, 178; of the Left registers bad deeds, 51; of the Right registers good deeds, 51; referred to as *sàyyìdnâ*, 47
Angels: are pure spirit and intellect, 45; commit murder, 55; created of light, 45; inhabit the sky, 27; leave person when he sins, 51; perceived as males, 47; seduced by woman, 55; teach people magic, 55; invincible, 46; belief in, required for being Muslim, 45; creation of, preceded that of Adamites, 45; guardian, fall off when person trips, 51; union between fallen, and human females, 104
Angels': habitat is seven-layers of heaven, 45
Anger: extreme, or wrath (*sùkhṭ*), 187; God's, or wrath, 186–87; unfulfilled pledges, God (saint), 19
Animal: possessed by jinni, 58; prayer on behalf of, 139; soul of, vanishes at death, 128
Animals: have souls but will not be resurrected, 129–30; cruel pleasure involving, tabu, 139; to undergo judgment/trial, 128 n. 454
Animistic: force labeled *mana*, 183
Ankle [*¿arqûb*]: as in a cow's, 162
Anonymity: in public-*zâr*, 96
Ant: "spoke" in the presence of Solomon, 116
Ants: supernatural qualities of, 116; Valley of, 116
Anthropomorphic: representations of affective and intellectual states, 100, 235; perceiving of inanimate objects and abstracts, 210; good and evil as, entities, 194
Antichrist: appearance of, 39, 150–51

Anubis: (attends weighing of heart), 33 n. 100; role of, in Hall of Double Justice, 51 n. 161
Anxiety, 96 n. 314; converted into *fear* or anger, 92; -generating sentiments expressed publicly, 92
Apparent (*see also* Overt), 166
Appearance: (coming) of the Antichrist, 39; (features) of cardinal angels, 46; frightening, of ogres, 104; physical, of angel, 49
Appeasing: *zâr* concentrates on, possessing spirits, 91
Aquatic: jinn residents of, habitat, 65
Arabic: as language spoken in Paradise, 141; classical, 83 n. 270; no feminine form in, for "*malâk*", 47
Archangel: ¿Izrâ'îl/(Azrael), 'Isrâfîl/(Israfil), 46, 48–49, 77
Archangels: four, 46
Arch-saints: report on affairs of Kingdom, 169; each, has half the power of his immediate superior, 161; division of power among, 162; four, 41, 163, 166; hierarchy of, 161–62
Arch-saint's: domain located between Earth and the sky, 42
Ark: animal waste on the, 114; crow knows whereabouts of Noah's, 185
Armageddon: Battle at Latter Days, 39
Arrogance (*see also* Conceit), 48 n. 152, 174
Ascent: Prophet Mohammad's, to Heaven, 116
Ascribed: social roles (behavioral expectations), 157
'asmâ' 'Allâh al-ḥusnâ, see God's beautiful names:
Ass: in ancient Egyptian religious beliefs, 108; Esdras's, 57 n. 185
Association (*see also* Connection): between jinn and wind, 118; free, under controlled conditions, 98, 100
Associations: mechanical, within the supernatural, 197–211; voluntary, in Arab society are few, 152
Astrology (*¿ìlm en-nùgûm/tangîm*): as deductive inference, 177; science of stars, 37; key doctrine of, 36
Aswad (el-), el-S., 30 n. 89, 51 n. 161
Attitude: maintaining positive, toward the afflicted, 59
Attitudes: toward manuscripts, 61 n. 203; toward "the word", 29; interpersonal, 156 n. 574; social, toward practitioners of magic, 78
Attribute: of letters and names put to use, 28; of *sharîf* inherited from mother, 156; physical, as bases for stereotyping, 156–57
Atum: has union with his shadow, 54 n. 175; Eye of, sent to search for lost children, 207
Audible: cries of dead, to animals, 52
Autonomous: Evil Eye, of owner's will, 208
Awakening: husband's sexual desire for wife, 76
Axes (*'aqṭâb*),149
Axis/(*qùṭb*): as sea of knowledge, 178; one exists during every period or era, 149, 161
Azrael/¿Izrâ'îl: as archangel, 46, 77; disguises as feeble old man, 123; portrayed as vulnerable, 46; weeps, 123; Adam made of Earth crust fetched by, 133–34

ba: (soul), 80 n. 259, 113 n. 384, 121–22
Babylonian: account of Deluge, 111 n. 371; hero-god Gilgamesh, 143
Badawî (el-): battle with Bint-Birrî, 21 n. 56, 22 n. 59, 284; *es-sayyìd*, 12, 162, 284; cult of, 165, 171
Badawi, el-S. and M. Hinds: identify *akhkh* (Brother), 84
bàkht: Luck, 190
Balance: set up simultaneously with raising of sky, 33
banî/'Âdam: (Adam's progeny/children), 133
barakàh (grace): as sacred entity, 159, 186; brought by reciting Koran, 17; constituted of efficiency and God's help, 186; equated with *mana*, 183; in anthropological writings, 183; is diffusible, 186; is not hereditary, 186; localized in parts of body, 185; Saints endow community with, 145
Barakât, M.K., 100
Barrenness: fear of, 199; induced, 201–203
Barrier-to-gnosis, 22, 39–40; affects only the body, 177

Bàrzàkh (el-) (Isthmus/Purgatory): between Earth and sky, 41–42; meanings of, 41; souls of the dead congregate in, 125
baṣîrah: insight, 180
Bast/(Bastet): cat-goddess of Bubastis, 115
bâṭìn rule: covert or internal (government), 166
bâṭiniyyàh (School of interpretation), 166 n. 615
Battle: at Latter Days (cf. Armageddon), 40; between Bint Birrî and el-Badawî, 12 n. 56, 284; females doing, 39
bà¿th: (Resurrection), 128
Bearer: of traditions, 134 n. 475; active (of tradition), 4 n. 12; passive, 4 n. 12
Beauty: jinn enamored with, 59
Bebrothering: *mikhawìyyàh*, 63
Behavior: beliefs treated as, 2
Behavioristic: nature of belief, 2, 5; religious formula, 35
Bekhten: legend of possessed princess of, 89 n. 299
Belief, 2 n. 4 characters, 1; in honorific death, 173; in omens, 188
Belief-practice: systems, 3, 6, 29, 30 n. 89, 40, 75, 182, 193, 195; behavioristic nature of, system, 3
Beliefs: expressed in truisms, 54; treated as behavior, 2
Believing: in preliminary judgment, 52; that magic works without God's permission is *kùfr*, 78; that word is active entity, 210
Berlo, D.K.: (on reward), 35 n. 107
Bible: (*'Ingîl (al-)*), 12 n. 25, 141; (the Bible/ the New Testament) as God's Book, 141
Biblical: accounts of male superiority, 137; literature, 142; texts (on first marriages), 138 n. 500
bìd¿àh: irreverent innovation (deviant fad), 24 n. 65; *zìkr* judged as, 19, 20–24
Bier: becomes unmanageable, 73 n. 241; flying, 127
Birth (*'ibn-ḥalâl*): legitimacy of, as bases for judging character, 158
"Black": magic, 67
Blackmailed: clients of sorcerer, 75
Blackman, Winifred S., 82 n. 269, 83, 86, 125 n. 438, 172 n. 635, 185–86, 202 n. 710, 285 n. 777
Blame: Koran sets, on Adam and Eve evenly, 138 n. 497; *malâmâtìyyàh* (those who, themselves), 150; shielding afflicted from, 92
Blessed: animals, 115; birds, 111; British lady, 185; directions (orientations), 184; limbs and sides of person's body, 184; times, 183–84
Blessedness, 183–86; -bringing animals, 114; -bringing birds, 111; -bringing ritual, 93; -bringing saints, 145; Koran reciting, 17; with food, 114; with Christian or Jewish professional, 185
Blood: bond repulses incestuous desires, 159; stain indicates slaying of possessing spirit, 91; defloration, must not fall on ground, 201; mystical bond exists among, relatives, 159
Body: ties soul to earth, 121; barrier-to-gnosis affects only the, 177; blessed limbs and sides of, 184; soul freed from, during sleep, 179
"Bogeyman": (cf. *Abu-Rìgl-Màslûkhàh*/ "Skinned-leg"), 104 n. 342
Bond: brother-sister, overrides father-daughter bond, 97; mystical, among blood relatives, 159
Book: desecrating Holy, 74; Egyptian, of the Dead, 34 n. 103; The holy, 12 n. 25; opening Holy, 179, 191; People of the, *'ahl al-kitâb* (*see also kitabiyyîn*), 140–41; reciting passages from Holy, 209
Brains: diligence in applying rationally (*'ìgtihâd*), 177
Bread: and salt placed with deceased, 124–25; hair baked in (cake), 66 n. 248
Breast: thrown over shoulders, 104 n. 342; *el-Mùzayyaràh* has iron, 64
Bride of the *zâr*-[ceremony]: *¿arûsàt-ez-zâr*, 95
Brother: spirit (*'Akhkh*), 61, 79 n. 257, 80–81, 83–84
Brotherhood: switching from one ("path") to another not permitted, 154
Brotherhoods: *ṣûfî*, 20, 33, 151, 152–55, 162
Brothers: troika of two, and sister, 167

Brother-sister: incest not possible due to blood bond, 159; marriage in ancient Egypt, 138; tie eluded scholars of *zâr*, 97; Earth and Heaven as, 27
Budge, E.A. Wallis, 29 n. 86, 33 n. 100, 80 n. 259, 88 n. 292, 89 n. 299
Bullfights: sinful, 139
bûmàh: (owl) bird of ill-omen, 111; soul in (owl) form, 111
Bûnî (al-), A. bin-¿Alî, 12 n. 25, 28, 62 n. 205, 69, 72 n. 239, 91 n. 303
Bùrâq (el-): mare or mare-like winged animal, 106–7; ridden by Prophet Mohammad to Heavens, 116
Burial: of brother and sister together, 123 n. 429; of corpses in "earth crust", 134; practices that isolate corpse from earth, 30; corpse mystically moved from, place to another, 128 n. 452; grave-side, ritual, 52; instructing the dead at, 124, 134; place of predestined, 124
Burton, R., 32 n. 97, 57 n. 185, 107 n. 357, 145 n. 526, 167 n. 618, 172 n. 635, 177 n. 645, 178 n. 647, 183 n. 663, 190 n. 684
bushrâ: (herald of good news), 180 n. 653
bù¿bù¿: fearsome creature without definable description, 105

Cain, *see* Qâbîl
Caliph: ¿Alî Ibn 'Abî-Ṭâlib, 167; culture-hero of near divine proportions, 144; plays two distinct roles, 164; Prophet's cousin and son-in-law, 163; ¿Uthmân Ibn ¿Affân, 167; *See also* ¿Umar (Omar)
Caliphate: Omayyads in the, 167; requirements of, Office, 166
Caliphs: successors to the Prophet (*khulafâ'*), 143
Cardinal: sins (*kabâ'ir*), 15 n. 33, 31, 74, 159; angels, 46–48, 142, 166; saints, 149 n. 552
Carnal: love-charm, 76 n. 248; terms for paradise, 30 n. 89
Cat: as enemy of snakes and rodents, 114; as woman's supernatural-'Ukht (Sister), 86; bites girl and makes her sick, 60 n. 197; has seven souls, 114; supernatural qualities of, 114–15
Catalyst: gold jewelry, for *mushâhràh*, 201; haircut, for *mushâhràh*, 201; menstruous woman, in *mushâhràh*, 200, 202–3; object, for mechanical associations, 201, 205
Catastrophe (*see also* disasters): destruction by (prodigy), 113
Cat-goddess: of Bubastis, 115
Cause-effect: in phallic depression, 204; in superstitions, 197; spoken word embodies its own mechanisms, 210
Celebration: of *¿Âshûrâ'*, 170; Coptic-Islamic, 169 n. 623; of *as-sayyidàh* Zàynàb's Day is ancient Egyptian, 169 n. 623
Cemeteries (*see also* graveyards): activities at, 126 n. 445; addressing the dead in, 119 n. 410; religious holidays spent at, 127; soul assumes form of fly around, 121
Censure or reproach (those who): *¿awâzìl (el-)*, 205
cha, 80 n. 259
Chain: of command among angels, 48; Qâf Mountains, 37–38
Chair: God's, 42; moon derives his light from God's, 36; *zâr-* (stool), 101 n. 333
Challenge: to nonexistence of *Akhkh* (spirit-Brother), 83; to woman's role as wife, 86
Chancellor: of the Divan (*sàyyidàh* Zainàb), 169
Changeling: (*badàl*), 60; has full set of teeth and insatiable appetite, 60; "barring-out", 60 n. 198
Character: factors in perceiving supernatural, 11; kinship as bases for judging, 158–59; legitimacy of birth as bases for judging, 158; line of descent as bases for judging, 158; *màkhwàl* as basis for judging, 158; process of judging, 156–58
Characteristics: of humans reflect attributes of Earth's clay, 38; of *zâr*-spirits community, 96–97; physical, of classes of angels, 49–50
Characters: names of supernatural, treated, 138 n. 257

Chaste: martyrdom by, love, 172
Child of Sin, *see ḥarâm (el-)*
Childbirth: jinn multiply by, 54; martyrdom by, 172
Children: born from wedlock of jinni and human, 63; not to be left unattended, 60; of Imam ¿Alî, 165–67; of same mystical source for support (*'awlâd-madàd*), 153; Adam's, 52, 133, 138, 140; circumcision of, 201, 204 n. 719; creatures invoked by adults to scare, 105; one's deeds affect one's, 35; wife's status strengthened by bearing male, 66
Choice: retribution in this world or in the hereafter, 55; undertaken by pious person (*'istikhâràh*), 181; evil and harm are of man's own, 193; asking God to show His choice, 189; asking God to show right, 190–91; prophets granted, of time and place of deaths, 123
Christ (*see also* Jesus): was not crucified (but elevated to Heaven), 151; creation of, through God's breathing of His "Spirit", 117–18
Christian: -Moslem relations, 75; saints venerated also by Moslems, 151–52; blessedness with, or Jewish professional, 185; Koran acknowledges, martyrs, 172; Osirian and, tragedies are emotionally identical, 171
Christianity: was the right religion, 141
chu: (intelligence), 80 n. 259
Circumcision: of children, 201, 204 n. 719
Classes: of *jihâd*, 178; of martyrs, 171–72; Islam's egalitarianism concerning social, 139
Classical: Arabic, 83 n. 270
Classification: according to temperament or character, 156; by para-religious Sufi organizations, 151; of saints, 146 n. 523
Clay: figure (of person/ghost), 129 n. 457; brought from Earth crust, 53 n. 167, 135, 157; Khnum fashioned gods and men from, 134; man created of, 134
Clients: view nether-magic as necessary evil, 79; female, of sorcerer secretly videotaped, 75; responsiveness of, to rituals, 96
Coercion: of jinn into forced-labor, 66; gentle, as healing technique, 92
Coffee: foretelling future from, residuals, 190; how, is drunk (prepared), 190 n. 683
Cognitive clusters, 203; of indigo and sexual activities, 203
Cognitive isolate: 2 n. 2, 36, 198
Cognitive subsystem, 59
Cognitive system, 2, 41
Cohesion: among members Sufi brotherhoods, 153; success in maintaining group, 155
Coins: placed with deceased to pay ferryman, 125
Coition (*see also* sexual intercourse): "avoiding", with menstruous woman, 203; cleansing self after, 16 n. 37; female may not top the male during, 137; jinn procreate through, 54
Collin, G.S., 183 n. 660
Command: God's, 175; prophet's *ru'yàh/manâm* is divine, 180–81
Commandments: God's, as motivation, 35; violation of God's, 14, 16
Commemoration: (celebration) of el-Ḥusain's martyrdom (*¿Âshûrâ'*), 170; in Egypt, 170 n. 630
Communal: cult institutions, 67 n. 225; "formal magic" as cult institution, 72
Communicate: ability to verbally, with the dead, 119; dead, with living through dreams, 181; summoning soul to, with it, 130
Community: of the dead, 119; of saints, 166; reorganized to accommodate the afflicted, 102; Alexander comes across a utopian, 38; characteristics of, of *zâr*-spirits, 96–97; crowded, of saints, 165; imams as leaders of entire, 149–50; of angels, 166; saints protect the, 145
Companion: of Moses kills boy, 20; el-Khiḍr as, of Alexander, 163
Companions: of Prophet Mohammad, 141, 143–44; Era (days) of the, 143
Compartment: private, of Isthmus for soul of arch-saint, 41
Compression: of reproductive organs, 200; stone, 202

Conceit (*see also* arrogance/self-admiration): equated with Eblis's behavior, 48
Condemn: formal institutions, cult of saint, 152; leading on so as to, oneself, 177
Condemned: belief in omens, 188; *zâr*-cult, 101
Conflict: between Horus and Seth over rule, 54 n. 175, 195 n. 694; between siblings, 30 n. 90, 36, 140 n. 509; between soul and body, 207 n. 727; between western institutions and religious beliefs, 101; conflict of interest, 140
Confusion: due to multiplicity of meanings of words, 88; academic, concerning angels and jinn, 50
Congruence: and interconnectedness, 156, 198, 210; of ogres' roles as paternal or maternal figures, 105; lack of, between self-concepts and experience, 101
Connection (*see also* Association): between the soul and its body, 125; between supernatural Sister (Brother) and emotional instability, 85; mechanical, 146
Consciousness: knowledge through states of altered, 176; state of altered, 20–22
Consonance, 2 n. 2
Constituted: *barakàh*, of efficiency and God's help, 186; day, of nighttime followed by daytime, 27
Contact: between soul and entombed body, 127; with soul of dead person, 130, 132; with jinn tabu, 65 n. 216, 79; illness due to, initiated by jinni, 87; magic of (touch), 70–71; no direct, with universe behind Veil, 52; prophet's soul is never in, with Satan, 180
Contagious: magic case reported, 77 n. 248; magic, 27, 70–71 n. 232
Contextual: role assigned to personal supernatural entity is, 82
Contextualism: psychological implications of, 82 n. 264
Contract: with jinn (*¿ùqâd/¿àqd*), 93; marriage, between jinni and human, 63
Control: by leader-chanter of *zîkr* event, 21; of entire universe, 175, 190; of *zâr*-rituals by (*kùdyàh*), 98; over reptiles, 37; magic seeks to, the supernatural, 68
Controlled: free association under, conditions, 98
Conversion: of anxiety into fear, 92
Copts: refer to saint as *shahîd* (martyr), 145; riot against scandal, 74–75; view el-Khiḍr as Moslem variant of Mâr Girgìs, 164; ancient celebration continued by Egypt's, 169 n. 623
Corpse: buried in ground unseparated from earth, 38; immovable, 127; transferred supernaturally to another location, 128; coins placed with, in grave, 125; laid on its right side, 184 n. 667
Correct: knowledge is "light", 177–78; leading to, path by divine or mystical power, 176; the, religion, 141
Correlating: physical attributes and behavior, 157; blood of menstruation and harm (hurt), 203
Cosmogony: Heliopolitan, of ancient Egypt, 207
Cosmological: dimensions (measurements) of angels, 49; stratigraphy, 26; angels with lesser, functions, 50
Cosmology, 24–43; ancient Egyptian, 162
Council: of saints presides over affairs of world, 163, 167; of nine gods, 169; views of, of Senior Ulama on *zâr*, 101
Counsel (*shûrâ*): *ṣâḥibàt esh-* (zàynàb), 169; *'ìstikhâràh* by asking God for, 180
Counter-spirits (*'Aqrân*): opposite in sex to humans', 80
Covert: rule (or parallel government), 167; division of power into overt and, 166–67
Craft: of harnessing jinn (and minor angels), 62; jargon of the shamanistic, 70, 74
Crafts: Gabriel taught Adam and Eve the, 138
Craftsmanship: jinn's inimitable, 56
Created: each of, things has own supernatural servants, 62; Knowledge, *a priori*, 176
Creation: as doctrine in science curricula, 176; of Adam, 26, 157; of angels, 45; of animals through degeneration, 9, 187; of Eve, 157; of Christ, 117; original (Genesis), 133; sequence of, 26
Credibility: as function of source of report, 147; derived from formal religion, 2

Cremation: bodies destroyed by, will be reconstituted, 128
Criteria: for stratifying the bulk of people, 155
Criterion: for identifying soul and ghost, 129; woman's fertility as most important, 199
Crooked: Why women are, 135; rib, 136 n. 488
Crow (raven): as bird of ill omen, 111; deviously harbors "his" knowledge, 185; devoid of *barakàh*, 185
Cruel: treatment of animals, 16; pleasure involving animals tabu, 139; roles of parents and teachers, 105
Cucumber/s: and phallus are cognitively correlated, 203; as an agent causing *mushâhràh*, 203
Cult: institutions, 67 n. 225; of Imam ¿Alî, 164; of Martyrdom, 167–71; of saints (*¿ibâdàh*), 152; of supernatural illness and healing, 87–103; *zâr*, 89–95
Culture-hero: Arch-saint as, 161; ¿Alî as, 144, 164
Culture-heroes: arch-saints continue to exist as, 161
Curing: of sore by snake charmers, 61 n. 201; effects of envy or Evil Eye, 209
Curse (Wrath): *la¿nàh*, 186–88; of (by) the weak, 187

Dâbbàt al-'àrḍ: The Earth's Animal, 108
dàhr: course of time, 189 n. 678; (Time-epochs), 190 n. 679
dàhriyyàh (ad-): school of atheistic, 189
dàqqàh: musical beat, 93, 95, 98
daragàh/*darajàh*: stratum or level, 34
daràk: saint's precinct (domain of power), 162; level of a pit, 35
Dark: (*ẓalâm*) Quarter of Earth, 37, 163
"*dàstûr*": "Permission!" or "Apology!", 58
dawlàt al-mùbtalîn: "nation of the afflicted", 156
Day: begins with sunset of previous day, 27; linked to activity, 28
Day of Judgment, 33, 46, 52, 57, 124, 128, 142, 151, 154; John the Baptist leads martyrs at, 173
Days: of the week, 26; "of the Companions", 143; latter (*'Âkhir al-Zamân*), 39; passage of Time (*el-'ayyâm*), 189; battle at Latter, 39; Creation lasted for six, 27
Dead: communicate with living through dreams, 181; community of (*'ahl al-qubûr*), 119; in ancient Egyptian beliefs, 119; how a, person interacts with the living, 119; soul of, may not possess living person, 120
Death: of Abraham, 123; of Mohammad, 123; of Moses, 123; of perfect martyr, 171; of Solomon remained unknown to jinn, 58; rituals, 126 n. 446; prophets granted choice of time and place of, 123; sleep as lesser, 121; star falls to Earth at person's, 36
Deceased: belief that, grant and deprive is sinful, 126 n. 446; granting one's religious credit to, person, 15
Deeds: judged according to intentions, 17, 69; rendered into corporal or tangible form, 34
Defender: of deceased against Nâkir and Nakîr, 124
Defenders: of home against malevolent jinn, 59
Defensive: devices against envy and the Eye, 208; mechanism in Sunni Islam, 54
Defloration: blood and *mushâhràh* by jinn, 201; punishment: suffering, pains, 137 n. 494
Defrocked: Coptic monk as magician, 74–75
Deified: Concept of power and right to rule, 166–67; Four Axes [of Earth], 161–63; humans (idolized), 161–71
Deluge (The), 111, 138, 143, 185
Demographic: community of *zâr*-spirits as, model, 96
Demons (*see* Sengers), 50 n. 158, 53 n. 169, 63 n. 210, 78 n. 254, 91 n. 303, 99 n. 325, 152
Deprives: body, soul of etherial capabilities, 121
Descent: line of, as bases for judging character, 158

Desecration: of holy books (scriptures), 74
Desires: awakening husband's sexual, 76; jihâd against one's own sinful, 171
Desperation: venturing everything out of (*'ìstìbyâ¿*), 191
Deus-nymics, 13 n. 26
"Devil": exorcised, 89 n. 299; citing, as possessing spirit, 100
Dice: *zàhr*, 190
Digwî (al-), Y., 152 n. 563
Disasters: as Divine "trials and tribulations", 19; four (*maṣâ'ib*) received daily, 194
Dismemberment: bodies destroyed by, will be reconstituted, 128
Disorder: localized, illness in part of body, 87; mental, related to belief in jinn, 55, 59; physical, believed to be caused by jinn, 60
Dissipation: of bent-in energies through *zìkr* and *zâr*, 103
Dissociative: knowledge through induced, states, 176; reaching, state, 98
Dissonance: in cognitive system, 2 n. 2
"Discotheque": public-"*zâr*" resembles Euro-American, 103
Disûqi (ed-), Ibrâhîm: (arch-saint), 162
Divan (*see dîwân*):
Divine: Justice, 128 n. 454; Knowledge, 177; leading to correct path, 176; angels as, soldiers, 48; prophet's *ru'yàh/manâm* is, command, 180–81; ¿Alî as culture-hero of near, proportions, 144
Division: of labor according to gender, 39; of livelihoods, 182; quadruple, of Earth, 37; of power among arch-saints, 162; of power into overt and covert, 166
diwân/Divan: Council of Saints, 165; not known outside Nile Valley, 168–69; head of the, 169
Domain: God's, knowledge from (*¿ìlm ladùnnî*), 177
Dominance: of the brother-sister relationship among *zâr*-spirits, 97; of patriarch, 199
Dream/(*ḥìlm*) (*see also* vision): and *manâm* (sleeper's vision), 180–81; Stella, 181–82; *'ìstikhâràh* though, 180; soul of dead may visit the living in, 127; trap, 179
Dreaming: factors affecting (dreamer), 181
Dreams: as source of truth, 179; dead communicate with living through, 181; symbolism and, 179
Drowning: martyrdom by, 172; Osiris murdered by, 173
Duality: between formal religion and subcultural practices, 6; of meanings of the word "*roaḥ*", 118–19
Dyadic: communication with soul of dead person, 127
Dynamics: of social organizational in truisms, 54

Earth: *'Arḍ (el-)*, 37–39; crust of (*'adîm al-'arḍ*), 53 n. 167, 133; Dark Quarter of, 163; fetched by Archangel, 134; receives four catastrophes daily, 194; was joined with skies, 27; body ties soul to, 121; flat, 24; four quarters of, 37; jinn became despotic on, 56; primordial marriages on, 138; Ruined Quarter of, 162–63
Earthly: paradises or utopias, 38
Eating: bread and salt with angels, 124–25; pregnancy due to, 54; protection against, sinful food, 148
Eblis (*see also* Satan): as leader (*shaikh*) of women, 53; cast out of paradise, 28, 53; declares that fire is superior to clay, 53; frolics with Adam's "hollow" figure, 135; led armies of angels against Earth jinn, 48; not associated with horses, 108; presented as an angel, 53 n. 167; secured God's promise of eternal life, 53; stripped of former angelic name, 56; agents and allies of, 194; evicted at last hour of creation week, 28; instigation by, as defensive mechanism, 53–54
Ecclesiastical: cult institutions, 67 n. 225, 71–72; religion, 3
Efficiency: *barakàh* constituted of, and God's help, 186
Eggplant: and phallus cognitively correlated, 203; cannot withstand defilement, 202; jinn's testicles, 203; varieties of, 203 n. 715

Egypt: centrality of the dead in ancient, 119; dead communicates with the living in ancient, 181–82; death ritual in ancient, 125; detective practice in ancient, 73; Heliopolitan "cosmogony" of ancient, 207; Osiris as judge of the dead in ancient, 163
Egyptian/ancient: account of fashioning of men by Khnum, 134; account of struggle between Good and Evil, 195; beliefs about the Eye, 143; belief in honorific death, 173; belief systems about deities, 162; brother-sister marriage, 138; celebration, 169 n. 623; cosmology, 36, 162; counterpart of weighing of deeds, 33; *Ka*, 80; religious rituals, 126–27; serpent responsible for stability of universe, 26; triad composed of two gods and one goddess, 169; ancient, superstition reported, 110; ass in, religious beliefs, 108; exorcism in, literature, 90; holidays spent with dead in, 126; practices associated with death in, 126
Elias/Elyâs: Elijah, 164
Enactment: of what has been ordained, 25; of spirits' role (psychodrama), 99; of martyrdom tragedy, 170
Enamorment: with God, types of (*¿ishq 'Allâh*), 176 n. 642
Encounter: referred to as entering upon someone, 200; with angels in human form, 50; nature of supernatural being emerges in, 85; with female in certain physiological condition, 200; with jinni in form of mule or donkey, 107
Enculturation: beliefs affect process of, 60
Energy: dissipation of bent-in, promotes mental heath, 103
Ennead: council of nine gods (ancient), 169
Envy: condemned, 207; as sinful desire instigated by Satan, 208; due to benign intent occurs unintentionally, 206; is cited in Koran, 207; is mostly deliberate, 206; soul of dead may, those still alive, 125
Erotic: nature of possession, 89; nature of spirit-"Sister", 84; physical movements of *zâr*-ritual, 94, 101; attempting to affect, behavior, 78; implicit, nature of *Qarînàh* (Spouse), 82
Ethereal (*'athîrî*), 118
Euphemism: and meaning of word, 53, 59, 120; for dying, 173 n. 639; Satan in man's blood as, 21 n. 169; *nîlah* as, 203 n. 717; "yellow-palace", 23
European: scientific (experimental) practices on the soul, 131; wars between Moslems and, Christians, 171
Eve: bore twins regularly, 138; daughter of, *see* ¿Unâq; gets Adam drunk, 136; suffered traits peculiar to women only, 137; Adam and, taught necessary crafts, 138; first wife for Adam before, 138; nature of (crooked), 135; punishment of, 136–37
Evil: *shàrr*, 193–94; word mispronounced to evert its, effect, 188; Good and, not clearly delineated independently, 195; *sùflî*-magic as necessary, 79
Evil Eye: (*el-¿àyn*), 205–8; may also affect animals and objects, 207; reported only in Prophet's Tradition, 207; threatened, 208 n. 731
Evokes: music, words, 100; belief character, specific sentiment, 2 n. 3; description, image of waiters in restaurant, 30
Exhaustion: has preventive and therapeutic effects, 103
Exorcism: cult of possession and, 90, 120; in ancient Egyptian literature, 89–90
Expectations: behavioral (ascribed social roles), 157
Extremity: of the universe (location), 42–43; Lote-tree of the, 42–43
Eye: belief more pronounced among females, 208; may act independently, 207; of Ra sent to search, 207–8; reflexes of, believed to be due to guardian angel, 51; "strong (blunt) eye" as bases for stereotyping (*¿ain qawiyyàh*), 158; Toth mollifies the Evil, 143

fâ'idàh: benefit or usefulness, 186
Factors: affecting dreaming, 181; affecting knowledge of the system, 5; contributing to increase of woman's influence, 199; in judging a person's character, 158; underlying supernatural illness, 88–89
Falls: charm uttered when infant trips and, 84; if person, on ground he becomes in jinn's domain, 51; star, with person's death, 36
Family: of afflicted person participate in treatment, 92; healer observes client's typical, life, 92, 96; network of ties within, of Imam ¿Alî, 168; new patterns of, organization, 199; new wife has shaky position in husband's, 86; running away from, and friends, 34
Fatalistic: attitudes toward acquisition of material possessions, 31
fàtḥ el-kitâb: bibliomancy, 190
Father's sister (*¿ammàh*): as bases for judging girl's character 158
Fatwa: deliverance of religious legal edicts, 5; on "karâmât al-'awliyâ", 152 n. 563; on addressing the dead, 119, 122; on the *zâr*, 101
Faulkner, R.: (on left hand), 34 n. 103
Favored: strata in Paradise, 35; Adamites are, by God, 135; saints are, by God, 147; Satan pledges to corrupt Adam if, over him, 135; the afflicted are, by God, 156
Fear: cup–object and ritual, 60; God, 33; of barrenness, 199; of coming of the Hour, 39; of envy and the Evil Eye, 208; conversion of anxiety into, or anger, 92
Features: soul's, and character conform to owner's, 117
Fee: for attending public-*zâr*, 39; for crossing river to hereafter, 125; magician's exorbitant, 74
Female bird with human face: *¿ànqâ' (al-)*, 111–12
Femaleness: stereotyped, 157
Females: as "daughters of Eve", 53, 104; in high offices partake in *zâr*, 102; 3 percent of saints are, 147; effects of *mushâhràh* not restricted to humans, 202; Evil Eye belief more pronounced among, 208; parlance of, 202; riding warhorses and doing battle, 39; (*shàbshabàh*) as magic ritual conducted by, 74–76; spirit-Brother belief seems confined to, 84; vipers perceived as, 109
"ferryboat": ("*mi¿addiyyàh*") fee left with dead crossing to hereafter, 125
Fertility: married woman judged by her, 199; child's (or fecundity) during adulthood, 201
Fieldwork: effect of fear of Evil Eye on, 206
Fiery: type character (*nârî*), 156
firâsàh: physiognomy, 156–57
Fire: -breathing serpent (*tennîn*), 110; Eblis created from, 54; *el-Mùzayyaràh* has iron breast that squirt, 64; Hell as bottomless, pit, 31; jinn created from pure smokeless, 52, 56; martyrdom for death by, 172; punishment by, 34
First: blowing of the "Horn", 41, 46; day of Creation, 26; wife for Adam before Eve, 138; Eve was, to succumb to temptation, 136; ritual undertaken after, menstruation, 76
"Fix" or work: (*¿amàl*), 70, 200
Flat: Earth, 24; top of house for undertaking ritual, 76
Folk: cultures portray stratified society, 139; sources, 3; theater, 170; religion, 68; majority of population are, groups, 6
"Folkloric": behavior, 3 n. 6; expressions, 98; role of Imam ¿Alî as saint, 164
Foretelling: future on deductive basis, 177
Formal: "magic", 67–69, 72, 77, 79; institutions condemn cult of saints, 152; institutions condemn cult of *zâr*, 101; Institutions endorse *'istikhâràh*, 190–91; institutions tolerate "formal magic", 78
Formalized: ritual, 71; ¿Alî's feats, in Shiite sect in Islam, 144; martyrdom of el-Ḥusain, in Shiite Sect, 170
Fornication: with wall of sinner's house, 19; by substitute (as magic ritual), 74
Foster-sibling (*see mikhawìyyàh*/ bebrothering), 24–25, 32, 62

Foundations: for cult of martyrdom in Egypt, 171; affective, of Sunni Islam different from Shiite's, 170–71
Four: Axes (Arch-saints), 167; calamities sent to Earth daily, 194; Islamic Schools of Sunni Jurisprudence, 154; Quarters of Earth, 37–39
"Fraction of Decision": 35 n. 107
Frame: of reference determines nature of entity, 82; time, 201
Free: association, 98, 100; self-expression during the *zâr* process, 100
Friendship: bond of, with interrogative angels, 125
Fruit: symbolically associated with male genitalia, 203; life-spans corresponding to, 43
Functions: assigned to Osiris as judge of the dead, 163; of supernatural characters, 11; fulfilling both sacred and secular, 166
Fundamentalism: as social movement, 167; practicing *zâr* curtailed under, 102; neo-, came into power during the 1970s, 61
Future: foretelling, on deductive basis, 177; no one knows the, 40

Gabriel: communicates God's instructions to man, 47; conveyer of God's revelations, 178; dims moon with his wing, 36; roles compatible with his office, 47; taught Adam and Eve crafts, 138; will be in charge of holding the Balance, 33
gâhilyyah: practices of pre-Islamic (paganism), 77
gannàh (el-), see Paradise: as place of *¿àdn* (Eden) and *khùld* (eternal-life), 29
Garment: as token of visit in dream, 127 n. 449; white, worn in exorcism ritual, 91
Gawhary (el-), M., 66
Geb: brother of goddess Nut, 27; god, as earth, 27
Gender: as bases for stereotyping, 157; of sun and moon incorrectly translated, 72 n. 239; of moon (masculine), 36; of sun (feminine), 36
Genesis (*'àwwàl (al-), al-khàlq*): *See al-khàlq al-'àwwàl*, 133
Genitalia: abuse of female, as Satan-pleasing act, 76; fruit symbolically associated with male, 203; skin excised from, 71
ghibṭàh: as wishing to have someone's good asset, 207; differentiated from envy, 207; sanctioned, 207
Ghost: (*¿àfrît*), 114; (ghost) haunts spot of violent death, 129; (ghost) of person who suffered violent death, 118; jinni (*afrit*), 61; soul turns to (ghost) after three days, 129 n. 455; how a (ghost) comes into being, 129
Ghosts: of the dead (*'efreets, see also* Afrit/*¿ifît*), 129 n. 456; absence of, of animal, 129
Gilgamesh: traces of, epic, 143
Gindî (al-), ¿A., 109 n. 364
gìnnìyyàh: female water spirit, 62
Girgis: Church of Mar, 91; el-Khiḍr as Moslem variant of Mar, 164; Mar, devil slayer, 152, 257–58
Girl's: father's sister as bases for judging, character, 158
Given only to males: (*¿àbd*-names), 13
Glance: at (*yibùṣṣ lì*), 205; from saint heals (gives strength), 207 n. 729
Gnosis: (knowledge), 176–78; proportionate to position within stratification, 178; instructive sleeper's vision, 179–82; sources of, and truth, 178–82
God: al-Khumaynî/(Khumaini), as sign from, 167; has no second (*thânî*), 12; if God wills, *see 'ìn-shâ'a-'Allâh*; is *Wâḥid* (One), 12; is unlike whatsoever may occur to mind, 13; is greater (meaning of), 210 n. 738; of the underworld (serpent), 26; ordered angels to prostrate before Adam, 139; preferred man over all other creatures, 138; relying on (*¿ala-Allâ*), 191; revelation from God [minor], '*ìlhâm*, 178; sent his eye to search for lost deities, 207–208; sign from God (*'Âyàtù-Allâh*), 167; *'ìstikhâràh* by asking, for counsel, 180; before, there was God, 14; exists in the Sky, 24; as the central point in Islam, 11–20

Goddess: Nut as "Heaven", 27. *See* ¿Uzza (al-); cat-, of Bubastis, 115; triad of two gods and one, 169
God's: beautiful names (*'asmâ' 'Allâh al-ḥusnâ*), 11; day worth one thousand years, 28; name created by God, 14; oneness, 12; she-slave or servant (*'amàtu-llâh*), 13; support acquired by worship and obedience, 17; Throne, 45; wisdom (*ḥìkàm*), 193; *barakàh* constituted of efficiency and, help, 186; God's Book, *see* the Bible/the New Testament; God's Volition (*'ìrâdàh*), 175; moon derives his light from, Chair, 36; opposites in, names, 13; sun derives her light from, Throne, 36; water will flow from under, Throne, 46
Gog and Magog: 39, 106; as recently devolved race, 187
Goldziher, Ignác: 152 n. 564, 284 n. 774
Good: and evil not clearly delineated, 195; and evil as anthropomorphic entities, 194; and evil are brothers, 194; person, hearted and compassionate if not excited, 157
Government: legitimacy of, 153–54; parallel (covert), 167–68
Graves (*see also* Tomb): visiting, and talking to the dead, 126 n. 446
Greater: jihâd against own sinful desires, 171; knowledge of jinn, 40, 72; Sinner, 16 n. 37; God is ("Allâhu *'akbar*!"), 210; trait of, beauty, 16
Ground: is jinn's domain, 51; breeding, for reptiles, 37; burying the dead in, 38; defloration blood must not fall on, 201–2; "Earth's Animal" will come from whole in, 108
Grouping: humans according to *ṭibâ¿* (temperament), 156
Guardian: -genius for each quarter of Cairo, 110; Ràḍwân, of Paradise, 47
Guilt: as agent of social control, 55 n. 176, 235 n. 753; contrasted with shame, 170 n. 632; -generating ethos, 170; emotional consequences of, are minimal, 55; Sunni Islam promotes no, feelings toward major figures, 171

Hâbîl (Abel)): became shepherd, 138; killed by brother, 138
Habitat: of angels, 45; of jinn, 58; aquatic, of jinn, 65
ḥaḍràh: being in the (Presence) of God via *zìkr*, 22; remembrance in God's Presence, 21 n. 54
ḥadîth: as Prophets' "Tradition", 3 n. 7; *al-nàfs* (soul's talk/dream), 180 n. 653
ḥagàr: *eṭ-ṭàrafàh* (abrasion/tamarisk stone), 202; *el-kàbbâs* (compression stone), 202
ḥalâl: is what God deemed legitimate, 14; *'ibn-*, as bases for judging character, 158; *sìḥr* ("legitimate magic"), 72
ḥalb en-nùgûm: (milking-the-stars), 75
Hallucination: drugs in *zâr*, 92; as false perception, 178 n. 649; origins of jinn concept in, 89
Halo-of-power: (*ṭàqìt-el-qàdr*), 184
Ḥâm: (Hem), 138
hâmàh: cries for revenge, 113 n. 385 and 386; ghost in owl-form, 113 n. 386; person's soul in bird form, 113
Ḥanafî: School, 65 n. 215
Ḥanbalî: School, 65 n. 215
ḥarâm (el-): is what God deemed sinful, 14, 16; *'ibn-harâm* (child of sin or bastard); as bases for judging character, 158; killing certain flies in cemetery is, 121; trafficking with black magic is, 69, 72
Harnessing: jinn and minor angels, 65–72; craft of, jinn, 62
Hârût and Mârût: 104, 142; as two fallen angels, 55–56
ḥasàd: as malicious envy, 206–7; differentiated from *ghibṭàh*, is condemned, 207
Ḥasan (al-): absent in oral traditions, 168–69; not a possessing spirit, 120; poisoned by his wife, 170; unsuccessful in quest for Caliphate, 168; inclusion of, in the Divan is honorary, 168

ḥasanàh: as act of charity or benevolence, 14, 193; freckle-like mole (deed of benevolence), 15
Ḥasanyan (al-): The Two Ḥasans, 130 n. 461
Hashemite: vein as bases for stereotyping, 157; lineage, 155 n. 573, 169 n. 626
Hashish: in *zâr*, 98 n. 324, 100
hâtìf: as *'ìlhâm* (minor revelation), 178; supernatural voice, 178
Haunt: soul of dead can only, or obsess the living, 120
Haunts: *¿àfrît* (ghost), spot of violent death, 129
hawâ'î: (aerial) whimsical type personality, 72, 156
Hâwiyah: seventh stratum of Hell, 35 n. 106
Ḥawwâ' (Eve): created of Adam's rib, 135; and *ḥàyyàh* (viper), 109; *banât* (females), 53
ḥawwâshîn (preventers): absorb most of daily calamitous events, 194; those who shield or prevent disaster, 161–62
ḥayâh (al-) al-bàrzakhìyyàh: isthmusian life (purgatory), 125
Haykal, M. Ḥusayn: "*Zaynab*", 22 n. 61
ḥàyyàh (viper): and Ḥawwâ (Eve) as words, 109; invariably feminine, 109; surrounds God's Throne, 25–26
ḥaẓẓ/*bàkht*: (luck), 190; nonsacred entity, 190
Healing: by Koran, 100–101; conditions lacking in public-*zâr*, 102; through nonconfrontational technique, 92
Healthy: attaining mentally, self-concept, 209; jinn steal, human infant, 60; why evil person seems, 194
Heart: bestowing peace and serenity on, 20; looking into people's, by deity-king, 73; sinless, is light, 33; sinner, is heavy/weighty, 33; weighing of, 33 n. 100
Heaven/(sky): highest, closer to God's Throne, 45; lowest, closer to Earth, 45
Heavens: ascent to, 106; composed of seven layers, 27; created from steam or vapor, 26; martyrs are alive in, 172; Satan cast out of, 208; Tablet-of-destiny safeguarded in, 177
Hell: as infinite place in sky, 29; exists in the sky, 24; Mâlik as warden of, 46; used to be in seventh earth, 29; will be populated by humans and jinn, 29
Helpers (*'à¿wân*), *see* Aids
Henoch (Idrîs): deceives angel of death, 46; intercedes on behalf of sinning angels, 55, 142
Hereafter: *'âkhiràh (al-)*, 41; belongs to us (belief), 31; evaluation of deeds in the, 33; judge of the dead in the, 163; rewards and punishments deferred until the, 35; road connecting the here-and-now with the, 41; *shafâ¿àh* in the, 151, 154; sinful for Hell to touch pilgrim's body in the, 18
Here-and-Now (*'ûlâ (al-)*), 41
Hermaphroditic: Eblis, 54 n. 175
Hero: -god seeks immortality, 143; war, rebels against commander in chief, 48
Heyob, S.K.: 169 n. 625
hidâyàh: divine leading to correct path, 176; natural capabilities as divine gifts, 116
Hierarchical: power structure of jinn, 62; stratification of *zâr*-spirits community, 96; stratification of angel and jinn, 68; stratification, 5; classification without, structure, 156
Hierarchies: of jinn societies, 62; of saints, 144–45
Hierarchy: of arch-saints, 161; pyramidal, in Sufis organizations, 153–54
ḥigâb (Veil): as Barrier to gnosis, 22, 39–40, 52; protective amulet as, 70; temporarily suspended, 40
Holiness: (*qùdsìyyàh*) assigned to Moslem "saints", 145
Holy: book, 74, 76, 209; -land (Hejaz), 128; -One (God), 12; war, 171–72; Arab's, site, 112; saintess—with, implications, 145; religious legends of, war, 171
Homeopathic: (sympathetic) magic, 71 n. 232
Honey: as cure, 116; bees' ability to construct, combs, 176; wine becomes, 148
Honorific: ancient belief in, death, 173
Hoopoe bird (*see hùdhùd*), 111
Horn: -locking, 82 n. 267; blowing of, signals Resurrection, 41

Incense: -fumigators, 93 n. 306; imported (from Yemen), 92; smoke, 77; types of, for rituals, 92–93, 98
Incestuous: blood bond repulses, desires, 159; tendency in brother-sister relationship, 97–98
Incongruence: between self and experience, 101
Indicator: of femininity, 94 n. 311, 203; needle-, of Balance, 33; repeated occurrence of *manâm* as, of validity, 180
Indicators: of prophethood (*dalâ'il al-nùbuwwàh*), 180
Indigenous: music, 20; one arch-saint, Egyptian by birth, 162; rituals concentrate on expelling possessing spirits, 91
Indignity: *zìkr/dhìkr* as an, 24
Indigo: as barrenness-generating agent, 203; as inauspicious substance, 203; associated negatively with sexual activities, 201
Individual: jinni servant may serve certain, 62; *zìkr* as an indignity to the, 24
Individualistic: cult institutions, 67 n. 225; ritual as, cult institutions, 76
Induced: dissociative state, 176; impotence as "magical" ritual, 78; infertility (barrenness), 200–205; knowledge (acquired), 176; means of acquiring knowledge used to foretell future, 177; patient, to express self freely, 91–92
Inebriation: mystical, 22
Inference: foretelling future as, 70, 177; inaccurate, 53 n. 169
Infertility: 199–205; temporary (infecundity), 199
Infidels (*see also kùfr*): and sinners granted power, 78; lesser jihâd against (holy war), 171; persons practicing *zâr* become, 101
Inhabited: Jinn, Earth before humans, 56; quarter of Earth, 37; soul will seek the body it had, 128
Inspired: *Tâbi¿*, poets, 83
Instructs: angel in human form, pious person, 178; officiating cleric, the deceased, 52
Intent: behind acts, 22, 34, 78, 104, 206
Intentions: deeds judged by their, 17, 69, 78
Interaction: angels', 48; behavioral patterns in social, 160; between dead person and the living, 119; between jinn and man, 63, 79; between soul and corpse, 125
Intercession: in behalf of sinners, 55, 142, 151, 154
Interconnectedness: among components and larger system, 9, 64, 198 n. 2
Intercourse: female may not top male during sexual, 137; reference to sexual, by euphemisms, 203; sexual, granted to beggar, 19 n. 38; with oneself, 54; with female client, 74
Intermediary: between man and God (absent in Islam), 152; in oracular rituals, 72
Intermediate: agent between cause and effect, 197; life (world), 41
Internal: agreement (within cognitive system), 2 n. 2; covert (inner) rule, 166; senses, 180
Interpersonal: attitudes within family, 156 n. 574; components (responses) in *mushâhràh*, 201
Interpretation: literal, misleading, 53; of al-Khiḍr story, 20; of omens, 177, 179 n. 651; of being "Dual-horned", 143
Interval: between death and resurrection, 41, 125
Intervals: danger during postnuptial and postpartum, 200
Interviewing: and fear of the Evil Eye, 206
Invaders: miraculously defeated, 112–13
Invoked: creatures, by adults to scare children, 105; incantation, to protect children, 84
Ions, V.: 80 n. 258, 125 n. 435, 162 n. 594
Isaac: "father of the Hebrews", 142
Ishmael: father of the Arabs, 142
¿ishq 'Allâh, see enamorment
Isis: Osiris-, and Horus triad, 169; *sayyidàh*-Zàynàb replaced pagan, 169; tricks Seth into eating semen-stained lettuce, 54 n. 175
Islam: as religion and legal code (*¿aqîdàh wa sharî¿àh*), 166; condemns the *zâr*, 101; condemns *taṭayyùr* (belief in omens), 188;

five pillars of, 17; influence of, on sub-Saharan Africa, 8
Islamic: account of male superiority, 137; burial practices, 38, 134; dogma on envy, 207; fundamentalism tide, 102; highest, authority, 20; mysticism, 21; stand of formal, institutions on "magic", 88
Ismâ¿îl, ¿A.: 66, 70 n. 230, 76, 83, 110 n. 365, 202–3
'Isrâfîl/(Israfil), *see* Archangel
Isthmus (*see also Bàrzàkh*): abode of arch-saint, 41; as road connecting here-and-now with hereafter, 41; Purgatory, 41–42
Isthmusian: life, 41, 125, 140
¿Izrâ'îl, *see Azrael*

Jabrîya[h]: School (view on predestined evil), 193 n. 687
Jaḥîm: sixth stratum of Hell, 35 n. 106
Jâḥiẓ (al-), 'Abû-¿Uthmân: 89 n. 295 and 297, 114 n. 387 and 389, 176 n. 641
Jahannam: first stratum of Hell, 35 n. 106
Jerusalem: Prophet Mohammad's *'isrâ'* to, 106; Well (*Bîr el-Qùds*), 125
Jesus (*see* Christ): as Messenger of God, 141; "- died for you" (as guilt-generating ethos), 170
Jewish: and Christian traditions about Lilith, 85; blessedness with Christian or, professional, 185; saints also venerated by, Moslems and Christians, 151–52
jihâd: against injustice and infidelity, 171; dyning "on God's path", 172; greater, against own sinful desires, 171; martyrdom companion of, 171; not one of the five "pillars" of Islam, 171; righteous struggle in the cause of God, 171–73
Jinn: Adamites and, will be resurrected, 46; are invisible to humans, 56; capabilities revealed in their titles, 57; consume food, 61 n. 201; created from pure smokeless fire, 52, 56; described as fond of filth, 59; dig out seas and pile up mountains, 56; disobedient, evoked, 76; exist everywhere on Earth, 58; exist independently of humans, 79; exist side-by-side with humans, 56; fought by Imam ¿Alî, 165; have no knowledge of future, 57; have own world (*¿âlàm*), 56; have strong inclination toward sin and evil, 56; household jinn coexist with humans, 59; less powerful than angels, 57; live longer, 40; love also beauty and pure humans, 59; may steal healthy human infant, 60; obligated to observe the precepts of religion, 57; reports that, are catalysts for Eye inaccurate, 205; similar to humans, 56; societies mirror human societies, 56–57; were driven off to remote areas by angel armies, 56
Jinni: believed to enter and reside in body, 87; defiant (*¿âṣ*), 62 n. 205; dream generated by, 180; giant or afrit (*¿oan*), 61; in form of cat, 60 n. 197; in form of mule or donkey deceives lone travelers, 107; *nàdr* (pledge) not made to, or devil, 19; remains in the form assumed if killed, 56, 104, 130; sacrifice to, or devil sinful, 139
Jinn's: capabilities differ from humans' only in degree, 40; inimitable industry (craftsmanship), 56; knowledge, 40; shape-shifting abilities, 130 n. 461; social and cultural institutions, 56–57
Job (*'Ayyûb*): the major figure in "nation of the afflicted", 156
John the Baptist: lord and leader of all martyrs, 173
Judaism: fanatical convert to, 172 n. 637; refusal to convert to, 172; was the right religion (until appearance of Christ), 141
Judge: Imam al-Shâfi¿î as supreme, until today, 163; Osiris as, of the dead, 163
Judging: *'aṣl* (nobility) as bases for, character, 158; by analogy or syllogism, 177; character (physiognomy/*firâsàh*), 156–57; kinship as bases for, character, 158–59; legitimacy of birth as bases for, character, 158; *màkhwàl* as basis for, character, 158
Jurisprudence: Islamic, 33, 78, 65, 78, 154, 208
Justice: God's, not always readily discernible, 19; Hall of [Dual], 33

Juxtaposing (*see* wiles): two Koranic assertions about women is illogical, 157 n. 579
Ka: as "genius" of the deceased, 80 n. 259; compared to *Qarînàh*, 80; continues to live inside the mummy, 80
kabâ'ir: (cardinal sins), 15, 101–2
kàbsàh: "compression" (induced infertility), 78, 200
kâbûs: stifler (nightmare), 179
kàf (el-): reading the palm of the hand, 190
kafâ'àh: legal doctrine of (equality of status in marriage), 139
kalimàh (al-): the word—spoken or written as active entity, 210
karâmàh: and miracle (*mù¿gizàh*), 149; as violation of natural order, 146; as used by Copts (*shafâ¿àh*), 151; as used by Moslems, 151; inaccuracy of translation as miracle, 4 n. 16; is miracle-*like* manifestation, 146–47
kàrfàh (cold-sore): as proof that jinn consume food, 61 n. 201; caused by she-Sniffer, 60
khâdim: (servant/aid) *sùflî* typically jinni, 62; *¿ùlwî* typically minor angel, 62
khair/*khàyr*: goodness, 193
khâl: maternal-uncle (mother's brother), 82; (maternal uncle) as bases for judging boy's character, 158; (mole), 16 n. 38
khalîfàh: (successor) assistant-*shaikh*, 153
Khalîfah, M. ¿A., 125 n. 437 and 439, 126 n. 445 and 446, 128 n. 452 and 454, 129 n. 455
khalîfàt al-khulafâ: (head assistant-*shaikh*) he is appointed, 153
khàlq (el-): [human] creatures (Humans), 133
Khiḍr (al-): as companion of Alexander, 163–64; as prophet receiving divine revelation, 20; as helper, 164 n. 606; as son of sister of Moses, 164; kills boy, 20
khìtm el-'awlyâ': seal of saints (the Messiah), 150
Khnum: fashioned men and gods on potter's wheel, 134
Khonsu: expels possessing spirit, 89 n. 299
khulafâ' (al-): *al-râshidîn* ([four] Rightly Guided Successors), 166; (caliphs) successors to the Prophet, 143
Khumaynî (al-): *'Âyàtù-Allâh*, found not to be the Messiah, 167
"*khunnâq*": (SIDS), 82 n. 268
khùrâfât: myths or false beliefs, 198
khuzà¿balât: as exoteric term involving value judgment, 198; (superstitions), 198
Kinetic-hymn (*see zìkr*), 19–20, 41
Kinship: relationship as bases for judging character, 158–59; ties in *zâr*-spirits organization, 96; to the Prophet, 155, 168
Kisâ'î (al-), M., 138 n. 502
kitâb (al-) al-muqàddàs: bibliomancy by, 179 n. 651; desecrated for magic ritual, 74; The Holy Book, 12 n. 25
Kline, Nathan S.: 88 n. 292
Klunzinger, C.B.: 90 n. 301, 82 n. 268
"Knowledge": and "belief", 2 n. 3; created *a priori*, 176; crow has, of the whereabouts of Noah's ark, 185; Divine, 177; of Axis/(*qùṭb*), 178; of people-of-the-testimony, 178; through induced dissociative states, 176; through meditations, 176; through visions (dreams), 176; types of (natural and induced), 177; varied amounts of, of components of system, 5
Koran (*al-Qur'ân*): 3, 12 n. 25, 16 n. 39, 29 n. 85, 30 n. 87 and 88, 31 n. 92 and 93, 32 n. 95, 33 n. 99, 42 n. 132, 50 n. 157, 55 n. 177, 56 n. 182, 65 n. 216, 106 n. 351, 108 n. 362, 111 n. 373, 116 n. 396, 118 n. 401, 126 n. 446, 129 n. 458, 133 n. 473, 138, 147 n. 530, 173, 179 n. 652, 189 n. 678, 193 n. 688, 207
Koranic: healing, 101; pronouncements set blame on both Adam and Eve, 138; interpretation of, sentence (12:28), 157 n. 579
Koran Healing/Treatment: (*¿ilâg bi-al-Qur'ân*), 93 n. 306
kùdyàh: as root-cluster (*zâr* shamaness), 94; cites lists of *zâr*-spirits, 97; induces free expression under her control, 98; *zâr*-priestess, 50 n. 158

kùfr: as injustice, 171; (being an infidel), 34, 65, 76, 78; practice of *zâr*-cult is (sacrilege), 101–2; rejecting belief in tomb trial is, 52
kùrsî-ez-zâr: *zâr*-chair/stool, 101 n. 333

Lailìt el-Qàdr: (the Eve of [Divine] Power), 183–84
làms/màss: illness (mere touch), 87
Lane, E.: 20 n. 53, 22 n. 61, 22 n. 58, 27 n. 77, 42–43 n. 135, 51 n. 160, 66, 110, 118 n. 404, 130, 164
Language: created *a priori*, 62; of animals, 143; spoken in Paradise (Arabic), 141; utilitarian use of, in magic, 62
Latter Days: (*'Âkhir al-Zamân)*, 39; battle at (Armageddon), 39
Laẓâ: second stratum of Hell, 35 n. 106
Leading on (*'ìstìdrâg*), 78; practitioner of sacrilege given power to condemn themselves, 146–47, 177
Leaves: life-spans corresponding to, on tree, 42–43; placing palm-, on tombs, 126
Left: Angel of the [side], 51; hand unclean (bad), 34 n. 103; wailing for receiving records in, had, 34
Legal: innovations in Islamic jurisprudence, 139–40; Islam as religion and, legal code, 166; religious, edicts (fatwas), 5; secular, systems sanctioned belief in magic, 79; usage of the words "soul" and "self", 117
Legend: cycles, 37–38, 143, 165; of the Greater Sinner, 16 n. 37; "- of the Possessed Princess", 89 n. 299; religious, about emergence of Islam, 171; saint's, 16 n. 37, 22 n. 59
Legitimacy: of one's birth, 158; shamans' claim of, of their craft, 88
Legitimate (the): and the sinful, 6, 14, 35, 101, 136, 153, 172; birth, 158; martyrdom: death while seeking, employment, 172; power (political), 158, 166; witchcraft, 72 n. 237
Legs: donkey-like, 104; jinni posing as riding animal lengthens its, 107; support for, of Nut (sky in form of cow), 161; viper used to have, 136
Lesser: angels, 48, 149; Death, 121; *jihâd* against infidels (holy war), 171; saints (in Divan), 167, 169; Sins, 34
Letters: soliciting deceased Imam's justice, 163; science of (*¿ìlm el-ḥùrûf*), 14, 66, 68–69, 71; were created, 24, 210
Levels: of being closer to God, 22; of supernatural illness, 87
Life: *¿îshàh (el-)*, 189; -Giver, 12; history of hero (*sîràh*), 171; in the Isthmus, 41; intermediate life, 41; the World, 189; fountain of ("Fountain of Youth"); *¿ain el-ḥayâh*, 37; on Earth, 38; rendering into debased form of, 187; selling one's, 191
Life-span: God offers to extend, of Moses, 123; new (*¿ùmr gdîd*), 124; predestined, 182
Life-spans: God created, 27; tree of, 43–44
Lifestyle: ideal, in utopia, 38; opulent, 144
Light: angels created of, 45; correct knowledge is, 177; sources of moon's and sun's, 36
Lilith (*see also* ¿Unâq), 30 n. 90
Limbs: blessed, 184; one's own, will testify on Judgment Day, 34
Lion: cat from sneezing (nostrils) of, 114
Littmann, E.: 4 n. 15, 18 n. 48, 63 n. 208, 97 n. 316
Living: able to hear the dead, 119; dead communicate with the, in dreams, 181; would the dead befit from deeds by the, 15 n. 36
Love: carnal, charm, 76 n. 248; martyrdom by chaste, 172; song (*mawwâl*), 122 n. 423
Luck: *ḥaẓẓ/bàkht*, 190
Lunar: condition of sainthood comes with, month of Ragab, 150; eclipse, 30 n. 88; fasting during, month of Ramaḍân, 17, 94; rituals at middle of, month of Sha¿bân, 42

madhâhìb: Islamic Schools of Jurisprudence, 154
mâ'î: (aquatic/"watery") personality type, 156

Magic: taught by angels, 55; "black", 67; contagious, 71; "Er-rooḥânee" (spiritual), 66; "Es-Seemiyâ" (satanic), 66; formal, 67–69, 72, 77, 79; formal, is not magic at all, 68; formal, as para-religious, 68; practitioner of formal, esteemed, 79; "white", 67
màgnûn/gunûn: jinn-stricken or ridden, 58
Màg'ûg: (*see also* Yà'gûg), 106
maḥâsîb: (proteges) of a certain saint, 151
màhdî (al-) al-mùntaẓàr: anticipated Messiah, 167
Maḥfouẓ, N.: 98 n. 322, 151 n. 560
makhwàl: ("maternal-unclehood") as basis for judging character, 158
Male: female-, stereotypes, 56; moon as (masculine), 36; no, component of certain supernatural female beings, 64
Maleness: corresponds to God's-names, 13; stereotyped, 157
Males: "¿Abd- . . . " given to, only, 13; angels perceived as, 47; snakes perceives as, 109
Malignant: martyrdom by, disease, 172
Mâlik: (angel) as warden of Hell, 47; (Imam) quoted, 41
Mâlikî: School (*madhhab*), 65 n. 215
màmlakàh (el-) er-ràbbâniyyàh: (the Divine Kingdom), 167
Màmmàh: has sister and son but no wife, 97; sultan of *zâr*-spirits, 97
Man (*see also* Adamites): created of clay, 134; preferred by God, 138; ogre and ogress are, -eaters, 104
mana: equated with *barakàh*, 183
manâm: Abraham's, 180; recurrence of, as indicator of validity, 180; sleeper's-vision, 179–80; *'ìstikhâràh* via, 190–91
màndàl: *b-el-qullàh* (divination via pottery-water-bottle), 73; images of persons constituted by, jinn, 130; requirements of, -opening process, 73, 130
Mantis: "The Prophet's mare", 116
Manuals: for interpreting dreams existed for millennia, 179; magic (handbooks), 4, 49, 61, 69
Marital: discord, 59 n. 195; infidelity, 204–5; regulating, relations to jinn, 89
Marriage: between primordial brothers and sisters, 138; contract at outset of relation between jinni and human, 63; exchange, of twin brothers and sisters, 84–85; first, on Earth, 138; *kafâ'àh* in, 139; morning after consummation of (*ṣabâḥiyyàh*), 95
Martyrdom (*'istìshhâd*): being witness, 171; by malignant disease, 172; by chaste love, 172; by drowning, 172–73; by violent death, 172; by death while pursuing noble cause, 172; by childbirth, 172; encompasses more than holy wars, 171; of el-Ḥusain formalized in Shiite Sect, 170; companion of *jihâd*, 171; foundations for cult of, in ancient Egypt, 171; types of, 171–72
Martyrs: are alive in heaven, 172; classes of, 171–72; leader of all (John the Baptist), 173
masâkhîṭ: devolved beings, 202
Masîḥ (al-): *al-mùntaẓàr* (the Messiah), 150; *ad-dàggâl* the impostor Christ (Antichrist/ *al-Masîkh*), 39 n. 122, 150–51
mashî'àh: God's Will, 175
màskh (*see also sakhṭ*): degenerative punishment, 187; Maspero, G.C.: 89 n. 299, 119 n. 411, 173 n. 639, 179 n. 651
màss: ("touch") from Satan or evil jinn, 101
Maternal-uncle (*see also khâl*): can swear "This is my sister's son", 71 n. 234; beautiful, 82; Moses as, of el-Khiḍr (folk belief), 163–64
"Maternal-unclehood": (*makhwàl*) as bases for judging character, 158
Matriarchal: influence, 199; role, 105
Matrilineal: descent identifies person, 70
Matrilocal: residence (initial), 199
Màymûn/(el-): hybrid stallion, 106–7; ¿Alî's war horse, 165
Mechanism: of envy, 203; cause-effect, 210; defensive, in Sunni Islam, 54–55, 183; healing, through nonconfrontational techniques, 92
Medical Association: Egyptian, and case of shamanism, 79 n. 256
Meditations: knowledge through, 40, 176

Medium: in shamanistic ritual, 7, 130–31, 158–59; must be of the "aerial" character, 72 n. 239, 156
Melancholic: type character (*tùrâbî*), 156
Membership: in a Sufi-brotherhood is lifelong commitment, 154–55; bases for, in ¿Âshurâ (martyrdom) tragedy, 170
Memory: phrase to aid, 211
Menopause: termed "age of despair (hopelessness)", 199
Menstruous: woman catalyst in *mushâhràh*, 200, 202–203; avoiding coition with, woman (*maḥîḍ*), 203
Mental: asylum ("¿Abbâsiyyah"), 59; deficiency, 119; illness (disorder), 18 n. 44, 38, 58–59, 85, 100; images, 22; nature of, illness and possession, 58–59; dissociated mental and emotional state (*'ìngizâb*/ *'ìngidhâb*), 22
Mercy: (*raḥmah*), 15, 139 n. 504; act of, to benefit a deceased, 15; divine, saves from Evil Eye, 209; killing as act of, 20
Microbes: jinn reinterpreted as (germs), 60
Midnight-afrit: *¿àfrît nùṣṣ-el-lail*, 105
Mîkâ'îl (Michael): as archangel, 46; as trustee at "weighing" of deeds, 33; controls nature, 47; recurrent male name among Copts only, 48; name of, in para-religious "work", 77
mikhawìyyàh/(*mu'âkhâh*): taking supernatural foster-sibling (bebrothering), 62–63, 83
Military: birds never seen after, event, 107; Imam ¿Alî's, feats, 107, 165; -like chains of command in angel community, 48; -like power hierarchies in jinn community, 62; ranks of Gog and Magog, 106
Milk: cow's, is pure (*ṭâhìr*), 14; used for cleansing (in latrine), 76; he-sparrow's, 92 n. 305
Milking: -the-stars (*ḥalb en-nùgûm*), 75–77; Venus, 76
Minimizing: effect of abstracts by personification, 182; sense of responsibility, 183
Minor: angels (angel-like) serve in Paradise, 29–30; minor female jinn or jinn-like beings, 64; signs of Day of End of World, 39; sins (*ṣaghâ'ir*), 14–15 n. 33, 39, 102; zoological beings used to discipline children, 61; *'ìlhâm* as, revelation, 178; harnessing, angels, 65–72
"*miqàysàh*/(*mùqâyasàh*)": venturing all, 191
Miracle: (*mù¿gizàh*), 142, 146, 149; *karâmàh* and (*mù¿gizàh*), 149
Miracle-*like* manifestation: (*karâmàh*), 4, 22, 146–47, 151–52, 183
Miracles: as indicator of validity of prophethood, 142; suited to arts of prophets' times, 142; Mohammad's, miracles (linguistic), 142
Mirror: jinn societies, human societies, 56–57; liquid, 72 n. 240, 130; community of souls is, of community of Paradise, 126
Mischief: of jinn, 200; of saint, 149 n. 549
Mischievous: possessing "*afrît*" is only mischievous Puck, 120; roles of birds, 198; *¿àfrîtàh* signifies, female jinni (not female ghost), 129
Misleading: information by Satan (jinni), 179 n. 652; literal interpretation, 53
Misleads: ¿Unâq, her brothers, 84–85; Eblis, Adam and Eve, 109, 136; Eblis, Adam's children, 194; Satan, and corrupts (but does not possess), 88
Mispronounced: saint's name typically, 162; word, deliberately to avert its evil, 188
Mite (*sûsàh*): bored holes in Solomon's cane (he collapsed), 58
mîzân (al-) (Balance/Scale): weighing of deeds in, 32–33
"*mi¿addiyyàh*": "ferryboat" fee placed with corpse, 125
Mohammad: as third Messengers of God, 141; as "the seal of prophets", 150; death of, 123; descendants of, 90; founded monotheistic faith and headed political state, 166; has right to the "great-intercession", 142, 151; messenger of God, 17; Qarîn of Prophet, 80; sayings and deeds of Prophet, 3

Mohammad's: Birthday, 183–84; Bùrâq, 106 n. 355; Companions, 143–44; daughter (Fâṭimah), 167; miracles (linguistic), 142; visit to Jerusalem and ascent to Heavens, 106, 116
Moietic: division of universe (two realms), 40, 53, 176
Monotheism, 142, 171, 166
Moon: and sun were equal in light and heat, 36; as masculine, 72 n. 239; derives light from God's Chair, 36; practice reckoned according to position of, 201
Morphologically: pronunciation varies, 11 n. 23; gender of Koranic words specified, 72 n. 239; "w" and "y" are, interchangeable, 135 n. 487
Moses: as *kalîmu-Allâh* (the One-who-Spoke-with-God), 142; as maternal uncle of el-Khiḍr, 163–64; as Messengers of God, 141; strikes Azrael, 46; death of, 123
Moslems (*see also* Muslims): ancient Egyptian celebration adopted by, 169 n. 623; appellations for nation of, 140; Christian and Jewish saints revered by, 186; as a human stratum, 140; qualities, believe must characterize conduct of rulers, 144; type of fasting not practiced by, 73; wars between, and European Christians, 171
Mother: children of man and jinni woman belong with, 63; attribute of *sharîf* inherited from, 155; identification through, and mother's mother, 71; (mother-of male-children) injurious spirit (*'Omm-eṣ-Ṣùbyân*), 83, 86, 204; self-esteem for being a, 199
Mother's: craving, 17 n. 38; prayer (or curse), 18, 187; martyrdom due to her death during childbirth, 172
Motifs: as analytical classificatory device, 8–9
Motivation: for injurious ritual, 204; in cognitive behavioristic formula, 5; person's wants and God's commandments as, 35
Mountains: created to stabilize the Earth, 26; chain of, called Qâf, 37; jinn piled up, 56, 58
mubtalîn (al-)/ *'aṣḥâb el-balâwî*: the afflicted, 150, 156
mùddàrrakîn)/ (*mudàrrakîn*): saints assigned own precincts, 161–62, 162 n. 592
mùkallafîn (obligated): animals are not, 116, 128, 129–30; humans and jinn are, 57
mûlìd (*màwlìd*): saint's [birth]-day celebration, 184 n. 664
Multiplex: system, 2 n. 2; systems with numerous components, 197
Multiplicity: of meaning leads to confusion in some academic studies, 88
"*mùnaggiyât (al-)*" / *al-mùnjiyât*: [soul]-rescuers/savers, 15–16, 124
mùnshid: lead-chanter, 21
muqaddàr (el-): the preordained (predestined), 182
mùqâmaràh: gambling (taking a gamble), 191
murîd: "aspirant" (candidate or novice), 153
mùṣḥàf (al-) ash-sharîf: ("*The Glorious/Noble Koran*"), 69
mushâhràh/*kàbsàh*: and new moon, 201 n. 707; (induced barrenness), 78, 199–205; affects eggplant, 201; as process triggered by specific catalysts, 200; name derived from the Arabic word *shàhr* (month), 200; precautionary measures taken against, 95
mùshrikîn: worshippers of a god other than God, 141
Music (*see also nidâ, dàqq'àh*): conveyed message in verbal utterance, 100; indigenous, 20; in *zìkr*-performances, 20; in *zâr*-performances, 95
Muslim (*see also* Moslem): jinn pay *zakâh*, 108; basic requirement for being, 45
Muslims (*see also* Moslems): receive wrong lot from bad messenger, 31
Mùzayyaràh (el-): female water-spirit, 64
mù¿gizàh/*mù¿gizât* (*see karâmàh*): (miracle), 142, 146, 149
mù¿taqàd: "belief" (with no value judgment), 198
Mu¿tazilah/ (rationalists): views of, on possession by jinn, 89; views of, on *shafâ¿àh*, 151 n. 560
Mystical: bond among blood relatives, 159; bond connects soul with body, 126;

contexts (and personification), 116; inebriation, 22; romancing (love talk), 142; children of same, source for support, 153; divine or, power of guidance, 176
Mysticism: (Sufism), 21

Nabhânî (al-), Y., 147, 154 n. 570
nàdr/(*nàdhr*): conditional vow or pledge, 18
nàfs: self (or psyche), 117, 206
nagâsàh: (defilement), 202
nàḥs: as nonsacred personified entity, 188; inauspicious ("*nà¿s*"), 188
Nâkir: and Nakîr (two interrogating angels), 52; as angel scribe for good deeds, 52
Nakîr: as angel scribe for sins, 52
Name: has real independent existence, 14; of entity is relativistic and contextual, 82; organically connected to object, 28; meaning of the, *Ḥawwâ'*, 135
Names: of dangerous things not to be spoken, 210; confusion from different meanings of, 50; God's beautiful, 11, 213
nàmnàm: (cannibals), 105
naqîb: (marshall), 153
Nâr (en-): Fire (Hell), 31
nârî: (fiery) character, 156
naṣîb (en-): one's due, 182
Nation: of "There is no god but Allah", 140; worships the Sun, 111; Calif leads the Moslem, 143, 166; God may punish entire, or race, 187; head of Sufi brotherhood will lead his, on Judgment Day, 33; jihad required when, is in peril, 171; tree in Heaven each leaf of which shades a, 42
Natural: knowledge bestowed by God, 176; purity of all of God's prophets, 134; blessed, medicine, 116; breaking of, order, 146; cat as, enemy of snakes, 114; means of acquiring, knowledge, 176; spoiling of Earth or, resources tabu, 17
Nature: cognitive behavioristic, of the system, 2; Mìkâ'îl control, and weather, 43; of character as factor in how perceived, 11; of Eve and her daughters (womankind), 138; varying, of various peoples, 157
"*nazîl*": shaman's familiar, 87
nàz¿: wrenching soul from body (at death), 122
Need: of many "believers" to be followers, 54; martyrdom: dying while helping person in, 172
Negative: attitudes toward psychiatries, 59; attitudes toward women, 137; expressing, feelings presumably impersonally, 92
negìs/(*najìs*): (impure or profane), 14
Nelson, Admiral Lord: soul of, summoned, 130
Neo-fundamentalism, *see* fundamentalism
Neolocal: residence, 199
Nether: -magic, 74–78; servant (*khâdim sùflî*), 62, 66; -works (black magic/sorcery), 69; (satanic) rituals, 70, 77; generating love by, magic rituals, 77
New Testament, *see* Bible
Newlyweds: to dwell with bride's parents, 199
nidâ: ("call") summons or beat (*dàqqàh*), 95, 98
nigìs: (profane), 59
nîlàh: (indigo) agent of barrenness, 201, 204 n. 718
Nile: dead ferried across, 184; helping ships sail against, current, 184
Ninety-nine: praise names of God, 11, 213
Noah: (prophet), 111–12, 114
Noah's: three sons, 138; crow knows the whereabouts of, ark, 185
Noble (*'aṣîl*), 158
Noncognitive: contradictions, 116
Nonconfrontational: healing technique, 92
Nonsacred: Days, 189; forces and concepts, 189–91; luck as, entity, 307; Time/Days as, entity, 189; World/Life as, entity, 189
Non-twin: each male married his, sister, 138
"Normal abnormality": as traditional concept, 71–72
Nullify: activities that can, shackles of mind and body, 176; common ancestry can (reduce) differences, 140; good deeds, sinful ones, 15; how to, effects of *rabṭ*, 205

Number: of beads in rosary, 20; One (1) as creature, 29; titles indicating, of jinn in group, 61
nûr: *min, i-llâh* (of God's light), 177; The Pen is made of, 25; used to denote ("light"), 36 n. 108
nûrânî: (light-bound), 69; the soul is (*nurânyyah*), 117 n. 400
Nut: as goddess (sky in form of cow), 161; goddess, joined with brother Geb, 27

Oath: repeated till "servant" comes, 72 n. 239; to be read seven times, 77; punishment for breaking, 73; Solomon's, 143
Objections: to practice of soul summoning, 132; to *zâr*-cult, 101
Obligated: creatures that are not, 57, 116–17
Offspring: of ordinary mare and a sea-jinni horse, 107; of a mother is verifiable, 71; of Adam and Eve (Adamites), 133; without mate, 54 n. 175
Ogres: have goat- or donkey-like legs and hoofs, 104
Okasha, A., 88 n. 292
Olympian: psychological pattern, 165, 171; ¿Alî's (military) feats, 165 n. 609
Omar (¿Umar): Caliph, 167; in narrative lore, 143
Omayyads: in the Caliphate, 167, 170
Omen: interpretation as deductive inference, 177; bad, 188, 195, 198; birds of ill, 111
Omens: belief in (*taṭayyùr*) condemned, 188
'Omm-Hâshim: nickname for *sàyyidàh* Zaynab, 169 n. 626
One: God is, 12; number (1) as creature, 29; there can be only, Axis during an era, 149
Oneness: of God, 12, 20, 178; God's, and unity, 11
One's: own limbs will testify against him, 34; fusion of, self with the Beloved, 22
Opium (*'afyûn*), 23
Opposites: in God's names, 13; union of, 13 n. 26
Oracular: gods, 73; ritual, 73; services, 73–74
Organized: professional clergy, into bureaucracy, 67 n. 225; saints, into hierarchies, 144–45
Origin: of precious stones, 37; of the unknown (the veiled), 40; of pig, 114; of characteristics of humans, 38; of human soul, 117–18; of cat, 114
Osirian: and Christian "tragedies" are emotionally identical, 171; Horus, 169; weighing of heart, 33
Osiris: as judge of the dead, 163; as martyr, 173; murdered by his brother Seth, 169; murdered by drowning, 173; al-Ḥusayn replaced, 171; closeness to, in the afterlife, 35
Overt: economic and status power, 199; division of power into, and covert, 166
Owl: as bird of ill omen, 111 n. 386; ghost of murdered person in, -form, 113 n. 386

Pact: of no-remarriage with wife, 127 n. 449; People of the, 141
Padwick, C.E., 38 n. 118, 59 n. 193, 82 n. 269
Pagan: Arab's holy site, 112; illegal character of, ritual, 77; Zàynàb replaced, Isis, 171
Palm branches: at cemeteries, 126 n. 445
Pantheon: of *zâr*-spirit (*'asyâd*), 90; published lists of *zâr*-spirits, 97, 258–60
Para-religious: accounts, 4; literature (sources), 46, 112; oracular service, 73; practitioner, 78; rituals, 29, 65, 67, 72; Sufi organizations, 151; teachers of, ritual, 28
Paradise (*el-gànnàh*): absence of excessive eroticism in, 30 n. 89; admittance into, before or at death, 126 n. 441; ancient Egyptian counterpart of, 35 n. 105; as field or grove ("*ghaiṭ*"), 29; as infinite places in sky (*es-samâ*), 29; exists in the sky, 24; higher and lower classes in, 34–35; populated by humans and jinn, 29; Ràḍwân guardian of, 48; sensual pleasures in, 30; (*wìldân mukhàlladûn*) serve inhabitants of, 29–30
Parallelism: between the Islamic trio and ancient Egyptian triad, 169 n. 628
Parents': approval, 159; curse or discontent, 159; prayers, 159
Parent-son: relationships present among *zâr*-spirits, 97

Parties: political, imitate Sufi-brotherhoods' ways, 155
Passive: amulet of (defensive) nature, 70; bearing of traditions, 4, 134 n. 475
Patriarchal: authority lessened, 199; role, 105; society (authority), 199; martyrdom of, figure, 171; ogres appear in, roles, 105
Patricide: (Freud's view), 171 n. 633
Patrilineal: descent (unverifiable), 70–71; society, 199
Pattern: of distribution of saints, 145; new, of family organization, 199
People: "types" or sorts of (*'anwâ¿*), 156
Perfect: martyr, 171–72; time for answered prayer, 37
Peripheral: beliefs, 2, 5, 124, 194; members of group of characters, 114, 116; role, 47 n. 148
Permanent: departure of the soul, 122; jinn as, component of the individual, 79
Personality: folk theories of, 155–60; four, types, 37 n. 114; whimsical, type, 72
Personification: of concepts, 182; of deeds, 186; of entities (good and evil), 186; of *nàḥs* as nonsacred entity, 188; of "something", 178
Persons: deified, 161–71
Phallic: depression induced, 204
Philosophical (*see shàṭḥ*): folktales, 43; debates over creation of good and evil, 188; unorthodoxy due to ascetic immersion, 23 n. 64
Phoenix: *al-¿ànqâ'* as, 111–12
Physical: attributes and behavior correlated, 156; attribute as bases for stereotyping, 156–57; characteristics of angels, 49; stratification on basis of, qualities, 140
Physiognomy (*firâsàh*): has generated stereotypical characters, 156–57
Pilgrimage: elevates pilgrim's status, 18 n. 44; one of five pillars of Islam, 6; seven times, 18; to Mecca, 17; to Jerusalem, 12 n. 25
Pillars: five, of Islam, 17
Plants: susceptible to *mushâhràh*, 202
Pledges: to saints, 19; to God, 18
Polarity: Principle of, in learning/recall, 120 n. 416
Political: quietism, 155 n. 571; Mohammad founded monotheistic faith and headed, state, 166; titles of jinni with potent, powers, 61
Pope Shenoudah the III, 132 n. 471
Position: of the moon, 201; of the afflicted in community, 156 n. 574; of lesser characters, 5; gnosis proportionate to, within stratification, 178
Possess: jinn's ability to, person's body and mind, 58; soul of dead can not, the living, 120
Possessing: spirit responds to musical "beat", 120; spirit responds to, call (*nidâ*), 98–99
Possession: affects whole person (body and mind), 87; by Satan possible in formal Islamic and Coptic dogmas, 87
Postnuptial: and postpartum intervals of danger, 200
Postpartum: and postnuptial intervals of danger, 200
Potter's: men fashioned on, wheel (by Khnum), 134
Power: contrasted, to nobility, 158 n. 585; division of, among arch-saints, 162; division of, into overt and covert, 166; God grants, even to infidels and sinners, 78; God's (suspends planets in heavens, etc.), 175; structure of, within community of saints, 166; types of (rule), 166
Practical: and utilitarian aspects of *barakàh*, 186; no, difference between *karâmàh* and *mù¿gizàh*, 146
Praise: song (hymn) addressed at Zàynàb, 168; ninety-nine names of God, 11
Prayer: time as means for setting appointments, 17 n. 42; time for a prayer to be heard and answered, 37; devices that ensure an answered, 185; on behalf of animal, 139
Precautions: taken against offending jinn, 58
Precinct: as domain for saint's responsibility and power, 162

Predestination: provides defensive mechanism, 54; concepts involving, only implicitly, 189; owl denies, 111–12
Preferred: God, man over all other creatures, 48, 138; right side, over left, 51; unanimity, in Islam's political ideology, 155
Preparing: coffee (way of), 190 n. 683; sweet delicacy of wheat pudding (called *¿ashûrâ*), 170; *barakàh* in, food, 185
Presence: mere, of *mushâhràh* catalyst doesn't cause infertility, 201; how possessing spirit manifests its, 102; in the, of God (*galâlah or ḥaḍrah*), 22, 177; soul is responsible for, of life in creature, 116
Preventive: amulet (charm), or as a cure, 202; devices are either, or therapeutic, 209; hiding one's good assets as, measure, 209
Primordial: (first) marriages on Earth, 138; brother-sister marriage, 138
Principle: of soul summoning not disputed, 132; "of polarity", 120 n. 416; of divine justice, 19
Private: compartment of Isthmus occupied by soul of arch-saint, 42; form of *zìkr*, 23; true *zâr* as, and individualized ritual, 92, 95
Privileges: of *'asharâf*, 155 n. 573; a mother's, 199; adult male's, 96 n. 314
Professional: blessedness with a Christian or a Jewish, 185
Professional practitioners ("*¿amalât*"): by professional shaman-*shaikh*s, 197; ungrammatical plural of "*¿amàl*", 70
Projection: interpretations of divination figures matter of, 132 n. 467; *zâr*-spirits represent, of demographic model, 96
Promoting: one's self-esteem, 209
Propensity: grouping humans according to, 156; predestined, toward violence, 28
Prophet (*see* Mohammad): Mohammad's *Qarîn* (male Counter-spirit), 80; Mohammad's visit to Jerusalem and ascent to Heavens (*al-'ìsrâ' w-al-mì¿râg*), 106; Muhammad (as guardian of Paradise), 47 n. 147; Sulaymân, 56 n. 182; titled as *sayyìdnâ* (our lord/master), 142
Prophethood: and sainthood, 149; miracles as indicator of, 142; *rù'yàh/manâm* as indicator of, 180
Prophet's: foretelling future is by reading Tablet of Destiny, 70; *ḥadîth*, 61 n. 201; Mare, 116 n. 397; *ru'yàh/manâm* is divine command, 180–81; utterance, 17 n. 40; Birthday (celebrating of), 184 n. 664; Evil/Eye is reported only in, utterances, 207
Prophets: *'anbiyâ'*, 141; cast into different "race", 134; corpses of, suffer no decay, 135; created of white heart of Earth, 134; granted choice of time and place of death, 123
Proportionate: gnosis, to position within stratification, 178
Protect: saints, the community, 145; two angels, every person, 51
Protective: devices (precautionary measure), 210; measures against danger, 202; amulet as barrier, 29, 111
Proteges of God, *see* Saints
Protocol: royal court, governs angels' interaction, 48
Prym, E. and A. Socin, 86 n. 286
Psalms (*see* hymn): in *zìkr*, 21
Psychiatries: negative attitudes toward, 59
Psychiatry: and disregard for local cultures, 101
Psychodrama: as folk therapeutic technique, 99, 231
Psychological: and emotional traits peculiar to women, 136–37; implications of bebrothering, 62; Olympian, pattern, 165
Psychosocial: anthropomomorphic, realities, 2; realities expressed symbolically, 100; *zâr* character duplicates, condition of afflicted, 261
Psycho-therapeutic: institutions opposing religious beliefs, 101
Psychedelic: public-"*zâr*" resembles, musical activities, 103
Ptah: Lord of Truth, 73
Public-*zâr*: lacks several healing conditions, 102; offers conditions of anonymity and pleasantness, 96

Punishment: of Adam, 136; for breaking oath made to formal deity, 73; of Eve, 136–37; of Hârût and Mârût, 55 n. 180; of the new sinners in Paradise, 136; of viper, 136; illness as, 87; sinners stripped of their names as, 56; transformation into planet as, 55
Purgatory: *Bàrzàkh* (Isthmus), 41, 125
Pyramidal: hierarchy in Sufi organizations, 153

Qâbîl: (Cain) became farmer, 138; given jinni as wife, 30 n. 90; killed Hâbîl over marriage to their sisters, 138; wanted to keep his twin sister as wife, 138
qabîlàh: (tribe) of jinn, 61
qaḍâ': differentiated from *qadàr*, 182 n. 658
qadàr (el-): (destiny), 25, 182
"Qadarites": School, 193 n. 687
qâḍî al-quḍâh: (chief justice), office, 153
Qâf: Mountains on surface of Earth, 37–38
qânûn ¿urfi: (customary law), 89
"*qarâfah*": (cemetery), 126 n. 445
Qarîn/Ḳarîn: male Counter-spirit, 61, 79 n. 260, 80, 82
Qarînàh/Ḳarîneh: causes death of her human man for intending to marry human girl, 82; compared to ancient Egyptian *Ka*, 80 n. 260; dies along with the person, 80; female Counter-spirit, 79; of same sex as the human to whom it belongs, 80; (Counter-spirit, Spouse, Correlative), 200; *'Ukht* and, may stand for the same thing, 82; female Counter-spirit, may also be perceived as the *'Ukht*, 82
qismàh (el-): (kismet), 182
qiyâs: as judging by analogy or syllogism, 177; syllogism, 177 n. 643
Quarter: Dark, of Earth, 163; Empty, of Earth, 37; Ruined, of Earth, 162
Quarters: four, of Earth, 37
qùdràh: God's Omnipotence, 175
Questions: God answers Moses', 142
Quests: fools', 92 n. 305
Quietism: political, 155 n. 571
Qur'ân (*see also* Koran): as God's [final] Book, 141; blames Adam and Eve evenly, 138 n. 497; healing with, 65 n. 214, 93
qùrbân: ritual sacrifice, 18, 101
qùṭb (Axis or "Pole"): at top of community of saints, 165; there can be only one, during an era, 149

Ra: comes to prince Thutmosis in dream, 181–82; sent his Eye to search for lost children, 208
ràbṭ: affects adversely male's potency, 204; induced phallic depression, 78
Race: each of Noah's three sons represents a, 138; Islam's egalitarianism concerning, 139; prophets cast into different, 134
Races: jinn belong to different, 62
raḍwàh: (reconciliation/appeasement) ritual, 94
Ràḍwân/(Ruḍwân): gatekeeper of Paradise, 48
Ragabìyyîn (er-): ("Ragabites") sainthood comes to them with the month of Ragab, 150
raḥmânee: divine magic, 66
Ramaḍân: lunar month of fasting, 108; *zâr* not held during, 139 n. 504
ràqwàh/rùqyàh: religious incantation, 93
Real culture: 3 n. 6
Realities: of daily life, 11, 26; psychosocial, expressed symbolically, 100
Realm: of the supernatural, 116; distinct, labeled "nation of the afflicted", 156; heavenly, 40; para-religious, 65; transparent, is timeless and infinite, 40; worldly, 40
Recall: process of, 211
Recitations: from Koran bring blessedness, 7, 17, 19; from Koran used as remedy, 93, 185
Reckoned: basic types of character, according to the elements, 156 n. 575; descent, patrilinially, 71; saint's day, according to date of death, 184 n. 664
Reconstituted: bodies destroyed by cremation or dismemberment will be, 128

Redemption: by performing additional credit-worthy deeds, 15–16
Reflexes: of eyelid attributed to guardian angel, 51
Regression: as psychoanalytic term, 167
Reinterpretation: of "jinn" to mean germs (microbes), 60
Relationship: between man and God, 13; between *¿amàl* and its compelling effects, 197; mechanical, between cause and effect, 202
Relativistic: nature of role assigned to personal supernatural entity, 82
Reliance: on diverse and historical sources, 82
Relic: of ancient Egyptian superstition cited, 110
Relief: those who bring (*'àhl el-ghàwth*), 161
Religion: solicits aid of sacred supernatural, 68; credibility derived from formal, 3; ecclesiastical, 3; Islam as, and legal code (*¿aqîdàh/wa sharî¿àh*), 166
Religious: Literature, views envy as caused by spiritual effect, 205; behavioristic, formula, 35
Removed: Veil between man and God, via ritual, 22
*Re*organized: social system, to accommodate the afflicted, 92
Replaced: al-Ḥusayn, Osiris, 171; During its absence Atum, the eye, 207; Zàynàb, pagan Isis, 171; ¿Alî/Zayn-el-¿Âbidîn, Horus, 171
Report: arch-saints, on affairs of Kingdom to Divan, 169
Reptiles: may be jinn assuming form of animal, 60; supernatural, 109; Ruined Quarter of Earth is breeding ground for, 37, 162
Repulses: blood bond, incestuous desires, 159
Required: sacred ritual services (*furûḍ*), 15, 17; *jihâd* is, when nation is in peril, 171; shrouds are, in ordinary death, 171; visiting eggplant field, to cure *mushâhràh*, 202–203
Requirements: for *màndàl*-opening, 73; of office of the Caliphate, 166; of slaughtering animal or bird, 139
Residuals: trace (*'aṭàr/ 'athàr*), 70; reading, in coffee cup, 190; "time"-bound concepts, of earlier arguments, 189
Resorting: to higher and more powerful supernatural agent, 91; to profane and fallacious practices, 79
Responsible: person under influence of jinn not, for own actions, 79
Responsibility: for an evil act, 193–94; minimizing an individual's sense of, 183
Restore: social movements seeking to, original state, 167
Resurfacing: of Gog and Magog as sign of Day of End of World, 106
Resurrected: Adamites and jinn will be, 46; certain animals will be, 128
Resurrection: on, Day every soul will seek and enter its body, 128; when special water flows from under God's Throne, 46
Returning: to earth at death, 38
Revelation: *wàḥy*, 178; *'ilhâm* as minor, from God, 178; final, from God, 141
Revenant: how a (*¿àfrît*) comes into being, 129–30
Revenge: ghost of murdered person cries for, 113 n. 385; *hâmàh* will cry for, until it is accomplished, 113
Reversal: of the established social order, 39; of the sun's course, 36; causes for gradual, of fortunes, 189
Revitalization: of old beliefs under impact of neo-fundamentalism, 60
Reward: or punishment delayed until the hereafter, 35; to be spared for one's descendants, 35–36
Rib: crooked, 135–36; Eve created out of Adam's, rib, 135, 157
riḍâ: contentment, 186–87
Rifâ¿î (er-): Aḥmad, 37, 162; resides in Ruined Quarter, 37; rank of, in hierarchy of arch-saints, 162
Rifâ¿iyyah: Brotherhood, 37, 162
Right: angel of, side, 51; corpse laid on its, side, 184 n. 667; receiving record with,

hand, 34; side blessed, 184; two, hands for the sinlessness, 34
Rightly: The, Guided Successors, 166
rîḥ: wind or wind-like spirit, 101, 118, 121
Rising: by lengthening legs, 107; of sun and moon from the west, 36; Day of (Resurrection), 26 n. 74
Ritual: dancing, 7; seeks aid of jinn in providing information, 72; extinct, 77; para-religious, 28, 77–79; *zìkr* as, 20–21
Rituals: of life and death at middle of Sha¿bân, 42; death, 126 n. 446; do it yourself, 209; sacrilegious, 77
roaḥ/rûḥ: soul, 116–28; confused with *rîḥ* (wind), 121
Role: belief character plays determines character's nature (name), 86; name and, assigned to supernatural entity relativistic, 82; nature of, assigned is determined by frame-of-reference, 82
Roles: of foster-sisterly relation, 64–65; ascribed social (behavioral expectations), 157; Imam ¿Alî plays two completely distinct, 170; social, of ogres in tales, 105
Romer, John, 73
"Rooḥânee (Er-)": *spiritual* magic, 66
Roots: of martyrdom, 173; of *màndàl*-ritual in Coptic period, 74
Rosary: *'ìstikhâràh* by, 190; number of beads in, 20
Rosenthal, Franz (*see* Ibn Khaldûn), 3 n. 11
ru'â/marâ'î: five types of (sleeper's visions), 180 n. 653; prophet's, is divine command, 180–81; sleeper's-vision, 180
Ruḍwân: as word in Koran, 47 n. 147; deceived by Eblis and viper, 109, 136; guardian of Paradise, 47
Ruined: Quarter of Earth, 37, 162
rùkhkh: (roc) as legendary bird, 111
rùkûb: spirit riding person as if an animal, 87
Rule: general, of effect (reward [and punishment]), 35; the right to, 166–67; two types of (power), 166
Rules: of "brotherhood" conduct, 154; of royal court protocol govern angels' interaction, 48; universally applied, concerning dying, 123
Rushdî, I., 82 n. 268, 200 n. 701
rùsùl: rank of apostles (messengers of God), 141
rù'yàh: and prophethood, 180; *malakìyyah* (of the *malkât* faculties, propensities), 180 n. 653; requesting (as instructive dream), 190

ṣabâḥiyyàh (eṣ-): morning after consummation of marriage/*zâr*-ritual, 95
Sacred: *barakàh* as, entity, 186; fulfilling both, and secular functions, 166; irrevocable violation of, tabus, 74; *zâr*-ritual never held during, times, 94
Sacrifice: to possessing spirit, 92; to jinni or devil sinful, 139; semi- (*shìbh-qùrbân*), 18 n. 48; "slaughtering" for pledge is not ritual, 18
Sacrificial: ram from Paradise, 180; God's name not mentioned on, animal offered to *zâr-'asyâd*, 94; required qualities in, animal or bird, 92 n. 305; *¿ùqâd* as, ritual, 93
Sacrilegious: acts please Satan, 74, 76–77; persons allowed power to condemn themselves, 146–47; via anti-sacred agents, 68
ṣadâ: ghost of murdered person in bird-form (cries for revenge), 113 n. 386
Sadat (el-), Anwar, 19 n. 51
Safety: of afflicted provided by shielding him/her from blame, 92; of female during postpartum/postnuptial intervals, 95; guardian snake ensures, of household, 110
ṣaff: line or file (platoon) of jinn, 61
ṣaghâ'ir: (minor infringements), 14–15, 102
ṣaḥâbàh: ("Companions" of Prophet) as a class, 143
ṣâḥibàt/esh-shûrâ: Zainàb as the Chancellor, 169
sâḥìr/sàḥḥâr: (sorcerer or true magician) 68, 74
Saint: George's "devil-slaughtering" ritual, 91; titled *sîdî* (my lord/master), 142; community cannot remain without a, 145

Saintess: *qiddîsàh* (title with holy implications), 145; being protege of, 151 n. 560
Sainthood: and prophethood mutually complementary, 149–51; persons marked for, 68; claim of, for preserved corpse, 135; concept of, pivotal force, 144; accompaniments of, 145–46
Saints: are sheer blessedness, 185; assume form of birds and fly as flock, 119–20; believed to protect the community, 145; Moslem *'awliyâ* and Coptic *shuhdâ* ("Martyrs"), 144; organized into hierarchies, 144–45; proteges of God (*'awaliyâ* [u-Allâh]), 144; about three percent of Nabhânî's list are female, 147; categories of, 144 n. 523; names of, uttered in *zâr*-ritual (not possessing spirits), 120; structure of power within community of, 166; veneration of, belonging to all three denominations, 151
sàkhṭ: rendering into debased life form, 187
Sakr, A.H., 121 n. 420
ṣalâh: (prayers), 17
Salient: experiences proving indelible, 6; physical characteristic of Azrael, 46 n. 141; male pregnancy as, theme, 54 n. 175; most, belief about brother and sister, 84
Ṣâliḥ's/(Salih's): she-camel, 57 n. 185, 128
Salt: and bread placed with deceased inside grave, 124–25; as spell against ghosts, 129 n. 456
Sâm: (Sem), 138; son of Noah, 164 n. 606
Sand cutting: (*ḍarb er-ràml*), 190
Saqar: fifth stratum of Hell, 35 n. 106
"*sarâyâ/ṣafra*": "yellow-palace" (mental asylum), 59
ṣarîkh: belief character that parallels *hâmàh*, 113
sarûkh/(*ṣârûkh*): shooting flame (spirit), 113 n. 385
Satan (*see also* Eblis): as "feeler-licker", 61 n. 201; confused with other belief-characters, 53 n. 169; pausing in form of man as cook, 119; prevented from eavesdropping on heavens, 37; -pleasing act, 76; substituted for she-Sniffer, 61 n. 201; dream generated by, 179; evil jinni may be called (*sheṭân*), 54; *nàdr* (pledge) not be made to, 19; reciting Koran drives away, 17
Saturday: first day of Islamic week, 26; eve of (Friday night), 27, 169; not first day of Creation, 26
"Savage-faced Messenger": (death), 46 n. 141
Sayce, A.H., 120, 129 n. 456
sayyi'àh: (sin/bad deed) is from man himself, 193
sàyyìd: as proper name, 120 n. 416; as adj.: descendant of the Prophet (*sharîf*), 120 n. 416, 155
sayyidàh-Zàynàb: and Isis, 169; characteristics and titles of, 169
"*sayyidna*": Our lord (prophet or saint), 47 n. 149
sa¿âlî: as ogres (hybrid), 104
Sa¿îr: fourth stratum of Hell, 35 n. 106
sà¿lùwwàh/si¿lâh: ogress, 105 n. 348
Scales (*see also* Balance), 33
Scarab: and "the gods of hours of the night", 36
Scarcity: of knowledge of arithmetical calculations among women, 68; of use of concept of "holiness", 12 n. 25
Scare: creatures invoked by adults to, children, 105
School: *ad-dàhriyyàh* as, of atheistic, 189; Mu¿tazilah, of Islamic philosophy (rationalist), 89; Shafiite, of sharia, 163
Schools: of Islamic Jurisprudence (*madhâhìb*), 33, 65, 154
Schrempp, G., 13 n. 26
Science: curricula in schools, 176; of letters (*¿ìlm el-ḥùrûf*), 14 n. 28–29, 66, 68–69, 71, 210
"Scientific": stand on folk practices, 5; European, and experimental practices on the soul, 131
Scripture (*see also* biblical), 138 n. 500
Sea: -jinni horse, 107; -maiden (-bride) as water-spirit (*¿Arûsìt-el-Bàḥr*), 64; suspended between sky and earth, 36; cosmological, 26, 49; direction of the, 184; Moses parts the, 149; reading, shells, 190

Seance (*see* Summoning of souls), 131
Seas: jinn dug out, 56, 58; Roc wreaks havoc on ships on high, 111; seven, 38
Secret: of marriage to *gìnnìyyàh* must never be revealed, 63; "soul" as the divine, 118
Secretly: sex acts by female clients of sorcerer, videotaped, 75
Secrets: spying on heaven and learning its, 40
Secular: school system, 245 n. 760; fatalistic attitudes toward acquisition of, power, 31; fulfilling both sacred and, functions, 166; stand of, legal systems toward magic, 79
Seduced: angels, by woman (Venus), 55
Seemiyâ (*Es-*): is satanic magic, 66
Sees: God, whatsoever any creature does, 17; sleeper, the truth, 179
Seker: necropolis deity of Memphis, 31 n. 92
Self-admiration/conceit: (*el-?igb*) is from Satan, 48
Self-concept: and Evil Eye belief, 209; woman's, 199
Self-confidence: not differentiated from arrogance (conceit), 48
Self-esteem: and "spiritual" illness, 88, 209; woman's, is being a mother, 199
Self-transformation: capability of shape-shifting and, 104, 130, 148
Seligman, B.: sex of Qarinah, 82 n. 269
Semantic: evolution (of interpretation of Koranic verse), 189 n. 678
Semen: in love philtre, 76 n. 248; -stained lettuce, 54 n. 175; -stained clothing, 70 n. 230
Sengers, Gerda, 24 n. 65, 47 n. 149, 50 n. 158, 53 n. 169, 57 n. 187, 63 n. 210, 78 n. 254, 85 n. 284, 91 n. 303, 92 n. 305, 99 n. 325, 100 n. 328, 102 n. 336, 151 n. 561, 183 n. 660
Sensory: deprivation and hallucination, 89
Sentiment, 2 n. 3
Sentiments: as learned feelings, 3, 92, 170; structure of, within traditional Egyptian family, 98
Sentries: stars as, 37
Separate: cognitive systems for father (¿Alî) and his children, 165; cognitive subsystem, 59
Sequence: of acts of Creation, 26; word (stability of syntax), 120 n. 416
Serpent: responsible for stability of the universe, 26; Agathodaemon in form of, 110; flying (*'âf*), 110; winged viper or, 110
Servants: female water spirits not used as ("aids"), 64–65; *zâr-'asyâd* not used as ("aids"), 90
Seth: as paternal/maternal uncle, 195 n. 694; in conflict with Horus, 54 n. 175; murdered Osiris by drowning, 173; trickster deity linked to ass, 108; Horus and, 195; Osiris murdered by his brother, 169
Seven: layers of heaven as Angels' habitat, 45; planets, 65; provinces of Earth, 38; seas, 38; bride of *zâr* must stay home for, days, 96; cat has, souls (life-spans), 114; dog of the, Sleepers, 57 n. 185
Sex: (gender) of personal supernatural entity in relation to human's, 80
Sexual: inability to experience, arousal (erection), 78; liaison between jinn and humans as reality, 89; liaisons with the afflicted in *zâr* possession, 90; needs and possession, 89; sorcerer has, intercourse with female clients, 74
shàbshabàh: ("slippering") sorcery through use of slipper, 6, 74–76, 67, 77 n. 250
shâfâ¿àh: for copts denotes performing "miracle" (*karâmàh*), 151; intercession in behalf of sinners, 142, 151; *al-*, *al-¿ùẓmâ* (the great-intercession), 142; Sufi-*shaikh* given power of, 154
Shâfi¿î (al-), "Imam" Moḥammad ibn Idrîs: held as supreme judge until today, 163; defines "magic", 65; opinion of, on magic constituting *kùfr*, 76; magic and sorcery according to, 65
shagaret el-'a¿mâr: (tree of life-spans), 43
shahâdàh: Testimony, 17, 178
shaikh-el-mashâyìkh: Sufi sheik over the sheiks (uppermost sheik), 153
shaikh-siggâdàh: sheik of the [prayer]-rug, 153
shaikhìt-ez-zâr: the she-shaikh of the *zâr* (*kùdyàh*), 94

Shaman-*shaikh/mashâyìkh*: faith healer or "magician", 5, 7, 49, 51, 57, 61, 68–69, 96, 156, 197, 209
Shaman-*shaikhàh* (*see also zâr*-priestess), 76, 98, 102, 96 n. 315; effeminate male assistant (*'ùdyàh*) to (*zâr*-priestess), 94
Shamanistic: cult institutions, 67 n. 225; "sciences" as deductive inference, 177
Shaman's: proficiency judged by appeal spirits he/she offers, 96; techniques that seem effective, 92
Shame: as agents for social control, 55 n. 176
Shamhûrish: deceased king of jinn, 61 n. 202; sultan (ruler) of all jinn, 61
Shàmmâmàh: she-Sniffer, 105
Shamy (el-), H., 2 n. 3, 4 n. 15, 9 n. 22, 12 n. 25, 13 n. 26, 16 n. 37, 18 n. 47, 42 n. 134, 47 n. 148 and 149, 54 n. 175, 55 n. 176, 59 n. 196, 82 n. 264, 88 n. 292, 89 n. 296, 91 n. 303, 93 n. 306, 98 n. 322, 100 n. 329, 106 n. 355, 110 n. 365, 112 n. 376 and 379, 115 n. 391, 122 n. 423, 123 n. 429, 133 n. 473, 138 n. 497 and 500, 151 n. 561, 154 n. 570, 157 n. 577, 158 n. 585, 160 n. 589, 164 n. 606, 165 n. 609, 178 n. 650, 195 n. 694, 204 n. 718, 235 n. 753, 275 n. 772
Shape-shifting: capability of, and self-transformation, 67, 104, 130, 149
Shared: characteristics among public-*zâr* and *zìkr*, 103; healing depends on beliefs and attitudes, 92
sharî¿àh (shria), 24 n. 65, 33, 153, 89, 101, 152 n. 564, 163, 166
sharîf, see Hashemite
shàrr: (evil), 78, 193–94
shàṭḥ (*see* unorthodoxy), 23 n. 64; going into the Beyond, 176
shayâṭîn/'abâlisàh: devils or satans as sons and descendants of Eblis, 54
shayṭân: confused with other belief-characters (academic lit.), 53 n. 169; euphemistic use of (as satan), 83
"Shayṭânee": (satanic) magic, 66
She-mule: of the tenths ("*bàghlìt-el-¿ashr*"), 107–108
Shegaret al-Muntahâ: tree of Extremity of the universe, 43
Sheik, 78 n. 254, 91 n. 303, 131, 145, 153, 155
Sheik's: heart appears as cock, 154 n. 570
Shells: divination by sea (*el-wadà¿*), 190
"Shem hamme forash": (the unspoken name of God), 61 n. 202
Shenoudah/Shenûda, the Third: Pope (head of Church), addresses rioters and nation, 75, 132
Sheṭân (esh-): (devil) jinni, 61; Satan, 14, 17; Eblis as, 53; to be ridden by, 88
Shiite: Sect, 71, 165; martyrdom of el-Ḥusain formalized in, Sect, 170–71; ¿Alî in, Islam, 144
Shine: sun and moon, over Earth from behind a sea, 36
shùhadâ/'àhl esh-shahâdàh: knowledge of (people-of-the-testimony), 178
Shumays, ¿Abd al-Mun¿im, 56 n. 181, 94 n. 311, 97 n. 318, 259
Shu: deities, and Tefnut were lost, 207
shù'm/shûm (*see also* disgrace): bad-omened, 188
sibḥah/misbaḥàh: rosary, 20, 179, 190
Sides: blessed limbs and, of a person's body, 190; feather has seventy thousand, 26
sidi/sîdî: saint or prophet labelled (my lord/master), 47 n. 149, 142, 145
Sìdràt al-Mùntahâ: Lote-tree of the Extremity, 42–43
SIDS: (Sudden Infant Death Syndrome) "*khunnâq*", 82 n. 268
ṣiddîqîn; Knowledge of (instantaneous true-believers), 178
Signs: (*¿alâmât*) heralding coming of End of World, 26 n. 47, 36, 39; major, of coming of Day of End of World, 106, 109; ogress', of anger or peacefulness, 104
sìḥr: (magic) according to early Moslem jurists, 65; *ḥalâl* (legitimate magic), 72; *ràsmî* ("formal magic"), 67; *shà¿bî* ("folk magic"), 67; *suflî* (nether magic or sorcery), 74 n. 244

"*sijjîl*-rocks": ("stones of baked clay"), 113
sijjîn: Hell, 35 n. 106
simplex: systems with few components, 2 n. 2, 197–98
Sin: (*'âthâm/dhànb/ 'ìthm/ sàyyi'ah*), 14, 16–17, 19; and forgiveness, 22; differentiated from shame, 170 n. 632; Adam's, 137; cardinal, 159; redeeming, 15
Sindâs: jinni all-knowing of vaginas, 76
Sinful: bullfights, 139; for earth to "eat" a prophet's corpse, 135; practice of witchcraft, 72; belief in beings that call for revenge is, 113; jihâd against one's own, desires, 171; sacrifice to jinni or devil, 139; usury is, 17
Sinner: Greater, 15–16 n. 37; heart of, would be "heavy", 33
Sinners, 31–32, 34, 52, 78, 136, 142, 151, 154
Sins: attributed to external entities and forces, 54–55; ranking of, 14–15
ṣirâṭ (al-) al-mùstaqîm: (straight path) described, 32
Sister (*'Ukht*): spirit Sister, 60 n. 197, 83, 200; 'Um-Kulthûm younger, of Zàynàb, 170; each male married his non-twin, 138; el-Khiḍr as son of the, of Moses, 163–64; human, jealous of affection between her brother and his wife, 86; punishment for desire to marry foster-, 61 n. 207; troika of two brothers and their, 168
Skies: were joined with Earth, 27
Skinned-leg/[One-with-a-]: ("*Abu-Rìgl-Màslûkhàh*") evoked to frighten children, 105
Sky: raised and suspended without pillars, 26; is seven strata (skies), 37; spanned by the "Straight Path", 29; angels sexist in, 24; God exists in, 24; Hell is in the, 24, 29, 112; Paradise exists in, 24
"Slaughtering": own son, 181 n. 655; to appease *¿ummâr* (jinn inhabitants), 93 n. 307; *nàdr-*, is not a ritual sacrifice, 18; requirements of, animal or bird, 139
Sleep: as lesser death or its brother, 121; soul freed from body during, 179
Sleeper: sees the truth, 179
Sleeping: arrangements in large families, 159–60; *Shàmmâmàh* sniffs unwashed mouths of, humans, 60 n. 589
Snake: perceived as male, 109; beneficent, protects certain locale, 110; dead saint assumes form of, 120; household-jinni in, form protects, 59
Social: control (through shaming), 55 n. 176; domination by adult male, 96 n. 314; stratification (the Western system), 140 n. 508
Socializing: through belief characters, 61
Social-system: ability of healer to *re*organize the, 92
Soldiers: Eblis', 54; angels as, of God (*'agnâd 'ilâhiyyàh*), 48
Sole: guide in deliberations (*ṣâḥibàt esh-shûrâ*/Zàynàb), 169; possessor of at least one enviable quality, 209; ruler, 180 n. 635
"Soliciting": aid of sacred supernatural (deity), 68; God's choice (*'ìstikhâràh*), 190–91; letters, deceased Imam's justice, 163
Solomon: commanded jinn to manufacture inimitable things, 56; understood language of animals, 143; jinn disobedient to, evoked, 76; Thoth's role assigned to Prophet, 208
Solomon's: answered prayer, 65 n. 216; death revealed by mite (*sûsàh*), 58; Oath, 143; Seal, 143; similarities between, song and *zìkr*-songs, 22 n. 58
Sorcerer: *sâḥìr*, 68, 74; view of Islamic jurisprudence toward, 78
Sorceress: addressing jinni (Sindâs), 76; beats own vulva with slipper, 75
Soul: (*rûḥ*) as eternal, 16, 40; and ghost as two facets of same entity, 129; *cannot* possess another person, 121; can converse with living person during sleeper's vision, 130; freed from body during sleep, 179; joins its likes after death, 126; leaves the body permanently at death, 122

Soul (*cont.*)
may assume form of green or blue fly, 121; of dead person in form of certain animals (snake), 119; of dead person may visit the living in dream, 127; of Admiral Lord Nelson summoned, 130; originated when God "breathed" of his "Spirit" into Adam, 118–28; perceived as feminine, 118; provides tangible proof of contact with living person, 127; -vs.-self, 117 n. 400; abstention from consuming whatsoever
; has, 73; adversarial relations between, and body, 34; beliefs about, central in both Moslem and Coptic systems, 116; God's, 118; human, cannot possess another human soul, 121; inaccuracy of argument that, of dead may possess living person, 120; proving existence of, tangibly, 117 n. 398
Soul-savers: are multiple and varied, 15–16
Source: dreams as, of truth, 179
Sources: of knowledge and truth, 178–82
Spans: "straight path", Hell and Paradise, 29
Speaks: Sphinx, to Prince Thutmosis in vision, 181
Sphinx: Dream stella found between the paws of the, 181–82; in vision asks Thutmosis to clear sand away, 181
Spirit: angels are pure, 45; el-Khiḍr as benevolent, 20; factors in how the, is perceived, 82; four water, categories, 65; God "breathed" of his, into Adam, 117–18; the Holy, 12
Spirits: personal, represent realities (not fictions), 100
Spiritual: envy is, effect of the *nàfs* (the psyche), 206
"Spirituals": chants/hymns, 21
Spoken: word embodies its own cause-effect mechanisms, 210
Spreading: women *zìkr*-circles emerged and are, 24; *zâr* sub-cult is, 90, 102
Spying: on inhabitants of heavens, 37, 40
Squeezed: soul, out of corpse, 125
Stability: of syntax (word sequence, word order), 120 n. 416
Stabilize: four gods stabilize the legs of Nut (sky), 162 n. 596; Mountains created to, Earth, 27, 56
Stand: of formal religious institutions on soul-summoning, 132; of secular legal systems toward magic, 79; taken by formal institutions vis-a-vis folk practices, 5
Star: falls to Earth at person's death, 36
Stars *See also* astrology (*¿ìlm nùgûm (en-)/tangîm*): as sentries, 37; Milking-the-, 74–76; power of, or planets, 75
Status: equality in, and wealth between couple to be married, 139–40
Steam: heavens created of (vapor), 26
Steering: client to express self freely, 98
Stella: Dream, 181–82
Stereotypes: systemic nature of female–male, 54
Stereotypical: physiognomy maintains, characters, 156
Stereotyping: gender (male–female), 157; patterns of culturally sanctioned, 160
Stone of tamarisk, 202 n. 710
Stones: from Hell, 112; origin of precious, 37; semiprecious, in charm, 202
Straight-path: euphemistic usage, 32; leads to Paradise, 29; spans over Hell, 29
Strata: Hell divided into, 31; highest, in Heaven are closest to God, 34; humans comprise three, 140; occupants of highest, in after life, 126; seven, of the sky, 122
Stratification: of souls in isthmusian life, 126; on basis of physical qualities, 140; pervasiveness and stability of saint, 153; hierarchical, 5; hierarchical, of angel and jinn communities, 68; no social, in utopian community, 38; organization of angels reflects political, 48
Stratified: Hell community, 31; Paradise as community, 34–35; Society is, in folk cultures, 139–40
Stratigraphy: Cosmological, 26
Strength: of Sufi religious organizations, 153
Structure: of entire field of the supernatural, 1; of power within community of saints,

Systems: belief-practice (motivation-organism-response), 5; separate cognitive, for father and for his children, 165

ṭabaqât (classes): of saints, 149–50; three, of people, 141
Tâbi¿ (Follower): as jinni or satan who inspired poets, 82; as *shàyṭân* ("satan"), 83 n. 270; does not exist in Egypt, 83
tâbi¿î et-tâbi¿în: successors of the successors of the Companions, 144
tâbi¿în (et-): successors of the Companions, 144
Tâb¿àh/*Tâbi¿àh*: (she-Follower), 83
tàfqîr: ritual dancing in *zìkr* or *zâr*, 20, 23 n. 63
tàfqîràh: [joining in] one ritual-dance, 102 n. 335
tàgsîm: deeds rendered tangible, 34
tàḥdîr/*'ìstid¿â' el-'arwâḥ*: (the summoning of souls), 130
ṭâhìr/*ṭâhràh*: ritually immaculate or pure, 14, 59; Zàynàb as (*ṭâhràh*), 169
tàḥwîṭàh: protective amulet, 70
takhwîf: fear-evoking (dream), 180 n. 653
Tale-types: as analytical classificatory device, 8–9
Talking: to the dead, 126; *dâbbàh* as, hybrid, 18
Tàll Baṣṭàh/(Bubastis): ancient site, 199 n. 700
tàlqîn, 38 n. 120, 134 n. 477; "prompting" the deceased, 52; negates need for grave trial, 124
ṭàqìt-el-qàdr: halo-of-power, 184
tàqwâ: (piety) as criterion for social differentiation, 139
ṭarîqàh: religious brotherhood or "path", 152
taṣawwùf: Sufism (Islamic mysticism), 21
tàsbîḥ: exaltation of God, 20
"*taskhîr al-gân*": coercing jinn into forced-labor, 66
ṭaṣṣ/(*ḍàrb*): illness (dealing a blow), 87
taṭáyyùr: belief in omens, 188 n. 675
"*Ṭayr'abâbîl*": *'abâbîl*-birds, 112
ṭàyyâr: jinni ("Flyer"), 57
Te Velde, Herman, 108 n. 361
Techniques: that seem effective, 92; of free association under controlled conditions, 98; nonconfrontational healing, 92; psychodrama as folk therapeutic, 99
Tefnut: deities Shu and, were lost, 207
Temperament: classification according to (character), 156
Temporarily: effects of Veil, suspended, 40; soul, freed from body during sleep, 121, 179; vulnerability when angels, leave the person, 51
Tendency: to perceive inanimate objects and abstracts in anthropomorphic terms, 210; incestuous, underlies brother-sister relationship, 97–98
tennîl/*tànnîl*: dragon-like serpent, 110
Test: of the strength of person's faith in God, 194; God puts individuals and groups to, 193; illness as, of strength of faith, 87
Tha¿labî (al-), A. Ibn M., 29 n. 82, 30 n. 90, 36 n. 108, 54 n. 175, 164 n. 606, 208 n. 732
Theater: folk, in Islamic cultures, 170
Theban: Kingdom, 73
Therapeutic: practices (countermeasures) for the Evil Eye, 209; preventive and, effects of exhaustion, 103; *zâr* as drama played on, stage, 98
Thompson, Stith, 9 n. 21, 20 n. 52, 271 n. 770
Thoth: the moon god, was sent to fetch and mollify Ra's Eye, 208
Thoth's: role assigned to Prophet Sulaymân (Solomon), 208
Three: folk groups view humans as comprising, strata, 140; major types of people, 156; races after (Noah's sons), 138; sets of religious figures constitute the Divan, 168
Three hundred sixty-six: number of existing sufi paths is, 153
Throne: highest heaven (sky) closer to God's, 45; sun derives her light from God's, 36; water will flow from under God's (Resurrection follows), 46

Thutmosis: freed Sphinx from sand and is rewarded, 182; Sphinx addresses Prince, in vision as "My son", 181
thu¿bân: (snake) always masculine, 109; bites bride, 109 n. 364
ṭibâ¿: temperament or character, 156
Time: passage of (*'ayyâm/(el-)*), 189; *ez-zamàn/ez-zamân*, 189; of the month is instrumental in *mushâhràh*, 201
Time-bound: concepts residuals of older counter-religious arguments, 189
Time-epochs: *dàhr*, 189
Times: blessed, 183–84; Certain days and, have special significance, 28
Tipping: down the scales in favor of the individual being judged, 33
Titles: characteristics and, of *sayyidàh*-Zàynàb, 169; indicating number of jinn groups, 61; of jinni with potent political powers, 61; referring to jinn in their relationship to humans, 61
Tomb: -people ("*'ahl al-qubûr*"), 119; trial fundamental aspect of required faith, 52
Top: female may not, the male during sexual intercourse, 137
Toth: mollifies the Evil Eye, 143
Traditional: diagnostic techniques, 98; healing practice identical with modern psychodrama, 99; wedding nomenclatures utilized in *zâr* jargon, 95; choice of site according to, architecture, 184–85; sentiments within, Egyptian family, 98
Tragedies: Osirian and the Christian were emotionally identical, 171
Tragedy: bases for membership in ¿Âshurâ, 171
Transcontinental: Adam was of, size, 135
Transferred: buried corpse, supernaturally to another location, 128
Transient: jinni may interact with Adamite in, manner, 79
Transitory (*¿âriḍ/¿awâriḍ*): harmful intruder(s), 87; some angels have, relationship with all humans, 51
Translation: accuracy of, 145 n. 526
Transparent: realm, 40, 172; realm ends with angels category, 52
Tree: of Extremity of the universe, 43; of life-spans, 43
Triad: of triads, 169; with a cult different from their father's (¿Alî), 165; Osiris-Isis-Horus, 169
Trial: and error, 127; by ordeal, 32; judge asserts that jinn do exist, 79; final, on Judgment Day, 124, 154; tomb, not needed, 124; tomb (*ḥisâb al-qàbr*), 52, 57
Trials: disasters as Divine, and tribulations, 19, 155
Tribulations: disasters as Divine trials and, 19
Trilogy: N. Maḥfouẓ's, 156 n. 574
Trinity: contradistinction to the doctrine of, in Christianity, 12
Troika: of two brothers and their sister, 168
True: "believer [always] afflicted", 194; death may come to, believers in soft peaceful form, 122–23; folk theater in Islamic cultures, 170; *sùflî*-magic, 75; *zâr* conducted by female (*kùdyàh*), 94; *zâr* has become less overt, 102; *zâr* includes diagnostic phase, 92; *zâr* lasts for several days, 95; *zâr* requires sacrificing living being to jinn, 93
Truisms: representing beliefs, 54; "[If you stack] one brick on top of another, [this] will . . . ", 198
Trumpet: of light, 46–47 n. 138
Trustee, *see 'amîn*
Truth: dreams as source of, and instruction, 179; means of acquiring, 176; Ptah Lord of, 73; sleeper sees the, 179
Truthfulness: of visions is one of forty-six indicators of prophethood, 180
ṭûfân: (Deluge), 111
Twin: Cain wanted, sister for himself, 138; marriage to non-, sister/brother, 138; ¿Unâq born without, brother, 84
Twins: Eve bore, regularly, 138
Types: of knowledge, 176; of manifesting supernatural feats (deeds), 146; of martyrdom, 171–72; of saints' miracle-like manifestations, 147–49; five, of dreams (*ru'â*), 180 n. 653; three major, of people, 156; two, of objects and deeds, 14

Types (*cont.*)
two, of magic, 66; two, of power (rule), 166; two, of supernatural, 146

Ulama: views of, 6, 69, 78, 101, 146, 167
'Um-Kulthûm: unheard of in folk oral traditions, 170; younger sister of Zàynàb not included in Divan, 168
¿Umar (Omar), *see* Omar
¿ùmmâr, *see* jinn
¿Unâq: becomes wicked, 30 n. 90; daughter of Adam and Eve without twin brother, 84–85; misled her brothers and sisters, 85
Umpires: people acting as, rule in favor of Evil, 194
Un-Islamic: death (funerary) practices, 125
Unanimity (*'ijmâ¿*), 155 n. 571
Unbelievers: (*kùffâr*), 109, 112, 141, 146
Unchanged: attitudes toward magical fertility ritual, 74
Undoing: of *mushâhràh*, 202
Unequivocal: condemnation of *zâr*-cult, 102; violation of sacred taboos, 74
Unfulfilled: pledges anger God (saint), 18
Uniformity: *'ìjmâ¿* (unanimity), 155
Union: of opposites, 13 n. 26; with own shadow, 54 n. 175
Unity: of the universe (*wiḥdìt ek-koan/al-wugûd*), 177; God's oneness and, 11
Universality: of belief in the soul, 131; of belief in malice of envy and Evil Eye, 205
Universe: divided into ten portions, 58; control of entire, 175; typical image of, 24; unity of the, 177
Unknown: read off the Tablet of Destiny, 70; how the, came into existence, 40
Unorthodoxy: philosophical, 23 n. 64, 176 n. 724
Usage: of God's creatures is to be only as ordained, 36
¿Uthmân Ibn ¿Affân: Caliph, 167; in narrative lore, 143
Utilitarian: functions of jinn extends to language, 62; objectives of magic, 66
Utopian: otherworld, 38
¿Uzza (al-): (ancient Arabian goddess) described, 104 n. 342

Vaginas: jinni (Sindâs) all-knowing of, 76
Validity: repeated occurrence of *manâm* as indicator of, 180; Sunni institutions recognize, of sainthood, 152
Valley: of Ants, 116; the Holy (sacred), 12 n. 25
Value: judgment applied mostly by the "learned", 198; terms that bear no, judgment, 198
Variations: Western, on Middle Eastern sacred belief system, 8
Varieties: of eggplant, 203 n. 715
Varying: nature of various peoples, 157
Veil, *see ḥigâb*
Veiled: things that God intended to be, 40
Veneration: of ¿Alî in folk culture, 144; of martyred mortal, 173 n. 639; of planets, 65; of saints, 152; of shrine, 12 n. 25; of spirits, 101
Venturing all out of desperation: (*'ìstìbyâ¿*), 191
Venus (planet): seduces angels, 55 n. 179; milking, 76
Verifiable: link to one's own mother is, 71
Vertically: *zâr* is spreading both, and horizontally, 102
Videotaped: female clients of sorcerer secretly, 75
Violent: martyrdom by, death, 179
Viper: agrees to smuggle Eblis into Paradise, 136; invariably feminine, 109; with seventy thousand wings, 26; punishment of, 136; similarity between the words *ḥàyyàh*, and Ḥawwâ (Eve), 109
Virgin: danger at deflowering, 201; pubescent, required for magical ritual, 76
Vision: knowledge acquired through (dream), 176; Sphinx speaks to Prince Thutmosis in, 181
Visiting: graves, 126 n. 446
Voice: supernatural (*hâtìf*), 178
Voluntary: associations in Arab Society, 152

Voodoo: -doll, 71 n. 232
Vulnerability: to anxiety and disorganization, 101
Vulva: slapped repeatedly with slipper in magical ritual, 75–76

wadà¿ (el-): [casting] sea shells, 190
wâdî (al-) al-muqàddàs, 12 n. 25
Wagdî, M.F., 117 n. 398, 131
wàhb: granting (bestowing) one's own religious credit to another, 15
wahbàh: donation (price) for religious object, 102 n. 335
wàḥmah: "birthmark" due to craving by a pregnant woman, 16 n. 38
wàḥy: revelation [from God], 178; through the Archangel Gabriel, 178
wakîl: (deputy), 153
Walker-Ismâ¿îl, 61 n. 201, 70 n. 230, 76 n. 248, 110 n. 365, 170 n. 630
Walker, J., 82 n. 268 and 269, 83
Wallace, Anthony F.C., 67 n. 225, 71–72, 76
War: hero rebels against supreme commander in chief, 48; of 1973, 132; prediction about World, III, 132 n. 469
Wars: between Moslems and European Christians, 171–72
Washing-of-the-dead: rituals of, not required for perfect martyr, 171
waswasàh: instigation, 53; temptation of Eblis, 194
Water: carrier's she-mule, 107–8; Resurrection occurs when, flows from under God's Throne, 46
Water-Spirit: (*'Omm-esh-Shu¿ûr*): (the one-with-[long-]hair) as water-spirit, 64
wathàniyyîn: idol-worshippers, 141
Waugh, E.H., 22 n. 58
wàzz: inciting, 53
wà¿d (el-): that which has been promised [by fate], 182
Wealth: equality in status and, between couple to be married, 139
Weaning: and subsequent circumcision of children, 202, 204 n. 719
Weasel: supernatural qualities of, 114
Wedges/Pegs (*'awtâd*): four of them exist during each era, 150
Weighing: of heart, 33–34; 33 n. 100; of deeds in Balance (Scale), 33; worth of one's deeds in life, 32–33
Well: souls of the dead congregate in, 125
West: sun and moon will rise from the, 36
Westermarck, Edward, 205
Western: psycho-therapeutic institutions, 101; religions being variations on Middle Eastern sacred belief system, 8
Whale: Earth created on back of, 26
Wheel: with three hundred and sixty notches (days), 36
Whimsical: type character *hawâ'î*/(aerial), 72, 156
Whirlwind: *zàwba¿àh*, 83 n. 270
Whisky: in *zâr*, 98 n. 324
White: heart of Earth, 134; magic, 67
Why: differences in appearances and temperaments, 134; women are crooked, 135
Wife: has more freedom at her own home, 199; husband-, tie absent among *zâr*-spirits, 97; female jinni becoming, of human male, 63; new, has shaky position in her husband's family, 86
wiḥdàt al-kàwn: unity of the universe, 177
wilâyàh/(sainthood): closely associated with *khawârìq* (supernatural), 146
"*wìldân mukhàlladûn*": serve inhabitants of Paradise, 29–30
Wiles (*see* juxtaposing): (*kàyd*/machination) misapplied by interpreters, 157 n. 579
Willmore, J. Seldon, 39 n. 123
Winds/jinn (*'aryâḥ*); confused with *'arwâḥ* (souls), 121
Wings: fail (refuse) to carry sinning angels, 55; of viper (surrounding God's Throne), 26; of Ḥizqyâ'îl, 49; of Gabriel block the east and the west, 49; angels have, and dwell in trees, 42
Woman: will always be "under the male", 137
Woman's: self-concept, 199; self-esteem is being a mother, 199; supernatural Sister destroys husband's/wife's affectionate ties, 86

Women: in *zìkr*-circles, 24
World: of ether-like beings (*¿âlàm al-'athîr*), 56; Life (*dùnyâ/ed-dìnyâ/(ed-)*), 189
Worshipper: cat as, 114; of a god other than God, 141
Wrath (*see also* curse): almsgiving prevents God's, 18; extreme anger or (*sùkhṭ*), 187; God's anger or, 186–87
Wrenching: soul from body at death, 122

"Yà'gûg/wa/Màg'ûg": (Gog and Magog), 106
yâ-naṣîb (el-) (lùtariyyàh): lottery, 190
Yablonsky, Lewis, 99 n. 325, 235 n. 754
Yâfeth: (Japhet), 138
Yaḥyâ Ḥqqî, 169 n. 626
Yemen: as source for required incense, 92 n. 305
yetshàyṭàn: act like a devil (naughty or unruly), 120 n. 417
yit¿afràt: acting like an afrit (naughty or unruly), 120 n. 417
Yosaih: son of Sultan Màmmàh, 97; Mùstaghîtàh is sister of, 97
Youth: fountain of, in Dark Quarter, 37, 163
yùkhùshsh/yùdkhùl ¿alâ: (to enter upon), 200

zabâniyàh: are Hell's angels (keepers), 31
ẓâhìr rule: overt or apparent (government), 166
zàhr: dice, 190
Zàhràh/(az-): (Venus) seduces angels, 55
zakâh: (required alms-tax) paid by Muslim jinn, 108; alms-tax or tithe, 17
zàkkîr/dhakkîr: lead-chanter in ritual, 21
zamàn/(ez-)/zamân: Time, 189
zâr: as therapeutic drama, 100; concentrates on appeasing spirit, 91 ; condemned as veneration of spirits, 101; dissipates bent-in energies, 103; is relatively newcomer to Egypt, 91; not held during Ramaḍân, 42; sub-cult has limited distribution, 90; utilizes all devices involved in lesser rituals, 94; the word "*afrît*"/(ghost) in, explained, 120
zâr-jinn: category of jinn associated exclusively with *zâr*, 90; masters or lords of (*'asyâd-ez-zâr*), 90–91; never used as "helpers" or "servants", 90; Pantheon, of, 95–103
zâr-spirit: proper way of referring to, 90
zâr-spirits: have specific well-known names and characteristics, 90; jinni, and the "malayka ardiyyah", 50 n. 158
Zàynàb (Zaynab/Zainab): as immaculate, 169; as mother of the disabled, 169; referred to as *es-sayyidàh*, 165; replaced "pagan" Isis, 171; hymn to, 168
Zayn-el-¿Âbidîn ¿Alî: equated with the Osirian Horus, 169; replaced Horus, 171
Zbinden, Ernest, 56 n. 181
zìkr: allows for dissipation of bent-in energies, 103; as kinetic-hymn, 19, 20, 41; as remembrance [of God], 20–24; as ritual, 19; as sinful *bìd¿àh*, 19, 21
zìkr-circle: holding *ḥàlqàt-dhìkr* (group "kinetic-hymns"), 19; overlaps with modernized public *zâr*, 24
Zizyphus lotus, 43 n. 135
Zodiac: horoscope, 190
Zoolatry, 113 n. 384
Zoological: minor, beings used to socialize children, 61

About the Author

HASAN M. EL-SHAMY is Professor of Folklore in the Department of Folklore and Ethnomusicology, the Department of Middle Eastern Languages and Cultures, and the African Studies Program at Indiana University. His research and publications introduced a number of innovative approaches to the study of traditional cultures in general and Arabic communities in particular. Among these are the concepts and research methodology of "Folkloric Behavior" and "The Brother Sister Syndrome" in Arab family life and psychological practices. His works apply principles of cognitive psychology and social structure as analytical tools for the identification and classification of sociocultural phenomena by motif and tale-type. His publications include several interdisciplinary reference works and scores of articles in English, German, and Arabic.